Lecture Notes in Computer Science 11295

Commenced Publication in 1973
Founding and Former Series Editors:
Gerhard Goos, Juris Hartmanis, and Jan van Leeuwen

Ioannis Kompatsiaris · Benoit Huet
Vasileios Mezaris · Cathal Gurrin
Wen-Huang Cheng · Stefanos Vrochidis (Eds.)

MultiMedia Modeling

25th International Conference, MMM 2019
Thessaloniki, Greece, January 8–11, 2019
Proceedings, Part I

Springer

Editors
Ioannis Kompatsiaris 🆔
Information Technologies Institute
Centre for Research and Technology Hellas
Thessaloniki, Greece

Benoit Huet 🆔
EURECOM
Sophia Antipolis, France

Vasileios Mezaris
Information Technologies Institute
Centre for Research and Technology Hellas
Thessaloniki, Greece

Cathal Gurrin
Dublin City University
Dublin, Ireland

Wen-Huang Cheng
National Chiao Tung University
Hsinchu, Taiwan

Stefanos Vrochidis
Information Technologies Institute
Centre for Research and Technology Hellas
Thessaloniki, Greece

ISSN 0302-9743   ISSN 1611-3349   (electronic)
Lecture Notes in Computer Science
ISBN 978-3-030-05709-1   ISBN 978-3-030-05710-7   (eBook)
https://doi.org/10.1007/978-3-030-05710-7

Library of Congress Control Number: 2018963821

LNCS Sublibrary: SL3 – Information Systems and Applications, incl. Internet/Web, and HCI

This Springer imprint is published by the registered company Springer Nature Switzerland AG
The registered company address is: Gewerbestrasse 11, 6330 Cham, Switzerland

Preface

These two-volume proceedings contain the papers presented at MMM 2019, the 25th International Conference on MultiMedia Modeling, held in Thessaloniki, Greece, during January 8–11, 2019. MMM is a leading international conference for researchers and industry practitioners for sharing new ideas, original research results, and practical development experiences from all MMM-related areas, broadly falling into three categories: multimedia content analysis; multimedia signal processing and communications; and multimedia applications and services.

MMM 2019 received a total of 204 valid submissions across five categories; 172 full-paper regular and special session submissions, eight demonstration submissions, eight industry session submissions, six submissions to the Video Browser Showdown (VBS 2019), and ten workshop paper submissions. All submissions were reviewed by at least two and, in most cases, three members of the Program Committee, and were carefully meta-reviewed by the TPC chairs or the organizers of each special event before making the final accept/reject decisions. Of the 172 full papers submitted, 49 were selected for oral presentation and 47 for poster presentation. In addition, six demonstrations were accepted from eight submissions, five industry papers from eight submissions, six workshop papers from ten submissions, and all six submissions to VBS 2019. Overall, the program of MMM 2019 included 119 contributions presented in oral, poster, or demo form.

MMM conferences traditionally include special sessions that focus on addressing new challenges for the multimedia community; five special sessions were held in the 2019 edition of the conference. In addition, this year's MMM hosted a workshop as part of its program. Together with the conference's three invited keynote talks and two tutorials, one industry session, and the Video Browser Showdown, these events resulted in a rich program extending over four conference days.

The five special sessions of MMM 2019 were:

- SS1: Personal Data Analytics and Lifelogging
- SS2: Multimedia Analytics: Perspectives, Tools, and Applications
- SS3: Multimedia Datasets for Repeatable Experimentation
- SS4: Large-Scale Big Data Analytics for Online Counter-Terrorism Applications
- SS5: Time-Sequenced Multimedia Computing and Applications

The workshop hosted as part of the MMM 2019 program was:

- Third International Workshop on coMics ANalysis, Processing and Understanding (MANPU)

We wish to thank the authors of all submissions for sending their work to MMM 2019; and, we owe a debt of gratitude to all the members of the Program Committee and all the special events organizers (Special Sessions, Industry Session, Workshop,

VBS) for contributing their valuable time to reviewing these submissions and otherwise managing the organization of all the different sessions.

We would also like to thank our invited keynote speakers, Daniel Gatica-Perez from the IDIAP Research Institute and Ecole Polytechnique Federale de Lausanne (EPFL), Switzerland, Martha Larson from Radboud University Nijmegen and Delft University of Technology, The Netherlands, and Andreas Symeonidis from the Aristotle University of Thessaloniki, Greece, for their stimulating contributions. Similarly, we thank our tutorial speakers, Lucio Tommaso De Paolis from the University of Salento, Italy, and Xavier Giro-i-Nieto from the Universitat Politecnica de Catalunya, for their in-depth coverage of specific multimedia topics.

Finally, special thanks go to the MMM 2019 Organizing Committee members, our proceedings publisher (Springer), and the Multimedia Knowledge and Social Media Analytics Laboratory of CERTH-ITI – both our local organization and support team, and the conference volunteers – for their hard work and support in taking care of all tasks necessary for ensuring a smooth and pleasant conference experience at MMM 2019.

We hope that the MMM 2019 participants found the conference program and its insights interesting and thought-provoking, and that the conference provided everyone with a good opportunity to share ideas on MMM-related topics with other researchers and practitioners from institutions around the world!

November 2018

Ioannis Kompatsiaris
Benoit Huet
Vasileios Mezaris
Cathal Gurrin
Wen-Huang Cheng
Stefanos Vrochidis

Organization

Organizing Committee

General Chairs

Ioannis Kompatsiaris	CERTH-ITI, Greece
Benoit Huet	EURECOM, France

Program Chairs

Vasileios Mezaris	CERTH-ITI, Greece
Cathal Gurrin	Dublin City University, Ireland
Wen-Huang Cheng	National Chiao Tung University, Taiwan

Panel Chair

Chong-Wah Ngo	City University of Hong Kong, SAR China

Tutorial Chair

Shin'ichi Satoh	NII, Japan

Demo Chairs

Michele Merler	IBM T.J. Watson Research Center, USA
Tao Mei	JD.com, China

Video Browser Showdown Chairs

Werner Bailer	Joanneum Research, Austria
Klaus Schoeffmann	University of Klagenfurt, Austria
Jakub Lokoc	Charles University in Prague, Czech Republic

Publicity Chairs

Lexing Xie	Australian National University, Australia
Ioannis Patras	QMUL, UK

Publication Chair

Stefanos Vrochidis	CERTH-ITI, Greece

Local Organization and Webmasters

Maria Papadopoulou	CERTH-ITI, Greece
Chrysa Collyda	CERTH-ITI, Greece

Steering Committee

Phoebe Chen	La Trobe University, Australia
Tat-Seng Chua	National University of Singapore, Singapore
Kiyoharu Aizawa	University of Tokyo, Japan
Cathal Gurrin	Dublin City University, Ireland
Benoit Huet	EURECOM, France
Klaus Schoeffmann	University of Klagenfurt, Austria
Meng Wang	Hefei University of Technology, China
Björn Thór Jónsson	IT University of Copenhagen, Denmark
Guo-Jun Qi	University of Central Florida, USA
Wen-Huang Cheng	National Chiao Tung University, Taiwan
Peng Cui	Tsinghua University, China

Special Sessions, Industry Session, and Workshop Organizers

SS1: Personal Data Analytics and Lifelogging

Xavier Giro-i-Nieto	Universitat Politecnica de Catalunya, Spain
Petia Radeva	University of Barcelona, Spain
David J. Crandall	Indiana University, USA
Giovanni Farinella	University of Catania, Italy
Duc Tien Dang Nguyen	Dublin City University, Ireland
Mariella Dimiccoli	Computer Vision Centre, Universitat de Barcelona, Spain
Cathal Gurrin	Dublin City University, Ireland

SS2: Multimedia Analytics: Perspectives, Tools, and Applications

Björn Þór Jónsson	IT University of Copenhagen, Denmark
Laurent Amsaleg	CNRS-IRISA, France
Cathal Gurrin	Dublin City University, Ireland
Stevan Rudinac	University of Amsterdam, The Netherlands

SS3: Multimedia Datasets for Repeatable Experimentation

Cathal Gurrin	Dublin City University, Ireland
Duc-Tien Dang-Nguyen	Dublin City University, Ireland
Klaus Schoeffmann	University of Klagenfurt, Austria
Björn Þór Jónsson	IT University of Copenhagen, Denmark
Michael Riegler	Center for Digitalisation and Engineering and University of Oslo, Norway
Luca Piras	University of Cagliari, Italy

SS4: Large-Scale Big Data Analytics for Online Counter-Terrorism Applications

Georgios Th. Papadopoulos	Centre for Research and Technology Hellas, Greece
Ernesto La Mattina	Engineering Ingegneria Informatica SpA, Italy
Apostolos Axenopoulos	Centre for Research and Technology Hellas, Greece

SS5: Time-Sequenced Multimedia Computing and Applications

Bing-Kun Bao	Nanjing University of Posts and Telecommunications, China
Shao Xi	Nanjing University of Posts and Telecommunications, China
Changsheng Xu	Institute of Automation, Chinese Academy of Sciences, China

Industry Session Organizers

Panagiotis Sidiropoulos	Cortexica Vision Systems Ltd./UCL, UK
Khalid Bashir	I. University of Madinah, KSA
Gustavo Fernandez	Austrian Institute of Technology, Austria
Jose Garcia	Universidad de Alicante, Spain
Carlo Regazzoni	University of Genoa, Italy
Eduard Vazquez	Cortexica Vision Systems Ltd., UK
Sergio A Velastin	Universidad Carlos III, Madrid, Spain
M. Haroon Yousaf	UET Taxila, Pakistan
Qiao Wang	SouthEast University, China

MANPU Workshop Organizers

General Co-chairs

Jean-Christophe Burie	University of La Rochelle, France
Motoi Iwata	Osaka Prefecture University, Japan
Yusuke Matsui	National Institute of Informatics, Japan

Program Co-chairs

Alexander Dunst	Paderborn University, Germany
Miki Ueno	Toyohashi University of Technology, Japan
Tien-Tsin Wong	The Chinese University of Hong Kong, SAR China

MMM 2019 Program Committees and Reviewers

Regular and Special Sessions Program Committee

Esra Acar	Middle East Technical University, Turkey
Laurent Amsaleg	CNRS-IRISA, France
Martin Aumüller	IT University of Copenhagen, Denmark
Werner Bailer	Joanneum Research, Austria

Liqiang Nie	Shandong University, China
Naoko Nitta	Osaka University, Japan
Noel O'Connor	Dublin City University, Ireland
Neil O'Hare	Yahoo Research, USA
Vincent Oria	NJIT, USA
Tse-Yu Pan	National Cheng Kung University, Taiwan
Georgios Th. Papadopoulos	Information Technologies Institute, CERTH, Greece
Cecilia Pasquini	Universität Innsbruck, Austria
Stefan Petscharnig	AIT Austrian Institute of Technology, Austria
Konstantin Pogorelov	Simula, Norway
Manfred Jürgen Primus	University of Klagenfurt, Austria
Yannick Prié	LINA - University of Nantes, France
Athanasios Psaltis	CERTH, Greece
Jianjun Qian	Nanjing University of Science and Technology, China
Georges Quénot	Laboratoire d'Informatique de Grenoble, CNRS, France
Miloš Radovanović	University of Novi Sad, Serbia
Amon Rapp	University of Turin, Italy
Stevan Rudinac	University of Amsterdam, The Netherlands
Mukesh Saini	Indian Institute of Technology Ropar, India
Borja Sanz	University of Deusto, Spain
Shin'Ichi Satoh	National Institute of Informatics, Japan
Klaus Schöffmann	University of Klagenfurt, Austria
Wen-Ze Shao	Nanjing University of Posts and Telecommunications, China
Xi Shao	Nanjing University of Posts and Telecommunications, China
Jie Shao	University of Science and Technology of China, China
Xiangjun Shen	Jiangsu University, China
Xiaobo Shen	Nanjing University of Science and Technology, China
Koichi Shinoda	Tokyo Institute of Technology, Japan
Mei-Ling Shyu	University of Miami, USA
Alan Smeaton	Dublin City University, Ireland
Li Su	UCAS, China
Lifeng Sun	Tsinghua University, China
C. Sun	Central China Normal University, China
Yongqing Sun	NTT Media Intelligence Labs, Japan
Pascale Sébillot	IRISA, France
Estefania Talavera	University of Groningen, The Netherlands
Sheng Tang	Institute of Computing Technology, Chinese Academy of Sciences, China
Georg Thallinger	Joanneum Research, Austria
Vajira Thambawita	Simula Research Laboratory, Norway
Christian Timmerer	University of Klagenfurt, Austria
Daniele Toti	Roma Tre University, Italy
Sriram Varadarajan	Ulster University, UK

Stefanos Vrochidis	CERTH-ITI, Greece
Xiang Wang	National University of Singapore, Singapore
Lai Kuan Wong	Multimedia University, Malaysia
Marcel Worring	University of Amsterdam, The Netherlands
Hong Wu	UESTC, China
Xiao Wu	Southwest Jiaotong University, China
Hongtao Xie	University of Science and Technology of China, China
Changsheng Xu	Institute of Automation, Chinese Academy of Sciences, China
Toshihiko Yamasaki	The University of Tokyo, Japan
Keiji Yanai	The University of Electro-Communications, Japan
You Yang	Huazhong University of Science and Technology, China
Yang Yang	University of Science and Technology of China, China
Zhaoquan Yuan	University of Science and Technology of China, China
Matthias Zeppelzauer	University of Applied Sciences St. Pölten, Austria
Hanwang Zhang	Nanyang Technological University, Singapore
Tianzhu Zhang	CASIA, China
Jiang Zhou	Dublin City University, Ireland
Mengrao Zhu	Shanghai University, China
Xiaofeng Zhu	Guangxi Normal University, China
Roger Zimmermann	National University of Singapore, Singapore

Demonstration and VBS Program Committee

Werner Bailer	JRS, Austria
Premysl Cech	MFF, UK
Qi Dai	Microsoft, China
Xiangnan He	National University of Singapore, Singapore
Dhiraj Joshi	IBM Corporation, USA
Sabrina Kletz	University of Klagenfurt, Austria
Andreas Leibetseder	University of Klagenfurt, Austria
Jakub Lokoč	Charles University Prague, Czech Republic
Michele Merler	IBM, USA
Bernd Münzer	University of Klagenfurt, Austria
Ladislav Peska	Charles University Prague, Czech Republic
Jürgen Primus	University of Klagenfurt, Austria

MANPU Workshop Program Committee

John Bateman	University of Bremen, Germany
Ying Cao	City University of Hong Kong, SAR China
Wei-Ta Chu	National Chung Cheng University, Chiayi, Taiwan
Mathieu Delalandre	Laboratoire d'Informatique, France
Seiji Hotta	Tokyo University of Agricultural and Technology, Japan
Rynson Lau	City University of Hong Kong, SAR China

Jochen Laubrock	University of Potsdam, Germany
Tong-Yee Lee	National Cheng Kung University, Taiwan
Xueting Liu	The Chinese University of Hong Kong, SAR China
Muhammad Muzzamil Luqman	University of La Rochelle, France
Mitsunori Matsushita	Kansai University, Japan
Tetsuya Mihara	University of Tsukuba, Japan
Naoki Mori	Osaka Prefecture University, Japan
Mitsuharu Nagamori	University of Tsukuba, Japan
Satoshi Nakamura	Meiji University, Japan
Nhu Van Nguyen	University of La Rochelle, France
Christophe Rigaud	University of La Rochelle, France
Yasuyuki Sumi	Future University Hakodate, Japan
John Walsh	Indiana University Bloomington, USA
Ying-Qing Xu	Tsinghua University, China

Additional Reviewers

Elissavet Batziou
Lei Chen
Long Chen
Luis Lebron Casas
Gabriel Constantin
Mihai Dogariu
Jianfeng Dong
Xiaoyu Du
Neeraj Goel
Xian-Hua Han
Shintami Chusnul Hidayati
Tianchi Huang
Wolfgang Hürst
Benjamin Kille
Marios Krestenitis
Yuwen Li
Emmanouil Michail

Tor-Arne Nordmo
Georgios Orfanidis
John See
Pranav Shenoy
Liviu Stefan
Gjorgji Strezoski
Xiang Wang
Zheng Wang
Stefanie Wechtitsch
Qijie Wei
Wolfgang Weiss
Pengfei Xu
Xin Yao
Haoran Zhang
Wanqing Zhao
Yuanen Zhou

Contents – Part I

Contents – Part II

Industry Papers

Demonstrations

MANPU 2019 Workshop Papers

Regular and Special Session Papers

Sentiment-Aware Multi-modal Recommendation on Tourist Attractions

Junyi Wang[1], Bing-Kun Bao[2(✉)], and Changsheng Xu[1,3,4]

[1] Hefei University of Technology, Hefei, China
jywang921@gmail.com
[2] College of Telecommunications and Information Engineering,
Nanjing University of Posts and Telecommunications, Nanjing, China
bingkunbao@njupt.edu.cn
[3] National Lab of Pattern Recognition, Institute of Automation, CAS,
Beijing, China
csxu@nlpr.ia.ac.cn
[4] University of Chinese Academy of Sciences, Beijing, China

Abstract. For tourist attraction recommendation, there are three essential aspects to be considered: tourist preferences, attraction themes, and sentiments on themes of attraction. By utilizing vast multi-modal media available on Internet, this paper is aiming to develop an efficient solution of tourist attraction recommendation covering all these three aspects. To achieve this goal, we propose a probabilistic generative model called Sentiment-aware Multi-modal Topic Model (SMTM), whose advantages are four folds: (1) we separate tourists and attractions into two domains for better recovering tourist topics and attraction themes; (2) we investigate tourists sentiments on topics to retain the preference ones; (3) the recommended attraction is guaranteed with positive sentiment on the related attraction themes; (4) the multi-modal data are utilized to enhance the recommendation accuracy. Qualitative and quantitative evaluation results have validated the effectiveness of our method.

Keywords: Tourism recommendation · Multi-modal computing Topic model · Sentiment analysis

1 Introduction

With the acceleration of globalization and fast development of technologies for travel needs, personalized tourism become more and more popular especially among younger generations. Nowadays, the opinions and sentiments shared on travel websites act an important role for tourists on attraction selection. TripAdvisor[1], one of the most popular ones in its kind, is being checked by many tourists for the multi-modal comments, including text and image, on the attractions they plan to visit. However, due to the fast growth of these travel websites,

---

[1] [online]. Available https://www.tripadvisor.in/.

© Springer Nature Switzerland AG 2019
I. Kompatsiaris et al. (Eds.): MMM 2019, LNCS 11295, pp. 3–16, 2019.
https://doi.org/10.1007/978-3-030-05710-7_1

the overwhelming and sometimes unorganized information become a hurdle to the tourists to find the pieces that values most to them. Therefore, it is not hard to see that a sharp increasing demand of customizable and automatic tourist attraction recommendation solutions.

To design a satisfying tourist attraction recommendation method, the mining on following three aspects from multi-modal data is crucial. The first one is "tourist preferences", which are the tourist topics that a tourist truly interested on among all those he/she visited, commented, followed, liked and so on. The second one is "attraction themes", which are the types of experience that tourists would received through visits. For example, the theme of Disney Land seems most likely to be "entertainment" over "historical site". Of course, an attraction could have multiple themes. And the last one is "sentiment on a theme of the attraction", which measures the quality of attraction on a certain theme by the view of tourists. Based on these three aspects, the task of recommending a tourist with the most suitable attractions can be decomposed into mining the preferences of this tourist, then selecting the most similar attraction themes, and at last returning the attractions with positive sentiments on selected themes.

Existing works on personalized tourism recommendation mostly ignore the sentiment analysis on both tourist preferences and attraction themes, and also lack of processing of multi-modal data [1,8]. [9,10] directly work on tourist topics instead of mining of tourist preferences. Without analyzing the sentiments of a tourist over the topics, there is a high chance that some of the recommended attractions are not what the tourist is looking forward. [11,15] recommend top searched attractions on the selected themes. This only reflects the popularity of the attractions but fails to reveal the sentiments from the tourists who actually visited them. [20] analyzes the sentiments yet neglects to separate tourists and attractions into two domains and identify tourist topics with attraction themes. Moreover, [9,10,20] only focus on text modality, and leave image modality out of consideration.

This paper emphasizes on mining all above mentioned three aspects, and proposes a Sentiment-aware Multi-modal Topic Model (SMTM), which is capable of discovering topics/themes of tourists/attractions conditioned on multi-modal tourism data and analyzing their sentiments for better recommendation results. Specifically, we divide tourists and attractions into two domains. As shown in Fig. 1, the left side is topic mining and sentiment analysis on tourist domain, while the right side is those on attraction domain. The inputs of two sides are the multi-modal corpus from tourist and attraction domains respectively. The outputs of two sides include topics/themes of each tourist/attraction, and their corresponding sentiments. The middle of Fig. 1 shows the applications of SMTM, including personalized attraction recommendation and potential tourist recommendation.

In summary, the contributions of this work are as follows:

– We analyze the three essential aspects on attraction recommendation, and propose Sentiment-aware Multi-modal Topic Model (SMTM) whose advantages are four folds: (1) we separate tourists and attractions into two domains for better recovering tourist topics and attraction themes; (2) we investigate tourist sentiments on topics to retain those with actual preference; (3) the recommended attraction is guaranteed with positive sentiment on the related attraction themes; (4) the multi-modal data are utilized to enhance the recommendation accuracy.

- We present two applications on SMTM, including personalized attraction recommendation and potential tourist recommendation. We also construct a large scale tourism recommendation dataset including 14,648 tourists and 8,724 attractions with multi-modal data. The experiments on this dataset show the effectiveness of our proposed approach, and the high accuracies on two applications.
- The proposed model has great potential for other recommendation applications, including movie, goods recommendations, and so on.

The rest of this paper is organized as follows. In Sect. 2, we briefly review the related work. Section 3 presents the details of Sentiment-aware Multimodal Topic Model. Section 4 introduces the above mentioned two applications. Section 5 reports and analyzes experimental results. Finally, we conclude the work in Sect. 6.

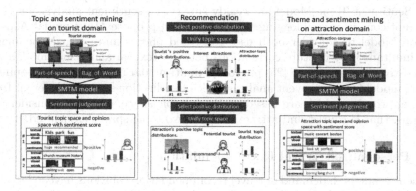

Fig. 1. Framework of sentiment-aware multi-modal recommendation

2 Related Work

Our work is related to two main research areas, that is, probabilistic topic models and personalized travel recommendation.

2.1 Probabilistic Topic Models

The Probabilistic Topic Model (PTM) is proposed to explore a set of topics from a document set, where a topic is a distribution over a fixed vocabulary and a document is a distribution over topics. The simplest probabilistic topic model [2] is Latent Dirichlet Allocation (LDA) [17]. In order to extend the LDA model to learn the joint correlations between data of different modalities, such as the texts and images, some variants of topic models are developed, such as multimodal-LDA and correspondence LDA [3]. They use a set of shared latent variables to explicitly model images and annotated text to capture correlations between the data of two modalities.

In order to mine subjective emotion, some works focus on studying topic models on sentiment/opinion mining [5–7,18,24,26–28]. Topic Sentiment Mixture model is proposed by Mei *et al.* [18] to reveal the latent topic facets in a Weblog collection, and their associated sentiments. In [27], Alam *et al.* propose a domain-independent topic-sentiment model called Joint Multi-gain Topic Sentiment to extract quality semantic aspects automatically, thereby eliminating the requirement for manual probing. These works are the pioneer studies on topic sentiment analysis. However they just consider limited states on sentiment spaces like "negative, positive, neutral" in [18]. To improve this, Titov [21] propose Multi-Aspect Sentiment model which can aggregate sentiment texts for the sentiment summary of each rating aspect. [23] propose Contrastive Opinion Modeling to present the opinions of the individual perspectives on the topic and furthermore to quantify their difference. Latter, some works research on sentiment topic model with multi-modal data. In [26], Huang *et al.* propose Multi-modal Joint Sentiment Topic Model for weakly supervised sentiment analysis on texts and emoticons in microblogging. Fang *et al.* [19] propose Multi-modal Aspect-opinion Model to consider both user-generated photos and textual documents and simultaneously capture correlations between textual and visual modalities. Extend to [23], Qian *et al.* [25] propose a multi-modal multi-view topic opinion mining model for social event analysis multiple collection sources. Different from above approaches which are based on single topic space, our work consider two domains, that is tourist and attraction, and two topic spaces associated.

2.2   Personalized Travel Recommendation

In recent years, high demand of travel recommendation solutions have led to a lot of researches. Some works [12–14,16] consider that the reviews contain diverse information which can mitigate sparse problems, and some of them also use reviews to extract sentiments for recommendation. But they ignore the theme of attractions. Some other works focus on mining the themes of attractions to facilitate trip planning [4,9,15]. By considering the tourist topics and attraction themes, Leal *et al.* [9] propose Parallel Topic Modelling to extract information and utilize semantic similarity to identify relevant recommendation. However, majority of those methods lack of analysis of sentiment on themes of attractions. [20] proposes a user interest modeling method called LSARS to represent the user's interest. [11] designs a personalized similarity (PAS) model which utilizes the heterogeneous travel information for recommendations. This method takes sentiments of the attraction themes into consideration and uses a multi-modal data, but fails to reveal the sentiments from the tourists who actually visited them.

3 Sentiment-Aware Multi-modal Topic Model

This section introduces the proposed Sentiment-aware Multi-modal Topic Model (SMTM), which is composed of theme and sentiment mining on tourist domain, topic and sentiment mining on attraction domain, and correlation analysis between tourist and attraction topic spaces, as shown in Fig. 2.

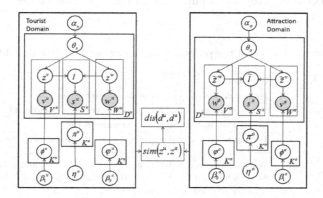

Fig. 2. Representation of sentiment-aware multi-modal topic model.

3.1 Problem Definition

Supposing that we are given a collection of tourist documents $\mathcal{U} = \{d_1^u, ..., d_{D^u}^u\}$ and a collection of attraction documents $\mathcal{A} = \{d_1^a, ..., d_{D^a}^a\}$, where $d_i^u = \{U_i^W, U_i^V, U_i^S\}$, $d_i^a = \{A_i^W, A_i^V, A_i^S\}$ are composed of three components: textual component U_i^W, A_i^W, visual component U_i^V, A_i^V, and sentiment component U_i^S, A_i^S. Table 1 lists the key notations. As discussed in Sect. 1, tourist preferences, attraction themes, and sentiments on themes of attraction are the three essential aspects for tourist attraction recommendation. We separate tourist and attraction into two domains, seek their associated theme spaces, analyze the sentiment of each topic for every tourist and attraction, and at last, find the correlation between tourist topic space and attraction theme spaces for recommendation. Thus, the problem of SMTM can be defined as follows:

Definition 1 *(Sentiment-aware Multi-modal Topic Model). Given two collections of tourists and attractions from travel websites, that is, $\mathcal{U}$ and $\mathcal{A}$, the goal of SMTM is to learn: (1) tourists topic space φ^u, ϕ^u and attraction theme space φ^a, ϕ^a; (2) corresponding sentiment space π^u and π^a; (3) the distributions of tourist domain document-topic θ^u and attraction domain document-theme θ^a; (4) the correlation between tourist and attraction topic spaces is measured by all the similarities between tourist topics and attraction themes, that is, $sim(z^u, z^a)$, for $z^u \in \{1, 2, \cdots, K^u\}$ and $z^a \in \{1, 2, \cdots, K^a\}$.*

3.2 Topic and Sentiment Mining on Tourist Domain

Topic and sentiment mining on tourist domain is to determine the preferences of each tourist. Specifically, each tourist document contains texts and images. By using our model, the textual and visual words are generated following document-topic distributions θ^u, while the sentiment words are generated from the sentiment distribution conditioned on the corresponding topics. Accordingly, the generative process of a tourist document d^u in SMTM can be described as follows.

Table 1. The key notations of the proposed sentiment-aware multi-modal topic model

Notations	Description
$\mathcal{U}, \mathcal{A}$	Tourist document set, attraction document set
D^u, D^a	Number of tourist documents and attraction documents
K^u, K^a	Number of tourist topics and attraction topics
U^W, U^V, U^S	Textual word vocabulary, visual word vocabulary and sentiment word vocabulary in tourist document set
A^W, A^V, A^S	Textual word vocabulary, visual word vocabulary and sentiment word vocabulary in attraction document set
$W^u, V^u, S^u, W^a, V^a, S^a$	Number of word in $U^W, U^V, U^S, A^W, A^V, A^S$
φ^u, ϕ^u, π^u	The multinomial distributions over textual words, visual words and sentiment words for tourist topics
φ^a, ϕ^a, π^a	The multinomial distributions over textual words, visual words and sentiment words for attraction topics
θ^u, θ^a	The multinomial distributions over topics for tourists and attractions
z^w, z^v, l	Topic assignment for textual word, visual word, and sentiment word on tourist domain
$\tilde{z}^w, \tilde{z}^v, \tilde{l}$	Topic assignment for textual word, visual word, and sentiment word on attraction domain
$\alpha^u, \alpha^a, \beta_0^u, \beta_0^a$ $\beta_1^u, \beta_1^a, \eta^u, \eta^a$	Dirichlet priors to multinomial distribution $\theta^u, \theta^a, \varphi^u, \varphi^a, \phi^u,$ ϕ^a, π^u, π^a
$\mathbf{w}_{-i}, \mathbf{z}_{-i}, \mathbf{v}_{-i}, \mathbf{s}_{-i}, \mathbf{l}_{-i}$	Vector values of $\mathbf{w}, \mathbf{z}, \mathbf{v}, \mathbf{s}, \mathbf{l}$ on all the other dimensions except i

1. For each tourist topic $z^u \in \{1, 2, \cdots, K^u\}$ including textual topic z^w and visual topic z^v, draw a multinomial distribution over topic words, $\varphi^u \sim Dir(\beta_0^u)$ and $\phi^u \sim Dir(\beta_1^u)$.
2. For each tourist topic $z^u \in \{1, 2, \cdots, K^u\}$, draw a multionmial sentiment word distribution $\pi^u \sim Dir(\eta^u)$.
3. For each document d^u:
   (a) draw a multinonmial distribution $\theta_d^u \sim Dir(\alpha^u)$ for document.
   (b) for each textual word w in document d^u: draw a topic $z_d^w \sim Multi\left(\theta_d^u\right)$, a textual word $w \sim Multi\left(\varphi_{z_d^w}^u\right)$.
   (c) for each visual word v in document d^u: draw a topic $z_d^v \sim Multi\left(\theta_d^u\right)$, a visual word $v \sim Multi\left(\phi_{z_d^v}^u\right)$.

(d) for each sentiment word s in document d^u: draw a topic assignment $l \sim Uniform\,(z_1^u, z_2^u, ..., z_{K^u}^u)$, a sentiment word $s \sim Multi\,(\pi_l^u)$.

We assume that the priors $(\alpha^u, \beta_0^u, \beta_1^u, \eta^u)$ follow symmetric Dirichlet in modeling learning process, where the symmetric Dirichlet are conjugate priors for multinomial distribution.

After modeling the tourist domain of SMTM, we use Gibbs sampling [25] for model inference. There are three sets of variables involved, that is, textual topic assignment $\mathbf{z}^w$, visual topic assignment $\mathbf{z}^v$ and sentiment distribution l. In a Gibbs sampler, one iteratively samples new assignments of latent variables by drawing from the distributions conditioned on the previous state of the model. For tourist domain of SMTM model, the update rules for latent variables are as follows.

The rule for the latent variables $\mathbf{z}^w$, $\mathbf{z}^v$ and l:

$$p(z_i^w = k^u | \mathbf{w}, \mathbf{z}_{-i}^w) \propto \frac{n_{kd,-i}^u + \alpha^u}{\sum_{k=1}^{K^u} n_{kd,-i}^u + K^u \alpha^u} \times \frac{n_{wk,-i}^u + \beta_0^u}{\sum_{w=1}^{W^u} n_{wk,-i}^u + W^u \beta_0^u} \quad (1)$$

$$p(z_i^v = k^u | \mathbf{v}, \mathbf{z}_{-i}^v) \propto \frac{n_{kd,-i}^u + \alpha^u}{\sum_{k=1}^{K^u} n_{kd,-i}^u + K^u \alpha^u} \times \frac{n_{vk,-i}^u + \beta_1^u}{\sum_{v=1}^{V^u} n_{vk,-i}^u + V^u \beta_1^u} \quad (2)$$

$$p(l_i = m^u | \mathbf{s}, \mathbf{l}_{-i}) \propto \frac{n_{sm,-i}^u + \eta^u}{\sum_{s=1}^{S^u} n_{sm,-i}^u + S^u \eta^u} \times \frac{n_{md}^u}{N_{kd}^u} \quad (3)$$

where the symbol $-i$ means a counting variable that excludes the i-th word index in the corpus. $n_{kd,-i}^u$ denotes the times of words for topic k^u being generated from document d^u except the current assignment. $n_{wk,-i}^u$ denotes the times of word w being generated from topic k^u except the current assignment. $n_{vk,-i}^u$, $n_{sm,-i}^u$, n_{md}^u, is similar. N_{kd}^u means the times of all topic words in document d^u.

After sampling, the tourist domain parameters can be estimated as follows:

$$\theta_{kd}^u = \frac{n_{kd}^u + \alpha^u}{\sum_{k=1}^{K^u} n_{kd}^u + K^u \alpha^u}, \varphi_{wk}^u = \frac{n_{wk}^u + \beta_0^u}{\sum_{w=1}^{W^u} + W^u \beta_0^u},$$

$$\phi_{vk}^u = \frac{n_{vk}^u + \beta_1^u}{\sum_{v=1}^{V^u} + V^u \beta_1^u}, \pi_{sm}^u = \frac{n_{sm}^u + \eta^u}{\sum_{s=1}^{S^u} n_{sm}^u + S^u \eta^u} \quad (4)$$

In this paper, the SentiWordNet, a popular linguistics based sentiment model, is used to set a sentimental value (between -1 and 1) to every sentiment word. The value of is closer to 1, it is more likely to be positive, otherwise to be negative. Then the sentiment score of each tourist topic is,

$$Q\,(\mathbf{z}^w, \mathbf{l}) = \frac{1}{2} \left[\sum_{w=1}^{Nwk} p\,(w|z^w = k) \cdot Q_w + \sum_{s=1}^{Nsk} p\,(s|l = k) \cdot Q_s \right] \quad (5)$$

In this equation, $Q\,(s)$ and $Q\,(w)$ are the individual sentiment scores of a word. $Q\,(\mathbf{z}_w, \mathbf{l})$ represents the overall sentiment tendency of the topic.

3.3 Theme and Sentiment Mining on Attraction Domain

Theme mining on attraction domain is to determine attraction themes, while sentiment mining is to determine sentiments on themes of attraction. Similar to those on tourist domain, we use the same process. So we just express the key formulas below. The update rules are as follows.

$$p(\tilde{z}_i^w = k^a | \mathbf{w}, \tilde{\mathbf{z}}_{-i}^w) \propto \frac{n_{kd,-i}^a + \alpha^a}{\sum_{k=1}^{K^a} n_{kd,-i}^a + K^a \alpha^a} \times \frac{n_{wk,-i}^a + \beta_0^a}{\sum_{w=1}^{W^a} n_{wk,-i}^a + W^a \beta_0^a} \quad (6)$$

$$p(\tilde{z}_i^v = k^a | \mathbf{v}, \tilde{\mathbf{z}}_{-i}^v) \propto \frac{n_{kd,-i}^a + \alpha^a}{\sum_{k=1}^{K^a} n_{kd,-i}^a + K^a \alpha^a} \times \frac{n_{vk,-i}^a + \beta_1^a}{\sum_{v=1}^{V^a} n_{vk,-i}^a + V^a \beta_1^a} \quad (7)$$

$$p(\tilde{l}_i = m^a | \mathbf{s}, \tilde{\mathbf{l}}_{-i}) \propto \frac{n_{sm,-i}^a + \eta^a}{\sum_{s=1}^{S^a} n_{sm,-i}^a + S^a \eta^a} \times \frac{n_{md}^a}{N_{kd}^a} \quad (8)$$

After sampling, the attraction domain parameters can be estimated as follows:

$$
\begin{aligned}
\theta_{kd}^a &= \frac{n_{kd}^a + \alpha^a}{\sum_{k=1}^{K^a} n_{kd}^a + K^a \alpha^a}, \varphi_{wk}^a = \frac{n_{wk}^a + \beta_0^a}{\sum_{w=1}^{W^a} + W^a \beta_0^a}, \\
\phi_{vk}^a &= \frac{n_{vk}^a + \beta_1^a}{\sum_{v=1}^{V^a} + V^a \beta_1^a}, \pi_{sm}^a = \frac{n_{sm}^a + \eta^a}{\sum_{s=1}^{S^a} n_{sm}^a + S^a \eta^a}
\end{aligned}
\quad (9)
$$

3.4 Correlation Analysis Between Tourist and Topic Space and Attraction Theme Space

To correlate tourist topic space and attraction theme space, we calculate all the similarities between tourist topics and attraction themes. Inspired by [22], we use symmetric Kullback-Leibler (KL) to measure the similarity, that is,

$$sim(z^u, z^a) = \sum_i p(i|z^u) \, log \frac{p(i|z^u)}{p(i|z^a)} + \sum_i p(i|z^a) \, log \frac{p(i|z^a)}{p(i|z^u)} \quad (10)$$

where i indexes the word which occurs in both domains.

4 Applications

In this section, we introduce how to leverage the learned SMTM to enable two interesting applications: personalized attraction recommendation and potential tourist recommendation.

4.1   Personalized Attraction Recommendation

For a tourist d_i^u and a query attraction d_i^a in $\mathcal{A} = \{d_1^a, d_2^a ..., d_n^a\}$, the topic and theme distribution $\theta_{d_i}^u$, $\theta_{d_i}^a$ and the topic and theme space $\mathbf{z}^u$, $\mathbf{z}^a$ can be obtained by model. Taking into account the sentimental factors, we use the Eq. (5) in Sect. 3.2 to learn sentiment score $Q(z)$ of a topic z. Then use it to compute sentiment binary variable q^z of topic z for further comparison recommendation using the following equation:

$$q^z = \begin{cases} 1, \text{ if } Q(z) \geq \sigma \\ 0, \text{ if } Q(z) < \sigma \end{cases} \tag{11}$$

where σ is threshold parameter. We calculate the distance between d_i^u and each document of $\mathcal{A}$ to rank the recommended attractions by following equation:

$$
\begin{aligned}
dis(d_i^u, d_i^a) &= \sum_z \sqrt{(q^z \cup q^{z'}) \times [p(z|d_i^u) - p(z'|d_i^a)]^2} \\
&= \sum_z \sqrt{(q^z \cup q^{z'}) \times \left(\theta_{d_i,z}^u - \theta_{d_i,z'}^a\right)^2}
\end{aligned}
\tag{12}
$$

Where z is the topic in $\mathbf{z}^u$. z' is a corresponding theme to z in $\mathbf{z}^a$, which is calculated by semantic similarity according to Sect. 3.4.

4.2   Potential Tourist Recommendation

Potential tourist recommendation is similar to the interest attraction recommendation. Specifically, given an attraction d_i^a and a tourists d_i^u in set $\mathcal{U} = \{d_1^u, d_2^u ..., d_n^u\}$. The theme and topic distribution $\theta_{d_i}^a$, $\theta_{d_i}^u$ and the topic and theme space $\mathbf{z}^a$, $\mathbf{z}^u$ can be learned by model. q^r and $q^{r'}$ are obtained using the method mentioned in Sect. 4.1. Then we calculate the distance between d_i^a and each tourist from $\mathcal{U}$ to rank the recommended tourists by follows:

$$dis(d_i^a, d_i^u) = \sum_r \sqrt{(q^r \cup q^{r'}) \times \left(\theta_{d_i,r}^a - \theta_{d_i,r'}^u\right)^2} \tag{13}$$

Where r is the theme in $\mathbf{z}^a$. r' is a corresponding topic to r in $\mathbf{z}^u$, which is also calculated by semantic similarity according to Sect. 3.4. The *topk* of the potential tourists is recommended to tourist attraction d_i^a .

5   Experiment

5.1   Experimental Settings

The evaluation dataset was constructed from TripAdvisor, an online travel website. We collected multi-modal data from tourist and attraction domains respectively. For tourist domain, we collected 14,648 tourists, including their comments, descriptions and images. For attraction domains, we collected 8724 attractions with at least 30 comments and 1 image. In total, we have 459,160 textual comments or descriptions, and 43,944 images in tourist domain, while 392,580 textual comments and 26,172 images in attraction domain.

For each image from both domains, we represent image visual content by SIFT-Bow feature with 968 visual words. With the assumption similar to that used in [23,25], we extract all the nouns in the documents as the textual words and the adjectives, verbs, adverbs as the sentiment words. To classify tokens into nouns, adjectives, verbs, and adverbs, we use the Part-of-Speech tagging function provided by Stanford NLP toolkits[2]. Here we set Dirichlet hyper parameters of $\alpha^u = \alpha^a = 50/K$ and $\beta_0^u = \beta_1^u = \beta_0^a = \beta_1^a = 0.02$, $\eta^u = \eta^a = 0.01$ for all the experiments.

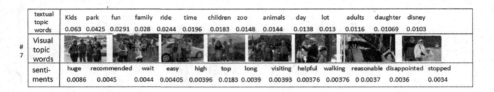

Fig. 3. Sample of topic words with corresponding sentiment words.

5.2 Evaluation of Sentiment-Aware Multi-modal Topic Model

Qualitative Analysis. We demonstrate the effectiveness of SMTM by examining the extracted topics with their sentiments and visualize them by providing the top ranked words. Both tourist and attraction domains are represented by a set of topic and theme distributions with textual words, visual words and corresponding sentiment words. Figure 3 presents a sample of topic words composed of textual words and visual words, and sentiment words, among which positive ones are in red while negative ones are in green, on tourist domain.

Figure 3 shows the partial results of the tourist domain. Here, topic #7 is about the topic "family travel", where textual words are closely related to the image patches. Sentimental words that describe the topic reflect the tourist's preferences, such as "recommended" and "disappointed".

Quantitative Evaluation. To evaluate our model, the perplexity is used as the metric. The perplexity score can be used to measure the generalization ability of a model, the lower the score is, the better capacity the topic model has. The perplexity for a set of test documents D_t is calculated as follows:

$$perplexity(D_t) = \exp - \frac{\sum_{d \in D_t} log\, p\,(\mathbf{w}_d, \mathbf{v}_d, \mathbf{o}_d)}{\sum_{d \in D_t} (N_{w,d} + N_{v,d} + N_{o,d})} \tag{14}$$

where $p\,(\mathbf{w}_d, \mathbf{v}_d, \mathbf{o}_d) = p\,(\mathbf{w}_d) + p\,(\mathbf{v}_d) + p\,(\mathbf{o}_d|\mathbf{w}_d, \mathbf{v}_d)$.

---

[2] [online]. Available http://nlp.stanford.edu/software/index.shtml.

In our experiment, the data sets are divide into two parts separately: 80% are set as the training set and the rest are set as the test set. Figure 4(a) and (b) shows the perplexity of SMTM model in different topic numbers. It can be seen that, as the number of iterations increases, the degree of perplexity decreases, and it tends to stabilize when iterating about 100 times.

The baselines include: LDA, which treats all words as topic words. multi-modal LDA(mm-LDA), which model extends LDA by considering two modality of textual and visual. Topic-Sentiment(TS), which mines topic and sentiment on single domain. Figure 4(c) and (d) show the perplexity scores of all models in both data sets. From the result we can see LDA get a highest score which means the worst ability. This is because LDA only models textual words and sentiment words but does not distinguish them. The mm-LDA and TS model get a better performance than LDA, because of the additional dependencies of visual or sentiment information. The proposed SMTM model achieves the best results than other topic models on both domains.

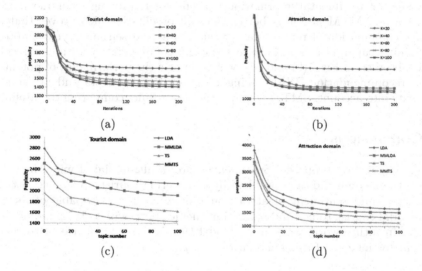

(a)   (b)

(c)   (d)

Fig. 4. Perplexity of different topic numbers and different models

5.3   Evaluation of Cross-Domain Multi-modal Recommendation

To evaluate the validity of the two recommendations, two test sets are created. 1,261 tourists who have visited at least 15 attractions are selected from all tourists. And a total of 2411 tourist destinations, which have been visited by at lease 15 tourists, are selected from all the attractions. After the model is completed, the formula obtained in Sect. 4 was used to make two recommendations. Referring to traditional search metrics, $Precision@k$ and $MAP@k$ are used to measure two recommendations.

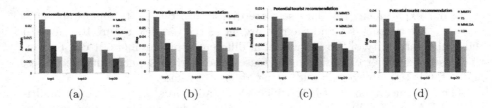

Fig. 5. Precision and MAP of two recommendations

We report the *Precision@k* and *MAP@k* for two settings when K is 5, 10 and 20. Figure 5(a) and (b) show the performance comparison for personalized travel recommendation. It can be observed that LDA performance is the worst because it lacks the ability to mine the potential relationship between multi-modal topics and sentiments. The mm-LDA and TS perform better than LDA because they capture the consistency between different modalities. This indicates that visual or sentimental information is useful for improving recommendation performance. SMTM performs better than all baselines, which proves that an effective combination of textual data, visual data, and sentiments can improve data mining capabilities and help to achieve recommendations. Similar results can be observed in Fig. 5(c) and (d), which reports the performance of potential tourist recommendation. With taking both tourists' interests and attraction' comments into account, SMTM achieves the best results comparing to baselines.

6　Conclusions

In this paper, we proposed Sentiment-aware Multi-modal Topic Model to address the recommendation problem by considering tourist preference, attraction theme, and sentiment of attraction theme. SMTM is capable of mining multi-modal tourist topics and attraction themes both with corresponding sentiments. In future work, we plan to model the shared topic space to correlate two domains instead of using similarities.

Acknowledgement. This work is supported by the National Key Research & Development Plan of China (No. 2017YFB1002800), by the National Natural Science Foundation of China under Grant 61872424, 61572503, 61720106006, 61432019, and by NUPTSF (No. NY218001), also supported by the Key Research Program of Frontier Sciences, CAS, Grant NO. QYZDJ-SSW-JSC039, and the K.C.Wong Education Foundation.

References

1. Adomavicius, G., et al.: Toward the next generation of recommender systems: a survey of the state-of-the-art and possible extensions. IEEE Trans. Knowl. Data Eng. **17**(6), 734–749 (2005)

2. Blei, D., Carin, L., Dunson, D.: Probabilistic topic models. IEEE Signal Process. Mag. **27**(6), 55–65 (2010)
3. Blei, D.M., Jordan, M.I.: Modeling annotated data. In: Proceedings of the 26th Annual International ACM SIGIR Conference on Research and Development in Information Retrieval, pp. 127–134 (2013)
4. Huang, C., Wang, Q., Yang, D., et al.: Topic mining of tourist attractions based on a seasonal context aware LDA model. Intell. Data Anal. **22**(2), 383–405 (2018)
5. Bao, B.K., Xu, C., Min, W., Hossain, M.S.: Cross-platform emerging topic detection and elaboration from multimedia streams. TOMCCAP **11**(4), 54 (2015)
6. Bao, B.-K., Liu, G., Changsheng, X., Yan, S.: Inductive robust principal component analysis. IEEE Trans. Image Process. **21**(8), 3794–3800 (2012)
7. Bao, B.-K., Zhu, G., Shen, J., Yan, S.: Robust image analysis with sparse representation on quantized visual features. IEEE Trans. Image Process. **22**(3), 860–871 (2013)
8. Borras, J., Moreno, A., Valls, A.: Intelligent tourism recommender systems: a survey. Expert Syst. Appl. **41**(16), 7370–7389 (2014)
9. Leal, F., González–Vélez, H., Malheiro, B., Burguillo, J.C.: Semantic profiling and destination recommendation based on crowd-sourced tourist reviews. Distributed Computing and Artificial Intelligence, 14th International Conference. AISC, vol. 620, pp. 140–147. Springer, Cham (2018). https://doi.org/10.1007/978-3-319-62410-5_17
10. Yang, D., Zhang, D., Yu, Z., et al.: A sentiment-enhanced personalized location recommendation system. In: ACM Conference on Hypertext and Social Media, pp. 119-128. ACM (2013)
11. Shen, J., Deng, C., Gao, X.: Attraction recommendation: towards personalized tourism via collective intelligence. Neurocomputing **173**, 789–798 (2016)
12. Kurashima, T., Iwata, T., Irie, G., Fujimura, K.: Travel route recommendation using geotags in photo sharing sites. In: Proceedings of the 19th ACM International Conference on Information and Knowledge Management, Toronto, Canada, pp. 579–588. ACM, October 2010
13. Wu, Y., Ester, M.: FLAME: a probabilistic model combining aspect based opinion mining and collaborative filtering. In: Eighth ACM International Conference on Web Search and Data Mining, pp. 199–208. ACM (2015)
14. Arbelaitz, O., Gurrutxaga, I., Lojo, A., Muguerza, J., Perez, J.M., Perona, I.: Web usage and content mining to extract knowledge for modelling the users of the Bidasoa Turismo website and to adapt it. Expert Syst. Appl. **40**(18), 7478–7491 (2013)
15. Hao, Q., et al.: Equip tourists with knowledge mined from travelogues. In: Proceedings of the 19th International Conference on World Wide Web, pp. 401–410. ACM (2010)
16. Jiang, K., Wang, P., Yu, N.: ContextRank: personalized tourism recommendation by exploiting context information of geotagged web photos. In: 2011 Sixth International Conference on Image and Graphics, Hefei, Anhui, China, pp. 931–937. IEEE, August 2011 (2011)
17. Blei, D.M., Ng, A.Y., Jordan, M.I.: Latent Dirichlet allocation. J Mach. Learn. Res. **3**, 993–1022 (2003)
18. Mei, Q., Ling, X., Wondra, M., et al.: Topic sentiment mixture: modeling facets and opinions in weblogs. In: Proceedings of the 16th International Conference on World Wide Web, pp. 171–180 (2007)

19. Fang, Q., Xu, C., Sang, J., et al.: Word-of-mouth understanding: entity-centric multimodal aspect-opinion mining in social media. IEEE Trans. Multimedia **17**(12), 2281–2296 (2015)
20. Xiong, H., Xiong, H., Xiong, H., et al.: A location-sentiment-aware recommender system for both home-town and out-of-town users, pp. 1135–1143 (2017)
21. Titov, I., McDonald, R.: A joint model of text and aspect ratings for sentiment summarization. In: ACL-08: HLT, pp. 308–316. Association for Computational Linguistics (2008)
22. Olszewski, D.: Fraud detection in telecommunications using Kullback-Leibler divergence and latent Dirichlet allocation. In: Dobnikar, A., Lotrič, U., Šter, B. (eds.) ICANNGA 2011. LNCS, vol. 6594, pp. 71–80. Springer, Heidelberg (2011). https://doi.org/10.1007/978-3-642-20267-4_8
23. Fang, Y., Si, L., Somasundaram, N. Yu, Z.: Mining contrastive opinions on political texts using cross-perspective topic model. In: Proceedings of the fifth ACM international conference on Web search and data mining, pp. 63–72. ACM (2012)
24. Lin, C., He, Y., Everson, R., et al.: Weakly supervised joint sentiment-topic detection from text. IEEE T. Knowl. Data En. **24**(6), 1134–1145 (2012)
25. Qian, S., Zhang, T., Xu, C., et al.: Multi-modal event topic model for social event analysis. IEEE Trans. Multimedia **18**(2), 233–246 (2016)
26. Huang, F., Zhang, S., Zhang, J., et al.: Multimodal learning for topic sentiment analysis in microblogging. Neurocomputing **253**(C), 144–153 (2017)
27. Alam, M.H., Ryu, W.J., Lee, S.K.: Joint multi-grain topic sentiment: modeling semantic aspects for online reviews. Inf. Sci. **339**, 206–223 (2016)
28. Min, W., Bao, B.K., Mei, S., et al.: You are what you eat: exploring rich recipe information for cross-region food analysis. IEEE Trans. Multimed. 1 (2017)

SCOD: Dynamical Spatial Constraints for Object Detection

Kai-Jun Zhang[1], Cheng-Hao Guo[2], Zhong-Han Niu[1], Lu-Fei Liu[1],
and Yu-Bin Yang[1(✉)]

[1] State Key Laboratory for Novel Software Technology, Nanjing University,
Nanjing 210023, China
yangyubin@nju.edu.cn
[2] Science and Technology on Information System Engineering Laboratory,
Nanjing 210007, China

Abstract. One-stage detectors are widely used in real-world computer vision applications nowadays due to their competitive accuracy and very fast speed. However, for high resolution (e.g., 512×512) input, most one-stage detectors run too slowly to process such images in real time. In this paper, we propose a novel one-stage detector called Dynamical Spatial Constraints for Object Detection (SCOD). We apply dynamical spatial constraints to address multiple detections of the same object and use two parallel classifiers to address the serious class imbalance. Experimental results show that SCOD makes a significant improvement in speed and achieves competitive accuracy on the challenging PASCAL VOC2007 and PASCAL VOC2012 benchmarks. On VOC2007 test, SCOD runs at 41 FPS with a mAP of 80.4%, which is 2.2× faster than SSD that runs at 19 FPS with a mAP of 79.8%. On VOC2012 test, SCOD runs at 71 FPS with a mAP of 75.4%, which is 1.8× faster than YOLOv2 that runs at 40 FPS with a mAP of 73.4%.

Keywords: Object detection · Spatial constraints · Class imbalance Non-maximum suppression

1 Introduction

Recently, we have witnessed significant improvements in the generic object detection area, thanks to the success of ImageNet classification models [1,11,12,25,27] and region proposal networks (RPN) [22]. Current state-of-the-art object detectors could divide into two branches: two-stage detectors and one-stage detectors. Compared with two-stage detectors, one-stage detectors run very fast and achieve competitive accuracy.

In more recent works of one-stage detectors, YOLO [19–21] applies a custom base network and strong spatial constraints, running very fast but at the expense of its accuracy [13]. SSD [7,17] uses multi-scale feature maps to predict objects of different scales and achieves a better speed/accuracy trade-off.

© Springer Nature Switzerland AG 2019
I. Kompatsiaris et al. (Eds.): MMM 2019, LNCS 11295, pp. 17–28, 2019.
https://doi.org/10.1007/978-3-030-05710-7_2

Because of the matching strategy [8, 17] that matches multiple default boxes to one ground-truth box, a one-stage detector must spend much time to fix multiple detections of the same object during reference. When the number of default boxes is small (e.g., 8732 in SSD300), multiple detections have slight implications on the speed of detectors. However, when we increase the resolution of the input image and simultaneously use multi-scale feature maps [16] to detect objects of different scales, a much larger set of default boxes need to be processed. Liu et al. [17] argues that we spent much time to address multiple detections, almost equaling to the total time spent on all newly added layers. For high resolution inputs, multiple detections have become the main issue that results in a sharp drop in detector speed.

Many works have been proposed to address multiple detections. Lin et al. [16] keeps at most 1k top-ranking proposals per feature pyramid level. Kong et al. [14] uses an extra objectness prior map to reduce the searching space. Redmon et al. [19] applies strong spatial constraints to fix multiple detections.

In this paper, we apply dynamical spatial constraints to address multiple detections, which is more effective than previous methods. During training, we apply dynamical spatial constraints on all class-agnostic positive boxes, select several best boxes and filter out most of the positive boxes by their confidence scores and the overlap. The remaining positive boxes have a higher confidence score and a lower overlap between them. Our method makes a significant improvement in speed without loss of accuracy. Compared with the strong spatial constraints in [19], our method has a notable advantage that can detect small objects appearing in groups, for instance, flocks of birds. After applying dynamical spatial constraints, the number of positive samples decreases by 75%, which makes the class imbalance between positive and negative samples more serious.

One-stage detectors produce a large set of default boxes while most of default boxes don't contain an object. What's more, the number of default boxes per positive category is much smaller. Previous methods often use hard example mining [6, 17, 24, 26] or focal loss [16] to address class imbalance. We encounter a more serious class imbalance. If we only use the previous method in [16, 17] to address class imbalance, we will achieve a considerably inferior accuracy. We use two parallel classifiers to mitigate the serious class imbalance. During training, we first apply a 2-class (object or not) classifier on all default boxes and then apply C-class classifier on all positive boxes to predict the specific category of each positive box. Compared with previous methods that apply a $(C + 1)$-class classifier to directly predict the specific category of each box, our method treats all positive boxes containing an object as a whole, which mitigates class imbalance and achieves better performance.

To verify the effectiveness of our method, we design a one-stage detector, called SCOD. Experimental results show that with high-resolution 512×512 input SCOD achieves 80.4% mAP and runs at 41 FPS on VOC2007 test, outperforming its counterpart SSD with a mAP of 79.8% at 19 FPS. The accuracy of our method is slightly better than SSD by 0.6% mAP. Furthermore, our method is 2.2× faster than its counterpart SSD, which is a significant improvement in the speed of high-quality detectors.

Our major contributions are summarized as follows.

- We propose SCOD, a efficient one-stage detector which applies dynamical spatial constraints to fix multiple detections of the same object, which makes a significant improvement in speed (41 FPS on VOC2007 test, vs. SSD 19 FPS).
- We introduce two parallel classifiers to address the class imbalance, which achieves better performance. (80.4% mAP on VOC2007 test, vs. SSD 79.8% mAP).
- We evaluate our method on the Pascal VOC2007 and VOC2012 datasets. Our method makes a significant improvement in speed and achieves competitive accuracy (41 FPS with a mAP of 80.4% on VOC2007 test, vs. SSD 19 FPS with a mAP of 79.8%). Compared with YOLOv2 that uses the strong spatial constraints, SCOD outperforms YOLOv2 in both speed and accuracy (71 FPS with a mAP of 75.4% on VOC2012 test, vs. YOLOv2 40 FPS with a mAP of 73.4%).

2 Related Work

R-CNN [9] is the first modern two-stage detector based on the convolutional neural network. Compared with the classic methods based on SIFT [18] or HOG [3], R-CNN uses a state-of-the-art convolutional neural network to extract features and achieves significant improvement in accuracy. After the original R-CNN, many methods are proposed to improve it. Fast R-CNN [8] speeds up R-CNN by sharing computation. Faster R-CNN [22] further improves Fast R-CNN by Region Proposal Network (RPN) that takes place of the computationally expensive approach (e.g., Selective Search or EdgeBoxes), which yields a large gain in the speed and accuracy. R-FCN [2] removes region-wise layers and shares all convolutional layers to further improve training and testing efficiency, which is 2.5–20× faster than the Faster R-CNN counterpart. Compared with the original R-CNN, two-stage detectors have achieved significant improvements in speed. However, they still run too slowly for real-time applications.

One-stage detectors [7,17,19–21], which are an order of magnitude faster than two-stage detectors, reject the region-wise subnetwork and directly predict the category and coordinates of each bounding box by a single fully convolutional network (FCN). YOLO [19–21] is one of the fastest object detectors but trades its accuracy for speed. Originated from YOLO, SSD uses a multi-scale feature maps to detect objects of different scales. SSD improve the accuracy significantly and still runs very fast. In SSD [17] and its variants [7,14,23], multiple detections are not addressed and limit their speed, especially for high-resolution inputs.

YOLO applies strong spatial constraints to address multiple detections, which divides an entire input image into a $S \times S$ grid ($S = 7$ in YOLOv1) and only selects one default box per grid cell to be responsible for the ground-truth box. The approach is a special case of Multibox [4] that selects only the

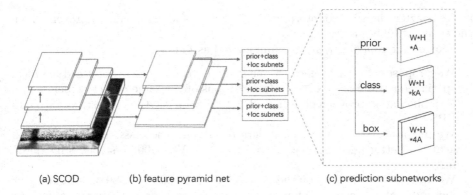

(a) SCOD   (b) feature pyramid net   (c) prediction subnetworks

Fig. 1. SCOD framework. We use VGG as its base network and attach extra convolutional layers to generate feature pyramids. Three subnetworks are in parallel to attach the end of each level of feature pyramids. One subnetwork is responsible for bounding box regression and the left two are responsible for classification.

one with maximum overlap. YOLO runs very fast but sacrifices its accuracy. What's more, YOLO has a notable drawback that it cannot detect small objects appearing in groups, for instance, flocks of birds.

Current two-stage detectors [2,10,22] use two cascade classifier: one for its Region Proposal Networks (RPN) and one for its classification subnetwork. Two-stage detectors have top accuracy but run too slowly, hard to deploy in real-time applications. One-stage detectors often use one $(C+1)$-class classifier to directly predict the positive label of each box, which makes significant improvement in speed. Based on these methods, we propose two parallel classifiers for a one-stage detector. Compared with one $(C+1)$-class classifier used in one-stage detectors, our method adds a small computational overhead and improves its accuracy.

Inspired by previous work, we design SCOD that solves multiple detections by dynamical spatial constraints and solves class imbalance by tow parallel classifiers. Our method achieves better performance.

3 SCOD

SCOD is a one-stage detector that consists of two components: a backbone network for extracting multi-scale feature maps and three task-specific subnetworks for prediction over multi-scale response maps, see Fig. 1. The three subnetworks are in parallel with each other. One subnetwork is responsible for bounding box regression, and the left two are responsible for classification. For each default box, we first predict whether it contains an object and then predict C class probabilities conditioned on the default box containing an object.

Each proposal box predicts 1 object probability $Pr(object)$, C conditional class-specific probabilities $Pr(Class_i|Object)$ and 4 offsets relative to the ground-truth box ($C = 20$ in the PASCAL VOC dataset). The object probability

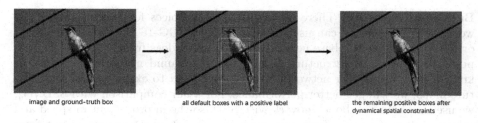

image and ground-truth box   all default boxes with a positive label   the remaining positive boxes after
                                                                                      dynamical spatial constraints

Fig. 2. Dynamical spatial constraints. Dynamical spatial constraints only select a part of positive default box to train the network, which is helpful to reduce redundant proposals. The selected boxes have a higher confidence score and a lower overlap between them.

indicates the likelihood that the proposal box contains an object. If no object exists in the proposal box, the object probability should be 0. Otherwise, it should be close to 1. During reference, we calculate the class-specific probability by $Pr(object) \times Pr(Class_i|Object)$.

Matching Strategy: During training, we need to determine the category label per default box and then train the network based on these positive and negative samples. We apply the matching strategy [17] to determine whether a default box contains an object but change its thresholds. Specifically, one default box is treated as a ground-truth box if its intersection-over-union (IoU) overlap with one ground-truth box is higher than 0.5, and a background box if its IoU overlap is lower than 0.3. If its overlap lies in [0.3, 0.5), the default box is ignored and makes no contribution to the training objective.

Dynamical Spatial Constraints: Different from Multibox [4] that selects only one default box with maximum overlap, our method matches multiple default boxes to one ground-truth box, which improves the detection accuracy but results in multiple detections of the same object. To address multiple detections, we use dynamical spatial constraints on all positive boxes and only select a part of them to train the network, see Fig. 2. We make sure that the selected boxes have a higher confidence and a lower overlap between them. In this paper, we simply apply non-maximum suppression (NMS) with a threshold of 0.5 IoU on all positive boxes, which filters out most of the positive boxes and makes the remaining positive boxes have a higher confidence score and a lower overlap. These positive boxes filtered out are ignored during training.

Two Parallel Classifiers: One-stage detectors produce a large number of default boxes while most of default boxes do not contain an object. We first use a 2-class (object or not) classifier on all default boxes and then use a C-class classifier on all positive boxes to predict the final category per default box. Compared with the methods [7, 17, 23] that directly use a $(C + 1)$-class classifier on all default boxes, our method treats all default boxes containing an object as a whole, which is helpful to mitigate the serious class imbalance and achieves better accuracy.

Backbone Network: There are many design choices for the backbone network. For example, we can use Darknet-19 [20], VGG-16 [25], ResNet-100 [11] or ResNeXt [27] as the base network. Many recent ideas from [7,14,15] are proposed to improve the structure of the feature pyramid network (FPN). As is known, if we use deeper networks and a better FPN to extract multi-scale feature maps, we will get better performance. For a fair comparison with SSD [17], we use the same backbone network with SSD, so the improvement in speed and accuracy does not come from the innovation in network frameworks but from our method of addressing multiple detections and class imbalance.

Prediction Subnetwork: Each subnetwork is a small FCN attached to each FPN level. The regression subnet applies one 3×3 conv layer with $4A$ filters, where A is the number of anchors per spatial position. The design of the two classification subnetworks is identical to the regression subnetwork, except that they end with CA and A filters per spatial position respectively.

Training Object: During training time, we optimize the following multi-task loss:

$$\lambda_{loc} \frac{1}{N_{obj}} \sum_i x_i^{obj} L_{loc}(l_i, g_i)$$

$$+ \lambda_{conf} \frac{1}{N_{obj}} \sum_i x_i^{obj} L_{conf}(c_i)$$

$$+ \lambda_{obj} \frac{1}{N_{obj}} \sum_i x_i^{obj} L_{obj}(p_i)$$

$$+ \lambda_{nobj} \frac{1}{N_{nobj}} \sum_i (1 - x_i^{obj}) L_{nobj}(p_i) \tag{1}$$

where x_i^{obj} denotes whether the i-th proposal box in a mini-batch contains an object and N_{obj} and N_{nobj} denote the number of positive samples and negative samples, respectively.

We perform a Smooth $L1$ loss L_{loc} for the bounding box regression and a Softmax loss L_{conf} for the conditional classifier, which are commonly used in modern object detectors. L_{obj} and L_{nobj} are defined as a $L2$ loss between the predictive score p and its target $\hat{p}$. If an object appears in a proposal box, its target $\hat{p}$ is 1 and 0 otherwise.

The hyper-parameters $\lambda_{loc}, \lambda_{conf}, \lambda_{obj}$ and λ_{nobj} adjust the balance among these losses. $\lambda_{loc} = 1, \lambda_{conf} = 2, \lambda_{obj} = 2$ and $\lambda_{nobj} = 2$ work best.

3.1   Training and Inference

Initialization: We apply the pre-trained SSD to initialize our backbone network. The prediction subnetworks are initialized with a Gaussian weight filling with $\sigma = 0.01$ and different biases. The initial biases of conditional classification subnetwork and regression subnetwork are set to $b = 0.05$ and

$b = 0.0$ respectively. The initial bias of object classification subnetwork is set to $b = -log((1 - \pi)/\pi)$, where π indicates that the prior probability of each proposal box containing an object is $\pi = 0.01$ at the begin of training.

Optimization: We train SCOD by stochastic gradient descent (SGD) with a weight decay of 0.0005 and a momentum of 0.9. Each mini-batch contains 16 images densely covered with default boxes of different scales and aspect ratios. We fine-tune SCOD with the initial learning rate of 10^{-3}. Proposal boxes are dominated by negative proposals. Instead of using all negative proposals, we only use a part of negative proposals so that the ratio between negative and positive proposals is at most 10:1.

Inference: Our method generates a larger number of default boxes per image, covering objects with various scales and shapes. Although our method can drastically reduce the number of proposal boxes exceeding the confidence threshold of 0.15, it is crucial to carry out non-maximum suppression (NMS) during inference. For all proposals, we first filter out most of the proposals by the class-specific probability of 0.15, then perform NMS with the IoU overlap of 0.40 per class to yield the final proposals.

4 Experimental Results

We evaluate the effectiveness of SCOD on the widely used PASCAL VOC2007 and VOC2012 [5]. Results show that SCOD achieves competitive accuracy and simultaneously makes significant improvement in speed. All object detectors are measured by mean average precision (mAP) and frame per second (FPS).

Table 1. Results on Pascal VOC2007 test. Compared to the previous methods, SCOD improve the speed dramatically and achieve better accuracy. All are trained on the union of VOC2007 trainval and VOC2012 trainval. The sign "*" denotes that the method uses data augmentation tricks for the small object.

Method	mAP	FPS	# Boxes	Input resolution
Faster R-CNN	73.2	7	~6000	~1000 × 600
RON384	75.4	15	30600	384 × 384
YOLOv2	73.7	81	605	352 × 352
YOLOv2	76.8	67	845	416 × 416
YOLOv2	78.6	40	1445	544 × 544
SSD300*	77.2	46	8732	300 × 300
SSD512*	79.8	19	24564	512 × 512
SCOD300 (ours)	78.0	71	8732	300 × 300
SCOD512 (ours)	80.4	41	24564	512 × 512

Table 2. Ablation study on Pascal VOC2007 test. DSC denotes the dynamical spatial constraints.

Method	mAP	FPS	# Boxes	Input resolution
SSD300*	77.2	46	8732	300×300
SSD300* + DSC	70.9	83	8732	300×300
SCOD (ours)	78.0	71	8732	300×300

4.1 PASCAL VOC2007

Our method is trained on the union of VOC 2007 trainval and VOC 2012 trainval. We follow the settings of SSD for default boxes and apply pre-trained SSD to initialize our network. We fine-tune our model with the initial learning rate of 10^{-3} for the first 80k iterations, 10^{-4} for the next 50k iterations, 10^{-5} for the last 30k iterations.

Table 1 shows that with 300×300 input image SCOD outperforms SSD by a margin of 0.8% mAP. When we increase the input size to 512×512, SCOD obtains 80.4% mAP which surpasses SSD by 0.6% mAP. SCOD not only yields a slight gain in accuracy but also makes a significant improvement in speed. With high resolution 512×512 input, SCOD512 is 2.2× faster than SSD512 (41 FPS vs. SSD 19 FPS). YOLOv2 [20] is one of the fastest detectors but sacrifices its accuracy. Compared with YOLOv2, our method achieves a better tradeoff between accuracy and speed. Our method runs at 71 FPS with a mAP 78.0%, surpassing YOLOv2 running at 67 FPS with a mAP 76.8%. When the accuracy of YOLOv2 exceeds 78%, it only runs at 40 FPS, much slower than our method. Our method relies on VGG-16 as its base network, which is a complex network requiring 30.69 billion operations for a single pass over a 224×224 input image. However, YOLOv2 relies on a custom network named Darknet-19, faster than VGG-16 as it uses only 8.52 billion operations for a single forward pass. If we use a faster base network, SCOD could achieve better performance in speed.

4.2 Model Analysis

To understand SCOD better, we perform controlled experiments to study how each component affects performance. Results are shown in Table 2. The standard SSD runs at 46 FPS and achieves 77.2% mAP. When combining dynamical spatial constraints with the standard SSD [17], we get a much faster speed of 83 FPS and a drastically lower mAP of 70.9%. The comparison validates that dynamical spatial constraints can significantly improve the speed. The lower accuracy may be caused by the serious class imbalance. If we add our two parallel classifiers to deal with the serious class imbalance, we achieve a faster speed of 71 FPS and a higher mAP of 78.0%, surpassing the standard SSD 46 FPS with mAP 77.2%. This comparison validates the effectiveness of our approach for dealing with the class imbalance.

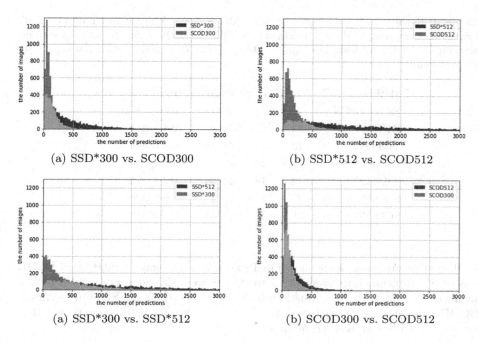

(a) SSD*300 vs. SCOD300   (b) SSD*512 vs. SCOD512

(a) SSD*300 vs. SSD*512   (b) SCOD300 vs. SCOD512

Fig. 3. Results on Pascal VOC2007 test. The number of images vs. the number of candidate proposals per image. Compared to its counterpart SSD, our method generates a smaller number of candidate proposals per image, especially for high resolution input. For SSD512, 8% of images on VOC2007 test contain at least 3000 candidate proposals and they are not shown in the plot above.

We have validated the effectiveness of dynamical spatial constraints. To understand dynamical spatial constraints better, we analysis the distribution of the number of candidate proposals per image on VOC2007 test in Fig. 3. The histograms of candidate proposals yielded by all methods have a similar shape. With low-resolution input, our method reduces the number of candidate proposals by 33% compared to SSD. With high-resolution input, our method gets better performance. Specifically, For SCOD512 80% of images contain at most 289 candidate proposals while for SSD512 images containing at most 1200 proposals only count for 62.9%. Our method greatly reduces the number of candidate proposals. Its effectiveness will increase as the input resolution increases, as shown by the experiments on the VOC2007 test.

4.3 PASCAL VOC2012

We train our models on the union of VOC2012 `trainval` and VOC2007 `trainval+test`. We fine-tune our models with the initial learning rate of 10^{-3} for the first 160k iterations, 10^{-4} for the next 100k iterations, 10^{-5} for the last 60k iterations. Other settings keep consistent with our VOC2007 experiments.

Table 3. Results on Pascal VOC2012 test. All are trained on the union of VOC2007 `trainval+test` and VOC2012 `trainval`. SCODs keep the same performance trend showing on VOC2007 test. The sign "-" denotes that this method does not supply its FPS officially.

Method	mAP	FPS	# Boxes	Input resolution
Faster R-CNN	70.4	-	~6000	~1000 × 600
RON384	73.0	15	30600	384 × 384
YOLOv2	73.4	40	1445	544 × 544
SSD300*	75.8	46	8732	300 × 300
SSD512*	78.5	19	24564	512 × 512
SCOD300 (ours)	75.4	71	8732	300 × 300
SCOD512 (ours)	78.2	41	24564	512 × 512

Experimental results are shown in Table 3. Results again validate that SCOD makes a significant improvement in speed and gets similar accuracy. SCOD512 achieves 41 FPS with 78.0% mAP, which is 2.2× faster than SSD. Furthermore, SCOD runs at 71 FPS with a mAP of 75.0%, 1.8× faster than YOLOv2 that runs at 40 FPS with a mAP of 73.4%.

5   Conclusions

We propose SCOD, a novel one-stage detector. SCOD uses dynamical spatial constraints to address multiple detections and uses two parallel classifiers to mitigate the serious class imbalance. Our method gets slightly better accuracy and simultaneously makes a significant improvement in speed. For a fair comparison with SSD, SCOD uses VGG-16 as its base network and uses FPN to detect objects of different scales. On the challenging PASCAL VOC2007 and PASCAL VOC2012 benchmarks, our method gains state-of-the-art speed and competitive accuracy, making it a better tradeoff between accuracy and speed.

Acknowledgments. This work is funded by the Natural Science Foundation of China (No. 61673204), State Grid Corporation of Science and Technology Projects (Funded No. SGLNXT00DKJS1700166).

References

1. Chollet, F.: Xception: deep learning with depthwise separable convolutions. In: Proceedings of the IEEE Conference on Computer Vision and Pattern Recognition, pp. 1800–1807. IEEE (2017)
2. Dai, J., Li, Y., He, K., Sun, J.: R-FCN: object detection via region-based fully convolutional networks. In: Advances in Neural Information Processing Systems, pp. 379–387 (2016)

3. Dalal, N., Triggs, B.: Histograms of oriented gradients for human detection. In: IEEE Computer Society Conference on Computer Vision and Pattern Recognition, CVPR 2005, vol. 1, pp. 886–893. IEEE (2005)

4. Erhan, D., Szegedy, C., Toshev, A., Anguelov, D.: Scalable object detection using deep neural networks. In: Proceedings of the IEEE Conference on Computer Vision and Pattern Recognition, pp. 2147–2154 (2014)

5. Everingham, M., Van Gool, L., Williams, C.K., Winn, J., Zisserman, A.: The PASCAL visual object classes (VOC) challenge. Int. J. Comput. Vis. **88**(2), 303–338 (2010)

6. Felzenszwalb, P.F., Girshick, R.B., McAllester, D.: Cascade object detection with deformable part models. In: 2010 IEEE Conference on Computer Vision and Pattern Recognition (CVPR), pp. 2241–2248. IEEE (2010)

7. Fu, C.Y., Liu, W., Ranga, A., Tyagi, A., Berg, A.C.: DSSD: deconvolutional single shot detector. arXiv preprint arXiv:1701.06659 (2017)

8. Girshick, R.: Fast R-CNN. In: Proceedings of the International Conference on Computer Vision (ICCV) (2015)

9. Girshick, R., Donahue, J., Darrell, T., Malik, J.: Rich feature hierarchies for accurate object detection and semantic segmentation. In: Proceedings of the IEEE Conference on Computer Vision and Pattern Recognition (CVPR) (2014)

10. He, K., Gkioxari, G., Dollár, P., Girshick, R.: Mask R-CNN. In: 2017 IEEE International Conference on Computer Vision (ICCV), pp. 2980–2988. IEEE (2017)

11. He, K., Zhang, X., Ren, S., Sun, J.: Deep residual learning for image recognition. In: Proceedings of the IEEE Conference on Computer Vision and Pattern Recognition, pp. 770–778 (2016)

12. Huang, G., Liu, Z., van der Maaten, L., Weinberger, K.Q.: Densely connected convolutional networks. In: Proceedings of the IEEE Conference on Computer Vision and Pattern Recognition (2017)

13. Huang, J., et al.: Speed/accuracy trade-offs for modern convolutional object detectors. arXiv preprint arXiv:1611.10012 (2016)

14. Kong, T., Sun, F., Yao, A., Liu, H., Lu, M., Chen, Y.: RON: reverse connection with objectness prior networks for object detection. arXiv preprint arXiv:1707.01691 (2017)

15. Lin, T.Y., Dollár, P., Girshick, R., He, K., Hariharan, B., Belongie, S.: Feature pyramid networks for object detection. In: Proceedings of the IEEE Conference on Computer Vision and Pattern Recognition (2017)

16. Lin, T.Y., Goyal, P., Girshick, R., He, K., Dollar, P.: Focal loss for dense object detection. In: Proceedings of the IEEE Conference on Computer Vision and Pattern Recognition, pp. 2980–2988 (2017)

17. Liu, W., et al.: SSD: single shot MultiBox detector. In: Leibe, B., Matas, J., Sebe, N., Welling, M. (eds.) ECCV 2016. LNCS, vol. 9905, pp. 21–37. Springer, Cham (2016). https://doi.org/10.1007/978-3-319-46448-0_2

18. Lowe, D.G.: Distinctive image features from scale-invariant keypoints. Int. J. Comput. Vis. **60**(2), 91–110 (2004)

19. Redmon, J., Divvala, S., Girshick, R., Farhadi, A.: You only look once: Unified, real-time object detection. In: Proceedings of the IEEE Conference on Computer Vision and Pattern Recognition, pp. 779–788 (2016)

20. Redmon, J., Farhadi, A.: YOLO9000: better, faster, stronger. arXiv preprint arXiv:1612.08242 (2016)

21. Redmon, J., Farhadi, A.: YOLOv3: an incremental improvement. arXiv preprint arXiv:1804.02767 (2018)

22. Ren, S., He, K., Girshick, R., Sun, J.: Faster R-CNN: towards real-time object detection with region proposal networks. In: Neural Information Processing Systems (NIPS) (2015)
23. Shen, Z., Liu, Z., Li, J., Jiang, Y.G., Chen, Y., Xue, X.: DSOD: learning deeply supervised object detectors from scratch. In: Proceedings of the IEEE Conference on Computer Vision and Pattern Recognition, pp. 1919–1927 (2017)
24. Shrivastava, A., Gupta, A., Girshick, R.: Training region-based object detectors with online hard example mining. In: Proceedings of the IEEE Conference on Computer Vision and Pattern Recognition, pp. 761–769 (2016)
25. Simonyan, K., Zisserman, A.: Very deep convolutional networks for large-scale image recognition. In: Neural Information Processing Systems (NIPS) (2015)
26. Viola, P., Jones, M.: Rapid object detection using a boosted cascade of simple features. In: Proceedings of the 2001 IEEE Computer Society Conference on Computer Vision and Pattern Recognition, CVPR 2001, vol. 1, p. I-I. IEEE (2001)
27. Xie, S., Girshick, R., Dollár, P., Tu, Z., He, K.: Aggregated residual transformations for deep neural networks. In: Proceedings of the IEEE Conference on Computer Vision and Pattern Recognition (2017)

STMP: Spatial Temporal Multi-level Proposal Network for Activity Detection

Guang Chen[1], Yuexian Zou[1,2(✉)], and Can Zhang[1]

[1] ADSPLAB, School of ECE, Peking University, Shenzhen, China
zouyx@pkusz.edu.cn
[2] Peng Cheng Laboratory, Shenzhen, China

Abstract. We propose a network for unconstrained scene activity detection called STMP to provide a deep learning method that can encode effective multi-level spatiotemporal information simultaneously and perform accurate temporal activity localization and recognition. Aiming at encoding meaningful spatial information to generate high-quality activity proposals in a fixed temporal scale, a spatial feature hierarchy is introduced in this approach. Meanwhile, to deal with various time scale activities, temporal feature hierarchy is proposed to represent activities of different temporal scales. The core component in STMP is STFH, which is a unified network implemented Spatial and Temporal Feature Hierarchy. On each level of STFH, an activity proposal detector is trained to detect activities in inherent temporal scale, which allows our STMP to make the full use of multi-level spatiotemporal information. Most importantly, STMP is a simple, fast and end-to-end trainable model due to its pure and unified framework. We evaluate STMP on two challenging activity detection datasets, and we achieve state-of-the-art results on THUMOS'14 (about 9.3% absolute improvement over the previous state-of-the-art approach R-C3D [1]) and obtains comparable results on ActivityNet1.3.

Keywords: Activity detection · Spatiotemporal feature hierarchy
Multi-level proposal detector

1 Introduction

Activity detection is a very challenging task, because it not only requires precise activity localization but also accurate classification in untrimmed videos. Current state-of-the-art activity detection approaches can be roughly divided into three categories: (1) *Regression-based approaches*. Inspired by the great success of Faster R-CNN [2] and YOLO [3] in object detection, most existing wonderful works, such as R-C3D [1] and SSAD [4], regarding activity detection as a regression problem. These methods usually contain three stages: C3D [5] as the backbone network for extracting features, following by a region proposal network for generating activity proposals, and finally a classifier is used for labeling. (2) *2D CNN based methods*. These approaches usually consist of several parts, and these parts are solved independently. Take the most successful framework for example, SSN [6] contains three separate parts, including frame-level actionness score generation, proposals generation [7] and action classification. (3) *Encoding temporal information with LSTM*, such as SST [8].

© Springer Nature Switzerland AG 2019
I. Kompatsiaris et al. (Eds.): MMM 2019, LNCS 11295, pp. 29–41, 2019.
https://doi.org/10.1007/978-3-030-05710-7_3

In this paragraph, we will make a brief analysis of advantages and disadvantages of the above methods. Regression-based approaches are end-to-end trainable frameworks. However, these methods lose spatial information and are not suitable for multi-scale activity scenarios (activities with various temporal durations). Because they down sample the spatial resolution to 1×1 and detect activity instances in a fixed temporal resolution. 2D CNN based approaches learn deep and effective representation of spatial information by utilizing hand-crafted features [8, 9] or deep features (*e.g.* VGG [10] and ResNet [11]). Unfortunately, these approaches are the framework of multi-stages and learned separately on image/video classification tasks. Such off-the-shelf representations may not be optimal for detecting activities in diverse video domains. From the results of existing experiments, 2D CNN based methods usually achieves better performance, owing to its good representation of spatial information.

Based on the above analysis, we propose a fast, end-to-end trainable network, named Spatial Temporal Multi-level Proposal Network (STMP). In our approach, a spatiotemporal feature hierarchy network is introduced to extract multi-level spatiotemporal features. For multi-level spatiotemporal features, a multi-level activity proposal detector network is designed to handle different temporal scale activities.

We summarize our contributions as follows:

(1) To learn the effective representation of spatial information, Spatial Multi-level Proposal (SMP) network with spatial feature hierarchy and multi-level proposal detector is introduced.
(2) To deal with various time scale activities, we add a temporal feature hierarchy in SMP, which is called STMP. This capacitate our model to represent multi-level spatiotemporal information simultaneously.
(3) Our STMP model achieves the state-of-the-art results on THUMOS'14 and obtains comparable results on ActivityNet1.3.

2 Related Work

2.1 Action Recognition

Action recognition is a core computer vision task that has been studied for decades. Just as image classification network can be used in object detection, action recognition models can be used in activity detection for feature extraction. Before the breakthrough of deep learning, Improved Dense Trajectories (iDT) [9] achieves remarkable performance by using SIFT and optical flow to eliminate the influence of camera motion. Later, two-stream network [12, 13] is proposed to learn both spatial and temporal features with single frame and stacked optical flows using 2D CNN [10, 11]. Although these methods achieve higher accuracy, they are extremely time-consuming and difficult to transform to end-to-end activity detection frameworks. Other approaches try to capture spatiotemporal information directly from raw video frames with 3D convolution, e.g. C3D and P3D [14]. These methods are very efficient and can be trained end-to-end. Therefore, we adopt C3D as our backbone network.

2.2   Object Detection

Object detection is a major breakthrough of deep learning in computer visions. There are two mainstream methods. Faster R-CNN [2] and its variants are typically "detection by classification" framework, which can be categorized as proposal-based methods. Proposal-free methods like SSD [15] make the most of multi-level spatial information in order to detect different scale objects. Compared to SSD, Faster R-CNN achieves better performance due to its high quality proposals.

The consensus of all these methods is to detect objects via regression, owing to the prior knowledge that each type of object has their own size and aspect ratio. This is also the maximum commonality with temporal activity detection. Each type of activity usually has its own duration, for example, drinking water usually lasts 10 s, rather than 10 min or more. This prior knowledge allows us to detect activities through the methods of object detection.

2.3   Temporal Activity Detection

This task needs to locate when and which type of activity happens in untrimmed diverse videos. Typical datasets such as THUMOS'14 [16] and ActivityNet [17] including thousands untrimmed videos and tens thousands of activity instances with various duration scales.

RNN and its variants are widely used in temporal activity detection [18–21]. Although these methods are successfully used in natural language processing, e.g. machine translation, they are not applicable to activity detection because they do not maintain long-term memory in practice [19]. Furthermore, textual information is regular and predictable, which is completely different with video temporal information.

Aside from approaches related to RNN, many researches adopt "detection by classification" framework. For example, S-CNN [22] separates the whole work into three stages: candidate segment generation, action classification and temporal boundary refinement. SSN [6] is also a multi-stage framework, containing frame-level actionness scores generation, candidate segments generation and action recognition. These discrete frameworks are often very difficult to train. Recently, an end-to-end trainable network named R-C3D [1] was proposed. It is a representative approach to detect activity via Faster R-CNN framework. Similar to R-C3D, we adopt Faster R-CNN framework and generate activity proposals from multi-level spatiotemporal feature maps. Compared with R-C3D, our model not only can encode effective spatiotemporal information, but also has better robustness for different temporal scale activities.

3   Our Approach

In this section, we will elaborate on our Spatial Temporal Multi-level Proposal (STMP) network. The framework of our approach is shown in Fig. 1, consisting of four components: a shared 3D ConvNet feature extractor as backbone network, spatiotemporal feature hierarchy network, multi-level proposal detector and classification network. More details of each component are shown as following.

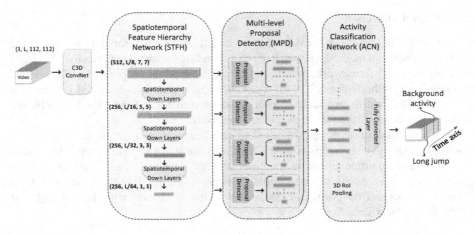

Fig. 1. Our STMP architecture. The C3D ConvNet is the backbone network and is used to extract spatiotemporal features from raw video frames. The spatiotemporal feature hierarchy is created for extracting hierarchical spatiotemporal features. On each level of the spatiotemporal feature hierarchy, an activity proposal detector is learned to detect candidate activity segments in a fixed temporal scale. These candidate segments are stacked and fed into a shared activity classification subnet, which outputs activity categories and refines temporal boundaries.

3.1 Backbone Network

We adopt the `conv1a` to `conv5b` layers from C3D ConvNet as backbone network for extracting spatiotemporal features. The input of 3D ConvNet is a sequence of RGB video frames with dimension $\mathbb{R}^{3 \times L \times H \times W}$. The output is the feature maps $C_{conv5b} \in \mathbb{R}^{512 \times \frac{L}{8} \times \frac{H}{16} \times \frac{W}{16}}$ (512 is the channel dimension), which is the shared input to spatiotemporal feature hierarchy and classification subnet. The number of input frames L can be arbitrary and is only limited by GPU memory. Typically, the height (H) and width (W) of the video frames are taken as 112.

Training: We pre-train the C3D network [5] on UCF101 [23].

3.2 Spatiotemporal Feature Hierarchy

In the unconstrained environment, activities in videos have various temporal scales. Besides, because of the movement of camera or object, the interest object in video often present different scales with time. Nevertheless, current mainstream solutions (*e.g.* [1, 6]) completely ignore these two facts. R-C3D down-samples spatial resolutions to 1×1, and utilizes a fixed temporal length feature for activity detection. SSN connects small basins into proposal regions by watershed algorithm.

In contrast, we introduce a network called Spatiotemporal Feature Hierarchy (STFH) that can encode multi-level spatiotemporal information simultaneously. As shown in Fig. 1, STFH takes `conv5b` feature maps as input, and outputs four hierarchical spatiotemporal feature maps. The spatial resolution of `conv5b` feature maps in the C3D ConNet is 7×7, and the temporal stride is 8. To learn hierarchical spatial features, we add three branches with spatial feature maps size of 5×5, 3×3 and 1×1. Meanwhile, in order to detect activities of longer durations, we add three branches with temporal strides of 16, 32 and 64. Thus, there are 4 levels of the spatiotemporal feature hierarchy, each feature map $C_{stfh} \in \mathbb{R}^{256 \times \frac{L}{L_l} \times S_s}$, $L_l \in \{8, 16, 32, 64\}$, $S_s \in \{7 \times 7, 5 \times 5, 3 \times 3, 1 \times 1\}$.

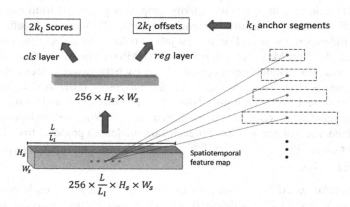

Fig. 2. A proposal detector consists of two ConvNet with kernel of size $1 \times H_s \times W_s$ and filters of $2k_l$ (one for classification, the other for regression).

3.3 Multi-level Proposal Detector

Inspired by SSD [15], a proposal detector is learned to generate high quality activity proposals for each level of spatiotemporal feature hierarchy. Similar to the RPN of Faster R-CNN, the anchor segments are pre-defined multi-scale windows centered at L/L_l uniformly distributed temporal locations. Whereby $L_l \in \{8, 16, 32, 64\}$, indicates 4 level temporal scales. Each temporal location specifies $K_l (l \in \{1, 2, 3, 4\})$ anchor segments. Thus, the total number of pre-defined anchor segments is $\sum_{l=1}^{4} K_l * \frac{L}{L_l}$.

As illustrated in Fig. 2, the $256 \times H_s \times W_s$ feature at each temporal location in C_{stfh} is fed into two sibling fully-connected layers: a segment-regression layer (*reg*) and a segment-classification (*cls*). Because the fully-connected layers are shared across all temporal locations, each proposal detector is naturally implemented with two sibling $1 \times H_s \times W_s$ convolutional layers. The first convolution layer is used to predict proposal score (background or activity), the second is used to predict a relative offset $\{\delta c_i, \delta l_i\}$ to the center location and the length of each anchor segment $\{c_i, l_i\}$, $i \in \{1, 2, ..., K_l\}$.

Training: Each level of spatiotemporal feature hierarchy and its corresponding proposal detector are considered an activity proposal network (APN). Typically, for training each APN, we assign a binary class label (of being an object or not) to each anchor segment. We assign an anchor segment with a positive label if it has the highest Temporal Intersection-over-Union (tIoU) for a given ground-truth activity or it has a tIoU higher than 0.7 with any ground-truth activity. If the anchor segment has tIoU overlap lower than 0.3 with all ground-truth activities, given a negative label. We sample balanced batches with a positive/negative ratio of 1:1.

3.4   Activity Classification Network

Our STMP is a typical "detection by classification" network. Therefore, ACN have two main jobs: (1) Selecting high quality activity proposals generated from every feature map and getting fixed-size features for each proposal. (2) Activity classification and temporal boundaries refinement. For the first job, similar to the object detection [2], we employ a greedy Non-Maximum Suppression (NMS) strategy to eliminate highly overlapping and low confidence proposals from each proposal detector (the NMS threshold is set as 0.7). Then, we stack all the proposals (after NMS) from every proposal detector and employ a highly NMS thresh (such as 0.9 or 0.999). After that, following the standard practice in activity detection, a 3D RoI pooling layer is used to extract the fixed-size volume features for each variable-length proposal from the shared convolution features $C_{conv5b} \in \mathbb{R}^{512 \times \frac{L}{8} \times \frac{H}{16} \times \frac{W}{16}}$. For the second job, we design two simple full-connected layers.

Training: Similar to APN, we need to assign activity labels to each proposal for training the classifier. Our tIoU thresh is set to 0.5, that means we assign an anchor segment with an activity (positive) label if it has the highest tIoU for a given ground-truth activity or it has a tIoU higher than 0.5 with any ground-truth activity. If the anchor segment has tIoU overlap lower than 0.5 with all ground-truth activities, given a background (negative) label. We sample balanced batches with an activity/background ratio of 1:3. And, the batch size is set to 64.

3.5   Loss Function

For each activity proposal network (there are 4 APN), softmax loss is used for classification (activity or not), and smooth L1 loss is used for regression. Specifically, our loss function for an APN is defined as:

$$L(\{a_i\}, \{t_i\}) = \frac{1}{N_{cls}} \sum_i L_{cls}(a_i, a_i^*) + \lambda \frac{1}{N_{reg}} \sum_i a_i^* L_{reg}(t_i, t_i^*) \tag{1}$$

Here, i is the index of an anchor segment in a batch and a_i is the predicted probability of anchor segment i being an activity. The ground-truth label a_i^* is 1 if the anchor segment is positive, and is 0 if the anchor segment is negative. $t_i = \left\{ \delta\widehat{c_i}, \delta\widehat{l_i} \right\}$ is the predicted relative offset to anchor segments. $t_i^* = \{\delta c_i, \delta l_i\}$ is the coordinate transformation of ground-truth segments to anchor segments. λ is the loss trade-off parameter. By default, we set $\lambda = 5$, and thus both cls and reg terms are roughly equally weighted.

Above is the single loss for a subnet. In our approach, there are 4 sub activity proposal network (APN) and one activity classification network (ACN). Thus, our joint loss function for a video is defined as:

$$\text{Loss} = \sum_{k=1}^{K} \gamma_k L(\{a_{ki}\}, \{t_{ki}\}) \tag{2}$$

Where K is the number of subnets (here is 5). γ_k balances the importance of models at different branch, here is set to 1 for each γ.

4 Experiments and Analysis

For studying the influence of multi-level spatial information on detection, we add an experiment (SMP) with temporal stride of each layer in STFH as 8. SMP denotes Spatial Multi-level Proposal network. We evaluate SMP and STMP on two challenging activity detection datasets: THUMOS'14 [16] and ActivityNet1.3 [17]. For both datasets, Average Precision (AP) and mean AP (mAP) are adopt for evaluation. More details are introduced from the following aspects: (1) implementation details of two experiments. (2) Experimental settings and evaluation on these public benchmarks.

4.1 Implementation Details

Experiments Settings. Table 1 shows the APN architecture (Spatiotemporal Feature Hierarchy and Multi-level Proposal Detector) of SMP and STMP. Here, each term of STFH and MPD denote the kernel size and filters of the convolutional layer.

Table 1. APNs architecture of SMP and STMP

#	Layer name	Output size	STFH	MPD
	Conv5b	$512 \times L/8 \times 7 \times 7$		$1 \times 7 \times 7, 2k$
SMP	APN_conv1_x	$256 \times L/8 \times 5 \times 5$	$1 \times 1 \times 1, 256$ $3 \times 3 \times 3, 256$	$1 \times 5 \times 5, 2k$
	APN_conv2_x	$256 \times L/8 \times 3 \times 3$	$3 \times 3 \times 3, 256$	$1 \times 3 \times 3, 2k$
	APN_conv3_x	$256 \times L/8 \times 1 \times 1$	$3 \times 3 \times 3, 256$	$1 \times 1 \times 1, 2k$
STMP	APN_conv1_x	$256 \times L/16 \times 5 \times 5$	$1 \times 1 \times 1, 256$ $3 \times 3 \times 3, 256$	$1 \times 5 \times 5, 2k$
	APN_conv2_x	$256 \times L/32 \times 3 \times 3$	$3 \times 3 \times 3, 256$	$1 \times 3 \times 3, 2k$
	APN_conv3_x	$256 \times L/64 \times 1 \times 1$	$3 \times 3 \times 3, 256$	$1 \times 1 \times 1, 2k$

Training Setup. We create a video buffer of 512 frames for THUMOS'14 and 768 frames for ActivityNet1.3, each frame in a video is resized to 172×128 (width $\times$ height) pixels, and we randomly crop regions of 112×112 from each frame. These buffers of frames act as input, and are generated by a sliding window.

Hyper-parameters. The weights of the filters of ACN and APNs are initialized by randomly drawing from a zero-mean Gaussian distribution with standard deviation 0.01. Biases are set to 0.1. All other layers are initialized from C3D model pre-trained on UCF-101. SGD algorithm with a momentum of 0.9 and a weight decay of 5×10^{-4} was adopted to train our model. Most importantly, we divided the whole network into two parts: backbone network and the rest (APNs and ACN), and take turns training the two parts alternately. The learning rate is initially set to 10^{-4} and then reduced by a factor of 10 after every 80k.

4.2   Experiments on THUMOS'14

THUMOS'14 is a widely used benchmark. The training set is the UCF-101 [23] dataset including 13320 trimmed videos of 101 categories while the validation and the test sets contain 200 and 213 untrimmed videos. In our experiments, all 200 videos are used as the training set and the results are reported on 213 test videos.

Experiments Setup. Since the GPU memory is limited, we create a video buffer of 512 frames and sample the frames at 25 fps to fit it in the GPU memory. As shown in Table 2, the number of anchor segments K in each level of STFH chosen for SMP (STMP) is 26 (7) with scale range 1:56 (1:7, 3:8, 4:8, 4:8). At 25 fps, the anchor segments of SMP (STMP) correspond to segments of duration between 0.64 and 17.92 s ([0.32, 2.24), [1.92, 5.12), [5.12, 10.24), [10.24, 17.92)).

Table 2. Anchor segments settings on THUMOS'14 for SMP and STMP.

Layer name	SMP		STMP		
	Strides	Anchor segments scale	Strides	Anchor segments scale	Temporal scale ranges
Conv5b	8	1:56	8	1:7	8–56
APN_conv1_x	8	1:56	16	3:8	48–128
APN_conv2_x	8	1:56	32	4:8	128–256
APN_conv3_x	8	1:56	64	4:8	256–512

Results. In Table 3, we present a superior activity detection performance of our SMP and STMP with existing state-of-the-art approaches. Our SMP (STMP) model shows about 8.4% (9.3%) absolute improvement @mAP 0.5 over R-C3D model, which clearly confirm that our model can encode effective spatiotemporal information simultaneously. Moreover, in Table 4, we present the Average Precision (AP) for each class in THUMOS'14 at tIoU threshold 0.5. Our STMP outperforms all the methods in most classes and achieves significant improvement (by more than 10% absolute AP over the R-C3D) for activities *e.g.* Crick Bowling, High Jump, Long Jump and Volleyball Spiking, which indicates the robustness of our model to multi-scale activities.

4.3 Experiments on ActivityNet

ActivityNet [17] is a recently released large-scale activity detection benchmark. We use the latest release (1.3) which has 10024, 4029 and 5044 videos containing 200 different types of activities in the training, validation and test respectively. Compared to THUMOS'14, ActivityNet1.3 is a large-scale dataset with longer activity instances and more classes.

Experimental Setup. Considering the long duration of activity instances of ActivityNet1.3, we create a video buffer of 768 frames and sample the frames at 3 fps to fit the GPU memory. The duration of the buffer is approximately 256 s covering 99.99% training activities. Similar to THUMOS'14, Table 5 shows the anchor segments settings on ActivityNet1.3.

Table 3. Activity detection results on THUMOS'14 test dataset (in percentage), measured by the mean average precision (mAP) of different tIoU thresholds α.

Method	α				
	0.1	0.2	0.3	0.4	0.5
Oneata et al. [24]	36.6	33.6	27.0	20.8	14.4
Richard et al. [25]	39.7	35.7	30.0	23.2	15.2
Yeung et al. [20]	48.9	44.0	36.0	26.4	17.1
Yuan et al. [21]	51.4	42.6	33.6	26.1	18.8
S-CNN [22]	47.7	43.5	36.3	28.7	19.0
CDC [26]	–	–	40.1	29.4	23.3
SSAD [4]	50.1	47.8	43.0	35.0	24.6
TCN [27]	–	–	–	33.3	25.6
R-C3D [1]	54.5	51.5	44.8	35.6	28.9
SSN [6]	**66.0**	59.4	51.9	41.0	29.8
SMP (ours)	60.4	58.8	55.7	48.7	37.3
STMP (ours)	62.5	**60.8**	**56.9**	**50.5**	**38.2**

Results. The comparison results between our SMP/STMP and other state-of-the-art methods [1, 19, 28, 29] published recently are shown in Table 6. Our SMP and STMP model achieve a significant improvement (about 2.8% and 3.5% absolute improvement in the average mAP of tIoU thresholds from 0.5:0.05:0.95) over R-C3D [1], which demonstrates the effectiveness of our method. Our STMP shows inferior performance over MSN [19], which using a deeper two-stream (RGB and optical flow) network. However, C3D is a simple 3D ConvNet, only uses low resolution RGB information. In Table 7, we compare detection speed of our model with R-C3D and two other state-of-the-art methods. S-CNN is similar to MSN and uses two-stream network to extract features. Despite the comparable results on ActivityNet1.3, our model is dozens of times faster than other framework (about 16x faster than S-CNN and 7x faster than DAP), which demonstrates the great potential of our model in future applications. Furthermore, our backbone network is relatively independent and can be replaced by other action recognition networks, e.g. I3D or P3D.

Table 4. Per-class AP at tIoU threshold α = 0.5 on THUMOS'14 test dataset (in percentage)

	[24]	[20]	[21]	R-C3D	SMP (ours)	STMP (ours)
Baseball pitch	8.6	14.6	14.9	**26.1**	16.8	25.7
Basketball dunk	1.0	6.3	20.1	54.0	**56.1**	55.3
Billiards	2.6	9.4	7.6	8.3	20.6	**23.9**
Clean and Jerk	13.3	**42.8**	24.8	27.9	35.5	30.4
Cliff diving	17.7	15.6	27.5	49.2	52.2	**57.1**
Crick bowling	9.5	10.8	15.7	30.6	42.2	**44.9**
Cricket shot	2.6	3.5	13.8	10.9	**21.0**	**21.0**
Diving	4.6	10.8	17.6	26.2	28.1	**29.4**
Frisbee catch	1.2	10.4	15.3	20.1	19.6	**21.3**
Golf swing	**22.6**	13.8	18.2	16.1	18.4	15.3
Hammer throw	34.7	28.9	19.1	43.2	45.9	**51.8**
High jump	17.6	33.3	20.0	30.9	46.3	**48.8**
Javelin throw	22.0	20.4	18.2	47.0	63.9	**66.7**
Long jump	47.6	39.0	34.8	57.4	72.8	**74.8**
Pole vault	19.6	16.3	32.1	42.7	**48.2**	44.2
Shotput	11.9	16.6	12.1	19.4	34.0	**35.1**
Soccer penalty	8.7	8.3	19.2	15.8	**32.4**	25.2
Tennis swing	3.0	5.6	19.3	16.6	23.4	**23.9**
Throw discus	36.2	29.5	24.4	29.2	**44.9**	42.3
Volleyball spiking	1.4	5.2	4.6	5.6	23.7	**25.6**
mAP@0.5	14.4	17.1	19.0	28.9	37.3	**38.2**

Table 5. Anchor segments settings on ActivityNet1.3 for SMP and STMP

Layer name	SMP		STMP		
	Strides	Anchor segments scale	Strides	Anchor segments scale	Temporal scale ranges
Conv5b	8	1:64	8	1:16	8–128
APN_conv1_x	8	1:64	16	8:12	128–192
APN_conv2_x	8	1:64	32	6:8	192–256
APN_conv3_x	8	1:64	64	4:8	256–512

Table 6. Activity detection results on ActivityNet1.3 validation dataset. The performance are measured by mean average precision (mAP) at different tIoU thresholds α and the average mAP of tIoU thresholds from 0.5:0.05:0.95.

Method	α			
	0.5	0.75	0.95	Average
UPC [28]	22.5	–	–	–
R-C3D [1]	26.45	11.47	1.69	13.3
Wang et al. [29]	**42.48**	2.88	0.06	14.62
MSN [19]	28.67	**17.78**	**2.88**	**17.68**
SMP (ours)	27.30	14.70	1.45	15.10
STMP (ours)	34.23	13.96	2.40	16.88

Table 7. Activity detection speed during inference.

Methods	FPS
S-CNN [22]	60
DAP [30]	134.1
R-C3D (Titan X Pascal)	**1030**
SMP (ours on Titan X Pascal)	719
STMP (ours on Titan X Pascal)	972

5 Conclusion

In this paper, we propose a spatial temporal multi-level proposal (STMP) network for activity detection. We evaluate our approach on two benchmark datasets: THUMOS'14 and ActivityNet1.3. Experimental results demonstrate that STMP outperforms other approaches in terms of detection and computation on THUMOS'14. However, our method is superior to R-C3D on ActivityNet1.3, but inferior to MSN because C3D and 3D RoI pooling cannot encode long-term spatiotemporal information. Our future research will focus on developing a better video representation network for improving the performance of detecting on large multi-scale activities.

Acknowledgement. This paper was partially supported by the Shenzhen Science & Technology Fundamental Research Program (No: JCYJ20160330095814461) & Shenzhen Key Laboratory for Intelligent Multimedia and Virtual Reality (ZDSYS201703031405467). Special acknowledgements are given to Aoto-PKUSZ Joint Research Center of Artificial Intelligence on Scene Cognition & Technology Innovation for its support.

References

1. Xu, H., Das, A., Saenko, K.: R-C3D: Region convolutional 3D network for temporal activity detection. In: The IEEE International Conference on Computer Vision (ICCV), p. 8. (2017)
2. Girshick, R.: Fast R-CNN. arXiv preprint arXiv:1504.08083 (2015)
3. Redmon, J., Divvala, S., Girshick, R., Farhadi, A.: You only look once: unified, real-time object detection. In: Proceedings of the IEEE Conference on Computer Vision and Pattern Recognition, pp. 779–788 (2016)
4. Lin, T., Zhao, X., Shou, Z.: Single shot temporal action detection. In: Proceedings of the 2017 ACM on Multimedia Conference, pp. 988–996. ACM (2017)
5. Tran, D., Bourdev, L., Fergus, R., Torresani, L., Paluri, M.: Learning spatiotemporal features with 3D convolutional networks. In: 2015 IEEE International Conference on Computer Vision (ICCV), pp. 4489–4497. IEEE (2015)
6. Zhao, Y., Xiong, Y., Wang, L., Wu, Z., Tang, X., Lin, D.: Temporal action detection with structured segment networks. In: The IEEE International Conference on Computer Vision (ICCV) (2017)
7. Roerdink, J.B., Meijster, A.: The watershed transform: definitions, algorithms and parallelization strategies. Fundamenta informaticae **41**, 187–228 (2000)

8. Buch, S., Escorcia, V., Shen, C., Ghanem, B., Niebles, J.C.: SST: Single-stream temporal action proposals. In: 2017 IEEE Conference on Computer Vision and Pattern Recognition (CVPR), pp. 6373–6382. IEEE (2017)

9. Wang, H., Schmid, C.: Action recognition with improved trajectories. In: 2013 IEEE International Conference on Computer Vision (ICCV), pp. 3551–3558. IEEE (2013)

10. Simonyan, K., Zisserman, A.: Very deep convolutional networks for large-scale image recognition. arXiv preprint arXiv:1409.1556 (2014)

11. He, K., Zhang, X., Ren, S., Sun, J.: Deep residual learning for image recognition. In: Proceedings of the IEEE Conference on Computer Vision and Pattern Recognition, pp. 770–778 (2016)

12. Feichtenhofer, C., Pinz, A., Wildes, R.P.: Spatiotemporal multiplier networks for video action recognition. In: 2017 IEEE Conference on Computer Vision and Pattern Recognition (CVPR), pp. 7445–7454. IEEE (2017)

13. Simonyan, K., Zisserman, A.: Two-stream convolutional networks for action recognition in videos. In: Advances in Neural Information Processing Systems, pp. 568–576 (2014)

14. Qiu, Z., Yao, T., Mei, T.: Learning spatio-temporal representation with pseudo-3D residual networks. In: 2017 IEEE International Conference on Computer Vision (ICCV), pp. 5534–5542. IEEE (2017)

15. Liu, W., et al.: SSD: single shot multibox detector. In: Leibe, B., Matas, J., Sebe, N., Welling, M. (eds.) ECCV 2016. LNCS, vol. 9905, pp. 21–37. Springer, Cham (2016). https://doi.org/10.1007/978-3-319-46448-0_2

16. Jiang, Y., et al.: THUMOS challenge: action recognition with a large number of classes (2014)

17. Caba Heilbron, F., Escorcia, V., Ghanem, B., Carlos Niebles, J.: ActivityNet: a large-scale video benchmark for human activity understanding. In: Proceedings of the IEEE Conference on Computer Vision and Pattern Recognition, pp. 961–970 (2015)

18. Ma, S., Sigal, L., Sclaroff, S.: Learning activity progression in LSTMs for activity detection and early detection. In: Proceedings of the IEEE Conference on Computer Vision and Pattern Recognition, pp. 1942–1950 (2016)

19. Singh, B., Marks, T.K., Jones, M., Tuzel, O., Shao, M.: A multi-stream bi-directional recurrent neural network for fine-grained action detection. In: 2016 IEEE Conference on Computer Vision and Pattern Recognition (CVPR), pp. 1961–1970. IEEE (2016)

20. Yeung, S., Russakovsky, O., Mori, G., Fei-Fei, L.: End-to-end learning of action detection from frame glimpses in videos. In: Proceedings of the IEEE Conference on Computer Vision and Pattern Recognition, pp. 2678–2687 (2016)

21. Yuan, J., Ni, B., Yang, X., Kassim, A.A.: Temporal action localization with pyramid of score distribution features. In: Proceedings of the IEEE Conference on Computer Vision and Pattern Recognition, pp. 3093–3102 (2016)

22. Shou, Z., Wang, D., Chang, S.-F.: Temporal action localization in untrimmed videos via multi-stage CNNs. In: Proceedings of the IEEE Conference on Computer Vision and Pattern Recognition, pp. 1049–1058 (2016)

23. Soomro, K., Zamir, A.R., Shah, M.: UCF101: a dataset of 101 human actions classes from videos in the wild. arXiv preprint arXiv:1212.0402 (2012)

24. Oneata, D., Verbeek, J., Schmid, C.: The LEAR submission at Thumos 2014 (2014)

25. Richard, A., Gall, J.: Temporal action detection using a statistical language model. In: Proceedings of the IEEE Conference on Computer Vision and Pattern Recognition, pp. 3131–3140 (2016)

26. Shou, Z., Chan, J., Zareian, A., Miyazawa, K., Chang, S.-F.: CDC: convolutional-de-convolutional networks for precise temporal action localization in untrimmed videos. In: 2017 IEEE Conference on Computer Vision and Pattern Recognition (CVPR), pp. 1417–1426. IEEE (2017)
27. Dai, X., Singh, B., Zhang, G., Davis, L.S., Chen, Y.Q.: Temporal context network for activity localization in videos. In: 2017 IEEE International Conference on Computer Vision (ICCV), pp. 5727–5736. IEEE (2017)
28. Montes, A., Salvador, A., Pascual, S., Giro-i-Nieto, X.: Temporal activity detection in untrimmed videos with recurrent neural networks. arXiv preprint arXiv:1608.08128 (2016)
29. Wang, R., Tao, D.: UTS at activitynet 2016. AcitivityNet Large Scale Activity Recognition Challenge 2016, 8 (2016)
30. Escorcia, V., Caba Heilbron, F., Niebles, J.C., Ghanem, B.: DAPs: deep action proposals for action understanding. In: Leibe, B., Matas, J., Sebe, N., Welling, M. (eds.) ECCV 2016. LNCS, vol. 9907, pp. 768–784. Springer, Cham (2016). https://doi.org/10.1007/978-3-319-46487-9_47

Hierarchical Vision-Language Alignment for Video Captioning

Junchao Zhang and Yuxin Peng[✉]

Institute of Computer Science and Technology, Peking University, Beijing, China
pengyuxin@pku.edu.cn

Abstract. We have witnessed promising advances on video captioning in recent years, which is a challenging task since it is hard to capture the semantic correspondences between visual content and language
descriptions. Different granularities of language components (e.g. words,
phrases and sentences), are corresponding to different granularities of
visual elements (e.g. objects, visual relations and interested regions).
These correspondences can provide multi-level alignments and complementary information for transforming visual content to language descriptions. Therefore, we propose an Attention Guided Hierarchical Alignment
(AGHA) approach for video captioning. In the proposed approach, *hierarchical vision-language alignments*, including **object-word**, **relation-
phrase**, and **region-sentence alignments**, are extracted from a well-
learned model that suits for multiple tasks related to vision and language, which are then embedded into parallel encoder-decoder streams
to provide multi-level semantic guidance and rich complementarities on
description generation. Besides, *multi-granularity visual features* are also
exploited to obtain the coarse-to-fine understanding on complex video
content, where an attention mechanism is applied to extract comprehensive visual discrimination to enhance video captioning. Experimental
results on widely-used dataset MSVD demonstrate that AGHA achieves
promising improvement on popular evaluation metrics.

Keywords: Video captioning · Hierarchical vision-language alignment
Multi-granularity

1 Introduction

Video captioning aims to generate natural language descriptions for video
content automatically, which has become an attractive research topic with
widespread practical applications, such as video retrieval and assisting the
visually-impaired. Recent years have witnessed its advances [1–4] with the development of deep learning. Inspired by the recent advances in machine translation
[5], most works take the encoder-decoder structures with recurrent neural networks (RNNs), to directly generate sentences from the video content.

As a complex media, video conveys diverse and dynamic information in both
spatial and temporal dimensions, and different frame regions and time segments

© Springer Nature Switzerland AG 2019
I. Kompatsiaris et al. (Eds.): MMM 2019, LNCS 11295, pp. 42–54, 2019.
https://doi.org/10.1007/978-3-030-05710-7_4

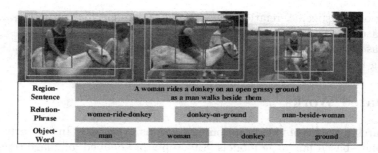

Fig. 1. Illustration of hierarchical alignment between visual content and language descriptions.

play different roles in understanding video content. Thus, many researchers focus on applying attention mechanism [2,6] and designing complicate encoder-decoder structures [3,7], which help to determine the interested content and salient temporal structures.

However, video captioning is challenging because it needs to not only understand the complex visual content, bust also tackle the correspondence relationships between visual content and language semantics, which are important to provide the accurate guidance on description generation. In fact, the vision-language correspondences indicate multi-level alignments among different granularities of visual elements (e.g. objects, visual relations, and the interested regions) and language components (e.g. words, phrases, and the sentence). For a video with its sentence description, as shown in Fig. 1, first, the visual objects in video content are usually presented by individual words in the sentence, which is the **object-word alignment**. Second, the visual relations, including relative spatial relations or interactions of objects, can be described by subject predicate phrases in the sentence, which is the **relation-phrase alignment**. Third, the whole sentence usually describes the main content conveyed by the interested regions in video frames, which is the **region-sentence alignment**.

In this paper, we propose an **Attention Guided Hierarchical Alignment (AGHA)** approach to address above problems, which exploits multi-level vision-language alignment information and multi-granularity visual features to boost the accurate generation of video descriptions. The main contributions of the proposed approach are as follows: (1) *Hierarchical vision-language alignments* are exploited to boost video captioning, including object-word, relation-phrase and region-sentence alignments. They are extracted from a well learned-model that can capture vision-language correspondences from object detection, visual relation detection and captioning tasks. We establish three parallel encoder-decoder streams with attention mechanism, which take these multi-level alignments to provide coarse-to-fine guidance on video description generation. As well, the rich complementarities among multi-level alignments are also mined to further improve the video captioning performance. (2) *Multi-granularity visual features* are exploited for comprehensive video content understanding, including object-specific, relation-specific and region-specific features as well as global features. We introduce the attention-based encoder, which takes global features as attention guidance to learn comprehensive visual discrimination for enhancing the video description generation.

2   Related Works

The research progress of video captioning contains two stages. In the early stage, the template-based language models [8,9] apply pre-defined language templates on detect objects and semantic concepts to generate sentences. However, the template definition limits the diversities of generated sentences. Recently, sequence learning based models [1–3] achieve great advances on video captioning. These methods adopt an encoder-decoder framework that can be trained in an end-to-end manner.

Li et al. [6] and Venugopalan et al. [1] construct encoder-decoder frameworks and process consecutive video frames by 3D CNN and LSTM respectively. Following works [2,3,7] make further improvements by modelling more flexible and complex temporal structures, as well as adaptively capture the salient regions in each frame for better video understanding. There are also some works [10–12] that exploit multi-modal features to improve video captioning, including motion and audio features.

While our work focus on the correspondences between visual content and language descriptions, which we argue can provide accurate guidance on captioning. Recent work [13] exploits visual attributes, such as object and action categories, to improve video captioning, which explores similar object-word alignment as our work. However, there are multi-level vision-language correspondences that should be specifically distinguished and fully exploited for better description generation.

3   Our AGHA Approach

Our AGHA approach takes the encoder-decoder framework to address video captioning problem. As shown in Fig. 2, for the input video, we first extract multi-granularity visual features including global features, as well as region-specific, relation-specific, and object-specific features. These features are then fed into three parallel encoder-decoder streams to capture coarse-to-fine visual information and hierarchical vision-language alignment information. All three streams have the same structure that includes an attention-based encoder and an alignment-embedded decoder. Finally, the hierarchical alignments from three streams are integrated to obtain the description sentence.

3.1   Multi-granularity Visual Feature Extraction

As shown in Fig. 2, given an input video V with N frames, four different granularities of visual features are extracted for each frame. At each time t, we extract global feature g_t, region-specific features $REG_t = (reg_1^t, reg_2^t, \cdots, reg_k^t)$, relation-specific features $REL_t = (rel_1^t, rel_2^t, \cdots, rel_m^t)$, and object-specific features $OBJ_t = (obj_1^t, obj_2^t, \cdots, obj_q^t)$, where k, m, q denote the numbers of different specific features.

The **global feature** is extracted from GoogLeNet [14] with Batch Normalization [15] that is pre-trained on ImageNet dataset. We feed the entire frame into GoogLeNet and take the output of its last pooling layer as global feature vector. For the other three kinds of specific features, we take the Multi-level Scene Description Network (MSDN) [16] as feature extractor, which is designed for object detection, visual relation detection and region captioning [16]. MSDN is constructed based on Faster RCNN [17] with 16-layer VGGNet [18], where there are two region proposal networks (RPNs) to produce object and region proposals. These proposals are fed into three different branches for object prediction, predicate prediction and region captioning. We denote these three branches as object branch, predicate branch and region branch for simplicity, and the specific features are constructed based on them.

Specifically, for **object-specific features**, we first extract multiple object features A^{obj} and object prediction scores S^{obj} from object branch, then select top-q features according to the prediction scores as object-specific features. For **relation-specific features**, we obtain a group of relation triplets, as well as the corresponding predicate features A^{pred} and predicate predication scores S^{pred}. For a relation triplet $< O_1 - P - O_2 >$[1], we compute its score $s^{rel} = s_1^{obj} * s^{pred} * s_2^{obj}$, where $s_1^{obj}, s_2^{obj} \in S^{obj}$ and $s^{pred} \in S^{pred}$ denote the prediction scores of objects O_1, O_2 and predicate P. The corresponding relation feature is computed as the weighted sum of two object features and one predicate feature:

$$a^{rel} = a_1^{obj} * s_1^{obj} + a^{pred} * s^{pred} + a_2^{obj} * s_2^{obj} \tag{1}$$

where $a_1^{obj}, a_2^{obj} \in A^{obj}$ and $a^{pred} \in A^{pred}$. We select top-m relation features according to relation scores s^{rel} as relation-specific features. For **region-specific features**, we obtain multiple region candidate features and their objectness scores, which indicate the probabilities of a region being an interested region for captioning. We select top-k region features according to the objectness scores as region-specific features.

The MSDN model [16] is trained on Visual Genome [19] dataset, which is a large-scale image dataset with rich annotations, including object categories, bounding boxes, attributes, relations over object pairs and region descriptions. The MSDN model learns rich visual information from Visual Genome dataset, which benefits the discriminative visual feature extraction.

So far, we extract multiple granularities of visual features, where the global features describe the global content of video frames; the region-specific features focus on the interested content that may receive the main attention from human; the relation-specific features describe the interaction information among objects, while the object-specific features describe the relatively fine-grained object

---

[1] We denote a visual relation as a $< object1 - predciate - object2 >$ triplet.

information. These four granularities of visual features contain coarse-to-fine visual information of a video frame.

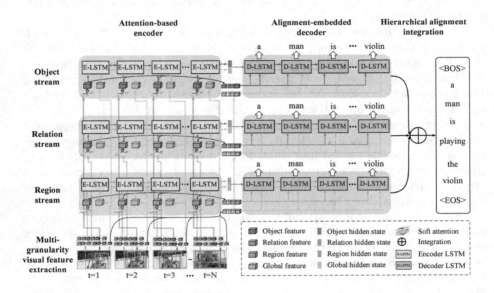

Fig. 2. Framework of our AGHA approach.

3.2 Attention-Based Encoder

For three kinds of specific features, we construct three parallel encoder-decoder streams, as shown in Fig. 2. Every stream has the same attention-based encoder and alignment-embedded decoder but with different specific features as inputs. We first introduce the detailed structure of attention-based encoder in this subsection. Inspired by [2], we utilize the LSTM structure with double memory cells and double hidden states. Meanwhile, we take the soft attention mechanism to encoding the coarse-to-fine visual information from different granularities of visual features.

In the multi-granularity visual feature extraction stage, for each video frame, we extract one global feature and multiple features of each finer granularity. Although we preliminarily select the features with high corresponding prediction scores, it is hard to ensure that all of them are discriminative or irrelevant to the interested semantic. Thus following [2], with taking the global feature as attention guidance, we apply the soft attention mechanism on each stream to learn the discriminative and relevant visual features of finer granularity. Taking object-specific features as example, the soft attention mechanism evaluates their discrimination according to the relevance score between object-specific features with global feature. Specifically, at time t, the relevance score between global feature g_t and object-specific feature obj_i^t is computed as follows:

$$r_i^t = w^T tanh(W_g g_t + W_{obj} obj_i^t) \tag{2}$$

where $i = 1, 2, \cdots, q$, and w, W_g, W_{obj} are parameters to learn. Then the attention weights are computed as the normalized relevance score over all q object-specific features:

$$\alpha_i^t = \frac{exp(r_i^t)}{\sum_{j=1}^{k} exp(r_j^t)} \tag{3}$$

As the attention weight α_i^t indicates the discrimination of the object-specific feature, we compute a weighted sum of all the object-specific features and obtain: $obj_t^\alpha = \sum_{i=1}^{k} \alpha_i^t obj_i^t$, where obj_t^α denotes the discriminative object-specific feature for the frame at time t. Similarly, we can obtain discriminative relation-specific and region-specific features by the same soft attention mechanism.

Then, we use the LSTM structure with double memory cells and double hidden states to encode the visual information. Taking the object stream as example, the encoder LSTM unit has three control gates, at time t, they are computed as follows:

$$i_t = \sigma(W_{ih} h_{t-1}^g + U_{ih} h_{t-1}^{obj} + W_{ix} g_t + U_{ix} obj_t^\alpha)$$
$$f_t = \sigma(W_{fh} h_{t-1}^g + U_{fh} h_{t-1}^{obj} + W_{fx} g_t + U_{fx} obj_t^\alpha) \tag{4}$$
$$o_t = \sigma(W_{oh} h_{t-1}^g + U_{oh} h_{t-1}^{obj} + W_{ox} g_t + U_{ox} obj_t^\alpha)$$

where $W_{*h}, U_{*h}, W_{*x}, U_{*x}$ are learned parameter matrices. σ denotes the sigmoid function. Based on the control gates, the two memory cells and two hidden states are updated as follows:

$$c_t^g = f_t \odot c_{t-1}^g + i_t \odot tanh(W_{ch} h_{t-1}^g + W_{cx} g_t)$$
$$c_t^{obj} = f_t \odot c_{t-1}^{obj} + i_t \odot tanh(U_{ch} h_{t-1}^{obj} + U_{cx} obj_t^\alpha) \tag{5}$$

$$h_t^g = o_t \odot tanh(c_t^g), \quad h_t^{obj} = o_t \odot tanh(c_t^{obj}) \tag{6}$$

where c_t^g, h_t^g are the memory cell and hidden state corresponding to the global feature, while c_t^g, h_t^g are corresponding to the discriminative object-specific feature. $W_{ch}, U_{ch}, W_{cx}, U_{cx}$ are learned parameter matrices. $\odot$ denotes the element-wise multiplication. After t time steps, we concatenate the two hidden states as the initial hidden state of the following encoder:

$$h_{obj}^{d0} = Concat(h_N^g, h_N^{obj}) \tag{7}$$

The encoders in relation stream and region stream are the same as object stream, similarly, we also obtain h_{rel}^{d0} and h_{reg}^{d0}.

3.3   Alignment-Embedded Decoder

As stated in above subsections, three kinds of specific features are extracted from three different branches of MSDN, which learn rich knowledges about the correspondences between visual content and language semantics. Specifically, the object branch is corresponding to object category semantics, which can be expressed by words; the predicate branch is corresponding to visual relations, which can be expressed as phrases; and the region branch is corresponding to captioning task, which is to generate description sentences. Consequently, the extracted object-specific, relation-specific and region-specific features provide object-word, relation-phrase and region-sentence alignments, respectively, which we called hierarchical vision-language alignments and are exploited in the decoder to boost the generation of video descriptions.

In the decoding stage, for each stream, we introduce an alignment-embedded decoder to exploit the specific vision-language alignment information. Specifically, we utilize the temporal attention mechanism to process the discriminative features of finer granularities obtained in the encoding stage, so as to embed the hierarchical vision-language alignment information into the decoder.

Taking the object stream as example, after above encoding stage, for an input video with N frames, we obtain N global features $G = (g_1, g_2, \cdots, g_N)$ and N discriminative object-specific features $OBJ^\alpha = (obj_1^\alpha, obj_1^\alpha, \cdots, obj_N^\alpha)$. The temporal attention mechanism is as follows:

$$z_i^t = w^T tanh(W_h h_t^d + W_g g_i + W_{obj} obj_i^\alpha) \tag{8}$$

where h_t^d denotes the hidden state of decoder LSTM unit in time t, the superscript d denotes "decoder". w^T, W_h, W_g, W_{obj} are parameters to learn. Then the attention weights are computed as follows:

$$\beta_i^t = \frac{exp(z_i^t)}{\sum_{j=1}^N exp(z_j^t)} \tag{9}$$

Thus, the temporal attention weighted global feature and discriminative object-specific feature are obtained as follows:

$$g_t^\beta = \sum_{i=1}^N \beta_i^t g_i, \quad obj_t^\beta = \sum_{i=1}^N \beta_i^t obj_i^\alpha \tag{10}$$

Then we use g_t^β and obj_t^β to update the control gates, memory cell and hidden state of the decoder LSTM unit:

$$
\begin{aligned}
i_t &= \sigma(W_{ih} h_{t-1} + W_{ix} x_t + U_i^g g_t^\beta + U_i^{obj} obj_t^\beta) \\
f_t &= \sigma(W_{fh} h_{t-1} + W_{fx} x_t + U_f^g g_t^\beta + U_f^{obj} obj_t^\beta) \\
o_t &= \sigma(W_{oh} h_{t-1} + W_{ox} x_t + U_o^g g_t^\beta + U_o^{obj} obj_t^\beta)
\end{aligned}
\tag{11}
$$

$$c_t = f_t \odot c_{t-1} + i_t \odot tanh(W_{ch} h_{t-1} + W_{cx} x_t + U_c^g g_t^\beta + U_c^{obj} obj_t^\beta) \tag{12}$$

$$h_t = o_t \odot tanh(c_t) \tag{13}$$

where x_t denotes the word embedding at time t. W, U are parameter matrices to learn. It's noted that, for simplicity, we omit the superscript d in above equations. The decoders in relation and region streams are the same as object stream.

To obtain the description sentence, following [1,2], we compute the conditional probability of next word with a softmax layer, and adopt the cross-entropy loss as the objective function while generating words.

3.4 Hierarchical Alignment Integration

The three different streams in our AGHA approach take different vision-language alignments, which provide semantic guidance on description generation from different aspects. The object stream can assist the accurate word generation with object-word alignment. While the relation and region streams provide discriminative guidance from phrase and the whole sentence aspects. For further exploiting the complementarities among the three different streams, we conduct integration on the results of three streams. Specifically, at each time t in the decoding stage, we merge the prediction scores of next word by late fusion, and then decide the predicted word according to the merged prediction score. In such an integration way, the rich complementarities among multi-level hierarchical vision-language alignments are mined to further improve the video captioning performance.

4   Experiment

In this section, we present comparison experimental results and analyses on Microsoft Video Description Corpus (MSVD) dataset [20], taking **BLEU@N** [21], **METEOR** [22], and **CIDEr** [23] as evaluation metrics.

4.1   Experimental Settings

Video Preprocessing. For each input video, we sample 30 frames. For each video frame, the global feature is extracted from the pre-trained GoogLeNet, taking the output of $pool5/7x7\_s1$ layer as feature vector with $1,024$ dimensions. The object-specific, relation-specific and region-specific features are extracted from the MSDN [16] model, which all have $1,024$ dimensions. We set $q = 10, m = 50, k = 5$ respectively, which means we select 10 objects, 50 relations and 5 regions for each frame, according to the corresponding prediction scores.

Sentence Preprocessing. Following [1,2], we convert ground truth captions to lower case, tokenize sentences and remove punctuations. The collection of word tokens for MSVD dataset contains $12,593$ words. Each word is encoded by a one-hot vector.

Training Details. For the training video/sentence pairs, we filter out the sentences with more than 30 words. During training, begin-of-sentence <BOS> tag and end-of-sentence <EOS> tag are added at the beginning and the end of each sentence. The encoder for each stream has 512 hidden units, while the decoder has 1024 hidden units. Following [2], we set the attention size as 100. We utilize the RMSPROP algorithm to update model parameters, which can achieve better convergence. The learning rate is initialized to be 2×10^{-4}, and the training batch size as 64. We apply dropout on the outputs of fully connected layers and decoder LSTM, with dropout rate of 0.5. We also apply gradient clip of $[-5, 5]$ to prevent gradient explosion.

Table 1. Comparisons with state-of-the-art methods on MSVD dataset. "-" indicates that the authors do not report their performance on this dataset.

Methods	BLEU@1	BLEU@2	BLEU@3	BLEU@4	METEOR	CIDEr
Our AGHA approach	**83.1**	**73.0**	**64.3**	**55.1**	**35.3**	**83.3**
mGRU+pre-train (ResNet-200) [7]	82.5	72.2	63.3	53.8	34.5	81.2
M&M-TGM (IR+C+MFCC) [10]	-	-	-	48.8	34.4	80.5
RecNet-SA-LSTM (I) [24]	-	-	-	52.3	34.1	80.3
MCNN+MCF (G) [25]	-	-	-	46.5	33.7	75.5
MA-LSTM (G+C) [11]	82.3	71.1	61.8	52.3	33.6	70.4
DMRM (G) [2]	-	-	-	51.1	33.6	74.8
LSTM-TSA (V+C) [13]	82.8	72.0	62.8	52.8	33.5	74.0
TDDF (V+C) [26]	-	-	-	45.8	33.3	73.0
HRNE with attention (G) [27]	79.2	66.3	55.1	43.8	33.1	-
h-RNN (V+C) [28]	81.5	70.4	60.4	49.9	32.6	65.8
Boundary-aware encoder (C+ResNet-50) [3]	-	-	-	42.5	32.4	63.5
Attentional fusion (V+C+MFCC) [12]	-	-	-	53.9	32.2	67.4
LSTM-E (V+C) [29]	78.8	66.0	55.4	45.3	31.0	-
S2VT (V+O) [1]	-	-	-	-	29.8	-

4.2   Comparisons with State-of-the-art Methods

Comparison results of the proposed AGHA approach and state-of-the-art methods are shown in Table 1. The short names in brackets indicate the frame/motion features used in corresponding method, where IR, I, G, C, V and O denote Inception-ResNet [30], Inception-v4 [30], GoogLeNet, C3D [31], VGGNet and Optical flow features, respectively. MFCC [32] denotes the audio feature.

As shown in Table 1, in general, our AGHA approach achieves the best performances on popular evaluation metrics, which demonstrates its effectiveness with integrating hierarchical vision-language alignments as well as exploiting multi-granularity visual information. Among all the compared methods, S2VT [1] is the fundamental sequence-to-sequence method, which applies LSTMs to construct both encoder and decoder for video captioning. Then elaborate temporal structures [3, 7, 27] are explored and multi-modal features [10–12] are exploited to improve video description generation. Our AGHA approach outperforms them by embedding the hierarchical vision-language alignments into the temporal attention mechanism, which makes the decoder more "intelligent" with capturing semantic correspondences between video content and language descriptions. In addition, our AGHA approach also exploits different granularities of features, which provide complementary video content understanding from coarse-to-fine granularities.

One recent work worth noting is LSTM-TSA [13], which exploits similar object-word alignment as the object stream in the proposed AGHA, by predicting some nouns and verbs that represent objects and actions. From Table 1, although LSTM-TSA obtains similar BLEU@1 score as AGHA, while the proposed AGHA achieves higher results on BLEU@2, BLEU@3 and BLEU@4 scores, because the integration of relation-phrase and region-sentence alignments in AGHA further improves the performance effectively. As well, we can also observe the increments on METEOR and CIDEr scores, which further demonstrate the effectiveness of exploiting hierarchical vision-language alignments and their intrinsic complementary.

4.3   Effectiveness of Components in AGHA

In this subsection, we present the comparison results of three streams in AGHA as well as the integration of them. The experimental results are listed in Table 2. The "LSTM" denotes the plain LSTM-based encoder-decoder framework with temporal attention, which only takes the global features as input. While the "Region Stream", "Relation Stream" and "Object Stream" take different extra visual features as region-specific, relation-specific, and object-specific features respectively. These three streams take different granularities of visual information, as well as exploit different levels of vision-language alignment information.

Table 2. Experimental results of three streams and their integration in AGHA on MSVD dataset.

Methods	BLEU@1	BLEU@2	BLEU@3	BLEU@4	METEOR	CIDEr
LSTM	78.6	67.5	58.1	47.8	32.1	71.4
Region stream	81.2	70.1	61.3	52.3	34.0	77.0
Relation stream	81.3	70.6	61.9	53.1	34.2	79.1
Object stream	81.7	70.6	61.7	52.5	34.1	77.3
Object + relation + region	**83.1**	**73.0**	**64.3**	**55.1**	**35.3**	**83.3**

From Table 2, we can observe that, compared to the baseline LSTM, all the three streams achieve clear improvements, which demonstrates the effectiveness of the vision-language alignments. Compared to the region stream, the

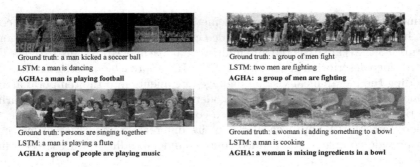

Fig. 3. Video description examples generated by AGHA and the baseline LSTM. The sentence in the first row is the ground truth reference.

relation and object streams obtain better performance. It is because that the region stream takes coarse-grained features, while the other two streams exploit fine-grain features with more detailed visual information and finer alignment information. Compared to the object stream, the relation stream obtains higher BELU@4, METEOR, and CIDEr scores. It results from that the relation stream can seek for the correspondence between visual content and phrases, while the object stream focuses more on the accurate word generation. In "Object + Relation + Region", we integrate three individual streams to further improve the performance of video captioning with clear increments on all the metrics, which demonstrates that there exist strong complementarities among multi-level hierarchical vision-language alignments as well as coarse-to-fine visual features, and our AGHA approach is effective to generate better descriptions by mining these complementarities.

4.4 Qualitative Analysis

Figure 3 shows some captioning examples generated by our approach. We also present the comparison results of baseline LSTM. From Fig. 3, we can observe that our AGHA approach can generate more accurate and detailed descriptions. For the example in the top-left, the baseline LSTM generates the wrong description ("dancing"), while our AGHA approach generates the description of "playing football", which is semantically consistent with the ground truth reference ("kicked a soccer ball"). For the example in the bottom-right, compared to baseline LSTM, the sentence generated by our approach not only expresses the correct semantic, but also describes more details ("in a bowl"). That is because our approach exploits finer granularities of visual features and multi-level hierarchical vision-language alignments. Overall, these examples illustrate the effectiveness of our proposed AGHA approach.

5   Conclusion

In this paper, we propose an attention guided hierarchical alignment approach for video captioning. It exploits multi-level vision-language alignments and mines their complementarities to capture the semantic correspondences between visual content and language descriptions. In addition, our proposed approach also explores multi-granularity visual features, which capture coarse-to-fine visual information to obtain comprehensive understanding of complex and dynamic video content. Evaluation on the widely-used MSVD dataset demonstrates the effectiveness of our proposed approach. For the future work, on one hand, we intend to employ transfer learning to obtain more accurate vision-language alignment information leveraging existing large-scale datasets; on the other hand, we intend to explore the interactions among multi-level alignments to boost each other, which will further improve the video description generation.

Acknowledgment. This work was supported by National Natural Science Foundation of China under Grant 61771025.

References

1. Venugopalan, S., Rohrbach, M., Donahue, J., Mooney, R., Darrell, T., Saenko, K.: Sequence to sequence-video to text. In: ICCV, pp. 4534–4542 (2015)
2. Yang, Z., Han, Y., Wang, Z.: Catching the temporal regions-of-interest for video captioning. In: ACM MM, pp. 146–153 (2017)
3. Baraldi, L., Grana, C., Cucchiara, R.: Hierarchical boundary-aware neural encoder for video captioning. In: CVPR, pp. 3185–3194 (2017)
4. Wang, J., Wang, W., Huang, Y., Wang, L., Tan, T.: M3: multimodal memory modelling for video captioning. In: CVPR, pp. 7512–7520 (2018)
5. Bahdanau, D., Cho, K., Bengio, Y.: Neural machine translation by jointly learning to align and translate. In: ICLR, pp. 1–15 (2015)
6. Yao, L., et al.: Describing videos by exploiting temporal structure. In: ICCV, pp. 4507–4515 (2015)
7. Zhu, L., Xu, Z., Yang, Y.: Bidirectional multirate reconstruction for temporal modeling in videos. In: CVPR, pp. 1339–1348 (2016)
8. Guadarrama, S., et al.: Youtube2text: Recognizing and describing arbitrary activities using semantic hierarchies and zero-shot recognition. In: ICCV, pp. 2712–2719 (2013)
9. Rohrbach, M., Qiu, W., Titov, I., Thater, S., Pinkal, M., Schiele, B.: Translating video content to natural language descriptions. In: ICCV, pp. 433–440 (2013)
10. Chen, S., Chen, J., Jin, Q., Hauptmann, A.: Video captioning with guidance of multimodal latent topics. In: ACM MM, pp. 1838–1846 (2017)
11. Xu, J., Yao, T., Zhang, Y., Mei, T.: Learning multimodal attention LSTM networks for video captioning. In: ACM MM, pp. 537–545 (2017)
12. Hori, C., et al.: Attention-based multimodal fusion for video description. In: ICCV, pp. 4203–4212 (2017)
13. Pan, Y., Yao, T., Li, H., Mei, T.: Video captioning with transferred semantic attributes. In: CVPR, pp. 6504–6512 (2017)
14. Szegedy, C., et al.: Going deeper with convolutions. In: CVPR, pp. 1–9 (2015)

15. Ioffe, S., Szegedy, C.: Batch normalization: accelerating deep network training by reducing internal covariate shift. In: ICML, pp. 448–456 (2015)
16. Li, Y., Ouyang, W., Zhou, B., Wang, K., Wang, X.: Scene graph generation from objects, phrases and region captions. In: CVPR, pp. 1261–1270 (2017)
17. Ren, S., He, K., Girshick, R., Sun, J.: Faster R-CNN: Towards real-time object detection with region proposal networks. In: NIPS, pp. 91–99 (2015)
18. Simonyan, K., Zisserman, A.: Very deep convolutional networks for large-scale image recognition. arXiv preprint arXiv:1409.1556 (2014)
19. Krishna, R., et al.: Visual genome: connecting language and vision using crowd-sourced dense image annotations. Int. J. Comput. Vis. **123**(1), 32–73 (2017)
20. Chen, D.L., Dolan, W.B.: Collecting highly parallel data for paraphrase evaluation. In: ACL, pp. 190–200 (2011)
21. Papineni, K., Roukos, S., Ward, T., Zhu, W.: BLEU: a method for automatic evaluation of machine translation. In: ACL, pp. 311–318. Association for Computational Linguistics (2002)
22. Banerjee, S., Lavie, A.: METEOR: An automatic metric for MT evaluation with improved correlation with human judgments. In: Proceedings of the ACL workshop on intrinsic and extrinsic evaluation measures for machine translation and/or summarization, pp. 65–72 (2005)
23. Vedantam, R., Lawrence Zitnick, C., Parikh, D.: CIDEr: consensus-based image description evaluation. In: CVPR, pp. 4566–4575 (2015)
24. Wang, B., Ma, L., Zhang, W., Liu, W.: Reconstruction network for video captioning. In: CVPR, pp. 7622–7631 (2018)
25. Wu, A., Han, Y.: Multi-modal circulant fusion for video-to-language and backward. In: IJCAI, pp. 1029–1035 (2018)
26. Zhang, X., Gao, K., Zhang, Y., Zhang, D., Li, J., Tian, Q.: Task-driven dynamic fusion: Reducing ambiguity in video description. In: CVPR, pp. 6250–6258 (2017)
27. Pan, P., Xu, Z., Yang, Y., Wu, F., Zhuang, Y.: Hierarchical recurrent neural encoder for video representation with application to captioning. In: CVPR, pp. 1029–1038 (2016)
28. Yu, H., Wang, J., Huang, Z., Yang, Y., Xu, W.: Video paragraph captioning using hierarchical recurrent neural networks. In: CVPR, pp. 4584–4593 (2016)
29. Pan, Y., Mei, T., Yao, T., Li, H., Rui, Y.: Jointly modeling embedding and translation to bridge video and language. In: CVPR, pp. 4594–4602 (2016)
30. Szegedy, C., Ioffe, S., Vanhoucke, V., Alemi, A.A.: Inception-v4, inception-Resnet and the impact of residual connections on learning. In: AAAI, pp. 4278–4284 (2017)
31. Tran, D., Bourdev, L., Fergus, R., Torresani, L., Paluri, M.: Learning spatiotemporal features with 3D convolutional networks. In: ICCV, pp. 4489–4497 (2015)
32. Xu, Z., Yang, Y., Tsang, I., Sebe, N., Hauptmann, A.G.: Feature weighting via optimal thresholding for video analysis. In: ICCV, pp. 3440–3447 (2013)

Task-Driven Biometric Authentication of Users in Virtual Reality (VR) Environments

Alexander Kupin, Benjamin Moeller, Yijun Jiang,
Natasha Kholgade Banerjee, and Sean Banerjee[✉]

Clarkson University, Potsdam, NY 13699, USA
{kupinah,moellebr,jiangy,nbanerje,sbanerje}@clarkson.edu

Abstract. In this paper, we provide an approach for authenticating users in virtual reality (VR) environments by tracking the behavior of users as they perform goal-oriented tasks, such as throwing a ball at a target. With the pervasion of VR in mission-critical applications such as manufacturing, navigation, military training, education, and therapy, validating the identity of users using VR systems is becoming paramount to prevent tampering of the VR environments, and to ensure user safety. Unlike prior work, which uses PIN and pattern based passwords to authenticate users in VR environments, our approach authenticates users based on their natural interactions within the virtual space by matching the 3D trajectory of the dominant hand gesture controller in a display-based head-mounted VR system to a library of trajectories. To handle natural differences in wait times between multiple parts of an action such as picking a ball and throwing it, our matching approach uses a symmetric sum-squared distance between the nearest neighbors across the query and library trajectories. Our work enables seamless authentication without requiring the user to stop their activity and enter specific credentials, and can be used to continually validate the identity of the user. We conduct a pilot study with 14 subjects throwing a ball at a target in VR using the gesture controller and achieve a maximum accuracy of 92.86% by comparing to a library of 10 trajectories per subject, and 90.00% by comparing to 6 trajectories per subject.

1 Introduction

Head mounted virtual reality (VR) systems, such as the HTC Vive, Oculus Rift, and PlayStation VR, while traditionally used for recreational purposes, are now rapidly permeating a variety of mission critical applications ranging from therapy [16,25,35], manufacturing [4,6], flight simulations [26], military training [5,28], and education [9,19]. It is becoming increasingly important to authenticate the identity of people using mission-critical VR systems in order to prevent tampering of virtual training environments and to guarantee the safety of users working in single- and multi-user VR environments. Unfortunately, work in the

© Springer Nature Switzerland AG 2019
I. Kompatsiaris et al. (Eds.): MMM 2019, LNCS 11295, pp. 55–67, 2019.
https://doi.org/10.1007/978-3-030-05710-7_5

area of VR authentication has been limited. Existing approaches to authenticate users in VR environments rely on personal identification number (PIN) or pattern matching [10,37] similar to mobile authentications systems [3], and do not allow continual seamless authentication. Head motions and blink patterns [29], head movements to music [14], and bone conduction of sound through the skull [30] have been used to authenticate users wearing Google Glass. However, these approaches have limited scalability for continuous authentication in large user groups due to the restricted degrees of freedom in the analyzed actions.

In this paper, we provide the first approach to authenticate users from natural goal-oriented tasks in VR environments by tracking 3D trajectories of VR gesture controllers. Due to their experience with the real-world, humans develop innate consistencies in average everyday tasks such as throwing a ball, lifting a chair, lowering a potted plant, swinging a golf club, or driving a car, which when translated to VR environments can provide a unique signature for a person. Unlike approaches that perform authentication using cameras by tracking the trajectories of a large group of points on the body of a person [1,2,11,12,24,36], our approach uses a sparse point set from a single trajectory corresponding to the gesture controller, which can prove insufficient for authentication. To address the sparseness, our work draws inspiration from behavior-based authentication systems in mobile devices [7,34] and matches complex multi-part actions, e.g., lifting a ball, poising it above the shoulder, throwing it at a target, and returning the hand back to neutral. Over multi-part actions, each user shows unique spatial placements of the gesture controller and temporal durations of controller motions, enabling multi-part actions to be specific to the user.

While approaches exist to authenticate users in real-world environments from sparse trajectories obtained using body-mounted or non-invasive sensors, these approaches require single actions [18], use user-dependent signatures [15,18], or perform recognition based on gait [8,13,22,23,32,38] or device shaking [27]. Unlike these approaches, our work on using multi-part goal-oriented actions can be used to perform continual authentication in VR environments where users perform a large number of tasks. Our challenge is that multi-part actions contain natural unavoidable differences in wait times between various segments of the actions. For instance, successive throws by a ball pitcher may show variations in the amount of time the pitcher holds a knee lift before pitching the ball. These variations prevent matching using a simple distance metric between corresponding trajectory points. Our approach addresses this challenge by identifying nearest neighbors between 3D points on a query trajectory and 3D points on a library trajectory, and using Euclidean distance between the nearest neighbors to match the trajectories.

We present results from a pilot study in which we capture 14 male and female subjects ranging in age from 18 to 37 years throwing a ball at a target in VR. To prevent over-fitting to trajectories, the test dataset actions for a particular user are captured on a different day from the library dataset actions for the same user, with 10 trajectories per user captured on each day. Our accuracy averaged over 10 trajectories from the second day is 92.86% when we use a library of all 10 trajectories from the first day, and 90.00% when we use a reduced library of 6 trajectories from the first day. Our results demonstrate that the accuracy of matching converges within 6 trajectories indicating that user behavior becomes consistent in 6 captures. Our work enables seamless authentication without requiring the user to stop their activity and enter specific credentials, and can be used for continual authentication.

2   Related Work

Current approaches in VR authentication largely extend traditional pattern and PIN-based techniques to VR environments. Yu et al. [37] provide users with 3D patterns, 2D sliding patterns, and PINs to authenticate themselves in a virtual environment. They determine 3D patterns to be most effective through a user study involving 15 participants. In George et al. [10], the authors use various virtual input surface sizes with both pattern and PIN based authentication systems to regulate in-game purchases in a 25 participant user study. However, these approaches require the user to stop their activity and interact with a virtual PIN pad or pattern entry surface. Our approach provides continual interaction by using the user actions to authenticate users.

Several approaches have attempted to use the hardware on Google Glass to perform user authentication. Rogers et al. [29] capture blink and head movements of users viewing a series of rapidly changing images using the infrared, gyroscope, and accelerometer sensors built into the Glass device. Similar to the PIN and password based authentication, this approach diverts users from their natural interactions. Li et al. [14] track head movements of users in response to external audio stimuli. Their approach depends on the variation in properties such as frequency and amplitude for periodic motions in response to music. Head movements in goal-oriented tasks such as throwing a ball or swinging a golf club may have limited diversity for use in continual identification of users in VR systems. In Schneegass et al. [30], the authors use the integrated bone conduction speaker and an external microphone to collect data on transmission of white noise through the skull of a user in a noise-free environment, which is unrealistic in a typical VR environment consisting of varying audio input. Unlike these approaches, our approach identifies users using actions such as lifting and throwing a ball that are natural in everyday environments, without constraints on their gestures.

Our work is related to authentication of users using bodily motions in real-world environments. There exists a large body of work in using cameras to authenticate users from their real-world motions. However, several of these approaches rely on the presence of a dense set of spatial points on the body of the person [1, 2, 11, 12, 24, 36]. While work exists on using sparse samples from a single body-mounted sensor, most approaches focus on authentication based on gait [8, 13, 22, 23, 32, 38], which is not suitable for continual authentication using gesture controllers in VR environments, since users spend a large portion of time performing tasks such as picking, throwing, shooting, or exploring, and the hand controllers have more recognizable tracks during non-walking actions. Okumura et al. [27] perform authentication on users shaking a smartphone, while Mendels et al. [18] and Liu et al. [15] use free-form gestures to perform authentication using user-dependent signatures. Device shaking [27] and user-dependent signatures [15,18] cannot be used for uninterrupted continual authentication.

While Mendels et al. [18] also show authentication using user-independent gestures as analyzed in our work, their approach performs authentication using single-action gestures such as drawing a shape, which precludes continual authentication in VR environments where users change their tasks regularly. Additionally, while they collect samples for 18 users, they provide recognition in groups of 3 to 7 users, with an average recognition rate of 85% and lower for user independent gestures in groups of 4 or more users using 28 samples per shape. The approach of Matsuo et al. [17] requires 12 users to submit 30 to 100 samples per day for a six week period before performing authentication, which is unrealistic for immediate authentication in mission critical systems. In contrast, our approach provides recognition rates of 92.86% and 90.00% when run on all 14 users used in our work with smaller sets of 10 and 6 samples per trajectory from a single day tested against 10 samples collected on a second day.

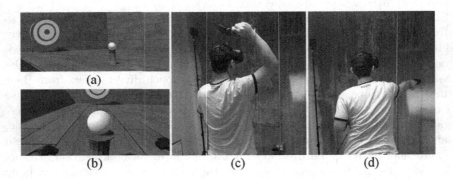

Fig. 1. (a) Ball throwing game showing target, ball on pedestal, and red 'X' on the floor for subject to stand on. (b) Perspective view from a subject preparing to pick up the ball. (c) Subject wearing the HTC Vive headset preparing to throw the ball. (d) Subject after completing the ball throw. (Color figure online)

In using data from a sparse set of time-samples to perform task-based authentication, our work resembles traditional behavioral biometrics, such as keystroke and gesture. Fixed password based keystroke dynamics relies on hold times and delay times for 26 alphabetic, 10 numeric, and 10 special character keys to generate the user model, with the number of samples per user depending on the length of the password [20,21,33]. Gesture based approaches for authentication use swipe behavior to authenticate users on smartphones [31,34]. In Serwadda et al. [31], the authors used 80 strokes to authenticate users, while in Syed et al. [34], the authors used 300 strokes per subject for authentication. Unlike traditional gesture-based biometrics in smartphones, we use 3D trajectories that provide higher constraints on matching due to the extra third dimension. Additionally, unlike mobile authentication approaches that require high prior device usage in order to develop consistency of behavior for authentication, our approach of task-driven authentication requires minimal prior use for high recognition accuracy due to the direct translation of everyday tasks to VR environments.

Table 1. Demographic and pre-interview summary of the 14 subjects tested.

Total number of subjects	14
Total number of male subjects	8
Total number of female subjects	6
Subjects with no VR experience	6
Subjects with VR experience	8
Subjects with experience in throwing sports	6
Subjects with no prior throwing sports experience	8

3   Data Collection

We gather our data by having users interact with a ball throwing VR experience developed in Unity for an HTC Vive headset and hand controllers. Figures 1(a) and 1(b) show views of the interaction. During the interaction, the subject picks up a white ball placed on a pedestal placed in front of the subject and attempts to throw it at a circular target on the wall directly in front. To reduce variability caused by the position of the subject in relation to the target, each subject is asked to stand on the red 'X' marked on the floor of the virtual space.

Our pilot study dataset consists of 14 subjects, both male and female, ranging in age from 18 to 37 years. Prior to data capture, we conducted a brief pre-interaction interview to solicit prior experiences with VR systems and throwing based sports. The following information was collected from each subject:

– Has the subject had prior experience with VR systems,
– If yes, what VR systems has the subject used,
– Has the subject had experience playing throwing sports,
– If yes, what sports has the subject played.

After interviewing the subject, we noted down their dominant throwing hand, gender, and age. The subjects in our dataset show varying degrees of familiarity with VR systems, with some subjects having never used a VR system before, and other subjects being regular users and owners of VR systems. The subjects in our dataset also show varying degrees of experience playing throwing sports, with some having never played a throwing sport, and others having actively played sports such as baseball or tennis. Due to the low prevalence of left handed subjects, all 14 subjects in our dataset were right handed. We summarize subject demographics in Table 1. As shown in the table, we maintain a near 50-50 split for gender, VR experience, and throwing sports experience, thus reducing biases due to these factors.

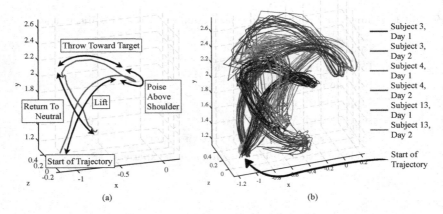

(a)   (b)

Fig. 2. (a) Description of trajectory for the right controller. (b) Right controller trajectories of ball throwing actions for Subjects 3 (blue), 4 (green), and 13 (red) for Day 1 (dark color) and Day 2 (light color). Despite the lag in capture between the two days, subject still show consistent behavior, enabling gesture-based authentication. (Color figure online)

For each subject, we capture two data collection sessions on two different days to enable cross-day analysis. To reduce priming, where a subject learns the objective of the interaction, we asked each subject to wait one or more days between each session. During each session, we captured 10 trajectories corresponding to 10 attempts made by the subject at hitting the target, similar to a carnival game. We captured the x, y, and z positional information for the dominant hand controller at 45 frames per second for 3 s to obtain a total of 135 samples per trajectory. As shown in Fig. 2(a), each action consists of four parts: picking the ball, poising the ball above the shoulder, throwing the ball toward the target, and returning the controller to the neutral position. Example right controller trajectories for three of the subjects used in our analysis are shown in Fig. 2(b). As shown by the figure, intra-class (i.e., within user) consistency in the pattern of the action is retained across the two capture days.

4 Trajectory Based User Authentication

While all trajectories start near a common spatial point, i.e., the location of the ball on the pedestal, differences in the extension of the arm of the user may

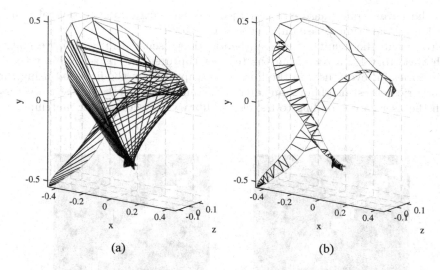

Fig. 3. (a) Corresponding points in two trajectories for the same user deviate from each other over time due to differences in wait times between actions, (b) Our approach handles the deviation by identifying nearest point neighbors between both trajectories. (Color figure online)

induce translational offsets in the trajectories. To handle these offsets, we re-center each trajectory at the center of the bounding box for that trajectory prior to matching. While each trajectory contains an equal number of time samples, differences in time delays between multiple parts of an action (e.g., lifting the ball and throwing the ball toward the target) prevent the use of a distance metric between corresponding points of the trajectories. As shown by two trajectories for a single user in Fig. 3(a), points earlier in the blue trajectory correspond to points further along in red trajectory since the user is slower during the blue trajectory. Due to the differences in length of time for which the controller is poised over the shoulder, the deviation in correspondence increases over the latter parts of the trajectory. To address this issue, our approach computes the distance $d(\mathbf{T}_1, \mathbf{T}_2)$ between two trajectories $\mathbf{T}_1 \in \mathbb{R}^{N \times 3}$ and $\mathbf{T}_2 \in \mathbb{R}^{N \times 3}$ with N time samples as the symmetric sum-squared distance between nearest point neighbors given as

$$d(\mathbf{T}_1, \mathbf{T}_2) = \tfrac{1}{2}\sum_{i=1}^{N} \min_j (\mathbf{T}_1(i) - \mathbf{T}_2(j))^2 + \tfrac{1}{2}\sum_{j=1}^{N} \min_i (\mathbf{T}_1(i) - \mathbf{T}_2(j))^2. \quad (1)$$

The nearest neighbor in $\mathbf{T}_2$ to the ith 3D point in $\mathbf{T}_1$ is represented by the argument of $\min_j(\mathbf{T}_1(i) - \mathbf{T}_2(j))$ in Eq. 1, and vice versa. As shown in Fig. 3(b), matches between the nearest point neighbors provides an accurate matching between the various parts of the two trajectories. While our approach shares features with bipartite graph matching, unlike bipartite graph matching, our matches are not bijective, i.e., a single point in one trajectory may match to multiple points in the other trajectory. We allow repetitive matches since a point in a short wait time phase on one trajectory may correspond to several points in a longer wait time phase on a second trajectory.

To obtain the results of user authentication discussed in Sect. 5, we match each trajectory for a user from the test set captured on the second day to all trajectories for every user in the library set captured on the first day using the symmetric nearest neighbor sum-squared distance. We label each test trajectory with the user corresponding to the closest library trajectory after matching.

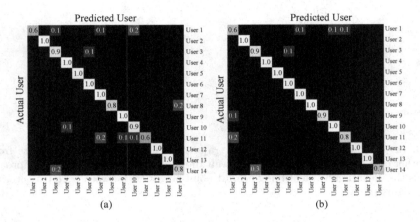

Fig. 4. Confusion matrices for classifying the trajectories of 14 users using (a) all 135 time samples, and (b) the first 95 time samples.

5   Results

Figure 4 shows the confusion matrices for performing authentication of 10 trajectories per user for 14 users using (a) all 135 time samples, and (b) the first 95 time samples. The average accuracy with all 135 time samples is 90.00%, while the average accuracy with the first 95 time samples is 92.86%. The higher accuracy with fewer time samples may be attributed to low information content toward the end of the trajectory as users' hands follow less predictable trajectories toward the end of the return phase. For instance, at the end of a return, the user may dangle their hand, or external factors such as gravity may induce the user to follow an alternative trajectory during the return.

Table 2 provides comparisons of our approach of symmetric nearest neighbor matching using trajectories re-centered around the bounding box center against 5 other matching methods for classifying using 95 time samples in the first column and 135 time samples in the second column. Results of our approach are provided in the first row. The second and third rows show classification results with re-centering of the trajectory using the centroid of the trajectory points, and without re-centering. As shown by the third row, without re-centering, the accuracy is low, indicating that users may change the location of the hand from the first day to the second. Despite the change in hand location, the higher accuracy of results in the first row demonstrates that the pattern of throw remains consistent within the user from one day to another.

The results in the second row obtained by re-centering using the centroid are lower than in the first row as the centroid is weighted toward regions of the trajectory with high point concentrations. The point concentration is higher in regions representing wait times during, for instance, the shoulder poise or the end of the return. Variations in wait times change the centroid position, due to which the translation offsets are not zeroed out. The last three rows in Table 2 provide authentication accuracies using matching of points at corresponding time samples between the two trajectories without identifying spatial nearest neighbors, i.e., using the correspondences shown in Fig. 3(a). The matches are significantly lower due to the differences in temporal shift in the trajectories induced by the variations in wait times during the shoulder poise phase.

Table 2. Accuracy with 95 time samples and 135 time samples using multiple matching approaches. We achieve the highest accuracy using of 92.86% using 95 points and re-centering around the bounding box center with symmetric nearest neighbor matching.

Approach	95 pts	135 pts
Re-center around bounding box center, symmetric nearest neighbor matching	92.86%	90.00%
Re-center around centroid, symmetric nearest neighbor matching	83.57%	83.57%
No re-centering, symmetric nearest neighbor matching	82.14%	80.00%
Re-center around bounding box center, corresponding points matching	62.86%	63.57%
Re-center around centroid, corresponding points matching	57.86%	60.00%
No re-centering, corresponding points matching	56.43%	58.57%

Figure 5 shows plots of average accuracy using increasing numbers of trajectory points ranging from the first 5 time samples to the complete set of 135 samples in steps of 5. Each plot represents classification using the first n library trajectories for each user, where n varies from 1 to 10. As shown by the figure, classification using 6 trajectories and higher approaches the classification using 10 trajectories. The plots demonstrate that we can authenticate users using a reduced set of trajectories, indicating that users use their natural interactions in the real world to rapidly develop consistency to actions in virtual environments. For all plots, increasing the number of time samples improves accuracy in the initial phase, after which the accuracy remains steady. For plots corresponding to matching with between 6 and 10 throws, peak accuracies are obtained at between 95 and 115 trajectory points, demonstrating that time samples later than 115 points, or around 2.56 s may contribute reduced information content due to the noise during the return phase. With 6 trajectories, we achieve a recognition accuracy of 90.00% within 115 points, which matches the recognition accuracy with 10 trajectories using all 135 points. Using 5 trajectories, we receive an accuracy of 87.14% within 105 points.

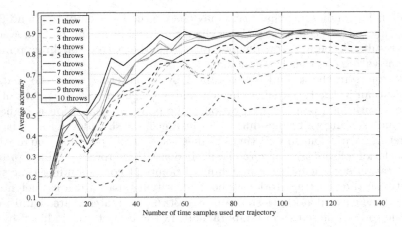

Fig. 5. Plots of the average accuracy of authentication against increasing numbers of time samples included per trajectory. Each plot corresponds to using the first n library throws, where n varies from 1 to 10 as shown by the legend.

6   Discussion and Future Work

In this paper we provide the first approach for authenticating users using their natural behavior in VR environments using the 3D trajectories obtained from the dominant hand controller. Our approach does not require any external devices, such as RGB-D cameras or smartphones. Using our approach, users can continually authenticate themselves in VR environments without needing to stop their activity and enter credentials in a PIN or pattern based password system. We validate our 3D trajectory-based authentication approach by collecting data from a pilot study involving 14 subjects throwing a virtual ball at a target across two independent sessions. Using 135 3D trajectory points we achieve an overall accuracy of 90.00%, while using 95 points, we achieve an accuracy of 92.86%.

Our authentication approach relies on the notion that the trajectories of each user are unique. In future work, we will develop attack strategies that utilize trained actors to mimic the action trajectories of a genuine user to determine how long it takes an attacker to mimic the physical behavior of a genuine user. The authentication task used in our approach was a purely physical task with limited cognitive requirements. In future, we will create a broader range of authentication tasks ranging from physical tasks, such as swinging a golf club, to cognitive tasks, such as solving a puzzle. As part of these experiments, we will include changes in the position and orientation of the subject in the virtual space, and investigate matching techniques such as iterative closest point to address offsets in rotation and translation between user trajectories. Our current work focuses on the dominant hand gesture controller. As part of future work, we are interested in analyzing the influence of the subtle motions of the head and the non-dominant hand on user authentication.

Acknowledgements. This work was partially supported by the National Science Foundation (NSF) grant #1730183. We acknowledge the support of NVIDIA Corporation with the donation of the Titan Xp GPU used for this research.

References

1. Ahmed, F., Paul, P.P., Gavrilova, M.L.: DTW-based kernel and rank-level fusion for 3D gait recognition using kinect. Vis. Comput. **31**, 915–924 (2015)
2. Andersson, V., Dutra, R., Araújo, R.: Anthropometric and human gait identification using skeleton data from kinect sensor. In: ACM SAP (2014)
3. Andriotis, P., Tryfonas, T., Oikonomou, G.: Complexity metrics and user strength perceptions of the pattern-lock graphical authentication method. In: Tryfonas, T., Askoxylakis, I. (eds.) HAS 2014. LNCS, vol. 8533, pp. 115–126. Springer, Cham (2014). https://doi.org/10.1007/978-3-319-07620-1_11
4. Berg, L.P., Vance, J.M.: Industry use of virtual reality in product design and manufacturing: a survey. Virtual Reality **21**, 1–17 (2017)
5. Bhagat, K.K., Liou, W.K., Chang, C.Y.: A cost-effective interactive 3D virtual reality system applied to military live firing training. Virtual Reality **20**, 127–140 (2016)
6. Choi, S., Jung, K., Noh, S.D.: Virtual reality applications in manufacturing industries: past research, present findings, and future directions. Concurrent Eng. **23**, 40–63 (2015)
7. Feng, T., et al.: Continuous mobile authentication using touchscreen gestures. In: IEEE HST (2012)
8. Frank, J., Mannor, S., Precup, D.: Activity and gait recognition with time-delay embeddings. In: AAAI (2010)
9. Freina, L., Ott, M.: A literature review on immersive virtual reality in education: state of the art and perspectives. In: The International Scientific Conference eLearning and Software for Education (2015)
10. George, C., et al.: Seamless and secure VR: Adapting and evaluating established authentication systems for virtual reality. In: NDSS (2017)
11. Haque, A., Alahi, A., Fei-Fei, L.: Recurrent attention models for depth-based person identification. In: IEEE CVPR (2016)
12. John, V., Englebienne, G., Krose, B.: Person re-identification using height-based gait in colour depth camera. In: IEEE ICIP (2013)
13. Kwapisz, J.R., Weiss, G.M., Moore, S.A.: Cell phone-based biometric identification. In: IEEE BTAS (2010)
14. Li, S., Ashok, A., Zhang, Y., Xu, C., Lindqvist, J., Gruteser, M.: Whose move is it anyway? authenticating smart wearable devices using unique head movement patterns. In: IEEE PerCom (2016)
15. Liu, J., Zhong, L., Wickramasuriya, J., Vasudevan, V.: uWave: accelerometer-based personalized gesture recognition and its applications. Pervasive Mobile Comput. **5**(6), 657–675 (2009)
16. Lohse, K.R., Hilderman, C.G., Cheung, K.L., Tatla, S., Van der Loos, H.M.: Virtual reality therapy for adults post-stroke: a systematic review and meta-analysis exploring virtual environments and commercial games in therapy. PloS one **9**, e93318 (2014)

17. Matsuo, K., Okumura, F., Hashimoto, M., Sakazawa, S., Hatori, Y.: Arm swing identification method with template update for long term stability. In: Lee, S.-W., Li, S.Z. (eds.) ICB 2007. LNCS, vol. 4642, pp. 211–221. Springer, Heidelberg (2007). https://doi.org/10.1007/978-3-540-74549-5_23

18. Mendels, O., Stern, H., Berman, S.: User identification for home entertainment based on free-air hand motion signatures. IEEE Trans. Syst., Man, Cybern. Syst. **44**, 1461–1473 (2014)

19. Merchant, Z., Goetz, E.T., Cifuentes, L., Keeney-Kennicutt, W., Davis, T.J.: Effectiveness of virtual reality-based instruction on students' learning outcomes in K-12 and higher education: a meta-analysis. Comput. Educ. **70**, 29–40 (2014)

20. Monrose, F., Reiter, M.K., Wetzel, S.: Password hardening based on keystroke dynamics. Int. J. Inf. Secur. **1**(2), 69–83 (2002)

21. Monrose, F., Rubin, A.D.: Keystroke dynamics as a biometric for authentication. Future Gener. Comput. Syst. **16**(4), 351–359 (2000)

22. Muaaz, M., Mayrhofer, R.: Orientation independent cell phone based gait authentication. In: Proceedings of the 12th International Conference on Advances in Mobile Computing and Multimedia (2014)

23. Muaaz, M., Mayrhofer, R.: Smartphone-based gait recognition: from authentication to imitation. IEEE Trans. Mob. Comput. **16**, 3209–3221 (2017)

24. Munsell, B.C., Temlyakov, A., Qu, C., Wang, S.: Person identification using full-body motion and anthropometric biometrics from kinect videos. In: Fusiello, A., Murino, V., Cucchiara, R. (eds.) ECCV 2012. LNCS, vol. 7585, pp. 91–100. Springer, Heidelberg (2012). https://doi.org/10.1007/978-3-642-33885-4_10

25. North, M.M., North, S.M., Coble, J.R.: Virtual reality therapy: an effective treatment for the fear of public speaking. IJVR **3**, 1–6 (2015)

26. Oberhauser, M., Dreyer, D.: A virtual reality flight simulator for human factors engineering. Cogn., Technol. Work **19**, 263–277 (2017)

27. Okumura, F., Kubota, A., Hatori, Y., Matsuo, K., Hashimoto, M., Koike, A.: A study on biometric authentication based on arm sweep action with acceleration sensor. In: ISPACS (2006)

28. Pallavicini, F., Toniazzi, N., Argenton, L., Aceti, L., Mantovani, F.: Developing effective virtual reality training for military forces and emergency operators: from technology to human factors. In: International Conference on Modeling and Applied Simulation, MAS 2015 (2015)

29. Rogers, C.E., Witt, A.W., Solomon, A.D., Venkatasubramanian, K.K.: An approach for user identification for head-mounted displays. In: ACM ISWC (2015)

30. Schneegass, S., Oualil, Y., Bulling, A.: Skullconduct: biometric user identification on eyewear computers using bone conduction through the skull. In: ACM CHI (2016)

31. Serwadda, A., Phoha, V.V., Wang, Z.: Which verifiers work?: a benchmark evaluation of touch-based authentication algorithms. In: IEEE BTAS (2013)

32. Sprager, S., Zazula, D.: A cumulant-based method for gait identification using accelerometer data with principal component analysis and support vector machine. WSEAS Trans. Sig. Process. **5**, 369–378 (2009)

33. Syed, Z., Banerjee, S., Cheng, Q., Cukic, B.: Effects of user habituation in keystroke dynamics on password security policy. In: IEEE HASE, pp. 352–359 (2011)

34. Syed, Z., Helmick, J., Banerjee, S., Cukic, B.: Effect of user posture and device size on the performance of touch-based authentication systems. In: IEEE HASE (2015)

35. Wiederhold, B.K., Wiederhold, M.D.: Virtual reality therapy for anxiety disorders: advances in evaluation and treatment. American Psychological Association, Worcester (2005)
36. Wu, J., Konrad, J., Ishwar, P.: Dynamic time warping for gesture-based user identification and authentication with kinect. In: IEEE ICASSP, pp. 2371–2375 (2013)
37. Yu, Z., Liang, H.N., Fleming, C., Man, K.L.: An exploration of usable authentication mechanisms for virtual reality systems. In: IEEE APCCAS (2016)
38. Zhong, Y., Deng, Y., Meltzner, G.: Pace independent mobile gait biometrics. In: IEEE BTAS (2015)

Deep Neural Network Based 3D Articulatory Movement Prediction Using Both Text and Audio Inputs

Lingyun Yu, Jun Yu$^{(\boxtimes)}$, and Qiang Ling$^{(\boxtimes)}$

Department of Automation, University of Science and Technology of China,
Hefei 230027, Anhui, China
yuly@mail.ustc.edu.cn, {harryjun,qling}@ustc.edu.cn

Abstract. Robust and accurate predicting of articulatory movements has various important applications, such as human-machine interaction. Various approaches have been proposed to solve the acoustic-articulatory mapping problem. However, their precision is not high enough with only acoustic features available. Recently, deep neural network (DNN) has brought tremendous success in many fields. To increase the accuracy, on the one hand, we propose a new network architecture called bottleneck squeeze-and-excitation recurrent convolutional neural network (BSERCNN) for articulatory movement prediction. On the one hand, by introducing the squeeze-and-excitation (SE) module, our BSERCNN can model the interdependencies and relationships between channels and that makes our model more efficiency. On the other hand, phoneme-level text features and acoustic features are integrated together as inputs to BSERCNN for better performance. Experiments show that BSERCNN achieves the state-of-the-art root-mean-squared error (RMSE) 0.563 mm and the correlation coefficient 0.954 with both text and audio inputs.

Keywords: Deep Neural Network · Squeeze-and-excitation module
Bottleneck network · Articulatory movement prediction

1 Introduction

Synthetic 3D articulatory animation, with human-like appearance and articulatory movements, is a popular topic in interactive multimedia. For instance, in pronunciation training, 3D articulatory animations, generated by the 3D facial mesh model [1] and articulatory movements, can assist people to learn correct pronunciation in language tutoring. In medical treatment based on multimedia, 3D articulatory animations can be used as an adjuvant treatment for patients with hearing impairment [2]. Moreover, in human-machine interaction, 3D articulatory animations use visual cues, such as lip and tongue movements, to improve the capability of expressing and recognizing feelings [3]. To generate 3D articulatory animations, a most important issue is the articulatory movement prediction. However, it is difficult to predict the movements of articulators, because this

© Springer Nature Switzerland AG 2019
I. Kompatsiaris et al. (Eds.): MMM 2019, LNCS 11295, pp. 68–79, 2019.
https://doi.org/10.1007/978-3-030-05710-7_6

regression problem is ill-posed [4]. Meanwhile, coarticulation is also a great challenge in this task. To solve these problems, various methods have been proposed and a few of the most relevant examples are as follows.

For acoustic-articulatory mapping, Toda et al. [5] adopt a Gaussian mixture model (GMM) to model the joint probability density of acoustic and articulatory parameters, achieving the root-mean-squared error (RMSE) of 1.43 mm. Zhang et al. [6] present a hidden Markov model (HMM) based inversion system to recovery articulatory movements from speech. Recently, due to the tremendous success in speech recognition [7] and synthesis [8], deep neural network (DNN) also has been introduced to this mapping. Uria et al. [9] implement a deep belief network (DBN) [10] and a deep trajectory mixture density network (TMDN). Their work provides a first demonstration of applying deep architectures to a complex, time-varying regression problem. Furthermore, Zhu et al. [11] investigate the feasibility of using deep bidirectional long short-term memory (BLSTM). Their approach indicates that recurrent neural network (RNN) is capable of learning long time-dependencies, obtaining the lowest RMSE of 0.565 mm. For text-to-articulatory-movement prediction, Wei et al. [12] propose to combine the stacked bottleneck features and linguistic features as inputs to improve accuracy. More importantly, compared to that only acoustic features or text information is used as input, the performance can be improved when they are integrated together [13].

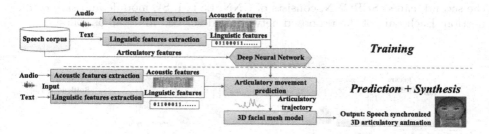

Fig. 1. The overall framework of this paper.

According to the analysis above, we can conclude two points. First, DNN can bring a clear RMSE reduction than traditional methods [11]. Second, the prediction performance can be improved with both text and audio inputs [13]. To improve the accuracy, we introduce the DNN-based articulatory movement prediction by fusing text and audio inputs. The overall framework of the proposed method is shown in Fig. 1. Indeed, DNN has brought tremendous success in many fields. For example, RNN, especially long short-term memory (LSTM), can retain an internal memory to learn the context information for sequential problems [11]. Convolutional neural network (CNN), using local connectivity and weight sharing, can learn translational invariant features and achieves excellent performance on speech recognition [14]. However, for each convolutional layer, a set of filters are merely learned to express local spatial connectivity patterns along input channels. In order to better model spatial dependence and incorporate spatial attention, the squeeze-and-excitation (SE) module [15] is introduced to model the interdependencies between the channels of convolutional features. Our major contributions are summarized as follows.

(1) We introduce DNN-based articulatory movement prediction with both text and audio inputs for the first time. The linguistic features extracted from text contain broad context information. The acoustic features extracted from audio have high synchronous and high dependent relationship with articulatory movements. Thus, the combination of them can make full use of different inputs to achieve excellent results.
(2) The SE module is introduced to articulatory movement prediction. This module can make the network more powerful by emphasizing important features and suppress useless features among the channels. We find that adding the module can improve the performance.

2   The Proposed Approach

We propose a new network architecture bottleneck squeeze-and-excitation recurrent convolutional neural network (BSERCNN) for articulatory movement prediction. The proposed BSERCNN consists of two networks (shown in Fig. 2). The first is the bottleneck network with a narrow bottleneck hidden layer. And the second, called SERCNN, consists of CNN, LSTM, SE module and skip connection. Each part of the proposed network is described in detail as follows.

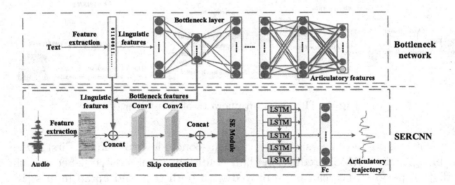

Fig. 2. (a) The proposed BSERCNN for articulatory movement prediction with both text and audio inputs.

2.1   Bottleneck Features

Bottleneck features are the activation at a bottleneck layer in DNN. Since there are far fewer hidden units in a bottleneck layer, this small layer can force the input information into a low dimensional representation. It means that these bottleneck features can represent a nonlinear transform and dimensionality reduction of input features [16]. Furthermore, the bottleneck features capture information that is complementary to input features [16]. Inspired by the superiority mentioned above, the bottleneck features are introduced as the supplementary input features when text and audio are integrated as inputs.

In this paper, the bottleneck network is designed as a typical architecture of DNN with a narrow bottleneck hidden layer (Fig. 2). It is trained with the linguistic features as input and articulatory features as output. Then the bottleneck features are combined with the acoustic features and the original linguistic features as inputs of SERCNN for articulatory movement prediction.

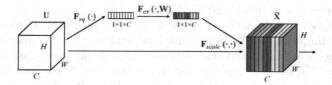

Fig. 3. The SE module.

2.2 The SE Module

Inspired by the SENet [15], the SE module is adopted to articulatory movement prediction. This module can make the network more powerful by modeling the interdependencies among channels and reweight the features [17]. Specifically, the SE module [15] can be split into two parts (shown in Fig. 3): the squeeze and excitation. For the squeeze part, it can squeeze global spatial information of each channel into a channel descriptor. This operation can be achieved by using global average pooling to generate channel-wise statistics. Formally, a statistic z is generated by shrinking $U = [u_1, u_2, ..., u_c]$ through spatial dimensions $H \times W$, where the c-th element of z is calculated by:

$$z_c = F_{sq}(u_c) = \frac{1}{H \times W} \sum_{i=1}^{H} \sum_{j=1}^{W} u_c(i,j) \tag{1}$$

where $F_{sq}(.)$ is the squeeze function and z_c is the c-th element of the squeezed channels. u_c is the c-th channel of the input. H and W denote the height and width of the input. For the excitation part, it is capable of capturing channel-wise dependencies and reweighting the features. To meet these demands, a simple gating mechanism, with a sigmoid activation, is employed as:

$$s = F_{ex}(z, W) = \sigma(g(z, W)) = \sigma(W_2 \sigma(W_1 z)) \tag{2}$$

where $F_{ex}(.)$ is the excitation function and σ denotes the sigmoid function. $W_1 \in \mathbb{R}^{\frac{c}{r} \times c}$ and $W_2 \in \mathbb{R}^{c \times \frac{c}{r}}$ denote the 1×1 convolutional layer with reduction ratio r. The final output of the SE module is obtained by rescaling the transformation output U as:

$$\tilde{x}_c = F_{scale}(u_c, s_c) = s_c.u_c \tag{3}$$

where $\tilde{X} = [\tilde{x}_1, \tilde{x}_2, ..., \tilde{x}_c]$, and $F_{scale}(u_c, s_c)$ denotes the channel-wise multiplication between the feature map u_c and the scale s_c.

2.3   The Architecture of BSERCNN

The overall network architecture-BSERCNN (Fig. 2) is proposed for articulatory movement prediction with both text and audio inputs. It consists of two main parts, the bottleneck network and SERCNN.

First, the bottleneck network, with a narrow bottleneck hidden layer, is trained with linguistic features as input and articulatory features as output. Six hidden layers are used, and the bottleneck layer is on the second layer. Each layer contains 256 units except for the 32 units of the bottleneck layer. Each convolution layer is followed by Rectified Linear Unit (ReLU) operation.

Second, the bottleneck features are combined with the acoustic features and the original linguistic features as the input of SERCNN to predict articulatory movements. In SERCNN, combining CNN with LSTM can extract local spatial features and store the temporal state. Besides, the SE model can make the network more powerful by emphasizing important features and suppress useless features among channels [17]. Enhancing the input representation learned from different layers, skip connection can improve the accuracy by preserving the feature information. In this paper, the SERCNN includes 2 convolutional layers with 128 features maps, a SE model, a LSTM layer with 1024 feature maps and a skip connection between convolutional layers. Among them, in the SE module, the squeeze was done by global average pooling. We reduce the number of output channels to 16 and then increase the number of channels to 256. We then use the sigmoid layer to model the correlations between the channels. The weights for channels are then multiplied with the transformation output.

3   Experiments

In this section, we describe dataset and input features, implementation details. Besides, to verify the superiority of fusing text and audio as inputs, we also make contrast experiments with only text and only audio input.

3.1   Dataset and Input Features

Our experiments are carried out on MNGU0 dataset with 1263 English utterances from a male British English speaker [18]. Parallel recordings of acoustic data and EMA data are available. Six EMA sensors are used, located at Tongue

Tip (T1), Tongue Blade (T2), Tongue Rear (T3), Lower Incisor (LI), Upper Lip (UL) and Lower Lip (LL) of the speaker. Each sensor records data in 3 dimensions. Only the data in x-axis (front to back) and y-axis (bottom to top) are used in the experiment because the movements in z-axis (left to right) are very small. In order to compare with other methods, the dataset is partitioned into three sets as [9,11,13]: validation and testing sets comprising 63 utterances each, and a training set consisting of the other 1137 utterances.

The waveforms are in 16kHz PCM format. The acoustic features are extracted including 60-dimensional Mel-Cepstral Coefficients (MCCs), 1-dimensional band aperiodicities (BAPs) and 1-dimensional log-scale fundamental frequency (logF0) with deltas and delta-delta features. Moreover, the linguistic features are extracted from text by Merlin [19]. The linguistic features consist of 416-dimension binary features and 9-dimension numerical features [12]. Among them, the 416-dimensional features, derived from the fully-context labels, represent the context information. The 9-dimensional numerical features represent the frame position information.

3.2   Implementation

We carry out the experiments based on Intel i7-6700K 4.0G, 16G memory and NVIDIA GTX1080. All the networks are trained using stochastic gradient descent (SGD) with a batch size of 60, implemented in Caffe [20]. The bottleneck network is trained with a learning rate of 0.0015 and a momentum of 0.9. And the SERCNN is trained with a learning rate of 0.0001, a momentum of 0.9 and a weight decay of 0.0005. The weights are initialized based on a Gaussian distribution. We train all the networks for 50 epochs from scratch. During Training, the validation set in MNGU0 dataset is used to refine and select the best model including the weights and bias. Furthermore, we explore the performance based on DNN with different inputs. The detailed processes are expounded as follows.

3.3   Articulatory Movement Prediction from Audio Input Alone

Two metrics are used to measure the performance of our systems. The first metric is the RMSE that reflects the difference between the predicted value and the real value integrally:

$$\text{RMSE} = \sqrt{\sum_{i=1}^{n} (y_i - \hat{y}_i)^2 / n} \tag{4}$$

where y and $\hat{y}$ represent the predicted articulatory trajectories and the real articulatory trajectories recorded by EMA. n represents the number of frames.

The second is the correlation coefficient r:

$$r = \sum_{i=1}^{n} (y_i - y')(\hat{y}_i - \hat{y}') / \sqrt{\sum_{i=1}^{n} (y_i - y')^2 \sum_{i} (\hat{y}_i - \hat{y}')^2} \tag{5}$$

where y' and $\hat{y}'$ are the mean values of y and $\hat{y}$.

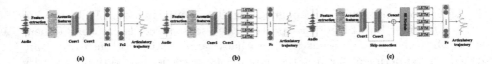

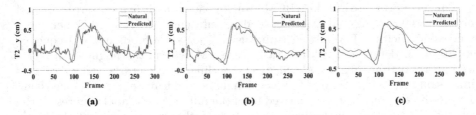

Fig. 4. The network architectures of (a) CNN (b) CNN-LSTM, and (c) SERCNN for articulatory movement prediction with audio input alone.

Fig. 5. The comparisons for articulatory trajectories predicted from (a) CNN, (b) CNN-LSTM and (c) SERCNN with only audio input.

In this section, we investigate the SERCNN for acoustic-articulatory mapping (Fig. 4(c)). Besides, to compare with the prediction performance of SERCNN, the combination of CNN and LSTM (CNN-LSTM, Fig. 4(b)) and CNN alone (Fig. 4(a)) are also utilized. In CNN-LSTM, 2 convolutional layers and a LSTM are directly combined. The network CNN alone includes 2 convolutional layers with each 128 features maps and 2 fully-connected layers.

The results are shown in Table 1 and Fig. 5. The RMSE predicted from CNN-LSTM is lower than that predicted from CNN and the articulatory trajectory predicted from CNN-LSTM is smoother and closer to the real one. These results demonstrate that CNN can learn local higher-level features, but it fails to acquire sequential correlations. Whereas, the LSTM, following CNN, can learn proper context information from purpose-built memory cells for better performance. Besides, compared to CNN-LSTM and CNN, SERCNN brings a clear RMSE reduction and the articulatory trajectory predicted from SERCNN is smoother and closer to the real one. These results indicate that the SE module can make the network more powerful by reweighting the features among channels and the skip connection can enhance the input representation learned by different layers to boost the performance significantly.

3.4   Articulatory Movement Prediction from Text Input Alone

In this section, SERCNN is proposed for text-to-articulatory mapping (Fig. 6(a)). The DNN approach [12], consisting of fully-connected networks, achieves the mean RMSE with 0.737 mm. As far as we know, this is the best result publicly ever reported. From Table 2 and Fig. 6(b), the SERCNN achieves the lowest RMSE with 0.695 mm. Meanwhile, the articulatory trajectory predicted from SERCNN is smooth and close to the real one. These results demonstrate

Table 1. The comparison of the RMSE and the correlation coefficient for different network architectures with audio input alone.

	RMSE	Correlation coefficient
CNN	1.191 mm	0.822
CNN-LSTM	1.001 mm	0.883
SERCNN	**0.747 mm**	**0.924**

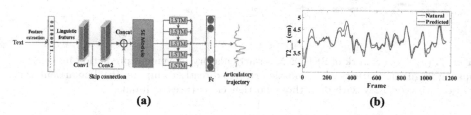

(a)   **(b)**

Fig. 6. (a) The network architecture of SERCNN for articulatory movement prediction with text input alone. (b) Articulatory trajectories predicted from SERCNN with only text input for T2_x.

that SERCNN, including SE module, CNN, LSTM and skip connection, has high expression capability for sequential problems and make full use of the features.

Table 2. The comparison of the RMSE and the correlation coefficient for different methods with text input alone.

	RMSE	Correlation coefficient
HMM [21]	0.872 mm	\
DNN [12]	0.737 mm	\
SERCNN	**0.695 mm**	**0.944**

3.5 Articulatory Movement Prediction from Text and Audio Inputs

Effect of Bottleneck Network. In this section, we explore BSERCNN (Fig. 2(a)), including bottleneck network and SERCNN, for articulatory movements by fusing text and audio inputs. The bottleneck features, extracted from bottleneck network, can be considered a dimensionality reduction and nonlinear feature transformation. To verify the effectiveness of the bottleneck network, we make a contrast experiment when linguistic features are concatenated with acoustic features directly (without bottleneck features, Fig. 7(a)). Table 3 shows that BSERCNN achieves a lower RMSE and higher correlation coefficient. Figure 7(c) shows that the predicted articulatory trajectory is closer to the real one when the input is with bottleneck features. These results demonstrate that bottleneck features, as the supplementary of input features, can boost the performance significantly.

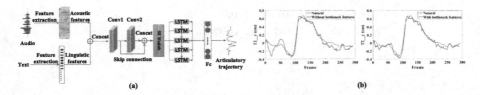

(a)   (b)

Fig. 7. (a) The network of SERCNN for articulatory movement prediction by concatenating linguistic features and acoustic features directly as inputs. (b) The articulatory trajectories for T2_y with or without bottleneck features as input.

Table 3. The comparison of the RMSE and the correlation coefficient whether the input features are with the bottleneck features.

	RMSE	Correlation coefficient
SERCNN (without bottleneck features)	0.635 mm	0.941
BSERCNN (with bottleneck features)	**0.563 mm**	**0.954**

Fusing Text and Audio Inputs. In this part, we explore the effectiveness of fusing text and audio input. Figure 8 compares the predicted articulatory trajectories when the input is (a) only audio input, (b) only text input, and (c) both text and audio inputs. Table 4 shows the comparison of different methods for articulatory movement prediction on MNGU0 dataset. In Fig. 8, articulatory trajectories predicted from both text and audio are the smoothest and achieve the highest consistency with the real one. Table 4 shows that BSERCNN achieves the state-of-the-art RMSE 0.563 mm and the correlation coefficient 0.954 with both text and audio inputs. These results demonstrate that the combination of text and audio contains not only the phoneme-level context information but also spectral features, which are all essential for articulatory movement prediction.

Table 4. The RMSE and the correlation coefficient predicted from different methods on MNGU0 dataset.

	TMDN [22]	HMM [13]	DRMDN [23]	BLSTM [23]	DNN [12]	BLSTM [11]	**BSERCNN**
RMSE	0.99 mm	0.90 mm	0.832 mm	0.816 mm	0.737 mm	0.565 mm	**0.563 mm**
Correlation coefficient	\	0.812	0.914	0.921	\	\	**0.954**

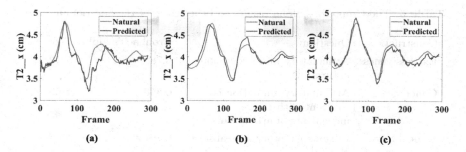

Fig. 8. The comparison of the real and predicted articulatory trajectories for T2_x with (a) only audio input, (b) only text input, (c) both text and audio inputs.

4 Perceptual Evaluation of Networks

The performance of the network can be evaluated by 3D articulatory animations[1] which are generated by the 3D facial mesh model [24] and the predicted articulatory movements. Figure 9 shows the movements of articulators for the latter phoneme 'a' in 'Sarah' and the phoneme 'b' in 'subject'. The main goal of the evaluation is to decide whether the 3D articulatory animation is consistent with the corresponding real articulatory movements. We adopt the similar method as [24]. In the experiment, one hundred volunteers are selected randomly who can speak English fluently. Table 5 shows the constructs and questions of the survey. Besides, a Cronbach's alpha test [25] is also carried out to reflect the reliability between constructs. The answers to these questions are given from 'absolutely disagree' to 'totally agree' on a ten-point scale, where the maximum score is 10 and the minimum score is 0. Table 5 shows the mean scores after evaluation. The alpha values are higher than 0.7, indicating that the questionnaire is suitable for the evaluation. And the scores of all constructs are higher than 8.0, proving the articulatory animation is consistent with the corresponding real movements.

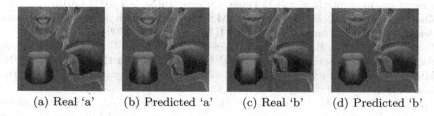

(a) Real 'a'   (b) Predicted 'a'   (c) Real 'b'   (d) Predicted 'b'

Fig. 9. The positions of articulators for the latter phoneme 'a' in 'Sarah' and the phoneme 'b' in 'subject'. (a)–(b) represent the real and predicted phoneme of 'a'. (c)–(d) represent the real and predicted phoneme of 'b'.

---

[1] The demo can be downloaded from https://pan.baidu.com/s/1q0YLvdqq8WVU 5OOLj0ru1w.

Table 5. The Cronbach's alpha results and the scores of the questionnaire.

Construct	Question	Cronbach's alpha	Score
Expressiveness	Articulatory movements look natural	0.789	8.12
Coherence	Articulatory animation is coherent with the real movements of articulators	0.850	8.53
Appearance	I like articulatory appearance	0.761	8.27

5 Conclusions

In this paper, the overall architecture BSERCNN, combining CNN, LSTM, SE module and bottleneck network, is proposed for articulatory movement prediction with both text and audio inputs. Our approach BSERCNN achieves the state-of-the-art results with the RMSE 0.563 mm and the correlation coefficient 0.954. Besides, we also analyze the performance when the input is text alone and audio alone, respectively. Our network also achieves the lowest RMSE 0.695 mm in text-to-articulatory movement prediction. Comprehensive experimental results further prove that both text and audio are essential for this prediction.

Acknowledgement. This work is supported by the National Natural Science Foundation of China (U1736123, 61572450), Anhui Provincial Natural Science Foundation (1708085QF138), the Fundamental Research Funds for the Central Universities (WK2350000002).

References

1. Yu, J., Wang, Z.-F.: A video, text, and speech-driven realistic 3-D virtual head for human-machine interface. IEEE Trans. Cybern. **45**(5), 991–1002 (2015)
2. Zhao, G., Barnard, M., Pietikainen, M.: Lipreading with local spatiotemporal descriptors. IEEE Trans. Multimedia **11**(7), 1254–1265 (2009)
3. Fanelli, G., Gall, J., Romsdorfer, H., Weise, T., Van Gool, L.: A 3-D audio-visual corpus of affective communication. IEEE Trans. Multimedia **12**(6), 591–598 (2010)
4. Mitra, V.: Articulatory information for robust speech recognition, Ph.D. dissertation (2010)
5. Toda, T., Black, A.W., Tokuda, K.: Statistical mapping between articulatory movements and acoustic spectrum using a gaussian mixture model. Speech Commun. **50**(3), 215–227 (2008)
6. Zhang, L., Renals, S.: Acoustic-articulatory modeling with the trajectory HMM. IEEE Signal Process. Lett. **15**, 245–248 (2008)
7. Deng, L., Hinton, G., Kingsbury, B.: New types of deep neural network learning for speech recognition and related applications: an overview. In: IEEE International Conference on Acoustics, Speech and Signal Processing, pp. 8599–8603 (2013)

8. Qian, Y., Fan, Y., Hu, W., Soong, F.K.: On the training aspects of deep neural network (DNN) for parametric TTS synthesis. In: IEEE International Conference on Acoustics, Speech and Signal Processing, pp. 3829–3833 (2014)
9. Uria, B., Murray, I., Renals, S., Richmond, K.: Deep architectures for articulatory inversion. In: Thirteenth Annual Conference of the International Speech Communication Association (2012)
10. Uria, B., Renals, S., Richmond, K.: A deep neural network for acoustic-articulatory speech inversion. In: NIPS 2011 Workshop on Deep Learning and Unsupervised Feature Learning (2011)
11. Zhu, P., Xie, L., Chen, Y.: Articulatory movement prediction using deep bidirectional long short-term memory based recurrent neural networks and word/phone embeddings. In: INTERSPEECH, pp. 2192–2196 (2015)
12. Wei, Z., Wu, Z., Xie, L.: Predicting articulatory movement from text using deep architecture with stacked bottleneck features. In: 2016 Asia-Pacific Signal and Information Processing Association Annual Summit and Conference (APSIPA), pp. 1–6. IEEE (2016)
13. Ling, Z.H., Richmond, K., Yamagishi, J.: An analysis of HMM-based prediction of articulatory movements. Speech Commun. **52**(10), 834–846 (2010)
14. Abdel-Hamid, O., Mohamed, A.-R., Jiang, H., Deng, L., Penn, G., Yu, D.: Convolutional neural networks for speech recognition. IEEE/ACM Trans. Audio, Speech, Lang. Process. **22**(10), 1533–1545 (2014)
15. Hu, J., Shen, L., Sun, G.: Squeeze-and-excitation networks, arXiv preprint arXiv:1709.01507, vol. 7 (2017)
16. Yu, D., Seltzer, M.L.: Improved bottleneck features using pretrained deep neural networks. In: Twelfth Annual Conference of the International Speech Communication Association (2011)
17. Cheng, X., Li, X., Tai, Y., Yang, J.: SESR: Single image super resolution with recursive squeeze and excitation networks, arXiv preprint arXiv:1801.10319 (2018)
18. Schönle, P.W., Gräbe, K., Wenig, P., Höhne, J., Schrader, J., Conrad, B.: Electromagnetic articulography: use of alternating magnetic fields for trackingmovements of multiple points inside and outside the vocal tract. Brain Lang. **31**(1), 26–35 (1987)
19. Wu, Z., Watts, O., King, S.: Merlin: an open source neural network speech synthesis system. Proc. SSW, Sunnyvale, USA (2016)
20. Jia, Y., Shelhamer, E., Donahue, J., et al.: Caffe: Convolutional architecture for fast feature embedding. In: Proceedings of the 22nd ACM International Conference on Multimedia, pp. 675–678. ACM (2014)
21. Ling, Z.-H., Richmond, K., Yamagishi, J.: HMM-based text-to-articulatory-movement prediction and analysis of critical articulators. In: Proc. Interspeech, pp. 2194–2197, Sep. 2010
22. Richmond, K.: Preliminary inversion mapping results with a new EMA corpus (2009)
23. Liu, P., Yu, Q., Wu, Z., Kang, S., Meng, H., Cai, L.: A deep recurrent approach for acoustic-to-articulatory inversion. In: 2015 IEEE International Conference on Acoustics, Speech and Signal Processing (ICASSP), pp. 4450–4454. IEEE (2015)
24. Yu, J., Li, A., Hu, F., et al.: Data-driven 3D visual pronunciation of Chinese IPA for language learning. In: 2013 International Conference on Oriental COCOSDA Held Jointly with 2013 Conference on Asian Spoken Language Research and Evaluation (O-COCOSDA/CASLRE), pp. 1–6. IEEE (2013)
25. Marcos, S., Gómez-García-Bermejo, J., Zalama, E.: A realistic, virtual head for human-computer interaction. Interact. Comput. **22**(3), 176–192 (2010)

Subjective Visual Quality Assessment of Immersive 3D Media Compressed by Open-Source Static 3D Mesh Codecs

Kyriaki Christaki$^{(\boxtimes)}$, Emmanouil Christakis, Petros Drakoulis,
Alexandros Doumanoglou[iD], Nikolaos Zioulis[iD], Dimitrios Zarpalas,
and Petros Daras

Visual Computing Lab, Information Technologies Institute,
Centre for Research and Technology Hellas, Thessaloniki, Greece
{kchristaki,manchr,petros.drakoulis,aldoum,nzioulis,zarpalas,
daras}@iti.gr
http://vcl.iti.gr

Abstract. While studies for objective and subjective evaluation of the visual quality of compressed 3D meshes has been discussed in the literature, those studies were covering the evaluation of 3D-meshes either created by 3D artists or generated by a computationally expensive reconstruction process applied on high quality 3D scans. With the advent of RGB-D sensors operating at high frame-rates and the utilization of fast 3D reconstruction algorithms, humans can be captured and reconstructed into a 3D representation in real-time, enabling new (tele-)immersive experiences. The produced 3D mesh content is structurally different in the two cases. The first type of content is nearly perfect and clean while the second type is much more irregular and noisy. Evaluating compression artifacts on this new type of immersive 3D media, constitutes a yet unexplored scientific area. In this paper, we conduct a survey to subjectively assess the perceived fidelity of 3D meshes subjected to compression using three open-source static 3D mesh codecs compared to the original uncompressed models. The subjective evaluation of the content is conducted in a Virtual Reality setting, using the forced-choice pairwise comparison methodology with existing reference. The results of this study are two-fold; first, the design of an experimental setup that can be used for the subjective evaluation of 3D media, and second, a mapping of the compared conditions to a continuous ranking scale. The latter can be used when selecting codecs and optimizing their compression parameters to achieve optimum balance between bandwidth and perceived quality in tele-immersive platforms.

Keywords: Subjective visual quality study · 3D · Compression
Tele-immersion · Forced pairwise comparison · Virtual reality (VR)

© Springer Nature Switzerland AG 2019
I. Kompatsiaris et al. (Eds.): MMM 2019, LNCS 11295, pp. 80–91, 2019.
https://doi.org/10.1007/978-3-030-05710-7_7

1 Introduction

Nowadays, advances in the fields of 3D capturing, imaging and processing technologies have allowed the advent of new forms of interactive immersive experiences. Mixed reality and tele-immersive platforms [6,17], are now investigated as applications that increase user engagement and immersion by embedding 3D reconstructed human representations in virtual environments. These 3D representations usually take the form of 3D meshes. A 3D mesh is a collection of vertices and faces (triangles) that defines the surface of an object in three dimensions. In the previous decades, 3D meshes were mostly created in specialized modeling software by 3D expert artists or generated by 3D reconstruction algorithms operating on real world depth data acquired by 3D scanners. In both scenarios, the 3D mesh outcomes are perfect and clean, as in the first case they are manually crafted and in the second, they are produced off-line by computationally expensive algorithms on high precise depth data acquired by the aforementioned 3D scanners. The real-time production of human 3D meshes in modern mixed reality and tele-immersive platforms, conceptually undergo a similar automatic process as mentioned previously, with the fundamental difference of utilizing computationally cheaper reconstruction algorithms operating on depth data of lower precision, acquired at high frame rates. Contrariwise to the above mentioned perfect and clean meshes, the latter are highly irregular and noisy.

To realize the tele-immersion experience, the human 3D meshes are required to be transmitted in real-time to remote parties, often not without compression. However, in that case, an overly aggressive compression scheme can negatively impact the content quality and the viewer's quality of experience. Oftentimes, the assessment of the geometrical similarity between 3D meshes via objective metrics is used to measure the fidelity of a compressed model to the original. However, objective metrics might not correlate well with viewers' perceived visual quality that may also be related to psychophysical factors. While subjective studies on the visual quality of compressed 3D meshes have been extensively discussed in the literature, the overwhelming majority of those works studied compression artifacts on clean and perfect 3D meshes. Subjectively evaluating compression artifacts on immersive 3D media (3D meshes produced in mixed reality and tele-immersive platforms) is a field not yet thoroughly explored.

In this paper, we try to investigate the impact of the chosen 3D mesh codec and the value of geometric distortion parameter on the subjective visual quality of compressed immersive 3D media. In particular, we examine the geometric distortion artifacts induced by three open-source static 3D mesh codecs on watertight meshes of reconstructed human models, produced in mixed reality platforms. In order to examine possible effects of the mesh production process on the subject's opinion, we perform two independent subjective experiments by using the same codecs and compression parameters but different datasets. The first dataset is composed of human 3D meshes generated by a real-time 3D reconstruction algorithm used in a mixed-reality platform, while the second one consists of samples taken from an open repository containing high quality 3D reconstructed meshes of precisely 3D scanned real world objects.

Tested conditions include various codec and compression parameter combinations. Instead of using the conventional approach of a 2D monitor, we chose to use a virtual reality (VR) headset as our display medium. A VR headset allows for realistic and natural viewing of the surveyed content as the (human) 3D models can be observed in real-life sizes. In addition, it is also very aligned with the envisaged applications of tele-immersive content that focus on an elevated feeling of presence and natural interactions.

The main contributions of this paper are:

- The setup of a consistent experiment for subjective evaluation of compressed immersive 3D media in a VR setting.
- To provide a concise analysis of the collected subjective data, leading to an overall ranking of the compared conditions, implicitly capturing the subjective preference on the compression algorithm and distortion levels.
- To provide a side-by-side comparison on how the same compression conditions affect subjective preference depending on the source type of the 3D meshes, being either immersive 3D media or meshes generated by 3D reconstructing high quality 3D scans of real objects.

The rest of the paper is organized as follows. Firstly, in Sect. 2, we present existing works related to objective and subjective quality assessment, where the effect of one or multiple distortion parameters on 3D mesh and point cloud geometry is examined. Section 3 presents this survey's experimental setup. In Sect. 4 we present and analyze the survey's results and discuss on the relation between an objective metric (Hausdorff distance) and the acquired subjective ratings. Finally, in Sect. 5 we conclude by highlighting the main findings of this study.

2   Related Work

There exist a number of objective metrics that are used to measure the geometric error between 3D meshes, as there is not a single more appropriate way to measure the difference between 3D geometries [10]. One of the most widely accepted ones, also typically used when comparing the performance of 3D compression methods, is the Hausdorff distance [9]. While objective metrics results might not necessarily agree with the perceived - by the viewers - quality, they are commonly used for evaluating degradation effects on 3D meshes, as subjective evaluation can be time expensive. Nonetheless there are also works that focus on evaluating the quality of 3D meshes and point clouds, affected by distortions, on a subjective basis.

Subjective quality assessment of mesh distortions, other than compression: In [27], the authors perform a subjective evaluation survey to determine how down-sampling or adding coordinate/color noise in 3D point cloud affects the perceived quality using a Mean-Opinion-Score (MOS) methodology. A subjective study of 3D point cloud denoising algorithms with the use of Double-Stimulus-Impairment-Scale (DSIS) methodology is presented in [15] and the correlation with objectives metrics is investigated. However, the focus of this study is to assess the performance of denoising algorithms rather than the quality of the geometry of the compressed meshes. In a later work [8], a subjective evaluation with the use of DSIS methodology and Mean-Opinion-Scores of 3D point cloud models with different noise distortion levels and geometry resolution in an Augmented Reality (AR) environment, is presented. The study concludes that the geometric complexity of the model affects the evaluation score and that there is low correlation between objective and subjective metrics. While relevant, this study is focused on clean models as opposed to immersive 3D media. Another study [25] in VR assesses the impact of the number of mesh triangles on the perceived quality using a pairwise comparison with forced choice. An interesting conclusion is drawn, which is that by displaying the meshes either using a VR headset or a regular monoscopic display, there are no significant differences in the choices of the subjects. This result, however, cannot be safely extrapolated to the effects of compression.

Subjective quality assessment of mesh distortions related to compression: In [16], a subjective and objective evaluation of two point cloud compression schemes, Octree-based and Graph-based compression, is attempted. The authors correlate the subjective results obtained using the DSIS methodology, with two different types of objective metrics, namely, Point-to-Point and Point-to-Plane metrics. However, a typical LCD monitor was used as the display medium during the user study. In a similar context [7], performs a study in order to correlate objective and subjective metrics for the evaluation of point clouds subjected to realistic degradations. An interesting finding is that although there is a strong correlation between subjective and objective metrics in noise related distortions, they do not correlate well in the case of compression related distortions. While relevant to our work, their study is focused on clean point clouds and the evaluation is performed on a flat screen. In [20], an objective and subjective evaluation of different compression algorithms applied on reconstructed 3D human meshes in a virtual environment is presented. This work, while in the same application area with ours, is focusing on compression of immersive 3D-media without investigating compression artifacts on clean models. Furthermore, the real-time 3D reconstruction method used to produce the human 3D meshes in [20] is one of the first in the field, while in the current paper we use 3D meshes produced by a more recent and higher quality method [6]. Additionally, while the meshes used in [20] are textured, we choose to exclude texturing from our meshes in an effort to eliminate the unwanted effects of texturing on the subjects' choices, as texture masking can greatly reduce the perception of geometric distortions and degradations [11]. Finally, in the present work we consider more recent and open-sourced 3D mesh codecs than [20].

3 Experiment

In this section we present the implementation details of the conducted survey by describing the evaluation methodology, dataset generation, compared conditions and details of the experiment.

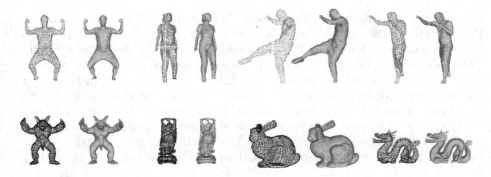

Fig. 1. The 3D models comprising the survey's content. The human 3D reconstructions are presented on top while the scanned objects are presented on the bottom. For each 3D model, a wireframe representation is depicted on the left, followed by a shaded one on the right.

Evaluation Methodology: In both of our experiments we chose a pairwise comparison methodology [21] to evaluate the fidelity of the various conditions to the reference undistorted 3D mesh. More specifically, during the experiment every subject was presented simultaneously with two distorted versions as well as the reference one. Then, each subject was asked to choose which of the two distorted versions bests resembles the reference. The forced choice pairwise comparison method was preferred over standard methodologies recommended by ITU [13,14] because recent works have shown its superiority in terms of producing statistically robust results with smaller variance [19,26]. Furthermore, this method is easier to implement and is less mentally demanding for the subjects. However, a significant drawback of this method is that the number of the required comparisons can quickly get prohibitively large if the number of examined conditions is also large. Various ways to mitigate this problem have been investigated [12]. As mentioned in [21], an effective way to deal with this issue is to only consider comparisons between conditions that do not have a big difference in terms of quality.

Datasets: As already discussed in Sect. 1, in order to study the effect of compression distortion in different types of content, mostly related to the mesh production techniques, we use two distinct 3D content groups. The first group ("Model Group #1"), comprises a selection of four 3D reconstructed human meshes that were produced by the tele-immersive platform of [6] during four human performance captures. As in most typical cases of tele-immersive application settings, these models suffer from visual artifacts and the presence of noise is apparent. The second group ("Model Group #2'), comprises four models taken from the widely acknowledged and used Stanford 3D Scanning Repository [5], namely the "Bunny", "Happy Buddha", "Dragon" and "Armadillo" models. These higher quality models, were created via a 3D reconstruction process on higher accuracy 3D scans of real world objects. All the reference models of the two datasets are illustrated in Fig. 1.

Compared Conditions: All 3D mesh codecs compress connectivity losslessly and any visual distortions come from geometric loss that is controlled by a quantization parameter expressed in number of bits. Different codecs may use different quantization schemes. While there are four available open source 3D mesh codecs, more specifically, Draco [2,24], Corto [1,22,23], O3DGC [3,18] and OpenCTM [4], we select the first three, Draco, Corto and O3DGC for this study. From the selected three codecs, Draco and O3DGC use the same quantization strategy leading to visually identical models for the same compression parameters. The only aspect in which those two codecs differ, is in compression performance which is out of this paper's scope. Thus, while we explicitly use Draco in our experiments, the results equivalently apply to O3DGC. The reason why OpenCTM was excluded from our experiments is two-fold. First, and most importantly, including one more codec in the study would result into a much more expensive experiment in terms of time while we would have to take additional measures to counter potential subjects' fatigue. Second, based on an extensive benchmarking we have conducted in our lab, OpenCTM was found to be the least performant codec among the rest in rate-distortion terms.

A forced pairwise comparison methodology comes with a set of restrictions. These are related to the way the number of comparisons scales with the increase in the different levels that are compared. As a result, in order to reduce the burden and stress of the survey on the subjects to obtain higher quality results, three compression levels were selected. These are directly mapped to the quantization bits of each codec, and more specifically, 10, 11 and 12 bits were the target of this study. This choice was based on the empirical assessment that 9 bits produced unpleasing visual results, but even more importantly, it produced a bigger difference in visual quality when compared to the results of 10 bits than the other incremental combinations of the higher quantization bit levels. This would manifest in a clear and universal selection of the higher quality (10 bits), that would in turn create biased or even erroneous results, as reported in [21]. Further, as aforementioned, adding yet another compression bit into the comparisons, would significantly increase the required comparisons for every subject and make it a lot more demanding. Overall, we evaluate 2 codecs in 3 quantization levels, with comparisons being limited among codecs and neighboring quantization levels. This results in a total number of 11 comparisons for each data sample, compared to 15 when comparing between all possible condition combinations. Since we used 4 models in each dataset, the total number of comparisons required for each model group was 44.

Survey: The user study was realized by a VR application, developed in Unity3D[1], that implemented the pairwise methodology for comparing the visual

---

[1] https://unity3d.com.

quality of compressed 3D content. We used an HTC Vive head mounted display (HMD) that each subject wore. Within the VR environment, each subject was able to view the undistorted (i.e. uncompressed) 3D model in the middle, and the two distorted (i.e. compressed) on its left and right sides. The models were displayed in life size, effectively simulating realistic tele-immersive scenarios. The content was viewed freely as a combination of natural navigation (i.e. physical movement in the real-world) and user interaction. Exploiting the HMD's tracking system, the users were allowed to freely move into the tracking area and thus, inspect the models in a natural manner. In addition, by using the headset's controllers, they were also able to rotate the models around their origin simultaneously to aid them in inspecting their visual fidelity and compare them to the reference. Overall, the study subjects could view and inspect the models in a free viewpoint fashion within the VR environment.

Inside the VR environment, the subjects would vote for the least distorted mesh by choosing one of the side (left/right) models. Left/right positioning was randomized to avoid any bias in the selection process. The 3D content was rendered un-textured, with flat shading, so as to accentuate differences in lighting, therefore allowing surface normal information to influence the perceived quality.

Moreover, we conducted the study using two different control groups, each one paired with a model group. As a result, half the subjects (Control Group #1) only viewed and assessed 3D content of captured human performances (Model Group #1), while the other half (Control Group #2) focused on the widely used high quality scanned objects models (Model Group #2).

There was no time limit imposed on the subjects, instead they could take their time in inspecting the content in their own pace. The average study session duration was 25 min, thereby minimizing fatigue which the subjects are more prone to, due to the use of VR headsets. In total, 40 subjects participated in the study, 8 females and 32 males evenly divided in the 2 Control Groups.

Fig. 2. Screenshot from the VR application showing the reconstructed human meshes. The reference model is in the middle while the two distorted are to its left and right.

4   Results

After collecting the responses from all the subjects in our pairwise comparison survey, we processed these data using the toolbox provided by Perez-Ortiz and Mantiuk [21]. This results in an assignment of a rating in a continuous scale to each of the compared conditions. By default, a zero rating is given to the worst, as perceived by the subjects, condition. No voting outliers were detected in our subjects for either of the control groups, as reported by the use of the toolbox [21]. The final ratings for both groups are illustrated in Fig. 3 as heat-maps. Moreover, Fig. 4 presents the rankings and their corresponding 95% confidence intervals for both control groups (*left and middle* for Control Group #1 & #2 respectively). The scores can be interpreted as such: a rating difference of a single unit between two conditions means that in a hypothetical comparison between these conditions, the probability of a subject to choose the one with the higher rating is 75%. A detailed mapping between probabilities and quality scores are depicted in Fig. 4 (Figure re-printed with permission from [21]).

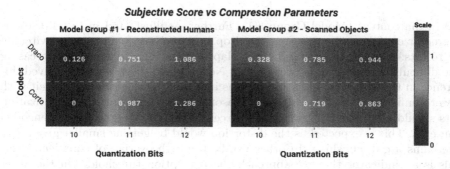

Fig. 3. Survey Results: subjective ranking score for every compression condition and for both Model Groups. Values are smoothly interpolated in each heat-map. Interpolation used only for visualization purposes. The underlying domain is discrete.

During the experiment, the majority of the subjects commented on the difficulty in distinguishing the differences between the compared conditions and the reference mesh. Despite this fact, it is obvious from the results that they had a clear preference towards meshes compressed with a higher number of quantization bits across codecs and model contents. This difficulty in making a confident vote, interestingly aligns with a similar outcome presented in [25], where subjects were asked to subjectively evaluate the visual quality of simplified meshes (meshes with less number of triangles compared to the original). In [25], despite the subjects reporting a guessing behavior in their votes, their choices actually aligned with the true quality of the meshes (i.e. meshes with higher number of triangles were consistently voted preferable).

In our case, the transition from 10 to 11 bits had a higher impact on subjective visual quality than the one from 11 to 12, especially for the immersive

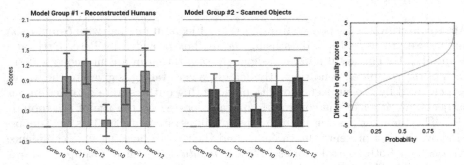

Fig. 4. (a, b) Survey Results: quality scores of the compared conditions and their confidence intervals. (c) Mapping of the difference in the rating between two conditions into the estimated probability of a random subject to select the condition with the higher rating. Reprinted from "A practical guide and software for analysing pairwise comparison experiments." by Perez-Ortiz and Mantiuk [21]. Reprinted with permission.

3D media content (Model Group #1). Further, as illustrated in Fig. 4, there is a greater confidence in assessing the drop in perceived quality when switching to 10 bits. Instead, there is a high overlap between 11 and 12 bits, showcasing the difficulty in selecting between them. Nonetheless, there was a perceived difference in the upper quantization bits, as indicated by the rankings, albeit with lower confidence. One hand, this is reasonable as increasing the quantization bits should progressively lead to less perceived differences between the encoded contents. This is expected as the distortion would be getting smaller given that the gains are diminishing. In other words, the high overlap of confident intervals is an indicator that we approach the perception threshold. On the other hand, understanding where the first jump in perceived quality happens is a very important indicator when choosing the quantization level.

For the "noisy" models (Model Group #1), Draco was preferred for the lowest bits (10) but Corto was scored as more visually pleasing for the 11 and 12 quantization bits. However, for the "clean" models (Model Group #2), the compressed representation produced by Draco was always preferable to the one produced by Corto for the same number of quantization bits. For the scanned objects (Model Group #2), the difference in the relative score between the lowest and the highest rated condition was smaller than in the case of the human meshes. Effectively, there was a larger distribution of the scores, and by extension a wider ranking, for Control Group #1. This points to an increased sensitivity to distortions for the Model Group #1 that can be attributed to the content itself being actual persons' 3D reconstructions and the fact that we are highly attuned to the human body and face forms. Consequently, such content requires higher presentation quality as it is more susceptible to perceived distortions.

Correlation with Objective Metrics: Interestingly, the correlation between objective metrics and subjective score is not consistent in the two model sets. The average Hausdorff distances across all models for the same quantization parameters and their Relative Standard Deviations (RSDs) for both Model Groups are presented in Table 1. In the scanned objects group, we notice a strong correlation between Hausdorff distance and the subjective score. Draco codec has smaller Hausdorff distance compared with the Corto one, for the same quantization bits. Therefore, the preference of Draco over Corto among user study subjects, can be easily explained. The human meshes experiment does not seem to follow this pattern. There, users seems to prefer Corto over Draco in all quantization levels, apart from the lowest one. The fact that Corto compressed meshes receive higher subjective score, despite having a greater Hausdorff distance from the original mesh, implies that the human perceived quality does not correlate well with the objective metrics for that Model Group. The high presence of noise in the human meshes may influence the subjects' preference towards Corto compressed meshes, as in that case Corto's quantization scheme may produce subjectively more pleasant forms. This may also mean that codec choice matters for subjective visual quality, depending on the production process of the 3D meshes.

Table 1. Average distortion across models (measured in Hausdorff distance with respect to the bounding box) and its relative Standard Deviation (RSD) for the two model groups for all compression parameters.

Codec-parameter	3D Reco. human meshes		Scanned objects	
	Hausdorff distance	RSD	Hausdorff distance	RSD
Corto-10	0.0012025	10%	0.00111425	15%
Corto-11	0.00060775	9%	0.00062375	30%
Corto-12	0.00030325	11%	0.00027675	13%
Draco-10	0.000594	11%	0.00073425	56%
Draco-11	0.00030525	10%	0.000279	17%
Draco-12	0.00015	8%	0.0001365	13%

5 Conclusion

In this work, we performed a survey to evaluate the effects of compression on the subjectively perceived quality of 3D meshes generated by two different processes: (a) human meshes produced by a real-time 3D reconstruction algorithm used in a tele-immersive platform and (b) meshes produced by computationally expensive 3D reconstruction algorithms applied on high quality 3D scans of real objects. The evaluation of three open-source static 3D mesh codecs was conducted with two of them producing an exact visual output and only differing in compression performance. The reference meshes were compressed by all codecs in three different distortion levels, controlled by a quantization parameter. The experimental results showed that the quantization scheme applied by each individual codec matters to the subjective visual quality of the compressed mesh and the preferred codec generally depends on the generation process that produced the 3D mesh. While the distortion levels on the output meshes that were induced by the quantization parameters were distinguished from the subjects, for higher values of the quantization parameter the differences are less apparent. The study was conducted in Virtual Reality to better emulate tele-immersive experience and followed the forced choice pairwise methodology with full reference.

Based on the findings of this work, future studies for tele-immersive applications may discuss on making codec and distortion level choices based on rate-distortion performance of the codecs and the subjectively perceived visual quality of the 3D meshes.

Acknowledgement. This work was supported and received funding from the EU H2020 Programme under Grant Agreement no 762111 VRTogether.

References

1. Corto. https://github.com/cnr-isti-vclab/corto. Accessed 07 June 2018
2. Google Draco. https://github.com/google/draco. Accessed 07 June 2018
3. Open 3D Graphics Compression (O3DGC). https://github.com/amd/rest3d/tree/master/server/o3dgc. Accessed 07 June 2018
4. OpenCTM. http://openctm.sourceforge.net/. Accessed 07 June 2018
5. The Stanford 3D Scanning Repository. http://graphics.stanford.edu/data/3Dscanrep/. Accessed 07 June 2018
6. Alexiadis, D.S., et al.: An integrated platform for live 3D human reconstruction and motion capturing. IEEE Trans. Circ. Syst. Video Technol. **27**(4), 798–813 (2017)
7. Alexiou, E., Ebrahimi, T.: On subjective and objective quality evaluation of point cloud geometry. In: 2017 Ninth International Conference on Quality of Multimedia Experience (QoMEX), pp. 1–3, May 2017. https://doi.org/10.1109/QoMEX.2017.7965681
8. Alexiou, E., Upenik, E., Ebrahimi, T.: Towards subjective quality assessment of point cloud imaging in augmented reality. In: 2017 IEEE 19th International Workshop on Multimedia Signal Processing (MMSP), pp. 1–6, October 2017. https://doi.org/10.1109/MMSP.2017.8122237
9. Aspert, N., Santa-Cruz, D., Ebrahimi, T.: Mesh: measuring errors between surfaces using the hausdorff distance. In: Proceedings of IEEE International Conference on Multimedia and Expo, vol. 1, pp. 705–708 (2002). https://doi.org/10.1109/ICME.2002.1035879
10. Berjón, D., Morán, F., Manjunatha, S.: Objective and subjective evaluation of static 3D mesh compression. Sig. Process.: Image Commun. **28**(2), 181–195 (2013). https://doi.org/10.1016/j.image.2012.10.013. http://www.sciencedirect.com/science/article/pii/S0923596512002019. mPEG-V
11. Bulbul, A., Capin, T., Lavoué, G., Preda, M.: Assessing visual quality of 3-D polygonal models. IEEE Sig. Process. Mag. **28**(6), 80–90 (2011). https://doi.org/10.1109/MSP.2011.942466
12. Silverstein, D.A., Farrell, J.E.: Efficient method for paired comparison. J. Electron. Imaging **10**, 10–10-5 (2001). https://doi.org/10.1117/1.1344187

13. International Telecommunication Union: Recommendation ITU-T P.910: subjective video quality assessment methods for multimedia applications (2008)
14. International Telecommunication Union: Recommendation ITU-R BT.500: methodology for the subjective assessment of the quality of television pictures (2012)
15. Javaheri, A., Brites, C., Pereira, F., Ascenso, J.: Subjective and objective quality evaluation of 3D point cloud denoising algorithms. In: 2017 IEEE International Conference on Multimedia Expo Workshops (ICMEW), pp. 1–6, July 2017. https://doi.org/10.1109/ICMEW.2017.8026263
16. Javaheri, A., Brites, C., Pereira, F., Ascenso, J.: Subjective and objective quality evaluation of compressed point clouds. In: 2017 IEEE 19th International Workshop on Multimedia Signal Processing (MMSP), pp. 1–6, October 2017. https://doi.org/10.1109/MMSP.2017.8122239
17. Karakottas, A., Papachristou, A., Doumanoglou, A., Zioulis, N., Zarpalas, D., Daras, P.: Augmented VR, IEEE Virtual Reality, 18–22 March 2018. https://www.youtube.com/watch?v=7O_TrhtmP5Q
18. Mamou, K., Zaharia, T., Prêteux, F.: TFAN: a low complexity 3D mesh compression algorithm. Comput. Animat. Virtual Worlds 20, 343–354 (2009). https://doi.org/10.1002/cav.v20:2/3
19. Mantiuk, R., Tomaszewska, A., Mantiuk, R.: Comparison of four subjective methods for image quality assessment, vol. 31, November 2012
20. Mekuria, R., Cesar, P., Doumanis, I., Frisiello, A.: Objective and subjective quality assessment of geometry compression of reconstructed 3d humans in a 3d virtual room. In: Proceedings of the SPIE Applications of Digital Image Processing XXXVIII, vol. 9599, p. 95991M, September 2015. https://doi.org/10.1117/12.2203312
21. Perez-Ortiz, M., Mantiuk, R.K.: A practical guide and software for analysing pairwise comparison experiments. ArXiv e-prints, December 2017
22. Ponchio, F., Dellepiane, M.: Fast decompression for web-based view-dependent 3d rendering. In: Proceedings of the 20th International Conference on 3D Web Technology, Web3D 2015, pp. 199–207. ACM, New York (2015). https://doi.org/10.1145/2775292.2775308
23. Ponchio, F., Dellepiane, M.: Multiresolution and fast decompression for optimal web-based rendering. Graph. Models 88, 1–11 (2016). https://doi.org/10.1016/j.gmod.2016.09.002. http://www.sciencedirect.com/science/article/pii/S152407031 6300285
24. Rossignac, J.: Edgebreaker: connectivity compression for triangle meshes. IEEE Trans. Vis. Comput. Graph. 5, 47–61 (1999)
25. Thorn, J., Pizarro, R., Spanlang, B., Bermell-Garcia, P., González-Franco, M.: Assessing 3d scan quality through paired-comparisons psychophysics test. CoRR abs/1602.00238 (2016). http://arxiv.org/abs/1602.00238
26. Zerman, E., Hulusic, V., Valenzise, G., Mantiuk, R., Dufaux, F.: The relation between MOS and pairwise comparisons and the importance of cross-content comparisons. In: Human Vision and Electronic Imaging Conference, IS&T International Symposium on Electronic Imaging (EI 2018), Burlingame, United States, January 2018. https://hal.archives-ouvertes.fr/hal-01654133
27. Zhang, J., Huang, W., Zhu, X., Hwang, J.N.: A subjective quality evaluation for 3d point cloud models, pp. 827–831, January 2015

Joint EPC and RAN Caching of Tiled VR Videos for Mobile Networks

Kedong Liu[1,2], Yanwei Liu[1,2]($\boxtimes$), Jinxia Liu[3], Antonios Argyriou[4], and Ying Ding[1,2]

[1] State Key Laboratory of Information Security,
Institute of Information Engineering, Chinese Academy of Sciences, Beijing, China
liuyanwei@iie.ac.cn
[2] School of Cyber Security, University of Chinese Academy of Sciences,
Beijing, China
[3] Zhejiang Wanli University, Ningbo, China
[4] University of Thessaly, Volos, Greece

Abstract. In recent years, 360-degree VR (Virtual Reality) video has brought an immersive way to consume content. People can watch matches, play games and view movies by wearing VR headsets. To provide such online VR video services anywhere and anytime, the VR videos need to be delivered over wireless networks. However, due to the huge data volume and the frequent viewport-updating of VR video, its delivery over mobile networks is extremely difficult. One of the difficulties for the VR video streaming is the latency issue, i.e., the necessary viewport data cannot be timely updated to keep pace with the rapid viewport motion during viewing VR videos. To deal with this problem, this paper presents a joint EPC (Evolved Packet Core) and RAN (Radio Access Network) tile-caching scheme that pushes the duplicates of VR video tiles near the user end. Based on the predicted viewport-popularity of the VR video, the collaborative tile data caching between the EPC and RAN is formulated as a 0-1 knapsack problem, and then solved by a genetic algorithm (GA). Experimental results show that the proposed scheme can achieve great improvements in terms of the saved transmission bandwidth as well as the latency over the scheme of traditional full-size video caching and the scheme that the tiles are only cached in the EPC.

Keywords: VR · Cache · EPC · RAN · Video tiles

1 Introduction

Recently, the 360-degree VR video applications are becoming more and more popular with the increasing maturity of VR technology. At the same time, the

This work was supported in part by National Natural Science Foundation of China under Grants 61771469 and 61572497, and Zhejiang Provincial Natural Science Foundation of China under Grant LY17F010001.

© Springer Nature Switzerland AG 2019
I. Kompatsiaris et al. (Eds.): MMM 2019, LNCS 11295, pp. 92–105, 2019.
https://doi.org/10.1007/978-3-030-05710-7_8

rapid development of wireless communication has made it possible to distribute 360-degree VR videos over wireless networks.

To create an immersive experience for the end users, panoramic VR video provides a 360×180 degree field of view with a high resolution (4K or beyond), and thus usually tends to consume a large amount of storage space and transmission bandwidth. Furthermore, due to the particularly interactive nature of the viewport data delivery, VR video systems have very strict latency requirements [11]. This brings a great pressure on the network especially the wireless part. It is quite challenging to transmit VR videos over mobile networks.

Since VR video consumes bandwidth, a number of VR video coding and transmission approaches were proposed by researchers to reduce the data volume by applying source data compression. In [4], a region-adaptive video smoothing approach was proposed to improve the encoding efficiency by considering the particular characteristics of sphere-to-plane projection. To enhance the ability of spatial random access, VR video tiling was also used during streaming. In [7], Gaddam et al. applied a tiling scheme to deliver different quality levels for different parts of the panoramic VR videos. In [14], Skupin et al. proposed an alternative approach to 360° video facilitating HEVC (High Efficiency Video Coding) tiles. To reduce the necessary data amount for the user, an approach was presented by Guntur et al. in [8] to transmit the tiled regions of a video to support RoI (Region of Interest) streaming. By taking a step further, Corbillon et al. in [5] proposed a viewport-adaptive 360-degree video streaming system to transmit VR videos by reducing the transmitted bit-rates of tiles. From the video networking perspective, the Dynamic Adaptive Streaming over HTTP (DASH) for 360-degree VR videos can also reduce the transmitted VR video data [9,10]. The above-mentioned approaches can reduce the transmitted VR video data amount significantly. However, due to multi-user concurrent requests, current VR video applications still consume higher bandwidth that incurs large transmission delay.

To deal with the latency issue of video streaming, video caching has been proposed to push duplicate videos near the user ends. This way can reduce the duplicate content transmissions and relieve the pressure on mobile networks as well. In [16], Xie et al. studied the effects of different access types on Internet video services and their implications on Content Delivery Network (CDN) caching. Franky et al. in [6] studied a video cache system which can reduce the video traffic and the loading time. In [18], Zhou et al. proposed a QoE-driven video cache allocation scheme for mobile cloud server. These methods are very effective in reducing the delivery latency in the fixed broadband networks, but in mobile networks, they cannot achieve the same results.

To further reduce the latency, cache servers can be deployed to the RAN that is closest to the user end. In [15], Wang et al. studied the caching techniques for both the EPC and RAN. In [12], Shen et al. designed an information-aware QoE-centric mobile video cache scheme. In [1], Ahlehagh et al. introduced a video-aware caching scheme in the RAN. Ye et al. in [17] studied the quality-aware DASH video caching scheme at mobile network edge. These approaches can further reduce the video streaming latency by caching the content in mobile networks. However, they neglected the collaboration between the EPC and RAN during the video data caching. In addition, these video caching approaches were originally designed for full-size videos and they cannot efficiently work for the VR videos due to the particular characteristic of VR videos, i.e., the tremendous size of video data, which might take up too much cache space.

Usually, people watch only a part of the VR video spatially not the full-size video, and thus the VR video can be cached with the tiled-chunk representation to reduce the occupied cache space. The VR video sequence is first segmented into several tiles spatially and then a number of chunks temporally. The tiled-chunk data is deployed in the EPC and RAN beforehand according to the prediction of user's viewport popularity. Additionally, taking account of the differences in transmission distance between the RAN cache and the EPC cache, the joint RAN and EPC caching scheme needs to designed. On the one hand, caches in the RAN are close to the end-user which can save the content transmission latency and relieve the bandwidth pressure for the backhaul network. However, the cache space in the RAN is strictly limited and each eNodeB (evolved NodeB) in the RAN may only serve a few users, which results in low cache hit rate in some cases. On the other hand, caches in the EPC aggregate many UEs (User Equipments) and the cache hit rate is higher, but it will incur higher latency than that in the RAN. To deal with these issues mentioned above, we propose to tile the VR video and cache the tiled VR video chunks in the EPC and RAN collaboratively.

By making full consideration of the characteristics of VR videos and the architecture of mobile networks, this paper presents a joint EPC and RAN tile-caching scheme for mobile networks. The contributions of this paper are summarized below.

- Taking into account the fact that only a small portion of the complete 360-degree VR video is visible to a viewer, a tile-caching scheme is proposed. By segmenting VR videos into several tiles spatially and a series of chunks temporally, the tiles within the users' viewports are more likely to be cached than the tiles out of the viewports. This can significantly save the cache space compared to the full-size video caching strategy.
- To reduce the user-perceived latency as well as the redundant traffic over the network, caches are deployed in both the EPC and RAN. Moreover, the joint EPC and RAN tile-caching scheme is proposed to maximize the saved system bandwidth cost subject to the constraint of viewport-requesting latency. The caching optimization process is formulated as a 0-1 knapsack problem, and then solved by a GA.

The rest of the paper is organized as follows. In Sect. 2, the proposed joint EPC and RAN tile-caching scheme is described. Experimental results are provided in Sect. 3. Finally, Sect. 4 concludes the paper.

2 Joint EPC and RAN Tile-Caching Scheme

The proposed joint EPC and RAN tile-caching scheme is shown in Fig. 1. Based on the architecture of mobile networks, the EPC and each RAN are equipped with a cache respectively, and they are regarded as the cache nodes. The cache in the EPC is deployed in the Packet Data Network Gateway (P-GW) and the caches for each RAN are deployed in eNodeBs. In addition, there is a logically centrally-deployed entity (Content Controller) which is connected to the P-GW. The Content Controller is responsible for recognizing VR video request from the UEs and then performs the caching optimization algorithm in terms of the collected information from each cache node. To improve the cache hit rate for different tiles in the video, a collaborative caching approach is used to optimize the caching placement of tiles among the EPC and RAN. The cache nodes cache the VR video tiles based on the optimization computation results.

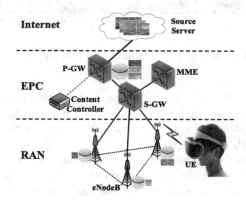

Fig. 1. Joint EPC and RAN tile-caching scheme.

In the optimization, the VR video tiles within users' viewports are more likely to be cached near the UE. Once a viewer requests a VR video viewport using a UE, the eNodeB will check whether the requested viewports were already existed in the RAN cache. If the requested data is available, the RAN cache node will serve the request and the requested VR video tiles will be transmitted to the UE through the wireless radio access network. If the requested data is not available locally in the RAN, the request will be transferred to the Content Controller to check whether the EPC and the other RAN cache nodes have had already cached the requested VR video tiles. If cached, the VR video tiles will be transmitted to the corresponding eNodeB through wired connections from EPC cache node or through wireless connections (e.g., interface X2 [15]) from the other RAN cache nodes, and finally transmitted to the UE. If none of the cache nodes had cached the requested VR video viewports, the request can only be served by the source server on the Internet.

2.1   Tile-Caching Problem Formulation

According to the limitation of the field of view (usually 120°) for human eyes, only a small part of the full frame VR image is watched in one moment which is called the viewport. That means only the VR video tiles within the viewport can be displayed on UE for watching. As shown in Fig. 2, the areas in the orange rectangles are frequently watched by the users that they can be predicted in terms of the popularity of viewport. The popularity of viewport in the whole image is obtained via the saliency map prediction approach [13].

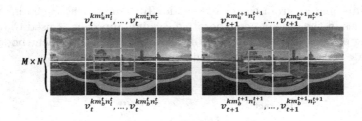

Fig. 2. Tile partition and viewport moving.

We define $\mathcal{T} = \{0, 1, \ldots, t, \ldots, T\}$ the set of the time slots and $\mathcal{K} = \{1, 2, \ldots, k, \ldots, K\}$ the set of VR videos. For a VR video k, $M \times N$ VR video tiles were obtained after the tiling process. v_t^{kmn} denotes the VR video tile at the mth row and nth column ($0 < m \leq M$, $0 < n \leq N$) in the kth video at the time slot t. Similarly, in the temporal dimension, the tiles were also divided into many chunks. Because the user's viewport varies with time and one chunk is with very short time, we can use an enlarged and unchanged viewport to denote the viewports for all frames in the whole chunk. The request from UE for the VR video k at the time of t denotes the request for a set of VR video tiles V_t^{kmn} covered by the enlarged viewport ($m_u^t \leq m \leq m_b^t$, $n_l^t \leq n \leq n_r^t$) at the time of t. m_u^t, m_b^t, n_l^t and n_r^t denote the tile number of the up row, bottom row, left column and right column that the viewport occupies, respectively. As a consequence, once the set of VR video tiles V_t^{kmn} are cached, the whole VR video is supposed to be cached technically because the tiles out of the viewport in the chunk are usually not necessarily watched.

In the joint EPC and RAN tile-caching scheme, caches are deployed inside both the EPC (P-GW) and the RAN (eNodeB). The caching network architecture is abstracted as the graph in Fig. 3. Denote c_i as the unit cost for transferring VR video tiles from the P-GW to eNodeB i, c_0 as the unit cost when transferring VR video tiles from the source server to P-GW and c_{ij} as the unit cost when transferring VR video tiles between eNodeBs i and j. To formulate the tile-caching problem, the transmission bandwidth cost of VR videos is utilized as the optimization metric. The optimization goal of the scheme is to minimize the total bandwidth cost for serving all VR video requests subjecting to the overall

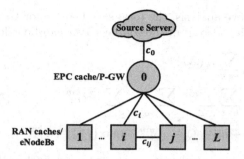

Fig. 3. The joint EPC and RAN tile-caching network architecture.

disk storage limitation of cache nodes and the system latency constraint. Easily, the problem can be transformed into an equivalent problem of maximizing the saving cost subjecting to the cache space limitation and latency constraint compared to the way that obtains VR video tiles from the source server.

Denote the 0-1 variable $x_{t,i}^{kmn}$ as the indication of whether the VR video tile v_t^{kmn} is cached in the cache node i. If node i had already cached the VR video tile v_t^{kmn}, $x_{t,i}^{kmn} = 1$; otherwise $x_{t,i}^{kmn} = 0$. Based on the above definition, there are basically four ways to fetch a VR video for viewers:

- If the cache node eNodeB i can fulfill the request from the UE locally for the VR video tile v_t^{kmn}, the unit cost saving is $c_0 + c_i$.
- If the request cannot be fulfilled locally by eNodeB i but can be fulfilled by the other eNodeBs, e.g., the node j ($i \neq j$), the unit cost saving can be written as $c_0 + c_i - c_{ij}$.
- If the request can be fulfilled by the EPC cache at the P-GW, the unit cost saving is c_0.
- If the request can only be fulfilled from the source server on the Internet, the unit cost saving is 0.

In the following, we define the saved bandwidth cost $P_{t,i}^{kmn}$ when the request for the VR video tile v_t^{kmn} at node i is fulfilled by the EPC cache. $P_{t,i}^{kmn}$ is given by

$$P_{t,i}^{kmn} = c_0 \times x_{t,0}^{kmn}. \tag{1}$$

Also, the maximal saved cost $Q_{t,ij}^{kmn}$ when the request for VR video tile v_t^{kmn} at node i is fulfilled by another eNodeB j is defined as

$$Q_{t,ij}^{kmn} = \max_{j \in \mathcal{L} \backslash \{i\}} \{(c_0 + c_i - c_{ij})y_{t,ij}^{kmn}\}, \tag{2}$$

where $\mathcal{L}$ is the set of the cache nodes which can be expressed as $\mathcal{L} = \{0, 1, \ldots, i, \ldots, j, \ldots, L\}$, and $y_{t,ij}^{kmn}$ is also a 0-1 variable which indicates whether the request for the VR video tile v_t^{kmn} from the UE connecting to eNodeB i is transferred to eNodeB j.

Based on the above analysis, the total saved cost τ for UEs compared to the way that obtains VR video from the source server can be calculated as:

$$\tau = \sum_{t \in \mathcal{T}} \sum_{k \in \mathcal{K}} \tau_k(\boldsymbol{X}_t)$$

$$= \sum_{t \in \mathcal{T}} \sum_{k \in \mathcal{K}} \sum_{i \in \mathcal{L}} \sum_{m_u^t \leq m \leq m_b^t} \sum_{n_l^t \leq n \leq n_r^t} \lambda_{t,i}^{kmn} \cdot s_t^{kmn} \cdot [x_{t,i}^{kmn} \cdot$$

$$(c_0 + c_i) + (1 - x_{t,i}^{kmn}) \cdot \max\{P_{t,i}^{kmn}, Q_{t,ij}^{kmn}\}], \tag{3}$$

where $\tau_k(\cdot)$ is a function to calculate the saved bandwidth cost for the VR video k. $\boldsymbol{X}_t$ is a set of 0-1 variable $x_{t,i}^{kmn}$ that denotes the caching result of a VR video k at the time of t, and $\boldsymbol{X}_t$ can be expressed as

$$\boldsymbol{X}_t = (x_{t,0}^{k11}, x_{t,0}^{k12}, \ldots, x_{t,0}^{kmn}, \ldots, x_{t,i}^{kmn}, \ldots, x_{t,L}^{kMN}). \tag{4}$$

where s_t^{kmn} denotes the file size of the VR video tile v_t^{kmn}. The request probability $\lambda_{t,i}^{kmn}$ for the VR video tile v_t^{kmn} from the UE connecting to eNodeB i is given by

$$\lambda_{t,i}^{kmn} = \xi_i^k \cdot \theta_t^{kmn}, \tag{5}$$

where ξ_i^k indicates the probability of requesting for the VR video k from the UE connecting to eNodeB i. θ_t^{kmn} denotes the probability of requesting for the tile v_t^{kmn} in VR video k, which can be obtained from the viewport popularity data of the VR videos.

Finally, the tile caching optimization problem of maximizing the saving cost τ can be mathematically formulated as

$$\max_{\boldsymbol{X}_t} \tau \tag{6}$$

$$s.t. \sum_{t \in \mathcal{T}} \sum_{k \in \mathcal{K}} \sum_{m \in \{1,2,\ldots,M\}} \sum_{n \in \{1,2,\ldots,N\}} s_t^{kmn} x_{t,i}^{kmn} \leq B_i \tag{7}$$

$$x_{t,i}^{kmn} \in \{0,1\}, \forall i \in \mathcal{L}, t \in \mathcal{T}, k \in \mathcal{K},$$
$$m \in \{1,2,\ldots,M\}, n \in \{1,2,\ldots,N\} \tag{8}$$

$$\begin{cases} \max_i \left\{ \dfrac{x_{t,i}^{kmn} \cdot s_t^{kmn}}{w_i} \right\} \leq T, & \text{when } \sum_i x_{t,i}^{kmn} \neq 0, \\ \dfrac{s_t^{kmn}}{w_s} \leq T, & \text{otherwise,} \\ \forall t \in \mathcal{T}, k \in \mathcal{K}, m_u^t \leq m \leq m_b^t, n_l^t \leq n \leq n_r^t, \end{cases} \tag{9}$$

where B_i denotes the cache space of the cache node i, w_i and w_s denote the available bandwidth from RAN cache node i to the UE and from the source server to the UE, respectively. T denotes the maximum limitation of transmission latency.

We know that, constraint (7) is used for cache space optimization. It guarantees that the space which the cached VR video tiles occupies doesn't exceed the cache space limitation. Constraint (8) indicates that the VR video tiles cannot be further divided anymore. 1 and 0 denote whether the cache node cached the VR video tile or not, respectively. Constraint (9) shows that the request for the tiles within the user's viewport should be responded and fulfilled timely under the constraint of transmission latency T. Specifically, the latency for transmitting the requested VR video tiles should be less than or equal to the maximum limitation of transmission latency T. In the caching system, the delivery distances for the tiles that the viewport covers are different because they are probably located in different cache nodes. Obviously, the delivery latency for the viewport depends on the maximum delivery latency for all the tiles within the user's viewport.

2.2 Solution

Based on the formulations from (6) to (9), the tile-caching problem is in line with the definition of the 0-1 knapsack problem. Due to its combinatorial nature, 0-1 knapsack is a NP-hard problem. As we all know, the GA has the advantage of the global optimization and the parallelism in seeking the solutions to the optimization problem, which indicates the solution-searching process can be implemented in parallel. Thus, to find the final result of placing VR video tiles in the cache nodes, we adopt the GA, a kind of heuristic algorithm, to solve the proposed optimization problem.

In the GA for joint EPC and RAN tile-caching optimization, the final optimization result X that has the highest fitness value is a set of X_t ($t \in \mathcal{T}$) for all the videos in $\mathcal{K}$. To represent the solution space in GA, we use the binary coding string X as the chromosome. The chromosome length l denotes the number of the 0-1 variables $x_{t,i}^{kmn}$ in one of the solution results X. Firstly, the population size s_{pop}, the chromosome length l, the probability of performing crossover p_c, probability of mutation p_m and the termination criteria (the fixed number of generations n_{ge}) are initialized. Then, the first generation of population is initialized by generating the candidate solutions of the caching result X. Next, the fitness value τ of each population X is calculated in terms of Eq. (3). If the individual X doesn't satisfy the constraints (7), (8) or (9), the fitness value τ will be zero. In step 4, roulette wheel selection is used to select a portion of population to breed a new generation. In order to avoid the problem of premature convergence, scale factor is introduced to update p_c in step 5 [2]. In steps 5–6, the operations of crossover and mutation are performed to generate a second generation. Finally, after n_{ge} loops, we can get the optimal caching result X. Since the GA belongs to a non-deterministic class of algorithms, the optimal solution may vary for each run of the algorithm with the same input parameters. Thus the final result X is rather sub-optimal. The specific GA for joint EPC and RAN tile-caching optimization is shown in Algorithm 1.

Algorithm 1. GA for the joint EPC and RAN tile-caching optimization

---

Input: The population size s_{pop}, the chromosome length l, the probability of performing crossover p_c, probability of mutation p_m and the termination number of generations n_{ge}.

Output: The optimal caching result X.

1: Initialization: generate the population of X. The number of generation $g \leftarrow 0$.
2: **repeat**
3:    **Selection:** calculate the fitness function according to Eq. (3), specially $\tau \leftarrow 0$ if the X cannot satisfy the constraints.
4:    **Sort** the individuals according to τ in a decending order and select a portion of population using roulette wheel selection to breed a new generation.
5:    **Crossover:** update p_c, calculate the number of crossover $s_{pop} \times p_c$, and do the crossover operation to generate a new generation.
6:    **Mutation:** calculate the number of mutation $s_{pop} \times p_m$, and mutate to generate a second generation.
7:    $g \leftarrow g + 1$.
8: **until** $g = n_{ge}$.
9: **return** X of the highest τ.

---

3   Experimental Results

3.1   Experimental Setup

To evaluate the proposed joint EPC and RAN tile-caching scheme, we developed a custom software in Java to realize the optimization algorithm. HEVC reference software HM 15.0 was used to encode the VR videos. The five 360-degree VR video test sequences with spatial size of 3840×1920 (AerialCity, DrivingInCity, DrivingInCountry, Harbor and PoleVault_le) were obtained from JVET [3]. They were divided into 4×2 tiles for the caching optimization scheme. The popularity of the VR videos (ξ in Eq. (5)) is assumed to follow a Zipf popularity distribution and the VR video k is requested with the probability $\xi^k = \beta/k^\alpha$, where $\beta = (\sum_{k=1}^{K} k^{-\alpha})^{-1}$. The Zipf parameter α was initialized as 0.75. The capacity ratio, which means the ratio of the aggregate size of video tiles to the total cache size was set to 60%. The key experimental parameters are shown in Table 1. To verify the performance of the proposed Joint EPC and RAN Tile-Caching (JERTC) scheme, we compared the proposed JERTC scheme with the scheme of Full-size VR video Caching without tiling (FC). Also, the Only EPC Caching (OEC) scheme was compared with the FC scheme. As the benchmark scheme, the FC scheme is based on the well-known Least Recently Used (LRU) caching algorithm [1].

Table 1. Experimental parameters

Tile size	Viewport size	Chunk length	RAN cache number (L)	Cache size in eNodeB	UE number per eNodeB	T	c_0	c_i
960×960	1920×1080	$1\,\mathrm{s}$	40	$10G$	100	$15\,\mathrm{ms}$	100	5

c_{ij}	w_i	w_s	s_{pop}	l	p_c	p_m	n_{ge}	
2–10	$600\,\mathrm{Mbps}$	$150\,\mathrm{Mbps}$	50	2000	0.7–0.9	0.02	500	

3.2 An Illustration of the Caching Optimization Result

Figure 4 illustrates one example of the caching optimization result. X_t is an example extracted from the optimization result X for the VR video k at the time of t. 0 means that the corresponding video tile should not be cached in the cache node i. On the contrary, the video tile marked 1 should be cached in the cache node i. It can be seen from Fig. 4 that the tiles within the viewport are more probable to be cached locally in the wireless access network.

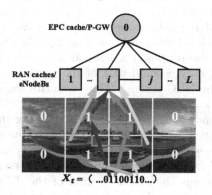

Fig. 4. One example of tile placement in the ith eNodeB.

3.3 Bandwidth and Latency Performances

Figure 5(a) shows the saved bandwidth cost curves with the increasing cache hit rates for the JERTC scheme, the OEC scheme and the FC scheme. Due to the limitation of the cache space in the eNodeB, the cache hit rate of the FC scheme can reach only to about 40% ($\alpha = 0.75$, capacity ratio is 60%). It can be seen from Fig. 5(a) that the proposed JERTC scheme can save more bandwidth cost than the OEC scheme at the same cache hit rate. It highlights the great effectiveness and advantages of the JERTC scheme against the OEC and FC. With the increasing of the cache hit rate, all the three schemes can save more bandwidth because more VR video tiles were found in the cache nodes in the

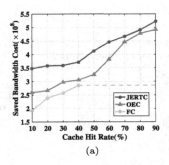 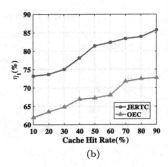

(a)   (b)

Fig. 5. (a) The curves of the saved bandwidth cost vs. the cache hit rate for the JERTC, OEC and FC scheme. (b) The curves of the saved latency vs. the cache hit rate for the JERTC scheme and the OEC scheme against the FC scheme.

mobile network. Besides, in Fig. 5(a) the gap between JERTC and OEC curves at the low cache hit rate is larger than that at high cache hit rate. With the increasing cache hit rate, the gap between the two schemes is gradually reduced. This is because at low cache hit rate, the requests from UE are mostly served by the source server besides the EPC cache node for the OEC scheme, and comparably most of the requests are served by RAN cache nodes and the EPC cache node for the proposed scheme. Consequently, the OEC scheme consumes more bandwidth than the proposed scheme at low cache hit rate. In contrast, at high cache hit rate, only a small part of the requests need to be served by the source server for the OEC scheme. Thus, a narrowing gap between the two schemes arises at high cache hit rate in Fig. 5(a).

The streaming latency is also a key factor affecting the VR video viewing experience. The saved percentage of the latency η_t for each scheme against the FC scheme is defined as $\eta_t = (t_f - t_s)/t_s \times 100\%$, where t_f and t_s are the latencies for the FC scheme and for the scheme to be compared, respectively. The curves of the saved latency versus the cache hit rate of the JERTC scheme and the OEC scheme are shown in Fig. 5(b). In the figure, when the cache hit rate of the scheme to be compared was more than 40%, the comparisons were performed with the result of FC at the cache hit rate of 40%. It is obvious that the proposed JERTC scheme can save more latency than the OEC scheme at the same cache hit rate. Averagely, the proposed scheme can save the latency by 10% over the OEC scheme and 80% over the FC scheme. What's more, the saved latencies of the both schemes grow with the increasing of the the cache hit rate because more VR video tiles were found in the cache nodes in the RAN and EPC.

3.4 Effects of Capacity Ratio and Zipf Parameter on Performance

The capacity size affects the cache performance directly. The saved bandwidth and the cache hit rate were measured with a set of capacity ratios varying from 20% to 80% as shown in Fig. 6. In the experiments, the request routing followed

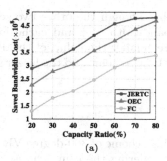 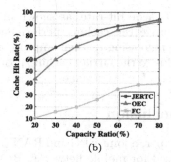

(a)   (b)

Fig. 6. (a) The curves of the saved bandwidth cost vs. the capacity ratio and (b) the curves of the cache hit rate vs. the capacity ratio for the JERTC, OEC and FC schemes.

the description in the second paragraph in Sect. 2. It can be seen from Fig. 6 that all three schemes can save more bandwidth and achieve higher cache hit rate with the increasing of the capacity ratio. It illustrates that larger capacity size will significantly increase the cache hit rate and correspondingly save more bandwidth cost. In Fig. 6(a), the proposed JERTC scheme can save the most bandwidth cost among all three schemes. It indicates that the tile caching scheme can increase the cache hit rate of tiles due to its smaller cache size to cater for the viewport-requesting way against the full-size caching. This is also verified by the cache hit rate to capacity ratio comparisons among the JERTC, OEC and FC schemes, as shown in Fig. 6(b).

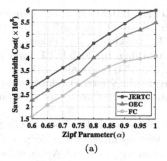 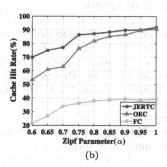

(a)   (b)

Fig. 7. (a) The curves of the saved bandwidth cost vs. the Zipf parameter and (b) the curves of the cache hit rate vs. the Zipf parameter for the JERTC, OEC and FC scheme.

Zipf distribution parameter α also affects the performance of the caching schemes. It can be seen from Fig. 7(a) that the proposed JERTC scheme can save more bandwidth cost than the OEC and FC schemes with the increasing α. It is because larger α value increases the hit-rate of viewport requesting for each VR video in the caches for the JERTC scheme. It is finally evidenced by the increased cache bit-rate, as shown in Fig. 7(b). Though the other two schemes both improve the caching performance in bandwidth cost and cache hit rate with the increasing α, their improvements are smaller than that of the JERTC scheme due to the farther caching position for OEC scheme and the larger spatial caching size for FC scheme.

4   Conclusion

In this paper, a joint EPC and RAN tile-caching scheme of 360-degree VR videos is proposed for mobile networks. By fully considering the tiling characteristics of VR videos and the restriction nature of the cache space in mobile networks, 360-degree VR video tiles are jointly cached in both EPC and RAN using the 0-1 knapsack optimization. Experimental results show that the proposed joint EPC and RAN tile-caching scheme can significantly reduce the duplicate video tile transmissions which relieves the pressure on mobile networks and at the same time reduces the latency to ensure the requirements of VR applications. In our future work, a network-adaptive data scheduling will be studied and integrated with the scheme to further improve the VR video streaming performance.

References

1. Ahlehagh, H., Dey, S.: Video-aware scheduling and caching in the radio access network. IEEE/ACM Trans. Networ. **22**(5), 1444–1462 (2014)
2. Andre, J., Siarry, P., Dognon, T.: An improvement of the standard genetic algorithm fighting premature convergence in continuous optimization. Adv. Eng. Softw. **32**(1), 49–60 (2000)
3. Boyce, J., Alshina, E., Abbas, A., Ye, Y.: JVET-D1030 r1: JVET common test conditions and evaluation procedures for 360° video, October 2016
4. Budagavi, M., Furton, J., Jin, G., Saxena, A., Wilkinson, J., Dickerson, A.: 360 degrees video coding using region adaptive smoothing. In: 2015 IEEE International Conference on Image Processing (ICIP), pp. 750–754, September 2015
5. Corbillon, X., Simon, G., Devlic, A., Chakareski, J.: Viewport-adaptive navigable 360-degree video delivery. In: 2017 IEEE International Conference on Communications (ICC), pp. 1–7, May 2017
6. Franky, O.E.A., Perdana, D., Negara, R.M., Sanjoyo, D.D., Bisono, G.: System design, implementation and analysis video cache on internet service provider. In: 2016 International Seminar on Intelligent Technology and Its Applications (ISITIA), pp. 157–162, July 2016
7. Gaddam, V.R., Riegler, M., Eg, R., Griwodz, C., Halvorsen, P.: Tiling in interactive panoramic video: approaches and evaluation. IEEE Trans. Multimedia **18**(9), 1819–1831 (2016)
8. Guntur, R., Ooi, W.T.: On tile assignment for region-of-interest video streaming in a wireless LAN. In: Proceedings of the 22nd International Workshop on Network and Operating System Support for Digital Audio and Video, pp. 59–64. ACM (2012)
9. Hosseini, M., Swaminathan, V.: Adaptive 360 VR video streaming based on MPEG-DASH SRD. In: 2016 IEEE International Symposium on Multimedia (ISM), pp. 407–408, December 2016

10. Lim, S.Y., Seok, J.M., Seo, J., Kim, T.G.: Tiled panoramic video transmission system based on mpeg-dash. In: 2015 International Conference on Information and Communication Technology Convergence (ICTC), pp. 719–721, October 2015
11. Ohl, S., Willert, M., Staadt, O.: Latency in distributed acquisition and rendering for telepresence systems. IEEE Trans. Visual. Comput. Graph. **21**(12), 1442–1448 (2015)
12. Shen, S., Akella, A.: An information-aware QoE-centric mobile video cache. In: Proceedings of the 19th Annual International Conference on Mobile Computing & Networking, pp. 401–412. ACM (2013)
13. Sitzmann, V., et al.: Saliency in VR: how do people explore virtual environments? IEEE Trans. Visual. Comput. Graph. **24**(4), 1633–1642 (2018)
14. Skupin, R., Sanchez, Y., Hellge, C., Schierl, T.: Tile based HEVC video for head mounted displays. In: 2016 IEEE International Symposium on Multimedia (ISM), pp. 399–400, December 2016
15. Wang, X., Chen, M., Taleb, T., Ksentini, A., Leung, V.C.M.: Cache in the air: exploiting content caching and delivery techniques for 5G systems. IEEE Commun. Mag. **52**(2), 131–139 (2014)
16. Xie, G., Li, Z., Kaafar, M.A., Wu, Q.: Access types effect on internet video services and its implications on CDN caching. IEEE Trans. Circ. Syst. Video Technol. **28**(5), 1183–1196 (2018)
17. Ye, Z., Pellegrini, F.D., El-Azouzi, R., Maggi, L., Jimenez, T.: Quality-aware dash video caching schemes at mobile edge. In: 2017 29th International Teletraffic Congress (ITC 29), vol. 1, pp. 205–213, September 2017
18. Zhou, X., Sun, M., Wang, Y., Wu, X.: A new QoE-driven video cache allocation scheme for mobile cloud server. In: 2015 11th International Conference on Heterogeneous Networking for Quality, Reliability, Security and Robustness (QSHINE), pp. 122–126, August 2015

Foveated Ray Tracing for VR Headsets

Adam Siekawa, Michał Chwesiuk, Radosław Mantiuk$^{(\boxtimes)}$, and Rafał Piórkowski

West Pomeranian University of Technology, Szczecin,
al. Piastów 17, 70-310 Szczecin, Poland
rmantiuk@zut.edu.pl

Abstract. In this work, we propose a real-time foveated ray tracing system, which mimics the non-uniform and sparse characteristic of the human retina to reduce spatial sampling. Fewer primary rays are traced in the peripheral regions of vision, while sampling frequency for the fovea region traced by the eye tracker is maximised. Our GPU-accelerated ray tracer uses a sampling mask to generate a non-uniformly distributed set of pixels. Then, the regular Cartesian image is reconstructed based on the GPU-accelerated triangulation method with the barycentric interpolation. The temporal anti-aliasing is applied to reduce the flickering artefacts. We perform a user study in which people evaluate the visibility of artefacts in the peripheral region of vision where sampling is reduced. This evaluation is conducted for a number of sampling masks that mimic the sensitivity to contrast in the human eyes but also test different sampling strategies. The sampling that follows the gaze-dependent contrast sensitivity function is reported to generate images of the best quality. We test the performance of the whole system on the VR headset. The achieved frame-rate is twice higher in comparison to the typical Cartesian sampling and cause only barely visible degradation of the image quality.

1 Introduction

Rendering algorithms use sampling in the regular Cartesian coordinates. Since the rendered image is supposed to be displayed on a flat and rectangular display it is an intuitive choice of sample distribution for raster images. With the increasing popularity of Virtual Reality (VR) and the head-mounted displays (HMD), often called *VR headsets*, non-uniform sample distribution strategies are applicable. HMDs use a spherically distorted image to compensate for the optical distortion of the lenses. It suggests that the sample distribution in HMDs can be combined with the *foveated rendering*, in which the number of samples is reduced in the peripheral regions of vision. The image is rendered with the highest sampling rate in the surrounding of the observer's gaze point but sampling is reduced with eccentricity (i.e. distance from the fovea). This degradation of the image quality is unnoticeable for the human observer because the human visual system (HVS) has a lower resolution at peripheral angles of view [23].

I. Kompatsiaris et al. (Eds.): MMM 2019, LNCS 11295, pp. 106–117, 2019.
https://doi.org/10.1007/978-3-030-05710-7_9

Foveated rendering is crucial for future VR headsets because their current resolution is well below the resolution of the human retina. For example, resolution of the HTC Vive headset is less than 5 cycles-per-degree (cpd) while the resolution of the human retina in fovea is almost 60 cpd [15]. Contemporary computer graphics technologies are not ready for a 12x increase in image resolution without significant degradation of the graphics quality [8]. VR headsets start to be equipped with the *eye trackers* that capture the gaze direction of the observer (e.g. FOVE, HTC VIVE with the SMI eye tracker, Oculus Rift with the Pupil Labs eye tracker). This information combined with the head position captured by the *head tracker* delivers an accurate location of the gaze point.

In this work, we present a foveated rendering system based on the ray tracing technique. We use information about the gaze direction captured by the eye tracker to render an image with spatially varying sample distribution. In the region surrounding the gaze point, the rays are traced for each pixel in the display but in the peripheral regions, some pixels are skipped. During reconstruction, vertices of the triangles are placed at corresponding sample positions in the screen space. Then, this triangle mesh is rendered using GPU and the sampling holes are filled by barycentric interpolation of the surrounding pixels.

Ray tracing generates high-quality images with accurate reflections, refractions and shadows, which results in photorealistic appearance and high emersion in the virtual environment. In this work, we propose our custom implementation of the ray tracer, which, due to the reduced number of samples, works in real time even for high-resolution display in the VR headset.

We perform an experiment, in which the Cartesian ray tracing is replaced with the foveated rendering in real time during the free-viewing task. Four different sampling scenarios have tested that increase the number of samples in fovea or at the periphery of vision. The results of the experiment show that more than the double reduction of samples can be acceptable for the human observers, even in the easy to notice the case of a dynamic change in the sampling method.

In Sect. 2, we present previous work on the foveated rendering. Section 3 describes our gaze-depended ray tracer - we present sampling and reconstruction techniques as well as details on the implementation of the ray tracer. Section 4 presents performed experiments that evaluate visible deterioration of the image quality caused by the reduced sampling in the peripheral regions of vision. The paper ends with conclusions and future work in Sect. 5.

2   Previous Work

A known approach is to use an eye tracker to reduce the computational complexity of the image synthesis.

An example is the gaze-driven level-of-detail (LOD) technique, in which simplification of the object geometry is driven by the angular distance from the object to gaze direction [14].

Watson et al. [24] studied a possible spatial and chrominance complexity degradation with the eccentricity in the screen space rather than the object space. They used different high detail inset sizes to generate a high-resolution inset within a low-resolution display field. The perception of a target object among distractors was tested for different peripheral resolutions. Experiments performed using head-mounted display revealed that the complexity can be reduced by almost half without perceivable degradation of the image quality.

Levoy and Whitaker in [9] proposed a ray tracer for volumetric data in which both distributions of rays traced through the image plane and distribution of samples along each ray are functions of local retinal acuity. As a result, the resolution of the rendered images varies locally in response to changes in the user's gaze direction. In a practical implementation, a 2D mipmap was generated by downsampling the original image. For each target pixel, which size varies according to the distance to the gaze position, rays are cast from four corners of each pixel from two MIP-map levels - falling just above and just below the desired target pixel size. A single colour is computed for the pixel by interpolating between colours returned by all rays. Traditional rendering of volume data involves the accumulation of voxel information along with a ray cast into the data set. In their ray tracer, the volume data was structured in a 3D mipmap. A sample for one ray was computed by interpolating between two adequate levels of this 3D mip-map (more precisely between the nearest eight voxels from each level). Again, the size of the 3D levels depends on the distance between the ray and gaze position.

For the ray casting, the gaze-dependent sampling was proposed by Murphy et al. [13]. A similar solution was used to accelerate the ambient occlusion algorithm [12]. The reduced number of rays was traced to approximate the occlusion coefficients in the peripheral regions. Günter et al. [7] proposed a rendering engine, which generates three low-resolution images corresponding to the different fields of view. Then, the wide-angle images are magnified and combined with the non-scaled image of the area surrounding the gaze point. Thus, the number of processed pixels can be reduced by 10–15 times, while ensuring the deterioration of image quality invisible for the observer. Another technique proposed by Stengel et al. [21] aims to reduce shading complexity in the deferred shading technique [2]. The spatial sampling is constant for the whole image but the material shaders are simplified for peripheral pixels. According to the authors, this technique reduces the shading time up to 80%. Programmable control of the shading rate, which enables efficient shading for the foveated rendering was also proposed in Vaidyanathan et al. [22]. In Patney et al. [16], a postprocess contrast enhancement in the peripheral region was introduced to reduce a sense of tunnel vision and further reduce the number of samples. They noticed that people tolerated up to 2x larger blur radius before detecting differences from a non-foveated ground truth. A novel multi-resolution and saccade-aware temporal antialiasing algorithm were also proposed.

A simple gaze-dependent ray tracer was presented at the non-peer-reviewed student conference [19]. In this ray tracer, spatial sampling of the primary rays is based on the shape of the gaze-dependent contrast sensitivity function. A similar approach was presented by Fujita and Harada [5]. More recently, Weier et al. [25] proposed combining foveated rendering based on the ray tracing with reprojection rendering using previous frames in order to reduce the number of new image samples per frame. In their work, the reprojection is also used to reconstruct the Cartesian image. Our solution has similar functionality but uses a much simpler approach. We reduce reconstruction to a simple barycentric interpolation.

3   Foveated Rendering

In this section, we present our gaze-dependent rendering system (see Fig. 1). The non-uniform sampling mask is used to trace primary rays with varying spatial distribution. Location of the mask centre is changed according to the gaze direction captured by the eye tracker. Rays are shot through vertices of the mask and traced using our real-time foveated ray tracer. Finally, the Cartesian RGB image is reconstructed from randomly and non-linearly distributed samples. This image is displayed in the VR headset. The camera is changed according to the head movement of the observer.

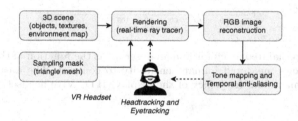

Fig. 1. High-level architecture of our gaze-dependent rendering system.

Non-uniform Sampling. The sampling mask is delivered as a mesh of triangles with samples located in the vertices of the triangles. Spatial distribution of the samples is defined based on the characteristic of the human retina. The mask is larger than the observer's field of view because it must compensate for the eye movements. The peripheral regions of the mask are uncovered when observers shift her/his eyes to the borders of the visual field. The centre of the mask is always located in the gaze position.

The eyes resolution at different viewing angles is measured using Gabor pattern (sinusoidal grating in the Gaussian envelope) presented to human observers in various eccentricities [17]. Observers are asked to guess the orientation of the stimulus (horizontal or vertical), while the contrast threshold (the contrast between light and dark bars of the sinusoidal grating) is decreased in the consecutive steps of the experiment. The threshold contrast sensitivity is indicated by the inability to distinguish the orientation of the stimulus. We repeated this experiment following the methodology presented in Chwesiuk and Mantiuk [3]. As explained in Loschky et al. [10], the resulting contrast thresholds can be expressed as the cut-off spatial frequency (see Fig. 2). This cut-off frequency defines the maximum number of samples visible for the human observer for a given eccentricity. We use this representation to create the sampling masks with varying spatial distribution of samples.

A mask prepared for HTC Vive display is presented in Fig. 3 (left). Because of the limited resolution of the headset display, there is a white spot in the centre of the mask, which covers all the available pixels.

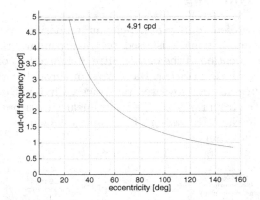

Fig. 2. Cut-off spatial frequency for human observer as the function of the eccentricity. Magenta line shows measured human sensitivity to contrast. The dashed horizontal line depicts the maximum frequency of the display (HTC Vive headset). (Color figure online)

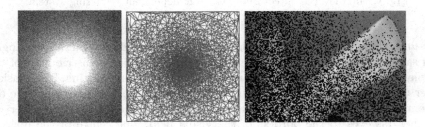

Fig. 3. Left: sampling mask corresponding to the function from Fig. 2. Centre: example triangle mesh used during rendering (for clarity of presentation, the number of vertices was reduced to below seven thousand). Right: inset of the RGB image consisting of the quasi-randomly distributed samples (the black areas indicate pixels for which no rays have been traced). (Color figure online)

Implementation Details. The basic assumption of the foveated rendering systems is real-time work. To accomplish this goal we implemented a custom ray tracer executed by a GPU. The ray tracer uses a non-uniform distribution of the primary rays depending on the observer's gaze direction, which changes continuously while using the VR headset. Actual ray tracing is performed by the OpenCL kernels and RadeonRays [1] routines. The sparse set of samples is converted into the RGB image during the reconstruction phase implemented in OpenGL. The final image is displayed by OpenVR [4]. To speed up rendering, we compute only one ray bounce.

The VR headset visualisation suffers from strong temporal aliasing, which is particularly visible in areas with a reduced number of samples. Therefore, we implemented a naïve temporal anti-aliasing (TAA) based on the depth information from both current and previous frames. The previous frame is accumulated, then, the TAA algorithm looks for pixel coordinates in this accumulation buffer that correspond to the same pixel in the current buffer. The colours from previous and current buffers are averaged.

Image Reconstruction. Ray tracing is not limited to the uniform sampling schema, because one has a full control over the ray origin and direction. This allows rendering images based on the non-uniform sampling algorithms with a negligible impact on the rendering performance. Since the ray tracing performance depends on the number of traced rays, a sample distribution that reduces the overall number of rays will benefit in the increased performance. However, the next step is required to transform the spatially non-uniform samples to the Cartesian coordinates, which can be displayed on the screen. The goal is to use a reconstruction technique, which introduces the lowest possible distortions to the original signal and does not affect the overall performance significantly.

The non-uniform map of samples can be triangulated and rendered using the standard forward rendering [20]. The triangulation is a time-consuming process, which is hard to execute in real time. Therefore, we generate the triangle mesh in the preprocessing and then this mesh is applied for image reconstruction during actual rendering.

The sampling mask is converted to the triangle mesh using the Delaunay triangulation technique. Each sample in the map becomes a vertex in the mesh (see example in Fig. 3 (centre)). This mesh is read from the file during initialisation of our real-time ray tracer. Ray tracer traces rays passing through the vertices of the mesh and stores colours of the corresponding pixels. During the actual triangle mesh rendering, colours inside the triangles are interpolated in screen space using the barycentric interpolation.

We also tested more complex reconstruction techniques: the push-pull reconstruction technique introduced by Gortler et al. [6] and the cell maps described in [20]. However, the mentioned techniques do not improve the image quality significantly but introduce a significant performance overload.

4   Experimental Evaluation

We performed perceptual experiments to explore whether the visible quality of foveated rendering and the quality of the full-resolution rendering are similar.

More precisely, the goal of the experiments was to find the larges sampling reduction that would be acceptable for people watching the rendered animation in VR headset.

Stimuli. We prepared two scenes - Air Shed and Bunny Box - that were displayed in subsequent sessions of the experiment. More realistic Air Shed scene (see Fig. 4, left) consisted of complex models and photorealistic textures. Bunny Box (see Fig. 4, right) was an artificial scene with simple objects and textures that do not mask deteriorations caused by the reduced sampling.

Fig. 4. Example rendering of Air Shed (left) and Bunny Box (right) scenes.

Fig. 5. From left: sampling masks with 54%, 27%, 18%, and 41% of samples.

During the experiment session, the spatial distribution of samples (i.e. primary rays) was modified using four different sampling masks. We also used the reference sampling mask with one ray per pixel, which did not require the reconstruction phase. The sampling masks presented in Fig. 5, correspond to functions plotted in Fig. 6. The 54% mask was created based on the measured gaze-dependent contrast sensitivity function. This function is plotted as the magenta line in Fig. 6. A value of 54% means that the mask defines 54% of the total number of the primary rays required for the full resolution/reference rendering. This 54% mask almost by half reduces the number of primary rays. The second mask defines 27% of samples, which means that the number of samples has been reduced more than three times. There are fewer samples in both fovea and peripheral regions (see blue line in Fig. 6). For the 18% mask, the number of samples has been reduced more than five times but the number of samples in the fovea is almost the same as for the 54% mask (see green line in Fig. 6). In the 41% mask, the densely sampled centre region was extended, while the number of samples in peripheral regions was strongly reduced (see black line in Fig. 6). These four masks were chosen to test different cases of the sampling distributions. Especially, different size of the fovea region was evaluated.

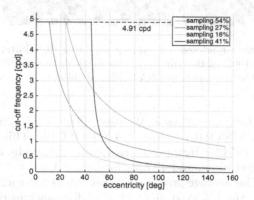

Fig. 6. Cut-off spatial frequency for human observer as the function of eccentricity. Magenta, blue, green, and black lines present simulated sensitivity for 54%, 27%, 18%, and 41% of samples, respectively. The dashed horizontal line depicts the cut-off frequency of the display (HTC Vive headset). (Color figure online)

Figure 7 shows example renderings of Air Shed and Bunny Box scenes for different sampling masks. As can be seen in the insets, the non-uniform distribution of samples causes visible degradation of the image quality increasing with the eccentricity.

Procedure and Participants. We asked observers to wear VR headset and freely look around the scene. At the beginning of the experiment, the reference image was displayed. After 20 s the reference image was replaced with the image generated using a randomly selected mask. The masks were changed at random intervals of about 5 s to the end of the session lasting 180 s. The observer task was to press the mouse button as soon as she/he noticed the change of the image quality caused by the change of the mask.

The experiment was performed on a group of 6 volunteer observers (age between 20 and 24 years, 4 males and 2 females). They declared normal or corrected to normal vision and correct colour vision. The participants were aware that the visualisation quality is tested, but they were naïve about the purpose of the experiment.

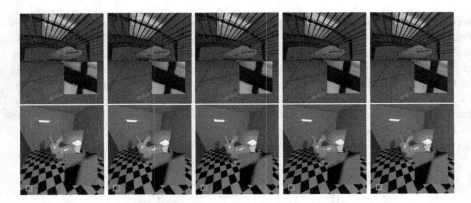

Fig. 7. Example images rendered for varying sampling distribution (from left: 18%, 27%, 41%, 54%, and 100% of the samples). The insets show magnification of the image regions depicted by the red rectangle. (Color figure online)

Apparatus and Performance Results. We used HTC Vive VR headset connected to PC computer with NVIDIA Geforce GTX 1080 GPU. This setup allows rendering two frames of 1512×1680 pixels resolution required by HTC Vive display in 66 ms for Air Shed scene, and 49.5 ms for Bunny Box.

Table 1 shows the average frame rendering times for each sampling mask. In the last column, the achieved increase in performance in comparison to the reference sampling is specified.

Table 1. Rendering performance.

Scene	Sampling mask	Rendering time [ms]	Speed-up
Air Shed	18%	18.1	3.7x
	27%	23.7	2.8x
	41%	37.5	1.8x
	54%	29.8	2.2x
Bunny Box	18%	15.0	3.3x
	27%	17.9	2.8x
	41%	27.6	1.8x
	54%	24.1	2.1x

We achieved more than 4-times speed-up for 18% sampling, however, this reduction of the samples is noticeable to observers (see Sect. 4). Acceptable quality was obtained for 41% and 54% sampling masks with double rendering time reduction.

Results. Figure 8 presents plots of the normalised detection rate for each sampling mask. The detection rate equal to one means that every observer managed to detect the change of the mask in all cases (i.e. pressed the mouse button at the right moment). The detection rate of zero means that observers noticed the change in 50% of cases, while −1 means that the change of the mask was unnoticed.

As can be seen in Fig. 8 (left), 18% and 27% sampling are above the zero detection threshold for both scenes, while 41% and 54% are below this threshold. It is worth noting that the experiment was performed for conservative assumptions because it is much simpler to notice image deterioration while the mask is replaced in real-time. It will be much harder to see image deteriorations if the same mask is used for the whole animation.

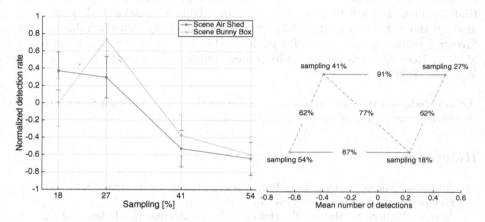

Fig. 8. Left: Normalized detection rate, the error bars depict the standard error of mean. Right: Ranking graph illustrating the statistical significance of the results achieved in the experiment. (Color figure online)

The tested the statistical significance of the achieved results using the multiple-comparison test, which identifies the statistical difference in ranking tests [12]. Figure 8 (right) presents a ranking of the mean detection rates for four tested sampling masks. They are ordered according to the detection rate, with the lowest detection on the left. The percentages indicate the probability that an average observer will choose the sampling on the right as worse than the sampling on the left. If the line connecting two samplings is red and dashed, it indicates that there is no statistical difference between this pair of samplings. The probabilities close to 50% usually result in the lack of statistical significance. For higher probabilities, the dashed-lines will start to be replaced by the blue lines. Figure 8 (right) shows that the ranking between 54% and 41% samplings cannot be trusted. However, 54% sampling generates significantly better results (fewer detections) than 18% sampling, and 41% sampling is better than 27% sampling.

5   Conclusions and Future Work

We have presented an efficient ray tracing system that renders the complex scenes on VR headset in real-time. The performance improvement was achieved with the use of non-uniform sample distribution, which by reducing the number of traced rays significantly decrease rendering time. Experiments that have been performed show that the reduction of the spatial sampling for the peripheral region of the image is barely noticeable, especially for the sampling mask, which mimics human sensitivity to contrast.

We did not manage to completely eliminate flickering in the periphery of vision. This flickering is caused by the temporal aliasing strengthened by the non-uniform and sparse sampling. In future work we plan to implement better anti-aliasing technique, e.g. the multi-sampling presented in [16]. We assume that the flickering can be further reduced by advanced fixation techniques that analyze the gaze data captured by eye tracker in a way more suitable for the foveated rendering. The essential work on this topic was done by Mantiuk et al. [11]. Recently, interesting findings were published by Roth et al. [18] and Weier et al. [25].

Acknowledgments. The project was funded by the Polish National Science Centre (decision number DEC-2013/09/B/ST6/02270).

References

1. Advanced Micro Devices, Inc.: Radeon-rays library, version 2.0 (2016). http://gpuopen.com/gaming-product/radeon-rays/
2. Akenine-Möller, T., Haines, E., Hoffman, N.: Real-Time Rendering, 3rd edn. A. K. Peters Ltd., Natick (2008)
3. Chwesiuk, M., Mantiuk, R.: Measurements of contrast detection thresholds for peripheral vision using non-flashing stimuli. In: Czarnowski, I., Howlett, R.J., Jain, L.C. (eds.) IDT 2017. SIST, vol. 73, pp. 258–267. Springer, Cham (2018). https://doi.org/10.1007/978-3-319-59424-8_24
4. V Corporation: Openvr library, version 1.0.10 (2017). https://github.com/ValveSoftware/openvr
5. Fujita, M., Harada, T.: Foveated real-time ray tracing for virtual reality headset. Technical report, Light Transport Entertainment Research (2014)
6. Gortler, S.J., Grzeszczuk, R., Szeliski, R., Cohen, M.F.: The lumigraph. In: Proceedings of the 23rd Annual Conference on Computer Graphics and Interactive Techniques, pp. 43–54. ACM (1996)
7. Guenter, B., Finch, M., Drucker, S., Tan, D., Snyder, J.: Foveated 3d graphics. ACM Trans. Graph. **31**(6), 164:1–164:10 (2012)
8. Hunt, W.: Virtual reality: the next great graphics revolution. Keynote Talk HPG (2015)
9. Levoy, M., Whitaker, R.: Gaze-directed volume rendering. ACM SIGGRAPH Comput. Graph. **24**(2), 217–223 (1990)
10. Loschky, L., McConkie, G., Yang, J., Miller, M.: The limits of visual resolution in natural scene viewing. Vis. Cogn. **12**(6), 1057–1092 (2005)

11. Mantiuk, R., Bazyluk, B., Mantiuk, R.K.: Gaze-driven object tracking for real time rendering. Comput. Graph. Forum **32**(2), 163–173 (2013)
12. Mantiuk, R.K., Tomaszewska, A., Mantiuk, R.: Comparison of four subjective methods for image quality assessment. Comput. Graph. Forum **31**(8), 2478–2491 (2012)
13. Murphy, H.A., Duchowski, A.T., Tyrrell, R.A.: Hybrid image/model-based gaze-contingent rendering. ACM Trans. Appl. Percept. (TAP) **5**(4), 22 (2009)
14. Ohshima, T., Yamamoto, H., Tamura, H.: Gaze-directed adaptive rendering for interacting with virtual space. In: 1996 Proceedings of the IEEE Conference on Virtual Reality Annual International Symposium, pp. 103–110. IEEE (1996)
15. Palmer, S.E.: Vision Science: Photons to Phenomenology, vol. 1. MIT Press, Cambridge (1999)
16. Patney, A., et al.: Perceptually-based foveated virtual reality. In: ACM SIGGRAPH 2016 Emerging Technologies, p. 17. ACM (2016)
17. Peli, E., Yang, J., Goldstein, R.B.: Image invariance with changes in size: the role of peripheral contrast thresholds. JOSA A **8**(11), 1762–1774 (1991)
18. Roth, T., Weier, M., Hinkenjann, A., Li, Y., Slusallek, P.: An analysis of eye-tracking data in foveated ray tracing. In: IEEE Second Workshop on Eye Tracking and Visualization (ETVIS), pp. 69–73. IEEE (2016)
19. Siekawa, A.: Gaze-dependent ray tracing. In: Proceedings of CESCG 2014: The 18th Central European Seminar on Computer Graphics (Non-peer-reviewed) (2014)
20. Siekawa, A.: Image reconstruction from spatially non-uniform samples. In: Proceedings of CESCG 2017: The 21th Central European Seminar on Computer Graphics (Non-peer-reviewed) (2017)
21. Stengel, M., Magnor, M.: Gaze-contingent computational displays: boosting perceptual fidelity. IEEE Sig. Process. Mag. **33**(5), 139–148 (2016)
22. Vaidyanathan, K., et al.: Coarse pixel shading. In: Proceedings of High Performance Graphics, pp. 9–18. Eurographics Association (2014)
23. Wandell, B.A.: Foundations of Vision, vol. 8. Sinauer Associates, Sunderland (1995)
24. Watson, B., Walker, N., Hodges, L.F., Worden, A.: Managing level of detail through peripheral degradation: effects on search performance with a head-mounted display. ACM Trans. Comput.-Hum. Interact. (TOCHI) **4**(4), 323–346 (1997)
25. Weier, M., et al.: Perception-driven accelerated rendering. Comput. Graph. Forum **36**(2), 611–643 (2017)

Preferred Model of Adaptation to Dark for Virtual Reality Headsets

Marek Wernikowski, Radosław Mantiuk$^{(\boxtimes)}$, and Rafał Piórkowski

West Pomeranian University of Technology, Szczecin,
al. Piastów 17, 70-310 Szczecin, Poland
rmantiuk@zut.edu.pl

Abstract. The human visual system has the ability to adapt to various lighting conditions. In this work, we simulate the dark adaptation process using a custom virtual reality framework. The high dynamic range (HDR) image is rendered, tone mapped and displayed in the head-mounted-display (HMD) equipped with the eye tracker. Observer's adaptation state is predicted by analysing the HDR image in the surrounding of his/her gaze point. This state is applied during tone mapping to simulate how an observer would see the whole scene being adapted to an arbitrary luminance level. We take into account the spatial extent of the visual adaptation, loss of colour vision, and time course of adaptation. Our main goal is to mimic the adaptation process naturally implemented by the human visual system. However, we prove in the psychophysical experiments that people prefer shorter adaptation while watching a virtual environment. We also justify that a complex perceptual model of adaptation to dark can be replaced with simpler linear formulas.

1 Introduction

Because the lighting conditions vary significantly from scene to scene, people evolved a mechanism, which allows seeing objects in both bright and dark conditions. This process within the human visual system (HVS) is called *visual adaptation* - it allows HVS to adjust to various light conditions ranging from very dark scenes lighted by the stars to the bright environments illuminated by millions of candelas [1]. Entering a dark room, people cannot see anything but after a time they begin to see the objects. During this time, the *adaptation luminance* is changing from a higher value to the average luminance of the objects and surfaces currently visible. People frequently change their gaze direction and adapt to different regions. As a result, HVS is permanently in the *maladaptation* state, in which the adaptation luminance is changing towards a target value but never reaches this value because in the meantime the target is changed.

Perceptual simulation of the dark adaptation is especially interesting from a virtual reality perspective. In this work we focus on simulating a virtual environment using the *head mounted displays* (HMD) (often called a *virtual reality* (VR) headsets) equipped with the eye tracker (Sect. 3). We model the adaptation to

© Springer Nature Switzerland AG 2019
I. Kompatsiaris et al. (Eds.): MMM 2019, LNCS 11295, pp. 118–129, 2019.
https://doi.org/10.1007/978-3-030-05710-7_10

dark taking into account the brightness of a scene region the observer is looking at. The goal is to simulate the visual adaptation process in a correct way in terms of the human perception so that it could reflect the real-world behaviour of HVS. We take into account both photopic and scotopic vision and accurately model the spatial extent of adaptation (Sect. 3.2), loss of color vision (Sect. 3.3) and maladaptation processes (Sect. 3.5).

We argue that from a usability perspective it is not necessarily desirable to strictly simulate the adaptation to dark process, which is rather slow. It takes tens of seconds to fully adapt from the bright environment to a very dark one. We perform a psychophysical experiment, which justifies that preferred speed of adaptation in the virtual environments is much shorter and that it is not needed to model this process with the same speed as in nature. We also investigate if the complex perceptual model of the adaptation to dark is noticeable to people. Another psychophysical experiment reveals that the perceptual model can be replaced with the simpler linear formulas (Sect. 4).

2   Background

The human eyes are able to adapt to luminance which differ greatly, even 14 orders of magnitude - from moonlight ($10^{-6} \frac{cd}{m^2}$) up to sunlight ($10^8 \frac{cd}{m^2}$) [2]. The *visual adaptation* process takes place when the lighting condition, to which the observer is currently adapted, changes. For example, she/he enters the darker room, turns on the light or just walks outside. The time for the eye to adapt to the new environment depends whether the cones or the rods are being activated/deactivated.

In the case of increasing the ambient luminance, the photopigment in rods gets bleached [3]. For a few seconds, they are completely blind and the sensitivity of cones begins to increase. The whole adaptation takes up to 5 min but the vision might be fully clear in even less than 1 s. During this short period, the vision is heavily impaired - the colours are barely visible and all objects seem to be too bright.

The adaptation to dark is a sustained process - depending on the amount of light it could take from 10 min to 2 h, sometimes even more. At the beginning of adaptation, when the bright light is switched off, it is hard to see anything. It is caused by the fact that cones are currently in the low sensitivity state and rods are bleached. Then, cones are regaining their sensitivity and rods are regenerated. When cones achieve the highest sensitivity, rods increase their sensitivity until are fully adapted. When the cones achieve more or less their lowest sensitivity level, rods are regenerated enough to start dark adaptation. The longer this process takes, the lower vision threshold gets - view becomes clearer and more objects emerge from the darkness. It also means, that dark adaptation takes a much longer time for very dark places then it does for a bit brighter ones.

Only a small part of the adaptation is due to changes in pupil size (from 1–2 mm to about 8 mm) [1,4]. Above a certain luminance level (of approximately 0.03 cd/m^2), the cone mechanism is involved in vision (called *photopic vision*).

Below this threshold, the rod mechanism is activated providing *scotopic vision*. In the mesopic range, there is a transition between these two mechanisms. A lot of the adaptation occurs in the photoreceptors themselves. Some of the photopigment in rods or cones can be bleached. Less photopigment means weaker response to light changes. Additionally, the *horizontal neural cells* in the retina can control the responsiveness of the photoreceptors. If the light changes strongly, they can reduce the sensitivity of the photoreceptors.

The human eyes mainly adapt to an area covering approximately 2–4° of the viewing angle around the gaze direction [5]. Other areas of the scene, observed not in foveal but in parafoveal and peripheral regions, have significantly less impact on the adaptation level, although, a human frequently changes his gaze direction and tries to adapt to different regions [6]. As the process of the luminance adaptation is slower than changes of gaze direction, the HVS is permanently in the *maladaptation* state, in which the adaptation luminance is changing towards a target value but never reaches this value because in the meantime the target is changed.

3   Simulation of Adaptation to Dark in Virtual Reality Headset

In this section, we present our virtual reality framework. We use this framework to implement the luminance adaptation models and provide a testbed for the perceptual experiments.

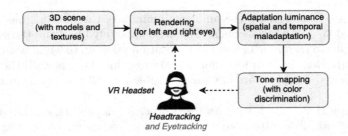

Fig. 1. High level scheme of our virtual reality framework.

The general scheme of the framework is presented in Fig. 1. The 3D scene is rendered to the texture buffers for both left and right eyes. The scene contains light sources and object materials of properties that enable rendering of the high dynamic range content. This HDR image data is used to compute the adaptation luminance taking into account the spatial extent of the visual adaptation (see Sect. 3.4) and current maladaptation state (see Sect. 3.5). The image is tone mapped using the adaptation luminance computed in the previous step (see Sect. 3.2), the difference in colour discrimination between scotopic, mesopic and photopic ranges are considered (see Sect. 3.3), and finally, the output RGB image is displayed in the VR headset. Movement of the observer's gaze direction results in redrawing of the image with new camera parameters and adequate change of the adaptation luminance. Details of the framework implementation are presented in Sect. 3.1.

3.1 Rendering

A modern graphics hardware generates computer images in real time using realistic lighting model. Calculations are performed with floating-point accuracy, which means that the dynamic range of the synthetic scenes can correspond to the dynamic range of the actual scene.

We prepared five complex scenes with the rapidly changing distribution of lighting (see example renderings in Fig. 2). The scenes contain the very bright object (e.g. lamps with a luminance of 800–1000 cd/m^2) and a number of the dark objects of more than 4-orders lower luminance.

Fig. 2. Example renderings of the test scenes. Dynamic range is expressed in log10 units. Presented images have been tone mapped assuming that observer is adapted to 600 cd/m^2 (top row) and 0.02 cd/m^2 (bottom row).

3.2 Tone Mapping

Rendered high dynamic range image must be transformed from the floating-point (or photometric) space to a fixed RGB space of the display. This is fundamentally a *tone reproduction* problem, which maps from scene to display in terms of physical limitations of the display system and psychophysical processes occurring in HVS as result of changing lighting conditions [2].

In our framework, we use Ward's concept of matching just noticeable difference for the world and display observers [7]. Word's contrast-based tone mapping operator seeks to match contrast visibility at the threshold and scales suprathreshold values relative to the threshold measure [8]. It is based on a *threshold-versus-intensity* (TVI) data, which shows the relationship between the adaptation luminance and the contrast detection threshold.

Ward's tone reproduction operator is defined as:

$$L_d = m * L_w, \tag{1}$$

where L_w is the *world* luminance of the rendered image pixels, and L_d is the luminance that L_w is mapped to on the display. Coefficient m is calculated with the equation:

$$m = t(L_{da})/t(L_{wa}), \tag{2}$$

in which L_{da} and L_{wa} are the adaptation luminance for the display observer and for the world observer, respectively. L_{da} depends on the maximum luminance of the display and for our VR headset can be set to approximately $85\,\text{cd/m}^2$ (half of the maximum screen luminance of approximately $170\,\text{cd/m}^2$). L_{wa} depends on the temporal scene luminance and is estimated taking into consideration the spatial extent of luminance in the observer's field of view (see Sect. 3.4), and time-course of the visual adaptation (see Sect. 3.5). $t(L_d)$ is the TVI function, which, after Ferwerda et al. [8], we apply separately for the cones ($t_s(L_a)$) and rods ($t_p(L_a)$) using the following approximations:

$$\log t_s(L_a) = \begin{cases} -2.86 & if \log L_a \leq -3.94, \\ \log L_a - 0.395 & if \log L_a \geq -1.44, \\ (0.405 \log L_a + 1.6)^{2.18} \\ -0.72 & otherwise. \end{cases} \tag{3}$$

$$\log t_p(L_a) = \begin{cases} -0.72 & if \log L_a \leq -2.6, \\ \log L_a - 1.255 & if \log L_a \geq 1.9, \\ (0.249 \log L_a + 0.65)^{2.7} \\ -0.72 & otherwise, \end{cases} \tag{4}$$

$t(L_{da})$ is computed only for cones. $t(L_{wa})$ is computed separately for rods and cones, and then combined together:

$$t(L_{wa}) = (1 - k(L_{wa})) * t_p(L_{wa}) + k(L_{wa}) * t_s(L_{wa}), \tag{5}$$

where k is a constant that goes from 1 to 0 as the scotopic adaptation goes from bottom to the top of the mesopic range (from $0.03\,\text{cd/m}^2$ to $3\,\text{cd/m}^2$ in our implementation).

3.3   Color Discrimination

In scotopic range, where only rods are active, colour discrimination is not possible. Inspired by Hunt [9], we model the sensitivity of rods σ with the following equation:

$$\sigma = \begin{cases} 1 & L_w < 0.03\,\text{cd/m}^2, \\ 0 & L_w > 3\,\text{cd/m}^2, \\ \frac{0.07}{0.069+1.409*e^{4.267*L_w}} & otherwise. \end{cases} \tag{6}$$

The $\sigma = 1$ denotes the perception using rods only (monochromatic vision) and $\sigma = 0$ perception using cones only (full colour discrimination). In the mesopic range, the sensitivity of rods is reduced following the sigmoidal function. We fitted this function assuming maximum and minimum sensitivity of rods at a luminance of $0.03\,\text{cd/m}^2$ and $3\,\text{cd/m}^2$, respectively. Figure 3 shows the plot of Eq. 6.

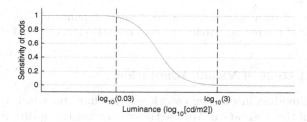

Fig. 3. Sigmoidal function approximating the sensitivity of rods.

The level of color discrimination is approximated as weighted sum of output luminance (L_d) and output RGB image after tone mapping [10]:

$$LDR_{RGB} = \sigma * L_d + (1 - \sigma) * \frac{HDR_{RGB}}{L_w} * L_d. \tag{7}$$

The output low dynamic range image (LDR_{RGB}) is gamma corrected and displayed in the VR headset.

Figure 4 presents examples of colour discrimination in the same scene but with different illumination. In the top row, only a few objects have faded colours because the average luminance is below cones sensitivity. The colours become more and more saturated as the scene luminance increases (i.e. the lights on the scene become brighter) (see middle and bottom rows). The right column in Fig. 4 shows the corresponding maps of the rod sensitivity. Brighter pixels means the higher sensitivity of rods, i.e. less saturated colours in the renderings.

Fig. 4. Examples of color discrimination for mesopic illumination (top row) and corresponding maps of the rod sensitivity (bottom row). (Color figure online)

3.4   Spatial Extent of Visual Adaptation

The important module in our framework is a mechanism, which computes the spatial extent of the adaptation. We use the eye tracker to capture the observer's gaze location and compute the adaptation luminance taking into account the surrounding pixels. More precisely, the weighted average of the luminance is computed, wherein the weights are delivered as a texture mask centred in the gaze point.

Vangorp et al. [5] proposed a nonlinear model, which estimates the local adaptation luminance using the pixels values in the 8-degrees surrounding of the gaze point. However, we notice that for wide fields of view (110° in our VR headset) this model underestimates the influence of light in peripheral areas. Therefore, in our framework, we apply an approach based on the gaze-dependent contrast sensitivity function [11]. This function roughly follows the distribution of the cones in the retina. As the number of cones decreases with the eccentricity, we assume that areas of the highest frequency affect the adaptation luminance at most [12]. Below equation models the spatial cutoff frequency f_c of the human retina, i.e. the highest frequencies that are still visible for the eccentricity d: $f_c = 43.1 * E_2/(E_2 + d)$, where E_2 denotes the eccentricity at which spatial frequency drops to half (we use a value of 3.118 cpd) [13]. We apply the above formula to create a mask, which is used to compute the weighted average of the luminance. We are aware that this solution does not model the spatial extent of visual adaptation accurately but, to the best of our knowledge, there are no better models available in the literature.

3.5   Temporal Adaptation

A recognized source in the literature describing how adaptation changes over time are the time-course of dark adaptation measured by Hecht [14] and published in Woodworth et al. [15] (see Fig. 5). It shows how the threshold contrast required to see the difference between objects reduces over time. Just after entering the dark environment, cones have the highest impact on the vision and the threshold contrast decreases rapidly. After approximately 7 min, rods start to support the vision. After a relatively long time (approx. 20 min), change of the sensitivity becomes insignificant. The curves in Fig. 5 show our fitting of the original data from Woodworth et al. to the equations:

$$\begin{cases} \Delta L_{cone} = 5.659 * t^{-0.051} - 7.431, \\ \Delta L_{rod} = -5.766 * e^{-0.0053*t} + 9.694 * e^{-0.1648*t}, \end{cases}$$

where ΔL_{cone} and ΔL_{rod} are contrast thresholds measured for an average human observer at a given moment in time t for cones and rods, respectively.

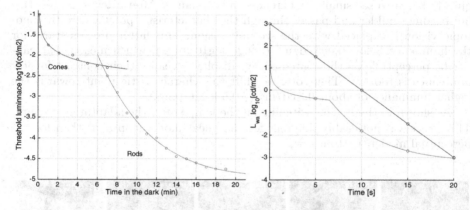

Fig. 5. Left: Dark adaptation process (after Woodworth et al. [15]). Right: The simulated change of the adaptation luminance over time. The circle markers correspond to images presented in Fig. 6. (Color figure online)

The relationship between the contrast threshold and adaptation luminance is explained by Weber's law [15] and gives the TVI function. Over a wide range of luminance (above -3 log10 (cd/m^2)), this relationship is linear in log-log space, i.e. the proportional decrease in threshold will decrease value of the adaptation luminance. Therefore, for simplicity, we assume that the inverse TVI function can be approximated by the inverse of this "linear" TVI:

$$\begin{aligned} log_{10}(L_a(t)) &= p1 * k + p2, \\ k &= \min(log_{10}(\Delta L_{cone}(t)), log_{10}(\Delta L_{rod}(t))), \end{aligned} \qquad (8)$$

where t is the time in dark in seconds, $p1 = 1.191$ and $p2 = 0.7075$. Inverse TVI function transfers contrast threshold to the adaptation luminance expressed in cd/m^2 (see example in Fig. 5 (right)).

From obvious reasons, in virtual reality simulations, the adaptation has to be shortened so that the observer would not need to wait minutes to see any information after entering the dark environment. We assume that after 20 min L_a is no longer reduced and we proportionally scale this time to obtain shorter adaptation periods up to 20 s (see Fig. 5 (right)). We compare the presented time-course of adaptation (we called it *perceptual* - magenta line in Fig. 5 (right)) with the linear model depicted as the blue line. It is worth noting that the latter model is linear in the logarithmic space and still mimics a non-linear decrease of the adaptation luminance.

Except shortening the adaptation time, we propose another modification presented in Fig. 5. The magenta line in the right plot is shifted towards higher luminance values in comparison to the curves presented in the left plot. During adaptation to dark, the sensitivity to contrast grows rapidly in the first few seconds. It is shown as a sharp drop in the threshold luminance - people quickly begin to see smaller differences in luminance. After a few minutes, this fall becomes milder and passes through the characteristic point where the photopic vision is replaced with the scotopic vision. This latter process starts for the luminance below $0.005\,cd/m^2$ (-2.25 log10 units), which means that cannot be perceptible on the contemporary displays because their contrast for low luminance is too low. Therefore, we shift this characteristic point towards the higher luminance of about $0.3\,cd/m^2$ (-0.5 log10 units).

As shown in the Fig. 6, switching off the lamp starts the adaptation to dark. This process is noticeably different for the linear model (top row) than for the perceptual model (bottom row).

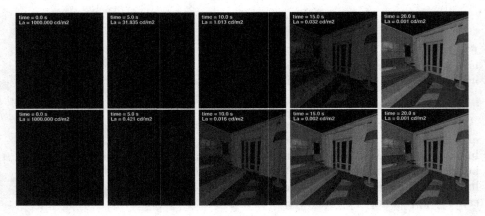

Fig. 6. Observer is fully adapted to the bright environment ($L_a = 1000\,cd/m^2$), then the lamp is switched off and adaptation to dark begins using linear (top row) or perceptual (bottom row) formulas.

4   Experimental Evaluation

We performed an experiment, which searches for a preferred speed of visual adaptation to dark. We also test the preference towards the perceptual or linear model of the adaptation.

Stimuli and Procedure. During the experiment, observers were asked to wear HTC Vive headset. They could freely look around the virtual environment. The scene was rendered with the lights switched on for 6 s. After this time the lights were switched off, which significantly reduced the scene lighting from about $600\,\mathrm{cd/m^2}$ to an average level of about $0.02\,\mathrm{cd/m^2}$ (see Fig. 2). At first, an observer could see only a black image because she/he was adapted to a high luminance level. Then, we simulated the adaptation to dark decreasing the adaptation luminance according to linear or perceptual formula (see Sect. 3.5).

In the first experiment, we tested the preferred time of adaptation to dark. The procedure described above was repeated twice one after another but using different adaptation times. Then, we asked the observer to choose the session, which she/he would prefer while watching simulation to dark in the virtual environment. We tested the adaptation periods of 5, 15 and 25 s. All cases were compared with each other and presented in random order.

In the second experiment, we compared the linear and perceptual adaptations. In the following sessions, we simulated linear or perceptual adaptation using the same adaptation time of 25 s. Each observer repeated the experiment twice for each scene.

Participants. The first experiment was performed on a group of 15 volunteer observers (age between 19 and 23 years). A different set of 9 observers was allocated to the second experiment (age between 20 and 23 years). All observers were recruited from IT students. They declared normal or corrected to normal vision and correct colour vision. They were aware that the visual adaptation is tested, but they were naïve about the purpose of the experiment. No session took longer than 20 min in the first experiment and 15 min in the second one.

Apparatus. The experiment was performed using HTC Vive headset. The images for the left and right eyes were rendered by Geforce GTX 1080 GPU.

Results. Figure 7 (left) presents a plot with the results of the first experiment, which shows the preference as a function of the adaptation time. This preference is a number of votes normalized by a number of times the condition has been tested. For the linear adaptation, 25 s is the most preferred adaptation period, while observers preferred 5 s in the case of the perceptual model of adaptation.

The differences in the number of votes between individual conditions are small, therefore we perform the multiple-comparison test, which identifies the statistical difference in ranking tests. Figure 7 (centre and right) presents a ranking of the mean number of votes for three tested adaptation times. They are ordered according to increasing number of votes, with the smallest number

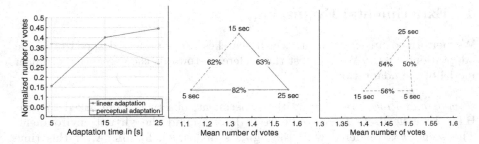

Fig. 7. Left: Preferred time of adaptation to dark. Ranking graphs illustrating the statistical significance of the experiment testing a preferred adaptation time for the linear (center) and perceptual (right) formulas. (Color figure online)

of votes on the left. The percentages indicate the probability that an average observer will choose the time on the right as better than the time on the left. If the line connecting two samplings is red and dashed, it indicates that there is no statistical difference between this pair of times. The probabilities close to 50% usually result in the lack of statistical significance. For higher probabilities, the dashed-lines will start to be replaced by the blue lines. The details on the interpretation of the graphs are presented in Mantiuk et al. [16].

The multiple-comparison test confirmed the significant statistical difference for 25 s for the linear adaptation. This adaptation time was preferred regardless of observers and scenes. However, for the perceptual adaptation, the ranking cannot be trusted. We tried to cluster the results according to selected groups of observers or scenes but the results were still not statistically significant.

The results of the second experiment indicated that people prefer the linear adaptation model (68 votes) against the perceptual model (32 votes). The multiple-comparison test confirmed the statistical significance of these results with the 65% probability. This interesting finding shows that nonlinearities of the adaptation model do not have to be preferred by people.

5   Conclusions and Future Work

We proposed a model of visual adaptation to dark designed for the virtual reality environments displayed in VR headsets. This model simulates how people see the HDR scene at a low level of luminance, while their adaptation changes from a low sensitivity to a high sensitivity. Our model simulates the change of the adaptation luminance in time in a manner that mimics the perceptual behaviour of the human visual system. It includes a variation of the colour discrimination for different levels of the adaptation luminance.

The model has been implemented in a virtual reality system with the VR headset. Based on this implementation we performed a perceptual experiment, which measures a preferred adaptation time. The results indicate a preference for a 25-seconds adaptation time for the linear adaptation. For the perceptual adaptation, the results are ambiguous. The second experiment proves that people prefer the linear adaptation rather than perceptual.

In future work, we plan to evaluate the perceptual model of adaptation for lower levels of luminance. It could be performed with the use of high-quality OLED displays equipped with the additional neutral density filters. We plan to add to our model a variation of the image acuity, which blurs the image for low luminance levels. It would be also interesting to evaluate how our virtual reality setup would benefit from using the eye tracker.

References

1. Palmer, S.E.: Vision Science: Photons to Phenomenology, vol. 1. MIT press, Cambridge (1999)
2. Reinhard, E., Heidrich, W., Debevec, P., Pattanaik, S., Ward, G., Myszkowski, K.: High Dynamic Range Imaging: Acquisition, Display, and Image-Based Lighting, 2nd edn. Morgan Kaufmann, Amsterdam (2010)
3. Davson, H.: Physiology of the Eye. Elsevier, Amsterdam (2012)
4. Graham, C.H.: Vision and Visual Perception. Wiley, Hoboken (1965)
5. Vangorp, P., Myszkowski, K., Graf, E.W., Mantiuk, R.K.: A model of local adaptation. ACM Trans. Graph. **34**, 166:1–166:13 (2015). Proceedings of ACM SIGGRAPH Asia
6. Mantiuk, R., Markowski, M.: Gaze-dependent tone mapping. In: Kamel, M., Campilho, A. (eds.) ICIAR 2013. LNCS, vol. 7950, pp. 426–433. Springer, Heidelberg (2013). https://doi.org/10.1007/978-3-642-39094-4_48
7. Ward, G.: A contrast-based scalefactor for luminance display. In: Graphics Gems IV, pp. 415–421 (1994)
8. Ferwerda, J.A., Pattanaik, S.N., Shirley, P., Greenberg, D.P.: A model of visual adaptation for realistic image synthesis. In: Proceedings of the 23rd Annual Conference on Computer Graphics and Interactive Techniques, pp. 249–258. ACM (1996)
9. Hunt, R.W.G.: The Reproduction of Colour. Wiley, Hoboken (2005)
10. Krawczyk, G., Myszkowski, K., Seidel, H.: Perceptual effects in real-time tone mapping. In: Proceedings of the 21st Spring Conference on Computer Graphics, Budmerice, Slovakia, pp. 195–202 (2005)
11. Peli, E., Yang, J., Goldstein, R.B.: Image invariance with changes in size: the role of peripheral contrast thresholds. JOSA A **8**, 1762–1774 (1991)
12. Mantiuk, R., Janus, S.: Gaze-dependent ambient occlusion. In: Bebis, G., et al. (eds.) ISVC 2012. LNCS, vol. 7431, pp. 523–532. Springer, Heidelberg (2012). https://doi.org/10.1007/978-3-642-33179-4_50
13. Loschky, L., McConkie, G., Yang, J., Miller, M.: The limits of visual resolution in natural scene viewing. Vis. Cogn. **12**, 1057–1092 (2005)
14. Hecht, S.: Vision: II. The Nature of the Photoreceptor Process, Clark University Press, USA (1934)
15. Woodworth, R.S., Schlosberg, H., Kling, J.W., Riggs, L.A.: Woodworth & Schlosberg's Experimental Psychology, 3rd edn. Holt, Rinehart and Winston, Houghton (1971)
16. Mantiuk, R.K., Tomaszewska, A., Mantiuk, R.: Comparison of four subjective methods for image quality assessment. Comput. Graph. Forum **31**, 2478–2491 (2012)

From Movement to Events: Improving Soccer Match Annotations

Manuel Stein[✉], Daniel Seebacher, Tassilo Karge, Tom Polk,
Michael Grossniklaus, and Daniel A. Keim

University of Konstanz, Konstanz, Germany
{manuel.stein,daniel.seebacher,tassilo.karge,
tom.polk,michael.grossniklaus,daniel.keim}@uni-konstanz.de

Abstract. Match analysis has become an important task in everyday
work at professional soccer clubs in order to improve team performance.
Video analysts regularly spend up to several days analyzing and summa-
rizing matches based on tracked and annotated match data. Although
there already exists extensive capabilities to track the movement of players and the ball from multimedia data sources such as video recordings,
there is no capability to sufficiently detect dynamic and complex events
within these data. As a consequence, analysts have to rely on manually created annotations, which are very time-consuming and expensive
to create. We propose a novel method for the semi-automatic definition and detection of events based entirely on movement data of players
and the ball. Incorporating Allen's interval algebra into a visual analytics system, we enable analysts to visually define as well as search
for complex, hierarchical events. We demonstrate the usefulness of our
approach by quantitatively comparing our automatically detected events
with manually annotated events from a professional data provider as well
as several expert interviews. The results of our evaluation show that the
required annotation time for complete matches by using our system can
be reduced to a few seconds while achieving a similar level of performance.

Keywords: Visual analytics · Sport analytics · Event analysis

1 Introduction

In numerous invasive team sports such as soccer, automatic video analysis is
increasingly being deployed to collect spatio-temporal data, consisting of player
and ball movement [10]. This data is collected to gain deeper insights into the
respective sport in order to increase the efficiency of players, analyze opposing
teams and, consequently, improve training and team performance. Without further processing and analysis, however, this data alone does not provide deeper
insights into a match. In order to take full advantage of the data, analyses must
be carried out and visualizations must be generated so that analysts can process
the large amounts of retrieved movement data.

© Springer Nature Switzerland AG 2019
I. Kompatsiaris et al. (Eds.): MMM 2019, LNCS 11295, pp. 130–142, 2019.
https://doi.org/10.1007/978-3-030-05710-7_11

Companies such as Stats and Opta manually annotate basic events, such as passes, ball possession times, and fouls or penalties, as well as more complex events such as offside determination. Here, analysts manually inspect and annotate vast amounts of multimedia data, mostly many hours of video, based on predefined criteria. In addition to being extremely time-consuming and expensive, this manual annotation is also susceptible to human error, thereby reducing the quality of the event data. Existing approaches to automate event detection are divided into two fields: Automatic video analysis and direct analysis based on previously recorded movement data in combination with existing, basic events. Automatic video analysis has been used, for example, to try to detect events in television broadcasts or video recordings of soccer matches [3,5,9,11,12,15–17]. Using these approaches, simple events such as corner balls or goals, can be easily detected. However, recognizing new kinds of events requires a considerable amount of effort, since separate algorithms have to be created for each event type. Furthermore, many algorithms rely on implicitly annotated data, such as the organizer's logo appearing before replays or specific camera movements, to detect certain events such as corner kicks or penalties. These techniques can typically only be applied in a narrow set of circumstances and do not represent a robust, generalizable approach. Several systems also use movement data directly in order to recognize events [6,7,13,18]. However, these concepts do not allow interactive definition of events and are typically designed for a narrow set of purposes, such as commenting on soccer matches. Consequently, de Sousa Júnior et al. [4] suggest the recognition of events in matches should be the core focus of current research on soccer analysis. The recognition of events based on underlying event patterns is mentioned as an example. In addition to automatically recording player and ball movement data at a reasonable spatio-temporal resolution, it is also necessary to automate event recognition in order to make the detection of events more cost-effective, faster, and more reliable. Automatic analysis can also reveal aspects that would not be found with manual analysis due to bias, human error, lack of time, or simple lack of knowledge. At the same time, intuition and expert knowledge are required to formulate a meaningful objective and to define event patterns that are interesting or important for the respective question, analyst, player, or team. Some event-types in soccer do not have a universally shared definition, but are instead defined differently depending on each team, and therefore cannot be recognized correctly without manual interaction.

In this paper, we propose an automated event detection system based solely on soccer movement data. Simultaneously, we enable analysts to efficiently and flexibly incorporate their intuitions in order to find complex patterns in events. The developed system gives the user the possibility to custom-define spatio-temporal patterns and then automatically search for them. In contrast to existing approaches, it allows expert knowledge and human intuition to be integrated into the automated analysis process. By directly using movement data to generate events, it closes the gap between raw multimedia data and event data and compensates the lack of flexibility and scalability of manual data annotation.

With the help of a visualization displaying identified events in combination with the associated movement data, the presented system allows the correction of existing event patterns, the creation of new patterns, and the general assessment of event data. Since the recognition of events is automated, the system therefore supports real-time analysis.

2   Detection of Complex Events

The processing of complex events is a broad field in computer science that includes not only their processing, but also the architecture for processing data or event streams and the recognition of (complex) events. The most important step in event processing consists of detecting *complex events* and is therefore the main focus of our proposed approach. The detection of complex events in large soccer data enables analysts to summarize the increasing amounts of gathered movement data by highlighting interesting occurrences. This helps soccer analysts and coaches interpret the data faster and more effectively, giving them more time to use the resulting knowledge. In the following, we define an *event* as a time interval or point containing associated objects and attributes. For example, a shot on goal event can be associated with the players specifically involved. Furthermore, we define *event types* as events with certain common characteristics. An *event type* has a name and contains a definition of the characteristics common to its events, enabling the user to identify all associated events. A constellation of event types is called a *temporal pattern* or an *event pattern*. A sequence of events that satisfies the event pattern is an instance of a complex event type, also called a *complex event*. Figure 1(a) shows an example event pattern involving the event types B, A and C. In the example shown, event type A is starting before B is fully finished. The identified locations of the user defined event pattern in the overall event data stream are highlighted in Fig. 1(b). Complex event types themselves can occur in event patterns, resulting in a hierarchy of event types as shown in Fig. 2. For a better understanding, all subsequent steps are explained using the example of the offside rule, since the rules for this event are generally known and many technical details of event detection can be explained using them.

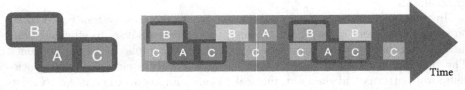

(a) Event Pattern of Event Types B, A and C

(b) Identified Locations of Event Pattern in Event Data Stream

Fig. 1. Event pattern and event data stream with pattern locations

The Laws of the Game of the International Football Association Board state that a player is in an offside position if a player is in the opponent's half of the pitch and closer to the goal line than both the ball and the second-to-last opponent [2]. In this description, we can see that several event types play a role in the offside rule and that they occur within a certain time constellation. Together, the event types form a complex event pattern including, for example, players and teams. Examples of involved event types in the offside rule are *player is in offside position* or *player is touching the ball*. The description of an event in natural language must be formalized in order to be usable for a program to find the event. One very similar and, therefore, intuitive formalism for describing temporal relationships of natural languages is given in *Allen's interval algebra* [1]. In this algebra, possible topological relations (*qualitative relations*) can be expressed between intervals which, in our case, translate to events. For example, the relationship between two events can describe whether both events happen at the same time or directly one after another.

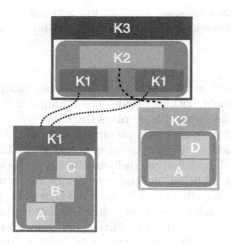

Fig. 2. Complex event patterns can be hierarchically composed by combining primitive or other complex events.

Some soccer events are not perceived as a time interval, but rather as a point in time. For example, the offside rule speaks about the *(...) point in time at which a ball is touched by a fellow team member (...)*. In order to use specific points in time, we need to extend Allen's interval algebra. However, these changes are not drastic, since a point in time can be understood as an interval whose start and end points are the same. There are some special cases that need to be considered, when including time points into Allen's interval algebra. For example, if A is an event that occurs at a point in time and B an event that has a time interval, not all relations can occur between these events, such as *DURING*, since $A_{start} = A_{end}$. An overview over all possible relations between time points and intervals is given in Fig. 3 and an overview of all possible relations between two time points in Fig. 4.

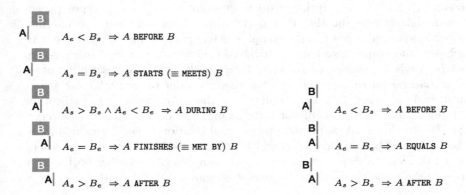

Fig. 3. Possible relations between a time point and a time interval

Fig. 4. Possible relations between two time points

These relations between the events allow us to create complex event patterns, as is the case, for example, with an offside. The example in Fig. 1(a) can serve as an illustration. B is the event "player plays the ball", which must overlap with or at least meet event A "player is in an offside position". This can be followed by another event C such as "Player A shoots at the goal". These events, such as "player is in the offside" position, can be hierarchically composed by small events, as shown in Fig. 2. In addition, multiple conditions can sometimes apply to a particular event pattern, as described by the IFAB laws of the game. For example, the player can be in an offside position before the ball is played, but also when both events start at the same time. In addition, multiple conditions may apply to a particular event. For example, the player can be in an offside position before the ball is played to him, but also if both events start at the same time. To create and visualize such ambiguous event patterns, we introduce the concept of whiskers. Whiskers are a graphical addition to the well-known rectangular representation of intervals, which makes it possible to model ambiguous relationships between intervals. In the example in Fig. 5(a) we use these whiskers to model that event A can start simultaneously with event B, but A must start before B is finished at the latest. This ambiguous relationship could not be represented by simple rectangles.

However, defining these patterns is only the first step in making the transaction data useful. These patterns must also be found in the data. This process can be very time-consuming, which is why it makes sense to check beforehand whether a sample can be found at all. An example of such an undetectable pattern of three intervals (I, J, K) is $(I\ BEFORE\ J,\ J\ BEFORE\ K,\ K\ BEFORE\ I)$.

With the help of the path consistency algorithm, such relations can be checked for consistency in polynomial time.

After checking the consistency of the patterns, they can be searched for in the dataset. For pattern identification, we proceed similarly to Kempe [8], which uses deterministic finite automata as pattern identifiers. The complete process is outlined in Fig. 5. We want to find the offside pattern from Fig. 1(a) in the set of events which are sorted by time. For this, we start with an empty pattern identifier (a). The first matching event is B1. We duplicate the pattern identifier and insert the event B1 (b). The same procedure applies to the remaining events. After several steps, we have processed the last event C3 and see that three pattern identifiers are complete and thus the complex event offside was found three times in our data set.

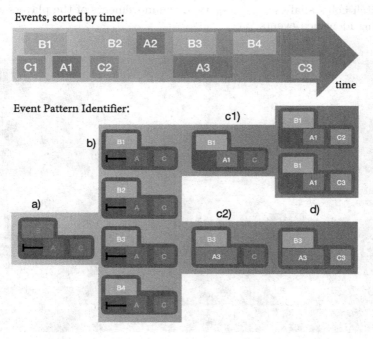

Fig. 5. Process of event detection: the starting point is an empty pattern identifier (a). The first event matching the pattern identifier is B1, the pattern identifier is duplicated and B1 is inserted into one of the duplicates (b). C3 is the last event and matches two pattern identifiers (c1, c2), which are therefore both duplicated. At the end, three pattern identifiers are complete, so the complex event was found three times (d).

3   System

We introduce a visual analytics system in order to define, search, and save events in soccer, based on the movement data of players and the ball. An overview about the system can be seen in Fig. 6. Based on the available position data, soccer-specific properties such as the speed of the players or their distance to the ball are calculated to generate the basic events. This allows the detection of instances of the event type *Player is less than 1 m away from the ball*. Basic event types can be graphically arranged by the user in the system to build event patterns and, therefore, define a complex event. The system then automatically interprets the graphically displayed patterns as expressions of Allen's interval algebra, which allows qualitative statements about the (temporal) order of events (like *Event A is before event B* or *Event A contains event B*). Created event patterns are searched in the data and the results of the search are visualized on a timeline as well as an abstract soccer pitch. The timeline allows the user to draw conclusions about when a pattern occurred in a match, and whether the definition of the pattern was correct or whether it needs to be adjusted. The visualization on the soccer pitch helps analysts to understand the movements of the players and the ball during identified events.

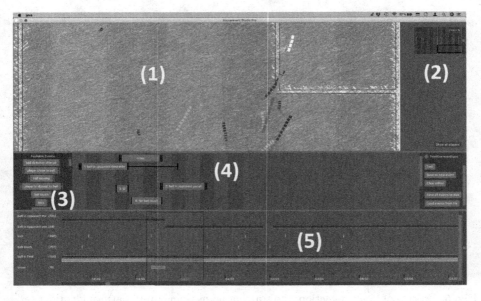

Fig. 6. System interface with abstract soccer pitch (1), mini map (2), library of events (3), event definition timeline (4) and timeline for displaying the results (5).

3.1   Defining and Detecting Basic Events

The starting point for the system is the movement data of the player and the ball during a soccer match. This data is not yet event data, unless we consider any recorded point as an event which, however, would not be practical. In our case, the movement data consist of two-dimensional coordinates for every tenth of a second of a match for every player and for the ball. The basic events are generated assuming that the available movement data is continuous, i.e., in a straight line or a slight curve from one recorded coordinate to the next. All implemented soccer-specific properties for basic events are listed in Table 1. The calculation of most features is straight-forward, such as the distance between a player and the ball and the features derived from it; such as the closest player to the ball. For features that have a temporal aspect, such as speed, we use linear interpolation between the individual points in time to calculate these features. The deflection of the ball, however, is more demanding. Here we use the algorithm of Visvalingam [14], which removes points from the trajectory of the ball, which lie approximately on a straight line. The remaining points are those where the ball has made a sufficiently strong turn or changed direction. To calculate *offside position* and *closest to ball*, naive detection algorithms were implemented, which sort the players according to their distance to the goal or the ball.

Table 1. Used properties for generating basic events

Property	Type	Generates an event, if...
Speed	Interval	...the speed has a certain value, or exceeds or falls below a certain threshold
Position	Interval	...the position is within a certain range. Some special positions on the soccer pitch are predefined, otherwise one or more rectangular areas can be defined
Closest to ball	Interval	...a player is at least as close to the ball as everyone else
Distance to ball	Interval	...a player has a certain distance to the ball, exceeds or falls short of it
Distance between players	Interval	...players have a certain distance to each other, exceed or fall short of each other
Offside position	Interval	...a player is in an offside position
Deflecting the ball	Point	...the ball changes direction

Due to the basic event types, no great gain in knowledge is yet to be expected. Complex event types are required to show hidden connections or find interesting situations more quickly in a match. Our proposed system provides a list of already defined events, both basic and complex, displayed in our system as interactive rectangles. If an event is an interval, the rectangle always has whiskers, which enable the modeling of ambiguous interval relationships such as *BEFORE ∧ STARTS WITH*. If it is a point, it has no whiskers. Existing events can be positioned and arranged on the integrated visual timeline via *Drag and Drop*. This interaction concept is based on video editing software in which users arrange video and audio snippets in time to create a more complex end product. By dragging the sides of the rectangle, these can be widened or narrowed and, as a consequence, the relation of the involved event types to each other can be defined. To modify the remaining parts of the event pattern, relationships to other event types can be set in the timeline as well as minimum and maximum duration time. Furthermore, it can be specified whether the new event type is to be an interval or a point, which either adds or removes the whiskers. After creating a new complex event, it is saved permanently in the event library. An example of a definition of a *cross* event can be seen in Fig. 7.

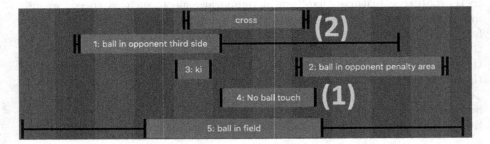

Fig. 7. Timeline enabling analysts to graphically define complex event types. All whiskers and rectangle sides in one of the strips are treated as if they had the same position (1). In the shown case, the reference interval is called "cross" (2).

3.2   Analyzing Identified Events

Complex events can be used both during their definition as well as afterwards to find and assess match situations in large amounts of soccer data. To provide an overview for the analyst, we visualize the locations of the identified event pattern in an additional, zoomable timeline, representing the entire match from kick-off to final whistle, as shown in Fig. 6(5). In this timeline, each interval is visualized by a rectangle, the left edge indicating where the event begins and the right edge of the rectangle indicating where the event ends. Since according to our event definition, point events are interval events where start and end time are the same, they are indicated by a rectangle with a very small width where the left edge is also at the point the event occurs. By giving the rectangles the respective team colors, we enable an efficient overview of the distribution of events and which team was responsible for which events at which time. The intervals or points displayed in the timeline are used, among other purposes, to quickly jump to match situations in which the event pattern occurs. In order to better assess the found complex events, the movement of the involved players and ball is visualized on an abstracted soccer pitch, when selecting a time period in the timeline. The trajectories are visualized as fragmented lines, as shown in Fig. 6(1). The color of a line corresponds to the team color. We use an additional color gradient on each trajectory, going from transparent at the start of the trajectory to opaque at the end, to indicate the direction of movement, without the need for animation. Additionally, we use the distance of the fragments in the line to indicate the speed of the players involved and the ball. In slower sections, the fragments are closer together. To see more precisely how player and ball trajectories progress or in order to get an overview, the abstracted soccer pitch can be zoomed in or out by scrolling and moved by clicking and dragging. When zooming, the displayed area of the soccer pitch is drawn as a rectangle on an additional mini-map to improve the user's orientation.

4   Evaluation

The goal of the evaluation is to show that most events, which are currently manually annotated, can be effectively defined and found with the system presented in this paper. Therefore, manually created event data sets of several matches are compared with their corresponding instances of event types defined in our system. The annotated event data has been collected by an established analysis company and consists of 43 manually annotated matches. First experiments have shown that the annotated events can partially lack accuracy due to human error and there is no detailed information available about the applied rules for annotation. For cross events, for example, it is not clear whether only successful crosses get annotated or an attempted cross is already enough to be annotated. In our definition for the automatic detection of cross events, we limit ourselves to only successful crosses. For quantitative analysis, statistical measures for the evaluation of proposed events are calculated. Afterwards, the differences between the data found and the manually generated data for individual cases are examined in more detail. To assess our method, we calculate the true positives (**TP**) (events found both manually as well as automatically), false positives (**FP**) (events that we found, but were not in the annotated data) as well as false negatives (**FN**) (manually annotated events that we did not find). The results of our quantitative evaluation, as displayed in Table 2, are very promising. All defined event types that are available both in the manually annotated datasets as well as our proposed system performed reasonably well, especially, considering that the rules

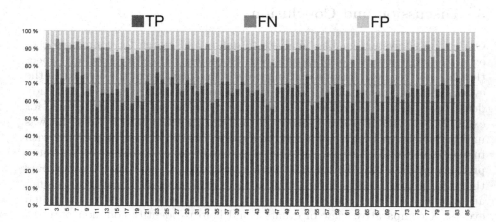

Fig. 8. Occurrences of true positives, false positives and false negatives for more than 36,000 passes in both half times of 43 matches (**Precision** = 87.5%, **Recall** = 75%, **F-Measure** = 80%)

and standards for manual annotation are not publicly available and might differ. Overall, the quantitative results of our proposed method demonstrate a good performance in detecting otherwise manually annotated events (Fig. 8).

Table 2. We assess our method quantitatively by comparing automatically detected events with manually annotated events from a professional data provider.

Event	No. of events	Precision	Recall	F-measure
Passing	36524	87.5%	75%	80%
Running with ball/dribbling	23874	68%	84%	75%
Ball out of the pitch	3012	78%	98%	87%
Goal	129	97.5%	91%	94%
Cross	1807	65%	70%	67%
Shot	1124	82%	49%	62%
Reception	28147	70%	78%	74%

Furthermore, we evaluated the possibility of our system to define complex, hierarchic events such as *linebreaking passes* within several open interviews with two experienced soccer experts. The experts, one former coach from the youth department of the German soccer club FC Bayern München and one coach from the first team of an Austrian first league soccer club, confirm the potential of our proposed system. Both experts state they would make extensive use of such a system in order to reduce manual effort as well as be able to dynamically define own complex events.

5 Discussion and Conclusion

Our proposed system enables analysts to define and search for complex soccer events in large amounts of player and ball movement data. An important aspect that has not yet been included in this work is the inclusion of the context in the event definition, visualization, and subsequent analysis. Our system can already detect events such as crosses, but not why these events were carried out, for example, whether a player passed the ball to his teammate because he was under pressure, or because of a good free space. Enriching identified events with further context information can help analysts in order to define events more precisely and to have better information available for analysis. Another part that will be improved in future work is the visual analysis. Currently, we offer an overview of found complex events as well as a detailed view of individual events. A comparative view of events could help to identify common patterns and help analysts during match summarization. Our automatic event detection is also centered on events around the ball. We plan to offer more ways to efficiently integrate the definition of events to annotate defensive player behavior in our system. Here, it would be interesting to define events when a player, for example, is blocking passing possibilities to other opposing players while attacking the ball possessing player. Another interesting set of events, according to our experts, would be to define complex events indicating when players are attacking in certain predefined pressing areas or when, for example, midfielders are too far away from the defenders of their team. Additionally annotating events when players are not close enough to opposing players would be helpful as well.

Finally, our work is an important step in the direction of automatic soccer analysis bridging the gap between movement data tracked by sensors or extracted from multimedia data and high-level analysis based on events. Our results are similar to manual event annotations but can be carried out in a fraction of the time and cost. Further improvements in the accuracy of event detection and the introduction of new events are planned for future work. Another main focus for subsequent research is not only on extending the detection of complex events but also on their assessment. For example, it should not only be detected that a pass has taken place, but also whether it was a good decision to pass to this specific player in the current state of the match. This would help soccer analysts and coaches analyzing large amounts of match data, efficiently making them aware of the relevant events for analysis and match preparation.

References

1. Allen, J.F.: Maintaining knowledge about temporal intervals. Commun. ACM **26**(11), 832–843 (1983)
2. International Football Association Board: Laws of the game (2018/2019). http://theifab.com/document/laws-of-the-game. Accessed 02 Aug 2018
3. Chen, M., Zhang, C., Chen, S.C.: Semantic event extraction using neural network ensembles, pp. 575–580. IEEE, September 2007. https://doi.org/10.1109/ICSC.2007.75
4. de Sousa Júnior, S.F., de Albuquerque Araújo, A., Menotti, D.: An overview of automatic event detection in soccer matches, pp. 31–38. IEEE, January 2011. https://doi.org/10.1109/WACV.2011.5711480
5. Ekin, A., Tekalp, A.M., Mehrotra, R.: Automatic soccer video analysis and summarization. IEEE Trans. Image Process. **12**(7), 796–807 (2003)
6. Gudmundsson, J., Wolle, T.: Towards automated football analysis: algorithms and data structures. In: Proceedings of the 10th Australasian Conference on Mathematics and Computers in Sport. Citeseer (2010)
7. Jensen, J.C.C.: Event detection in soccer using spatio-temporal data. Ph.D. thesis, Aarhus Universitet, Datalogisk Institut (2015)
8. Kempe, S.: Häufige Muster in zeitbezogenen Daten. Ph.D. thesis, Otto-von-Guericke University Magdeburg, Germany (2008). http://edoc.bibliothek.uni-halle.de/receive/HALCoRe_document_00005803
9. Kolekar, M.H., Palaniappan, K., Sengupta, S., Seetharaman, G.: Semantic concept mining based on hierarchical event detection for soccer video indexing. J. Multimed. **4**(5), 298–312 (2009). https://doi.org/10.4304/jmm.4.5.298-312
10. Stein, M., et al.: Bring it to the pitch: combining video and movement data to enhance team sport analysis. IEEE Trans. Vis. Comput. Graph. **24**(1), 13–22 (2018)

11. Wang, T., Li, J., Diao, Q., Hu, W., Zhang, Y., Dulong, C.: Semantic event detection using conditional random fields, p. 109. IEEE (2006). https://doi.org/10.1109/CVPRW.2006.190
12. Tavassolipour, M., Karimian, M., Kasaei, S.: Event detection and summarization in soccer videos using Bayesian network and copula. IEEE Trans. Circ. Syst. Video Technol. **24**(2), 291–304 (2014)
13. Tovinkere, V., Qian, R.: Detecting semantic events in soccer games: towards a complete solution, pp. 833–836. IEEE (2001). https://doi.org/10.1109/ICME.2001.1237851
14. Visvalingam, M., Whyatt, J.D.: Line generalisation by repeated elimination of points. Cartogr. J. **30**(1), 46–51 (1993)
15. Wickramaratna, K., Chen, M., Chen, S.-C., Shyu, M.-L.: Neural network based framework for goal event detection in soccer videos, pp. 21–28. IEEE (2005). https://doi.org/10.1109/ISM.2005.83
16. Tong, X.-F., Lu, H.-Q., Liu, Q.-S.: A three-layer event detection framework and its application in soccer video, pp. 1551–1554. IEEE (2004). https://doi.org/10.1109/ICME.2004.1394543
17. Yu, X., Xu, C., Leong, H.W., Tian, Q., Tang, Q., Wan, K.W.: Trajectory-based ball detection and tracking with applications to semantic analysis of broadcast soccer video, p. 10 (2003)
18. Zheng, M., Kudenko, D.: Automated event recognition for football commentary generation. Int. J. Gaming Comput.-Mediat. Simul. **2**(4), 67–84 (2010). https://doi.org/10.4018/jgcms.2010100105

Multimodal Video Annotation for Retrieval and Discovery of Newsworthy Video in a News Verification Scenario

Lyndon Nixon[1], Evlampios Apostolidis[2,3]([✉]), Foteini Markatopoulou[2],
Ioannis Patras[3], and Vasileios Mezaris[2]

[1] MODUL Technology GmbH, Vienna, Austria
nixon@modultech.eu
[2] Centre for Research and Technology Hellas, Thermi-Thessaloniki, Greece
{apostolid,markatopoulou,bmezaris}@iti.gr
[3] School of EECS, Queen Mary University of London, London, UK
i.patras@qmul.ac.uk

Abstract. This paper describes the combination of advanced technologies for social-media-based story detection, story-based video retrieval and concept-based video (fragment) labeling under a novel approach for multimodal video annotation. This approach involves textual metadata, structural information and visual concepts - and a multimodal analytics dashboard that enables journalists to discover videos of news events, posted to social networks, in order to verify the details of the events shown. It outlines the characteristics of each individual method and describes how these techniques are blended to facilitate the content-based retrieval, discovery and summarization of (parts of) news videos. A set of case-driven experiments conducted with the help of journalists, indicate that the proposed multimodal video annotation mechanism - combined with a professional analytics dashboard which presents the collected and generated metadata about the news stories and their visual summaries - can support journalists in their content discovery and verification work.

Keywords: News video verification · Story detection
Video retrieval · Video fragmentation · Video annotation
Video summarization

1 Introduction

Journalists and investigators alike are increasingly turning to online social media to find media recordings of events. Newsrooms in TV stations and online news platforms make use of video to illustrate and report on news events, and since professional journalists are not always at the scene of a breaking or evolving story, it is the content posted by users that comes into question. However the rise of social media as a news source has also seen a rise in fake news - the spread

© Springer Nature Switzerland AG 2019
I. Kompatsiaris et al. (Eds.): MMM 2019, LNCS 11295, pp. 143–155, 2019.
https://doi.org/10.1007/978-3-030-05710-7_12

of deliberate misinformation or disinformation on these platforms. Images and videos have not been immune to this, with easy access to software to tamper with and modify media content leading to deliberate fakes, although fake media can also be the re-posting of a video of an earlier event, with the claim that it shows a contemporary event.

Our InVID project[1] has the goal to facilitate journalists in identifying online video posted to social networks claiming to show news events, and verifying that video before using it in reporting (Sect. 2). This paper presents our work on newsworthy video content collection and multimodal video annotation that allows fine-grained (i.e. at the video-fragment-level) content-based discovery and summarization of videos for news verification, since the first step for any news verification task must be finding the relevant (parts of) online posted media for a given news story. We present the advanced techniques developed to detect news stories in a social media stream (Sect. 3), retrieve online posted media from social networks for those news stories (Sect. 4), fragment each collected video into visually coherent parts and annotate each video fragment based on its visual content (Sect. 5). Following, we explain how these methods are pieced together forming a novel multimodal video annotation methodology, and describe how the tailored combination of these technologies in the search and browsing interface of a professional dashboard can support the fine-grained content-driven discovery and summarization of the collected newsworthy media assets (Sect. 6). Initial experiments with journalists indicate the added value of the generated visual summaries (Sect. 7) for the in-time discovery of the most suitable video fragments to verify and present a story. Section 8 concludes the work reported in this paper.

2   Motivation

Even reputable news agencies have been caught out, posting images or videos in their reporting of news stories that turn out later to have been faked or falsely associated. It is surely not the last time fake media will end up being used in news reporting, despite the growing concerns about deliberate misinformation being generated to influence social and political discussion. Journalists are under time-pressure to deliver, and often the only media illustrating a news event is user-provided and circulating on social networks. The current process for media verification is manual and time-consuming, pursued by journalists who lack the technical expertise to deeply analyze the online media. The in-time identification of media posted online, which (claim to) illustrate a (breaking) news event is for many journalists the foremost challenge in order to meet deadlines to publish a news story online or fill a news broadcast with content.

Our work is part of an effort to provide journalists with a semi-automatic media verification toolkit. While the key objective is to facilitate the quicker and more accurate determination of whether an online media file is authentic (i.e. it shows what it claims to show without modification to mislead the viewer), a

---

[1] https://www.invid-project.eu/.

necessary precondition for this is that the user can identify the appropriate candidates for verification from the huge bulk of media content being posted online continually, on platforms such as Twitter, Facebook, YouTube or DailyMotion.

The time taken by journalists to select a news story and find online media for that news story, directly affects the time they have remaining to additionally conduct the verification process on that media. Hence, the timely identification of news stories, as well as the accurate retrieval of candidate media for those stories, is the objective of this work. Given that the journalistic verification and re-use (in reporting) of content only needs that part of the content which shows the desired aspect of the story (possibly combining different videos to illustrate different aspects), the fragmentation of media into conceptually distinct and self-contained fragments is also relevant.

The state of the art in this area would be e.g. using TweetDeck to follow a set of news-relevant terms continually (e.g. "just happened", "explosion" etc.), while manually adding other terms and hashtags when a news story appears (e.g. by tracking news tickers or Twitter's trending tags). Once media is found it has to be examined (e.g. a video played through) to check its content and identify the part(s) of interest. This is all still very time-consuming and prone to error (e.g. missing relevant media). Hence, this paper reports on our contribution - in the context of the journalistic workflow - to the content-based discovery and summarization of video shared on social platforms. The proposed system (see Fig. 1) combines advanced techniques for news story detection, story-driven video retrieval and video fragmentation and annotation, into a multimodal video annotation process which produces a rich set of annotations that facilitate the fine-grained discovery and summarization of video content related to a news story, through the interactive user interface of a professional multimodal analytics dashboard. This system represents an important step beyond the state of the art in the journalistic domain, as validated by a user evaluation.

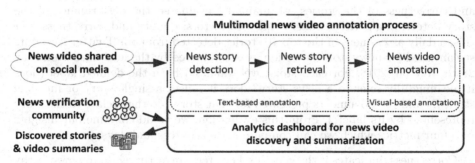

Fig. 1. The overall architecture of the proposed system.

The following Sects. 3, 4 and 5 describe the different components of the system and report on their performance using appropriate datasets. Section 6 explains how these components are pieced together into the proposed multimodal video annotation mechanism and the multimodal analytics dashboard to enable the content-based retrieval, discovery and summarization of the collected data. Finally, Sect. 7 reports the case-driven evaluations about the efficiency of the proposed system, made by journalists from two news organizations.

3   News Story Detection

The developed story detection algorithm uses content extracted from the Twitter Streaming API, modelling each tweet as a bag of keywords, clustering keywords in a weighted directed graph and using cluster properties to merge/split the clusters into distinct news stories [5]. The output is a ranked list of news stories labelled by the three most weighted keywords in the story cluster and explained by (up to) ten most relevant documents (i.e. videos) in our collection related to that story (based on keyword matching). Figure 2 shows the story detection in the dashboard: a story is given a label and the most relevant documents are shown underneath.

Fig. 2. Presentation of a story in the dashboard.

Guided by the fact that a human evaluator is required to assess the quality and correctness of the stories, we manually evaluated the performance of the story detection algorithm considering two factors: quality and correctness. For this, a daily assessment of the top-10 stories detected from our Twitter Accounts stream used for news story detection, was conducted by the lead author on May 28 to May 30, 2018. For each story, we evaluated both the defined label (does it meaningfully refer to a news story? does it reflect a single story or multiple stories?) and the documents presented for that story (do they relate to the story represented by its label?). From this evaluation, we could combine our insights into four metrics which we can compare across sources and days:

- Correctness: indicates if the generated clusters correctly relate to newsworthy stories;
- Distinctiveness: evaluates how precisely each individual cluster relates to an individual story;
- Homogeneity: examines if the documents in the cluster are only relevant to the newsworthy stories represented by the cluster;
- Completeness: assesses the relevance of the documents in the cluster with a single, distinct news story.

The results reported in Table 1 demonstrate that our method performs almost perfectly on providing newsworthy events and separating them distinctly. Sample size was n = 10 for the story metrics (correctness and distinctiveness) and n = 100 for the story document metrics (homogeneity and completeness).

Table 1. Story detection comparison for May 2018.

	Correctness	Distinctiveness	Homogeneity	Completeness
May 28, 2018	1	1	0.94	0.9
May 29, 2018	1	1	0.95	0.95
May 30, 2018	1	0.8	0.98	0.98
Three day average	1	**0.93**	**0.96**	**0.94**

4   News Video Retrieval

Given a set of detected news stories, the next step is to select from social networks candidate videos which claim to illustrate those stories. Multimedia Information Retrieval is generally evaluated against a finite video collection that is extracted from the social network data using some sampling technique, and then feature-based or semantic retrieval is tested on this finite collection. This is different from our goal, which is to maximize the relevance of the media documents returned for our Web-based queries, based on the news story detection.

On one hand, classical recall cannot be used since the indication of the total number of relevant documents on any social media platform at any time for one query is not possible. On the other hand, we should consider whether success in information retrieval only occurs if and only if the retrieved video is relevant to the story represented by the query, or if any newsworthy video being retrieved can be considered a sign of success. Indeed, videos related to a news story will keep being posted for a longer time after the news story initially occurred, and those videos can still be relevant for discovery in a news verification context. Thus, queries which reference keywords that persist in the news discussion, (e.g. "Donald Trump"), are likely to return other videos which are not relevant to the current story, but still reference an earlier newsworthy story. Classical "Precision" can indicate how many of the retrieved videos are relevant to the query itself, yet low precision may hide the fact that we still collect a high proportion of newsworthy video content. Still, it acts as an evaluation of the quality of our query to collect media for the specific story. We choose a second metric, titled "Newsworthiness", which measures the proportion of all newsworthy video returned for a query. Since this metric includes video not directly related to the story being queried for, it evaluates the appropriateness of our query for collecting newsworthy media in general. Finally, we define a "Specificity" measure as the proportion of newsworthy video retrieved that is relevant to the story being queried for, ergo our Specificity is the Precision divided by the Newsworthiness and assesses the specificity of our query for the news story.

After experimenting with different query-construction approaches based on how the stories are represented in our system (clusters of keywords) [5], we propose the story labels (top-3 weighted keywords in the cluster) as the basis for querying social networks for relevant videos. We used the story labels from the top-10 stories from Twitter Accounts in the dashboard for the period May 28–30, 2018 as conjunctive query inputs. We tested the results' relevance by querying the YouTube API, using the default result sort by relevance, and measuring "Precision at N", where N provides the cut-off point for the set of documents to evaluate for relevance. In line with the first page of search results, a standard choice in Web Search evaluation, we chose $n = 20$ for each story. Since each day we use the top-10 stories, the retrieval is tested on a sample of 200 videos. In Table 2 we compare the results from last year on 13 June 2017 (which acts as a benchmark for our work [5]) and the results for the aforementioned dates in May 2018 (and their average). It can be seen that our Specificity value has increased considerably, meaning that when we make a query for a newsworthy story we are more likely to only get videos that are precisely relevant to that story, than video of any newsworthy story. So, while Newsworthiness has remained more or less the same (the proportion of newsworthy video being collected into the developed platform is probably still around 80% for YouTube), our Precision at N value - that the collected video is precisely about the news story we detected - shows an over 20% improvement. Our news video retrieval technique collects documents from a broad range of stories with a consistent Precision of around 0.76 and Specificity of around 0.94, which indicate that document collection is well-balanced across all identified news stories. Since this video retrieval mechanism has been integrated in the InVID dashboard we add around 4000–5000 new videos per day, based on queries for up to 120 detected unique news stories.

Table 2. Our social media retrieval tested on the new story labels.

	13 June 2017	28 May 2018	29 May 2018	30 May 2018	2018 avg.
Precision	**0.54**	0.79	0.7	0.79	**0.76**
Newsworthiness	**0.82**	0.85	0.74	0.84	**0.81**
Specificity	**0.64**	0.93	0.95	0.94	**0.94**
F-score	**0.59**	0.82	0.72	0.81	**0.78**

5   News Video Annotation

Every collected video is analysized by the video annotation component which produces a set of human-readable metadata about the videos' visual content at the fragment-level. This component segments the video into temporally and visually coherent fragments and extracts one representative keyframe for each fragment. Following, it annotates each segment with a set of high-level visual concepts after assessing their occurrence in the visual content of the corresponding keyframe. The produced fragment-level conceptual annotation of the video can be used for fine-grained concept-based video retrieval and summarization.

The temporal segmentation of a video into its structural parts, called shots, is performed using a variation of [1]. The visual content of the frames is represented with the help of local (ORB [9]) and global (HSV histograms) descriptors. Then, shot boundaries are detected by assessing the visual similarity between consecutive and neighboring video frames and comparing it against experimentally defined thresholds and models that indicate the existence of abrupt and gradual shot transitions. These findings are re-evaluated using a pair of dissolve and wipe detectors (based on [12] and [11] respectively) that filter-out wrongly detected gradual transitions due to swift camera and/or object movement. The final set of shots is formed by the union of the detected abrupt and gradual transitions, and each shot is represented by its middle frame. Evaluations using the experimental setup of [1], highlight the efficiency of this method. Precision and Recall are equal to 0.943 and 0.941 respectively, while the needed processing time (13.5% of video duration, on average) makes the analysis over 7 times faster than real-time processing. These outcomes indicate the ability of this method to process large video collections in a highly-accurate and time-efficient manner.

When dealing with raw, user-generated videos the shot-level fragmentation is too coarse and fails to reveal information about their structure. A decomposition into smaller parts, called sub-shots, is needed to enable fine-grained annotation and summarization of their content. Guided by this observation, we define a sub-shot as an uninterrupted sequence of frames having only a small and contiguous variation in their visual content. The algorithm (denoted as "DCT") represents the visual content of frames using a 2D Discrete Cosine Transform and assesses their visual resemblance using cosine similarity. The computed similarity scores undergo a filtering process to reduce the effect of sudden, short-term changes in the visual content; the turning points of the filtered series of scores signify a change in the similarity tendency and therefore a sub-shot boundary. Finally, each defined sub-shot is represented by the frame with the most pronounced change in the visual content. The performance of this method was evaluated using a relevant dataset[2] and compared against other approaches, namely: (a) a method similar to [7], which assesses the visual similarity of video frames using HSV histograms and the x^2 metric (denoted as "HSV"); (b) an approach from [2], which estimates the frame affinity and the camera motion by extracting and matching SURF descriptors (denoted as "SURF"); and (c) an implementation of the best performing technique of [2], that estimates the frame affinity and the camera motion by computing the optical flow (denoted as "AOF"). The evaluation outcomes (see Table 3) indicate the DCT-based algorithm as the best trade-off between accurate and fast analysis. The analysis is over 30 times faster

---

[2] Publicly available at https://mklab.iti.gr/results/annotated-dataset-for-sub-shot-segmentation-evaluation/.

than real-time processing and results in a rich set of video fragments that can be used for fine-grained video annotation.

Table 3. Performance evaluation of the used sub-shot segmentation algorithm.

	DCT method	HSV method	SURF method	AOF method
Precision	0.22	**0.44**	0.36	0.27
Recall	**0.84**	0.11	0.29	0.78
F-Score	0.36	0.18	0.33	**0.40**
Proc. time (x video length)	**0.03**	0.04	0.56	0.08

The concept-based annotation of the defined video fragments is performed using a combination of deep learning methods (presented in [8] and [4]), which evaluate the appearance of 150 high-level concepts from the TRECVID SIN task [6] in the visual content of the corresponding keyframes. Two pre-trained ImageNet [10] deep convolutional neural networks (DCNNs), have been fine-tuned (FT) using the extension strategy of [8]. Similar to [4], the networks' loss function has been extended with an additional concept correlation cost term; giving a higher penalty to pairs of concepts that present positive correlations but have been assigned with different scores, and the same penalty to pairs of concepts that present negative correlation but have not been assigned with opposite scores. The exact instantiation of the used approach is as follows: Resnet1k-50 [3] extended with one extension FC layer with size equal to 4096 and GoogLeNet [13] trained on 5055 ImageNet concepts [10], extended with one extension FC layer of size equal to 1024. During semantic analysis each selected keyframe is forward propagated by each of the FT networks described above; each network returns a set of scores that represent its confidence regarding the concepts' occurrence in the visual content of the keyframe. The scores from the two FT networks for the same concept are combined in terms of arithmetic mean. The performance of this technique has been evaluated in terms of MXinfAP (Mean Extended Inferred Average Precision) on the TRECVID SIN 2013 dataset. The employed method achieved a MXinfAP score equal to 33.89%, thus proven to be a competitive concept-based annotation approach. After analyzing the entire set of extracted keyframes the applied method produces a fragment-level conceptual annotation of the video which enables concept-based video retrieval and summarization.

6   Concept-Based Summaries

The functionality of the aforementioned technologies is combined with a professional multimodal analytics dashboard, in a way tailored to the needs of journalists who want to quickly discover the most suitable newsworthy video content shared on social media platforms. The news story detection and retrieval components of the dashboard enable the creation of story-related collections of newsworthy videos. Then, a multimodal video annotation approach takes place for every collected video. It produces a set of text-based annotations at the video-level according to the associated metadata, and a set of concept-based annotations that represent the visual content of the video at the fragment-level. The dashboard provides a user interface to the aforementioned collected and generated metadata for every newsworthy video that is inserted to the system, allowing the users to quickly find (parts of) online video relevant to a news story. Based on the outcomes of the applied multimodal video annotation process the collected video content can be browsed at different levels of granularity - i.e. the story-level (groups of videos related to a story), the document-level (a single video about a story) and the fragment-level (a particular video fragment showing an event of interest) - through textual queries or by matching visual attributes with the visual content of the documents. In the latter case the user is able to retrieve and discover a summary of a video document that includes only the fragments that relate to a selected set of (event-related) visual concepts.

As a result, we have the possibility to offer concept-based summaries of videos of a news story. For example, a journalist looking for a video of the fire at Trump Tower, New York City (Jan 8, 2018) can text search for "trump tower fire" and find videos in that time period which reference this in their textual metadata (title + description). However, the videos do not necessarily show the fire (one observed phenonema on YouTube has been putting breaking news story titles into video descriptions as "clickbait" for views) and those who do, may be longer and the journalist still needs to search inside the video for the moment the fire is shown. With the visual concept search, a text search on "trump tower" can be combined with a concept-based search on EXPLOSION_FIRE. This would return a list of videos with their fragments where the fire is visible. The retrieved video fragments of each video, which form a concept-related visual summary of the video, are represented by their keyframes in the user interface of the dashboard, but can be also played back allowing the user to watch the entire fragment. Below in Fig. 3 we show a conceptual summary for a video returned for the story of the Thai cave rescue story with the visual concept of "Swimming".

7   Evaluation

A user evaluation is necessary to assess the efficiency of our story detection, video retrieval and summarization technologies. As opposed to the evaluation of the accuracy of these techniques through comparison with some benchmark, the "best" solution for a journalist is less the automatic achievement of 100% accuracy, and more the successful discovery in less time of relevant video material for verification. In our case, we have a clear use case for this and involve journalists in determining if the techniques, as provided through the dashboard, meet their expectations. We asked two journalists with verification expertise, one in Agence France Presse (AFP) and the other in Deutsche Welle (DW), to perform a number of queries for video documents associated to a news story detected by our story detection algorithm. For each of the selected stories, they used the multimodal analytics dashboard to select the top video documents associated with

Fig. 3. Video fragments with the "Swimming" concept for a "Thai cave rescue" video.

that story and to find a video snippet showing the desired visual component of the story (i.e. something which could be used in a news report after verification). In both cases, they can explore video documents either by conducting a textual search over the document set or generating a concept-based summary using the most appropriate visual concept. Finally, we surveyed which of the results were more useful for their journalistic work. Whereas we involved just two journalists in this initial evaluation, the evaluation methodology is based on previous discussions with the organizations and thus reflects adequately a real-life work scenario for journalists in general.

The journalist from AFP chose the story of the Thailand cave rescue, a story which was detected in the dashboard with the label CAVE + RESCUE + THAILAND. The system had retrieved 1317 videos for this story in the period 9–12 July. The visual component of interest in this story was a snippet of the divers in the cave undertaking the rescue operation. Firstly, we chose the term "divers" for further searching the 1317 videos, and got 142 matching videos which are ordered in the dashboard by a relevance metric. The journalist viewed seven videos until selecting an appropriate video snippet. In total, five video fragments were selected for viewing during the browsing process (from four distinct videos; the other three videos were previously discarded as irrelevant). The time needed was 8 min, mainly as the videos were presented in their entirety (all fragments) and time was spent on looking at videos which did not have any relevant content. Then, we chose as a visual concept that of "swimming", since in the context of the story only the divers would be swimming in the Thai cave. This returned 79 results. The journalist viewed seven videos until selecting an appropriate video snippet. In total, only two video fragments were viewed while browsing as they were now already filtered by the selected concept, and the displayed keyframes were already indicative of whether the video fragment actually showed divers in the cave or something else. The time needed was now 4 min as the videos were more relevant and could be more quickly browsed, as only potentially matching fragments were being shown in the dashboard. As a side note, at least one video could be considered as "fake" - it differed significantly from the other observed footage, contained other diving footage and was entitled with the Thai cave rescue story as "clickbait" - something that other verification tools developed in our project (e.g. the InVID Plug-in [14]) could help establish.

The journalist from DW tested on 21 July 2018 when one of the main news stories in the dashboard was the tragic sinking of a "duck boat" in Missouri, USA. The story was detected with the label BOAT + DUCK + MISSOURI. The system had retrieved 292 videos for this story in the period 21–22 July. The visual component of interest in this story was a snippet of the boat sinking in the lake. Firstly, we chose the term "sinking" to search the collection of 292 videos, getting 24 matching videos. In the results ordered by relevance, we had to discount three videos which were related with "sinking" but not with the Missouri duck boat story. The journalist viewed ten videos until an appropriate video snippet was selected. In total, five video fragments were viewed from three distinct videos. The time needed was 6 min, as it took some time to get to a video with an appropriate fragment. Then, we chose the visual concept of "boat-ship", since this would be the visual object doing the "sinking" in the video. This returned 137 videos. Actually the very first video in this case provided two usable fragments showing the boat, and thus less than one minute was actually needed in this case. However, we continued to analyse the remaining results (10 most relevant). A set of eleven fragments representing six videos was viewed as relevant, and two further usable fragments were identified (all coming from the same source, which is presumably a claimed user-recording of the sinking boat).

The evaluations, focused on the journalistic workflow, established that while both the text-based and concept-based searches could adequately filter video material for a detected news story, when searching for a specific visual event in the video the concept-based search was comparatively quicker. The returned videos were more relevant content-wise, as often in textual metadata the event is described but not necessarily shown in the video. The dashboard display of matching fragments (via their keyframes) could help the journalists quickly establish if the content of the video was what they were searching for, and the filtering of the fragments in a concept-based search brings the journalists quicker to the content they would like to use. The presence of a probable "fake" among the Thai cave rescue videos acted as a reminder of why journalists want to find content quickly: the time is needed to verify the authenticity of an online video before it should be finally used in any news reporting.

8 Conclusion

This paper described a novel multimodal approach for newsworthy content collection, discovery and summarization, that facilitates journalists to quickly find online media associated with current news stories and determine which (part of) media is the most relevant to verify before potentially using it in a news report. We presented a solution to news story detection from social media streams, we outlined how the news story descriptions are used to dynamically collect associated videos from social networks, and we explained how we fragment and conceptually annotate the collected videos. Then, we discussed a combination of these methods into a novel multimodal video annotation mechanism that annotates the collected video material at different granularities. Using a professional multimodal analytics dashboard that integrates the proposed news video content collection and annotation process, we provided a proof of concept-based summarization of those videos at the fragment-level. The evaluation of the proposed approach with journalists showed that the concept-based search and summarization of news videos allows journalists to find quicker the most suitable parts of the video content, for verifying the story and preparing a news report. The dashboard is now being tested with a larger sample of external journalistic users, which will provide more comprehensive insights into the value and the limitations of the work presented in this paper.

Acknowledgments. This work was supported by the EU's Horizon 2020 research and innovation programme under grant agreement H2020-687786 InVID.

References

1. Apostolidis, E., Mezaris, V.: Fast shot segmentation combining global and local visual descriptors. In: 2014 IEEE International Conference on Acoustics, Speech and Signal Processing, pp. 6583–6587 (2014)
2. Cooray, S.H., O'Connor, N.E.: Identifying an efficient and robust sub-shot segmentation method for home movie summarisation. In: 10th International Conference on Intelligent Systems Design and Applications, pp. 1287–1292 (2010)
3. He, K., Zhang, X., et al.: Deep residual learning for image recognition. In: 2016 IEEE Conference on Computer Vision and Pattern Recognition, pp. 770–778 (2016)
4. Markatopoulou, F., Mezaris, V., et al.: Implicit and explicit concept relations in deep neural networks for multi-label video/image annotation. IEEE Trans. Circuits Syst. Video Technol. 1 (2018)
5. Nixon, L.J.B., Zhu, S., et al.: Video retrieval for multimedia verification of breaking news on social networks. In: 1st International Workshop on Multimedia Verification (MuVer 2017) at ACM Multimedia Conference, MuVer 2017, pp. 13–21. ACM (2017)
6. Over, P.D., Fiscus, J.G., et al.: TRECVID 2013-An overview of the goals, tasks, data, evaluation mechanisms and metrics. In: TRECVID 2013. NIST, USA (2013)
7. Pan, C.M., Chuang, Y.Y., et al.: NTU TRECVID-2007 fast rushes summarization system. In: TRECVID Workshop on Video Summarization, pp. 74–78. ACM (2007)
8. Pittaras, N., Markatopoulou, F., Mezaris, V., Patras, I.: Comparison of fine-tuning and extension strategies for deep convolutional neural networks. In: Amsaleg, L., Guðmundsson, G., Gurrin, C., Jónsson, B., Satoh, S. (eds.) MMM 2017. LNCS, vol. 10132, pp. 102–114. Springer, Cham (2017). https://doi.org/10.1007/978-3-319-51811-4_9

9. Rublee, E., Rabaud, V., et al.: ORB: an efficient alternative to SIFT or SURF. In: 2011 International Conference on Computer Vision, pp. 2564–2571 (2011)
10. Russakovsky, O., Deng, J., et al.: ImageNet large scale visual recognition challenge. Int. J. Comput. Vis. **115**(3), 211–252 (2015)
11. Seo, K., Park, S.J., et al.: Wipe scene-change detector based on visual rhythm spectrum. IEEE Trans. Consum. Electron. **55**(2), 831–838 (2009)
12. Su, C.W., Tyan, H.R., et al.: A motion-tolerant dissolve detection algorithm. IEEE Int. Conf. Multimedia Expo. **2**, 225–228 (2002)
13. Szegedy, C., Liu, W., et al.: Going deeper with convolutions. In: IEEE Conference on Computer Vision and Pattern Recognition (2015)
14. Teyssou, D., Leung, J.M., et al.: The InVID plug-in: web video verification on the browser. In: 1st International Workshop on Multimedia Verification (MuVer 2017) at ACM Multimedia Conference, pp. 23–30. ACM (2017)

Integration of Exploration and Search: A Case Study of the M³ Model

Snorri Gíslason[1], Björn Þór Jónsson[1(✉)], and Laurent Amsaleg[2]

[1] IT University of Copenhagen, Copenhagen, Denmark
bjorn@itu.dk
[2] CNRS-IRISA, Rennes, France

Abstract. Effective support for multimedia analytics applications requires exploration and search to be integrated seamlessly into a single interaction model. Media metadata can be seen as defining a multidimensional media space, casting multimedia analytics tasks as exploration, manipulation and augmentation of that space. We present an initial case study of integrating exploration and search within this multidimensional media space. We extend the M³ model, initially proposed as a pure exploration tool, and show that it can be elegantly extended to allow searching within an exploration context and exploring within a search context. We then evaluate the suitability of relational database management systems, as representatives of today's data management technologies, for implementing the extended M³ model. Based on our results, we finally propose some research directions for scalability of multimedia analytics.

Keywords: Multimedia analytics · Exploration-search axis Scalability

1 Introduction

Multimedia analytics is a research field that grew from a desire to harness the information and insight that are embedded in today's media collections, which are growing both in scale and diversity. In multimedia analytics, supporting user interaction with media collections is particularly important, both in its own right and as a precursor to applying data mining methods. This user interaction can involve a number of distinct tasks, and Zahálka and Worring [14] defined an exploration-search axis with a range of tasks that multimedia analytics tools need to support in a single interface. Here, we focus on the two extremes of that axis: exploration and search.

Typically, exploration and search are implemented as two different operations that are grounded in disjoint informational contexts. On the Web, for example, exploration consists of clicking on links to jump from one document to the other, whereas searching consists of obtaining ranked lists of relevant documents. Once the user starts clicking on search results, the search context is lost and the only way to revisit that context is to go back to the original search and adjust the

© Springer Nature Switzerland AG 2019
I. Kompatsiaris et al. (Eds.): MMM 2019, LNCS 11295, pp. 156–168, 2019.
https://doi.org/10.1007/978-3-030-05710-7_13

query. Then the search starts again from scratch and the only way to observe the previous exploration context is via the color of hyperlinks. Similarly, in current file and media browsers search is implemented as a distinct operation that loses all context of the previous exploration session. To support the exploration-search axis, however, the two user interaction modes must be performed in the same context: we should be able to focus the exploration within search results, or search within the current exploration state.

Multidimensional Media Space. Today, media items are typically associated with a plethora of descriptive and administrative metadata. First, media is commonly generated with technical data about its creation, such as date and time, location, user, and technical specifications. Second, a multitude of methods have been developed to describe the media contents, for example based on deep learning. Third, as users see more and more benefits of annotating media, they likely become more willing to do so.

All this metadata can be seen as defining a multidimensional media space. Many multimedia analytics tasks then boil down to exploring, manipulating and augmenting that media space. Exploration can be seen as applying and updating a set of filters and predicates that outline the current set of multimedia items that a user is interested in. Search can be seen as a reorganization of the space from the reference point of the query.

Contributions. We define *browsing state* as the set of filters and reference points that the user is exploring. The browsing state is an abstract representation of the informational context of the currently displayed media items. Exploration and search tasks gradually update that browsing state, allowing users to alternate tasks while preserving the informational context. We believe that multimedia analytics suites can succeed in seamlessly integrating exploration and search tasks (as well as other tasks along the exploration-search continuum of [14]) if they implement something equivalent to a browsing state.

In this paper, we demonstrate such integration within the context of the Multidimensional Multimedia Model (M^3, pronounced emm-cube) [9]. M^3 was proposed as a way to interactively explore the multidimensional media space, merging concepts from business intelligence (online analytical processing (OLAP) and multidimensional analysis (MDA)) and faceted browsing. The M^3 model, however, was defined as a pure exploration interface, with no support for search. This paper is an initial exploration into the integration of search into the M^3 exploration model, showing that the M^3 model can be elegantly extended to support both extremes of the exploration-search axis.

This paper also highlights the difficulties that the underlying data-retrieval infrastructure runs into when trying to provide an *efficient* implementation of the browsing state and its maintenance. In short, the current state of the technology is unable to dynamically support the unpredictable user-defined sub-collections of media items involved in exploration and search tasks.

The remainder of this paper is organized as follows. We review background work in Sect. 2, and then summarize the M^3 model in Sect. 3. We then make the following contributions, before concluding the paper in Sect. 7:

- We extend the M^3 model to include search results as dynamic dimensions of the multidimensional media space (Sect. 4).
- Using a proof-of-concept implementation, we then show that relational systems are not suitable for the extended M^3 model (Sect. 5).
- Based on our experience, we present some research directions towards efficient exploitation of the multidimensional media space (Sect. 6).

2   Background

Zahálka and Worring [14] surveyed a collection of more than 800 research papers related to user interaction with multimedia collections and compiled into a model of user interaction for multimedia analytics. A key contribution of that work was the exploration-search axis, which consisted of a continuum of tasks that multimedia analytics users must be able to accomplish. In this paper we consider the two extremes of that axis. Here, we review key results related to multimedia search and exploration; this coverage is brief for space reasons.

Multimedia retrieval, in particular high-dimensional feature indexing, has received significant attention in the literature, including several highly scalable methods (e.g., [2,5,6,8]). None of these methods, however, offer any support for integration of search into a dynamic browsing state.

Multimedia exploration tools have typically considered various modes of interacting with static media collections (e.g., [10,11]). None of these tools consider the integration of dynamic search with exploration. Faceted media browsers create hierarchies (or DAGs) of tags and allow interactively traversing those structures, narrowing down the set of displayed items to match the user needs. Typically, faceted browsers present results in a linear list, thus losing the internal structure of the browsing set [3,4,12]. OLAP applications, on the other hand, have long been used to efficiently browse multidimensional numerical data, with support for slicing, drilling in, rolling out, and pivoting. Early applications of the OLAP model to multimedia include [1,7,15]. Neither the original OLAP systems, nor the referenced multimedia variants, consider search. Their efficiency is due to pre-computed indexes; including search in their interaction model would invalidate all their pre-computations, as it is impossible to consider all potential query reference points.

Zahálka and Worring also proposed interactive multimodal learning (IML) as an umbrella interaction model for multimedia analytics [14]. More recently, they and others proposed a very efficient system for IML over large-scale collections [13]. IML can be seen as a reorganization of the media space, just as search, and we plan to integrate IML with exploration and search in future work.

3   The M³ Model

The M³ model was proposed in 2015 by Jónsson et al. [9], as an interaction model for exploration of personal photo collections. The foundation of M³ is to consider media metadata as defining a multidimensional space that organizes the media items, and to use concepts from faceted browsing and OLAP to explore that space; much of the terminology for user interactions is indeed borrowed from OLAP. The basic data in the M³ model consists of *objects* and *tags*, which refer to the media items and their descriptive and administrative metadata, respectively. Originally, tags were defined as simple data items, such as alphanumerical strings, dates and timestamps, but tags might also be more complex, such as high-dimensional feature vectors.

The multidimensional aspects of the M³ model then arise from the ways the tags are organized among themselves. A *concept* in M³ groups related tags together into sets of tags, which may have an implicit ordering (e.g., for dates and numerical tags). A *hierarchy* then adds an explicit tree structure to (a subset of) the tags in single concept; hierarchies only contain tags from that concept. Together, the concepts and their hierarchies form the dimensions of a *hypercube*; the objects are conceptually present in the *cells* of this hypercube (or a subcube of it) if they are associated with each tag corresponding to the cell.

During exploration, the user uses *filters* over some of the dimensions to define a subcube of the complete hypercube; this subcube is the *browsing state* of M³. The filters may focus on a specific tag (tag filter), on a range of tags from a concept (range filter), or a subtree of a hierarchy (hierarchy filter). Applying a tag filter or range filter to a concept is called *slicing*, as each filter represents a slice of the entire hypercube; if a filter already exists on that concept it is replaced by the new filter. Traversing up or down a hierarchy is also tantamount to updating a corresponding hierarchy filter; called *rolling up* or *drilling down*, respectively. Note that each of these operations updates the browsing state.

Jónsson et al. [9] also proposed a user interface for the M³ model. The user interface consists of three axes (called *front*-axis, *up*-axis and *in*-axis for intuitiveness), and the user may assign any dimension from the browsing state with 1, 2 or 3 of these axes, resulting in projection of the browsing state onto a 1D, 2D or 3D representation, respectively. Replacing one visible dimension with another dimension is called *pivoting*; note that if the new visible dimension was already part of the browsing state, then pivoting does not change the browsing state. The following example demonstrates the common operations in the M³ model.

Example 1. *A mother is sitting down with her children in front of her computer to recall a hiking trip. She first selects the People dimension (a hierarchy over a sub-set of the people concept) as a starting point on the front-axis, which has two tags at the top level: "Adults" and "Kids". Then she selects the Location dimension, which has such nodes as "Cabin" and "River", as the up-axis. Being a photo nerd, she becomes interested in the light conditions and assigns the Aperture value to the in-axis. The current browsing state then has three dimensions, where each cell has (at least) one particular person in one particular location* *type with one particular aperture value. Note that photos containing kids and adults will show up in two cells (and, if a cabin were situated next to a river, it could show up in four cells) as the photos belong logically in all these cells.*

4   Integrating Exploration and Search

We have identified the following requirements for integrating search within the M^3 model:

Metadata-Based Search: In the M^3 model, the browsing state is based on media metadata, as represented by filters over concepts and hierarchies. The media items themselves are never considered directly in the browsing state, but are represented only through their metadata. Consequently, search operations should also focus on metadata. In order to consider content-based search, the content description must therefore first be extracted into a (new or existing) metadata concept.

Dynamic Result-Dimensions: User interaction in the M^3 model consists of maintaining and projecting the browsing state, which in turn is composed of dimensions. To integrate search into the browsing state, the results of each search operation must therefore define a new dimension in the browsing state. If the query is modified, then the previous result dimension must be replaced by the new result dimension, and the browsing state updated correspondingly.

Single-Concept Search: As described above, a browsing state is composed of dimensions, which are either concepts or hierarchies; hierarchies, in turn, are simply a (relatively) static representation of a concept. There is thus a direct correspondence between browsing state dimensions and concepts. To maintain that correspondence, each search operation should only apply to one tag concept.

Generality: Depending on the metadata type, different search operations may apply, e.g., text search for alphanumeric tags and similarity search for feature vectors. And depending on the search type, different indexes may be required in the media server. In all cases, however, search results should be ordered based on score (e.g., relevance, similarity, or distance). Set-based search can be implemented by assigning the same score to each result. Some search methods only assign scores to a subset of the objects, while others assign a score to each object; range filters can be used to reduce the number of objects returned.

To better illustrate how following these requirements leads to integration of exploration and search, consider the following example.

Example 2. *Recall the final browsing state of Example 1, which had three dimensions: People on the front-axis; Location on the up-axis; and Aperture on the in-axis. The mother now decides she wants to focus on images with colors similar to a particular image. She opens up a search form, where she selects the image, chooses a distance filter to focus on similar images, and assigns this*

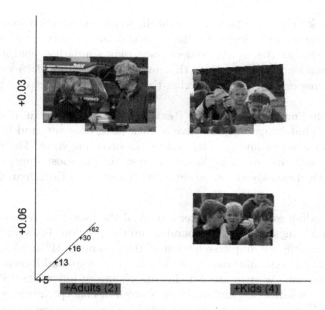

Fig. 1. 3D representation of the browsing state from the scenario in Example 2. See the text for a detailed description of the browsing state axes.

search concept to the in-axis. Note that the tags of this new temporary concept are the color distance values from the search. Also note that by assigning the search dimension to the in-axis she replaces the Aperture concept, but nevertheless only images with an aperture tag are included.

The mother now recalls a name from the trip and wants to focus on images tagged with that name. She opens up a second search form for the People dimension, types in the name "Mick Junior" and assigns the new search concept to the up-axis. The tags of this search concept are the similarity scores from the search. By assigning the search dimension to the up-axis she now replaces the Location hierarchy, but as before only images with a location tag are included.

Figure 1 shows the browsing state resulting from Example 2, which has one hierarchical dimension and two search dimensions. A few notes are in order.

- The scores on the up-axis indicate the relevance of image tags to the query, as computed by PostgreSQL (the relevance values are +0.03 and +0.06, presumably using some form of TFIDF scoring). Three participants in the family hike were named Mick (two kids, one adult), but only one was called Mick Junior. Images with Mick Junior receive higher relevance scores than images with one of the other Micks.
- The hierarchy on the front-axis divides the browsing state based on whether the Micks shown in images are adults or kids. In this case the images in the lower right corner contain Mick Junior, images in the upper left corner contain Mick Senior, and images in the upper right corner contain the third

(young) Mick. The collection does contain some images with two and three Micks, but these were filtered by the color similarity query.

- The distances on the in-axis reflect the color similarity, computed using squared Euclidean distance. Note that in this case a filter of 75 was applied, and hence images with distance higher than 75 are not reflected in the browsing state.
- The example image from the first (text) search has Euclidean distance of 0 from itself. That image did not have a Mick in it, however, and hence is not included in the set of images retrieved by the browsing state. Therefore there is no image with distance 0 in the browsing state. The most similar image has nearly identical average color, however, with a squared Euclidean distance of only 5.

In the preceding example, the interactions of the user were represented by a sequence of browsing states, each dependent on the previous browsing state. We believe that any efficient implementation of the extended M^3 model must take into account this incremental nature of the browsing state and interactions with users, but we are not aware of any existing algorithms or indexing strategies that do so. In Sect. 5 we describe and evaluate a proof-of-concept implementation of the extended M^3 model, using relational database technology as a representative of the current state of the art, and show why performance suffers when the previous browsing state is ignored. In Sect. 6 we then propose some research directions towards scalable implementation of the extended M^3 model.

5   Prototype Evaluation

The M^3 model was initially implemented by Jónsson et al. [9] as a server to deliver the objects in a browsing state (O^3) and a photo browsing client (P^3). We extended this prototype by integrating search functionality, as described below. As the O^3 server was implemented on top of a relational database management system (RDBMS), we decided to evaluate whether an RDBMS is a suitable technology for implementing this integration.

5.1   Proof-of-Concept Implementation

Following the requirements of Sect. 4, integrating search results into the browsing state of the M^3 model can conceptually be done in the following steps:

1. Create a temporary concept for the search results and add to browsing state:
   - Retrieve the relevant objects and their relevance score, applying a range filter if required.
   - Create new metadata tags for the relevance score and assign the appropriate objects to each score tag.
   - Update the browsing state description to include the search concept.
2. Retrieve the browsing state.

Since relational systems provide no efficient support for integrating knowledge of the previous browsing state into the first step, the query to retrieve the relevant objects is completely independent of the existing browsing state and only affected by the criteria applied to that particular search dimension, which leads to sub-optimal performance.

We decided to focus on two types of search that are well supported by many relational systems:

- Keyword search over alphanumeric tags, supported by an inverted index.
- Similarity search over low-dimensional features, supported by an R-tree.

For the latter, we use a very simple similarity-based search on color, using the average RGB color in each image (computed by averaging the R, G, and B values across all pixels). As feature vectors did not exist in O^3 as a tag type, we added a table to store these features, and used an R-tree to index the three-dimensional feature vectors.

5.2   Evaluation

In this section we evaluate the performance of our prototype for three extremely simple browsing states. Each of these three browsing states correspond to a user selecting search as the first (and only) operation to apply to the collection. The goal of these experiments is to gauge the potential performance of relational systems, to establish baseline performance numbers and to identify performance bottlenecks, with an aim towards inspiring and supporting subsequent research into indexing and query processing.

Experimental Collections. In the following we describe three experiments: keyword search with long text annotations; keyword search with short (name) tags; and color similarity search. For each experiment, a new collection with a single tag concept was created, allowing detailed control of the tag concept properties. We now describe the tag collections and concepts created for each experiment.

Text Search: In this experiment, we created collections with 1K, 10, 100K, and 400K objects, and used the Amazon review data set[1] to create a concept with one review tag associated with each object. Reviews exceeding 512 characters were truncated; as some reviews are shorter, the average tag length varied from 434 character for the smallest collection to 458 characters for the largest collection.

Tag Search: In this experiment, we created collections with 1K, 10K, 100K, and 1M objects. We then created a collection of 200 randomly chosen sur-names and associated each object with three surname tags. The surname tags were chosen by (a) assigning selected tags to 1, 10, 100 and 1,000 random objects, to facilitate the controlled experiment, and (b) randomly assigning the remaining tags to give three tags per object.

---

[1] Available at https://www.kaggle.com/bittlingmayer/amazonreviews.

Color Search: In this experiment, we again created collections with 1K, 10K, 100K, and 1M objects. We then created a random RGB tag for each image and inserted into the RGB concept.

Experimental Method. In each experiment, we consider retrieval of browsing states with 1, 10, 100 and 1,000 objects, and study how the performance of browsing state retrieval varies depending on both browsing state size and object collection size. In all cases, the experiments focus on the retrieval of the browsing state information and exclude the retrieval of the objects (images) themselves.

The experiments were run on a DELL Latitude E7440 laptop, with an Intel dual core i7-4600U 2.10 GHz processor, 4 MB CPU cache, 16 GB of RAM and a 256 GB solid state drive. The laptop runs Windows 8.1, but the experiment was run on a Linux Ubuntu 16.10 64-bit virtual machine with allocated base memory of 4 GB and 1 processor, running on Oracle VM VirtualBox Manager. In each experiment, we started with the smallest object collection and continued to the largest object collection. We repeated this process five times and report the average times from these five runs. Before each such run, the virtual machine was shut down and the laptop restarted.

Text Search. Figure 2(left) shows the performance of browsing state retrieval for long text tags, as the browsing state size varies from 1 object to 1,000 objects, and as the collection size grows from 1K to 400K. The figure shows that the time increases both with collection size and result size, but in all cases remains under 0.6 seconds, which is sufficient for interactive workloads.

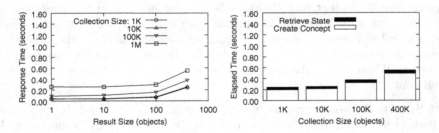

Fig. 2. Text search: performance of browsing state retrieval (left); Time breakdown for retrieval of 1,000 objects (right).

Figure 2(right) shows a more detailed analysis when the browsing state contains 1,000 objects, breaking the response time into (a) the creation of a temporary concept with the search results, and (b) the retrieval of the resulting browsing state. As the figure shows, the majority of the time is spent on the former. The increased time, as the collection grows, is due to the increased size of the inverted index; for even larger collections, the response time is likely to increase linearly.

Tag Search. Figure 3(left) shows the performance of browsing state retrieval for short name tags, as the browsing state size varies from 1 object to 1,000 objects, and as the collection size grows from 1K to 1M. As with the longer text tags, time increases both with collection size and result size, but remains interactive with less then 1 second to retrieve 1,000 objects from the 1M collection.

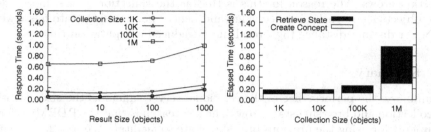

Fig. 3. Tag search: performance of browsing state retrieval (left); Time breakdown for retrieval of 1,000 objects (right).

Somewhat unexpectedly, however, retrieval from the 1M collection is significantly more expensive than before. Figure 3(right) shows the more detailed analysis when the browsing state contains 1,000 objects. As the figure shows, the creation of the new temporary concept is less expensive than with the larger text tags, due to the smaller inverted index. On the other hand, the creation of the resulting browsing state is significantly more expensive, for two reasons. First, the collection is larger (1M compared to 400K). Second, since each object is associated with more tags (3 name tags compared to 1 text tag), the number of tag-object associations is actually 7.5x larger for the short name tags, resulting in a more expensive query to assemble the browsing state.

Color Search. Figure 4(left) shows the performance of browsing state retrieval for RGB color tags, as the browsing state size varies from 1 object to 1,000 objects, and as the collection size grows from 1K to 1M. For the most part, time

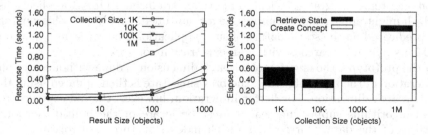

Fig. 4. Color search: performance of browsing state retrieval (left); Time breakdown for retrieval of 1,000 objects (right).

increases both with collection size and result size. The retrieval time is no longer interactive, however, when returning 1,000 objects from the 1M collection.

Figure 4(right) shows the detailed analysis when the browsing state contains 1,000 objects. As the figure shows, the creation of the new temporary concept is responsible for the majority of the response time, due to the inefficiencies of the R-tree index. Interestingly, the time to retrieve the browsing state shrinks as the collection grows. The reason for this is that as the collection grows, more and more objects share each distance value and hence the browsing state has fewer and fewer distinct distance tags, resulting in reduced computation time.

5.3   Summary

In summary, the performance of the relational server suffers as the size of both the collection and browsing state grow. The key reason is that the RDBMS offers no support for using the previous browsing state to facilitate the search, in some cases leading to high cost of computing the search, and in other cases to high cost of retrieving the browsing state.

6   Discussion

In this section we highlight the major lessons we have learned from this case study about integrating exploration and search for multimedia analytics.

- At the conceptual level, we have presented an elegant way to integrate exploration and search for multimedia analytics. As Example 2 shows, our model allows searching within an exploration context and exploring within a search context. This integration warrants further exploration, however, for example with respect to the meaning of k-NN search and approximate search within exploration contexts, as well as other modes of interaction, such as interactive multimodal learning. We believe that this field is ripe for investigation.
- The performance results show that relational database systems are not a suitable tool for multimedia exploration, as they do not support the multidimensional nature of the application well and fail to provide interactive performance, even with a relatively small collection of 1M objects. Note that some systems integrate efficient support for traditional OLAP applications, which might appear more appropriate for multimedia analytics. This support is predicated on the static nature of such applications, however, and does not address dynamic searches within an exploration context.
- In the prototype, the creation of a search dimension is done without any consideration of the browsing state; the browsing state is then updated using the new search dimension. For better integration, however, the index structures and algorithms supporting search must be aware of the multidimensional nature of the data. Currently, no such index structure or algorithms exist and developing those algorithms is another field that is ripe for investigation.

This paper highlights the difficulties that the underlying data-retrieval infrastructure runs into when trying to provide an *efficient* implementation of the browsing state and its maintenance. In short, the current state of the technology is unable to dynamically support the unpredictable user-defined subcollections of media items involved in exploration and search tasks. We believe that discovering the algorithms and index structures required to provide that support is a major research direction within the field of multimedia analytics.

7   Conclusion

Effective support for multimedia analytics applications requires exploration and search to be integrated seamlessly into a single interaction model. In this paper, have presented an initial case study of using the multidimensional media space of media metadata to integrate exploration and search. We have extended the M^3 model, initially proposed as a pure exploration tool for the multidimensional media space, and shown that it can be elegantly extended to allow searching within an exploration context and exploring within a search context. We have then presented and evaluated a proof-of-concept prototype and derived some major research directions for multimedia analytics.

References

1. Arigon, A.M., Miquel, M., Tchounikine, A.: Multimedia data warehouses: a multi-version model and a medical application. Multi. Tools Apps. **35**(1), 91–108 (2007)
2. Babenko, A., Lempitsky, V.S.: The inverted multi-index. IEEE Trans. Pattern Anal. Mach. Intell. **37**(6), 1247–1260 (2015)
3. Bartolini, I., Ciaccia, P.: Integrating semantic and visual facets for browsing digital photo collections. In: Proceedings of SEBD (2009)
4. Diao, M., Mukherjea, S., Rajput, N., Srivastava, K.: Faceted search and browsing of audio content on spoken web. In: Proceedings of CIKM (2010)
5. Guðmundsson, G.Þ., Amsaleg, L., Jónsson, B.Þ., Franklin, M.J.: Towards engineering a web-scale multimedia service: a case study using Spark. In: Proceedings of MMSys, Taipei, Taiwan (2017)
6. Jégou, H., Tavenard, R., Douze, M., Amsaleg, L.: Searching in one billion vectors: re-rank with source coding. In: Proceedings of ICASSP, Prague, Czech Republic (2011)
7. Jin, X., Han, J., Cao, L., Luo, J., Ding, B., Lin, C.X.: Visual cube and on-line analytical processing of images. In: Proceedings of CIKM (2010)
8. Amsaleg, L., Jónsson, B.Þ., Lejsek, H.: Scalability of the NV-tree: three experiments. In: Marchand-Maillet, S., Silva, Y.N., Chávez, E. (eds.) SISAP 2018. LNCS, vol. 11223, pp. 59–72. Springer, Cham (2018). https://doi.org/10.1007/978-3-030-02224-2_5
9. Jónsson, B.Þ., Tómasson, G., Sigurþórsson, H., Eiríksdóttir, Á., Amsaleg, L., Lárusdóttir, M.K.: A multi-dimensional data model for personal photo browsing. In: He, X., Luo, S., Tao, D., Xu, C., Yang, J., Hasan, M.A. (eds.) MMM 2015. LNCS, vol. 8936, pp. 345–356. Springer, Cham (2015). https://doi.org/10.1007/978-3-319-14442-9_41

10. Shneiderman, B., Bederson, B.B., Drucker, S.M.: Find that photo! interface strategies to annotate, browse, and share. Commun. ACM **49**(4), 69–71 (2006)
11. Worring, M., Koelma, D.C.: Insight in image collections by multimedia pivot tables. In: Proceedings of ACM ICMR, Shanghai, China (2015)
12. Yee, K.P., Swearingen, K., Li, K., Hearst, M.: Faceted metadata for image search and browsing. In: Proceedings of CHI (2003)
13. Zahálka, J., Rudinac, S., Jónsson, B.Þ., Koelma, D.C., Worring, M., : Blackthorn: large-scale interactive multimodal learning. IEEE Trans. Multi. **20**(3), 687–698 (2018)
14. Zahálka, J., Worring, M.: Towards interactive, intelligent, and integrated multimedia analytics. In: Proceedings of IEEE VAST, Paris, France (2014)
15. Zaïane, O.R., Han, J., Li, Z.N., Hou, J.: Mining multimedia data. In: Proceedings of CASCON (1998)

Face Swapping for Solving Collateral Privacy Issues in Multimedia Analytics

Werner Bailer[✉]

JOANNEUM RESEARCH Forschungsgesellschaft mbH, DIGITAL – Institute for
Information and Communication Technologies, Steyrergasse 17, 8010 Graz, Austria
werner.bailer@joanneum.at

Abstract. A wide range of components of multimedia analytics systems relies on visual content that is used for supervised (e.g., classification) and unsupervised (e.g., clustering) machine learning methods.
This content may contain privacy sensitive information, e.g., show faces
of persons. In many cases it is just an inevitable side-effect that persons
appear in the content, and the application may not require identification – a situation which we call "collateral privacy issues". We propose
de-identification of faces in images by using a generative adversarial network to generate new face images, and use them to replace faces in the
original images. We demonstrate that face swapping does not impact the
performance of visual descriptor matching and extraction.

1 Introduction

A wide range of components of multimedia analytics systems relies on visual
content that is used for supervised (e.g., classification) and unsupervised (e.g.,
clustering) machine learning methods, as samples for visualization etc. In some
applications the visual content may contain privacy sensitive information, e.g.,
show faces of persons. If the identification of persons is a task in the application, then handling those issues must be thoroughly addressed. However, there
are many cases where it is just an inevitable side-effect that persons appear in
the content, even if the application may not require identification. We refer to
such cases as "collateral privacy issues". Example application domains include
traffic and navigation, construction or tourism, where the objects of interest are
depicted in public space, and (identifiable) persons may also be visible.

For visualization purposes, to retrain machine learning tools (or migrate to
future technology) and to enable traceability the results of multimedia analytics
systems, it is useful to store the visual content and not discard it after its use for
training. It it obvious, that the related privacy issues must thus be taken into
account in the design and development process. The importance of privacy was
also one of the results of the discussion in the MAPTA special session at MMM
2018. In the European Union, the recently introduced General Data Protection Regulation (GDPR) legislation [7] further strengthens the rights of citizens,
allowing them to withdraw permissions about the use of data at any time. This

© Springer Nature Switzerland AG 2019
I. Kompatsiaris et al. (Eds.): MMM 2019, LNCS 11295, pp. 169–177, 2019.
https://doi.org/10.1007/978-3-030-05710-7_14

means that a system must be able to keep track of the provenance of every content item with potential privacy issues, and support its removal from the system, including any derived data, that cannot be considered already anonymized or aggregated. This extends the range of privacy issues also to content that is never displayed to users, but still retained for (re)training or matching purposes.

In order to address such collateral privacy issues due to identifiable persons in visual content, de-identification of faces is one option. We discuss related approaches in Sect. 2. Based on the analysis of the properties of different approaches, we propose the use of face swapping, i.e., the replacement of faces in content. In contrast to other work using a previously collected set of real faces for swapping, we use generative adversarial networks (GANs) to generate new face images of non-existent persons, and insert them into the target images. This approach is described in Sect. 3. While most existing work only considers face de-identification for displaying content to human viewers, we also investigate whether face swapping has any effect on automatic feature extraction. In particular, we evaluate in Sect. 4 the use of de-identified images for visual matching of landmark images. Section 5 concludes the paper.

2   Related Work

There is a range of methods that can be applied to support privacy protection of visual content. A recent survey that provides a good overview can be found in [23].

The most straight forward approach to de-identification of faces is blurring or pixelization. The authors of [11] propose an approach that preserves the key facial expression, but blurs parts of the face. It has been shown that people are still able to recognize familiar faces in blurred or pixelized images [10], and that moving faces are easier to recognize as static ones. This insight has also led to the development of face recognition approaches for blurred images, which eliminates the requirement of familiarity found in the human experiment, and makes blurring of faces an unreliable de-identification method at a larger scale. The approaches for blurred face recognition use descriptors in the frequency domain [2], or try to estimate the point spread function causing the blur in order to reconstruct a recognizable image [22]. In addition to deblurring, novel descriptors with higher robustness against blur have been proposed [8]. [20] show that pixelization and black masks on parts of the face hardly impact the performance of face recognition, if a classifier is trained on images with the same distortions.

Crypto-compression is an approach that applies encryption to specific parts of an image or video (e.g., faces), so that the content is concealed, but the resulting bitstream can still be read with a standard decoder. Such an approach has been recently standardized in the MPEG Visual Identity Management Application Format (VIMAF) [4]. While this is approach is secure due to strong cryptography, the encrypted parts introduce unwanted structures in the image, that may impact feature extraction and processing.

The MediaEval benchmark has organized a visual privacy task in the years 2012–2014 [3], with the aim to remove privacy-infringing cues from surveillance video, but allow a user to judge whether the action depicted is unlawful or requires an intervention. The approaches proposed included among others blurring, ghosting, cartooning or replacement with avatars. In 2018, MediaEval also launched a pixel privacy task to assess how effective modifications in visual content can prevent estimation of geo-locations.

The authors of [20] apply the concept of k-anonymity to face recognition. Using a training set, they average eigenface descriptors of the faces, so that discriminability of faces is reduced to groups of at least k individuals. One drawback of this approach is that it may require updates across many images, if new faces are added which are outliers wrt. the previous set of faces, and could thus break the k-anonymity. A similar approach of de-identification for content with a closed set of faces is described in [17], and performing the k-same test in real-time. In videos, this approach also ensures consistent de-identification of all appearances of one person.

In [5], an approach for face swapping for privacy preservation is proposed. The tool contains a library of previously collected faces, and performs replacement using face detection and registration of facial landmarks. The paper discusses different applications, but focuses on the display of images to users and does not address cases where content is used for automatic analysis. A more recent approach applying face swapping for privacy protection is described in [16], also using faces from a predefined database. In [21], an approach for face swapping under unconstrained conditions using a fully convolutional neural network for segmentation is proposed. A region-separative GAN (RSGAN) is used in [19] for face swapping based on latent face and hair representations. It has been recently shown that the use of face swapping can be detected with high accuracy [1,29], but no method enables the reconstruction of the original face and thus privacy is still preserved.

While we focus on faces in this work, there is other image content that may allow identification, e.g., clothes or accessories. In [18], the notion of privacy sensitive information (PSI) regions has been introduced. The authors propose to identify them via intended human objects, i.e., the content a human intends to capture in the image. However, this excludes background and passers-by, thus this approach would only detect PSI regions of persons that are the main object of the image, and leave the others identifiable. A model for privacy loss through content analysis beyond face identification, based on location (where), time (when), and activities (what) has been proposed in [26]. These issues are to be considered when re-identification is possible event without facial information (e.g., through grouping, clothes or gait), or when depicted actions alone may be sufficient to infer information about persons. However, in the still image dataset used in this work these issues do not apply.

We can draw the following conclusions from the analysis of the related work. Replacement of faces, i.e. face swapping, is one of the approaches that cannot be easily reverted, while still keeping the images aesthetically acceptable and avoiding the risk of introducing different structures in the content, that could bias feature extraction. However, replacement with a fixed set of real faces has limitations, if one of these persons decides to revoke the permission for using their image. Most of the works focus on privacy issues in the human review of content, while hardly any work addresses applying de-identification to images used for training or matching in automatic analysis algorithms. There is thus a lack of knowledge on the impact of de-identification on such methods.

3   Proposed Approach

We propose the following workflow for de-identification of images. We generate a set of new face images. In the images to be de-identified, we detect faces and extract their facial landmarks. For every face, a random replacement is selected, warped and composed into the target image. This is advantageous over inserting the same image into all targets, which would result in repeated content in the image set, and might potentially bias subsequent training processes. The selection process is entirely random, and does not try to preserve gender, age or any other characteristics, and does not try to preserve features such as glasses. This choice is made based on our assumption that we use the images for problems unrelated to the depicted persons. This section provides some details about the different steps in the process.

For the face generation, we use a Deep Convolutional Generative Adversarial Network (DCGAN) as proposed in [25]. The basic principle of GANs is to simultaneously train a generator network that produces samples of output data, trying to mimic the training samples, and a discriminator network that tries to classify between the distribution of the training data and the generated samples. We use a TensorFlow implementation of DCGANs[1] which makes more frequent updates to the generator, in order to avoid that the discriminator converges too fast. The DCGAN is trained on the CelebFaces Attributes (CelebA) dataset [13], which contains around 200 K images of more than 10K individuals. Figure 1 shows examples of generated faces. As apparent, the generation sometimes produces questionable results. We thus run the face detection and landmark extraction algorithm on the generated faces, and use the face only if we obtain a reliable result. This eliminates most of the generated outliers.

For face swapping, we use the DNN based face detector and landmark extractor from DLIB [9] on the target image. Between the source and target face the facial landmarks are registered, and 2D warping is performed. We used an existing face swapping implementation in Python[2] as a starting point. We integrate the random selection of generated faces to be used as source, and process all faces that can be detected in the image. Examples of images with replaced faces are shown in Fig. 2.

Some artifacts are visible, sometimes originating from the generated face image, sometimes from the warping/insertion process. One issue with the detec-

---

[1] https://github.com/carpedm20/DCGAN-tensorflow.
[2] https://github.com/wuhuikai/FaceSwap.

tor from DLIB is that small and non-frontal faces are not well detected. This component should thus be replaced, e.g. with a multi-task cascaded CNN as proposed in [28]. Some artifacts are caused by the fact that the DCGAN has been trained on very narrowly cropped faces, thus also only outputting a core face region, which then needs to be blended into the larger face region on the target image. Training the DCGAN with more hair and background leads to less stable results. This issue also needs to be addressed in future work.

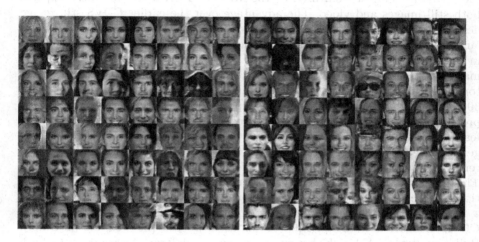

Fig. 1. Examples of generated faces, after two training epochs (left) and seven epochs (right).

Fig. 2. Example images from the Oxford Buildings dataset with replaced faces.

4 Evaluation

We evaluate the de-identified images by performing visual descriptor extraction and matching. This is only one example of automatic analysis, however, the feature extraction applied can be considered representative for a range of automatic analysis tasks. Tasks such as classification are typically based on very similar features as used in our experiment. We use the compact visual descriptor currently being standardized by the MPEG CDVA activity, which supports both still images and video. The advantage over the earlier CDVS still image descriptor is that it includes a component based on deep features. In particular, we use the global and deep feature descriptor components of the descriptor in our experiment, which are combined as specified by the standard in the matching process. The global descriptor is a Scalable Compressed Fisher Vector (SCFV) [12], obtained from extracting SIFT [15] descriptors around up to 300 detected interest points. These descriptors are aggregated to Fisher vectors, projected to a lower dimension space using PCA and then binarized. The deep feature descriptor is obtained from a VGG-16 network [27] trained on the ImageNet data set. As proposed in [14], the classification layers of the network are removed, and replaced by layers to perform nested invariance pooling (NIP). This improves the robustness of the descriptor to translation, scaling and rotation. The resulting descriptor has a dimension of 512, and is finally binarized.

We perform a pairwise matching experiment as described in the MPEG CDVA evaluation framework [6]. As dataset, we use the well-known Oxford Buildings dataset [24], which contains images of different locations in Oxford. For each of them, a set of queries and matching references are provided as ground truth. The references in the dataset are classified into good, ok, and junk, depending on how much of the location of interest is actually visible in the picture. It has to be noted, that not all images of a location are annotated, but only a subset is covered by the queries and reference images. Some of them are taken at locations with many persons around, such as Cornmarket. We thus construct the data for the experiment as follows: We create a set of matching image pairs, where one image is from the set of queries, and the other is from the set of references. This results in 65 pairs for Cornmarket. As many relevant images containing persons are not covered by the references, we also construct an extended version of the matching pairs by forming pairs from the queries against all images with "cornmarket" in their file name. This extended set contains 360 matching pair for Cornmarket. We also create a set of 650 non-matching pairs, from the queries for Cornmarket and random images from any of the other locations.

We extract the MPEG CDVA descriptors from the images and determine the similarity scores for the matching and non-matching image pairs. By varying the threshold for the similarity score, we can calculate the true positive rate (TPR) and false positive rate (FPR) for different working points. The results are shown in Fig. 3 as the solid lines (blue with square markers indicates the matching pairs using only the references in the ground truth, red with square markers indicates the extended pairs).

We then repeat the experiment using the de-identified images for Cornmarket. As we are interested in matching images with replaced faces with original images, we use for matching pairs the original queries, and use modified images for the references to match against. As we use only non-Cornmarket images as references in the non-matching pairs, we use the modified query images in this case. The results are also shown in Fig. 3 as the dashed lines with circle markers for the face images after two training epochs. The dash-dot lines with the x markers are the results with face images after 7 epochs. The results are identical for the original ground truth, and have small differences for the extended ground truth, with has more images with faces and containing larger faces.

In order to assess whether the use of random generated faces has significant impact, we have also performed the experiment, where every face was replaced with the same face image (a real face, different from any occurring in the Cornmarket images). The results are plotted as dotted lines with diamond markers in Fig. 3.

It is apparent that there are only minor differences between the original and the de-identified images. The images with swapped faces seem to yield the same performance in visual descriptor matching. While using faces generated after more training epochs may result in visually more pleasing results, the quality of the faces does not impact feature extraction.

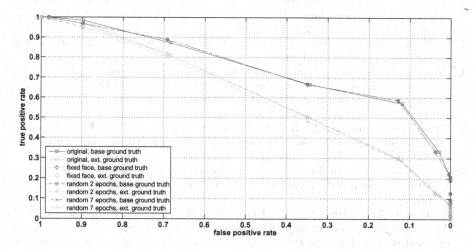

Fig. 3. Matching results for the original and de-identified face images for the Cornmarket location. (Color figure online)

5   Conclusion

In this work we have addressed the issue of de-identification of faces in images used in multimedia analytics applications, e.g. for training or visualization purposes. We have proposed the use of a DCGAN to generate new face images of non-existent persons, and use them to replace faces in the original images. We have shown in an experiment that the replacement of faces did not impact the performance of visual descriptor matching and extraction. We can thus conclude that the proposed processing pipeline is a suitable way to handle collateral privacy issues.

As noted in Sect. 3 the current implementation has deficiencies with handling small and lateral faces, which will be addressed in future work. In addition, hair, accessories and clothes may provide identification hints in some cases, so that also methods for replacing them should be considered.

Acknowledgments. The research leading to these results has received funding from the European Union's Horizon 2020 research and innovation programme under grant agreement no 761802, MARCONI ("Multimedia and Augmented Radio Creation: Online, iNteractive, Individual", https://www.projectmarconi.eu).

References

1. Agarwal, A., Singh, R., Vatsa, M., Noore, A.: Swapped! digital face presentation attack detection via weighted local magnitude pattern. In: 2017 IEEE International Joint Conference on Biometrics (IJCB), pp. 659–665. IEEE (2017)
2. Ahonen, T., Rahtu, E., Ojansivu, V., Heikkila, J.: Recognition of blurred faces using local phase quantization. In: 19th International Conference on Pattern Recognition, ICPR 2008, pp. 1–4. IEEE (2008)
3. Badii, A., Einig, M., Piatrik, T., et al.: Overview of the mediaeval 2013 visual privacy task. In: MediaEval (2014)
4. Bergeron, C., Sidaty, N., Hamidouche, W., Boyadjis, B., Le Feuvre, J., Lim, Y.: Real-time selective encryption solution based on ROI for MPEG-a visual identity management AF. In: 2017 22nd International Conference on Digital Signal Processing (DSP), pp. 1–5, Aug 2017
5. Bitouk, D., Kumar, N., Dhillon, S., Belhumeur, P., Nayar, S.K.: Face swapping: automatically replacing faces in photographs. In: ACM Transactions on Graphics (TOG), vol. 27, p. 39. ACM (2008)
6. Evaluation framework for compact descriptors for video analysis - search and retrieval - version 2.0. Technical report ISO/IEC JTC1/SC29/WG11/N15729 (2015)
7. Regulation (EU) 2016/679 of the European Parliament and of the Council of 27 April 2016 on the protection of natural persons with regard to the processing of personal data and on the free movement of such data, and repealing Directive 95/46/EC (General Data Protection Regulation). Official Journal of the European Union, L119:1–88, May 2016
8. Hadid, A., Nishiyama, M., Sato, Y.: Recognition of blurred faces via facial deblurring combined with blur-tolerant descriptors. In: 2010 20th International Conference on Pattern Recognition (ICPR), pp. 1160–1163. IEEE (2010)
9. King, D.E.: Dlib-ml: a machine learning toolkit. J. Mach. Learn. Res. **10**, 1755–1758 (2009)
10. Lander, K., Bruce, V., Hill, H.: Evaluating the effectiveness of pixelation and blurring on masking the identity of familiar faces. Appl. Cogn. Psychol. **15**(1), 101–116 (2001)

11. Letournel, G., Bugeau, A., Ta, V.T., Domenger, J.P.: Face de-identification with expressions preservation. In: 2015 IEEE International Conference on Image Processing (ICIP), pp. 4366–4370. IEEE (2015)
12. Lin, J., Duan, L.-Y., Huang, Y., Luo, S., Huang, T., Gao, W.: Rate-adaptive compact fisher codes for mobile visual search. IEEE Signal Process. Lett. **21**(2), 195–198 (2014)
13. Liu, Z., Luo, P., Wang, X., Tang, X.: Deep learning face attributes in the wild. In: Proceedings of International Conference on Computer Vision (ICCV) (2015)
14. Lou, Y., et al.: Compact deep invariant descriptors for video retrieval. In: Data Compression Conference (DCC), pp. 420–429, April 2017
15. Lowe, D.G.: Distinctive image features from scale-invariant keypoints. Int. J. Comput. Vis. **60**(2), 91–110 (2004)
16. Mahajan, S., Chen, L.J., Tsai, T.C.: SwapItUP: a face swap application for privacy protection. In: 2017 IEEE 31st International Conference on Advanced Information Networking and Applications (AINA), pp. 46–50. IEEE (2017)
17. Meng, L., Sun, Z., Collado, O.T.: Efficient approach to de-identifying faces in videos. IET Sig. Process. **11**(9), 1039–1045 (2017)
18. Nakashima, Y., Babaguchi, N., Fan, J.: Intended human object detection for automatically protecting privacy in mobile video surveillance. Multimed. Syst. **18**(2), 157–173 (2012)
19. Natsume, R., Yatagawa, T., Morishima, S.: RSGAN: face swapping and editing using face and hair representation in latent spaces. arXiv preprint arXiv:1804.03447 (2018)
20. Newton, E.M., Sweeney, L., Malin, B.: Preserving privacy by de-identifying face images. IEEE Trans. Knowl. Data Eng. **17**(2), 232–243 (2005)
21. Nirkin, Y., Masi, I., Tuan, A.T., Hassner, T., Medioni, G.: On face segmentation, face swapping, and face perception. In: 2018 13th IEEE International Conference on Automatic Face & Gesture Recognition, FG 2018, pp. 98–105. IEEE (2018)
22. Nishiyama, M., Takeshima, H., Shotton, J., Kozakaya, T., Yamaguchi, O.: Facial deblur inference to improve recognition of blurred faces. In: IEEE Conference on Computer Vision and Pattern Recognition, CVPR 2009, pp. 1115–1122. IEEE (2009)
23. Padilla-López, J.R., Chaaraoui, A.A., Flórez-Revuelta, F.: Visual privacy protection methods: a survey. Expert. Syst. Appl. **42**(9), 4177–4195 (2015)
24. Philbin, J., Chum, O., Isard, M., Sivic, J., Zisserman, A.: Object retrieval with large vocabularies and fast spatial matching. In: Proceedings of the IEEE Conference on Computer Vision and Pattern Recognition (2007)
25. Radford, A., Metz, L., Chintala, S.: Unsupervised representation learning with deep convolutional generative adversarial networks. CoRR, abs/1511.06434 (2015)
26. Saini, M., Atrey, P.K., Mehrotra, S., Kankanhalli, M.: W3-privacy: understanding what, when, and where inference channels in multi-camera surveillance video. Multimed. Tools Appl. **68**(1), 135–158 (2014)
27. Simonyan, K., Zisserman, A.: Very deep convolutional networks for large-scale image recognition. CoRR, abs/1409.1556 (2014)
28. Zhang, K., Zhang, Z., Li, Z., Qiao, Y.: Joint face detection and alignment using multitask cascaded convolutional networks. IEEE Sig. Process. Lett. **23**(10), 1499–1503 (2016)
29. Zhang, Y., Zheng, L., Thing, V.L.: Automated face swapping and its detection. In: 2017 IEEE 2nd International Conference on Signal and Image Processing (ICSIP), pp. 15–19. IEEE (2017)

Exploring the Impact of Training Data Bias on Automatic Generation of Video Captions

Alan F. Smeaton[✉], Yvette Graham, Kevin McGuinness, Noel E. O'Connor, Seán Quinn, and Eric Arazo Sanchez

Insight Centre for Data Analytics, Dublin City University, Dublin 9, Ireland
`alan.smeaton@dcu.ie`

Abstract. A major issue in machine learning is availability of training data. While this historically referred to the availability of a sufficient volume of training data, recently this has shifted to the availability of sufficient unbiased training data. In this paper we focus on the effect of training data bias on an emerging multimedia application, the automatic captioning of short video clips. We use subsets of the same training data to generate different models for video captioning using the same machine learning technique and we evaluate the performances of different training data subsets using a well-known video caption benchmark, TRECVid. We train using the MSR-VTT video-caption pairs and we prune this to reduce and make the set of captions describing a video more homogeneously similar, or more diverse, or we prune randomly. We then assess the effectiveness of caption-generating trained with these variations using automatic metrics as well as direct assessment by human assessors. Our findings are preliminary and show that randomly pruning captions from the training data yields the worst performance and that pruning to make the data more homogeneous, or diverse, does improve performance slightly when compared to random. Our work points to the need for more training data, both more video clips but, more importantly, more captions for those videos.

Keywords: Video-to-language · Video captioning
Video understanding · Semantic similarity

1 Introduction

Machine learning has now become the foundation which supports most kinds of automatic multimedia analysis and description. It is premised on using large-enough collections of training data, which might be labelled images, or captioned videos, or spoken audio with text transcriptions. This training data is used to train models of the analysis or description process and these models are used to analyse new and unseen multimedia data, thus automating the process.

I. Kompatsiaris et al. (Eds.): MMM 2019, LNCS 11295, pp. 178–190, 2019.
https://doi.org/10.1007/978-3-030-05710-7_15

Machine learning algorithms used to train the automatic process are improving with a current concentration on deep learning and a recent focus on multimodal learning, i.e. learning from multiple sources [5]. However, there is a veritable zoo of algorithmic techniques and possible approaches available [11] as well as a constant stream of new emerging ideas. It is reasonable to say that choosing the best machine learning algorithm from those available requires significant prior knowledge making the process akin to a "black art" with little underlying understanding of why different approaches work better in different applications, let alone a unified theory. Another issue is training data. While this used to refer to the availability of a sufficient *volume* of training data, recently this has shifted to the availability of sufficient *unbiased* training data, or rather an awareness of existing biases within training data.

In this paper we focus on the effect of training data bias on an emerging multimedia application, the automatic captioning of short video clips. We use variations of the same training data to generate different models for video captioning using the same machine learning techniques and we evaluate the performance of different training sets using the TRECVid benchmark.

This paper is organised as follows. Section 2 introduces related work covering data bias and training data, techniques used for automatic video captioning, and related work focused on data bias in training data for video captioning. Section 3 describes our experimental setup, training and test data used, the captioning models selected, and the metrics to assess caption quality. Section 4 presents our experimental results, and an analysis of those results is in the concluding section.

2 Related Work

2.1 Data Bias and Training Data

Bias exists in all elements of society, and in almost all data we have gathered. These biases are both latent and overt and influence the things we see, hear and do [4]. Biases are an intrinsic part of our society, and always have been, but so long as we are aware of such biases we can compensate and allow for them when we make decisions based on such biased data.

The data gathered around our online activities, our interactions with the web and its content and our interactions through social media is particularly prone to including biases. This is because much of our online activity is self re-enforcing, building on similarity and overlap by, for example, recommending products or services which we are likely to use because we use similar ones, or forming social groups where homogeneity rather than diversity is the norm.

Different forms of bias exist in our online data covering social and cultural aspects like gender, age, race, social standing, ethnicity as well as algorithmic bias covering aspects like sampling and presentation. While this may be undesirable as a general point, it becomes particularly problematic when we then use data derived from our online interactions, as a driver for some algorithmic process. In [4] the author points out that recommending labels or tags for images or videos is an extreme example of algorithmic bias when it is based on similarity with already tagged images or videos and/or used in collaborative filtering. In such a case, which is widespread, there is no novelty, no diversity, no and enlarging of the tag set, and this is a point we shall return to later.

2.2   Automatic Video Captioning: Video-to-text

Automatic video captioning or video description is a task whereby a natural language description of a video clip is generated which describes video content in some way. It is a natural evolution of the task of automatic image or video *tagging* which has seen huge improvement within the last few years to the extent that automatic techniques now replace manual tagging on a web-scale.

Video description or captioning has many useful applications including uses in robotics, assistive technologies, search and summarisation, and more. But video, or even image, description is extremely difficult because images and videos are so information-rich that reducing their content to a single caption or sentence is always going to fall short of capturing the original content with all its nuances. Issues of vocabulary usage, interpretation, bias from our background culture or current task or context, all contribute to it being almost impossible to get a universally agreed caption or description for a given video or image.

Broadly speaking, there are three approaches to automatic image and video captioning. The first, called *pipelined*, aims to recognise specific objects and actions in the images/videos and uses a generative model to create captions. This has the advantage that it builds on object/action detection and recognition whose quality is now quite good, and it can generate new captions not seen in the training data. The second approach involves projecting captions and videos from a training set into a common representation or space and *finding the closest existing video* to the target and using its caption. The disadvantage of this approach is that it cannot *create* new captions, it just re-uses existing ones. The third approach, which has become popular, is an *end-to-end solution*. It uses a pre-trained CNN such as VGG16, Inception or ResNet, to extract a representation and using this as input to a RNN-based caption generator. This approach can generate novel captions but it requires plentiful training data.

A good description of recent work in video description, including available training material and evaluation metrics, can be found in [1]. While this is a good survey, there is even more recent work appearing in the literature such as the convolutional image captioning work in [2], where they do away with the LSTM decoder altogether and show that you can generate good captions just using temporal convolutions. Other recent work focuses on dense video captioning, captioning longer videos with many captions, aiming to generate text descriptions for all events in an untrimmed video [21] as opposed to other work which sets out to caption short video clips of just a few seconds duration.

2.3   Data Bias in Video Captioning

Given the recognised existence of bias in almost all our data, and the dependence on training data for training machine learning algorithms, it is inevitable that biases will affect the performance of video captioning systems. This is especially so considering the open nature of the domain of video captioning where almost anything can be captioned, yet very little work has been reported on assessing the impact of data bias on the quality of generated captions.

Much of the work which tries to map video clips to natural language and vice-versa, sets out to map both language (text) and images (or videos) to a common space, such as in [16]. When working with such an approach it is important that the multimedia artifacts, whether images/videos or text fragments (captions) mapped into a common space are distinct and that there is "distance" between them. Separating the artifacts is essential to allow whatever kind of content-based operation is being developed. This also reveals that biases in the data, among any sets of objects, will yield clusters of similar objects in the common space and this will be unhelpful and so achieving diversity among the objects in the common space is important, a point highlighted in [12].

More recent work reported in [17] highlighted the difficulties in evaluating the quality of multiple captions for the same video. In an attempt to achieve diversity and coherence in training data in their work, the authors removed outlier captions from the MSR-VTT training dataset by using SenseEmbed, a method to obtain a representation of individual word *senses* [10] which allowed them to model different senses of polysemous words. Outlier captions are those whose semantic similarity among the set of captions for a single video clip make them different from the rest of the captions, or far removed from a centroid. Individual word sense embeddings are combined to create a global similarity between captions that is used to determine outliers, which are then pruned. The authors also added new captions that mix-and-match among subject, object and predicate in the original captions. Using the MSR-VTT training data [20], results indicate small improvements in generated captions when outlier captions are removed from the training data.

In this paper we take the work in [17] further by judiciously removing some captions from the training data, not just because they may be outliers but because they may help improve overall diversity or homogeneity of the training data.

3   Experimental Setup

Figure 1 outlines our experimental procedure. We start with a collection of 10,000 short videos (1) from the MSR-VTT collection [20]. Each has been manually captioned 20 times with a sentence descriptor (2) some of which may be duplicates. For each video, we computed inter-caption semantic similarity (190 pair-wise caption similarity computations per video) using the STS measure of semantic similarity described in [9,13]. STS similarities is based on distributional similarity and Latent Semantic Analysis (LSA) complemented with semantic relations extracted from WordNet. We use the STS similarity values to prune captions from each set of 20 captions per video.

Our first approach to pruning captions is to randomly remove them, reducing the 200,000 to about 160,000 overall, shown as step (5) in the diagram with

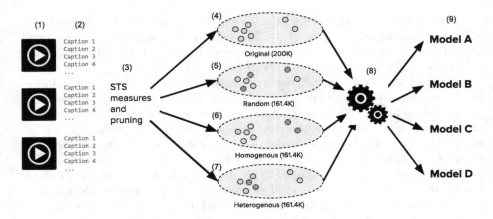

Fig. 1. Outline of experimental setup (Color figure online)

the red crosses indicating captions which are removed. A second approach we take is to remove captions which are semantically distinct from the set of other captions, resulting in a more homogeneous set of captions with stronger overall inter-caption similarity. We refer to this strategy as "homogeneous", shown as step (6). The inverse of this is to remove captions that are already semantically similar to other captions in the set of captions for a single video, an approach we refer to as generating a more "heterogeneous" collection of captions (step 7).

We use the four variations of the MSR-VTT training data [20], derived from the full collection and described in Sect. 4.1 – the full collection, randomly pruned collection, homogeneously pruned collection and heterogeneously pruned collection – to each train an individual model for caption generation (8), which in turn generates 4 models referred to as A, B, C, and D.

3.1   Training Data for Video Captions

There is already a host of training data available for generating video captions and currently the best source of information on this is in [1]. This presents details of publicly-available training datasets, covering MSVD, MPII Cooking, YouCook, TACoS, TACos-MLevel, MPII-MD, M-VAD, MSR-VTT, Charades, VTW and ActyNet Cap. These vary from 20,000 videos of 849 h duration (ActyNet CAP) to just 2.3 h (YouCook).

The data we use in this paper is from the Microsoft Research Video to Text (MSR-VTT) challenge [20] a large-scale video benchmark. The videos are of 41.2 h duration in total, each clip annotated with 20 natural sentences by 1,327 AMT workers forming the groundtruth for captions.

3.2   Video Caption Generation

To evaluate how the training data variations affect video captioning, we used an end-to-end stable model that generates natural language descriptions of short video clips from training data. We selected the S2VT model from [19] that consists of a stack of two LSTMs, one to encode the frames and another that uses the output of the first LSTM to generate a natural language caption. Both LSTMs have 1,000 hidden units. This is a sequence-to-sequence model that generates a variable length sequence that corresponds to the caption, given a video with a variable number of frames.

Video frames are encoded using VGG16 pre-trained on ImageNet with weights fixed during training. The resulting 4096D representation from $fc7$ (after the ReLU) are projected to 500D for input to the first LSTM, which encodes multiple frame representations into a single representation that captures the visual and temporal information from the clip. During this stage the output of the second LSTM is ignored. The output of the first LSTM is passed to the second LSTM together with a "beginning of sentence" tag to generate the first word of the caption. Subsequent words are generated by concatenating the previous predictions to the output of the first LSTM until the "end of sentence" tag is predicted.

To obtain the words we project the output of the second LSTM to a 22,939D vector. We built the vocabulary from the captions in MSR-VTT [20] without any pre-processing of the words. We then apply a softmax to find the predicted word in each step. The model is trained to minimise the cross entropy between the predicted words and the expected output using SGD on the MSR-VTT training set. We trained for 25,000 iterations, where an iteration consists of a batch of 32 videos. We sub-sample 1 in 10 frames to accelerate computation.

3.3 Evaluating Quality of Automatic Video Captions •

Evaluating the performance of automatic captioning in a way that balances accuracy, reliability and reproducibility is a challenge that may be irreconcilable. Current approaches assume there is a collection of video clips with a reference or gold standard caption against which to compare, yet we know there can be many ways to describe a video so who is to know what is and is not correct? As a default, most researchers work with a reference caption and use measures including BLEU, METEOR, or CIDEr to compare automatic vs manual captions but this is an active area of research and there are no universally agreed metrics.

BLEU has been used in machine translation to evaluate the quality of generated text. It approximates human judgement and measures the fraction of N-grams (up to 4-gram, so BLEU1, BLEU2, BLEU3 and BLEU4) in common between target text and a human-produced reference. BLEU's disadvantage is that it operates at a corpus level and is less reliable for comparisons among short, single-sentence captions. METEOR computes unigram precision and recall, extending exact word matches to include similar words based on WordNet synonyms and stemmed tokens. It is based on the harmonic mean of unigram precision and recall, with recall weighted higher than precision and like BLEU it also operates at a corpus level rather than at a set of independent video captions. CIDEr computes the TF-IDF (term frequency inverse document frequency) for each n-gram of length 1 to 4 and is shown to agree well with human judgement.

A number of benchmarks have emerged in recent years to assess and compare approaches to video caption generation and one of those is the VTT track in TRECVid in 2016 and 2017 [18]. In the 2017 edition [3], 13 groups participated and submitted sets of results including ourselves [15] and we re-used the infrastructure from that in the work reported here.

In the TRECVid 2017 VTT task, the STS measure [9], mentioned earlier and used by in this work to determine semantic outlier captions among the 20 manual captions assigned to each video in the MSR-VTT collection, was used to measure the similarity between captions submitted by participants and a manual reference. We include mention of STS as an evaluation measure but do not use this as a measure; however, we do use it to compute similarity among manual captions for the same video.

The final evaluation metric is known as direct assessment (DA) and it brings human assessment using Amazon Mechanical Turk (AMT) into the evaluation by crowdsourcing how well a given caption describes its corresponding video. The metric is described in [7] and includes a mechanism for quality control of the ratings provided by AMT workers via automatic degradation of the quality of some manual captions hidden within AMT HITs (Human Intelligence Tasks). In this way, DA produces a rating of the reliability of each human assessor and filters out any unreliable human assessors prior to producing evaluation results. It provides a reliable way to distinguish genuine human assessment from attempts to game the system by augmenting the training data similar to what was done in [17] but not to increase the amount of training data but to validate the accuracy of the AMT workers. A human assessor is required to rate each caption on a [0..100] rating scale and the ratings are micro-averaged per caption before computing the overall average for the system (called RAW DA). The average DA score per system is also computed after standardisation per individual crowdsourced worker's mean and standard deviation score (called Z-score).

In a recent analysis of metrics for measuring the quality of image captions [14], the authors introduced a variation of Word Mover's Distance (WMD) and compared this against the other "standard" metrics but not direct assessment, concluding that they are each significantly different to each other. Work described in [1] also examined different evaluation metrics and concluded that evaluation is more reliable when more reference captions are available to compare against, and that CIDEr and METEOR seem to work best in such situations.

To test this we took system rankings from 13 participants in the TRECVid 2017 VTT task according to the CIDEr, METEOR, BLEU, STS and DA metrics presented in [3] and calculated Spearman's correlation among pairs of rankings. The results (Fig. 2) show good agreement among the automatic metrics (CIDEr, METEOR and BLEU) with STS and DA being somewhat different both from each other and from the automatic systems, but with a lowest correlation of 0.736 there is still reasonable agreement among all metrics. What all this means in terms of evaluation metrics for this work is that we should consider all metrics when assessing the performance of a video caption generation system.

	CIDEr	METEOR	BLEU	STS	DA
CIDEr	1.000	0.819	0.923	0.868	0.857
METEOR	0.819	1.000	0.808	0.879	0.736
BLEU	0.923	0.808	1.000	0.835	0.736
STS	0.868	0.879	0.835	1.000	0.797
DA	0.857	0.736	0.736	0.797	1.000

Fig. 2. Metric correlations for evaluating video caption system performance in [3].

4   Experimental Results

4.1   Pruning the Training Data

Two strategies were developed to prune captions from our training data based on the semantic text similarity (ground) measure described in [13]. This method takes two segments of text and returns a score in the range [0..1], representing how similar the pieces of text are in their semantic meaning. Our training set contained 10,000 videos with 20 human captions per video. To implement our pruning of captions, we first calculated inter-caption STS scores for all caption pairings on each video. This resulted in 190 inter-caption similarity scores per video. We denote the inter-caption similarity between a caption A and caption B as as $sim(A, B)$. We then computed average similarity scores for each caption by averaging the 19 inter-caption scores for that caption. We denote the average inter-caption similarity for a caption A as $avgsim(A)$. We computed summary statistics on the entire populations of $avgsim$ and $sim(A, B)$ scores to allow us to establish appropriate thresholds for our pruning as outlined in the following.

Homogeneous Pruned Training Dataset. The homogeneous pruning strategy aimed to remove captions which were highly dissimilar to the other captions for a given video, thus removing the "outlier" captions in our training data. There are two requirements which must be met for caption X to be pruned under this strategy:

1. $avgsim(X)$ must be below the 30th percentile for our total population of $avgsim$ scorings. For the dataset used in this experiment the 30th percentile $avgsim$ threshold was 0.36099.

2. There must not exist any caption Y for the same video as X where $sim(X, Y)$ is greater than the 80th percentile for our total population of $sim(A, B)$ scorings. For the dataset used in this experiment the 80th percentile $sim(A, B)$ threshold was 0.610.

Requirement 1 asserts that caption X can be considered dissimilar to all the other captions for the video, while requirement 2 asserts that there is no other caption Y present for this video which is highly similar to this caption X. This strategy resulted in the pruning of 38,379 captions.

Heterogeneous Pruned Training Dataset. The heterogeneous pruning strategy aimed to reduce the size of clusters of captions which were highly similar to each other, thus enforcing greater diversity in our training data. Similar to the threshold used in our homogeneous pruning we define two captions X and Y to be highly similar or "neighbours" if $sim(X, Y)$ is greater than the 80th percentile for our total population of $sim(A, B)$ scorings, which for our dataset is 0.610. The procedure for heterogeneous pruning is as follows:

1. For each video rank the captions using the number of neighbours they have.
2. If the highest neighbour count is greater than 3, prune this caption and recalculate neighbour counts.
3. Continue pruning the caption with highest neighbour count until no caption has more than 3 neighbours.

This resulted in the pruning of 38,816 captions.

Random Pruned Training Dataset. Here we randomly chose 38,598 captions to be pruned from across the 10,000 videos. This is the average of the number pruned by heterogeneous and homogeneous strategies.

In terms of overall changes to the data as a result of pruning we did not compute whether the overall vocabulary has reduced and if so by how much. In terms of data availability, the original MSR-VTT-10k dataset is openly available and our prunings of this according to homogeneous, heterogeneous and random strategies, is available at https://github.com/squinn95/MMM_2018_Files/.

4.2   Performance Figures for Generating Video Captions

Tables 1 and 2 show results using the automatic metrics (BLEU1, 2, 3, 4, METEOR, and CIDEr) computed using the code released with the Microsoft COCO Evaluation Server [6] and the direct assessment (DA) evaluation for both the MSR-VTT and the TRECVid 2017 collections. When computing DA, we also compute DA scores for the manual (human) captions for both collections as reference points. In the case of TRECVid 2017 (Table 2) we reproduce the official DA values for the TRECVid assessment of human captions as well as the best-performing of the official submissions.

Table 1. Results for MSR-VTT17 videos using 4 different MSR-VTT training datasets

| | BLEU1 | BLEU2 | BLEU3 | BLEU4 | METEOR | CIDEr | DA | |
							Av	z
HOM	75.0	57.0	40.8	27.6	20.7	18.6	60.2	−0.066
DIV	73.7	56.2	40.2	26.8	20.2	16.3	59.1	−0.090
RAND	75.1	57.0	40.6	27.2	20.9	18.9	58.8	−0.110
ALL	73.5	57.2	41.9	29.2	20.7	18.0	57.8	−0.131
Human captions							88.6	0.690

Table 2. Results for TRECVID17 videos trained using 4 different MSR-VTT training datasets, manual (human) annotation evaluation and manual (human) and best automatic results from TRECVid 2017[3]

| | BLEU1 | BLEU2 | BLEU3 | BLEU4 | METEOR | CIDEr | DA | |
							Av	z
HOM	24.3	11.4	5.5	2.8	8.4	15.6	49.7	−0.151
DIV	22.3	9.9	4.6	2.1	8.1	13.8	48.5	−0.180
RAND	24.6	11.0	5.2	2.3	8.3	14.3	47.2	−0.205
ALL	24.5	11.1	5.2	2.5	8.6	16.1	50.1	−0.150
Human captions							82.8	0.723
TRECVid 2017 Human captions							87.1	0.782
TRECVid 2017 Best automatic performance (RUC_CMU)							62.2	0.119

In terms of human evaluation, raw DA scores for all runs range from 57.8 to 60.2% for the MSR-VTT dataset, with HOMogeneous training achieving highest absolute DA score, and from 47.2 to 50.1% for the TRECVid dataset, with training on ALL data achieving the highest DA score overall.

DA scores achieved by competing runs are close for all runs and tests for statistical significance should be carried out before concluding that differences in performance are not likely to occur simply by chance. We therefore carry out Wilcoxon rank-sum test for DA scores for both sets of test data. In the case of both datasets, as expected, all runs were significantly lower than ratings achieved by human captions. Competing runs also showed no significance difference in performance with the single exception of ALL on the TRECVid test set achieving a significantly higher DA score compared to that of RAND.

In contrast in terms of metric scores, competing runs showed mixed results in terms of ordering of performances. For the TRECVid-tested data collection BLEU indicates best performance for RAND and HOM, while ALL achieves best performance according to Meteor and CIDEr. On the MSR-VTT dataset, it is ALL that achieves best performance according to Meteor and CIDEr while BLEU indicates top performance for RAND. Although testing for statistical significant differences in BLEU and other metric scores is common in Machine Translation evaluation using Bootstrap resampling or Approximate Randomization for example [8], we do not report these here as the accuracy of such methods has not as yet been tested for the purpose of video captioning.

The best-performing automatic submission for the DA metric in TRECVid on TRECVid17 data was from Renmin University of China and Carnegie Mellon University (RUC_CMU) (Table 2) with DA values of Av = 62.2, z = −0.119. This is higher than the highest of our automatic systems, which had Av = 50.1, z= −0.150. While we would have liked to work with a better performing caption generation system and ours is not as good as the best possible but it was sufficient to allow us to experiment with different sets of training data and evaluate their effectiveness.

The DA values for our assessment of human captions in TRECVid 2017 are lower than the official TRECVid assessment of the same (Av 82.8 vs 87.1) but variance in DA scores from different sets of Mechanical Turk workers are to be expected. Additionally, there is a pool of human captions for each video in this dataset and human captions were chosen at random for each evaluation. Either way, as expected, human captions are significantly better than all other runs in each dataset, showing that automatic systems still need improvement.

5   Analysis and Conclusions

We expected that improving diversity in training data would achieve better performance in the resulting caption generation, as advocated in [12] as opposed to other work to improve the quality of training data which simply removed outliers in [17] for example. In practice we did not find this and like the work in [17] the improvements are minor for pruned datasets. Based only on statistical significance, all system variations are roughly the same performance with the exception that RAND performs significantly worse than ALL on the TRECVid dataset. It is possible that given a larger training set this difference (RAND and ALL) might increase and distinguish RAND from all other runs, but it could just as easily be that given a larger test set the difference disappears. Also, the biases we address here are based on semantic similarity between captions which is a limited form of bias and doesn't address biases as a result of gender, ethnicity, etc. which will require digging deeper into the semantics of homogeneity and diversity criteria.

With most of the work in machine learning applications there is a seemingly insatiable desire for more and better training data, and in our case this means more video clips, and increased volumes of manual captions for each clip. The availability of video clips is not a problem but we are unlikely to realise increases in manual captioning of these videos with the approaches used to date. Instead we could look at pre-processing existing manual captions to generate variations for the videos we already have using data augmentation techniques like synonym substitution and others used as part of the STS measure. This forms part of our planned future work.

Acknowledgements. This work is supported by Science Foundation Ireland under grant numbers 12/RC/2289 and 15/SIRG/3283.

References

1. Aafaq, N., Gilani, S.Z., Liu, W., Mian, A.: Video description: a survey of methods, datasets and evaluation metrics. arXiv preprint arXiv:1806.00186 (2018)
2. Aneja, J., Deshpande, A., Schwing, A.G.: Convolutional image captioning. In: Computer Vision and Pattern Recognition (CVPR), June 2018
3. Awad, G., et al.: TRECVID 2017: evaluating ad-hoc and instance video search, events detection, video captioning and hyperlinking. In: Proceedings of TRECVID 2017. NIST (2017)
4. Baeza-Yates, R.: Bias on the web. Commun. ACM **61**(6), 54–61 (2018)
5. Baltrušaitis, T., Ahuja, C., Morency, L.P.: Multimodal machine learning: a survey and taxonomy. IEEE Trans. Pattern Anal. Mach. Intell. (Early Access) (2018). https://doi.org/10.1109/TPAMI.2018.2798607
6. Chen, X., et al.: Microsoft COCO captions: data collection and evaluation server. CoRR, abs/1504.00325 (2015)
7. Graham, Y., Awad, G., Smeaton, A.: Evaluation of automatic video captioning using direct assessment. CoRR, abs/1710.10586 (2017)
8. Graham, Y., Mathur, N., Baldwin, T.: Randomized significance tests in machine translation. In: ACL 2014 Workshop on Statistical Machine Translation, pp. 266–274. Association for Computational Linguistics (2014)
9. Han, L., Kashyap, A., Finin, T., Mayfield, J., Weese, J.: UMBC EBIQUITY-CORE: semantic textual similarity systems. Joint. Conf. Lex. Comput. Semant. **1**, 44–52 (2013)
10. Iacobacci, I., Pilehvar, M.T., Navigli, R.: SensEmbed: learning sense embeddings for word and relational similarity. In: Proceedings of ACL, pp. 95–105 (2015)
11. Jordan, M.I., Mitchell, T.M.: Machine learning: trends, perspectives, and prospects. Science **349**(6245), 255–260 (2015)
12. Karpathy, A.: Connecting images and natural language. Ph.D. thesis, Stanford University, August 2016
13. Kashyap, A., et al.: Robust semantic text similarity using LSA, machine learning, and linguistic resources. Lang. Resour. Eval. **50**(1), 125–161 (2016)
14. Kilickaya, M., Erdem, A., Ikizler-Cinbis, N., Erdem, E.: Re-evaluating automatic metrics for image captioning. In: Proceedings of EACL, April 2017
15. Marsden, M., et al.: Dublin City University and partners' participation in the INS and VTT tracks at TRECVid 2016. In: Proceedings of TREVid, NIST, Gaithersburg, MD, USA (2016)
16. Pan, Y., Mei, T., Yao, T., Li, H., Rui, Y.: Jointly modeling embedding and translation to bridge video and language. In: Computer Vision and Pattern Recognition (CVPR), pp. 4594–4602 (2016)
17. Pérez-Mayos, L., Sukno, F.M., Wanner, L.: Improving the quality of video-to-language models by optimizing annotation of the training material. In: Schoeffmann, K., et al. (eds.) MMM 2018. LNCS, vol. 10704, pp. 279–290. Springer, Cham (2018). https://doi.org/10.1007/978-3-319-73603-7_23
18. Smeaton, A.F., Over, P., Kraaij, W.: Evaluation campaigns and TRECVid. In: MIR 2006: International Workshop on Multimedia Information Retrieval, pp. 321–330 (2006)

19. Venugopalan, S., Rohrbach, M., Donahue, J., Mooney, R., Darrell, T., Saenko, K.: Sequence to sequence – video to text. In: International Conference on Computer Vision (ICCV) (2015)
20. Xu, J., Mei, T., Yao, T., Rui, Y.: MSR-VTT: a large video description dataset for bridging video and language. In: Computer Vision and Pattern Recognition (CVPR), pp. 5288–5296, June 2016
21. Zhou, L., Zhou, Y., Corso, J.J., Socher, R., Xiong, C.: End-to-end dense video captioning with masked transformer. In: Computer Vision and Pattern Recognition (CVPR), June 2018

Fashion Police: Towards Semantic Indexing of Clothing Information in Surveillance Data

Owen Corrigan(✉)[iD] and Suzanne Little[iD]

The Insight Centre for Data Analytics, Dublin City University, Dublin, Ireland
{owen.corrigan,suzanne.little}@dcu.ie

Abstract. Indexing and retrieval of clothing based on style, similarity and colour has been extensively studied in the field of fashion with good results. However, retrieval of real-world clothing examples based on witness descriptions is of great interest in for security and law enforcement applications. Manually searching databases or CCTV footage to identify matching examples is time consuming and ineffective. Therefore we propose using machine learning to automatically index video footage based on general clothing types and evaluate the performance using existing public datasets. The challenge is that these datasets are highly sanitised with clean backgrounds and front-facing examples and are insufficient for training detectors and classifiers for real-world video footage. In this paper we highlight the deficiencies of using these datasets for security applications and propose a methodology for collecting a new dataset, as well as examining several ethical issues.

1 Introduction

In recent years (2012–2018), policing organisations in western europe have been forced to adapt to emerging factors. The first, and perhaps the most visible of these is a rise in the number of terrorist attacks [15,29]. Police have adapted in several ways, including community based policing [13] and inter-agency partnerships [3]. It is difficult to say whether these initiatives have been effective, as there is a lack of evaluation research on counter-terrorism interventions [20].

Secondly, Police have also been made more effective by a variety of Information Technology (IT) initiatives. Among these is the deployment of Surveillance Video (also known as CCTV) by city councils and private companies. This can be useful for solving crimes, as police can request footage in areas where a crime may have been committed. However, CCTV produces large amounts of data, which generally requires manual reviewing.

Thirdly, there has been a dramatic increase in the performance of machine learning algorithms in recent years. Machine learning is the discipline of giving computers the ability to "learn", without having been explicitly programmed. This has been particularly successful in the domain of analysing multimedia, with

I. Kompatsiaris et al. (Eds.): MMM 2019, LNCS 11295, pp. 191–201, 2019.
https://doi.org/10.1007/978-3-030-05710-7_16

tasks such as image classification [14], instance segmentation, object detection [6] and speech detection [8] becoming more accurate.

This performance improvement is both in terms of accuracy of predictions and speed of execution. These advancements have enabled new technologies to become rapidly embedded into daily life with features such as Facebook's facial recognition for face tagging, Google's photo search by concept and Apples IPhone assistant Siri. Clearly, performance has reached a threshold which has made it acceptable to be used by the general public. Along with this, there is now an awareness among the public of the impact of machine learning, with one study finding that 70% of young people in the United Kingdom "had seen or heard something about programmes which tailor web content based on browsing behaviour; voice recognition computers; facial recognition computers used in policing; and driverless vehicles" [9].

Given these three factors, a natural opportunity has arisen: to use machine learning techniques paired with the data generated from IT systems to assist police organisations to adapt to the challenge of counter-terrorism. In fact, several machine learning and statistical based products are currently deployed in other law enforcement contexts. These include an application to assess the likelihood of someone on probation from re-offending [26] and make decisions about custody arrangements [23]. There are also a number of start ups offering surveillance cameras with integrated deep learning capabilities [28].

This paper aims to bridge the gap between policing policy and machine learning practitioners, with a special focus on the application of indexing and searching videos by clothing. We have chosen a hypothetical application based on clothing search as it will be relevant to the issues we will raise shortly.

In Sect. 2 we briefly review the recent advancements in the state of machine learning. We will then describe the task of clothes classification in Sect. 3. This will serve as a typical example of a machine learning task in video surveillance. We will also give an overview of the publicly available datasets for surveillance and clothes detection tasks. We will highlight several deficiencies in currently existing datasets, which will motivate the discussion of gathering a new dataset in Sect. 3.3. We also note that if such a system were to be deployed, it would raise some ethical questions. We outline some of these in Sect. 4.

2   A Brief Summary of Recent Advances in Machine Learning

In this section we will outline a very brief summary of recent advances in machine learning. As a full description of this topic is out of the scope of this paper, we recommend [7, 16] for a more comprehensive view. We begin by describing four research tasks related to Object Recognition in images, in increasing order of difficulty.

Image Classification. The objective of this task is to take an image and to classify it into one of a set of predetermined labels. For example, this might be cats, dogs, types of food, etc. This task will assign a single class for the entire image. For an example dataset, see the MNIST database [5]

Image Localisation. Again, we classify an image into one of set of categories. The difference is that we also predict a bounding box in which the object appears. The mentioned ImageNet database contains these labels [14].

Object Detection. In this task our aim is to detect multiple objects in a single image, and for each one determine the bounding box in which it is contained. This type of label can be found in the COCO dataset [17].

Instance Segmentation. This task is similar to object detection, but we refine the bounding box down to pixel level segmentation. These labels are found in the COCO dataset.

A visual guide to these tasks can be found in Fig. 1.

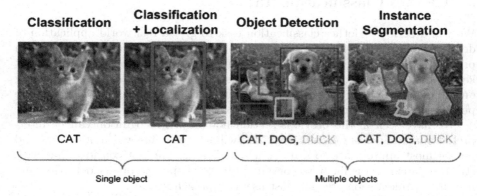

Fig. 1. Demonstration of the differences between different types of object recognition tasks. Downloaded from https://medium.com/comet-app/review-of-deep-learning-algorithms-for-object-detection-c1f3d437b852 in July 2018

In addition, we can also apply machine learning to video data sets. For example, we describe two tasks below.

Video Classification. Similar to a image classification task, we take a video and determine what class it belongs to. See the Youtube8M dataset [1] for an example.

Action Recognition. In this task, the goal is to predict what action is being performed in a video. For example, in the UCI101 dataset [27] some labels include "blowing candles","High Jump" and "Cricket Shot".

Applying deep learning techniques to video techniques is a more difficult problem. Although datasets do exist for this problem they have less individual data points (e.g. videos), while having far more information to process. The state of the art in images is more advanced, largely because there are larger data sets available for them. Even when there are large datasets for videos, they may not be as easy to label (in fact, it is harder to agree on what the labels should even be). For these reasons, in this paper we will examine our problem under both scenarios.

One common thread across all of the above tasks is that the state of the art performance in each of them is now held by methods based on deep learning [10–12,25]. This is a technique in which stacks of hidden layers (often convolutional layers in the case of image classification) are composed and trained to predict some target. This advance has been driven in recent years by a number of factors, including the availability of larger datasets, the ability to run models on a GPU and advancements in algorithms. Having briefly discussed some recent advancements in machine learning and their applications, we will now see how they can be used in a relevant practical application: clothes classification.

3   Clothes Classification Task

We will describe a clothes classification task to give a real world application of deep learning. We will first consider the problem in terms of an image recognition problem, and then extend it to video. To consider it an image problem, we extract key frames from the video and treat them as independent data points. Depending on the model of camera used, the frame rate may be anything between 1 image per 30 s or 1 frame per second.

We have seen in the previous section how object recognition can be interpreted in a number of different ways. We will now examine which of these would be the most appropriate to frame our question as. We first consider that each still from a camera is likely to contain multiple people. So object detection and instance segmentation are the most useful approaches.

Let us consider some potential applications of a clothes classifier that might be useful to the police

1. Searching for a known terrorist before they flee
2. Finding lost children, given a description of clothes
3. Given the description of clothes of someone who has committed a crime, search through a database at a given time to find evidence of this crime

Of the above examples, none require pixel-level segmentation. So of the four image related tasks discussed in Sect. 2, object detection is the most useful. Similarly, object detection in videos would be the most useful application of machine learning for videos.

3.1   Feasibility Considerations

To determine if such an application is possible, we must determine the rate at which videos can be processed to identify clothing features. In an early deep learning paper on object localisation, RCNN, object search took 5 s per image [6]. In later papers this latency has been reduced down $\frac{1}{5}$ of a second per image [24]. This has the potential to allow real time streaming of object detection. If an efficient streaming service were to be built and the frame rate of the cameras was one frame per second, we could even have one GPU service five individual cameras. This would enable a near real time location wide search of an area with minimal hardware.

We must also consider that even if the searching does not need to be performed live, the time taken to search must still be considered. For example, if we were told that a child wearing certain clothing went missing at some point 2 days ago, we would have to search a large amount of videos. Let us say for example, the child could have reasonably walked in an area large enough to contain 50 CCTV cameras. We would like to identify the child in as quick a time as possible. If we had a single GPU based machine, at a frame processing rate of 5 images per second, we would not finish an exhaustive search of the cameras for 240 h or 10 days. This would take too long to produce actionable information. This could be reduced if a policing unit were to use more than a single GPU machine, however the number of cameras could be larger or more than one such case be active at a time. Hence 5 frames per second may not be enough. Recent results have shown even higher throughput rates [10] and have more options for trade offs between processing time and predictive performance. We expect the trend of higher frames per second processing rates for object detection to continue for the foreseeable future.

We could also imagine a computing "fog", where each camera is equipped with a GPU [4]. The idea of a "fog" computing is in contrast to "cloud" computing, where the object detection processing takes place in the camera hardware. This will be made possible as GPU inference hardware becomes cheaper. However this is a trade off which will affect the security of the system, as it is easier to access the individual cameras, and more likely that some of them will break down.

In this section we have discussed the feasibility of designing a surveillance prediction system. However, we must consider another aspect: without training data, we will not be able to build such a system. In the next section we will examine publicly available datasets.

3.2   Available Datasets

Having outlined the problem of predicting the clothes that people are wearing, and some of the reasons for which police might want to do it, we will now describe some datasets which are available for that purpose.

For Clothes Classification there are several available datasets. We highlight some of these below.

– DeepFashion [18]. This is the most comprehensive and best labelled publicly available dataset. This dataset contains over 800,000 images. Each of these images is labelled with a category (from a choice of 50), multiple attributes (from a choice of 1000), and landmarks (e.g. left hem, right sleeve). It also contains pairs of images taken of the same item of clothing, one from social

media and one taken by the shop itself. This enables us to find a piece of clothing from a shop, based on an image from social media, for example.
- Fashion MNIST [30]. This is a dataset generated by Zalando, consisting of 70,000 greyscale images of size 28×28, with a choice of 10 categories. It is mostly of interest for testing machine learning algorithms.
- Fashion 10000 [19]. This paper contains 32000 images collected from Flickr across 470 fashion related categories.

We contrast this to publically available Video Surveillance Datasets.

- VIRAT Video Dataset [22]. This dataset consists of 23 event types (for example walking, running, getting into car, entering facility) with an average of between 10 to 1500 examples per event type. This dataset is made up of ground cameras and aerial vehicles.
- 3DPes [2]. This dataset consists of hundreds of videos of 200 people taken from multiple cameras. It also contains a 3D layout of the camera coverage. The labels allow us to do perform detection, people segmentation and people tracking tasks.

We note that there are a number of differences between these two types of datasets. For example, clothes and fashion datasets typically consist of images, whereas surveillance datasets typically consist of videos. We highlight some of these differences in Table 1.

Table 1. Characteristics of fashion datasets vs surveillance datasets

	Fashion	Video surveillance
Type	Photo	Video
Angle	Dynamic	Fixed
Source	Social media, retail websites	Video feeds
Datasets	Large, well annotated datasets available	Not many datasets available
Focus	Single person	Can be multiple people in shot, or none
Angle	Mostly from the front	From the top
Quality	High quality	Depends on camera. Often grainy, no colour

One important aspect to note is that there is far less data available in surveillance tasks than clothes tasks. This could be because it is easier to gather clothes data from the internet, and the difficulty of dealing with data privacy issues, which we shall discuss more in Sect. 4.1.

3.3 Proposals for Data Collection

In Sect. 3.2 we have examined some existing datasets for clothes classification and video surveillance. We have not been able to find a dataset which contains both videos and clothing annotations. In this section we will propose a collecting such a dataset.

This dataset should be composed of CCTV data. This could be acquired by partnering with a body such as a city council. An important choice to make initially is whether the dataset should be made public or not. Considering the nature of the collected data, it may be difficult to convince a stakeholder to release CCTV footage. However, if the dataset is made public, external researchers can compete to produce better models, which in turn improves the performance of the eventual application.

Another aspect that must be considered is whether to anonymise the faces in the dataset. An ideal dataset would have hundreds or thousands of hours of footage, with thousands of people walking in the shot. However, at this scale it would be difficult to get approval from all of them. One option might to anonymise the faces of the people in the video. However we must also remember that this may not be enough, as their clothes may be distinctive enough to de-anonymise them. We do not provide a solution to this problem, as laws and norms will vary region to region, however it is something to bear in mind.

How the data could be annotated depends on the task. We will consider some search tasks below, and then consider the annotations required. These have been selected to be useful for police agencies.

Keyword Search. The aim in this task would be to get a ranked list of images of people wearing a type of clothing based on searching for a list of pre-selected categories. For example, a search for "heavy coats". One aspect of this would be that we would like to suppress multiple images of the same person, so that multiple shots do not pollute the search results. The data here would contain multiple bounding boxes surrounding people, each associated with a category.

Reverse Image Search. The aim of this task would be to get a ranked list of images of people wearing clothes, which are similar to an image provided. An annotation scheme here might be to provide annotators with an example picture of clothes, and get them to select the image out of the dataset which most closely matches the image.

Text Search. In this task, the user enters some text to describe the clothes, and a list of the ranked best matches is returned. The difference between this task and the first task is that the text here is unconstrained. For example the user could enter "a blue heavy coat with a hood" and get a list of results. Similar to the reverse image search example this could be annotated by giving some pre-selected queries and asking the annotators to select the images which best match the query.

In all of the above cases, the annotation would require a lot of person-hours. One solution to this might be to outsource the labelling required, for example to Amazon's mechanical turk program. However, again due to data privacy issues related to this dataset, this may not be possible.

Having discussed practical issues regarding data collection and deployment of such a system, we will now discuss ethical issues related to it.

4   Ethics of Deep Learning and Surveillance Systems

In Sect. 1 we discussed the motivation for creating a machine learning clothes surveillance system. In Sect. 3.1 we have discussed the feasibility of creating such a system. We must now consider the social impact of such a system. It is important that such a system would not be deployed without public acceptance.

Of particular note, recently there has been a raised awareness of privacy issues (for example, see GDPR legislation) and the potential of machine learning algorithms to display bias [26]. In the following subsections we will outline some of these issues. We note that this is a growing field in artificial intelligence research, with topics such as accountability, transparency, explainability, bias, and fairness all topics of interest. We refer the reader to [21] for more information.

4.1   Data Protection

Managing data protection issues is a difficult topic. While collecting data, it would theoretically be possible, albeit difficult, to get consent from each participant. For example, by ensuring that everyone who walks through an area is asked to complete a brief survey. The data of those who opt out could be deleted from the collected database. Alternatively, signs could be put up alerting people to the fact that data is being collected.

To deploy the system live, however, it would be impossible to get people's consent to be filmed. We could argue that they give implicit consent by walking on roads with signage alerting them to CCTV cameras, but if the sign were to placed on a road which a person has no practical alternative to crossing, the person has effectively lost their ability to consent to being recorded.

One proposal would be to have the system off in most cases, and to only enable it if there is a special event, such as an imminent threat, or a missing child.

4.2   Bias

One obvious aspect of a person's identity, which is generally not obscured by blurring their face, is their gender. Often, you will be able to tell if a person is a man or a woman just based on their clothes. Similarly, it may be possible to identify someones religion, race or age.

It is possible to imagine a situation in which a deployed system is used in a way which could lead to mis-identification of a crime suspect for wearing similar clothing. In this case the clothes a person was wearing may have been be a proxy for gender, race or religion. In this hypothetical scenario, this system has introduced a dangerous bias. Avoiding this situation would be difficult, and perhaps the only mitigation strategy would be through training the human operator of the system.

4.3   Non Police Usage

Throughout this paper we have assumed that a deep learning surveillance system would be used responsibly by a policing organisation. We must also consider that such a system, once built, may be used by an organisation with less oversight. It could for example be produced by a commercial company, who then sell it on to shopping centres, marketing companies or directly to local councils, for example. Some examples of what might be considered unethical usage might include

- Searching areas to see if people an administrator knows personally is there currently
- Enforcing dress codes
- Sending marketing material to people based on what they are wearing

The only real protection against this is for people who have the ability to build such systems to refuse to work on them without some guarantees that the system will be deployed in an ethical manner.

5   Conclusions

In this paper we have investigated the possibility of using machine learning to detect clothes in surveillance videos. We have looked at publicly available datasets, and found that there is currently a lack of appropriate datasets to perform this task. We examined how an appropriate dataset might be collected. We also highlighted some privacy and ethical issues which might arise as a result of deploying such a system.

In future work we would like to expand on some of these issues, by collaborating with a broader range of stakeholders such as police officers and ethics researchers.

Acknowledgments. This project has received funding from the European Research Council (ERC) under the European Union's Horizon 2020 research and innovation programme (grant agreement number 700381) project ASGARD.

The Insight Centre for Data Analytics is supported by Science Foundation Ireland under Grant Number SFI/12/RC/2289.

References

1. Abu-El-Haija, S., et al.: YouTube-8M: a large-scale video classification benchmark. arXiv preprint arXiv:1609.08675 (2016)
2. Baltieri, D., Vezzani, R., Cucchiara, R.: 3DPeS: 3D people dataset for surveillance and forensics. In: Proceedings of the 2011 Joint ACM Workshop on Human Gesture and Behavior Understanding, pp. 59–64. ACM (2011)
3. Boer, M.D., Hillebrand, C., Nölke, A.: Legitimacy under pressure: the European web of counter-terrorism networks. JCMS: J. Common Market Stud. **46**(1), 101–124 (2008)

4. Bonomi, F., Milito, R., Zhu, J., Addepalli, S.: Fog computing and its role in the internet of things. In: Proceedings of the First Edition of the MCC Workshop on Mobile Cloud Computing, pp. 13–16. ACM (2012)
5. Deng, L.: The MNIST database of handwritten digit images for machine learning research [best of the web]. IEEE Signal Process. Mag. **29**(6), 141–142 (2012)
6. Girshick, R., Donahue, J., Darrell, T., Malik, J.: Rich feature hierarchies for accurate object detection and semantic segmentation. In: Proceedings of the IEEE Conference on Computer Vision and Pattern Recognition, pp. 580–587 (2014)
7. Goodfellow, I., Bengio, Y., Courville, A., Bengio, Y.: Deep Learning, vol. 1. MIT press, Cambridge (2016)
8. Graves, A., Fernández, S., Gomez, F., Schmidhuber, J.: Connectionist temporal classification: labelling unsegmented sequence data with recurrent neural networks. In: Proceedings of the 23rd International Conference on Machine Learning, pp. 369–376. ACM (2006)
9. Hamlyn, R., Matthews, P., Shanahan, M.: Science education tracker: young people's awareness and attitudes towards machine learning, February 2017. Accessed 26 July 2018
10. He, K., Gkioxari, G., Dollár, P., Girshick, R.: Mask R-CNN. In: 2017 IEEE International Conference on Computer Vision (ICCV), pp. 2980–2988. IEEE (2017)
11. He, K., Zhang, X., Ren, S., Sun, J.: Deep residual learning for image recognition. In: Proceedings of the IEEE Conference on Computer Vision and Pattern Recognition, pp. 770–778 (2016)
12. Karpathy, A., Toderici, G., Shetty, S., Leung, T., Sukthankar, R., Fei-Fei, L.: Large-scale video classification with convolutional neural networks. In: Proceedings of the IEEE Conference on Computer Vision and Pattern Recognition, pp. 1725–1732 (2014)
13. Klausen, J.: British counter-terrorism after 7/7: adapting community policing to the fight against domestic terrorism. J. Ethnic Migr. Stud. **35**(3), 403–420 (2009)
14. Krizhevsky, A., Sutskever, I., Hinton, G.E.: ImageNet classification with deep convolutional neural networks. In: Advances in Neural Information Processing Systems, pp. 1097–1105 (2012)
15. LaFree, G., Dugan, L.: Introducing the global terrorism database. Terror. Polit. Violence **19**(2), 181–204 (2007)
16. LeCun, Y., Bengio, Y., Hinton, G.: Deep learning. Nature **521**(7553), 436 (2015)
17. Lin, T.Y., et al.: Microsoft COCO: common objects in context. In: Fleet, D., Pajdla, T., Schiele, B., Tuytelaars, T. (eds.) ECCV 2014. LNCS, vol. 8693, pp. 740–755. Springer, Cham (2014). https://doi.org/10.1007/978-3-319-10602-1_48
18. Liu, Z., Luo, P., Qiu, S., Wang, X., Tang, X.: DeepFashion: powering robust clothes recognition and retrieval with rich annotations. In: Proceedings of the IEEE Conference on Computer Vision and Pattern Recognition, pp. 1096–1104 (2016)
19. Loni, B., Cheung, L.Y., Riegler, M., Bozzon, A., Gottlieb, L., Larson, M.: Fashion 10000: an enriched social image dataset for fashion and clothing. In: Proceedings of the 5th ACM Multimedia Systems Conference, pp. 41–46. ACM (2014)
20. Lum, C., Kennedy, L.W., Sherley, A.: Are counter-terrorism strategies effective? The results of the Campbell systematic review on counter-terrorism evaluation research. J. Exp. Criminol. **2**(4), 489–516 (2006)
21. Meek, T., Barham, H., Beltaif, N., Kaadoor, A., Akhter, T.: Managing the ethical and risk implications of rapid advances in artificial intelligence: a literature review. In: Proceedings of Portland International Conference on Management of Engineering and Technology: Technology Management For Social Innovation, p. 682 (2016)

22. Oh, S., et al.: A large-scale benchmark dataset for event recognition in surveillance video. In: 2011 IEEE Conference on Computer Vision and Pattern Recognition (CVPR), pp. 3153–3160. IEEE (2011)

23. Oswald, M., Grace, J., Urwin, S., Barnes, G.C.: Algorithmic risk assessment policing models: lessons from the Durham HART model and 'experimental' proportionality. Inf. Commun. Technol. Law **27**(2), 223–250 (2018)

24. Ren, S., He, K., Girshick, R., Sun, J.: Faster R-CNN: towards real-time object detection with region proposal networks. In: Advances in Neural Information Processing Systems, pp. 91–99 (2015)

25. Simonyan, K., Zisserman, A.: Two-stream convolutional networks for action recognition in videos. In: Advances in Neural Information Processing Systems, pp. 568–576 (2014)

26. Skeem, J., Eno Louden, J.: Assessment of evidence on the quality of the correctional offender management profiling for alternative sanctions (COMPAS). Unpublished report prepared for the California Department of Corrections and Rehabilitation. https://webfiles.uci.edu/skeem/Downloads.html (2007)

27. Soomro, K., Zamir, A.R., Shah, M.: UCF101: a dataset of 101 human actions classes from videos in the wild. arXiv preprint arXiv:1212.0402 (2012)

28. Vincent, J.: Artificial intelligence is going to supercharge surveillance. https://www.theverge.com/2018/1/23/16907238/artificial-intelligence-surveillance-cameras-security. Accessed 26 July 2018

29. Wang, J.: Attacks in western Europe. http://fingfx.thomsonreuters.com/gfx/rngs/EUROPE-ATTACKS/010042124ED/index.html. Accessed 03 July 2018

30. Xiao, H., Rasul, K., Vollgraf, R.: Fashion-MNIST: a novel image dataset for benchmarking machine learning algorithms. arXiv preprint arXiv:1708.07747 (2017)

CNN-Based Non-contact Detection of Food Level in Bottles from RGB Images

Yijun Jiang, Elim Schenck, Spencer Kranz, Sean Banerjee,
and Natasha Kholgade Banerjee[✉]

Clarkson University, Potsdam, NY 13699, USA
{jiangy,schencej,kranzs,sbanerje,nbanerje}@clarkson.edu

Abstract. In this paper, we present an approach that detects the level of food in store-bought containers using deep convolutional neural networks (CNNs) trained on RGB images captured using an off-the-shelf camera. Our approach addresses three challenges—the diversity in container geometry, the large variations in shapes and appearances of labels on store-bought containers, and the variability in color of container contents—by augmenting the data used to train the CNNs using printed labels with synthetic textures attached to the training bottles, interchanging the contents of the bottles of the training containers, and randomly altering the intensities of blocks of pixels in the labels and at the bottle borders. Our approach provides an average level detection accuracy of 92.4% using leave-one-out cross-validation on 10 store-bought bottles of varying geometries, label appearances, label shapes, and content colors.

Keywords: Food · Level detection
Deep convolutional neural networks · Training set augmentation

1 Introduction

The propagation of ubiquitous technologies in the consumer space has enabled a wide range of applications in kitchen environments to provide user-centric smart assistance [4,34]. The pervasion of ubiquitous sensing devices and intelligent monitoring of consumer activity has provided a further boost to smart kitchen applications, motivated by the need to provide nutrition awareness [10]. Successful monitoring of user food consumption in kitchens by understanding food levels in containers, recognizing food item counts, and detecting the age of food items has the potential to enhance intelligent kitchens by providing automatic person-centric shopping lists, and recommending user-aware diet choices.

However, existing approaches to detect food quantity are largely contact-based, making propagation of the approaches to average consumer spaces difficult. The approach of Chi et al. [10] requires weight sensors built into a countertop that sense weight change when the object makes contact with the countertop. Approaches that use capacitive sensors [5,32,37] only work with liquids,

© Springer Nature Switzerland AG 2019
I. Kompatsiaris et al. (Eds.): MMM 2019, LNCS 11295, pp. 202–213, 2019.
https://doi.org/10.1007/978-3-030-05710-7_17

and depend upon full immersion into the liquid, which can induce contamination. Work that detects content-based modulation of vibrational characteristics of objects [12,40] requires installation of sensors on the surface of the container. Non-contact approaches on food use character recognition to detect the expiry date [29], which is rarely visible in frontal viewpoints of containers. They estimate quantities of plated food from top-down cameras [14,38], which prove infeasible to install in multi-shelf environments, or provide a binary response on presence or absence of a food item [22,33] as opposed to estimating quantity.

In this paper, we provide the first approach to perform fully non-contact detection of the level of food such as salad dressing in store-bought bottles using deep convolutional neural networks (CNNs) on frontal images of the containers. The input to the CNNs consists of images of bottles with labels of a variety of shapes and appearances, while the output is one of four classes representing four different levels per bottle. We use bottles made of clear glass or plastic to enable visual level detection. While one method of level detection is to count the pixels in an image segment representing food contents, traditional image segmentation algorithms such as k-means clustering [30] or mean shift [11] yield incorrect segment boundaries in the presence of soft edges typical of real-world lighting and camera noise. While deep learning based segmentation algorithms show higher accuracy [9,26], real-world containers contain highly textured labels in addition to the food contents and may reveal various backgrounds, requiring a two-step process to first segment the image, and then recognize which segment represents food. Instead, our approach takes inspiration from at-a-glance approaches for recognition [7,31] and identifies food level directly from the image in one step.

Our work addresses three challenges to estimate food level from store-bought containers. First, store-bought containers show diversity in 3D geometry. Second, labels affixed to store-bought containers show a large variability in shape and appearance. Third, the contents of the containers demonstrate a range of color variations. To address these challenges, we augment the training sets used in learning the CNNs by (i) attaching physically printed labels with synthetic textures to the training bottles to provide invariance to label shape and texture, (ii) interchanging the contents of the training bottles to strengthen the invariance of the CNN to food color, and (iii) altering the intensities of images in random blocks in regions of the label and bottle border to prevent overfitting to bottle geometry, label shape, and label appearance. The random intensity alteration is inspired by the work of [41] which reduces overfitting in CNNs by changing pixel values in random rectangles in training images for object and person detection.

We use leave-one-out cross-validation on a set of 10 store-bought bottles with varying geometries and textures, where the training set contains no label, bottle, or food content from the test set. We use patches containing single containers extracted from bottle line-ups typical of real-world shelves and countertops. Our approach provides an average food level detection accuracy of 92.4%.

2   Related Work

Our work falls in the area of intelligent approaches to monitor food use and human behavior in kitchens. One approach of monitoring usage of food items is to use food identity recognition on an image of the item when a user scans the item before a camera after removing it from a storage location. Recognizing food identity requires pre-training of classification systems on a large group of food items. The success of deep learning approaches has motivated a number of approaches to perform food identity recognition with high accuracy. Liu et al. [24] and Hassanejad et al. [13] use CNNs to classify food images for dietary assessment. Kagaya et al. [17] use data expansion [21] to improve classification of food images using deep CNNs. Since pre-trained neural networks may not be tailored to food images, Martinel et al. [25] train deep residual networks and obtain 90.27% accuracy on the Food-101 dataset. Kawano and Yanai [18] combine features obtained from deep CNNs and conventional hand-crafted features. The approach of Sandholm et al. [33] builds food identity recognition into a cloud-based system to monitor food usage from a fridge. These identity recognition approaches require external accounting mechanisms to keep track of food counts, and do not inherently address level detection unlike our work.

To avoid external tracking of counts, several approaches perform holistic 'at-a-glance' estimation of discrete object counts in an image. Regressors [6,8,20] and CNNs [3,27,28,39] have been used to perform estimation of counts of people [6,8,28,39] and animals [3,27]. The work of Chattopadhyay et al. [7] uses CNNs trained on entire images and gridded cells in images to estimate discrete object counts. The work of Laput et al. [22] uses support vector machines (SVMs) trained on features obtained using correlation-based selection on sub-regions from images in a kitchen environment. The SVMs are used to perform classification of discrete quantities of objects in a sink, presence or absence of a food item, and general clutter on a countertop. Unlike discrete quantity estimation, our task handles estimation of the quantity of continuously varying food items. Approaches exist to use top-down cameras to estimate the volume of plated solid food [14,38] and the level of solid waste in trash cans [2]. Such approaches are impractical for consumer estimation of food level in containers, since the containers are required to be open, the camera may not be installable directly above the container when the containers are in multi-level shelves, and the approach may yield low accuracy for narrow-mouthed bottles which may occupy few pixels in the image space. In contrast to top-down camera approaches where the contents are unobscured, our task is rendered challenging by the significant obscuration of liquid content induced by the label, and the variation in this obscuration due to differences in label shape and appearance.

There exist a number of contact-based approaches on detecting the quantity of the contents in a container. Several approaches use capacitive sensors immersed in liquids in containers to detect levels based on the differences in dielectric constants of the liquid and the surrounding air [5,32,37]. Such immersive sensors can prove intrusive, potentially unsafe, and impractical to detect content levels in large container line-ups typical of home and store environments.

Approaches also exist to measure the differences in vibrational characteristics of containers due to the presence of varying quantities of contents. Zhao et al. [40] induce physical vibrations of waste bins using a DC motor, and measure the effect of vibration damping due to varying levels of garbage contents. Fan and Khai [12] provide a device that emits a sine wave probe sound using a speaker and classifies the impulse response received by a microphone to estimate food quantity. Both approaches require installation of sensors in contact with the container. Chi et al. [10] use a countertop-installed weight sensor in contact with a container to measure weight changes due to content reduction. Unlike the capacitive, vibrational, and contact-based weight detection approaches discussed here, our work provides fully non-contact level detection using an off-the-shelf RGB camera, improving the portability of our system to consumer environments.

Fig. 1. Original images captured for a variety of bottle line-ups composed from the ten bottles used in this work.

3   Data Collection

We use an off-the-shelf RGB camera of resolution 1920×1080 to capture an image dataset of 10 store-bought bottles with six different geometries. The camera is part of the Kinect sensor that flips images horizontally; however, to avoid overhead of extra operations, we do not perform unflipping. Five of the geometries correspond to bottles with salad dressings, while one corresponds to agave syrup. One geometry represents Ken's Steakhouse dressings, under which, we capture one set of three dressing types—Country French, Honey Mustard and Russian. Another geometry represents Kraft dressings, under which we capture a second set of three dressing types, namely Thousand Island, Honey Mustard and Italian. The remaining four geometries separately represent one bottle of Wish-Bone Caesar Dressing, one bottle of Hidden Valley Farmhouse Originals, one bottle of Southwest Chipotle Salad Dressing, and one bottle of Domino Light Organic Agave Nectar. We pour out varying quantities of liquid and leave 25% of liquid for Level 1, 50% for Level 2, 75% for Level 3, and 100% for Level 4.

To perform the capture, we place groupings of 3 or 4 of the 10 bottles at various levels in rows on a wooden plank against a concrete wall with texture. We perform between 15 to 21 small random real-world translations from left-to-right and from front-to-back to represent minute changes in position that occur when users have repeated interactions with containers on shelves or countertops. We use the camera to capture one RGB image per real-world translation at a resolution of 1920×1080. Figure 1 shows examples of images captured by the HD camera demonstrating the groupings captured in our work.

While the image captured by the camera contains several bottles, our objective in this paper is to use CNNs to perform level detection on a bottle-by-bottle basis. We perform a manual extraction of image patches containing individual bottles by specifying a region containing each bottle. While we do not perform automatic bottle extraction in this work, our goal is to make our approach directly pluggable into bottle extraction performed using off-the-shelf object detection algorithms. Since off-the-shelf algorithms may yield bounding boxes that are not perfectly centered around the bottle, we simulate offsets in bounding boxes by sliding the manually specified region left-to-right and top-to-bottom in the image to yield 36 translated patches per bottle instance. To ensure that all patches provided to the CNNs are of the same size, we resize them to a low resolution of 120×60, which accelerates training and prevents overfitting. Figure 2 shows examples of patches for four levels of one bottle on the left, and for various levels for the remaining nine bottles on the right.

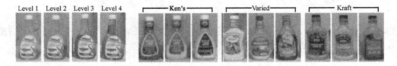

Fig. 2. Left: Four patches representing four different levels for a one bottle. Right: patches for remaining nine bottles. Note the differences in geometry within the 'Varied' group, and with respect to the 'Ken's' and 'Kraft' groups.

4   Classification Using CNNs

Network Architecture. Figure 3 shows the architecture of the CNNs used in our work. The network is made of three blocks. The first block includes two repeated Conv-BN-ReLU layers, that perform convolution using 32 filters, batch normalization (BN) of the feature maps [16], and activation of the normalized feature maps using the rectified linear unit (ReLU). We compared the accuracies of 3×3, 4×4, and 5×5 filters, and determined that filters of size 4×4 yielded the highest accuracy. The second block consists of another set of two repeated Conv-BN-ReLU layers where the number of 4×4 filters is doubled to 64 as recommended in [21,35], and [15]. The third block consists of two Conv-BN-ReLU layers using 128 filters, the first of which performs 4×4 convolution, and the second of which performs 1×1 convolution. The penultimate layer compresses 128 feature maps using four 1×1 convolutional filters for the four classes. At the output layer, we use global average pooling (GAP) [23] to minimize overfitting by reducing the number of parameters, and we use the softmax function to convert the GAP pooling results into classification probabilities.

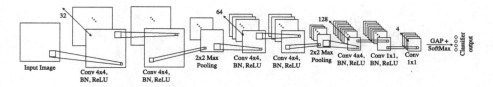

Fig. 3. CNN architecture used in our work. 'Conv' represents convolution, 'BN' represents batch normalization, and 'GAP' represents global average pooling.

Training Data Augmentation. To improve the invariance of our work to differences in bottle geometry, label shape, label appearance, and color of food contents, we use three strategies to augment the data used to train the neural network—expanding the label diversity by attaching new physically printed labels with synthetic texture to the training bottles termed 'Syn', interchanging the contents in the training bottles termed 'Int', and performing random image-based alterations to the training images termed 'Ran'. For the 'Int' approach, we interchange each liquid once to double the size of the training data, which enables the CNNs to avoid overfitting to liquid color. For the 'Syn' approach, we design and print 3 sets of labels for each bottle. The synthetic labels are of different shapes and colors, which reduces overfitting of the CNNs to the labels.

For the 'Ran' training strategy, we randomly choose half of all the training patches and augment each patch 20-fold by performing two types of transformations at random: domain-based transformations, including horizontal translation up to 3 pixels, horizontal flip, and scaling up to ±0.05, as recommended in [21] and [35], intensity transformations by performing global shifting of each RGB channel up to 30 in intensity values [35], and intensity alterations in random rectangles in half of the patches selected at random as suggested in [41]. Figure 4 shows examples of the training data augmented by the three strategies.

We train five CNNs using various combinations of the three training data augmentation strategies—'Int+Syn' that uses interchanging and physically printed labels with synthetic texture, 'Ran' that uses random intensity alterations only, 'Ran+Syn' that uses random intensity alterations with printed labels, 'Ran+Int' that uses random intensity alterations with liquid interchanging, and 'Ran+Int+Syn' that combines all three augmentation strategies. We also train two baseline CNNs for comparison—one based on the original training data without any augmentation strategy termed 'Orig', and one with the labels peeled off the bottles termed 'Bare' trained with the 'Ran' augmentation strategy.

Training and Testing. We generate train and test datasets by performing 1-fold cross validation based on bottles. We train the CNNs using Adam [19] as the adaptive gradient optimizer with cross entropy as the loss function. After each max pooling layer, we include dropout [36] with probability of 25% to prevent overfitting. We choose a batch size of 32 and train for 10 epochs. Our CNN architecture is implemented using the Keras API platform wrapped around the TensorFlow [1] library with GPU support. We perform training and testing using an Asus ESC4000-G3 server containing a single Intel Xeon E5-2660 v3 2.6 GHz

Fig. 4. Training data augmentation performed in this work. Top row: interchange of liquids (bottles correspond to their original countertops in Fig. 2), middle row: attachment of printed labels with synthetic texture, last row: random image-based alterations of intensities in randomly chosen rectangular patches in the images.

10-core processor, 256 GB of RAM, and two NVIDIA GeForce GTX 1080 Ti GPUs. The training takes 1.5 h per fold, while testing takes 0.24 ms per image. The small level detection runtime per image in comparison to 33.33 ms for 30 fps frame-rate enables our work to be readily deployed into real-time applications.

5   Results

Table 1 shows results of classification accuracies for all the CNNs. While the 'Orig' version receives an average accuracy of 69.9%, the various training augmentation strategies provide improvements in accuracy to 77.1% for 'Int+Syn', 78.9% for 'Ran', 81.7% for 'Ran+Syn', 85.2% for 'Ran+Int', and 92.4% for the combined 'Ran+Int+Syn' strategy. Figure 6 shows examples of the actual level and predicted class probabilities for a variety of bottles using the training approaches 'Ran+Int+Syn', 'Ran+Int', 'Int+Syn', and 'Orig'. As a baseline, the 'Bare' CNNs, where labels are peeled off the bottles in the training and testing set, provide 100% classification when trained with the 'Ran' strategy. Figure 5 shows the overall confusion matrices for CNNs trained without augmentation, and with the five augmentation approaches discussed in this work. Using randomized intensity alterations provides a boost in performance in Level 1, while improvement in classification of Level 2 to Level 4 is obtained using physical interactions of liquid interchanging and printed labels. This may be attributed to the ability of the synthetically printed labels placed in locations of the actual labels to learn the label appearance distribution, and for interchanging to boost invariance to color of the liquid behind the label.

For Bottles 3 and 5, the color similarity of the lower part of the label and the liquid prevents the CNNs from performing correct level prediction, even when trained with the 'Ran' strategy in the case of Bottle 5. The accuracy increases to

Table 1. Classification accuracy as percentages using CNNs trained with various combinations of augmentation strategies, as compared to CNNs trained with no augmentation ('Orig') and CNNs trained on label-free bottles ('Bare').

ID	1	2	3	4	5	6	7	8	9	10	Mean
Orig	68.8	50.0	73.8	100.0	54.2	100.0	25.0	91.1	68.1	67.7	69.9
Bare	100.0	100.0	100.0	100.0	100.0	100.0	100.0	100.0	100.0	100.0	100.0
Int+Syn	31.9	81.6	75.0	100.0	88.8	100.0	39.6	91.8	81.3	81.2	77.1
Ran	72.9	93.6	82.8	100.0	77.0	100.0	27.1	86.6	80.0	69.2	78.9
Ran+Syn	64.8	66.3	83.6	100.0	100.0	100.0	30.9	99.0	73.1	99.3	81.7
Ran+Int	83.2	88.3	93.3	100.0	98.6	100.0	31.9	99.6	90.1	67.0	85.2
Ran+Int+Syn	79.9	92.8	98.9	100.0	97.3	100.0	60.1	100.0	96.3	98.9	92.4

100% and 83.6% for Bottles 5 and 3 respectively when we train with 'Ran+Syn', since the diverse array of synthetic labels used in our approach ensures that the color similarities are modeled by combinations of synthetic labels and training bottles. For Bottle 2, although Bottles 1,2 and 3 have the same geometry, the label of Bottle 2 shows higher differences in label location and logo appearance compared to Bottles 1 and 3, due to which the 'Orig' strategy shows a low performance on Bottle 2. When trained with the 'Ran' approach, label occlusion improves the accuracy for Bottle 2 to 93.6%. For Bottles 4 and 6, similarity in liquid color and geometry enables all CNNs to predict 100% despite differences in label appearance.

In the combined augmentation strategy, i.e., 'Ran+Syn+Int', we observe a mis-prediction of Level 2 as Levels 1 or 3, and of Level 3 as Levels 3 and 4, due to the proximity of these levels. Our investigation reveals that 97.6% of the Level 3 mis-classifications as 2 or 4 and 56.1% of the Level 2 mis-classifications as Level 1 and 3 are due to Bottle 7, which shows a maximum of 60.1% correct average prediction. A small amount of confusion is also observed between Levels 1 and 3. This is due to the fact that the viscosity of the liquid causes it to stick to the container, inducing the appearance in moderate everyday lighting conditions at lower levels to resemble the appearance at higher levels. In future work, we will investigate the use of scene-specific illumination to resolve optical differences of liquids sticking to container walls with respect to the rest of the contents.

The similarity between agave syrup color on the label and in the contents of Bottle 10 influences level prediction in the 'Orig' strategy due to the closeness of the liquid color to part of the label appearance. The 'Ran+Syn' strategy improves the accuracy to 99.3% since synthetic labels enhance the invariance of the CNNs to the label contents. However, while the performance is likewise improved for Bottle 1 which shows color similarity within the white label writing and the liquid, the accuracy of Bottle 1 reaches a maximum of 83.2% and drops with synthetic label. As future work, we will investigate creating synthetic labels that model color similarities to the bottle liquid.

Orig

	Actual 1	2	3	4
Predicted 1	78.4%	20.6%	13.3%	13.7%
2	7.4%	58.3%	12.7%	8.4%
3	9.8%	16.0%	72.6%	7.6%
4	4.4%	5.1%	1.5%	70.2%

Int + Syn

	Actual 1	2	3	4
Predicted 1	84.2%	32.6%	17.1%	5.4%
2	7.9%	60.2%	1.9%	0%
3	5.9%	7.2%	80.8%	10.7%
4	1.9%	0%	0.3%	83.9%

Ran

	Actual 1	2	3	4
Predicted 1	93.6%	16.6%	10.2%	9.5%
2	1.6%	71.6%	2.5%	0.3%
3	0.7%	5.5%	69.7%	9.6%
4	4.1%	6.4%	17.7%	80.5%

Ran + Syn

	Actual 1	2	3	4
Predicted 1	92.5%	18.6%	13.5%	10.7%
2	0%	64.1%	3.3%	0.6%
3	6.2%	15.3%	83.3%	1.3%
4	1.3%	2%	0%	87.5%

Ran + Int

	Actual 1	2	3	4
Predicted 1	93.9%	15.5%	10.3%	7.5%
2	1.2%	76.3%	0.2%	0%
3	2.5%	3.5%	77.9%	0%
4	2.4%	4.8%	11.6%	92.5%

Ran + Int + Syn

	Actual 1	2	3	4
Predicted 1	95.1%	10%	2.4%	0.5%
2	0%	82.5%	3.8%	0.1%
3	3.6%	6.7%	93.7%	0.9%
4	1.3%	0.8%	0.1%	98.4%

Fig. 5. Confusion matrices for CNNs trained without augmentation ('Orig'), and with various combinations of the three augmentation strategies discussed in this work.

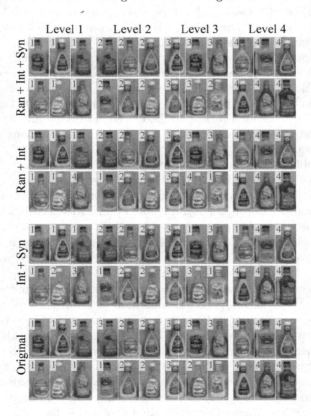

Fig. 6. Results using various training strategies in this work. Each row provides a training strategy, each column of represents the actual level, while the number in each image provides the predicted level.

6   Discussion

We have presented an approach in this paper to detect the level of food in store-bought food containers such as salad dressing bottles using convolutional neural networks trained on RGB images. To enable the neural networks to obtain invariance to bottle geometry, label shape, and label texture, we augment the training sets used to train the neural networks using printed labels with synthetic textures and random alteration of intensity blocks on the borders of the bottle, and the interior of the label. Our approach provides an average accuracy of 92.4% using a leave-one-out cross-validation with bottles containing opaque and semi-transparent liquids of several colors. While we have tested our approach with liquids, it can be readily extended to containers with solid contents.

One limitation of our approach is that it requires the optical properties of the container and food to be distinct, thereby preventing level detection in opaque containers. However, a large category of household containers fall within the realm of our approach, including translucent containers such as milk cans, and containers with microscopic perforations in the label that arise due to the process of printing label contents on plastic. While wrap-around labels preclude fine-grained level detection in the region of the label, our method can still be used to detect 'near full' if contents exist in the upper portion of the container above the label, and 'approaching empty' if the region below the label shows depleting contents. Another limitation is that while our approach handles bottles with variations in geometric structure, it requires them to be nearly the same height in order for consistent image sizes as input to the CNNs. In future work, we will investigate image resizing combined with container category detection to perform level percentage detection for containers of varying height.

Since our work performs food level detection on crops of containers from bottle line-ups found in shelves and on countertops, it can be deployed into consumer systems by combining sliding-window bottle detection with food level detection in the sliding window. As part of future work, we are expanding our dataset to contain wider array of container geometries, and solid and liquid food items with a range of opacities and mixture homogeneities, captured under varying illumination. We will also include slight rotations of containers which arise when users interact with them. To eliminate training dependence on physical activities such as attaching printed labels and interchanging liquids, we will investigate virtual approaches to alter liquid color and label appearance in the training set.

Acknowledgements. This work was partially supported by the National Science Foundation (NSF) grant #1730183.

References

1. Abadi, M., et al.: Tensorflow: a system for large-scale machine learning. In: OSDI (2016)
2. Arebey, M., Hannan, M., Begum, R.A., Basri, H.: Solid waste bin level detection using gray level co-occurrence matrix feature extraction approach. J. Environ. Manag. **104**, 9–18 (2012)

3. Arteta, C., Lempitsky, V., Zisserman, A.: Counting in the wild. In: Leibe, B., Matas, J., Sebe, N., Welling, M. (eds.) ECCV 2016. LNCS, vol. 9911, pp. 483–498. Springer, Cham (2016). https://doi.org/10.1007/978-3-319-46478-7_30

4. Bonanni, L., Lee, C.H., Selker, T.: Counterintelligence: augmented reality kitchen. In: ACM SIGCHI (2005)

5. Canbolat, H.: A novel level measurement technique using three capacitive sensors for liquids. IEEE Trans. Instrum. Meas. **58**, 3762–3768 (2009)

6. Chan, A.B., Liang, Z.S.J., Vasconcelos, N.: Privacy preserving crowd monitoring: counting people without people models or tracking. In: IEEE CVPR, pp. 1–7 (2008)

7. Chattopadhyay, P., Vedantam, R., Selvaraju, R.R., Batra, D., Parikh, D.: Counting everyday objects in everyday scenes. CoRR abs/1604.03505, **1**(10) (2016)

8. Chen, K., Loy, C.C., Gong, S., Xiang, T.: Feature mining for localised crowd counting. In: BMVC. vol. 1, 3 (2012)

9. Chen, L.C., Papandreou, G., Kokkinos, I., Murphy, K., Yuille, A.L.: DeepLab: semantic image segmentation with deep convolutional nets, atrous convolution, and fully connected CRFs. IEEE TPAMI **40**(4), 834–848 (2018)

10. Chi, P.-Y.P., Chen, J.-H., Chu, H.-H., Lo, J.-L.: Enabling calorie-aware cooking in a smart kitchen. In: Oinas-Kukkonen, H., Hasle, P., Harjumaa, M., Segerståhl, K., Øhrstrøm, P. (eds.) PERSUASIVE 2008. LNCS, vol. 5033, pp. 116–127. Springer, Heidelberg (2008). https://doi.org/10.1007/978-3-540-68504-3_11

11. Comaniciu, D., Meer, P.: Mean shift: a robust approach toward feature space analysis. IEEE TPAMI **24**(5), 603–619 (2002)

12. Fan, M., Truong, K.N.: SoQr: sonically quantifying the content level inside containers. In: ACM UbiComp (2015)

13. Hassannejad, H., Matrella, G., Ciampolini, P., De Munari, I., Mordonini, M., Cagnoni, S.: Food image recognition using very deep convolutional networks. In: MADiMa (2016)

14. Hassannejad, H., Matrella, G., Ciampolini, P., Munari, I.D., Mordonini, M., Cagnoni, S.: A new approach to image-based estimation of food volume. Algorithms **10**(2), 66 (2017)

15. He, K., Zhang, X., Ren, S., Sun, J.: Deep residual learning for image recognition. In: IEEE CVPR (2016)

16. Ioffe, S., Szegedy, C.: Batch normalization: accelerating deep network training by reducing internal covariate shift. arXiv preprint arXiv:1502.03167 (2015)

17. Kagaya, H., Aizawa, K., Ogawa, M.: Food detection and recognition using convolutional neural network. In: ACMMM (2014)

18. Kawano, Y., Yanai, K.: Food image recognition with deep convolutional features. In: ACM UbiComp (2014)

19. Kingma, D.P., Ba, J.: Adam: A method for stochastic optimization. arXiv preprint arXiv:1412.6980 (2014)

20. Kong, D., Gray, D., Tao, H.: A viewpoint invariant approach for crowd counting. In: IEEE ICPR. vol. 3, pp. 1187–1190 (2006)

21. Krizhevsky, A., Sutskever, I., Hinton, G.E.: Imagenet classification with deep convolutional neural networks. In: NIPS (2012)

22. Laput, G., Lasecki, W.S., Wiese, J., Xiao, R., Bigham, J.P., Harrison, C.: Zensors: adaptive, rapidly deployable, human-intelligent sensor feeds. In: ACM SIGCHI, pp. 1935–1944 (2015)

23. Lin, M., Chen, Q., Yan, S.: Network in network. arXiv preprint arXiv:1312.4400 (2013)

24. Liu, C., Cao, Y., Luo, Y., Chen, G., Vokkarane, V., Ma, Y.: Deepfood: deep learning-based food image recognition for computer-aided dietary assessment. In: ICOST (2016)
25. Martinel, N., Foresti, G.L., Micheloni, C.: Wide-slice residual networks for food recognition. arXiv preprint arXiv:1612.06543 (2016)
26. Noh, H., Hong, S., Han, B.: Learning deconvolution network for semantic segmentation. In: IEEE CVPR, pp. 1520–1528 (2015)
27. Norouzzadeh, M.S., et al.: Automatically identifying, counting, and describing wild animals in camera-trap images with deep learning. Proc. Nat. Acad. Sci. 115(25), E5716–E5725 (2018)
28. Oñoro-Rubio, Daniel, López-Sastre, Roberto J.: Towards perspective-free object counting with deep learning. In: Leibe, Bastian, Matas, Jiri, Sebe, Nicu, Welling, Max (eds.) ECCV 2016. LNCS, vol. 9911, pp. 615–629. Springer, Cham (2016). https://doi.org/10.1007/978-3-319-46478-7_38
29. Peng, E., Peursum, P., Li, L.: Product barcode and expiry date detection for the visually impaired using a smartphone. In: DICTA (2012)
30. Ray, S., Turi, R.H.: Determination of number of clusters in k-means clustering and application in colour image segmentation. In: Proceedings of the 4th International Conference On Advances in Pattern Recognition and Digital Techniques, pp. 137–143, Calcutta, India (1999)
31. Redmon, J., Divvala, S., Girshick, R., Farhadi, A.: You only look once: unified, real-time object detection. In: IEEE CVPR, pp. 779–788 (2016)
32. Reverter, F., Li, X., Meijer, G.C.: Liquid-level measurement system based on a remote grounded capacitive sensor. Sens. Actuators, A 138, 1–8 (2007)
33. Sandholm, T., Lee, D., Tegelund, B., Han, S., Shin, B., Kim, B.: Cloudfridge: a testbed for smart fridge interactions. arXiv preprint arXiv:1401.0585 (2014)
34. Sato, A., Watanabe, K., Rekimoto, J.: Mimicook: a cooking assistant system with situated guidance. In: TEI (2014)
35. Simonyan, K., Zisserman, A.: Very deep convolutional networks for large-scale image recognition. arXiv preprint arXiv:1409.1556 (2014)
36. Srivastava, N., Hinton, G., Krizhevsky, A., Sutskever, I., Salakhutdinov, R.: Dropout: a simple way to prevent neural networks from overfitting. JMLR 15, 1929–1958 (2014)
37. Terzic, E., Nagarajah, C., Alamgir, M.: Capacitive sensor-based fluid level measurement in a dynamic environment using neural network. Eng. Appl. Artif. Intell. 23, 614–619 (2010)
38. Xu, C., He, Y., Khannan, N., Parra, A., Boushey, C., Delp, E.: Image-based food volume estimation. In: Proceedings of the 5th International Workshop on Multimedia For Cooking & Eating Activities, pp. 75–80 (2013)
39. Zhang, C., Li, H., Wang, X., Yang, X.: Cross-scene crowd counting via deep convolutional neural networks. In: IEEE CVPR, pp. 833–841 (2015)
40. Zhao, Y., Yao, S., Li, S., Hu, S., Shao, H., Abdelzaher, T.F.: Vibebin: a vibration-based waste bin level detection system. ACM IMWUT 1, 122 (2017)
41. Zhong, Z., Zheng, L., Kang, G., Li, S., Yang, Y.: Random erasing data augmentation. arXiv preprint arXiv:1708.04896 (2017)

Personalized Recommendation of Photography Based on Deep Learning

Zhixiang Ji[1,2], Jie Tang[1,2(✉)], and Gangshan Wu[1,2]

[1] Department of Computer Science and Technology, Nanjing University,
Nanjing 210023, China
`tangjie@nju.edu.cn`
[2] State Key Laboratory for Novel Software Technology, Nanjing University,
Nanjing 210023, China

Abstract. The key to the picture recommendation problem lies in the representation of image features. There are many methods for image feature description, and some are mature. However, due to the particularity of the photographic works we are concerned with, the traditional recommendation based on original features or labels cannot get better results. In our topic problem, the discovery of image style features is very important. Our main job is to propose an optimized feature representation method in the unlabeled data set, and to train by the deep learning convolutional neural network (CNN), and finally achieve the recommended purpose. Combined with the latent factor model, the user features and image style features are deeply characterized. After a lot of experiments, we show that our method is better than other mainstream recommendation algorithms based on unlabeled data sets, and achieved better recommendation results.

Keywords: Photography · Recommendation · Image style

1 Introduction

Today, with the rapid growth of information, the number of pictures in the network is also growing exponentially. The research on image features is also a long-standing research. We focus on the category of photographic works in online image resources. On some photographic work sharing platforms, a large number of photographers are actively sharing their works and browsing works from other photographers at the same time. Due to the large number of works, users expect the platform to be personalized. But in practice, this recommendation does not meet the needs of users. Therefore, personalized photography recommendations are particularly important.

The recommended effect of collaborative filtering in real-world applications is usually better than content-based recommendations. However, collaborative filtering is limited by the cold-start problem: new images that have not been noticed before can't be recommended; because the data that is being watched

© Springer Nature Switzerland AG 2019
I. Kompatsiaris et al. (Eds.): MMM 2019, LNCS 11295, pp. 214–226, 2019.
https://doi.org/10.1007/978-3-030-05710-7_18

is scarce, images that are only liked by a small number of users are hard to recommend. In the process of recommending photography works, we pay more attention to the image style, content and other information of the works that users like, and there is not much relationship with the works themselves, so the collaborative filtering method is not fit in this recommendation and will limit the recommendation of a very suitable new work. Therefore, we expect to find a user's favorite features in the user's existing interest list, and explore the style features implied by each picture to provide users with personalized and accurate recommendations.

2   Related Work

From low-level features [1, 2] to advanced features [3], image content has evolved from shallow architecture to deep architecture to some extent. Image style [4], as a special image content information, plays a very important role in our research problems. Lu et al. [5] investigates problems of image style, aesthetics, and quality estimation, which require fine-grained details from high-resolution images, utilizing deep neural network training approach. They propose a deep multi-patch aggregation network training approach, which allows us to train models using multiple patches generated from one image. Tang et al. [6] proposed one kind of new image similarity measure operator and one kind of new acceleration algorithm to Difference small image. They have designed the image style study sorter effective enhancement image style study Efficiency. This has a guiding significance for the study of our image style. Sun et al. [7] propose a CNN architecture with two pathways extracting object features and texture features, respectively. The object pathway represents the standard CNN architecture and the texture pathway intermixes the object pathway by outputting the gram matrices of intermediate features in the object pathway.

The recommended methods can be divided into content-based filtering (CBF) method and collaborative filtering (CF) method [8]. CBF recommends images based on a comparison between image content and user profiles [9]. CF recommends images to users based on images shared by other users with similar interests [10]. However, when the network is very sparse, the performance of the CF can be unsatisfactory. In order to deal with this dilemma, some researchers have proposed CF models based on matrix decomposition, such as Singular Value Decomposition (SVD) [11], Weighted Matrix Factorization (WMF) [12], and probability matrix decomposition [13] and topic model combination [14]. Barragáns-Martínez et al. [15] eliminate the most serious limitations of collaborative filtering and resort to a well-known matrix factorization technique in the implementation of the item-based collaborative filtering algorithm, which has shown a good behavior in the TV domain.

Hu et al. [12] identify unique properties of implicit feedback datasets. They propose treating the Data as indication of positive and negative preference associated with vastly varying confidence levels. This leads to a factor model which is especially tailored for implicit feedback recommenders. Dieleman et al. [17]

are concerned with the issue of music recommendation, which is compared with our photography recommendations. Similarly, music recommendations mainly focus on discovering the underlying features of music, and photography needs to discover the style features of the picture. The commonality between the two problems is that they all need to discover the user's preference features, which is an implicit feedback. They propose to use a latent factor model for recommendation, and predict the latent factors from music audio when they cannot be obtained from usage data. Geng et al. [17] propose a novel deep model which learns the unified feature representations for both users and images. This is done by transforming the heterogeneous user-image networks into homogeneous low-dimensional representations, which facilitate a recommender to trivially recommend images to users by feature similarity.

3   Framework

3.1   Definition

Based on our main research questions, we give a formal definition. We have a collection U of users, a collection I of photographic works, and the aggregation of images will be divided into a training set I_{train} and a test set I_{test} according to the scale. Each user has a certain number of favorite pictures, and we construct a rating matrix G based on these data. Our goal is to design a kind of algorithm flow Γ, and finally realize the function of personalized recommendation picture for users, so the output is also a collection of some images I_{pred} we predict, we express as follows:

$$I_{pred} = \Gamma(U, I, I_{train}, I_{test}, G) \tag{1}$$

3.2   Image Style

In the recommendation of photography works, the traditional label does not play a big role. For example, a user likes a photo of a character, and the traditional label will mark the person, the weather, the place, the time and other information. It may not be the reason the user likes it. The user likes this picture just because it is a retro style. Of course, we can't completely discard other content information of the image, but the image style [4] factor should have a higher weight in our recommendation process.

Image style (see Fig. 1) is actually a kind of image texture feature, which is an important deep feature of image content. After studying this theme, we divided the style into many types: black and white, emotion, photo, macro, close-up, fresh, long exposure, synthesis, minimalist, sexy, impressionist and so on. We select a large number of images for training in different image styles. The training network uses the commonly used convolutional neural network. Finally, we can classify a picture and prepare for further feature extraction and learning recommendation.

Fig. 1. A examples list of common image styles.

3.3 Weighted Matrix Factorization

In the data set we get, the user's favorite data for the picture is expressed in the form of a matrix, which is similar to the representation of the scoring matrix, but each value in the matrix is the preference of a single user for a single picture, not a rating, which is a form of implicit feedback. Suppose the user u likes the picture i, we will set the corresponding value G_{ui} to 1 in the matrix, and if the user u does not like the picture i, the value G_{ui} will be set to 0. We expect to discover the user's preference features from the pictures that users like, and intuitively understand which style is preferred. But this preference may also include other image content, which requires mining the feature by a suitable algorithm.

For the form of this implicit feedback, the Weighted Matrix Factorization (WMF) algorithm proposed by Hu et al. [16] is more suitable for this application. The purpose of this algorithm is to generate a representation of the latent factors of all users and pictures. This is an improved matrix decomposition algorithm for implicit feedback data sets.

Let r_{ui} be the flag whether user u enjoys image i. For each user-image pair, we define a preference variable p_{ui}, $I(x)$ is the indicator function:

$$p_{ui} = I(r_{ui} = true) \tag{2}$$

The preference variable indicates whether user u enjoys image i. If it is 1, we will assume the user enjoys the image.

The WMF objective function is given by:

$$\min_{x_*,y_*} \sum_{u,i} (p_{ui} - x_u^T y_i)^2 + \lambda(\sum_u ||x_u||^2 + \sum_i ||y_i||^2) \tag{3}$$

where λ is a regularization parameter, x_u is the latent factor vector for user u, and y_i is the latent factor vector for image i. It consists of a mean squared error term and an L2 regularization term.

3.4 Latent Factor Model

The latent factor model (LFM) [18] is based on weighted matrix factorization, which decomposes the user's scoring matrix G of the image into the user's feature matrix multiplied by the image's feature matrix:

$$G_{m \times n} = X_{m \times k} Y_{k \times n} \tag{4}$$

G is the user scoring matrix. Suppose there are m users and n pictures. In the process of weight matrix factorization, an implicit parameter k is specified, which determines the dimensions of the user matrix X and the image matrix Y. This parameter is generally based on the actual application specification. The implicit meaning represents the implicit category generated in the matrix factorization process. The result of the factorization is the degree that m users like the k types image. The larger the value is, the higher the degree of preference is. The meaning of the matrix is the attribute of n pictures for the k types. The larger the value if, the more likely the picture may belong to this implicit category.

Based on the LFM model, we have made up for the shortcomings of the entire problem on Ground Truth. Since our recommendation is based on unlabeled recommendations and uses deep learning, the Ground Truth is missing. But now we construct the Ground Truth by using the LFM model, exactly the matrix $X_{m \times k}$.

3.5 Deep Learning CNN Network

Based on the X matrix and Y matrix decomposed by the LFM model, we use it as the Ground Truth of the CNN network [20] to train the network. After the network training is completed, we can use the network to predict the test images' implicit category and obtain the hidden vector y of the picture t, for a specific user x_t, simply multiply x_t and y_t to get the user's preference p_t (p_t is a value which denotes the preference degree of the user t.) for such an image, so that we can use the preferences to recommend images for users.

4   Algorithm

Combining the above theoretical basis, we designed a style-based feature learning and recommendation algorithm: Style-based Deep Leaning for User-Image Features (SUIF). The algorithm can be roughly divided into four steps.

The first step, select 50 common style categories from our photography website and select 1000 images under each category. Now we have 50,000 images with style tags. Then use CNN network (we call it $CNN\text{-}Style$) to learn. Finally we can use the trained network to predict style for new images, which is the basis for the following steps highlighting the importance of style in the recommendation of photography.

The second step, the LFM model is established and the WMF algorithm is used. For our test set, the user's preferences for the picture are organized into a matrix $G1$, assuming m users, n pictures, then the matrix is $m \times n$. We have made changes to the classic WMF algorithm to make the weight of the style larger. We use the trained $CNN\text{-}Style$ network to predict the style of each test image. Each image will get a 50-dimensional vector, corresponding to the possible weight of each style. The larger the weight is, the more likely this image may belong to this style. Now, we will get an $n \times 50$ matrix S, we will multiply $G1$ and S, and we will get a new matrix $G2(m \times 50)$, whose specific meaning is the degree of preference of each user for each style. Here we should adjust each weight to between 0 and 1. Next, we perform simultaneous weighted matrix factorization on the two matrices $G1$ and $G2$. We define the final objective function of the factorization process as follows:

$$\min_{x1_*, y1_*, y2_*} (1 - \alpha) \sum_{u,i} (p1_{ui} - x_u^T y1_i)^2 + \alpha \sum_{u,j} (p2_{uj} - x_u^T y2_j)^2 + \lambda R \quad (5)$$

$$R = \sum_u ||x_u||^2 + \sum_i ||y1_i||^2 + \sum_j ||y2_j||^2 \quad (6)$$

Where λ is a regularization parameter, x_u is the latent factor vector for user u, and $y1_i$ is the latent factor vector for image i and $y1_j$ is the latent factor vector for style j. It consists of Two mean squared error terms and an L2 regularization term R. α is the proportion of the style features in the total features, and the parameters are adjusted between 0 and 1. The matrix factorization yields three small matrices, $X(m \times k)$, $Y1(k \times n)$, and $Y2(k \times 50)$. The parameter k is manually specified before factorization. We set it 20, which means to set 20 hidden categories. The three matrices have the following relationship.

$$X \cdot Y1 = G1, X \cdot Y2 = G2 \quad (7)$$

The third step, the resulted matrix $Y1(k \times n)$ is used as Ground Truth to train the CNN network (we call it $CNN\text{-}Feature$). The objective function of the network is as follows:

$$\min_\theta \sum_i ||y_i - y_i'||^2 \quad (8)$$

Among them, y_i is the implied vector of image i, y_i' is the predicted value in the CNN network training process, and our goal is to make the prediction approximate the implied vector.

The fourth step, the trained $CNN\text{-}Feature$ network is used to predict the image feature in the test set, and each image will get a k-dimensional vector corresponding to the weight of the image belonging to the k implicit categories. For a single user, multiplying the user feature x_i and the image feature y_i will give the user a preference p_i(which is a value) for the image. For all test images to be calculated in the same way, you can select the most favorite ones for recommendation [19].

Algorithm 1. Style-based Deep Leaning for User-Image Features

Input: User set U, Image set I, Train image set I_{train}, Test image set I_{test}, Rating matrix $G1$.
Output: Predict image Set I_{pred}
1: Divide all the images into a training set and a test set according to a ratio of 6:4.
2: Set $I_{train} \leftarrow 60\% I$ and $I_{test} \leftarrow 40\% I$
3: //$ntrain$ is the number of I_{train} and $ntrain$ is the number of I_{train}.
4: Select 50 common styles and 1000 images under each style.
5: Train network CNN-$Style$.
6: **for** img in I_{train} **do**
7:     Predict $astyle(1 \times 50)$ for img by CNN-$Style$ network.
8: **end for**
9: Compute matrix S. //by predicted styles of images
10: $G2_{m \times 50} \leftarrow G1_{m \times ntrian} \cdot S_{ntrian \times 50}$
11: Adjust each weight in S to between 0 and 1.
12: $(X, Y1, Y2) \leftarrow Optimized\text{-}WMF(G1, G2, k = 20)$
13: Train network CNN-$Feature$ with Ground Truth $Y1$.
14: **for** img in I_{test} **do**
15:     Predict $afeature(1 \times k)$ for img by CNN-$Feature$ network.
16: **end for**
17: Compute matrix F.//by predicted features of images
18: $Result_{m \times ntest} \leftarrow X_{m \times k} \cdot F_{k \times ntest}$
19: **return** $I_{pred} \leftarrow TopN(Result)$

---

5   Experiments

Our dataset is selected from a website (http://www.tuchong.com/) which is one of Chinese mainstream photography. We choose 10,000 users and 500,000 images, covering 50 image styles. We divide all the images into a training set and a test set according to a ratio of 6:4. The training process is completed on the GPU. Our code is written in Python language based on tensorflow, where the style proportion λ is 50% and the hidden category parameter k is 20.

The experimental process compares our proposed algorithm (SUIF) with other mainstream algorithms. Content-based filtering (CBF), which generates user feature vectors by averaging all image features fixed by the user, and then recommends images based on the similarity of image features and user features; User-based collaborative filtering (UCF): It analyzes the user-image matrix to calculate similarity between users, and then recommends images to user with similar tastes and preferences; Item-based collaborative filtering (ICF): The technique first analyzes the user image matrix to identify the relationships between different images and uses these relationships to indirectly calculate recommendations for the user; Weighted Matrix Factorization (WMF) uses a weighted matrix decomposition algorithm to obtain implicit representations of users and images, and then learns this implicit indication. Finally do recommendation with the indications. We compare the results obtained by running the five algorithms.

Table 1. mAP values for five algorithms when the recommended number is 1, 5, 10, and 20.

Algorithm	Top1	Top5	Top10	Top20
CBF	0.0025	0.0079	0.0126	0.0196
UCF	0.0058	0.0105	0.0179	0.0235
ICF	0.0076	0.0236	0.0362	0.0427
WMF	0.0104	0.0365	0.0432	0.0497
SUIF	0.0128	0.0485	0.0508	0.0576

Table 2. AUC values corresponding to the five algorithms when the recommended number is 1, 5, 10, and 20.

Algorithm	Top1	Top5	Top10	Top20
CBF	0.526	0.603	0.681	0.715
UCF	0.532	0.625	0.672	0.708
ICF	0.563	0.701	0.724	0.736
WMF	0.526	0.605	0.689	0.727
SUIF	0.586	0.752	0.798	0.842

In the experiment, we calculated two evaluation indicators commonly used in the recommendation system, mAP (mean Average Precision) [21] and AUC (Area under ROC Curve) [22]. The experimental results are shown in Tables 1 and 2. As can be seen from the table, our algorithm SUIF performance is the best in both indicators. In detail, WMF performance is also very good on the mAP value, but is worse than our algorithm. The performance of ICF is at a medium level in this indicator, but this algorithm takes the relationship between images into account and plays a certain effect. It can achieve better results on some special images. The two algorithms of UCF and CBF do not perform well. The main reason is that the traditional image feature representation method is adopted separately, the features of the image or the similarity of the user is considered one-sidedly. The user's true preference for the image is shown. In terms of AUC indicators, CBF and UCF performance is still slightly worse, but ICF performance is better, which gives us a direction for thinking about future work. The relationship between images will play a role in feature extraction and

Fig. 2. The results of the five algorithms for User(a)'s photographic work recommendation, with red squares appearing in the user's favorite picture set I. It can be seen that the pictures that the user likes have obvious distinguishable style characteristics. (Color figure online)

recommendation. In addition, the performance of WMF is still good. Our SUIF algorithm performance is still the best.

In the specific image recommendation effect, we give two pictures. Figure 2 is a recommendation for User(a). The first line is the picture that the user liked, which belongs to our training set I_{test}. The recommendations given by each algorithm are listed below. The pictures with the red box indicates that they are indeed the picture that the user liked, which belong to the set of all images User(a) liked. Let's take a look at the first line. This user's favorite images have obvious features in both color and photographic style. We can see the difference in result from the image style recommended by various algorithms. The recommendation given by our SUIF algorithm is very similar to the style of the first line, and it can be seen from the number of red boxes that most of the recommended results belong to what the original user liked, so the recommended result is still relatively accurate. Of course, the results recommended by other algorithms are also good. For example, the results of the ICF algorithm are very close to the original style. However, it can be seen that only a small part of the results of other algorithms have red boxes, and the recommended result is not as accurate as SUIF. In addition, we found an interesting phenomenon. In the last picture that the user liked in the first line, there is a pet cat. We posted this picture separately, as shown in Fig. 3. When we look closely, we can see that this is not just a photo about a pet. There is actually a girl on the cat. This is actually a creative style of photography. In our recommendation, we found that the results of the three algorithms ICF, CBF, and UCF all have results about pet cats. However, we have seen that only one of all the favorite images of this user has a pet cat. After careful study, I found that there are exactly some similar creative styles among the images that users like. So when extracting the features of the pictures, the proportion of specific things in the pictures should not be too large, and we should consider the image style factor more. However, our SUIF algorithm and WMF algorithm, because they all contain the steps of matrix factorization, and the influence of specific things weakened in feature extraction, there is no pet cat in the recommendation results, and more recommended pictures that may belong to the creative category.

Fig. 3. The sixth picture of User(a) in Fig. 2. There is a pet cat in the picture and there is a girl on the cat.

Figure 4 is a recommendation for User(b). This user's favorite picture also has obvious features. One type is colorful, similar to the color of dusk or the color of maple leaves. But we found that there are some other styles of pictures. Given this example, we want to show the difference in recommended results under multi-styles user features. Our algorithm SUIF performs very well, and the number of red boxes in the results also accounts for a large number. Secondly, the ICF and WMF recommendations are also better. The recommended effects of CBF and UCF are slightly worse. There is also an interesting phenomenon. The third picture in the first line is a snapshot of a car driving on the grassland. We found that many algorithms recommend the same photo, such as SUIF's first, ICF's second, the third of UCF, the fifth of WMF. We also looked at all the user's favorite images, and compared the features of the two images, we found that the two images were taken in the same place, the angle and content are slightly different, but the overall similarity is very high, what is to say the image styles are very close. This verifies the correctness of the implementation of the five algorithms to a certain extent, and on the other hand, the superiority of the recommended results can be shown. For the recommendation of multiple styles, we carefully observed the recommended images and found that the SUIF's results are the most similar in style. The first and fourth pictures are very similar in color and style to the first line. The fourth one also appears in WMF. The sixth one is very similar to the last one in the first line, but it is quite different from other pictures. It can be seen that the recommended result is acceptable when multiple styles coexist.

Fig. 4. The results of the five algorithms for User(b)'s photographic work recommendation, with the red box representation appearing in the user's favorite picture set I. The figure shows that users like a variety of styles of pictures. (Color figure online)

6   Conclusion

After a lot of experiments, our proposed method has shown very good result in the recommendation of photography images, which is better than other common algorithms. On the other hand, under the photography topic, the factor of image style should play an important role in the feature extraction. In the subsequent research, we need to study the representation of image style features more deeply, and we will apply our algorithm to similar applications in real life to get more interesting applications. At the same time, the user's social relationship will be considered in our recommendation system to assist in the promotion of the recommendation result.

References

1. Dalal, N., Triggs, B.: Histograms of oriented gradients for human detection. In: IEEE Computer Society Conference on Computer Vision and Pattern Recognition, pp. 88–893 (2005)
2. Lowe, D.G.: Distinctive image features from scale-invariant keypoints. Int. J. Comput. Vis. **60**, 91–110 (2004)
3. Krizhevsky, A., Sutskever, I., Hinton, G.E.: ImageNet classification with deep convolutional neural networks. In: Proceedings of the 25th International Conference on Neural Information Processing Systems, pp. 1097-1105 (2012)
4. Gatys, L.A., Ecker, A.S., Bethge, M.: Image style transfer using convolutional neural networks. In: Computer Vision and Pattern Recognition, pp. 2414–2423 (2016)
5. Lu, X., Lin, Z., Shen, X., Mech, R., Wang, J.Z.: Deep multi-patch aggregation network for image style, aesthetics, and quality estimation. In: IEEE International Conference on Computer Vision, pp. 990-998 (2015)
6. Tang, L., Chang, J.Y., Li, J., Yu, R.W.: A new accelerated algorithm of image style study. In: International Conference on Multimedia Information Networking and Security, pp. 244–248 (2009)
7. Sun, T., Wang, Y., Yang, J., Hu, X.: Convolution neural networks with two pathways for image style recognition. In: IEEE Transactions on Image Processing: A Publication of the IEEE Signal Processing Society, pp. 4102–4113 (2017)
8. Balabanović, M., Shoham, Y.: Fab: content-based, collaborative recommendation. Commun. ACM **40**, 66–72 (1997)
9. Saveski, M., Mantrach, A.: Item cold-start recommendations: learning local collective embeddings. In: ACM Conference on Recommender Systems, pp. 89-96 (2014)
10. Su, X., Khoshgoftaar, T.M.: A survey of collaborative filtering techniques. Adv. Artif. Intell., 2 (2009)
11. Sarwar, B., Karypis, G., Konstan, J., Riedl, J.: Application of dimensionality reduction in recommender system-a case study. Technical report, DTIC Document (2000)
12. Hu, Y., Koren, Y., Volinsky, C.: Collaborative filtering for implicit feedback datasets. In: Eighth IEEE International Conference on Data Mining, pp. 263–272 (2009)
13. Salakhutdinov, R., Mnih, A.: Probabilistic matrix factorization. In: International Conference on Neural Information Processing Systems, pp. 1257–1264 (2007)
14. Wang, C., Blei, D.M.: Collaborative topic modeling for recommending scientific articles. In: ACM SIGKDD International Conference on Knowledge Discovery and Data Mining, pp. 448–456 (2011)
15. Barragáns-Martínez, A.B., Costa-Montenegro, E., Burguillo, J.C., Rey-López, M., Mikic-Fonte, F.A., Peleteiro, A.: A hybrid content-based and item-based collaborative filtering approach to recommend TV programs enhanced with singular value decomposition. Inf. Sci. **180**, 4290–4311 (2010)
16. Geng, X., Zhang, H., Bian, J., Chua, T.S.: Learning image and user features for recommendation in social networks. In: IEEE International Conference on Computer Vision, pp. 4274-4282 (2015)
17. Dieleman, S., Schrauwen, B.: Deep content-based music recommendation. In: Advances in Neural Information Processing Systems, pp. 2643–2651 (2013)
18. Jenatton, R., Roux, N.L., Bordes, A., Obozinski, G.: A latent factor model for highly multi-relational data. In: International Conference on Neural Information Processing Systems, pp. 3167-3175 (2012)

19. Schafer, J.B., Frankowski, D., Herlocker, J., Sen, S.: Collaborative filtering recommender systems. ACM Trans. Inf. Syst., 5–53 (2004)
20. Krizhevsky, A., Sutskever, I., Hinton, G.E.: ImageNet classification with deep convolutional neural networks. In: International Conference on Neural Information Processing Systems, pp. 1097-1105 (2012)
21. Liu, L., Özsu, M.T.: Mean average precision. In: Liu, L., Özsu, M.T. (eds.) Encyclopedia of Database Systems. Springer, Boston (2009). https://doi.org/10.1007/978-0-387-39940-9_3032
22. Baddeley, A.: Area under ROC Curve. http://www.packages.ianhowson.com

Two-Level Attention with Multi-task Learning for Facial Emotion Estimation

Xiaohua Wang[1,2], Muzi Peng[1], Lijuan Pan[1], Min Hu[1(✉)], Chunhua Jin[2], and Fuji Ren[1,3]

[1] School of Computer Science and Information Engineering,
Hefei University of Technology, Hefei, China
{xh_wang,jsjxhumin}@hfut.edu.cn
[2] The Laboratory for Internet of Things and Mobile Internet Technology
of Jiangsu Province, Huaiyin Institute of Technology, Huai'an, China
[3] Faculty of Engineering, University of Tokushima, Tokushima, Japan

Abstract. Valence-Arousal model can represent complex human emotions, including slight changes of emotion. Most prior works of facial emotion estimation only considered laboratory data and used video, speech or other multi-modal features. The effect of these methods applied on static images in the real world is unknown. In this paper, a two-level attention with multi-task learning (MTL) framework is proposed for facial emotion estimation on static images. The features of corresponding region were automatically extracted and enhanced by first-level attention mechanism. And then we designed a practical structure to process the features extracted by first-level attention. In the following, we utilized Bi-directional Recurrent Neural Network (Bi-RNN) with self-attention (second-level attention) to make full use of the relationship of these features adaptively. It can be concluded as a combination of global and local information. In addition, we exploited MTL to estimate the value of valence and arousal simultaneously, which employed the correlation of the two tasks. The quantitative results conducted on AffectNet dataset demonstrated the superiority of the proposed framework. In addition, extensive experiments were carried out to analysis effectiveness of different components.

Keywords: Facial emotion estimation · Attention mechanism Multi-task learning

1 Introduction

Affective computing has developed rapidly in recent years and gradually become an attractive field. It plays an important role in the field of human-computer interaction (HCI). With the rapid development of network, countless images with facial emotions are posted in the social media every second and the application scenario of HCI is mainly in reality. Therefore, facial emotion recognition

© Springer Nature Switzerland AG 2019
I. Kompatsiaris et al. (Eds.): MMM 2019, LNCS 11295, pp. 227–238, 2019.
https://doi.org/10.1007/978-3-030-05710-7_19

(FER) in-the-wild is closer to the application. Distinct from FER in the laboratory environment, FER in-the-wild can be impacted seriously by a variety of non-emotion factors, including occlusion, facial posture, illumination and diverse subjects. Besides, the continuous model represents feeling more accurately and reflects the relationship of different emotions compared with discrete model. And the facial emotion with slight changes can also be reflected by continuous numerical value effectively.

Previous works mainly focused on FER (discrete model), extracted features were applied to the appropriate classifier or ensemble method to achieve results [1–3]. Some continuous model works were based on video, speech, or physiological signals [4,5] to estimate emotions. In generally, Long and Short Time Memory network (LSTM) or support vector regression (SVR) is exploited to predict the labels with the usage of temporal information. However, the data of various modalities mentioned above is arduous to collect, while image is relatively capable of constructing a larger dataset. We employed static image to estimate facial emotion on the Valence-Arousal model [6]. The intensity of valence and arousal represent the degree of positive or negative, calming or exciting respectively. The prediction of both is essentially a regression problem. As far as the research we have discovered, Mollahosseini [7] replaced the last fully connection (FC) layer with linear regression and trained arousal and valence task respectively. Nonetheless, it overlooked the correlation of the two tasks. Multi-task learning (MTL) utilizes the relationship of tasks adequately to enhance the generalization ability of model through shared features of different tasks. Furthermore, the training time can be curtailed to a certain extent. So MTL is adopted in the following research.

In addition, it is critical to diminish the impact of non-emotion factors. Many prior studies used Convolutional Neural Networks (CNN) to learn features related to emotion through metric learning. Liu [8] proposed (N+M)-tuplet loss to calculate the distance between positive and negative samples to diminish the burden brought by different subjects. Li [9] proposed Deep Locality Preserving loss (DLP-loss) function which is able to preserve the compactness of intra-class samples, improve the discriminative ability of features, and weaken the influence brought by non-emotion factors relatively. However, these methods through enhancing intra-class discriminative ability are not applicable on continuous model. Sun [10] employed the attention mechanism before the last FC layer of the CNN to feature mapping. The author claimed that the method can extract features of the region of interest (ROI) automatically. But Sun took the features last layer into account merely and neglected the attention information among the previous convolution layers.

In this work, we proposed a two-level attention with MTL framework for facial emotion estimation. Firstly, the residual attention mechanism proposed by Wang [11] was adopted to extract the features of different layers as the first-level attention. For the features with different receptive fields, we used convolution layer with 1*1 filter and Global Average Pooling (GAP) to transform them into input of second-level attention. In the following, we proposed to use

Bidirectional-Recurrent Neural Network (Bi-RNN) with self-attention to capitalize the information of different layers with diverse receptive fields. In other word, second-level attention extracted the information of relationship of global and local features automatically. In addition, considering the correlation of arousal and valence, we used MTL to predict the value of the two. In order to verify the proposed framework, we have conducted extensive experiments on an open dataset (AffectNet [7]) and achieved a remarkable result.

The rest of this paper is organized as follows. In the next section, we introduce the related work of this paper. We describe the framework we designed in detail in Sect. 3. Section 4 shows the experiments results and related analysis. Finally, we conclude the paper in the last section.

2   Related Work

2.1   Facial Emotion Estimation

The common procedure of facial emotion estimation and FER is extracting features from images or video sequences. Traditional methods usually capture facial information as the features, such as geometry, appearance, texture and so on. In the real world, facial emotion generally has enormous variations in facial posture, illumination, background and subject. Consequently, the above feature extracted methods cannot deal with such non-emotion factors well. And the generalization ability under the environment is relatively impaired. Recently, with the growth of computing power, many fields developed deep learning (DL) to achieve state-of-the-art results. The challenges brought about by non-emotion factors in the real world can be solved to a certain extent through DL. The estimation of facial emotions on continuous models still is a troublesome task with DL technology.

The researches of facial emotion estimation are frequently based on video sequence. Earlier researches were conducted on highly controllable datasets. In the competition of AVEC2017, the winner [4] combined the features of text, acoustic and video features and utilized LSTM to extract temporal information for the final prediction. Chang [12] proposed an integrated network to extract face attribute action unit (AU) information and estimate Valence-Arousal values simultaneously and achieved winner in AFF-wild. Where facial attribute features are regarded as shallow features and AU information as the intermediate features. Dimitrios [13] put the final convolution layer, pooling layer, and fully connected layer into the gated recurrent unit and fused the final results.

In terms of static images, in addition to the method proposed by Mollahosseini which we mentioned in Sect. 1. Zhou [14] also conducted the experiments on the FER-2013 dataset. The original dataset is marked as seven categories, and the author labelled these images by crowd-sourcing (Since the author has not publicly disclosed the labels, this paper had not conducted experiment on this dataset). Zhou replaced the last layer of VGG16 and ResNet with GAP layer and adopted bilinear pooling to predict the value of V-A. In this paper, we also employed static images to predict the value of V-A, which is a rigorous problem.

2.2   Attention Mechanism

The process of human perception proves the importance of the attention mechanism [15]. Broadly, attention can be seen as a mechanism for allocating available processing resources to the most signal-fertile components [16]. Presently, attention mechanism is extensively used in various fields, machine translation [17], visual question answering [18], image caption [19]. In previous researches, most of the attention mechanisms were implemented in sequence processing and there were a few researches utilized attention mechanism for image classification. Hu [16] designed Squeeze-and-Excitation Network to learn the weight of feature map in line with loss, which makes the quality features can be improved, futile features can be diluted. It can be seen as engaging attention mechanisms to feature maps on channel dimension. Wang [11] proposed an attention model for image classification which used an hourglass model to construct trunk and mask branch, where mask branch is a Bottom-up Top-down structure. The mask branch is able to generate soft attention weight. In this paper, we exploited the residual attention block proposed by Wang to extract the features as the first-level attention.

2.3   Multi-task Learning

Multi-task learning is widely used in computer vision and natural language processing [20,21]. All of the papers mentioned above showed that MTL can train a unified system to carry out multiple tasks simultaneously (The premise is that there is a certain correlation between tasks.). In [5], the author proposed a multi-task model to adapt Deep Belief Network (DBN), in which the classification of emotion was regarded as the main task, and the prediction of V-A was regarded as the secondary task. The results showed that MTL utilized the additional information between different tasks and advanced the results of emotion estimation. In [12], the author constructed an end-to-end network and trained facial attribute recognition, facial action unit recognition and V-A estimation synchronously. In this paper, we exploited our proposed MTL framework to extract the shared features representation between tasks in view of the correlation of the two tasks.

3   A Valence-Arousal Predicted Framework

In this section, we will introduce our proposed framework. It mainly includes the overall framework, the two-level attention mechanism, the regression method of predicting valence and arousal and multi-tasking learning method.

3.1   Overall Framework

Figure 1 shows the overall framework for facial emotion estimation in this paper. The proposed framework mainly consists of three parts. First, as the first-level attention, the features of different receptive fields with attention are extracted by residual attention block. And then distill the information of relationship between different receptive field features by Bi-RNN with self-attention as second-level attention. Finally, the MTL method is used to predict the values of valence and arousal simultaneously.

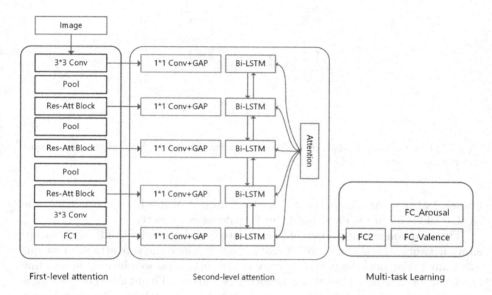

Fig. 1. An overview of our proposed framework. The framework is mainly contains three parts (first-level attention, second-level attention and multi-task learning).

3.2 First-Level Attention

The first-level attention features (attention-aware features) of this paper are extracted through residual attention block. The block adopts a bottom-up top-down structure to expand feedforward and feedback attention process into a single feedforward process, which makes it accessible to embed it into any end-to-end framework. As shown in the Fig. 2, the block has two branches: trunk branch and mask branch. The trunk branch has the same structure as the normal CNN and extracts the features by convolutional layers. The key component of the block is mask branch, which can generate soft weight attention. The mask branch utilizes several max pooling layers to expand the receptive field and obtains global information of the block. In the following, the same number of up-sample layers are manipulated to amplify feature map to the same size of input through the symmetric top-down structure (bilinear interpolation is adopted in up-sample layer). Finally, the sigmoid function is employed to regulate the output value to a range from 0 to 1, which is used as a control gate for trunk

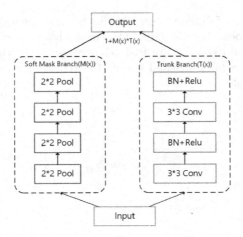

Fig. 2. The composition of attention block. The two branches were splitted from input and merged together finally.

branch features. At this point, the scale of output of mask branch is the same as that of trunk branch and both can be calculated directly.

The common attention model is calculated by dot product, but in the deepening network, the features will decay incredibly since the soft attention weight less than 1. Further, the potential error of soft attention weight may undermine the favorable features that trunk branch has learned. Therefore, the block constructs an approximate identical mapping structure to settle the above problems. The output of the entire block is as follow:

$$H_{i,c}(x) = (1 + M_{i,c}(x)) * T_{i,c}(x). \tag{1}$$

Where i denotes the ith pixel while c represents the cth channel of the feature maps. When $M_{i,c}(x)$ is close to zero, $H_{i,c}(x)$ is basically approximate to that of $F_{i,c}(x)$. $M(x)$ is capable to enhance the high quality features and weaken the non-significant features. In the forward process, it works as the feature selector with attention, and can easily update the gradient in the backward propagation. The gradient derivative formula is as follow:

$$\frac{\partial H(x; \theta, \phi)}{\partial \phi} = (1 + M(x; \theta)) \frac{\partial T(x; \phi)}{\partial \phi}. \tag{2}$$

Where ϕ is the parameter of trunk branch and θ is the parameter of mask branch. The presence of mask branch enhances the robustness of the network and prevents wrong gradients from noisy label to update the trunk branch parameters. Besides, the "1" in Eq. 1 enables trunk features to bypass soft mask branch and reach the output of block directly, which weakens the ability of feature selector of mask branch. Consequently, we can retain high quality features and suppress even discard some poor features appropriately through the block.

3.3 Second-Level Attention

To simulate the way human look at things, we're not looking at the whole image simply. Most grasp the target as a whole first, and scan the target in a order from global to local with the prior impression. In other words, people generally look at the outline and then perceive the details, combine global and local information to comprehend and judge the target. Abstractly, the way people look at images can also be seen as a sequence model, not only the order from global to local, but also combine global with local information which corresponding to different level features. The residual attention block mentioned in the previous part only extracted features for a certain size of receptive fields. Considered the above cognition, we judiciously adopted Bi-RNN to imitate this process. We exploited the self-attention mechanism to learn the features extracted from different receptive fields adequately. Merged with Bi-RNN, we assimilated the information both in a order from global to local and local to global. Therefore, Bi-RNN combined with self-attention model was utilized to extract features of different levels (the effectiveness analysis of this component will be presented in Sect. 4.4).

For the sequence to sequence problem, the input of Bi-RNN is vectors of multiple time steps. While the input in this paper is feature vectors of different levels (different receptive fields). In generally, most prior researches used the fully connected layer as the input vectors. Considered the huge amount of parameters in FC, we designed a simple structure as illustrated in Fig. 1. A convolution layer with $1*1$ filter was used to reduce or elevate dimensions to a fixed number for different layers. Followed by a GAP layer, the dimensions of output at each level were consistent. The input vectors can be represented as $X = (x_1, x_2, \ldots, x_l)$. We concatenate the hidden states (forward and backward process) of Bi-RNN to vectors $H = (h_1, h_2, \ldots, h_l)$. And the output of Bi-RNN can be represented as $Y = (y_1, y_2 \ldots, y_l)$. Therefore, the output with self-attention can be calculated:

$$Y_{att} = \sum_{i=1}^{l} y_i \frac{exp(score(h_i, y_i))}{\sum_{i=1}^{l} exp(score(h_i, y_i))}. \tag{3}$$

We implemented dot production as the score function here. The output vectors were utilized as the input of linear regression in the next part.

3.4 Regression Method

In generally, mean square error (MSE) is used as the loss function in the training phase for regression model. The calculate formula of mse is as follow:

$$L = \sum_{i=1}^{n} (y_i - \hat{y}_i)^2. \tag{4}$$

Where y_i represents the ground label and $\hat{y}_i$ represents the predicted label. Although MSE gives more punishment to samples with large error, it is sensitive to the outliers. The dataset (described in Sect. 4.1) was constructed by crowdsourcing method, and the labels of annotation are accurate to 1e−5. Owing to the subjective consciousness of annotators, the dataset may contains some inconsistent or imprecise labels. In this paper, we adopted Tukey's biweight function [22] as the loss function of our framework to overcome the problem. And the specific formula is as follow:

$$L_{tukey} = \begin{cases} \frac{c^2}{6} * \left[1 - (1 - \frac{y_i - \hat{y_i}}{c}^2)^3\right] & if |y_i - \hat{y_i}| \leq c \\ \frac{c^2}{6} & otherwise \end{cases} \tag{5}$$

Where c is a hyper parameter. It was set to 4.685 empirically. Unlike MSE, Tukey's biweight function is a non-convex function. The magnitude gradient of the noisy label sample can be reduced close to zero during back-propagation and the problem of human-labeled can be deal with effectively.

3.5 Multi-tasking Learning

Multi-task learning utilizes the correlation between multi-tasks and learns the shared feature representations of them. It raises the generalization ability of the model and shorten the training time tremendously. Due to the high correlation between the prediction of valence and arousal, we adopted multi-tasking learning to the framework to predict both simultaneously. In MTL, choosing which parts of framework as the shared layers will bring different effects. Excessive shared layers cannot reflect the distinction between tasks, but too few shared layers cannot learn the commonality of tasks. While appropriate shared layers maximize the use of the correlation of tasks and make them have certain independence.

In our proposed framework, the two tasks are separated after the feature extraction of the second-level attention. And two different fully connected layers are employed to predict the corresponding target tasks. In Sect. 4, the experiments of different shared parts were also carried out to demonstrate the effectiveness of our approach. In conjunction with Tukey's biweight loss, the training goal of our framework is to minimize:

$$L_{total} = \alpha L_{valence} + \beta L_{arousal}. \tag{6}$$

Where α and β are hyper parameters for balancing two tasks. In our framework, they were set to 0.5 and 1, respectively. The reason for the setting is that the valence task is easier to converge in our experiment.

4   Experiment and Analysis

4.1 Datasets and Performance Measures

Currently, AffectNet [7] is the largest dataset for facial emotion on the discrete and continuous models. The data was crawled under three search engines (Google Bing and Yahoo) with 1250 emotion-related tags. The collected images are widely distributed in most range of ages. In the dataset, nearly 10% of faces have glasses, 50% of faces have makeup on the eyes and lips and postures of faces are also various. Therefore, the distribution of the AffectNet is extraordinarily similar to the real world. About 300,000 face images are correctly labeled as continuous values by crowdsourcing. The values of valence and arousal are in the range of $[-1, 1]$. Since the author has not published the test set yet, we used the validation set to verify the approach proposed in the paper.

In order to evaluate our proposed framework, we calculated Root Mean Square Error (RMSE) and Concordance Correlation Coefficient (CCC). In the following, we briefly present the definitions of these measures.

Root Mean Square Error (RMSE) can heavily weigh the outliers, but does not take into account the correlation between the data, which is defined as follow:

$$RMSE = \sqrt{\frac{1}{n} \sum_{i=1}^{n} (y_i - \hat{y}_i)^2}. \tag{7}$$

Concordance Correlation Coefficient (CCC) measures the disparity of the data while taking into account the covariance of the data. Consequently, CCC is broadly used in various competitions (AVEC, OMG, Aff-Wild), the definition of CCC is as follow:

$$CCC = \frac{2s_{y\hat{y}}}{s_y^2 + s_{\hat{y}}^2 + (\bar{y} - \bar{\hat{y}})}. \tag{8}$$

Where s_y and $s_{\hat{y}}$ are the variances of the ground labels and predicted labels respectively, $s_{y\hat{y}}$ represents the covariance of the two. $\bar{y}$ and $\bar{\hat{y}}$ are the corresponding mean values.

4.2 Implement Details

In the aspect of image preprocessing, we adopted the current SOTA method, i.e. Multi-task Convolutional Networks (MTCNN) [23], to detect facial landmarks and align the faces base these points. The images were cropped and scaled to a size of 56 * 56. After gray scaled the images, we flipped them on the horizontal direction and random cropped to 48 * 48 as data augmentation. During the test, we did the same processing on the test set, averaging the predicted values of the two flipped images. For convolution layers and fully connection layers, we initialized with He and Xavier method, respectively. In order to optimize the parameters in the network, we chose RMSPROP as the optimization algorithm with a batch size 128. The initial learning rate was set to 1e−3, when the loss did not drop, the learning rate was divided by 10. We spent nearly 10 h to train the entire model for 10 epochs with Titan-X GPU support.

4.3 Results

Table 1 shows the experimental results of our framework on the validation set of AffectNet. For fair comparison, we used the same training set and validation set as in [7]. It can be seen that CCC of arousal was improved enormously than others, approximately 35% higher than the results in [24], but only 3% higher in valence. Since we found that the loss of valence decreased expeditiously in the beginning of training and quickly converged, while the loss of arousal declined slightly. The results of both SVR and CNN also demonstrated that the features of valence could be effortlessly learned, but the features of arousal were arduously to learn. The results also proved that our proposed framework can effectively utilize the correlation of the two tasks and enhance the prediction results of the two tasks. In addition, the input size of our framework is 48 * 48, which is one twenty-eighth of that in [7], hence the computation was greatly curtailed and training time was reduced by nearly half. It also evaluated that our approach is capable to achieve acceptable results with lower resolution images.

Table 1. Comparisons with current methods on AffectNet dataset.

Method	CCC		RMSE		Input size
	Valence	Arousal	Valence	Arousal	
SVR [7]	0.372	0.182	0.513	0.384	256 * 256
CNN [24]	0.600	0.340	0.410	0.370	256 * 256
Ours	0.618	0.460	0.393	0.360	48 * 48

4.4   Ablation Study and Effectiveness Analysis

We have also conducted extensive experiments to demonstrate the impact of different components in our framework. Our framework mainly consists of two components: the two-level attention and multi-task learning. The CCC performance of these experiments are presented in Table 2.

Table 2. Performance of ablation study and effectiveness analysis.

Method	CCC	
	Valence	Arousal
Baseline	0.589	0.423
1st-level attention	0.605	0.437
Without MTL	0.602	0.344
MTL until FC1	0.610	0.448
Ours	0.618	0.460

Two-Level Attention. Baseline represents the results adopted basic CNN with MTL. "1st-level" denotes the experiment implemented baseline with first-level attention. The enhancement of CCC compared with baseline exposed that the soft weight attention mechanism of mask branch boosted the ability of feature extracting spatial regions. "Ours" denotes the experiment with two-level attention. Self-attention mechanism was applied to the features of different receptive fields, which took advantage of the information represented the relationship of global and the local features. It also improved the results compared with the "1st-level".

Multi-task Learning. We carried on two additional experiments based on two-level attention: ablation multi-task learning and share features layers until the first FC. We can conclude that the CCC performance of arousal without MTL was significantly worse than ours. The main reason is that it did not take advantage of the correlation of different tasks. And when the two tasks shared features that included first FC and former layers, the performance of CCC in arousal had been improved. But the result was not as better as our method, mainly because it didn't mine enough shared features.

5 Conclusion

In this paper, we constructed a two-level attention with MTL framework for facial emotion estimation. In order to enhance the ability of neural network to extract features, we employed residual attention block to extract the features in the region of interest automatically. And Bi-RNN with self-attention was proposed to seize the relationship between the features of different size receptive fields and extract features adaptively. Finally, the labels of arousal and valence of facial emotions were predicted simultaneously through MTL method which consider the correlation information of both. The CCC performances in dataset were relatively high, 0.618 for valence and 0.460 for arousal. The experimental results were significantly improved. Besides, ablation study and effectiveness analysis also showed the superiority of proposed framework and the contribution of different components. In the future, we will apply our method to more datasets to verify its effectiveness.

References

1. Jung, H., Lee, S., Yim, J., Park, S., Kim, J.: Joint fine-tuning in deep neural networks for facial expression recognition. In: Proceedings of the IEEE International Conference on Computer Vision, pp. 2983–2991 (2015)
2. Kim, B.K., Dong, S.Y., Roh, J., Kim, G., Lee, S.Y.: Fusing aligned and non-aligned face information for automatic affect recognition in the wild: a deep learning approach. In: Proceedings of the IEEE Conference on Computer Vision and Pattern Recognition Workshops, pp. 48–57 (2016)
3. Zhang, K., Huang, Y., Du, Y., Wang, L.: Facial expression recognition based on deep evolutional spatial-temporal networks. IEEE Trans. Image Process. **26**(9), 4193–4203 (2017)
4. Chen, S., Jin, Q., Zhao, J., Wang, S.: Multimodal multi-task learning for dimensional and continuous emotion recognition. In: Proceedings of the 7th Annual Workshop on Audio/Visual Emotion Challenge, pp. 19–26. ACM (2017)
5. Xia, R., Liu, Y.: A multi-task learning framework for emotion recognition using 2D continuous space. IEEE Trans. Affect. Comput. **1**, 3–14 (2017)

6. Russell, J.A.: A circumplex model of affect. J. Pers. Socialpsychol. **39**(6), 1161 (1980)
7. Mollahosseini, A., Hasani, B., Mahoor, M.H.: AffectNet: a database for facial expression, valence, and arousal computing in the wild. arXiv preprint arXiv:1708.03985 (2017)
8. Liu, X., Kumar, B.V., You, J., Jia, P.: Adaptive deep metric learning for identity-aware facial expression recognition. In: CVPR Workshops, pp. 522–531 (2017)
9. Li, S., Deng, W., Du, J.: Reliable crowdsourcing and deep locality-preserving learning for expression recognition in the wild. In: 2017 IEEE Conference on Computer Vision and Pattern Recognition (CVPR), pp. 2584–2593. IEEE (2017)
10. Sun, W., Zhao, H., Jin, Z.: A visual attention based ROI detection method for facial expression recognition. Neurocomputing **296**, 12–22 (2018)
11. Wang, F., et al.: Residual attention network for image classification. arXiv preprint arXiv:1704.06904 (2017)
12. Chang, W.Y., Hsu, S.H., Chien, J.H.: FATAUVA-Net: an integrated deep learning framework for facial attribute recognition, action unit (au) detection, and valence-arousal estimation. In: Proceedings of the IEEE Conference onComputer Vision and Pattern Recognition Workshop (2017)
13. Kollias, D., Zafeiriou, S.: A multi-component CNN-RNN approach for dimensional emotion recognition in-the-wild. arXiv preprint arXiv:1805.01452 (2018)
14. Zhou, F., Kong, S., Fowlkes, C., Chen, T., Lei, B.: Fine-grained facial expression analysis using dimensional emotion model. arXiv preprint arXiv:1805.01024 (2018)
15. Mnih, V., Heess, N., Graves, A., et al.: Recurrent models of visual attention. In: Advances in Neural Information Processing Systems, pp. 2204–2212 (2014)
16. Hu, J., Shen, L., Sun, G.: Squeeze-and-excitation networks. arXiv preprint arXiv:1709.01507 **7** (2017)
17. Vaswani, A., et al.: Attention is all you need. In: Advances in Neural Information Processing Systems, pp. 5998–6008 (2017)
18. Das, A., Agrawal, H., Zitnick, L., Parikh, D., Batra, D.: Human attention in visual question answering: do humans and deep networks look at the same regions? Comput. Vis. Image Underst. **163**, 90–100 (2017)
19. Xu, K., et al.: Show, attend and tell: neural image caption generation with visual attention. In: International Conference on Machine Learning, pp. 2048–2057 (2015)
20. Chang, J., Scherer, S.: Learning representations of emotional speech with deep convolutional generative adversarial networks. In: 2017 IEEE International Conference on Acoustics, Speech and Signal Processing (ICASSP), pp. 2746–2750. IEEE (2017)
21. Duan, M., Li, K., Tian, Q.: A novel multi-task tensor correlation neural network for facial attribute prediction. arXiv preprint arXiv:1804.02810 (2018)
22. Black, M.J., Rangarajan, A.: On the unification of line processes, outlier rejection, and robust statistics with applications in early vision. Int. J. Comput. Vis. **19**(1), 57–91 (1996)
23. Zhang, K., Zhang, Z., Li, Z., Qiao, Y.: Joint face detection and alignment using multitask cascaded convolutional networks. IEEE Sig. Process. Lett. **23**(10), 1499–1503 (2016)
24. Mahoor, M.H.: AffectNet. http://mohammadmahoor.com/affectnet/. Accessed 27 July 2018

User Interaction for Visual Lifelog Retrieval in a Virtual Environment

Aaron Duane$^{(\boxtimes)}$ and Cathal Gurrin

Insight Centre for Data Analytics, Dublin, Ireland
aaron.duane@insight-centre.org, cathal.gurrin@dcu.ie

Abstract. Efficient retrieval of lifelog information is an ongoing area of research due to the multifaceted nature, and ever increasing size of lifelog datasets. Previous studies have examined lifelog exploration on conventional hardware platforms, but in this paper we describe a novel approach to lifelog retrieval using virtual reality. The focus of this research is to identify what aspects of lifelog retrieval can be effectively translated from a conventional to a virtual environment and if it provides any benefit to the user. The most widely available lifelog datasets for research are primarily image-based and focus on continuous capture from a first-person perspective. These large image corpora are often enhanced by image processing techniques and various other metadata. Despite the rapidly maturing nature of virtual reality as a platform, there has been very little investigation into user interaction within the context of lifelogging. The experiment outlined in this work seeks to evaluate four different virtual reality user interaction approaches to lifelog retrieval. The prototype system used in this experiment also competed at the Lifelog Search Challenge at ACM ICMR 2018 where it ranked first place.

Keywords: Virtual reality · Lifelog · Retrieval · User interaction

1 Introduction

The most prevalent form of lifelog data at present is visual data captured from wearable cameras. This data is typically captured continuously from the first-person perspective and a single lifelogger can produce thousands of images per day. Distilling this huge and ever-increasing dataset of images into actionable insights about the individual's life is a core aspect of lifelogging research. Most often this is assisted by automated image processing techniques such as concept detection and event segmentation. The enhanced metadata generated by these techniques then needs to be exposed intuitively to users alongside the visual imagery in order to support effective retrieval of lifelog information.

Previous research [1] in this area has focused on various hardware platforms such as desktops, tablets, and smart-phones; where each device was investigated for its impact on lifelog exploration use cases. In this paper we expand on that research by evaluating the potential of virtual reality (using the HTC Vive) as a

© Springer Nature Switzerland AG 2019
I. Kompatsiaris et al. (Eds.): MMM 2019, LNCS 11295, pp. 239–250, 2019.
https://doi.org/10.1007/978-3-030-05710-7_20

platform for visual lifelog retrieval. Though virtual reality has yet to become as ubiquitous as phones or tablet computers, the hardware is continually becoming more sophisticated and affordable. It is our hypothesis that visualising complex multi-faceted data in three dimensions alongside a broader field of view could be a more intuitive and efficient method of visual lifelog exploration.

While there are numerous potential benefits to interacting with a lifelog system in a virtual environment, the focus of this research is specifically on lifelog retrieval, defined as the ability of a lifelog system to "retrieve specific digital information" [2]. Unlike some other lifelogging use cases, such as reminiscence or reflection [2], retrieval is the most suitable due to the ease of evaluation and potential for use as a daily life assistance or memory support tool [3]. Evaluating these lifelog retrieval systems is most often accomplished by means of a known-item search task where a set of topics are defined based on events that appear in an individual's lifelog (e.g. waiting for a bus, drinking a coffee, etc.). Participants then attempt to search for these topics using their respective lifelog retrieval systems.

The goal of the experiment outlined in this paper was to determine a quantitative measure of the effectiveness of four different approaches to user interaction within a virtual environment and infer which one would be most suited, if any, to visual lifelog retrieval. In addition, we also wanted to determine a qualitative reflection of the system and interaction methodologies as a whole to help improve the virtual interface and user experience. To the best of our knowledge, this is the first lifelog interaction mechanism that has been developed for an environment in virtual reality [4]. This research is conducted as part of a larger study which also explores different data visualisation techniques for lifelog data in virtual reality.

2   Dataset

One of the largest obstacles in lifelogging research is the availability of test collections of sufficient quality and size. This is because there are significant technical challenges to overcome from the gathering of the data, its semantic enrichment and also ensuring the privacy of the individuals captured in the personal archive. The dataset utilised in this paper was sourced from the NTCIR conference [3] where it was originally released as part of the conference's lifelog tasks, which included a known-item search task referred to as the Lifelog Semantic Access Task (LSAT) [5]. The collection contains 90 days of data from 2 lifeloggers who together captured about 114,000 images. These images were then semantically enriched with automatic image processing techniques. The most valuable enrichment was the concept detection which resulted in each image in the dataset being tagged with an average of 5–10 concepts to describe its content (see Fig. 1). A total of 48 known-item topics were released alongside the test collection, 24 for each of the two lifeloggers present in the dataset. These topics encompassed a broad range of life experience from the mundane (e.g. eating pasta for lunch) to the unusual (e.g. being interviewed for television). For the scope of our experiment, we determined using one lifelogger and their corresponding 24 known-item topics would be sufficient.

concepts: {
"person",
"indoor"
"coffee",
"laptop",
"computer"
}

Fig. 1. Example image from test collection with concepts

3 Virtual Reality

The rationale for investigating the impact of virtual reality on visual lifelog exploration is based on its highly immersive quality. There are numerous benefits to operating in highly immersive environments; the most obvious being the ability for individuals to garner first-hand experience in an activity without actually engaging in said activity. For example in healthcare, a surgeon could practice an operation without risk of patient injury. However, there are other benefits to immersion that are less obvious. For example, actively using more of the human sensory capability and motor skills has been known to increase understanding and learning [6] and new research has suggested that immersion greatly improves user recall [7]. Also our ability to engage with digital elements directly in an open three dimensional environment more closely simulates our natural environment more so than a two dimensional analogue. This could suggest user interactions in virtual reality have the potential to be more intuitive, especially for novice users. It is difficult to speculate on every potential impact virtual reality might have on lifelog exploration, especially at this early stage, but we feel there is sufficient potential to warrant an exploratory examination of its applicability.

Virtual reality platforms, when compared to more conventional platforms such as laptops and phones, are in their relative infancy and this is compounded by the cost of the hardware to date. It still requires significant computing resources to generate high resolution virtual environments. However, the cost of the first generation of head-mounted displays has already notably reduced and more virtual reality platforms enter the consumer market each year, generating increased competition and more affordable pricing. It is reasonable to predict that as the hardware becomes more accessible to consumers, its application and use cases will become more sophisticated and nuanced. Using virtual reality to explore lifelog data may seem like a niche area today, but if we envision a future where virtual reality is as simple as equipping a mobile device and lightweight headset, it has potential to be preferable and more intuitive than previous conventional platforms.

Though there has been almost no research targeting the exploration of lifelogs in virtual reality, there has been some applications developed for the platform that could facilitate aspects of exploring and retrieving life experiences. One obvious example is the playback of 360° video which is considerably more immersive when viewed in virtual reality and is especially so when the footage is recorded from a more familiar first-person perspective. This evolution of immersion within virtual reality can extend to many interaction methodologies that could better facilitate lifelog exploration. This is not to suggest that explicit examples of lifelog interaction in virtual reality do not exist at all. For example, an art installation by Alan Kwan titled 'Bad Trip'[1] was developed in 2012 which enables users to explore a manifestation of the creator's mind and life experience within a virtual environment. There are also non-lifelog related image retrieval systems developed for virtual reality which do things like map the virtual environment's three axes to facets of image content [8].

For the scope of research carried out in this paper, it was decided to use the HTC Vive[2], developed by HTC and Valve, as the virtual reality (VR) platform. At the time of writing, it is one of the most technically sophisticated virtual reality platforms available to consumers. However, it is important to acknowledge that the work undertaken in this research area is intended to be applicable to virtual reality as a whole and not strictly limited to the scope of what is possible with the HTC Vive. Therefore where possible, the evaluation criteria implemented in this work has been adapted to account for any virtual reality platform, with the caveat that it should also be equipped with two wireless controllers that are tracked in real-time alongside the head-mounted display.

4   System Overview

As previously stated, the focus of this experiment was to determine a quantitative measure of the effectiveness of four different approaches (see Fig. 2) to user interaction performing lifelog retrieval tasks in a virtual environment. We also wanted to determine a qualitative reflection of the system and interaction methodologies to help address any notable flaws in the virtual user interface that may have been overlooked. The prototype system has two primary components, each of which needed to be optimised for virtual reality. The querying component was a virtual interface designed to provide a quick and efficient means for a user to generate a faceted query within the prototype system. While there are many approaches that one could take to input queries, a decision was made to focus on gesture-based interaction, as opposed to other forms of interaction.

The gesture-based querying interface consists of two sub-menus, one for selecting lifelog concepts of interest and the second for selecting the temporal aspect of the query (e.g. hours of the day or days of the week). A typical

---

[1] Alan Kwan's 'Bad Trip' - https://www.kwanalan.com/blank.

[2] HTC Vive - https://www.vive.com/eu/product/.

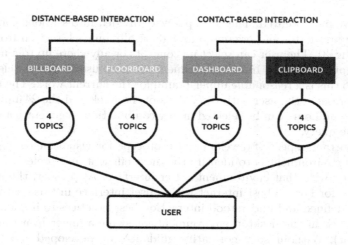

Fig. 2. Each user performed 4 topics on each of the 4 VR interaction modes

query to the system, such as "using the computer on a Saturday afternoon" would require the user to use the concept sub-menu to select the appropriate visual descriptors (e.g. computer or laptop) and the temporal sub-menu to select the time range (afternoon) and the day of the week (Saturday). The user then hits the submit button and the query is executed and the result is displayed for the user to browse. The concept sub-menu is shown in Fig. 3 and the temporal sub-menu is shown in Fig. 4. This querying interface is available for the user to bring up at any time by pressing a dedicated button on either of the two wireless controllers available with the HTC Vive. When the user submits their query, the interface disappears and the user is free to explore/browse the results inside the virtual environment.

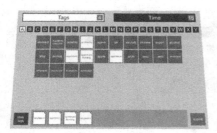

Fig. 3. The user can filter with up to 10 selected concepts at once

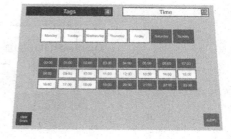

Fig. 4. The user can select any combination of days and hours to filter

The lifelog concepts that populate the concept sub-menu represent the original concepts that accompanied the dataset release; no additional computer vision outputs were incorporated. The concepts were divided into sections corresponding to their first letter and organised alphabetically on each section from left to right (see Fig. 3). The user can select no concepts or anywhere up to a maximum of 10 concepts per query. In our experimentation, no user has ever selected ten concepts, so this is a reasonable upper-bound for the current work. The temporal sub-menu presents the user with the 7 days of the week and the 24 h of the day. These days and hours can be selected in any combination to generate a temporal facet for the query.

An important aspect of developing a prototype for visual lifelog exploration in a virtual environment is to identify the most efficient and preferred methods of interacting with that environment's user interface. At present, there is not a clear answer for how to best interact with a user interface in this context; there are no well defined and understood interaction best practices to implement (e.g. point-and-click in the desktop environment, or swipe-a-finger in a touchscreen environment). Without such normative guidance, we developed two high-level interaction methodologies to interfacing with our prototype which we refer to as 'distance-based' and 'contact-based' user interaction. These two methodologies were further divided into two low-level variations for a total of four interaction modes in total.

4.1   Distance-Based Interaction

The distance-based approach utilises interactive beams which originate at the top of the user's wireless controllers. These beams are projected when the controllers are pointed at any relevant interface in the virtual environment and directly interact with that interface's elements (see Fig. 5). This method of interaction is comparable to a lean-back style of lifelog browsing as introduced in [9] and is functionally similar to using a television remote or other such device. Pressing a button on the controllers selects the concept or time-range that is being pointed

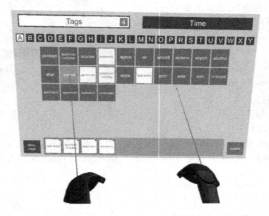

Fig. 5. Distance-based user interaction

at. Naturally, it is possible to use both hands to select concepts in parallel, should a sufficiently dexterous user be generating queries.

The low-level variations within the distance-based approach to interaction differ in the positioning of the user interface within the virtual environment. One variation orients the menu vertically and across from the user, which we refer to as the *billboard* style of interaction. The second variation places the menu horizontally and beneath the user, which we refer to as the *floorboard* style of interaction.

4.2   Contact-Based Interaction

The contact-based approach utilises a much more direct form of interaction where the user must physically touch the interface elements with their controllers. To facilitate this process, the controllers are outfitted with a drumstick-like device protruding from the head of each controller (see Fig. 6). This object was added to enhance precision and fidelity when contacting interface elements. This method of interaction is reminiscent of a more conventional style of lifelog browsing where the controller drumsticks mimic how our fingers interact with a keyboard or touchscreen. Tactile feedback is provided via the controllers to reflect hitting the keys.

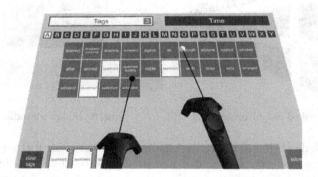

Fig. 6. Contact-based user interaction

Similar to before, the low-level variations within the contact-based approach to interaction differ in the positioning of the user interface. One variation orients the menu at a slight angle in front of the user and they have the option of interacting with it using both controllers. We refer to this as the *dashboard* style of interaction. The second variation attaches the menu directly to one of the user's controllers (their choice) and the user interacts with the menu using the opposing controller. We refer to this as the *clipboard* style of interaction.

The two high-level interaction methodologies, distance and contact, are based on real-world analogues (television, keyboard, touchscreen, etc.) and can be observed in various forms in industry-standard virtual reality applications such as the HTC Vive's main menu[3] or Google's popular Tilt Brush interface[4]. The low-level variations within these two methodologies were developed to further expand on how different interaction types impacted user experience.

4.3   Lifelog Data Ranking and Visualisation

As previously stated, after a faceted query is submitted to the system, the querying interface disappears and the user is presented with the highly-ranked filtered images (see Fig. 7) in decreasing rank order. These images are ranked using a combination of concept relevance and the time of capture (maintaining the temporal organisation of the data), where concept relevance takes precedence over the temporal arrangement. For example, if the user creates a query containing 3 different concepts, then images containing all 3 concepts will be ranked first in the list, followed by images containing 2, and then 1. When multiple images contain the same amount of relevant concepts, those images are ranked temporally according to the image capture time.

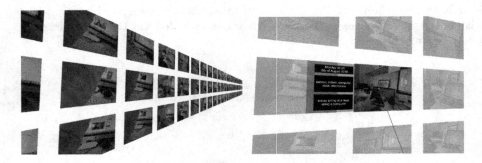

Fig. 7. Ranked list of images   **Fig. 8.** Image metadata

Any image displayed in the ranked list can be selected for further exploration by pointing the user's controller at it and pressing a button. This displays additional metadata about the image such as the specific capture date and time and what concepts have been detected (see Fig. 8). Additional filtering options are also made available along with this metadata. For example, the user can choose to see other images contained in the manually annotated event this image was labelled under or they can simply view all the images captured before and after the target image within a specific timespan.

5   Experiment Configuration

This experiment utilises known-item search tasks as the evaluation methodology to quantitatively compare different approaches to lifelog retrieval in virtual

---

[3] SteamVR - http://store.steampowered.com/steamvr.
[4] Google Tiltbrush - https://www.tiltbrush.com.

reality. Each participant also answers a post-experiment user feedback questionnaire (containing an open input field) to qualitatively evaluate how the system performed.

A total of 16 participants volunteered to take part in the experiment. The minimum criteria to participate was a strong understanding of the English language and rudimentary computer skills. It was not a requirement for participants to have any knowledge or experience with virtual reality prior to testing. To reduce any potential cognitive bias, each user was given a thorough walkthrough of the system prior to testing and needed to successfully complete a trial topic on each interaction type before proceeding with the experiment.

Each person attempted to identify a subset of 16 topics from the NTCIR test collection [3]. Since they were wearing a VR headset, the topics were described by an assistant. The description of each topic was taken directly from the test collection so every user received an identical definition of the topic prior to testing. The users were timed and given a maximum of 180 s to identify a relevant image from the dataset, reflecting the currently described topic, before moving onto the next topic.

To evenly assess each of the four interaction types (billboard, floorboard, dashboard and clipboard), the 16 topics were divided into four groups of four. Each user attempted to identify four topics on each interaction type until all four interaction types and all 16 topics were used. The experiment was purposefully configured so that each topic would be explored on each of the four interaction types a total of four times and that the ordering for each user would account for any learning bias.

6   Results

6.1   User Performance

The 180 s time limit per topic was imposed to prevent a topic taking an excessive amount of time and was also the same number of seconds allocated in the Lifelog Search Challenge [10] at ACM ICMR 2018 which used a subset of the NTCIR test collection employed in this work. If the user exceeded this limit, they would immediately stop and proceed to the next topic.

In Fig. 9 we can see a visualisation displaying the time taken to identify a topic on each of the four interaction types. Each of the 16 topics are labelled on the horizontal axis (with the topic ids taken from the test collection) and the vertical axis represents the average time in seconds each topic took to complete. The four interaction types are represented by four coloured bars for each topic and there is an indication beneath each topic of how many times a user failed to find relevant content (by exceeding the 180 s limit).

For the majority of topics, the interaction approaches performed similarly, suggesting that there is no clearly superior interaction approach. However there was some inconsistency in topics T2, T17 and T22. The fact that these are also the only topics which were failed by a number of users suggests this inconsistency is unrelated to the interaction type and is more likely the result of how some users interpreted the topic description. For example, T17 was a topic describing the lifelogger being recorded for a television show, and many participants correctly used 'camera' as a concept to filter with, as logically the lifelogger's personal camera would capture the television camera recording them. However, many participants failed to make this connection and instead used the 'television' concept which resulted in a significant number of false positives being returned.

It is immediately apparent that T7 proved the most difficult for participants with the highest average time across all interaction types and the most failed attempts. For this topic, the users were asked to locate an image where the lifelogger was presenting or lecturing to students in a classroom environment. However, there were no obvious concepts in the test collection related to this topic (i.e. 'classroom', 'presentation', etc. did not exist), so it was universally challenging for all users across all interaction types.

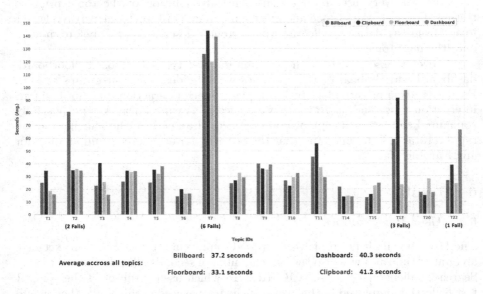

Fig. 9. Average seconds taken per topic on each interaction type

6.2 User Feedback

The experiment participants were asked to fill out a user experience questionnaire after each group of four topics, corresponding to the interaction type they had just used (billboard, dashboard, etc.). Each questionnaire contained usability statements which the users needed to state their level of agreement with on a five-point Likert [11] scale. Most importantly, the users were asked an open question about the usability of each interaction type and if they felt it could be improved. Finally, at the end of the experiment, the participants were asked to rank the four interaction types in order of their preference.

The most popular distance-based approach was the 'billboard' style interaction and the most popular contact-based approach was the 'dashboard' style interaction. There was a slight overall preference towards the distance-based approaches, which we suspect is due the familiar nature of the point-and-click interaction. Pointing and clicking came a lot more naturally to participants due to their experience with televisions and remote controls, whereas physically contacting digital interface elements required more practice to become accustomed with. Despite the general preference for the distance-based interaction, many users expressed positive sentiment for the contact-based approach for specific use cases, like selecting many interface elements in a short amount of time. However, there was notable discomfort using the 'clipboard' style interaction as it relied on controlling two separate interactive elements at once (the menu and the drumstick) which some users found challenging to coordinate.

Based on user feedback, we suspect a hybrid system utilising the elements of both the 'billboard' and 'dashboard' modes of user interaction would be the most effective interaction methodology. For example, a distance-based approach is most suited to more casual user interactions, such as browsing, whereas more complex user interactions, such as typing, would be most suited to a contact-based approach. Furthermore, ensuring that the user interface's position is static in the virtual environment, but adjustable by the user at any time, was a recurring sentiment.

7 Conclusion

In this paper we outlined our work developing a quantitative and qualitative evaluation methodology to develop a state of the art user interface for a lifelog retrieval system in virtual reality. This work did not extend to evaluating the data visualisation aspect of a virtual reality lifelog retrieval system as this will be addressed in a future work. Some of the key insights we determined during this study were to direct the attention of the users to newly exposed interface elements within the virtual environment to prevent any user getting lost in the virtual space. Also ensure all interface elements are resizeable and repositionable by the user to maximise content legibility and reduce eye strain. Where relevant, it is suggested to utilise a point and click interaction system for low precision tasks and a contact-based interaction system for high precision tasks. Clearly label and highlight the VR controller buttons when they are contextually relevant to the user interaction. These insights, and the remainder of the work outlined in this paper, contributed to the refinements of our virtual reality lifelog retrieval platform that enabled it to perform effectively at the Lifelog Search Challenge (LSC) [10] at ACM ICMR 2018 where it ranked first place among the other challenge participants [12]. It was the only virtual reality based system present at the conference; all other participants utilised conventional laptops or computers.

References

1. Yang, Y., Lee, H., Gurrin, C.: Visualizing lifelog data for different interaction platforms. In: CHI 2013 Extended Abstracts on Human Factors in Computing Systems on - CHI EA 2013, p. 1785 (2013). https://doi.org/10.1145/2468356.2468676
2. Sellen, A.J., Whittaker, S.: Beyond total capture. Commun. ACM **53**(5), 70 (2010). https://doi.org/10.1145/1735223.1735243. ISSN 0001-078
3. Gurrin, C., et al.: NTCIR lifelog: the first test collection for lifelog research. In: Proceedings of the 39th International ACM SIGIR Conference on Research and Development in Information Retrieval, pp. 705–708. ACM (2016). ISBN 978-1-4503-4069-4. https://doi.org/10.1145/2911451.2914680
4. Duane, A., Gurrin, C.: Lifelog exploration prototype in virtual reality. In: Schoeffmann, K., et al. (eds.) MMM 2018. LNCS, vol. 10705, pp. 377–380. Springer, Cham (2018). https://doi.org/10.1007/978-3-319-73600-6_36
5. Gurrin, C., et al.: Overview of NTCIR-13 lifelog-2 task. In: Proceedings of the 13th NTCIR Conference on Evaluation of Information Access Technologies, NTCIR, pp. 6–11 (2017). ISBN 978-4-86049-075-1
6. Dale, E.: Audio-Visual Methods in Teaching, 3rd edn, pp. 12–13. Dryden Press, New York (1969)
7. Krokos, E., Plaisant, C., Varshney, A.: Virtual memory palaces: immersion aids recall. Virtual Reality, 1–15 (2018). https://doi.org/10.1007/s10055-018-0346-3
8. Nakazato, M., Huang, T.S.: 3D MARS: immersive virtual reality for content-based image retrieval. In: Proceedings of 2001 IEEE International Conference on Multimedia and Expo (ICME2001) (2001)
9. Gurrin, C., Lee, H., Caprani, N., Zhang, Z.X., O'Connor, N., Carthy, D.: Browsing large personal multimedia archives in a lean-back environment. In: Boll, S., Tian, Q., Zhang, L., Zhang, Z., Chen, Y.-P.P. (eds.) MMM 2010. LNCS, vol. 5916, pp. 98–109. Springer, Heidelberg (2010). https://doi.org/10.1007/978-3-642-11301-7_13
10. LSC 2018: Proceedings of the 2018 ACM Workshop on the Lifelog Search Challenge. ACM, Yokohama (2018). ISBN 978-1-4503-5796-8
11. Likert, R.: A Technique for the Measurement of Attitudes, p. 55. The Science Press, New York (1932)
12. Duane, A., Huerst, W., Gurrin, C.: Virtual reality lifelog explorer. In: Proceedings of the 2018 ACM on International Conference on Multimedia Retrieval. ACM (2018)

Query-by-Dancing: A Dance Music Retrieval System Based on Body-Motion Similarity

Shuhei Tsuchida$^{(\boxtimes)}$ [iD], Satoru Fukayama$^{(\boxtimes)}$ [iD], and Masataka Goto$^{(\boxtimes)}$ [iD]

National Institute of Advanced Industrial Science and Technology (AIST),
Central 2, 1-1-1 Umezono, Tsukuba, Ibaraki, Japan
{s-tsuchida,s.fukayama,m.goto}@aist.go.jp

Abstract. This paper presents Query-by-Dancing, a dance music retrieval system that enables a user to retrieve music using dance motions. When dancers search for music to play when dancing, they sometimes find it by referring to online dance videos in which the dancers use motions similar to their own dance. However, previous music retrieval systems could not support retrieval specialized for dancing because they do not accept dance motions as a query. Therefore, we developed our Query-by-Dancing system, which uses a video of a dancer (user) as the input query to search a database of dance videos. The query video is recorded using an ordinary RGB camera that does not obtain depth information, like a smartphone camera. The poses and motions in the query are then analyzed and used to retrieve dance videos with similar poses and motions. The system then enables the user to browse the music attached to the videos it retrieves so that the user can find a piece that is appropriate for their dancing. An interesting problem here is that a simple search for the most similar videos based on dance motions sometimes includes results that do not match the intended dance genre. We solved this by using a novel measure similar to tf-idf to weight the importance of dance motions when retrieving videos. We conducted comparative experiments with 4 dance genres and confirmed that the system gained an average of 3 or more evaluation points for 3 dance genres (waack, pop, break) and that our proposed method was able to deal with different dance genres.

Keywords: Dance · Music · Video · Retrieval system · Body-motion

1 Introduction

Dancers often dance to music. They choose a dancing style that can match the genre or style of a musical piece, synchronize their movements with musical beats and downbeats, and change their movements to follow musical changes. When musical pieces are played on a dance performance stage, for example, the dancers just have to dance to match the piece being performed. On the

© Springer Nature Switzerland AG 2019
I. Kompatsiaris et al. (Eds.): MMM 2019, LNCS 11295, pp. 251–263, 2019.
https://doi.org/10.1007/978-3-030-05710-7_21

other hand, when dancers can select musical pieces for their dance performances, practices, or personal enjoyment, they spend a lot of time finding musical pieces appropriate for their intended performance. This is because selecting pieces of music is important for achieving successful dance performances and enjoying dancing. When searching for music to play while dancing, dancers sometimes find it by referring to online dance videos in which the dancers use motions similar to their own dance. They may also refer to dance events or showcases of their favorite dancers or dance groups for music. Since there has been no systematic support for finding certain kinds of dance music, such activities have been time consuming and difficult. Although many music retrieval systems have been proposed [2,7,9], none have focused on retrieving dance music.

Therefore, we developed a dance music retrieval system called Query-by-Dancing that enables a dancer (user) to use his/her dance motions to retrieve music. To find music for the dancer to dance to, our system first finds a dance music video that contains dancing similar to the motions of the user's dance. Our system can retrieve dance videos that include motions similar to an input query of a short video capturing dancing body motions. The musical pieces in the videos should be appropriate for the user to dance to.

Our Query-by-Dancing system does not need an expensive high-performance motion capture system or a camera that obtains depth information. It only needs a simple RGB camera like those installed in smartphones. We implemented a system that analyzes input query videos and a database of dance videos by using the OpenPose library by Cao et al. [1] to estimate body motions.

2   Related Work

A number of music retrieval and recommendation systems have been proposed, but none have allowed a dancer to search for music using dance motions. Our system, Query-by-Dancing, is equipped with a novel function based on the similarities between dance motions that enables the user to input their own dance video as a retrieval query. We surveyed studies on music retrieval and recommendation systems using various queries.

Ghias et al. [4] proposed a query-by-humming system that uses humming as a query. They claim that an effective and natural way of searching a musical audio database is by humming the song. Chen et al. [3] proposed a system for retrieving songs from music databases using rhythm. They use strings of notes as music information, and the database returns all songs containing patterns similar to the query. Jang et al. [5] proposed a query-by-tapping system. The system allows the user to search a music database by tapping on a microphone to input the duration of the first several notes of the query song. Maezawa et al. [6] proposed a query-by-conducting system. In this system, the interface allows a user to conduct during the playback of a piece, and the interface dynamically switches the playback to a musical piece that is similar to the user's conducting.

Some systems retrieve musical pieces by using a musical context, such as the artist's cultural or political background, collaborative semantic labels, and album cover artwork [10]. Turnbull et al. [11] presented a query-by-text system that can use a text-based query to retrieve relevant tracks from a database of unlabeled audio content. This system can also annotate novel audio tracks with meaningful words.

As described above, several retrieval methods using various queries have been proposed. However, to the best of our knowledge, this is the first study that has used dance motions as a query for retrieving music. Our system focuses on dance motions and acquires candidate musical pieces from a dance video database.

3   Dance Music Retrieval System

The system overview is shown in Fig. 1. Our system can be divided into two stages: pre-processing and similarity calculation. These two main stages are described below.

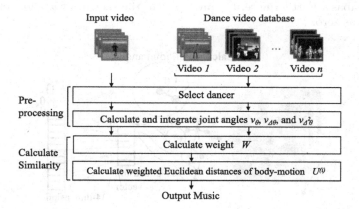

Fig. 1. System overview.

3.1   Pre-processing

Detect a Dancer. In this step, the system first estimates the person's skeleton information in all video frames using the OpenPose library [1]. Dance videos sometimes include frames of multiple people dancing or the OpenPose library sometimes detects skeleton information incorrectly on a frame that has no person. Therefore, the system selects the skeleton representing the main dancer by analyzing all of the skeletons detected in each frame. First, the area (A_o) occupied by each skeleton detected is computed by multiplying the width by the height of the area. The width is defined as the difference between the maximum and minimum values along the x-axis direction of the detected skeleton(s). The height is defined as the difference between the maximum and minimum values in the y-axis direction of the skeleton(s). Then, the position (P_d) of a dancer in a video is obtained by averaging the skeleton positions in all of the frames. The distance (D_c) from the center $(P_c(X_{\mathrm{mean}}, Y_{\mathrm{mean}}))$ of the entire frame image to P_d is computed for each dancer. Assuming the main dancer is located in the center, the skeleton that maximizes $R = \frac{A_o}{D_c}$ is selected as the main dancer.

Feature Extraction. To calculate the similarity between dance motions in the query video and each dance video in the database, we extracted the following motion features from the skeleton of the main dancer. Since both poses and motions are important elements that characterize dancing, the system first represents the poses by calculating 17 joint angles from the skeleton per frame. The angle is calculated clockwise from the upper side vertically across the image as zero. The joint angles are broken into the two dimensions θ_x and θ_y by calculating sine and cosine (as shown in Fig. 2), and we denote a 34-dimensional feature vector of angles at n-th frame of i-th video by $v_\theta^{(i)}(n)(1 \le n \le N^{(i)} and 1 \le i \le I)$, where N is the number of frames in the i-th video and I is the number of videos in the database. Furthermore, the angle where the skeleton was not detected is expressed as zero.

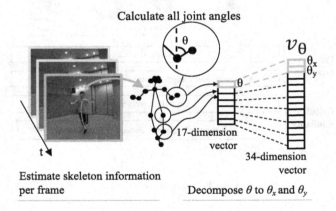

Fig. 2. All the joint angles are broken down per frame, and creating a 34-dimensional vector.

The system then represents the body motions by calculating the speed and acceleration of the change in joint angles between frames. It calculates $v_{\Delta\theta}^{(i)}(n)$ and $v_{\Delta^2\theta}^{(i)}(n)$ as follows:

$$v_{\Delta\theta}^{(i)}(n) = \mathrm{abs}(v_\theta^{(i)}(n) - v_\theta^{(i)}(n-1)) \tag{1}$$

$$v_{\Delta^2\theta}^{(i)}(n) = \mathrm{abs}(v_{\Delta\theta}^{(i)}(n) - v_{\Delta\theta}^{(i)}(n-1)) \tag{2}$$

where $\mathrm{abs}(x)$ denotes a vector containing the absolute value of each element of x. We concatenated the above 3 feature vectors, $v_\theta^{(i)}(n)$, $v_{\Delta\theta}^{(i)}(n)$, and $v_{\Delta^2\theta}^{(i)}(n)$, into one 102-dimensional vector $v^{(i)}(n)$.

3.2 Similarity Calculation

The system calculates the Euclidean distances $d(v^{\text{in}}(n), v^{(i)}(m))$ between all frames ($1 \leq n \leq N^{\text{in}}$) of an input video (in) and all frames ($1 \leq m \leq N^{(i)}$) of a video in the video database ($1 \leq i \leq I$), where $d(x, y)$ denotes an Euclidean distance between x and y, as shown in Fig. 3. The system computes these Euclidean distances in all frame combinations and divides them by the total number of combinations ($N^{\text{in}} N^{(i)}$). They are denoted by following formula:

$$R^{(i)} = \frac{1}{N^{\text{in}} N^{(i)}} \sum^{N^{\text{in}}} \sum^{N^{(i)}} d(v^{\text{in}}(n), v^{(i)}(m)). \tag{3}$$

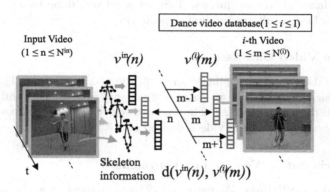

Fig. 3. The system computes the Euclidean distances in all frame combinations and divides them by the total number of combinations.

Now the system simply finds the most similar videos by using $R^{(i)}$ as the similarity of the dance motions per video, which leads to results that do not match the intended dance genre. We solved this problem by using a novel measure similar to tf-idf to weight the importance of dance motions when retrieving videos. The weight representing the importance of dance motions is calculated as follows:

$$W(n) = \frac{\frac{1}{N^{(i)}} \sum^{N^{(i)}} d(v^{\text{in}}(n), v^{(i)}(m))}{\max\limits_{i \in I}\{\frac{1}{N^{(i)}} \sum^{N^{(i)}} d(v^{\text{in}}(n), v^{(i)}(m))\}}. \tag{4}$$

where $\max(x)$ denotes a maximum value of x. To sharpen the weight gradient, the system calculates $W(n)$ to the 30-th power to obtain $W'(n)$. We determined the exponent 30 experimentally. Then, the system multiplied $W'(n)$ by all of the Euclidean distances. These distances are determined with the following formula:

$$U^{(i)} = \frac{\sum^{N^{\text{in}}} (W'(n) \sum^{N^{(i)}} d(v^{\text{in}}(n), v^{(i)}(m)))}{N^{\text{in}} N^{(i)}}. \tag{5}$$

The system finds the videos with the top k values among $U^{(i)}$ as the videos that contain dance motions similar to those in the input video. Finally, the system presents the candidate musical pieces from the dance videos searched.

4   Evaluation

We conducted two evaluation experiments to investigate whether the retrieval results are easy for dancers to use as dance music. In the first experiment, the system retrieved dance music based on whether the importance of each video was weighted or not. We adapted the calculated weights to the two methods; ADD method and DTW method, and retrieved dance music using each method. In the second experiment, the system retrieved dance music by using the dance videos of 4 dance genres as queries. This retrieval was done using the method that gave the best results in the first experiment.

4.1   Dance Video Database

We used 100 dance videos available on YouTube and Instagram. They were 25 videos per each dance genre we chose—break, hip-hop, waack, and pop—and their average duration was 82 s. The audio track of all these videos contained music that the dancers in the videos danced to.

4.2   Experiment I: Weighted or Unweighted

Experiment Conditions. We recruited 12 participants (4 males and 8 females) who were students belonging to a street dance club. All had between 1 to 15 years of dance experience (average = 8.5 years).

We compared 4 retrieval methods: ADD (unweighted), ADD (weighted), DTW (unweighted), and DTW (weighted). The ADD method, our proposed retrieval method using the Euclidean distance between frames, calculates one feature vector $v^{(i)}(n)$ of 102 dimensions by concatenating $v_\theta^{(i)}(n)$, $v_{\Delta\theta}^{(i)}(n)$, and $v_{\Delta^2\theta}^{(i)}(n)$ per frame. ADD (unweighted) does not use $W'(n)$, and it lists musical pieces in ascending order of $R^{(i)}$. ADD (weighted) uses $W'(n)$, and it lists musical pieces in ascending order of $U^{(i)}$.

The DTW method is a retrieval method that uses dynamic time warping, a sequence matching algorithm that considers longer-term similarity. This method creates a sequence $V_{\mathrm{dtw}}^{(i)}(n)(1 \leq n \leq N^{(i)} - 5$ and $1 \leq i \leq I)$ for every 6 frames by sliding $v_\theta^{(i)}(n)$ one frame at a time. The system calculates the dynamic time warping $\mathrm{dtw}(v_{\mathrm{dtw}}^{\mathrm{in}}(n), V_{\mathrm{dtw}}^{(i)}(m))$ between all sequences $(1 \leq n \leq N^{\mathrm{in}} - 5)$ of an input video (in) and all sequences $(1 \leq m \leq N^{(i)} - 5)$ of a video in the video database $(1 \leq i \leq I)$, where $\mathrm{dtw}(x, y)$ is the Euclidean distance between x and y calculated by FastDTW [8]. Then, $R_{\mathrm{dtw}}^{(i)}$ and $W_{\mathrm{dtw}}(n)$ are calculated using an equation in which the $d(v^{\mathrm{in}}(n), v^{(i)}(m))$ in Eq. (3) are replaced with $\mathrm{dtw}(v_{\mathrm{dtw}}^{\mathrm{in}}(n), V_{\mathrm{dtw}}^{(i)}(m))$. To sharpen the weight gradient, the system calculates

$W_{\mathrm{dtw}}(n)$ to the 40-th power to obtain $W'_{\mathrm{dtw}}(n)$. We determined the exponent 40 experimentally. Then, the system multiplies $W'_{\mathrm{dtw}}(n)$ by all the Euclidean distances and obtains $U^{(i)}_{\mathrm{dtw}}$. DTW (unweighted) does not use $W'_{\mathrm{dtw}}(n)$, and it lists musical pieces in ascending order of $R^{(i)}_{\mathrm{dtw}}$. DTW (weighted) uses $W'_{\mathrm{dtw}}(n)$ and lists musical pieces in ascending order of $U^{(i)}_{\mathrm{dtw}}$.

We asked a waack dancer with 15 years of dance experience to participate in the experiment and shot about 11 s of her waack dancing. With that video as a query, we used each of the 4 methods to retrieve musical pieces. We denoted the top 5 music groups in the retrieval results obtained with each of the 4 methods as MG-A, MG-B, MG-C, and MG-D. Each music group had 5 musical pieces.

Procedure. At the beginning of the session, participants filled out a pre-study questionnaire about their dance experience. Then, we gave them a brief explanation of the experiment. After watching a query of the waack dancer's 11-s video without music, they were asked to listen to the 5 musical pieces in each music group and evaluate them on a 5-point Likert scale ranging from 1 for "do not agree" to 5 for "totally agree." They were given the music groups MG-A, MG-B, MG-C, and MG-D in random order. We gave them the evaluation item below.

Q1: Given the assumption that "someone" dances with the choreography shown in this video while listening to music, is each of these 5 musical pieces easy to dance to according to its atmosphere and the atmosphere of the choreography?

Finally, they filled out a questionnaire about the dance music retrieval.

We prepared a MacBook Pro (Retina display, 15-in., mid-2015) and used the QuickTime Player to play the musical pieces and the video. The query dance video was set to "repeat play" beforehand and the participant selected and played the 5 musical pieces arranged next to it. The participants wore earphones to listen to the music and could play and re-evaluate the musical pieces as many times as they wanted. The participants could take breaks freely during the experiment. The experiment took about 40 min.

Results and Discussion. The averaged Q1 scores for each retrieval method are shown in Fig. 4. The vertical axis indicates the average of the Q1 scores given by all of the participants, and the vertical bars indicate standard errors. The horizontal axis represents retrieval methods. The gray rectangles show the averaged evaluation scores for each of the retrieval ranks. Each green rectangle shows the average of all evaluation scores within the retrieval method. We assessed the difference between the average Q1 scores with ANOVA. There was a significant difference ($F_{(3,236)} = 4.21, p < .05$). We also assessed the difference with Fisher's Least Significant Difference (LSD) test and found significant differences ($p < .05$) between ADD (weighted) and the other 3 methods. Thus, ADD (weighted) was the suitable retrieval method of searching for musical pieces that dancers can easily dance to.

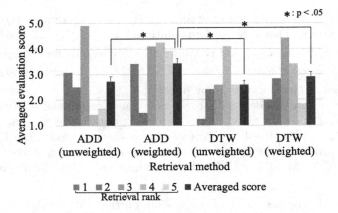

Fig. 4. The averaged Q1 scores for each retrieval method. The ADD (weighted) method was evaluated as significantly higher than the other 3 methods.

The retrieval results of ADD (weighted) had the same dance genres as the query more often than the other retrieval methods, which increased the evaluation score of ADD (weighted). The dance genres of each retrieval rank for each retrieval method are shown in Table 1. Focusing on the top 5 musical pieces in the retrieval results, we found that waack was 4 out of 5 musical pieces for ADD (weighted), which was the same dance genre as the query. For the other methods, 2 out of 5, 1 out of 5, and 3 out of 5 musical pieces were waack. The musical pieces used in videos of the same genre as the query's got higher evaluation scores.

Table 1. Top 5 retrieval results by retrieval methods. P in the table stands for the dance genre pop, and W stands for the dance genre waack.

Retrieval method	Dance genre	Retrieval rank				
		1	2	3	4	5
ADD (unweighted)	Waack	W	P	W	P	P
ADD (weighted)		W	P	W	W	W
DTW (unweighted)		P	P	W	P	P
DTW (weighted)		P	W	W	W	P

Next, we focused on the weights. Figure 4 shows that the scores of the weighted methods were higher than the unweighted methods', and that weighting is effective for retrieving dance music appropriate for dance motions. The calculated weight $W'(n)$ is shown in Fig. 5, where the vertical axis indicates the weight value and the horizontal axis represents the frame numbers in the video used as the query. The high-weight movements in the vicinity of frames 240 to 270 were movements such as the dancer swinging her arm above her head in long

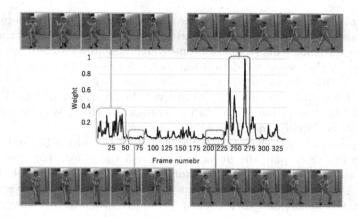

Fig. 5. Waack's characteristic movements were in the vicinity of a relatively high weight value. The movements common to other dance genres were in the vicinity of a relatively low weight value.

strides. Moreover, the movements in the vicinity of the first 50 frames with a relatively high weight value were movements such as the dancer swinging her arm to the left and right in long strokes. Swinging the arm in long strokes, a characteristic waack movement, had been highly weighted. On the other hand, the movements in the vicinity of frames 50 to 75 with a relatively low weight value were simple movements like moving backwards. Moreover, the movements in the vicinity of frames 200 to 225 with a relatively low weight value were movements such as the dancer shaking her waist to the left and right. These movements also occur in other dance genres. As the above shows, the system successfully weighted the movement particular to the dance motion in the query. In contrast, movements common to other dance genres were weighted low.

4.3   Experiment II: Retrieval Performance

Experiment Conditions. We recruited 12 participants (6 males and 6 females) who were students belonging to a street dance club. All participants had 1 to 15 years of dance experience (average = 5.9 years). We compared 4 dance genres: waack, break, pop, and hip-hop. We prepared the waack video used in the first experiment. The author who has 8 years of dance experience was in charge of a breakdancer, and we shot about 13 s of that author's breakdancing. To prepare other videos, we recruited two more dancers, a pop dancer and a hip-hop dancer. The pop dancer had 3 years of dance experience, and we shot about 16 s of his pop dance. The hip-hop dancer had 15 years of dance experience, and we shot about 16 s of her hip-hop dance. Using those videos as queries, we retrieved musical pieces by using the ADD (weighted) method. We denoted the top 5 music groups in the retrieval results obtained in each of the dance genres as DG-W, DG-B, DG-H, and DG-P. Each music group had 5 musical pieces.

Procedure. At the beginning of the session, participants filled out a pre-study questionnaire about their dance experience. Then, we briefly explained the experiment. After watching a query that was one of the randomly selected dance videos without music, they were asked to listen to the 5 musical pieces in each music group and evaluate them on a 5-point Likert scale ranging from 1 for "do not agree" to 5 for "totally agree." They were given the music groups DG-W, DG-B, DG-H, and DG-P according to the dance genre of the video. We gave Q1 as the evaluation item. Finally, they were orally interviewed.

We prepared a MacBook Pro (Retina display, 15-in., mid-2015) and used the QuickTime Player to play the musical pieces and the video. The query dance video was set to "repeat play" beforehand, and the participants selected and played the 5 musical pieces arranged next to it. The participants wore earphones to listen to the music, and they could play and re-evaluate the musical pieces as many times as they wanted. The participants could take breaks freely during the experiment. The experiment took about 40 min.

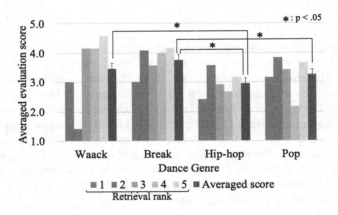

Fig. 6. The averaged Q1 scores for each dance genre.

Results and Discussion. Figure 6 shows the averaged Q1 scores for each dance genre. The vertical axis indicates the average of the Q1 scores from all of the participants, and the vertical bars indicate standard errors. The horizontal axis represents dance genres. The gray rectangles indicate the averaged evaluation scores for each retrieval rank. Each green rectangle indicates the average of all evaluation scores within the genre. We assessed the difference between the average Q1 scores with ANOVA. There was a significant difference ($F_{(3,236)} = 3.92, p < .05$). We also assessed the difference with Fisher's Least Significant Difference (LSD) test and found significant differences ($p < .05$) between waack and hip-hop, break and hip-hop, and break and pop.

Table 2 shows the Q1 evaluation scores and dance genres of each retrieval rank for each retrieval method. The hip-hop video had a comparatively bad performance as the query. The system returned musical pieces in the break genre. There are two reasons for this. Hip-hop is divided into more dance subgenres. The

Table 2. Top 5 retrieval results by dance genre. P in the table stands for pop, W for waack, and B for break.

Retrieval method	Dance genre	Retrieval rank				
		1	2	3	4	5
ADD (weighted)	Waack	W	P	W	W	W
	Break	B	B	B	B	B
	Hip-hop	B	B	B	B	B
	Pop	P	P	P	P	P

style of the hip-hop in our input video was middle hip-hop, but the hip-hop dance styles in the database were style hip-hop, girls hip-hop, jazz hip-hop, etc., dance styles slightly different from the query. Therefore, it was hard for the system to extract the musical pieces of hip-hop. The other reason is that middle hip-hop has some movements similar to those of break. One characteristic of break is when the dancer continues to dance while keeping their hands on the floor. However, before keeping their hands on the floor, breakdancers' movements are similar to middle hip-hop. Therefore, the system selected musical pieces for break. On the other hand, the system could extract motions similar to the query, which prevented the evaluation scores from markedly decreasing. For these two reasons, the system extracted musical pieces for break that were not the same dance genre of the query. In the future, we will divide the dance genres even further and add more dance genres into the database, which will improve evaluation scores.

The evaluation score for pop was worse than that of break and tended to be worse than that of waack. We interviewed the participants who gave a low score to pop to determine the reason for this. They said they scored it thus because the dance motions used as the query included a "vibration" technique in which the dancers move their bodies with a rapid trembling motion and a "wave" technique in which the dancers move their bodies like a wave. Those movements match specific sounds, and the participants decided that musical pieces that did not include those sounds were inappropriate for those movements. We can solve this problem by using interactive retrieval methods that let dancers adjust parameters according to their purposes. For example, if dancers want to search for specific musical pieces used in videos containing movements that closely resemble particular movements (like "waves"), the system will allow the dancers to search through a narrow range of musical pieces by adjusting parameters to match highly similar movements. In addition, if users want to search for musical pieces to practice to or to dance to in a club with many other dancers, the system will allow the users to search through a large range of various musical pieces by adjusting parameters to match the movements with a lower similarity. Users changing the parameters contextually could realize more efficient dance music retrieval.

5   Conclusion

We proposed Query-by-Dancing, which is a dance music retrieval system that enables a user to retrieve a musical piece using dance motions. We confirmed that the system's retrieval method is appropriate for dance music, that the system can find musical pieces that are easy to dance to, and that better music can be obtained by weighting the importance of dance motions when retrieving videos. Moreover, we conducted comparative experiments on 4 dance genres and confirmed that the system scored an average of 3 points or more evaluation points for 3 dance genres (waack, pop, and break), and our method can adapt to different dance genres. In the future, we plan to add a wider range of dance genres to the database of dance videos.

Acknowledgments. This work was supported in part by JST ACCEL Grant Number JPMJAC1602, Japan.

References

1. Cao, Z., Simon, T., Wei, S., Sheikh, Y.: Realtime multi-person 2D pose estimation using part affinity fields. In: The 2017 IEEE Conference on Computer Vision and Pattern Recognition (2017)
2. Casey, M.A., Veltkamp, R.C., Goto, M., Leman, M., Rhodes, C., Slaney, M.: Content-based music information retrieval: current directions and future challenges. Proc. IEEE **96**(4), 668–696 (2008)
3. Chen, J., Chen, A.: Query by rhythm: an approach for song retrieval in music databases. In: Proceedings of the 8th International Workshop on Research Issues in Data Engineering: Continuous-Media Databases and Applications, pp. 139–146 (1998)
4. Ghias, A., Logan, J., Chamberlin, D., Smith, B.C.: Query by humming - musical information retrieval in an audio database. In: Proceedings of ACM Multimedia 1995, pp. 231–236 (1995)
5. Jang, J.-S.R., Lee, H.-R., Yeh, C.-H.: Query by tapping: a new paradigm for content-based music retrieval from acoustic input. In: Shum, H.-Y., Liao, M., Chang, S.-F. (eds.) PCM 2001. LNCS, vol. 2195, pp. 590–597. Springer, Heidelberg (2001). https://doi.org/10.1007/3-540-45453-5_76
6. Maezawa, A., Goto, M., Okuno, H.G.: Query-by-conducting: an interface to retrieve classical-music interpretations by real-time tempo input. In: The 11th International Society of Music Information Retrieval, pp. 477–482 (2010)
7. Müller, M.: Fundamentals of Music Processing - Audio, Analysis, Algorithms, Applications. Springer, Cham (2015). https://doi.org/10.1007/978-3-319-21945-5
8. Salvador, S., Chan, P.: Toward accurate dynamic time warping in linear time and space. J. Intell. Data Anal. **11**(5), 561–580 (2007)
9. Schedl, M., Gómez, E., Urbano, J.: Music information retrieval: recent developments and applications. Found. Trends Inf. Retr. **8**(2–3), 127–261 (2014)

10. Smiraglia, R.P.: Musical works as information retrieval entities: epistemological perspectives. In: The 2nd International Society of Music Information Retrieval, pp. 85–91 (2001)
11. Turnbull, D., Barrington, L., Torres, D., Lanckriet, G.: Semantic annotation and retrieval of music and sound effects. IEEE Trans. Audio, Speech, Lang. Process. **16**(2), 467–476 (2008)

Joint Visual-Textual Sentiment Analysis Based on Cross-Modality Attention Mechanism

Xuelin Zhu[1], Biwei Cao[2], Shuai Xu[1], Bo Liu[1], and Jiuxin Cao[3(✉)]

[1] School of Computer Science and Engineering, Southeast University, Nanjing, China
{zhuxuelin,xushuai7,bliu}@seu.edu.cn
[2] ANU College of Engineering and Computer Science,
Australian National University, Canberra, Australia
tarasom0804@gmail.com
[3] School of Cyber Science and Engineering, Southeast University, Nanjing, China
jx.cao@seu.edu.cn

Abstract. Recently, many researchers have focused on the joint visual-textual sentiment analysis since it can better extract user sentiments toward events or topics. In this paper, we propose that visual and textual information should differ in their contribution to sentiment analysis. Our model learns a robust joint visual-textual representation by incorporating a cross-modality attention mechanism and semantic embedding learning based on bidirectional recurrent neural network. Experimental results show that our model outperforms existing the state-of-the-art models in sentiment analysis under real datasets. In addition, we also investigate different proposed model's variants and analyze the effects of semantic embedding learning and cross-modality attention mechanism in order to provide deeper insight on how these two techniques help the learning of joint visual-textual sentiment classifier.

Keywords: Sentiment analysis · Cross-modality analysis
Recurrent neural network · Attention mechanism

1 Introduction

The growing popularity of social networks makes significant influence on people's lifestyle, more and more people share experiences and express opinions on many events and topics in online social network platforms, thus large-scale images and posts are generated every day. Statistics indicate that about 25% of tweets contains image information [19] and 99% of image tweets contain textual information [20]. Due to complexity and variability of user-generated content, the performance of sentiment analysis based on single modality (image or text) still lags behind satisfaction. In this study, we focus on detecting user sentiment by jointly taking visual and textual information into consideration.

© Springer Nature Switzerland AG 2019
I. Kompatsiaris et al. (Eds.): MMM 2019, LNCS 11295, pp. 264–276, 2019.
https://doi.org/10.1007/978-3-030-05710-7_22

Joint visual-textual sentiment analysis is challenging since image and text may deliver inconsistent sentiment. Figure 1 shows several examples of image-text pair crawled from Flickr[1] and Getty[2]. In example (a), the text carries a positive sentiment while the corresponding image is neutral; in contrast, the image expresses a positive sentiment while the text is neutral in example (b); it is more troublesome in example (c) that the image seems to express a positive sentiment according to the people's smile, while the corresponding text carries a strong negative sentiment. Inspired by these examples, we consider that visual and textual information should differ in their contribution to sentiment analysis. In other words, for a given image-text pair, our model focuses on learning joint visual-textual representation by assigning different weights to visual and textual information according to their contribution on pair's sentiment polarity.

Fig. 1. Examples of images and corresponding descriptions from Flickr.

In this paper, we propose a advanced model for accurate sentiment classification. In specific, a bidirectional recurrent neural network (BiRNN) is designed to bridge semantic gap between visual and textual information, and a cross-modality attention mechanism is proposed to assigning reasonable weights to the visual and textual information. To the end, the contributions of our research work are as follows:

1. We show that BiRNN is capable of semantic embedding learning and bridging semantic gap between image information and text information.
2. A cross-modality attention mechanism is proposed to automatically assign weights to visual and textual information, then joint visual-textual semantic representation can be calculated for further training of sentiment classifier.
3. Extensive experiment results show that our model is more robust and has achieved best classification performance, especially when images and texts carry opposite sentiments.

2   Related Works

Joint visual-textual sentiment analysis has been researched many years, early fusion and late fusion are the mainstream strategies in early studies. Early fusion

---

[1]   https://www.flickr.com.
[2]   https://www.gettyimages.co.uk.

[7, 11, 16] employs feature fusion techniques to learn a joint visual-textual semantic representation for sentiment analysis afterward. Late fusion [8] treats image and text information separately by leveraging different domain-specific techniques, and subsequently utilize all modalities' sentiment label to obtain the ultimate results. Recently, You et al. [6] propose a cross-modality consistent regression (CCR) scheme for joint visual-textual sentiment analysis and achieve the best performance over previous fusion models. However, due to the semantic gap between visual and textual information, the performance of early fusion and late fusion is limited.

Recently, deep learning has made remarkable performance improvements in many visual and textual tasks [23]. Automatic image captioning [3, 12] and multimodal matching between image and sentence [1, 13] have shown the advance of deep neural networks in understanding and jointly modeling vision and text content. Notably, attention mechanism is widely studied in both vision and text tasks. Bahdanau et al. [17] introduce a novel attention mechanism that allows neural networks to focus on different parts of their input. Yang et al. [9] show that a well-trained context vector is capable of distinguishing key words from text for document classification. You et al. [2] propose vision attention to jointly discover the relevant local regions and build a sentiment classifier on the top of these local regions. Subsequently, You et al. [5] propose a bilinear attention model to learn the correlations between words and image regions for given image-pairs. However, practical results show that this model is failed to generalize to various datasets because there are much less correlations between words and image regions in real social networks. Chen et al. [4] utilize CNN to extract both image and text features, then concatenate them into a joint representation for further training. However, the performance of such simple feature fusion lags behind when image-text pairs carry opposite sentiments.

As far as we know, very few studies have considered that visual and textual information should differ in their contribution to sentiment analysis. In this paper, for a given image-text pair, we focus on discovering how the sequence of words and visual features are relevant to the pair's sentiment polarity and propose sentimental context to assign reasonable weights to them, then a reasonable representation is calculated as a weighted sum of the textual and visual information for the training of sentiment classifier. Meanwhile, visual semantic embedding is proposed to bridge semantic gap between image information and text information, and leads to a better cross-modality attention mechanism.

3   Long Short-Term Memory (LSTM) Networks

For completeness, we describe briefly the sequential LSTM model. Given the input sequence $\{x_1, x_2, ..., x_T\}$, traditional RNN is trying to predict the corresponding output sequence $\{y_1, y_2, ...y_T\}$. In specifically, at given time step t, RNN calculates the hidden state h_t to predict the output y_t according to the current input x_t, the formula is described as follows.

$$h_t = f(h_{t-1}, x_t) \tag{1}$$

where h_{t-1} is the previous hidden state, $f(\cdot)$ can be a nonlinear function or other unit, such as long short-term memory. Each LSTM memory cell c is controlled by an input gate i, an forget gate f and an output gate o. The specific updating process of these gates at time step t for given input x_t, h_{t-1} and c_{t-1} is as follows.

$$i_t = \sigma(W_{xi}x_t + W_{hi}h_{t-1} + b_i) \tag{2}$$
$$f_t = \sigma(W_{xf}x_t + W_{hf}h_{t-1} + b_f) \tag{3}$$
$$o_t = \sigma(W_{xo}x_t + W_{ho}h_{t-1} + b_o) \tag{4}$$
$$c_t = f_t \odot c_{t-1} + i_t \odot \tanh(W_{xc}x_t + W_{hc}h_{t-1} + b_c) \tag{5}$$
$$h_t = o_t \odot \tanh(c_t) \tag{6}$$

Where $W_{\cdot i}$, $W_{\cdot f}$, $W_{\cdot o}$ are the weighted matrices of the input, forget and output gate respectively, and $b.$ are bias vectors. σ is the sigmoid activation function, and $\odot$ denotes the element-wise multiplication between two vectors. Such multiplicative gates can deal well with exploding and vanishing gradients [3] which is a pretty common problem in deep neural network.

4   The Proposed Scheme

In this section, we propose a novel architecture for joint visual-textual sentiment analysis. The new architecture consists of a BiRNN as an encoder that bridge semantic gap between visual and textual information, and an attention model that assigns weights to visual and textual information and generates a joint visual-textual semantic representation, and finally a multi-layer perceptron is built for sentiment classification. The overall architecture of the proposed scheme is shown in Fig. 2. We describe the details of different components in the following sections.

4.1   Bidirectional RNN for Semantic Embedding

Unlike the usual RNN, which reads an input sequence of words in order starting from the first word to the last word, the BiRNN in proposed framework consists of a forward RNN and a backward RNN, so that it can summarize not only preceding words, but also the following words.

According to Fig. 2, the forward RNN reads an input sequence of words in its original order (from x_1 to x_T) and calculates a sequence of forward hidden states $(\overrightarrow{h_1}, \cdots, \overrightarrow{h_T})$. Similarly, the backward RNN reads the input sequence in the reverse order (from x_T to x_1) and generates a sequence of backward hidden state $(\overleftarrow{h_1}, \cdots, \overleftarrow{h_T})$. Subsequently, bidirectional RNN obtain an annotation h_j for each word x_j by concatenating the forward hidden state $\overrightarrow{h_j}$ and the backward hidden state $\overleftarrow{h_j}$, i.e., $h_j = \left[\overrightarrow{h}_j^T; \overleftarrow{h}_j^T\right]^T$. In this way, the annotation h_j can summarize the information of both the preceding words and the following words.

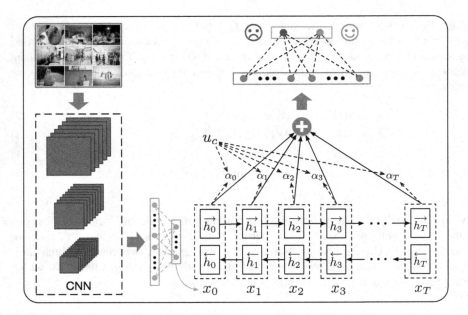

Fig. 2. The framework of the proposed model.

In order to bridge the semantic gap between image information and text information, visual features are extracted and fed into the BiRNN. Specifically, we use CNN for the representation of images, then the visual representation is projected into the specific dimension by a fully-connect layer, so that it can be used as the input of BiRNN.

$$x_0 = \sigma(W_m(CNN(I)) + b_m) \tag{7}$$

Where W_m and b_m are the weight and bias of fully-connect layer, $\sigma(\cdot)$ is non-linear activation function (e.g., Sigmoid or ReLU). Intuitively, visual semantic embedding enables the forward RNN to take visual information into consideration for computing textual hidden states and the backward RNN to factor textual information into computing visual hidden state. Thus BiRNN can calculate more reasonable hidden states for both image and text. Experiment results on real datasets demonstrate that visual semantic embedding can significantly improve the performance of the proposed model.

4.2   Cross-Modality Attention Mechanism

The previous attention models are commonly used to measure the relevance between words and sequence representation. In this section, we propose a cross-modality attention mechanism that is capable of automatically distinguishing the importance of image information and text information for sentiment analysis.

For a given image-text pair, we believe that not both text and image contribute equally to the pair's sentiment polarity. The intuition underlying our model is that visual information and several key emotional words in sequence mainly determine the sentiment polarity of the image-text pair. Therefore, we propose *sentiment context vector* u_c for discovering how relevant they are to the sentiment polarity. Note that the *sentiment context vector* u_c is not only used to extract these key emotional words in sequence, it also can automatically assign weights to visual and text information. Hence, the visual and textual information can be aggregated to form a joint visual-textual semantic representation.

For the hidden states $(h_0, h_1, \cdots, h_T)$ generated by the BiRNN mentioned before, a hidden representation u_i is calculated through a one-layer perceptron.

$$u_i = \tanh(W_w h_i + b_w) \quad i = 0, 1, ..., T \tag{8}$$

Where W_w and b_w are the parameters of the perceptron. Then, the similarity of u_i with the *sentiment context vector* u_c is utilized to measure the contribution of the words in sequence and the visual information, and a normalized weight α_i is obtained by a softmax function.

$$\alpha_i = \frac{\exp(u_i^T u_c)}{\sum_{i=0}^{T} \exp(u_i^T u_c)} \tag{9}$$

After that, a joint visual-textual semantic representation s is calculated as a weighted sum of the hidden states.

$$s = \sum_{i=0}^{T} \alpha_i h_i \tag{10}$$

Finally, a two-layer perceptron is built for sentiment classification.

$$logit = W_s(\sigma(W_h s) + b_h) + b_s \tag{11}$$

Where W_s, W_h, b_h, b_s are the parameters of the perceptron, σ is activation function $tanh(\cdot)$. The *sentiment context vector* u_c is randomly initialized and we parametrize the attention model as a feedforward neural network which is jointly trained with all the other components of the proposed scheme.

5   Experiments

In this section, we evaluate the proposed model on two real datasets. Specifically, we compare the performance of our model with several advanced models, including Early Fusion [6], Later Fusion [6], CCR [6], T-LSTM Embedding [5] and Deep Fusion [4]. In addition, we also add two our model's variants and analyze the effects of the cross-modality attention mechanism and semantic embedding learning. Table 1 shows a briefly description for our model and its variants.

Table 1. Summary of our model and its variants.

Model	Description
RNN embedding	Learn the BiRNN with semantic embedding
RNN-CA	Learn the BiRNN with cross-modality attention mechanism
RNN-CA embedding	Learn the BiRNN with cross-modality attention mechanism and semantic embedding simultaneously

Table 2. Statistics of the two datasets.

Datasets	Positive	Negative	Total
Getty	188028	181008	369036
VSO	118869	87139	206008

5.1 Datasets

To evaluate our model, we first build two datasets from Getty and Flickr, respectively. Followings are brief descriptions about these two datasets.

Getty Dataset. It was built by querying the GettyImage search engine with different sentiment keywords, such as happy, sad, smile and so on. In this way, we collected plenty of image-text pairs with sentiment label. Certainly, noise is unavoidable in the dataset, but the noise is tolerable due to the relatively formal and clean descriptions of images [5].

VSO Dataset. We built another weakly labeled dataset from Flickr to evaluate the proposed model. The dataset is obtained based on the Visual Sentiment Ontology (VSO) [22], which consists of more than 3,000 Adjective Noun Pairs (ANP), and each ANP has hundreds of images collected by querying in Flickr. However, this dataset only has the URLs of the images and lacks description for each image. Fortunately, the API provided by Flickr enables us to obtain the descriptions of the images by supplying its unique ID. In addition, similar to [5], we remove the invalid URLs and eliminate the images with descriptions that are more than 100 words or less than 5 words. Table 2 summaries the statistics of these two datasets.

5.2 Experimental Settings

To build the proposed model, we first need to choose feature representations for words and images. For word representation, we use the pre-trained 300-dimensional GloVe [18] features to represent words. For the representation of images, duo to the success of CNN in visual related tasks like object recognition and detection, we use CNN to extract visual feature. Our particular choice of

CNN is inception-V3 model [10], which is the improved version of the champion model on the ILSVRC 2014 classification competition [15].

The proposed model is trained on GPU machine, and the datasets are divided into three parts randomly, including training dataset, validation dataset and testing dataset at a ratio of 8:1:1, where validation dataset is used to select hyper-parameters and testing dataset is used to evaluate the proposed model. And the hidden layer size is 512, the proposed model is trained in a mini-batch mode, where 256 image-text pairs are randomly selected per batch. Dropout and L2-regularization are used to prevent model from overfitting, stochastic gradient descent (SGD) is utilized to optimize loss function.

Table 3. Results on the Getty testing dataset.

Models	Precision	Recall	F1	Accuracy
Early fusion	0.684	0.706	0.695	0.684
Later fusion	0.717	0.745	0.731	0.720
CCR	0.811	0.746	0.777	0.782
T-LSTM embedding	0.889	0.903	0.896	0.892
Deep fusion	0.895	0.919	0.907	0.905
RNN embedding	0.881	0.902	0.891	0.888
RNN-CA	0.877	0.896	0.886	0.884
RNN-CA embedding	**0.909**	**0.923**	**0.916**	**0.913**

5.3 Results Analysis

Results on the Getty Testing Dataset. Table 3 shows the performances of the different models on the testing dataset from Getty. Our model has significantly improved the performance on all metrics compared with all other models. Indeed, one observation is that the RNN-CA model is easily dominated by single modality. Compared to the RNN-CA model, the improvement of the performance of the RNN-CA Embedding model means that BiRNN based semantic embedding can bridge semantic gap between image information and text information effectively, and lead to better cross-modality attention. In addition, note that the RNN-CA Embedding has better performance than the RNN Embedding model, which proves that a well-learned sentiment context vector is capable of distinguishing visual and textual contribution to sentiment classification and generating more reasonable joint visual-textual semantic representation.

Results on the VSO Testing Dataset. We also test the proposed model on the VSO dataset and Table 4 summaries the results. Since the dataset built from VSO is pretty noisy, the performance of the all models declines compared

Table 4. Results on the VSO testing dataset.

Models	Precision	Recall	F1	Accuracy
Early fusion	0.636	0.800	0.709	0.620
Later fusion	0.645	0.885	0.746	0.652
CCR	0.653	0.661	0.657	0.668
T-LSTM embedding	0.823	0.834	0.828	0.829
Deep fusion	0.827	0.849	0.838	0.842
RNN embedding	0.813	0.831	0.822	0.827
RNN-CA	0.806	0.823	0.814	0.815
RNN-CA embedding	**0.838**	**0.856**	**0.847**	**0.851**

with the results on the testing dataset from Getty. However, the performance of the T-LSTM Embedding model decreases more remarkably, this may be caused by the fact that there are less correlations between words and image regions in VSO dataset. In contrast, our model still keeps better performance than the T-LSTM Embedding model and the Deep Fusion model. Namely, the RNN-CA Embedding model has consistently demonstrated the best performance by all metrics, which indicates that the RNN-CA Embedding model is capable of sentiment classification over various datasets.

Results on the Image-Text Pairs with Opposite Sentiments. In order to evaluate the performance of our model when images and texts carry opposite sentiments, we utilize RNTN [21] and Fine-tuned CaffeNet [14] to predict the sentiment labels of texts and images, respectively, then we can pick out 16461 and 7204 image-text pairs carrying opposite sentiments from Getty and VSO datasets. Possibly, these image-text pairs are noisy because of the limited prediction accuracy of RNTN and Fine-tuned CaffeNet. However, the noise is fair to all the candidate models since they are evaluated on the same testing datasets.

Table 5. Accuracy on the image-text pairs with opposite sentiments.

Datasets	Early fusion	Later fusion	CCR	T-LSTM embedding	Deep fusion	RNN-CA embedding
Getty	0.650	0.700	0.753	0.856	0.873	**0.911**
VSO	0.583	0.631	0.649	0.795	0.801	**0.849**

Table 5 provides the classification accuracy of different models on these image-text pairs with opposite sentiments from Getty and Flickr testing datasets. Note that all other models have varying degrees of performance degradation compared with their performance on full testing datasets, while our model still

1) [Image] Mother and daughter having fun time in bed room.
2) [Image] Shot of a happy senior woman spending quality time with her daughter outdoors.
3) [Image] Portrait of an attractive young woman enjoying a boat ride on the lake.

1) [Image] Breakup of a couple with bad girl and sad boyfriend.
2) [Image] A powerful EF-5 tornado rips through Greensburg, destroying most of the town.
3) [Image] Office worker stressed and upset in office.

(a) Top RNN-CA Embedding positive examples.

(b) Top RNN-CA Embedding negative examples.

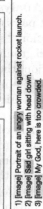

1) [Image] Little girl sleeping on her Father on the train.
2) [Image] Two men are busy working in office.
3) [Image] Young couple hugging each other in front of cars.

1) [Image] Portrait of an angry woman against rocket launch.
2) [Image] Sad girl sitting with head down.
3) [Image] My God, here is too crowded.

(c) Image dominating sentiment classification examples.

(d) Text dominating sentiment classification examples.

Fig. 3. Classification examples on the Getty and VSO datasets, the texts correspond to the images from left to right in each group.

maintains consistent classification accuracy. It indicates that our model still can assign reasonable weights to image and text information, and lead to a better joint visual-textual representation even if these image-text pairs may carry opposite sentiments. Indeed, BiRNN based visual semantic embedding enables cross-modality attention mechanism to consider visual and textual information comprehensively and assign reasonable weights, and lead to a more robust sentiment classification model.

Qualitative Attention Analysis. In this section, we try to visualize the attention weights of image-text pairs calculated by RNN-CA Embedding model. Note that in Fig. 3, the annotation "[image]" is used to indicate associated image for convenience, and the background colors of the words darken as the attention weights increase. In addition, the red and blue boxes of the images indicate positive and negative sentiment polarity of the corresponding pairs, respectively.

Examples (a) and (b) in Fig. 3 show several top ranked positive and negative examples of the RNN-CA Embedding model. It is obvious that our RNN-CA Embedding model prefers the images with clearly facial expression and the texts with strong emotional words like "fun", "happy", "attractive", "enjoying", "bad", "sad" and "upset". Overall, the RNN-CA Embedding model can capture crucial sentimental features in the image information and text information, and can assign reasonable weights for accurate sentiment classification.

In addition, another qualitative analysis is to check the proposed attention mechanism when images and texts carry opposite sentiments. In Fig. 3, example (c) shows several image-text pairs whose sentiment polarity is dominated by images. Our model can correctly recognize the pairs' sentiment according to the melancholy expression, the smile and the crashed car in the visual information, although some emotional words in the pairs' text, such as "little", "busy" and "hugging", are likely to cause the classifier to predict wrong sentiment. In contrast, example (d) provides several image-text pairs whose sentiment polarity is dominated by texts. The blue sky, the colorful background, and the people's smile in visual information seem to deliver positive sentiments, whereas combination of visual and textual information enables classifier to predict correct sentiment. Overall, our proposed cross-modality attention mechanism can flexibly assign weights to visual and textual information, and provides more accurate sentiment classification results. We attribute this flexibility to BiRNN based visual semantic embedding. Because of this, the RNN-CA Embedding model achieves the best performance of joint visual-textual sentiment classification.

6   Conclusion

In this paper, we propose a end-to-end framework for joint visual-textual sentiment analysis. A BiRNN is designed to bridge the semantic gap between visual and textual information, then a cross-modality attention mechanism is proposed to automatically assign weights to visual and textual information and generate a reasonable joint visual-textual representation for sentiment classification.

Experimental results have demonstrated that the proposed model has significantly improved the performance of joint visual-textual sentiment analysis on two new collected datasets, especially when images and texts carry opposite sentiments.

Acknowledgment. This work is supported by National Natural Science Foundation of China under Grants, No. 61772133, No. 61472081, No. 61402104, No. 61370207, No. 61370208, No. 61300024, No. 61320106007, Key Laboratory of Computer Network Technology of Jiangsu Province, Jiangsu Provincial Key Laboratory of Network and Information Security under Grants No. BM2003201, and Key Laboratory of Computer Network and Information Integration of Ministry of Education of China under Grants No. 93K-9.

References

1. Wang, L., Li, Y., Huang, J., et al.: Learning two-branch neural networks for image-text matching tasks. IEEE Trans. Pattern Anal. Mach. Intell. (2018)
2. You, Q., Jin, H., Luo, J.: Visual sentiment analysis by attending on local image regions. In: AAAI, pp. 231–237 (2017)
3. Vinyals, O., Toshev, A., Bengio, S., et al.: Show and tell: lessons learned from the 2015 MSCOCO image captioning challenge. IEEE Trans. Pattern Anal. Mach. Intell. **39**(4), 652–663 (2017)
4. Chen, X., Wang, Y., Liu, Q.: Visual and textual sentiment analysis using deep fusion convolutional neural networks. In: 2017 IEEE International Conference on Image Processing (ICIP), pp. 1557–1561. IEEE (2017)
5. You, Q., Cao, L., Jin, H., et al.: Robust visual-textual sentiment analysis: when attention meets tree-structured recursive neural networks. In: Proceedings of the 2016 ACM on Multimedia Conference, pp. 1008–1017. ACM (2016)
6. You, Q., Luo, J., Jin, H., et al.: Cross-modality consistent regression for joint visual textual sentiment analysis of social multimedia. In: Proceedings of the Ninth ACM International Conference on Web Search and Data Mining, pp. 13–22. ACM (2016)
7. Katsurai, M., Satoh, S.: Image sentiment analysis using latent correlations among visual, textual, and sentiment views. In: 2016 IEEE International Conference on Acoustics, Speech and Signal Processing (ICASSP), pp. 2837–2841. IEEE (2016)
8. Cao, D., Ji, R., Lin, D., et al.: A cross-media public sentiment analysis system for microblog. Multimedia Syst. **22**(4), 479–486 (2016)
9. Yang, Z., Yang, D., Dyer, C., et al.: Hierarchical attention networks for document classification. In: 2016 Proceedings of the Conference of the North American Chapter of the Association for Computational Linguistics: Human Language Technologies, pp. 1480–1489 (2016)
10. Szegedy, C., Vanhoucke, V., Ioffe, S., et al.: Rethinking the inception architecture for computer vision. In: Proceedings of the IEEE Conference on Computer Vision and Pattern Recognition, pp. 2818–2826 (2016)
11. Pang, L., Zhu, S., Ngo, C.W.: Deep multimodal learning for affective analysis and retrieval. IEEE Trans. Multimedia **17**(11), 2008–2020 (2015)
12. Xu, K., Ba, J., Kiros, R., et al.: Show, attend and tell: neural image caption generation with visual attention. In: International Conference on Machine Learning, pp. 2048–2057 (2015)

13. Ma, L., Lu, Z., Shang, L., et al.: Multimodal convolutional neural networks for matching image and sentence. In: Proceedings of the IEEE International Conference on Computer Vision, pp. 2623–2631 (2015)
14. Campos, V., Salvador, A., Giro-i-Nieto, X., et al.: Diving deep into sentiment: understanding fine-tuned CNNs for visual sentiment prediction. In: Proceedings of the 1st International Workshop on Affect and Sentiment in Multimedia, pp. 57–62. ACM (2015)
15. Ioffe, S., Szegedy, C.: Batch normalization: accelerating deep network training by reducing internal covariate shift. In: International Conference on Machine Learning, pp. 448–456 (2015)
16. Wang, M., Cao, D., Li, L., et al.: Microblog sentiment analysis based on cross-media bag-of-words model. In: Proceedings of International Conference on Internet Multi-media Computing and Service, p. 76. ACM (2014)
17. Bahdanau, D., Cho, K., Bengio, Y.: Neural machine translation by jointly learning to align and translate arXiv preprint arXiv:1409.0473 (2014)
18. Pennington, J., Socher, R., Manning, C.: Glove: global vectors for word representation. In: Proceedings of the 2014 Conference on Empirical Methods in Natural Language Processing (EMNLP), pp. 1532–1543 (2014)
19. You, Q., Luo, J.: Towards social imagematics: sentiment analysis in social multimedia. In: Proceedings of the Thirteenth International Workshop on Multimedia Data Mining, p. 3. ACM (2013)
20. Chen, T., Lu, D., Kan, M.Y., et al.: Understanding and classifying image tweets. In: Proceedings of the 21st ACM International Conference on Multimedia, pp. 781–784. ACM (2013)
21. Socher, R., Perelygin, A., Wu, J., et al.: Recursive deep models for semantic compositionality over a sentiment treebank. In: Proceedings of the 2013 Conference on Empirical Methods in Natural Language Processing, pp. 1631–1642 (2013)
22. Borth, D., Ji, R., Chen, T., et al.: Large-scale visual sentiment ontology and detectors using adjective noun pairs. In: Proceedings of the 21st ACM International Conference on Multimedia, pp. 223–232. ACM (2013)
23. Krizhevsky, A., Sutskever, I., Hinton, G.E.: ImageNet classification with deep convolutional neural networks. In: Advances in Neural Information Processing systems, pp. 1097–1105 (2012)

Deep Hashing with Triplet Labels and Unification Binary Code Selection for Fast Image Retrieval

Chang Zhou[1(✉)], Lai-Man Po[1], Mengyang Liu[1], Wilson Y. F. Yuen[2],
Peter H. W. Wong[2], Hon-Tung Luk[2], Kin Wai Lau[2],
and Hok Kwan Cheung[2]

[1] Department of Electronic Engineering, City University of Hong Kong,
83 Tat Chee Avenue, Kowloon, Hong Kong
chanzhou3-c@my.cityu.edu.hk
[2] TFI Digital Medial Limited, InnoCentre,
72 Tat Chee Avenue, Kowloon, Hong Kong

Abstract. With the significant breakthrough of computer vision using convolutional neural networks, deep learning has been applied to image hashing algorithms for efficient image retrieval on large-scale datasets. Inspired by Deep Supervised Hashing (DSH) algorithm, we propose to use triplet loss function with an online training strategy that takes three images as training inputs to learn compact binary codes. A relaxed triplet loss function is designed to maximize the discriminability with consideration of the balance property of the output space. In addition, a novel unification binary code selection algorithm is also proposed to represent the scalable binary code in an efficient way, which can fix the problem of conventional deep hashing methods that generate different lengths of binary code by retraining. Experiments on two well-known datasets of CIFAR-10 and NUS-WIDE show that the proposed DSH with use of unification binary code selection can achieve promising performance as compared with conventional image hashing and CNN-based hashing algorithms.

Keywords: Deep hashing · Unification binary code selection · Triplet loss

1 Introduction

With the popularity of mobile devices embedded with cameras and Internet connectivity, today thousands of digital photos are uploading on to the Internet every minute. The ubiquitous access to both digital images and the Internet provide the basis for many emerging applications with image search functionality. The purpose of image search is to retrieve similar visual documents for a textural or visual query from a large-scale visual database. Traditional image search methods usually index visual data based on the meta data information associate with the image such as tags and titles.

In practice, however, content-based image retrieval (CBIR) [3] is always preferred as textual information may be inconsistent with the visual content. Basically, CBIR retrieves images that are similar to a given query image in terms of visual or semantic similarities. Since the early 1990s, CBIR has attracted a lot of attentions from both

© Springer Nature Switzerland AG 2019
I. Kompatsiaris et al. (Eds.): MMM 2019, LNCS 11295, pp. 277–288, 2019.
https://doi.org/10.1007/978-3-030-05710-7_23

academia and industry. One of the common CBIR approaches is to represent images in the database and the query image by handcrafted real-valued features such as the invariant local visual feature of SIFT [20]. Then the image search is performed by ranking the database images according to their feature distances to the query image in the feature domain. The image with the smallest distance is returned as the most similar image. The main drawback of the real-valued feature approach is extremely high computational and memory requirements especially on large-scale image database with millions of images.

To tackle the complexity problem, compact binary codes are preferred to represent visual content of the images, which is possible to achieve high-speed searching as well as low memory requirement for database storage. The conversion of an image to compact binary code representation is commonly referred as image hashing. Conventional image hashing algorithms can be divided into data-independent and data-dependent approaches. For the data-independent approach, the hash function is independently generated without training data and the locality-sensitive hashing (LSH [2]) is a well-known example of the data-independent hashing algorithm. For the data-dependent approach, the hash function tries to learn from the training data and these algorithms are commonly referred as Learning to Hash (L2H) algorithms. In practical CBIR system implementation, L2H algorithms have become more and more popular, which is mainly due to L2H can achieve comparable or better image search accuracy with much shorter hash code length.

In general, L2H algorithms can be divided into unsupervised and supervised algorithms. Unsupervised L2H algorithms only use the feature information of training data without supervised information (label) during the training. However, supervised L2H algorithms use supervised information (label) to learn the hash codes during the training. The supervised information can be represented as pointwise labels, pairwise labels, and ranking labels. Recently, a lot of L2H algorithms have been developed such as CCA-ITQ [14], supervised discrete hashing (SDH) [21], fast supervised hashing (FastH) [22], and column sampling based discrete supervised hashing (COSDISH) [23]. However, most of these algorithms are still based on the traditional approach of using handcrafted features, in which the feature construction is independent of hash function learning such that the designed features might not be compatible with the hashing procedure.

On the other hand, the significant breakthrough of convolutional neural networks (CNNs) on image classification [1] and other computer vision tasks demonstrate that CNN can be used as a highly effective feature extractor. Recently some CNN-based deep hashing algorithms have been developed to perform simultaneous feature learning and hash code learning, which have been demonstrated could achieve better performance than the traditional handcrafted feature approach. Basically, these deep hashing algorithms are supervised L2H algorithms. Deep Pairwise-supervised Hashing (DPSH) [6] and Deep Supervised Hashing (DSH) [5] are two of the most recently proposed CNN based L2H algorithms. Both of them take pairs of images as training inputs and encourages the output of each image to approximate discrete values. While some deep hashing algorithms such as DTSH [7] and DNNH [8] are supervised by triplet labels which inherently contain richer information than pairwise labels.

Inspired by the online training strategy of DSH algorithm [5] and taking advantage of richer information on using triplet labels, we proposed to use triplet loss function to enhance DSH algorithm for learning the compact binary codes. The proposed binary code learning framework exploits the CNN structure based on triplet loss with a 3D online triplet generation training that can be realized by simple programming coding. Basically, the proposed network learns the similarity features from the triplet selection, which pulls the similar images together and pushes the dissimilar image apart. In addition, we also proposed a unification binary code selection method to handle the problem of binary code redundancy, which allows to train the network only once to obtain different lengths of hash code for achieving scalable hash code design without retaining of the model.

2   Deep Supervised Hashing (DSH)

The main idea of DSH [5] is to make use of CNN features for realizing a binary code learning framework. For mathematical representation, we denote the image RGB space as Ω, then the goal of the DSH is to learn a CNN-based mapping from Ω to k-bit binary code: $\mathcal{F}: \Omega \rightarrow \{+1, -1\}^k$. A typical network structure of the DSH learning framework is illustrated in Fig. 1, in which a CNN model is used to take image pairs along with labels indicating whether the two images are similar or not as training inputs, and produces binary codes as outputs. During the training, these image pairs are generated online and the loss function is designed to pull the network outputs of similar image pairs closer and push the outputs of dissimilar image pairs away. This loss function is designed to learn similarity-preserving binary-like image representations as it can achieve a good approximation of the semantic structure of images in the learned Hamming space. In addition, the network outputs are relaxed to real values for avoiding the non-differentiable loss function optimization in Hamming space. At the same time, a regularizer is imposed to boost the real-valued outputs to approach the desired discrete values. After training, new images can be encoded by propagating through the network and then quantizing the network outputs to generate binary code.

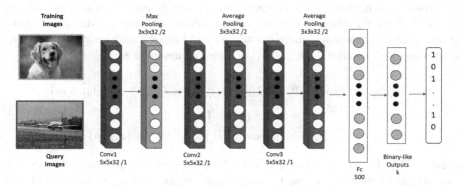

Fig. 1. The general network structure of the DSH with convolutional, average pooling and fully-connected layers.

3 DSH with Triplet Labels

To enhance the original DSH with image-pair loss function, we propose to use triplet loss function for simultaneously minimizing and maximizing the binary-code distances between similar and dissimilar images, respectively. In which three images instead of two images are used to calculate the loss. Basically, the proposed DSH has the same network structure as shown in Fig. 1, while the CNN is trained with triplet images combination and their corresponding similarity labels. We denote the training triplet images in the form of $(I_a\ I_p\ I_n)$, where I_a is an anchor image, I_p is a positive image that similar to I_a, and I_n is a negative image that dissimilar to I_a. Moreover, their corresponding output binary codes are given by $(b_a,, b_p,, b_n)$. In general, the triplet loss function $L(b_a, b_p, b_n)$ can be defined as:

$$L(b_a, b_p, b_n) = \max(0, dist(b_a, b_p) - dist(b_a, b_n) + m)$$
$$s.t.\ b_j \in \{+1, -1\}^k,\ j \in \{a, p, n\} \tag{1}$$

where the m is a margin of the triplet loss, the $dist(*, *)$ represents Hamming distance between two binary codes. The objective of this triplet loss function is to minimize the Hamming distance $dist(b_a, b_p)$ between similar images and maximize the distance $dist(b_a, b_n)$ between dissimilar images. In addition, the margin is used to make sure only the distances between positive pair and negative pair within a radius will contribute to the loss function.

Suppose that there are N triplet images selected from the training images $\{(I_{i,a}, I_{i,n}, I_{i,p})|i = 1, \ldots N\}$, our goal is to the minimize the overall loss function:

$$\mathcal{L} = \sum_i^N L(b_{i,a}, b_{i,p}, b_{i,n}).$$
$$s.t.\ b_{i,j} \in \{+1, -1\}^k,\ i \in \{1, \ldots N\},\ j \in \{a, p, n\}. \tag{2}$$

Theoretically, the triplet loss function of (2) can be used to provide output discrimination and binarization. However, it is intractable to train the network with backpropagation method due to the thresholding of the output. To tackle this problem, we try to relax the constraint of the output values by using L2 distance, impose constraint loss to reduce the quantization error and keep the hash code balance. A relaxed triplet loss function $L_r(b_a, b_p, b_n)$ is therefore designed as:

$$L_r(b_a, b_p, b_n) = \max\left(0, \|\mathcal{F}(I_a) - \mathcal{F}(I_p)\|_2^2 - \|\mathcal{F}(I_a) - \mathcal{F}(I_n)\|_2^2 + m\right)$$
$$+ \alpha\left(\big\|\,|\mathcal{F}(I_j)| - \mathbf{1}\big\|_1\right)$$
$$+ \beta|mean(\mathcal{F}(I_j))|,\quad s.t. j \in \{a, p, n\}. \tag{3}$$

where $\mathcal{F}(*)$ is the real-valued output the CNN, $\mathbf{1}$ is a vector of all ones, $\|*\|_2$ is the L2-norm of the vector, $\|*\|_1$ is the L1-norm of the vector, and $|*|$ is the element-wise absolute value operation. α and β are the weights for these two regularization terms.

The first term of (3) is similar to the general form of the triplet loss function for minimizing and maximizing similar and dissimilar image pairs with a margin m but L2-norm with real-valued CNN outputs are used to calculate the distances. To reduce the quantization error of the output instead of completely ignore the binary constraints, we impose the second term with output drawn between 1 and -1. This second term makes the codes binary-like. In the training process, we find that the contrastive and triplet loss will lead to slightly unbalance output. Thus, the third term is used to achieve balance output property, in which 50% of the values in the training samples are set to 0 and the other 50% are set to 1 for each bit. This term is also adopted in SSDH [17]. The α and β are hyperparameters for balancing the triplet loss, quantization error and the balance error. By substituting (3) into (2), we can express the relaxed overall loss function as:

$$L_r = \sum_{i=1}^{N} \{ \max \left(0, \left\| \mathcal{F}(I_{i,a}) - \mathcal{F}(I_{i,p}) \right\|_2^2 - \left\| \mathcal{F}(I_{i,a}) - \mathcal{F}(I_{i,n}) \right\|_2^2 + m \right)$$
$$+ \alpha \left(\left\| |\mathcal{F}(I_j)| - 1 \right\|_1 \right)$$
$$+ \beta |mean(\mathcal{F}(I_j))| \}, \quad s.t. \ j \in \{(i,a), (i,p), (i,n)\}. \tag{4}$$

The three gradients of the first term can be expressed as:

$$\frac{\partial Term1}{\partial \mathcal{F}(I_{i,a})} = 2 \left(\mathcal{F}(I_{i,n}) - \mathcal{F}(I_{i,p}) \right)$$
$$\frac{\partial Term1}{\partial \mathcal{F}(I_{i,p})} = 2 \left(\mathcal{F}(I_{i,p}) - \mathcal{F}(I_{i,a}) \right) \tag{5}$$
$$\frac{\partial Term1}{\partial \mathcal{F}(I_{i,n})} = 2 \left(\mathcal{F}(I_{i,a}) - \mathcal{F}(I_{i,n}) \right)$$

The gradients of the second terms can be expressed as:

$$\frac{\partial Term2}{\partial \mathcal{F}(I_j)} = a\delta(\mathcal{F}(I_j)). \tag{6}$$

where

$$\delta(x) = \begin{cases} 1, & -1 \le x \le 0 \ or \ x \ge 1. \\ -1, & otherwise. \end{cases} \tag{7}$$

The gradients of the third term can be expressed as:

$$\frac{\partial Term3}{\partial \mathcal{F}(I_j)} = \beta\mu(\mathcal{F}(I_j)). \tag{8}$$

where

$$\mu(x) = \begin{cases} 1/k, & x \ge 0. \\ -\frac{1}{k}, & x < 0. \end{cases} \tag{9}$$

With these computed sub-gradients over mini-batches, the rest of the backpropagation can be done in a standard manner to train the CNN-based DSH with triplet loss.

3.1 3D Online Triplet Generation

To speed up the training process, we use the online generation of triplets which is similar to the DSH's online image pairs generation [5] that exploit all the unique pairs in each mini-batch. However, the proposed online generation of triplets is denoted as 3D online generation method with three elements of 'anchor', 'positive', and 'negative' of the triplet loss. This 3D online triplet generation can alleviate the balance problem of the output space. Compared with the online training of contrastive loss which has more positive pairs against negative pairs in each batch. More specifically, we selected mini-batch images from the dataset in each iteration just like classification problem. In each mini-batch, we cover all the possibilities of triplets by building the whole triplet-wise similarity matrix. This method can significantly increase samples number in each iteration, which takes advantage of utilizing more images triplets that will make loss converge much faster. This approach is efficient and space saving as compared with offline training that generates image triplets randomly and stores the triplet combination in each iteration.

3.2 Unification Binary Code Selection

Most of the deep hashing methods are required to retrain their networks for generating the different lengths of the binary codes. However, we find that longer code lengths always have more redundant bits for the retrieval tasks. It means that every bit contributes unequally in term of the robustness and distinctiveness. As network retraining is computational expensive in most of cases, we propose to generate binary codes with different code lengths by selecting the most valuable bits from the binary codes with long code length. This can reduce the computational requirement as well as improve the efficiency of the shorter binary codes generation.

The proposed binary code selection strategy as described in Algorithm 1. Technically, the proposed binary code selection algorithm can be conducted in two stages. First, we obtain the representative binary code of classes H_j by taking the average of all the output $\mathcal{F}(I)$ where the label of image I belong to j th classes and then threshold by $sign(*)$. Figure 2 shows an example of three output bits with categories of Dog, Cat and Deer, in which we can easily realize that the Bit 3 is redundant. We input H_j to generate distinctiveness bit matrix $M_b^h[i,j] \leftarrow \{H_i^h! = H_j^h|1\}$, where the notion $\{a! = b|1\}$ mean that it will return 1 if $a! = b$ is true and $[i,j]$ denoting the entry in i-th row and j-th column of a matrix. The bit matrix $\{M_b^h|h \in 1.2\ldots K\}$ as shown in Fig. 2 which indicate the discriminable distance among classes for each binary bit. In other words, the h-th bit can discriminate class i from class j and make contribute to retrieval task if $M_b^h[i,j] = 1$, vice versa.

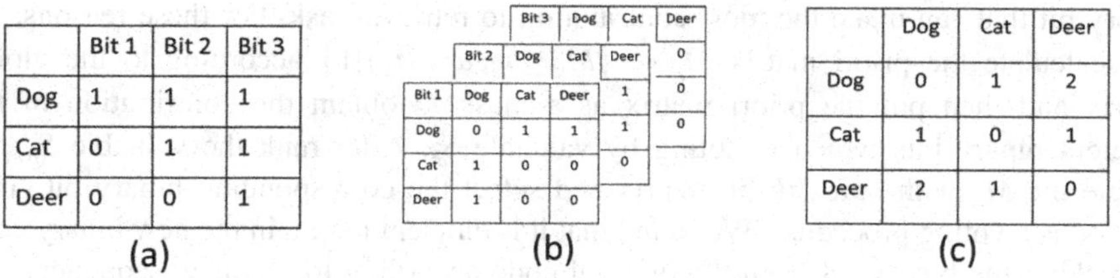

	Bit 1	Bit 2	Bit 3
Dog	1	1	1
Cat	0	1	1
Deer	0	0	1

(a)

			Bit 3	Dog	Cat	Deer
		Bit 2	Dog	Cat	Deer	0
	Bit 1	Dog	Cat	Deer	1	0
Dog	0	1	1	1	0	
Cat	1	0	0	0		
Deer	1	0	0			

(b)

	Dog	Cat	Deer
Dog	0	1	2
Cat	1	0	1
Deer	2	1	0

(c)

Fig. 2. (a) An example of binary codes for three different classes 'dog', 'cat', 'deer', (b) matrix M_b^k for the binary bit, and (c) the global matrix M_g with all binary bits.

Algorithm 1. Unification binary code selection
Input   representative binary code $\{H_j \mid j \in 1,2 \dots C\}$, the notion H_j^i indicates the ith bit from jth classes, C number of classes, K length of the binary code.
Output   a set of bit order $\{ index^v \mid v \in 1,2 \dots K\}$
{I. Compute output of the class-wise distance matrix for each bit}
  1: **for** h to K **do**
  2:    **for** i to C **do**
  3:      **for** j to C **do**
  4:        $M_b^h\, i,j \; \leftarrow \{ H_i^h\, ! = H_j^h \mid 1 \}$
  5:      **End for**
  6:    **End for**
  7: **End for**
{II. Select the valuable binary bit}
  8: Initialization: $M_g \leftarrow C \times C$ zero matrix
  9: **for** v to K **do**
 10:    $M_p \leftarrow \{ M_g \leq mean(M_g) \mid 1\}$ return $C \times C$ matrix.
 11:    **for** i to K **do**
 12:      $W_b^i \leftarrow M_b^i \circ M_p$ Hadamard product, return $C \times C$ matrix.
 13:      $S_b^i \leftarrow sum(W_b^i)$
 14:    **End for**
 15:    $index^v \leftarrow \underset{i}{\mathrm{argmax}} \{ S_b^i \mid i \in \{1,2 \dots K\}\}$
 16:    $M_g \leftarrow M_g + M_b^{index\,v}$
 17:    Select the $index^v$th binary code and set $M_b^{index\,v} \leftarrow 0$
 18: **End for**

Secondly, we select the valuable binary bit by iteratively updating the global matrix M_g which is initialized as $C \times C$ matrix with full of zero. Different from M_b^h, it indicates the sum of discriminable distance among classes for the selected binary code as shown in Fig. 2(c). In this stage, we consider two requirements for selecting binary code: (1) Making every entry in matrix close to the average value of matrix in order to keep the balance of the discriminable distance among classes, and (2) Choosing the binary bit that can make the most contribution to retrieval task. For these reasons, we first calculate the priori matrix $M_p \leftarrow \{M_g \leq mean(M_g)|1\}$ according to the global matrix and then put the priori matrix as a mask to obtain the contribution of the different binary bits which is noting by valuable S_b^i. After rank the valuable S_b^i, we update the M_g with $index^y th$ bit matrix and select the corresponding binary bit. This method is a voting procedure. We found that it is efficient to obtain the new binary code by picking the binary bit from the original code according to this new sequence.

4   Experimental Results

4.1   Implementation

In the implementation, all the experiments are built with Pytorch [18] and the network structure is same as the original DSH [5] as shown in Fig. 1, which only contains three convolutional layers and two fully-connected layers. The first fully-connected layer includes 500 nodes and the second contains k nodes, where k is the length of binary code. All the convolution layers and the first fully-connected layer are equipped with the ReLU activation function. In our implementation, SGD is the optimizer with momentum 0.9 for the network training. An online triplet training samples generation method as proposed in Sect. 3.1 is also used to train the network with mini-batch size of 256, learning rate of 0.001 at the beginning and decaying by 40% on every 50 epochs. The hyperparameters of α and β were set to 0.1 and 0.001, respectively. The margin m of triplet loss was set to 8 for the output code length of 48, and the other results with different code lengths are shorten from the 48-bit codes by the binary bit selection algorithm.

4.2   Dataset and Performance Evaluation

In our experiments, two widely used datasets of CIFAR-10 [9] and NUS-WIDE [10] are used. In the CIFAR-10 dataset, there are 10 object categories and each class consist of 6,000 images with a total of 60,000 images. We randomly selected 50,000 images as training set and the rest of 10,000 images are used as test set. All of these 10,000 test images are used as query images for the performance evaluation. In the NUS-WIDE dataset, there are 269,648 images among 81 classes collected from Flickr. Based on the experimental settings in [5] of DSH, we picked 21 most frequently used classes, each class with at least 5,000 images, and the total number of images from NUS-WIDE dataset is 195,834. Moreover, 10,000 images were randomly selected as test query images from these 195,834 images and the rest of them were used as training images. During the training, these images from NUS-WIDE were rescaled to the size of 64×64 for feeding the CNN model.

We compared our proposed DSH with triplet loss with original DSH and several state-of-the-art methods such as LSH [2], SH [13], ITQ [14], CCA-ITQ [14], MLH [4], BRE [19], KSH [16], CNNH [15], DLBHC [11], and DNNH [8]. Mean Average Precision (mAP) was used as performance metric for comparison. For a fair comparison with the original DSH, the same network structure of DSH as shown in Fig. 1 is used for the proposed DSH with triplet loss. Table 1 shows the mAP based performance comparison of the proposed method (DSH-TL) with the original DSH and other well-known hashing methods using different code lengths k as 12-bit, 24-bit, 36-bit, and 48-bit. From Table 1, we can observe that the CNN-based hashing methods outperform the conventional hashing methods of LSH, SH, ITQ, CCA-ITQ, MLH, BRE and KSH on both CIFAR-10 and NUS-WIDE datasets with a large margin. This demonstrates that the CNN-based learning image representations is advantageous against the traditional approach. In terms of CNN-based methods, CNNH, DLBHC, DNNH, and DSH generally have inferior performance. Furthermore, the proposed method of DSH-TL outperforms the original DSH. Compared with the original DSH with pair loss, the proposed DSH-TL improved the accuracy in terms of mAP by a large margin of 33.05%, 27.61%, 25.82% and 23.43% for 12-bit, 24-bit, 36-bit and 48-bit code lengths on CIFAR-10, respectively. For NUS-WIDE, we can see our method still outperforms DSH by about 3% on average.

Table 1. Performance comparison of the proposed DSH-TL with conventional learning hash methods and CNN-based hashing methods in terms of image retrieval mAP using CIFAR-10 and NUS-WIDE datasets.

Method	CIFAR-10				NUS-WIDE			
	12-bit	24-bit	36-bit	48-bit	12-bit	24-bit	36-bit	48-bit
LSH	0.1277	0.1367	0.1407	0.1492	0.3329	0.3392	0.3450	0.3474
SH	0.1319	0.1278	0.1364	0.1320	0.3401	0.3374	0.3343	0.3332
ITQ	0.1080	0.1088	0.2085	0.2176	0.3425	0.3464	0.3522	0.3576
CCA-ITQ	0.1653	0.1960	0.2085	0.2176	0.3874	0.3977	0.4146	0.4188
MLH	0.1844	0.1944	0.2053	0.2094	0.3829	0.3930	0.3959	0.3990
BRE	0.1589	0.1632	0.1697	0.1717	0.3556	0.3581	0.3549	0.3592
KSH	0.2948	0.3723	0.4019	0.4167	0.4331	0.4592	0.4659	0.4692
CNNH	0.5425	0.5604	0.5640	0.5574	0.4215	0.4358	0.4451	0.4332
DLBHC	0.5503	0.5803	0.5778	0.5885	0.4663	0.4728	0.4921	0.4916
DNNH	0.5708	0.5875	0.5899	0.5904	0.5471	0.5367	0.5258	0.5248
DSH	0.6157	0.6512	0.6607	0.6755	0.5483	0.5513	0.5582	0.5621
DSH-TL	**0.8192**	**0.8311**	**0.8315**	**0.8342**	**0.5758**	**0.5787**	**0.5798**	**0.5807**

4.3   Online Image Triplet Generation

In this subsection, we investigate the triplet online generation method which improving the training process of the proposed DSH with triple loss. To evaluate the contribution of the proposed online training strategy, we train the CNN network on CIFAR10 and compare with the offline train method. In which we randomly pick 1 million triplet combinations the same as the Siamese scheme and inputting the same number of images for both schemes in each iteration. These results are shown in Fig. 3(a). As can be seen, our proposed online triplet generation converges much faster than the offline training approach, since our scheme can sharply increase the samples number of triplet in each iteration, which offers the gradient the steepest direction and more information about the semantic relations between different images.

On the other hand, the latest research found that small batch size will have better performance on the classification problem. For this reason, we also investigate online triplet generation method with different batch size. We set batch sizes to 32, 64, 128, and 256 for evaluating their effects. Figure 3(b) shows the performance with different batch size on CIFAR-10. It can be found that as the batch size grows, the retrieval performance of DSH-TL consistently improves. The reason might be the rapid growth of samples number with the increment of batch size. Since 1.6×10^6 triplet will be generated from batch size 256 images compared with 2×10^2 from batch size 32 images.

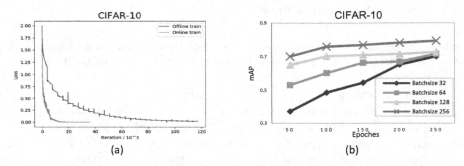

Fig. 3. (a) Comparison of train loss between the online triplet generation training method and offline training method. (b) Comparison of mAP with different batch sizes.

4.4   Unification Binary Code Selection and Extension

To verify the advantage of unification binary code selection. We investigate three DSH-TL variants: (1) F-DSH-TL is a DSH-TL variant with retraining network for different length of binary codes. (2) S-DSH-TL is DSH-TL variant replacing unification binary code selection with original sequence selection in order. (3) R-DSH-TL is a DSH-TL variant replacing unification binary code with random selection. For a fair comparison, all the re-selection strategy is based on the same 48-bit binary codes. The mAP results on the two benchmark datasets are shown in Table 2. It is observed that the proposed DSH-TL method yields the highest performance with different code lengths on NUS-WIDE and CIFAR-10 datasets. Individually, compared to the retrain method, DSH-TL achieve approximately increases of 2% and 1% in average on two datasets, respectively.

Furthermore, we notice that the redundancy of binary bits existing in most of the deep hashing method. We extend our method to DLBHC [11], they learn binary codes by employing a hidden layer for representing the latent concepts that dominate the class labels. We train the latent layer with 128 bits first based on VGG16 [12] and the rest length code will be selected by our proposed algorithm, compared with the method that retrains latent layer every time. The results are shown in Fig. 4. In general, the re-selected method can maintain the performance against the network retraining method with different code lengths of k, even surpass it on the node 8 bits. It can prove that the proposed binary bit selection method is efficient as the CNN network is only required to train once for long code length and its extensibility on other methods.

Table 2. Performance comparison of the proposed DSH-TL with three different strategies on CIFAR-10 and NUS-WIDE dataset.

Method	CIFAR-10				NUS-WIDE			
	12-bit	24-bit	36-bit	48-bit	12-bit	24-bit	36-bit	48-bit
F-DSH-TL	0.7922	0.8213	0.8244	0.8342	0.5501	0.5621	0.5711	0.5807
S-DSH-TL	0.7608	0.8049	0.8254	0.8342	0.4819	0.5460	0.5465	0.5807
R-DSH-TL	0.7517	0.8234	0.8261	0.8342	0.4518	0.4654	0.5580	0.5807
DSH-TL	**0.8191**	**0.8306**	**0.8312**	**0.8342**	**0.5758**	**0.5787**	**0.5798**	**0.5807**

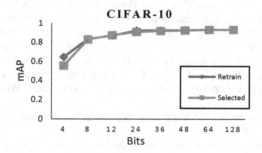

Fig. 4. The comparison on DLBHC with network retraining strategy and the proposed unification binary code selection strategy.

5   Conclusion

In this paper, we proposed to use triplet loss function to train the DSH convolutional neural networks for achieving simultaneous feature learning and hash code generation. A relaxed triplet loss function with two regularization terms is devised for avoiding the non-differentiable loss function optimization in Hamming space. To speed up the training, an online generation of triplet method is also adopted for the network training. In addition, a unification binary code selection method is also proposed to ease the redundant problem of hash code, which makes the binary code scalable and avoid retraining of the network for different code lengths. Experimental results on CIFAR-10 and NUS-WIDE datasets demonstrate that the proposed DSH with triplet loss can achieve higher quality hash codes than the original DSH using image pair loss and state-of-the-art image hashing algorithms.

References

1. Krizhevsky, A., Sutskever, I., Hinton, G.E.: ImageNet classification with deep convolutional neural networks. In: Advances in Neural Information Processing Systems, pp. 1097–1105 (2012)
2. Gionis, A., Indyk, P., Motwani, R.: Similarity search in high dimensions via hashing. In: VLDB, pp. 518–529 (1999)
3. Eakins, J., Graham, M.: Content-based image retrieval (1999)
4. Norouzi, M., Fleet, D.J.: Minimal loss hashing for compact binary codes. In: ICML 2011, pp. 353–360 (2011)
5. Liu, H., Wang, R., Shan, S., Chen, X.: Deep supervised hashing for fast image retrieval. In: IEEE Conference on Computer Vision and Pattern Recognition, pp. 2064–2072 (2016)
6. Li, W.-J., Wang, S., Kang, W.-C.: Feature learning based deep supervised hashing with pairwise labels. In: International Joint Conference on Artificial Intelligence (2016)
7. Wang, X., Shi, Y., Kitani, Kris M.: Deep supervised hashing with triplet labels. In: Lai, S.-H., Lepetit, V., Nishino, K., Sato, Y. (eds.) ACCV 2016. LNCS, vol. 10111, pp. 70–84. Springer, Cham (2017). https://doi.org/10.1007/978-3-319-54181-5_5
8. Lai, H., Pan, Y., Liu, Y., Yan, S.: Simultaneous feature learning and hash coding with deep neural networks. In: Computer Vision and Pattern Recognition, pp. 3270–3278 (2015)
9. Krizhevsky, A., Hinton, G.: Learning multiple layers of features from tiny images (2009)
10. Chua, T.S., Tang, J., Hong, R., Li, H., Luo, Z., Zheng, Y.: NUS-WIDE: a real-world web image database from national university of Singapore. In: Proceedings of the ACM International Conference on Image and Video Retrieval. ACM (2009)
11. Lin, K., Yang, H.-F., Hsiao, J.-H., Chen, C.-S.: Deep learning of binary hash codes for fast image retrieval. In: Computer Vision and Pattern Recognition Workshops (CVPRW), pp. 27–35 (2015)
12. Simonyan, K., Zisserman, A.: Very deep convolutional networks for large-scale image recognition. In: ICLR (2015)
13. Weiss, Y., Torralba, A., Fergus, R.: Spectral hashing. In: Advances in Neural Information Processing Systems, pp. 1753–1760 (2008)
14. Gong, Y., Lazebnik, S.: Iterative quantization: a procrustean approach to learning binary codes. In: Computer Vision and Pattern Recognition (CVPR), pp. 817–824 (2011)
15. Xia, R., Pan, Y., Lai, H., Liu, C., Yan, S.: Supervised hashing for image retrieval via image representation learning. In: Twenty-Eighth AAAI Conference on Artificial Intelligence (2014)
16. Liu, W., Wang, J., Ji, R., Jiang, Y.-G., Chang, S.-F.: Supervised hashing with kernels. In Computer Vision and Pattern Recognition (CVPR) 2012, pp. 2074–2081 (2012)
17. Yang, H.-F., Lin, K., Chen. C.-S.: Supervised learning of semantics-preserving hash via deep convolutional neural networks. IEEE Trans. Pattern Anal. Mach. Intell. 40(2), 437–451 (2018)
18. Paszke, A., et al.: Automatic differentiation in PyTorch (2017)
19. Kulis, B., Darrell, T.: Learning to hash with binary reconstructive embeddings. In: Advances in Neural Information Processing Systems, pp. 1042–1050 (2009)
20. Lowe, D.G.: Distinctive image features from scale-invariant keypoints. Int. J. Comput. Vis. 60(2), 91–110 (2004)
21. Shen, F., Shen, C., Liu, W., Tao Shen, H.: Supervised discrete hashing. In: Proceedings of the IEEE Conference on Computer Vision and Pattern Recognition, pp. 37–45 (2015)
22. Lin, G., et al.: Fast supervised hashing with decision trees for high-dimensional data. In: Proceedings of the IEEE Conference on Computer Vision and Pattern Recognition (2014)
23. Kang, W.-C., Wu-Jun, L., Zhou, Z.-H.: Column sampling based discrete supervised hashing. In: AAAI, pp. 1230–1236 (2016)

Incremental Training for Face Recognition

Martin Winter and Werner Bailer[✉]

JOANNEUM RESEARCH Forschungsgesellschaft mbH, DIGITAL – Institute for
Information and Communication Technologies, Steyrergasse 17, 8010 Graz, Austria
{martin.winter,werner.bailer}@joanneum.at

Abstract. Many applications require the identification of persons in
video. However, the set of persons of interest is not always known in
advance, e.g., in applications for media production and archiving. Additional training samples may be added during the analysis, or groups of
faces of one person may need to be identified retrospectively. In order
to avoid re-running the face recognition, we propose an approach that
supports fast incremental training based on a state of the art face detection and recognition pipeline using CNNs and an online random forest
as a classifier. We also describe an algorithm to use the incremental
training approach to automatically train classifiers for unknown persons,
including safeguards to avoid noise in the training data. We show that
the approach reaches state of the art performance on two datasets when
using all training samples, but performs better with few or even only one
training sample.

1 Introduction

Face recognition in images and video is a technology that has been widely
adopted in a range of applications such as media production and archiving,
surveillance, etc. A typical processing pipeline consists of face detection, i.e.,
identifying regions that contain faces, and the actual recognition, i.e., identifying the person being depicted. While face detection can be done without knowing
which persons to look for, face recognition requires to set up a database with
some example images of each of the persons to be identified. In this work, we
consider use cases in media production, where incoming content (both professional and user generated content) is analyzed, in order to obtain metadata
that will link it to topics, events and other content items. Identifying persons
is of course of high interest in such a use case. However, the persons of interest
may not be known in advance, in particular in emerging events. There are two
main problems: First, for persons to be added to the database, only few images
may be available initially. Especially the state of the art recognition approaches
using CNNs often require larger numbers of images for training. Second, while
face recognition could be performed for the set of persons known in advance,
recognition would need to be rerun for people added later. Alternatively, the
features of the detected faces could be indexed, so that they could be matched

© Springer Nature Switzerland AG 2019
I. Kompatsiaris et al. (Eds.): MMM 2019, LNCS 11295, pp. 289–299, 2019.
https://doi.org/10.1007/978-3-030-05710-7_24

to newly added persons later, which add considerable overhead over just storing the identifiers of recognized faces.

We thus propose an approach for face recognition capable of incremental learning. In particular, the contributions of this paper are the following two. First, we replace batch training with a support vector machine (SVM) by an online random forest as a classifier based on features extracted using a deep neural network. This enables bootstrapping a classifier with few (even a single) example image for a new person, to quickly react to user verification (e.g., correcting a false recognition) and to gradually improve as more samples are added. To the best of our knowledge, this is the first work to apply online random forests to features obtained from a neural network. Second, we describe how this approach can be used to automatically train new classifiers on the fly for persons not found in the database, so that they can be later associated with a name. This approach also enables efficient retrospective search for faces found in previous analysis.

The rest of this paper is organized as follows. Section 2 discusses related work on face detection and recognition. In Sect. 3 we describe the details of our incremental training approach, and in Sect. 4 its application to automatically training new classifiers on the fly. Section 5 presents the evaluation method and results and Sect. 6 concludes the paper.

2   Related Work

Traditional face detection approaches include the widely used Viola-Jones detector [26] or detectors using histograms of oriented gradients (HOG) [12]. However, these approaches are typically limited to a quite narrow range of variations around a particular pose (e.g., frontal). Other approaches use deformable part models (DPM, e.g. [15,28]), eliminating some of these limitations. Face detection using neural networks has already been proposed 30 year ago [19], but had been limited by the computational complexity and availability of training data. [14] proposes a cascaded neural network architecture, containing three CNNs for binary classification between face and non-face, and three CNNs for calibrating the bounding boxes, implemented as multi-class classification of different displacement patterns. CNN-based face detectors have also been built on top of generic object detectors such as R-CNN and Faster R-CNN [11]. A DNN-based multi-view face detector is proposed in [7], however, it does not provide features that can be used for alignment. [29] propose an approach using three stages of cascaded CNNs, applied to an image pyramid of the input image. The first uses a fully convolutional network to mine face candidates, followed by non-maxima suppression to eliminate overlapping candidates. The second stage performs rejection of false positives and regression of the bounding boxes. The third stage provides a refinement of the second, adding estimation of five facial landmark positions. The authors also show that jointly performing detection and alignment (based on the detected landmarks) improves the performance. [18] propose a single network for performing face detection, landmark localization, pose estimation, and gender classification by designing a network architecture that branches into different layers for the different tasks in the last layers of the network. [30] propose a multi-scale CNN, that also includes contextual information (such as a person's body) to guide the face detector.

Like for other visual detection/classification tasks, it has been shown that for face recognition deep convolutional neural networks outperform hand-crafted features. DeepFace [24] is one of the earlier works in this area. They propose a multi-stage approach, starting with face alignment, and then apply multiple neural networks on different alignments and color channels. The results are combined using a non-linear SVM. [31] use a DNN for performing alignment to a canonical front view, and train a CNN for face recognition. For verification of the recognition results, they use PCA on the facial features and SVM. FaceNet [21] is an approach to train a CNN for embedding faces into space, so that Euclidian distance corresponds to face similarity. The approach obtains a quite compact face descriptor, and classifiers such as SVMs can use these features for face recognition and verification. DeepID2+ [22] is another CNN-based face recognition approach, showing in particular the robustness of the obtained facial features, e.g. to partial occlusion. OpenFace [1] is a face recognition approach using CNNs, and aims to enable a low-complexity implementation for mobile devices. They use the face detector from [12] and perform 2D alignment. A modified version of FaceNet is trained for performing recognition. [3] also propose a very lightweight neural network architecture for face verification on mobile devices. However, this approach just supports inference, thus no training of new faces is supported with the lightweight network. [6] propose ArcFace, a face recognition approach using additive angular margin as a loss function to improve the separation of classes in feature space. The method performs at the state of the art or outperforms it on different face recognition databases, however, the outperformance is particularly clear on AgeDB, an in the wild face database containing images of more than 500 subjects with time annotations on year granularity.

An early approach for incremental training of face classifiers is described in [17]. It uses extended IPCA in the eigen-feature space and resource allocating networks with long-term memory, and learn both the feature representation and the classifier incrementally. However, the performance of this approach is limited. The authors of [4] use Gabor features, and incrementally train neural networks for face recognition. Similarly, a new incremental training method for a radial basis function neural network is described in [27] and applied to face recognition.

We can conclude that CNNs are both used in state of the art face detection and recognition approaches. For detection, cascade and multi-scale approaches seem to be among the most successful ones. As good alignment of input images is crucial for CNNs used for recognition, information about landmarks or pose is an important output of the detection step. Successful recognition approaches either perform classification using a CNN, or use the CNN as feature extractor and employ other classifiers such as SVMs. Incremental training approaches do exist, however, training additional faces is relatively costly.

3 Incremental Training Approach

For face detection, we use the approach proposed in [29] using multi-task cascaded CNNs. This approach does not only perform well in difficult cases (e.g., small faces, partial occlusion), but it enables also joint detection and alignment. The latter is an important prerequisite for the extraction of facial features using CNNs, which are quite sensitive to variations in cropping and pose of the input face images. We use a TensorFlow implementation[1] of this approach.

We then perform face feature extraction and embedding as described in [21] in order to obtain a feature representation suitable for classification. In particular, we use the TensorFlow[2]-implementation of FaceNet[3] to calculate proper feature representations of faces. The neural network architecture used by FaceNet is Inception-ResNet [23] which uses additional, residual connections to speed up the training process of Inception networks. This allows for the training on a larger amount of data resulting in a more powerful model. The FaceNet-model we use in our approach has been trained on the MS-Celeb-1M data set [10] to obtain a proper model for calculating the 128 dimensional face-features for each face detected.

We feed the obtained features into a random forest classifier. Random forest classifiers [2] are well known and studied classification methods. They show better or at least comparable performance in comparison to other state of the art classification algorithms such as support vector machines (SVMs) [25] or boosting technologies [8,9]. They have been successfully applied to a number of applications. Moreover, they have also recently been adapted to density estimation, manifold learning, semi-supervised learning and regression tasks in a very successful manner. Criminisi et al. [5] proposed a unified approach of random decision forests, which has been applied to a number of machine learning, computer vision and medical image analysis applications. Random classification forests are an ensemble combination of several binary decision trees where each binary decision tree is treated independently. The final output decision of the forest is obtained e.g. by a simple majority voting of all the individual leaf node predictions or more sophisticated combination strategies with respect to the individual leaf-probabilities. Each tree itself consists of a singular root node, which subsequently splits up into two child nodes in a hierarchical manner. A simple test function on a training sample is applied to decide about the path the sample moves down the tree. During the offline training, the best split for each individual tree node is calculated by globally optimizing several random test functions with respect to the overall information gain obtained by each split. Taking into account a large number of samples continuously arriving over time, the main disadvantages of such offline optimized classification forests are the increasing calculation time and the necessity for storing all samples. If boundary conditions

---

[1] https://github.com/davidsandberg/facenet/tree/master/src/align.
[2] https://www.tensorflow.org.
[3] https://github.com/davidsandberg/facenet.

change or if additional retraining is done the required execution time typically exceeds the processing capabilities of a system.

Online adaptation of classification forests has been introduced by Saffari et al. in [20]. The authors combined the ideas from online bagging and extremely randomized forests. They proposed a novel procedure (algorithm) for growing a decision tree in an online fashion for visual tracking and interactive real-time segmentation tasks. They use the basic idea of online bagging in a similar way like Oza and Russell [16] and model the sequential arrival of data by Poisson distribution sampling. This allows for continuous growing and updating the tree structure.

An important aspect is the proper choice of an objective function for maximizing information when splitting intermediate nodes during online training of the forest/tree. In the offline case, the optimal split can be determined during the global training step. In contrast to the offline case an early split decision has to be made during the samples arriving. The criteria for performing a split in the actual implementation are similar to the ones in Saffari's approach [20]. In particular a node only splits if

- a minimum number of samples has already passed the node (ensures statistical significance),
- the depth of the tree has not exceeded the predetermined maximum model complexity (ensures a final size model), and
- the minimal information gain required by a split is reached (avoids early growing).

The objective function for the information gain is the sum of all n labels' differences between actual (y) and the node's labels (m), for all parent (P) and left/right (L, R) child (C) nodes.

One problem introduced by this strategy is that it changes the tree configuration over time and the actual splitting criteria might no longer be optimal. Thus it is necessary to remove certain trees from time to time. Additionally we allow a novel tree to learn focusing optimally on novel examples with updated tree configuration. Therefore we introduce a jig-saw criterion, calculated on the out-of-bag error value calculation [16]. Thus we also are able to react on slightly changing boundary constraints of the problem. We have created our own C++ implementation of the online random forest.

4   Application to Auto-training for Unknown Persons

As we are able to start training a classifier from one or only few training images, we apply this approach to automatically training classifiers for persons not in the database. The online random forest is applied to every detected frame. If any of the faces detected receives a classification confidence below a minimal confidence threshold $minConf$, it is either an instance of a face of a new person, or the face image is heavily distorted w.r.t. previously encountered instances, e.g. due to strong viewpoint/lighting changes or large age difference. The main challenge in automatically training new classifiers is to avoid existing classifiers to become weaker (when $minConf$ is set too low, i.e., even strongly different faces are still considered as matching), and to avoid training new classifiers on noisy data, e.g., face images affected by short time distortions such as flashes, or becoming visible during a gradual transition. An overview of the algorithm is provided in Listing 1, where $features$ refers to the set of features from all faces detected in a recent time window.

In case a detected face has been successfully classified (i.e., with confidence above $minConf$), the features of the new face are stored for potential retraining, if the confidence is in an intermediate range (i.e., with confidence above $minConfStore$, but below $highConf$). The rationale is that features of very reliably classified faces will not add any new information, while those of faces classified with a confidence just above the threshold might help improving the classifier (this is basically the idea of boosting).

If a detected face has not been successfully classified, we create a (temporary) updated classifier for the encountered face which did not match any existing person. In order to support faster adaptation, we present new training samples multiple times. We then test the new classifier, and accept the update only if one of two conditions are met, that give an indication of the reliability of the classifier for the new person: (i) The confidence of the trained face is very high (confidence of match exceeds $highConf$ threshold), or (ii) the distance to the second possible match is very high. We do this check by calculating the ratio of confidences between the first and the second match against a threshold $ratio12Th$. If we do not accept the trained classifier, we revert to the previous version of the classifier, and store the unclassified face features for later investigation. One issue we might encounter is that the current configuration of the random forest prevents adding further classes. In this case a background thread will be started, which creates a tree with parametrization to support more classes, and retrain the forest from the existing data. Then the classifier can be switched to the new forest, and additional updates of the classifier could be done.

If any new features have been added (whether for a new or an existing face), we perform balancing the classifier to focus on samples that are not yet well classified. This is done by iteratively classifying the stored features, and presenting samples to update the classifier, until the convergence criterion or the maximum number of iterations for a class are reached. The order of the features and classes are randomized in order to avoid effects from a fixed presentation order. The convergence criterion is defined as reaching a classification confidence of $minConfStore$, and reaching a ratio of confidences between the first and the second match above threshold $ratio12Th$.

The values for the thresholds have been empirically determined on a development data set, and are set for the experiments reported in this paper to $minConf = 0.40$, $minConfStore = 0.70$ and $highConf = 0.90$; $ratio12Th$ is set to 4.0, and the maximum number of iterations to 10.

Algorithm 1. Handling a detected face in automatic training.

---

function AUTOTRAIN($currentFace, features$)
   $conf$ = classify($features[currentFace]$)
   if $conf < minConf$ **then**
      updateClassifier($features[currentFace]$)
      $personAdded$ = False
      for do $faceFeature_i \in features$
         ($conf_i, ratio_i$) = classify($faceFeature$)
         if $conf_i > highConf \lor ratio_i > ratio12Th$ **then**
            addPerson()
            storeFeatures($faceFeature_i$)
         else
            discardUpdatedClassifier()
      if $personAdded$ **then**
         for $numIterations$ **do**
            $features$ = getStoredFeatures()
            randomizeOrder($features$)
            for do $f_i \in features$
               ($conf_i, ratio_i$) = classify(f_i)
               while ($conf_i < minConfStore \land ratio_i > ratio12Th$) **do**
                  if $maxIterReached$ **then**
                     break
                  updateClassifier(f_i)
  else
     if $conf > minConfStore \land conf < highConf$ **then**
        storeFeatures($features[currentFace]$)

---

5   Results

We evaluate our approach on two commonly used and large datasets, Labeled Faces in the Wild (LFW) [13] and FERET v2[4]. First, we are interested in comparing the performance of our approach with [21], which uses the same feature extraction, but an SVM as classifier. Second, we are interested in the performance when only one or few training samples are provided.

5.1   LFW

The implementation using multi-task cascaded CNNs for detection, FaceNet as feature extractor and SVM as classifier, results in a correct classification rate of 99.9% using the train/classification set as proposed in [21]. With our approach we could manage to receive a notable correct classification rate of 94.4% when using the same test-setting. This is a feasible difference for a not globally optimizing classifier as used in our approach. There is a substantial difference in classification runtime, where the online random forest approach is about 10 to 100 times faster

---

[4] https://www.nist.gov/itl/iad/image-group/color-feret-database.

than the reference using SVM (see Table 1). Note, that the total training runtime required for the two approaches is comparable (in the magnitude of 10–20 ms per sample), but in contrast to the SVM, the online random forest approach can be trained incrementally. This means a constant cost of only 10–20 ms for each new face, while the SVM has to be trained from scratch (i.e., more than 26 s for the test-case with 1,680 training images).

To simulate cases of incremental learning, we compared our and the reference approach taking into account only between 1 up to 5 training images, and evaluated the resulting classifier for the remaining part of the whole LFW database. The results are shown in Table 1. As main conclusion we found, that our approach starts providing reliable results with 2 or more training images. It even reaches about 28% accuracy with a single image.

Table 1. Evaluation results on the LFW dataset using an Intel i7-4790 CPU @ 3.60 GHz, 16 GB RAM and NVIDIA GeForce GTX 970 graphic card.

Nr. training img.		Nr. test img.	Accuracy		Classification-time per sample	
Used	Total		Ours	[21]	Ours	[21]
1	1680	7484	27.59%	0.00%	1.37 ms	179.90 ms
2	1802	5804	68.00%	79.00%	0.82 ms	49.06 ms
3	1830	4903	74.16%	95.90%	0.59 ms	18.63 ms
4	1692	4293	86.05%	99.00%	0.45 ms	7.12 ms
5	1555	3870	88.68%	99.20%	0.40 ms	4.07 ms

5.2   FERET

We perform the same experiments on the FERET dataset. As some classes contain only 4 training images, we only test incremental training with 1 to 3 images. In this case we reach even nearly 90% accuracy with a single image while convergence of the SVM classifier fails. With the increasing number of images the accuracy of both methods converge, as shown in Table 2.

Table 2. Evaluation results on the FERET dataset.

Nr. training img.		Nr. test img.	Accuracy	
Used	Total		Ours	[21]
1	247	989	89.38%	0.00%
2	494	742	94.07%	83.20%
3	741	495	94.75%	95.60%

6   Conclusion

In this paper, we have shown how a state of the art face detection and recognition pipeline using CNNs for both steps can be modified to support fast incremental training. This is achieved by using the CNN as a feature extractor and using an online random forest as a classifier. This enables training an already usable classifier with just a single sample, and the performance converges quickly to the state of the art as more faces are added. Adding samples to a new or existing classifier is computationally inexpensive. We have also described an algorithm to use the incremental training approach to automatically train classifiers for unknown persons, including safeguards to avoid noise in the training data.

Acknowledgments. The research leading to these results has received funding from the European Union's Horizon 2020 research and innovation programme under grant agreements no 732461, ReCAP ("Real-time Content Analysis and Processing", http:// recap-project.com), and 761802, MARCONI ("Multimedia and Augmented Radio Creation: Online, iNteractive, Individual", https://www.projectmarconi.eu).

References

1. Amos, B., Ludwiczuk, B., Satyanarayanan, M., et al.: OpenFace: a general-purpose face recognition library with mobile applications. Technical Report CMU-CS-16-118, CMU School of Computer Science (2016)
2. Breimann, L.: Random forests. Mach. Learn. **45**, 5–32 (2001)
3. Chen, S., Liu, Y., Gao, X., Han, B.: MobileFaceNets: efficient CNNs for accurate real-time face verification on mobile devices. In: Chinese Conference on Biometric Recognition (2018)
4. Choi, K., Toh, K.-A., Byun, H.: Incremental face recognition for large-scale social network services. Pattern Recognit. **45**(8), 2868–2883 (2012)
5. Criminisi, A., Shotton, J., Konukoglu, E.: Decision forests: a unified framework for classification, regression, density estimation, manifold learning and semi-supervised learning. Found. Trends Comput. Graph. Vis. **7**, 81–227 (2012)
6. Deng, J., Guo, J., Zafeiriou, S.: Arcface: additive angular margin loss for deep face recognition. CoRR, abs/1801.07698 (2018)
7. Farfade, S.S., Saberian, M.J., Li, L.-J.: Multi-view face detection using deep convolutional neural networks. In: Proceedings of the 5th ACM on International Conference on Multimedia Retrieval, pp. 643–650. ACM (2015)
8. Freund, Y., Schapire, R.E.: A decision-theoretic generalization of on-line learning and an application to boosting. J. Comput. Syst.Sci. **55**(1), 119–139 (1997)
9. Freund, Y., Schapire, R.E.: A short introduction to boosting. J. Jpn. Soc. Artif. Intell. **14**(5), 771–780 (1999). English translation
10. Guo, Y., Zhang, L., Hu, Y., He, X., Gao, J.: MS-Celeb-1M: challenge of recognizing one million celebrities in the real world. Electron. Imaging **2016**(11), 1–6 (2016)
11. Jiang, H., Learned-Miller, E.: Face detection with the faster R-CNN. In: 2017 12th IEEE International Conference on Automatic Face and Gesture Recognition, FG 2017, pp. 650–657. IEEE (2017)
12. King, D.E.: Dlib-ml: a machine learning toolkit. J. Mach. Learn. Res. **10**(Jul), 1755–1758 (2009)

13. Learned-Miller, E., Huang, G.B., RoyChowdhury, A., Li, H., Hua, G.: Labeled faces in the wild: a survey. In: Kawulok, M., Celebi, M.E., Smolka, B. (eds.) Advances in Face Detection and Facial Image Analysis, pp. 189–248. Springer, Cham (2016). https://doi.org/10.1007/978-3-319-25958-1_8

14. Li, H., Lin, Z., Shen, X., Brandt, J., Hua, G.: A convolutional neural network cascade for face detection. In: Proceedings of the IEEE Conference on Computer Vision and Pattern Recognition, pp. 5325–5334 (2015)

15. Mathias, M., Benenson, R., Pedersoli, M., Van Gool, L.: Face detection without bells and whistles. In: Fleet, D., Pajdla, T., Schiele, B., Tuytelaars, T. (eds.) ECCV 2014. LNCS, vol. 8692, pp. 720–735. Springer, Cham (2014). https://doi.org/10.1007/978-3-319-10593-2_47

16. Oza, N.C., Russell, S.: Online bagging and boosting. In: Eighth International Workshop on Artificial Intelligence and Statistics, pp. 105–112 (2001)

17. Ozawa, S., Toh, S.L., Abe, S., Pang, S., Kasabov, N.: Incremental learning of feature space and classifier for face recognition. Neural Netw. 18(5–6), 575–584 (2005)

18. Ranjan, R., Patel, V.M., Chellappa, R.: Hyperface: a deep multi-task learning framework for face detection, landmark localization, pose estimation, and gender recognition. IEEE Trans. Pattern Anal. Mach. Intell. (2017)

19. Rowley, H.A., Baluja, S., Kanade, T.: Neural network-based face detection. IEEE Trans. Pattern Anal. Mach. Intell. 20(1), 23–38 (1998)

20. Saffari, A., Leistner, C., Santner, J., Godec, M., Bischof, H.: On-line random forests. In: 2009 IEEE 12th International Conference on Computer Vision Workshops, ICCV Workshops, pages 1393–1400. IEEE (2009)

21. Schroff, F., Kalenichenko, D., Philbin, J.: FaceNet: a unified embedding for face recognition and clustering. In: Proceedings of the IEEE Conference on Computer Vision and Pattern Recognition, pp. 815–823 (2015)

22. Sun, Y., Wang, X., Tang, X.: Deeply learned face representations are sparse, selective, and robust. In: Proceedings of the IEEE Conference on Computer Vision and Pattern Recognition, pp. 2892–2900 (2015)

23. Szegedy, C., Ioffe, S., Vanhoucke, V.: Inception-v4, inception-resnet and the impact of residual connections on learning. CoRR, abs/1602.07261 (2016)

24. Taigman, Y., Yang, M., Ranzato, M., Wolf, L.: Deepface: closing the gap to human-level performance in face verification. In: Proceedings of the IEEE Conference on Computer Vision and Pattern Recognition, pp. 1701–1708 (2014)

25. Vapnik, V.: The Nature of Statistical Learning Theory. Springer, Heidelberg (2013)

26. Viola, P., Jones, M.J.: Robust real-time face detection. Int. J. Comput. Vis. 57(2), 137–154 (2004)

27. Wong, Y.W., Seng, K.P., Ang, L.M.: Radial basis function neural network with incremental learning for face recognition. IEEE Trans. Syst. Man Cybern. Part B (Cybern.) 41(4), 940–949 (2011)

28. Yan, J., Lei, Z., Wen, L., Li, S.Z.: The fastest deformable part model for object detection. In: Proceedings of the IEEE Conference on Computer Vision and Pattern Recognition, pp. 2497–2504 (2014)

29. Zhang, K., Zhang, Z., Li, Z., Qiao, Y.: Joint face detection and alignment using multitask cascaded convolutional networks. IEEE Signal Process. Lett. 23(10), 1499–1503 (2016)

30. Zhu, C., Zheng, Y., Luu, K., Savvides, M.: CMS-RCNN: contextual multi-scale region-based CNN for unconstrained face detection. arXiv preprint arXiv:1606.05413 (2016)
31. Zhu, Z., Luo, P., Wang, X., Tang, X.: Recover canonical-view faces in the wild with deep neural networks. arXiv preprint arXiv:1404.3543 (2014)

Character Prediction in TV Series
via a Semantic Projection Network

Ke Sun[1], Zhuo Lei[2], Jiasong Zhu[1], Xianxu Hou[3],
Bozhi Liu[3], and Guoping Qiu[3,4(✉)]

[1] Shenzhen Key Laboratory of Spatial Information Smarting Sensing and Services,
Shenzhen University, Shenzhen, China
sk2093437@163.com, zhujiasong@gmail.com
[2] School of Computer Science, University of Nottingham Ningbo, Ningbo, China
zhuo.lei@nottingham.edu.cn
[3] Guangdong Key Laboratory of Intelligent Information Processing,
College of Information Engineering, Shenzhen University, Shenzhen, China
hxianxu@gmail.com, lucifer.bozhi@gmail.com, qiu@szu.edu.cn
[4] School of Computer Science, University of Nottingham, Nottingham, UK

Abstract. The goal of this paper is to automatically recognize characters in popular TV series. In contrast to conventional approaches which rely on weak supervision afforded by transcripts, subtitles or character facial data, we formulate the problem as the multi-label classification which requires only label-level supervision. We propose a novel semantic projection network consisting of two stacked subnetworks with specially designed constraints. The first subnetwork is a contractive autoencoder which focuses on reconstructing feature activations extracted from a pre-trained single-label convolutional neural network (CNN). The second subnetwork functions as a region-based multi-label classifier which produces character labels for the input video frame as well as reconstructing the input visual feature from the mapped semantic labels space. Extensive experiments show that the proposed model achieves state-of-the-art performance in comparison with recent approaches on three challenging TV series datasets (the Big Bang Theory, the Defenders and Nirvava in Fire).

Keywords: Video understanding · Character recognition
Convolutional neural network · Autoencoder · Semantic projection

1 Introduction

The booming of content-based video collections in recent years has created a strong demand to perform efficient video content understanding and retrieval. In the field of video understanding, a critical step is to recognize people's identities under unconstrained conditions [17]. In this regard, TV series, dramas, sit-coms and featured films have offered a representative test bed, where the objective is to recognize characters in given videos.

© Springer Nature Switzerland AG 2019
I. Kompatsiaris et al. (Eds.): MMM 2019, LNCS 11295, pp. 300–311, 2019.
https://doi.org/10.1007/978-3-030-05710-7_25

Video character recognition has it unique characteristics compared with traditional recognition tasks. Specifically, videos provide much more information than still images, which introduces extra character-level ambiguities caused by the variations of lighting, posing, occlusion, scenario and costume [25], etc. Besides, manually adding transcripts, subtitles [1–3] or facial data [11,19,35] to help recognize characters in videos is time-consuming and is susceptible to cognitive differences between different annotators.

In our work, we do not rely on transcript, subtitles or facial data to help recognize different characters, instead, we formulate this problem as the multi-label classification, where each character is treated as an independent label. Given a testing video frame, we first pass it into a pre-trained single-label convolutional neural network (CNN) to extract the visual feature activations from the last fully-connected layer, then take these features as the input of the trained semantic projection network (SPNet). The SPNet then produces the final character labels following a max-pooling strategy (see Fig. 1).

We conduct the character recognition experiments on three challenging TV series, namely *the Big Bang Theory* (US), *the Defenders* (US) and *Nirvana in fire* (China). The experimental results demonstrate the effectiveness and competitiveness of the proposed SPNet over other state-of-the-art multi-label classification methods.

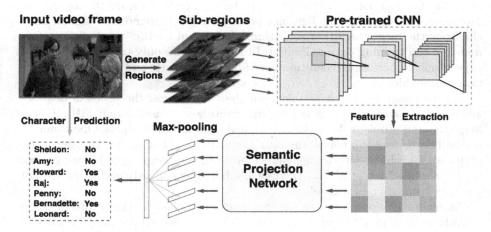

Fig. 1. The workflow of the proposed character recognition framework. Given an input video frame, we first generate a set of region proposals and then extract their visual features using a pre-trained single-label CNN. Next we feed the features into the trained semantic projection network and predict the existence of each targeted character. To obtain the final predicted results, we employ the max-pooling strategy over all the region proposals to aggregate their predictions.

The rest of this paper is organized as follows: Sect. 2 discusses the related work including character recognition in videos, and multi-label classification methods. Then Sect. 3 elaborates the architecture of semantic projection network for multi-label classification. Next, Sect. 4 exhaustively evaluates the proposed method on three different TV series. Finally, we summarize our work in Sect. 5.

2   Related Work

Recent years have witnessed increasing studies on character recognition in multi-media resources. Most previous approaches are aided by transcripts aligned with the subtitles to provide strong supervision for the task [4,28,29], however, transcripts and subtitles for all films or the entire seasons of a TV series are tough to find from the IMDB or social media sites. Besides, they often come in various styles and formats, results in much work on pre-processing and re-formatting. In contrast, only labeling the existence of every targeted characters in video frames are easy to achieve and does not introduces ambiguous information contained in transcripts and subtitles.

Some other transcript-free approaches tend to use face recognition algorithms to help capture the facial characteristics of actors in videos [6,9,15–17,30], and some also go beyond the frontal faces to also consider the profiles such as hair and poses [1,19,22]. Facial knowledge can benefit the character recognition algorithms, however, this requires extensive and tedious facial data annotation including the location and class labels of faces in order to train the algorithm. Moreover, the variations of lighting, posing and background also significantly challenge the face recognition algorithms, and would lead to dissatisfied performance if the training data is limited. In this work, we only uses the label-level supervision to perform recognition based on both holistic and regional information in the videos.

As the supervision is available from character labels, the problem of character recognition can be casted as the multi-label classification [31]. It is a long-standing problem and has been studied from multiple angles. One common method is the problem transformation. For example, Li et al. [14] transform the multi-label problem into a single-label problem by designing a binary coding strategy, while Nam et al. [18] treat each label independently and train a set of classifier to predict each label.

Many recent approaches tackle the multi-label classification problem using convolutional neural networks (CNNs). CNN has achieved promising results in many single label dataset [7,13,27] , such as the CIFAR10/100 [12] and ImageNet [5]. Many researchers have therefore adopted the CNN-based techniques to address multi-label classification problems. Wu et al. [36] design a weakly weighted pairwise ranking loss to tackle weakly labeled images and a triplet similarity loss to handle unlabeled images. Wang et al. [32] add a recurrent neural network (RNN) to the CNN backbone so as to predict multiple labels sequentially. Wei et al. [33] extend the single-label CNN to multi-label CNN which predicts all the labels at one time. All these methods can be formulated as a one-off mapping function which projects the visual (image) space to the semantic (label) space, however, such kind of projection strategy often suffers from the problem of imbalance data. This is, if some classes have very limited training samples, then the samples from these classes are likely to be classified as other classes which have many more training samples. In our work, we propose to solve this problem by encouraging mutual projection between the visual space and semantic space in order to learn more robust feature representation.

3   Character Recognition Using Semantic Projection Network

As depicted in Fig. 2, the semantic projection network (SPNet) consists of two stacked autoencoders with special constraints. Given the original visual features as the input (v), the first autoencoder (visual reconstruction subnet, VRNet) is used to learn robust visual embeddings (v_h) as well as reconstructing visual features from v_h. In the second autoencoder (semantic mapping subnet, SMNet), the learned visual embeddings (v_h) is employed to predict the character labels (s) while reconstructing the input v_h from s.

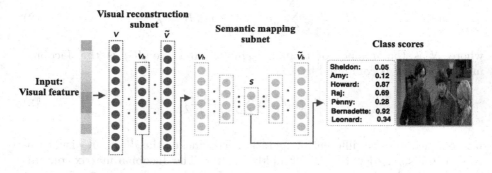

Fig. 2. The architecture of the semantic projection network (SPNet). The input visual features are refined by the visual reconstruction subnet and then mapped to the semantic space (represented by n class labels) in the semantic mapping subnet. We encourage the mapping from semantic space to visual space so as to learn robust semantic embeddings for the input visual feature.

3.1   Visual Reconstruction Subnetwork

The first subnetwork is the visual reconstruction subnetwork (VRNet) which aims to learn robust visual embeddings from the visual features. We start by introducing the formulation of the linear autoencoder and then extend it to the proposed one. An autoencoder is a feed-forward neural network with the same input vector and the target output. In its simplest form, an autoencoder is linear and only one hidden layer is placed between the encoder and decoder layers, compressing the input data into a low-dimensional representation. Formally, given an input data matrix $D \in \mathbb{R}^{n \times M}$ consisting of M feature vectors with the feature dimension of n, the encoder projects it into a k-dimensional $(k < n)$ latent space with an encoding matrix $W_{en} \in \mathbb{R}^{k \times n}$, resulting in a latent representation $H \in \mathbb{R}^{k \times M}$. The latent representation is then projected back to the input feature space via the decoding matrix $W_{de} \in \mathbb{R}^{n \times k}$ and becomes to the reconstructed data matrix $\hat{D} \in \mathbb{R}^{n \times M}$. For the learning objective, we minimize the reconstruction error, i.e. D and $\hat{D}$ should be as similar as possible. Hence, the objective function could be formulated as:

$$\min(W_{en}, W_{de}) = \|D - W_{de}W_{en}D\|_F^2 \tag{1}$$

The VRNet can be seen as a basic linear autoencoder with the contractive loss [24]. By adding such loss, it is aiming to learn more robust visual embeddings for the images of same class. To formulate, the VRNet projects the input visual feature vector v to the latent representation v_h, and then seeks to reconstruct v from v_h. Denoting reconstructed vector as $\hat{v}$, the model parameters are learned by minimizing the regularized reconstruction error:

$$L_v = \frac{1}{N} \sum_{1}^{N} \|v - \hat{v}\|^2 + \alpha \|J(v)\|_F^2 \tag{2}$$

where N is the number of training samples, and the $J(\cdot)$ is the Jacobian matrix [24] and is computed by:

$$\|J(v)\|_F^2 = \sum_{ij} (\frac{\partial v_h(j)}{\partial v(i)}) \tag{3}$$

where ∂ denotes the differential operation, $v(i)$ means the ith input visual feature vector, $v_h(j)$ denotes the jth hidden vector. The Jacobian matrix contains partial derivatives of the feature activations of neurons with respect to the input values, and so it is possible to inspect the impact of variations of the activation values and penalizing the representation accordingly. The α is a hyper-parameter controlling the proportion of the contractive loss during training.

3.2   Semantic Mapping Subnetwork

The second subnetwork is the semantic mapping subnetwork (SMNet) which is a multi-layer autoencoder with semantic constrains. In the SMNet, the encoder projects the learned visual embeddings to the semantic label space, similar to a conventional multi-label classification model. However, we also consider the semantic label space as an input to a decode in order to reconstruct the input original visual feature representation. This extra reconstruction task introduces a new constraint to the learning of the projection function from the semantic space to the visual space.

To formulate, the input of the SMNet is the visual feature activations v_h extracted from the hidden layer of the trained VRNet. The objective of SMNet is to first encode v_h to the latent semantic label space s and then decode it to the input visual feature space $\hat{v}_h$. The number of hidden neural in the semantic label space equals to the number of class labels. Hence, we wish to minimize the visual reconstruction error combined with the multi-label classification error:

$$L_s = \beta \frac{1}{N} \sum_{1}^{N} \|v_h - \hat{v}_h)\|^2 + \|\Phi(s)\|_F^2 \tag{4}$$

where N is the number of training samples and the parameter β controls the proportion of visual reconstruction loss in L_s. $\Phi(\cdot)$ denotes the multi-label soft margin error [8]:

$$\|\Phi(\hat{s}, s)\|_F^2 = -\sum_{i=1}^{N} \left[s_i \log \frac{e^{\hat{s}_i}}{1 + e^{\hat{s}_i}} + (1 - s_i) \log \frac{1}{1 + e^{\hat{s}_i}} \right] \tag{5}$$

where $\hat{s}_i$ and s_i is the predicted label vector and ground-truth label vector for i^{th} testing sample respectively. Combining Eqs. (2) and (4), we have:

$$L_{total} = L_v + L_s \tag{6}$$

To minimize L_{total}, we train the two subnetworks sequentially. In the first stage, we train the VRNet by minimizing L_v and then freeze the network parameters. In the second stage, we extract features from hidden layer (v_h) of the trained VRNet and use them as the input of the SMNet, then train the subnetwork by minimizing L_s.

3.3 Region-Based Multi-label Classification

In our work, the predicted class scores can be directly obtained from the hidden layer of the SMNet (as depicted in Fig. 2) because we force its content to be as similar as possible to the ground-truth label annotations during training.

Considering that each video frame may contain multiple labels and some labels may only apply to sub-regions, we add a region-based strategy to predict the character labels. More specifically, we first employ multi-scale combinatorial grouping (MCG) [21] method to extract hundreds of sub-regions from the given image, we then adopt the normalized cut algorithm [26] to cluster all region proposals into c clusters based on the IoU (Intersection-over-Union) affinity matrix. In each cluster, we select k region proposals with the largest predictive scores defined by the MCG approach and feed them into the trained SPNet. We also add the original image to the proposal group, and obtain $ck + 1$ region proposals for that image. The final prediction result is then obtained by max-pooling the predicted output of all the proposals (as depicted in Fig. 1). With max-pooling, large predicted class scores corresponding to targeted characters will be reserved, while the values from the noisy proposals will be ignored.

4 Experiment and Discussion

We evaluate the proposed SPNet on three challenging TV series, namely *the Big Bang Theory, (BBT)* from the US, *the Defenders, (TD)* from the US and *Nirvana in fire, (NIF)* from China. We also examine the importance of region-based strategy for character recognition.

Datasets. Consider the temporal redundancy of videos, for each TV series, we first sample five consecutive episodes every 5 frames and manually annotate these sampled frames with character labels. We then use the first four annotated episodes for training and the last one for testing. With such splitting strategy, the lighting, scenario, and costumes of characters could be totally different between the training samples and testing samples. More details about these datasets are shown in Table 1.

Table 1. Details of the three TV series video datasets.

Name	The Big Bang Theory	The Defenders	Nirvana in fire
Season no.	7	1	1
Training episodes no.	1–4	1–4	2–5
Testing episodes no.	5	5	6
No. of training samples	54,985	56,616	53,349
No. of testing samples	5,481	14,661	13,325

Visual Features. In our experiments, we use the ResNet (pre-trained on ImageNet for single-label image classification) [7] features which is the 2048D activation of the final fully-connected layer. The input video frame is first resized to 224×224 and then fed into the ResNet model to extracted visual features. For fair comparison with published results, we uniformly use the ResNet features as the input of the compared methods.

Parameter Settings. The length of layers in the VRNet (first subnetwork of SPNet) is $2048 \rightarrow 1024 \rightarrow 2048$, and the length of layers in the SMNet (second subnetwork of SPNet) is $1024 \rightarrow 512 \rightarrow n \rightarrow 512 \rightarrow 1024$, where n denotes the number of character labels.

Besides, the SPNet has two hyper-parameters: α in (see Eq. 2) and β (see Eq. 4). They are trade-off parameters for different loss components. As in [39], their values are set by class-wise cross-validation using the training data.

We train the two subnetworks in the SPNet separately. We employ the Adam algorithm [10] as the optimizer, the momentum is set to 0.9, the batch size is set to 128, the initial learning rate is set to 0.0001. We decrease the learning rate to one-tenth of its current value every 10 epochs. We execute 25 epochs to train the VRNet (first subnetwork) and 30 epochs to train the SMNet (second subnetwork).

Evaluation Metric. We use the f1 scores to throughly evaluate the performance of the proposed model. This score can be interpreted as a weighted average of the precision and recall, where an f1 score reaches its best value at 1 and worst value at 0. The formula for the f1 score is:

$$f1 = 2 \times \frac{precision \times recall}{precision + recall} \tag{7}$$

Competitors. We compare our method (SPNet-RP) with several recent multi-label classification approaches as follows.

CNN-SVM [23] and ML-KNN [38] serve as baseline methods which uses support vector machines and and k-nearest neighbor search to tackle the multi-label classification problem. Visual features are feature activations extracted from the pre-trained CNN.

HCP [34] is a novel CNN infrastructure, named hypotheses CNN pooling. In HCP, object segments hypotheses are taken as the input of the shared CNN, and the final predictions are obtained by max-pooling the results on all these hypotheses.

DeepBE [14] transforms the multi-label classification problem to single-label classification using the specially designed binary coding scheme. The transformed data can be learned by CNNs which are initially designed for single-label classification.

LGC [37] is a flexible deep CNN framework for multi-label classification. LGC consists of a local level multi-label classifier which takes object segment hypotheses as inputs to a local CNN, and a global CNN that is trained by multi-label images to directly predict the multiple labels from the input. The predictions of local and global level classifiers are fused together to obtain the final predicted results.

Besides, we also predict the character labels without the region-proposals in the SPNet to spot the differences.

Implementations. We implementate all the models using the Python programming language with the support of the PyTorch [20] deep learning toolkit. Codes were running on the GTX1080ti GPU with 11GB display memory.

Results and Discussion. The results of character recognition on the three TV series are shown in Tables 2, 3 and 4 respectively. From results, we can see that the proposed models (SPNet and SPNet-RP) outperform all the recent approaches and achieve a significant improvement over those two baseline methods (over ML-KNN [38] and CNN-SVM [23]). Only one observed exception is that the HCP [34] method achieves the best f1 score (0.791) on the *Bernadette* character in the *BBT* dataset.

We also notice that the best f1 scores obtained on the *BBT* and *TD* datasets (0.627 and 0.658 respectively) are lower than the one obtained on the *NIF* (0.788). This is because the video content in *NIF* contains many close-up views of individual characters which provide more detailed information in the corresponding visual features.

Besides, it can bee seen that the SPNet with region proposals (SPNet-RP) achieved very similar results as the vanilla SPNet on the *BBT* and *TD* datasets, however, the former exhibits significantly better performance than the latter on the *NIF* dataset. This is because its video content contains many big scenes like palaces and the battleground, in which the characters only appear in small regions. This demonstrates the effectiveness of region-based strategy for character recognition.

Table 2. The result of character recognition on *the Big Bang Theory, (BBT)*. We show f1 scores computed on each individual character and the average of them. The best values are highlighted using bold fonts.

Method	ML-KNN	CNN-SVM	HCP	DeepBE	LGC	SPNet	SPNet-RP
Sheldon	0.663	0.697	0.641	0.767	0.665	0.778	**0.795**
Amy	0.303	0.311	0.273	0.390	0.474	**0.587**	0.546
Howard	0.535	0.437	0.611	0.466	0.520	**0.660**	0.618
Raj	0.364	0.356	0.407	0.407	0.452	0.663	**0.670**
Penny	0.463	0.571	0.497	0.348	0.411	**0.628**	0.540
Bernadette	0.571	0.544	**0.791**	0.586	0.557	0.506	0.553
Leonard	0.348	0.380	0.440	0.549	0.403	0.566	**0.635**
Average	0.464	0.471	0.523	0.502	0.497	**0.627**	0.622

Table 3. The result of character recognition on *the Defenders, (TD)*. We show f1 scores computed on each individual character and the average of them. The best values are highlighted using bold fonts.

Method	ML-KNN	CNN-SVM	HCP	DeepBE	LGC	SPNet	SPNet-RP
Dare Devil	0.511	0.614	0.633	0.609	0.620	0.629	**0.716**
Jessica Jones	0.364	0.378	0.427	0.529	0.441	**0.531**	0.497
Luke Cage	0.486	0.476	0.561	0.531	0.570	**0.596**	0.591
Iron Fist	0.543	0.522	0.592	0.520	0.613	0.573	**0.649**
Alexandra	0.461	0.611	0.712	0.771	0.831	**0.858**	0.836
Average	0.473	0.520	0.585	0.592	0.615	0.637	**0.658**

Table 4. The result of character recognition on *Nirvana in fire, (NIF)*. We show f1 scores computed on each individual character and the average of them. The best values are highlighted using bold fonts.

Method	ML-KNN	CNN-SVM	HCP	DeepBE	LGC	SPNet	SPNet-RP
Changsu Mei	0.759	0.669	0.734	0.770	0.813	**0.834**	0.831
Jingyan Xiao	0.604	0.622	0.591	0.667	0.469	0.604	**0.725**
Nihuang Mu	0.596	0.579	0.579	0.617	0.585	0.683	**0.686**
Jinghuan Xiao	0.761	0.753	0.653	0.686	0.625	0.659	**0.839**
Emperor of Liang	0.610	0.605	0.705	0.751	0.773	0.775	**0.857**
Average	0.666	0.646	0.652	0.698	0.653	0.711	**0.788**

5   Concluding Remarks

In this work we propose a novel semantic projection network (SPNet) to address the problem of character recognition in TV series. The SPNet consists of two stacked subnetworks with specially designed constraints for different purposes. More specifically, the first subnetwork is a contractive autoencoder which focuses on reconstructing visual feature activations extracted from a pre-trained CNN, while the second subnetwork functions as a multi-label classifier with additional constraints which require to reconstruct input visual features from the projected semantic space. Considering that some character labels may only apply to the subregions of the video frames, we introduce the region-based strategy to further improve the classification performance. Experimental results on three challenging TV series show that the proposed method achieves state-of-the-art performance.

Acknowledgment. This work was jointly supported in part by the National Natural Science Foundation of China under Grant 61773414, and in part by the Shenzhen Future Industry Development Funding program under Grant 201607281039561400, and the Shenzhen Scientific Research and Development Funding Program under Grant JCYJ20170818092931604.

References

1. Bojanowski, P., Bach, F., Laptev, I., Ponce, J., Schmid, C., Sivic, J.: Finding actors and actions in movies. In: 2013 IEEE International Conference on Computer Vision (ICCV), pp. 2280–2287. IEEE (2013)
2. Cour, T., Sapp, B., Nagle, A., Taskar, B.: Talking pictures: temporal grouping and dialog-supervised person recognition. In: Proceedings of the IEEE Conference on Computer Vision and Pattern Recognition, pp. 1014–1021 (2011)
3. Cour, T., Sapp, B., Jordan, C., Taskar, B.: Learning from ambiguously labeled images. In: IEEE Conference on Computer Vision and Pattern Recognition, CVPR 2009, pp. 919–926 (2009)
4. Cour, T., Sapp, B., Nagle, A., Taskar, B.: Talking pictures: temporal grouping and dialog-supervised person recognition. In: 2010 IEEE Conference on Computer Vision and Pattern Recognition (CVPR), pp. 1014–1021. IEEE (2010)

5. Deng, J., Dong, W., Socher, R., Li, L.J., Li, K., Fei-Fei, L.: Imagenet: a large-scale hierarchical image database. In: IEEE Conference on Computer Vision and Pattern Recognition, CVPR 2009, pp. 248–255. IEEE (2009)

6. Dong, Z., Jia, S., Wu, T., Pei, M.: Face video retrieval via deep learning of binary hash representations. In: AAAI, pp. 3471–3477 (2016)

7. He, K., Zhang, X., Ren, S., Sun, J.: Deep residual learning for image recognition. In: Proceedings of the IEEE Conference on Computer Vision and Pattern Recognition, pp. 770–778 (2016)

8. He, Z., Chen, C., Bu, J., Li, P., Cai, D.: Multi-view based multi-label propagation for image annotation. Neurocomputing **168**(C), 853–860 (2015)

9. Iwata, M., Ito, A., Kise, K.: A study to achieve manga character retrieval method for manga images. In: 2014 11th IAPR International Workshop on Document Analysis Systems (DAS), pp. 309–313. IEEE (2014)

10. Kingma, D.P., Ba, J.: Adam: a method for stochastic optimization. In: International Conference on Learning Representations (2015)

11. Kostinger, M., Wohlhart, P., Roth, P.M., Bischof, H.: Learning to recognize faces from videos and weakly related information cues. In: IEEE International Conference on Advanced Video and Signal Based Surveillance, pp. 23–28 (2011)

12. Krizhevsky, A., Hinton, G.: Learning multiple layers of features from tiny images. M.Sc. thesis, University of Toronto (2009)

13. Krizhevsky, A., Sutskever, I., Hinton, G.E.: Imagenet classification with deep convolutional neural networks. In: Advances in Neural Information Processing Systems, pp. 1097–1105 (2012)

14. Li, C., Kang, Q., Ge, G., Song, Q., Lu, H., Cheng, J.: Deepbe: learning deep binary encoding for multi-label classification. In: Proceedings of the IEEE Conference on Computer Vision and Pattern Recognition Workshops, pp. 39–46 (2016)

15. Li, Y., Wang, R., Cui, Z., Shan, S., Chen, X.: Compact video code and its application to robust face retrieval in tv-series. In: BMVC (2014)

16. Li, Y., Wang, R., Shan, S., Chen, X.: Hierarchical hybrid statistic based video binary code and its application to face retrieval in tv-series. In: 2015 11th IEEE International Conference and Workshops on Automatic Face and Gesture Recognition (FG), vol. 1, pp. 1–8. IEEE (2015)

17. Nagrani, A., Zisserman, A.: From benedict cumberbatch to sherlock holmes: Character identification in tv series without a script. CoRR abs/1801.10442 (2017)

18. Nam, J., Kim, J., Loza Mencía, E., Gurevych, I., Fürnkranz, J.: Large-scale multi-label text classification—revisiting neural networks. In: Calders, T., Esposito, F., Hüllermeier, E., Meo, R. (eds.) ECML PKDD 2014. LNCS (LNAI), vol. 8725, pp. 437–452. Springer, Heidelberg (2014). https://doi.org/10.1007/978-3-662-44851-9_28

19. Parkhi, O.M., Rahtu, E., Zisserman, A.: It's in the bag: stronger supervision for automated face labelling. In: ICCV Workshop, vol. 2, p. 6 (2015)

20. Paszke, A., et al.: Automatic differentiation in pytorch. In: NIPS-W (2017)

21. Pont-Tuset, J., Arbeláez, P., Barron, J.T., Marques, F., Malik, J.: Multiscale combinatorial grouping for image segmentation and object proposal generation. IEEE Trans. Pattern Anal. Mach. Intell. **39**(1), 128–140 (2015)

22. Ramanathan, V., Joulin, A., Liang, P., Fei-Fei, L.: Linking people in videos with "their" names using coreference resolution. In: Fleet, D., Pajdla, T., Schiele, B., Tuytelaars, T. (eds.) ECCV 2014. LNCS, vol. 8689, pp. 95–110. Springer, Cham (2014). https://doi.org/10.1007/978-3-319-10590-1_7

23. Razavian, A.S., Azizpour, H., Sullivan, J., Carlsson, S.: CNN features off-the-shelf: an astounding baseline for recognition. In: Proceedings of the IEEE Conference on Computer Vision and Pattern Recognition, pp. 512–519 (2014)

24. Rifai, S., Vincent, P., Muller, X., Glorot, X., Bengio, Y.: Contractive auto-encoders: explicit invariance during feature extraction. In: ICML (2011)

25. Shan, C.: Face recognition and retrieval in video. Stud. Comput. Intell. **287**, 235–260 (2010)

26. Shi, J., Malik, J.: Normalized cuts and image segmentation. IEEE Trans. Pattern Anal. Mach. Intell. **22**(8), 888–905 (2000)

27. Simonyan, K., Zisserman, A.: Very deep convolutional networks for large-scale image recognition. arXiv preprint arXiv:1409.1556 (2014)

28. Sivic, J., Everingham, M., Zisserman, A.: "who are you?"- learning person specific classifiers from video. In: IEEE Conference on Computer Vision and Pattern Recognition, CVPR 2009, pp. 1145–1152. IEEE (2009)

29. Tapaswi, M., Bäuml, M., Stiefelhagen, R.: Story-based video retrieval in TV series using plot synopses. In: Proceedings of International Conference on Multimedia Retrieval, p. 137. ACM (2014)

30. Tapaswi, M., Bauml, M., Stiefelhagen, R.: Storygraphs: visualizing character interactions as a timeline. In: Proceedings of the IEEE Conference on Computer Vision and Pattern Recognition, pp. 827–834 (2014)

31. Tsoumakas, G., Katakis, I.: Multi-label classification: an overview. Int. J. Data Warehous. Min. (IJDWM) **3**(3), 1–13 (2007)

32. Wang, J., Yang, Y., Mao, J., Huang, Z., Huang, C., Xu, W.: CNN-RNN: a unified framework for multi-label image classification. In: 2016 IEEE Conference on Computer Vision and Pattern Recognition (CVPR), pp. 2285–2294. IEEE (2016)

33. Wei, Y., et al.: CNN: single-label to multi-label. arXiv preprint arXiv:1406.5726 (2014)

34. Wei, Y., et al.: HCP: A flexible CNN framework for multi-label image classification. IEEE Trans. Pattern Anal. Mach. Intell. **38**(9), 1901–1907 (2016)

35. Wohlhart, P., Köstinger, M., Roth, P.M., Bischof, H.: Multiple instance boosting for face recognition in videos. In: Mester, R., Felsberg, M. (eds.) DAGM 2011. LNCS, vol. 6835, pp. 132–141. Springer, Heidelberg (2011). https://doi.org/10.1007/978-3-642-23123-0_14

36. Wu, F., Wang, Z., Zhang, Z., Yang, Y., Luo, J., Zhu, W., Zhuang, Y.: Weakly semi-supervised deep learning for multi-label image annotation. IEEE Trans. Big Data **1**(3), 109–122 (2015)

37. Yu, Q., Wang, J., Zhang, S., Gong, Y., Zhao, J.: Combining local and global hypotheses in deep neural network for multi-label image classification. Neurocomputing **235**, 38–45 (2017)

38. Zhang, M., Zhou, Z.: ML-KNN: a lazy learning approach to multi-label learning. Pattern Recognit. **40**(7), 2038–2048 (2007)

39. Zhang, Z., Saligrama, V.: Zero-shot learning via joint latent similarity embedding. In: Proceedings of IEEE Conference on Computer Vision and Pattern Recognition, pp. 6034–6042 (2016)

A Test Collection for Interactive Lifelog Retrieval

Cathal Gurrin[1](✉), Klaus Schoeffmann[2], Hideo Joho[3], Bernd Munzer[2],
Rami Albatal[1], Frank Hopfgartner[4], Liting Zhou[1],
and Duc-Tien Dang-Nguyen[1,5](✉)

[1] Insight Centre for Data Analytics, Dublin City University, Dublin, Ireland
[2] Klagenfurt University, Klagenfurt, Austria
[3] University of Tsukuba, Tsukuba, Japan
[4] University of Sheffield, Sheffield, UK
[5] University of Bergen, Bergen, Norway
ductien.dangnguyen@uib.no

Abstract. There is a long history of repeatable and comparable evaluation in Information Retrieval (IR). However, thus far, no shared test collection exists that has been designed to support interactive lifelog retrieval. In this paper we introduce the LSC2018 collection, that is designed to evaluate the performance of interactive retrieval systems. We describe the features of the dataset and we report on the outcome of the first Lifelog Search Challenge (LSC), which used the dataset in an interactive competition at ACM ICMR 2018.

Keywords: Interactive retrieval · Lifelogging
Comparative evaluation · Test collection · Multimodal dataset

1 Introduction

Dodge and Kitchin [6] refer to lifelogging as 'a form of pervasive computing, consisting of a unified digital record of the totality of an individual's experiences, captured multimodally through digital sensors and stored permanently as a personal multimedia archive'. Technological progress and cheaper sensors has enabled people to capture such digital troves of life experiences automatically and continuously with ease and efficiency. Ongoing research is constantly optimising the user experience on these systems. A lifelog, according to the definition of Dodge and Kitchin, should consist of rich media data that captures, in so far as possible, a digital trace of the totality of an individual's experience. Such a lifelog should be a rich media archive of personal contextual data, which includes various forms of biometric data, physical activity data, wearable media, as well as data on the information creation and consumption of the individual.

In the spirit of Memex [2], it is our conjecture that a lifelog, if it is to be useful to the individual, must be '*continuously extended, it must be stored, and above all it must be consulted*'. Such lifelog consultation is likely to require both

I. Kompatsiaris et al. (Eds.): MMM 2019, LNCS 11295, pp. 312–324, 2019.
https://doi.org/10.1007/978-3-030-05710-7_26

ad-hoc and interactive retrieval mechanisms to support the variety of lifelog use-cases, as suggested in [20]. While we note significant efforts being made through various vehicles, such as NTCIR [10] and ImageCLEF [4], to support off-line ad-hoc search tasks, by the release of a first generation of lifelog test collection, until now, there was no dedicated benchmarking effort for interactive lifelog search, nor is there a test collection designed to support such benchmarking.

As reported in [5], the design and creation of a reusable lifelog test collection for any form of retrieval experimentation is not trivial. Jones and Teeven [12], in the context of personal information management (PIM), state that *"the design of shared test collections for PIM evaluation requires some creative thinking, because such collections must differ from more traditional shared test collections"*. In this paper, we report on the first such test collection, the LSC2018 collection, which was designed to support interactive lifelog search and was first used in the live LSC 2018 (Lifelog Search Challenge) competition at ACM ICMR 2018. We describe the test collection, motivate its development and report on the six experimental interactive retrieval systems that took part in the LSC and utilised the test collection. Hence, the contributions of this paper are as follows:

- A description of a new test collection that can be used to support interactive lifelog search, with associated details on how to access the collection.
- A review of the first interactive lifelog search systems that took part in the LSC 2018 workshop at ACM ICMR 2018.
- The introduction of a new type of query for interactive retrieval that is designed to become progressively easier during a time-limited interactive search competition.

2   Related Collections and Evaluation Forums

Collecting and organising lifelog data is clearly different from conventional data in many aspects. In 2010, Sellen and Whittaker [20] argued that rather than trying to capture everything, the so called "total capture", lifelog system design should focus on the psychological basis of human memory to reliably organise and search on personal life archives. The technical challenges arising from either focused or total capture, include the indexing and the organisation of hetero-geneous media, such as image, audio, video and sensor data, along with the development of a suite of interface tools to support access and retrieval. Many researchers have proposed lifelog retrieval systems, such as the eLifeLog system from Kim and Giunchiglia [14] and demonstrated the potential of their system on an archive of rich, multi-modal and event-based annotated data. However, in the majority of cases, such multimodal datasets were not released to the community.

In the last three years, large volumes of multimodal lifelog data have been gathered from several lifeloggers and released as part of the NTCIR collaborative benchmarking workshop series [13] in dedicated Lifelog tracks/tasks. To the best of our knowledge, as of October 2018, these collections (such as the NTCIR-12 Lifelog collection [8] and the NTCIR-13 Lifelog collection [10]) are the largest (in terms of number of days and the size of the collection) and richest (in terms of types of information) collections on lifelogging ever shared. These collections are summarised in Table 1.

Table 1. Statistics of the NTCIR Collections.

	NTCIR-12	NTCIR-13
Number of lifeloggers	3	2
Number of days	87	90
Size of the collection (GB)	18.18	26.6
Size of the collection (Images)	88,124	114,547
Size of the collection (Locations)	130	138

Based on the collections from NTCIR-12 and NTCIR-13, rigorous comparative benchmarking initiatives have been organised: the NTCIR 12 - Lifelog [9], and ImageCLEFlifelog2017 [3] exploited the NTCIR-12 collection and NTCIR-13 Lifelog 2 [10], ImageCLEFlifelog2018 [4] were proposed based on the NTCIR-13 collection. Typically, for each benchmarking initiative, based on the collection employed, several tasks were introduced which aim to advance the state-of-the-art research in lifelogging as an application of information retrieval.

Concerning only-visual collections of lifelog data, there have been a small number released in the last five years. For example, the UT Ego Dataset [15] contains four (3–5 h long) videos captured from head-mounted cameras, captured in a natural, uncontrolled setting; the Barcelona E-Dub dataset [23] contains a total of 18, 735 images captured by 7 different users during overall 20 days; and the Multimodal Egocentric Activity Dataset [22] contains 20 distinct lifelogging activities (10 videos for each activity and each video lasts 15 s) performed by different human subjects.

Related to interactive information retrieval efforts and datasets, the Video Browser Showdown (VBS) is an international video search competition with the goal to evaluate the state-of-the-art performance of interactive video retrieval systems on a large shared dataset [16] of video data. It is held as a special session at the International Conference on Multimedia Modeling (MMM), annually since 2012. In this competition several teams work in front of a shared screen and try to solve a given set of Known-Item Search (KIS) and Ad-Hoc Video Search (AVS) tasks as fast as possible, where the tasks are selected randomly on-site. The difference between the task types is that a KIS task would seek a specific single target clip in the entire collection – described either as a shown clip or as a textual description, while an AVS task would requite all shots belonging to a particular topic (e.g., "find all shots with cars on the street") to be found. The tasks are issued and scored by the VBS server, to which all teams are connected to. For scoring, the server evaluates the search time and correctness of each submission and computes a score for the team. In general, the scoring is higher the faster a correct submission has been sent (and the less false submissions were sent before) – for AVS tasks, however, it will also matter how many different instances were found and from how many different videos they are coming. The whole competition consists of expert and novice sessions, where in the latter kind volunteers from the conference audience work with the tools of the experts. The final score is computed as an average over all sessions (expert KIS visual, expert KIS textual, expert AVS, novice KIS visual, novice AVS). In VBS2018, the IACC.3 dataset has been used for the competition, which consists of 600 h of content and about 300,000 shots. For each session the participants had 5 min to solve an AVS or KIS task.

3 Justification for a New Test Collection

At the time of preparing the LSC workshop, both the NTCIR-12 and NTCIR-13 were the only readily available large-scale lifelog test collections. While, in theory, it was possible for any collection (large or small) to be employed for interactive retrieval, our conjecture was that in order to encourage participation of researchers from a variety of fields (MMIR, HCI, etc.), that we needed to provide a reasonably sized collection that contained real-world, multi-modal lifelog data, along with sufficient metadata, so as to reduce the barriers to entry for non-computer-vision researchers, who had heretofore been the main users of lifelog collections.

Both of the existing NTCIR test collections were (relatively) large lifelog collections with limited metadata and 24–48 ad-hoc topics with relevance judgements. While additional topics could have been generated for these test collections, it was decided that a test collection was needed with richer metadata, which would facilitate additional facets of retrieval to be integrated into an interactive querying engine. Hence, the LSC test collection was created, which was a subset of the NTCIR-13 collection, but with additional metadata, namely complete biometric data 24/7, detailed anonymised location logs, and the new source of informational data including information consumed and created on computer devices.

4 LSC 2018, A Test Collection for Interactive Lifelog Search

The conventional structure of a test collection requires three components, namely: (1) a collection of domain-representative documents, (2) a set of queries (called topics) that are representative of the domain of application, and (3) a set of relevance judgements that map topics to documents. The LSC test collection contains all three components, and since it was based on a subset of the NTCIR-13 collection, was it developed according to the same process outlined in [10].

4.1   Requirements for the Test Collection

Prior to generating the test collection we defined requirements for the collection based on our experiences of running the NTCIR 12 & 13 Lifelog tasks [9,10] and relevant literature concerning lifelogging and human memory, such as [20]. To summarise, these requirements were:

- be a valid test collect of real-world lifelog data and information needs from a wide variety of sensors.
- that appropriate metadata be included with the collection so as to reduce the barriers to use of the collection
- all user identifiable data must be removed from the collection.

The NTCIR-13 Lifelog test collection was created according to these requirements and included all day data gathering by volunteer lifeloggers using multiple devices. All data was then temporally aligned to UTC time (Coordinated Universal Time) and the data was filtered by firstly the lifelogger themselves and then by a trusted expert. This data was then enhanced by the addition of various forms of metadata before all user identifiable content was removed and the collection made available.

For the subsequent creation of the LSC test collection, 27 days of the NTCIR-13 Lifelog data from one lifelogger was extracted, due to the presence of the richest lifelog data from this period of time. Both GPS location (with work and home removed) and additional computer content access and creation data was added to the collection. We now describe the collection in detail.

4.2   Test Collection Description

Data. Although the collection is based on the NTCIR-13 Lifelog collection, there are a number of additions, as described above, so we summarise the collection thus:

- Multimedia Content. Wearable camera images were gathered using a Narrative Clip 2 wearable camera capturing about two images per minute and worn from breakfast to sleep, at a resolution of 1024×768, with faces blurred. Examples are shown in Fig. 1. Accompanying this image data is a timestamped record of music listening activities sourced from Last.FM.
- Biometric Data. Using the Basis smartwatch, the lifeloggers gathered 24×7 heart rate, galvanic skin response, calorie burn and steps, on a per-minute basis. In addition, daily blood pressure and blood glucose levels were recorded every morning before breakfast and weekly cholesterol and uric acid levels were recorded.
- Human Activity Data. The daily activities of the lifeloggers were captured on a per-minute basis, in terms of the semantic locations visited, physical activities (e.g. walking, running, standing) along with a time-stamped diet-log of all food consumed drinks taken, and a location record for every minute. An example of the locations is shown in Fig. 2.

- Information Activities Data. Using the Loggerman app, the information creation and consumption activities were provided, which were organised into blacklist-filtered, sorted, document vectors representing every minute.

In order to make the collection more suitable for interactive retrieval, the wearable camera images were annotated with the outputs of a semantic concept detector from Microsoft cognitive services (computer vision API) [21], which provided high-quality annotations of visual concepts from the visual lifelog data.

Fig. 1. Examples of wearable camera images from the test collection

Topics and Relevance Judgements. Being a test collection designed for interactive retrieval, the topics were selected to facilitate interactive retrieval and competitive benchmarking in a live setting. Hence we introduced a new type of interactive topic that was designed around the concept of temporal enhanced query descriptions. A topic was created based on the lifelogger selecting a memorable and interesting event that had occurred during the time period covered by the test collection. The guidance given to the lifelogger was that the event should ideally only occur either once or a few times in the collection. Each topic was represented by an information need that described the user context in detail, including locations, days of the week and visual elements of the image(s) that matched the topic. The rationale was that a user with an interactive system that included a range of facets would be able to quickly locate content of interest. However, since the topics were to be employed in a live search competition, the topics were designed to be temporally extended through six iterations, with

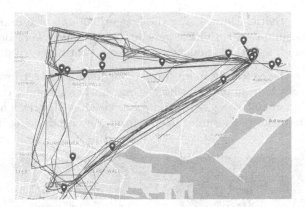

Fig. 2. Examples of the locations from the test collection.

Table 2. Statistics of LSC 2018 lifelog data

Number of lifeloggers	1
Number of Days	27
Size of the collection (GB)	9.40
Number of images	41,681
Number of locations	72
Number of development topics	6
Number of expert topics	6
Number of novice topics	12
Number of unique concepts	490

each iteration lasting for 30 s and providing increasing levels of contextual data to assist the searcher. With six iterations in total, this resulted in a total time allocation of three minutes per topic. An example of a topic is shown below.

```
<TopicID>LSC05</TopicID>
<TopicType>development</TopicType>
<Descriptions>
<Description timestamp="0">
I am walking out to an airplane across the airport apron. I stayed in an
    airport hotel on the previous night before checking out and walking a
    short distance to the airport.
</Description>
<Description timestamp="30">
I am walking out to an airplane across the airport apron. I stayed in an
    airport hotel on the previous night before checking out and walking a
    short distance to the airport. The weather is very nice, but cold,
    with a clear blue sky.
```

```
</Description>
<Description timestamp="60">
I am walking out to an airplane across the airport apron. I stayed in an
    airport hotel on the previous night before checking out and walking a
    short distance to the airport. The weather is very nice, but cold,
    with a clear blue sky. There is a man walking to the airplane in
    front of me with a blue jacket, green shoes and a black bag.
</Description>
<Description timestamp="90">
I am walking out to an airplane across the airport apron. I stayed in an
    airport hotel on the previous night before checking out and walking a
    short distance to the airport. The weather is very nice, but cold,
    with a clear blue sky. There is a man walking to the airplane in
    front of me with a blue jacket, green shoes and a black bag. Red
    airport vehicles are visible in the image also, along with a small
    number of passengers walking to, and boarding the plane.
</Description>
<Description timestamp="120">
I am walking out to an airplane across the airport apron. I stayed in an
    airport hotel on the previous night before checking out and walking a
    short distance to the airport. The weather is very nice, but cold,
    with a clear blue sky. There is a man walking to the airplane in
    front of me with a blue jacket, green shoes and a black bag. Red
    airport vehicles are visible in the image also, along with a small
    number of passengers walking to, and boarding the plane. I'm in Oslo,
    Norway and it is early in the morning.
</Description>
<Description timestamp="150">
I am walking out to an airplane across the airport apron. I stayed in an
    airport hotel on the previous night before checking out and walking a
    short distance to the airport. The weather is very nice, but cold,
    with a clear blue sky. There is a man walking to the airplane in
    front of me with a blue jacket, green shoes and a black bag. Red
    airport vehicles are visible in the image also, along with a small
    number of passengers walking to, and boarding the plane. I'm in Oslo,
    Norway and it is early in on a Monday morning.
</Description>
</Descriptions>
<RelevantImageIDs>
<ImageID>20160905_052810_000.jpg</ImageID>
</RelevantImageIDs>
</Topic>
```

There were three types of topic in the test collection. Six development topics
(as above), six test topics for experts (system developers) for the search challenge,
and twelve test topics for novice users, who were not knowledgeable about the
collection or how the systems worked. All three types of topic had the same
structure.

Associated with each topic were the relevance judgements generated manually by the lifelogger. As stated, there could be one or more relevant items in the collection, where relevant items could span multiple separate events or happenings. In this case, if a user of an interactive system found any one of the relevant items from any event, then the search is deemed to be successful. For the LSC collection, an item was assumed to be an image from the wearable camera.

4.3   Collection Applications

The LSC dataset was primarily developed to support comparative benchmarking of interactive lifelog retrieval systems. It was designed to be easy to employ, as well as to provide multi-level challenging topics. In addition to this primary application at LSC 2018, we also note that, due to the richness of the contextual data it provides, that the collection is already being employed by additional researchers to support:

- User Context Modelling, by identifying the tasks of daily life and modelling a user's life activities as a sequence of tasks.
- Hybrid Data Modelling, to develop various event detectors for daily life, such as fall event detection, or important moment detectors.
- Personal Data Engines, to provide prototype retrieval systems over personal data archives.

It is our conjecture that this collection can be employed for many other aspects of multimedia information retrieval, such as lifestyle activity detection, real-world task identification, multimodal retrieval systems, and so on.

4.4   Collection Limitations

While the LSC collection is the first interactive lifelog collection, there are a number of limitations that we wish to point out:

- The main limitation is the size of the collection, which is only 27 days of data. This time period was chosen because it gave the optimal trade-off between richness of gathered data and the duration of the collection. Ideally, this should be a longitudinal collection extending to several months at least. Small collections for interactive search can become familiar to expert searchers who can use this extra knowledge to assist in the search process.
- Another limitation of the collection is that the multimodal lifelog data does not include media such as contextual audio or non-written communications.
- A third limitation is the fact that the collection has been anonymised via a process that blurs faces and makes screens illegible. This was a necessary part of the data release process, but it restricts the type of queries that can be used with the collection.

5   Employing the Collection at the LSC

The LSC dataset was employed for the Lifelog Search Challenge (LSC), at ACM ICMR in June 2018. For the interactive search challenge, each of the six participants had developed an interactive search engine for the LSC collection and tested it using the six development topics. For the challenge, each participant was given a desk with a clear view of a large screen which showed the topics, the time remaining on each topic, as well as the current and overall scores of each team. When a participating team located a potentially relevant item from the collection, it was submitted to a host server which evaluated it and if it was successful, updated the team score, but if it was unsuccessful, the potential score of that team for that topic was down-weighted.

5.1   Overview of Participants at LSC

The LSC 2018 [11], which was the first time that the test collection was used, attracted six participating groups. To highlight the flexibility of the collection, we report on the six different approaches to interactive retrieval taken by the six participants:

- A multi-faceted retrieval system [18], based on the video search system div-eXplore [19]. Besides efficient presentation and summarisation of lifelog data, the tool includes searchable feature maps, concept and metadata filters, similarity search and sketch search.
- The LIFER retrieval system [25] that provided an efficient retrieval system based primarily on faceted querying using available metadata.
- An interactive retrieval tool [16], based on SIRET [17], that was updated to include enhanced visualisation and navigation methodologies for a high number of visually similar scenes representing repetitive daily activities.
- A Virtual Reality interactive retrieval system [7] that uses visual concepts and dates/times as the basis for a faceted filtering mechanism that presents results in a novel VR-interface.
- A clustering retrieval system [24] that groups images into visual shots and clusters, extracts semantic concepts on scene category and attributes, entities, and actions, and supports 4 main types of query conditions: temporal, spatial, entity and action, and extra data criteria.
- A faceted lifelog search mechanism [1] that introduced a four-step process required to support lifelog search engines and provided a ranked list of items as a sequential list of item clusters, as opposed to items themselves.

Four of the systems that took part performed comparatively well, with participants finding results within the time-limit for most of the topics. However, it is worth noting that the top two performing teams [7,18] were very close in performance, with a very minor separation in overall performance.

5.2 Description of the Experimental Infrastructure at LSC

During the Lifelog Search Challenge event, a similar infrastructure to that used at the VBS was employed to coordinate the competition. A host server coordinated, the display of the temporally advancing topics, the timer for each topic, evaluated the submissions from each team in real-time, calculated the points awarded to each team for a successful submission, and displayed a live scoreboard. The points awarded for a successful submission were based on a formula that rewarded the speed of submission, but also penalised an incorrect submission. An incorrect submission would result in a 20% reduction in the total available points for that topic, where the number of available points were decreasing every second. This added an element of excitement to the live competition.

6 Conclusions and Collection Availability

In this paper, we have introduced a new test collection for interactive lifelog retrieval. To the best of our knowledge, it is the most rich multimodal collection of lifelog / personal sensor data that has been released for comparative experimentation. The dataset extends for 27 days with data items for every minute of this time. We also introduced a new type of temporally-advancing topic for use in interactive retrieval experimentation and we reported on the types of interactive systems that were developed for this test collection and entered by participating research teams at the Lifelog Search Challenge competition at ACM ICMR 2018.

The LSC test collection (and associated documentation) is available for download from the LSC website[1]. Anyone using the dataset must sign two forms to access the datasets, an organisational agreement form for the organisation (signed by the research team leader) and an individual agreement form for each member of the research team that will access the data. This is requested in order to adhere to host data governance policies for lifelog data. The test collection is composed of a number of files; the core image dataset, the associated metadata, the information access dataset and the provided visual concept data for each image. Each zip file is additionally password protected.

Acknowledgements. We acknowledge the financial support of Science Foundation Ireland (SFI) under grant number SFI/12/RC/2289 and JSPS KAKENHI under Grant Number 18H00974.

References

1. Alsina, A., Giró, X., Gurrin, C.: An interactive lifelog search engine for LSC2018. In: ACM Workshop on The Lifelog Search Challenge, LSC 2018, pp. 30–32. ACM, New York (2018)
2. Bush, V.: As we may think. Interactions **3**(2), 35–46 (1996)

---

[1] Lifelog Search Challenge website: http://lsc.dcu.ie/. Last Visited 27th July 2018.

3. Dang-Nguyen, D.-T., Piras, L., Riegler, M., Boato, G., Zhou, L., Gurrin, C.: Overview of ImageCLEFlifelog 2017: lifelog retrieval and summarization. In: CLEF2017 Working Notes, Dublin, Ireland, 11–14 September 2017
4. Dang-Nguyen, D.-T., Piras, L., Riegler, M., Zhou, L., Lux, M., Gurrin, C.: Overview of ImageCLEFlifelog 2018: daily living understanding and lifelog moment retrieval. In: CLEF2018 Working Notes, CEUR Workshop Proceedings, Avignon, France, 10–14 September 2018. CEUR-WS.org (2018)
5. Dang-Nguyen, D.-T., Zhou, L., Gupta, R., Riegler, M., Gurrin, C.: Building a disclosed lifelog dataset:challenges, principles and processes. In: Content-Based Multimedia Indexing (CBMI) (2017)
6. Dodge, M., Kitchin, R.: Outlines of a world coming into existence: pervasive computing and the ethics of forgetting. Environ. Plan. B: Plan. Des. **34**(3), 431–445 (2007)
7. Duane, A., Gurrin, C., Huerst, W.: Virtual reality lifelog explorer: lifelog search challenge at ACM ICMR 2018. In: ACM Workshop on The Lifelog Search Challenge, LSC 2018, pp. 20–23. ACM, New York (2018)
8. Gurrin, C., Joho, H., Hopfgartner, F., Zhou, L., Albatal, R.: NTCIR lifelog: the first test collection for lifelog research. In: Proceedings of SIGIR 2016 Conference, pp. 705–708. ACM (2016)
9. Gurrin, C., Joho, H., Hopfgartner, F., Zhou, L., Albatal, R.: Overview of NTCIR-12 lifelog task. In: Proceedings of the 12th NTCIR Conference, pp. 354–360 (2016)
10. Gurrin, C., et al.: Overview of NTCIR-13 lifelog-2 task. In: Proceedings of the 13th NTCIR Conference, pp. 6–11 (2017)
11. Gurrin, C., Schoeffmann, K., Joho, H., Dang-Nguyen, D.-T., Riegler, M., Piras, L. (eds.): LSC 2018: Proceedings of the 2018 ACM Workshop on The Lifelog Search Challenge. ACM, New York (2018)
12. Jones, W., Teevan, J.: Personal Information Management. University of Washington Press, Seattle (2011)
13. Kato, M.P., Liu, Y.: Overview of NTCIR-13, pp. 1–5 (2017)
14. Kim, P.H., Giunchiglia, F.: The open platform for personal lifelogging: the elifelog architecture. In: CHI 2013 Extended Abstracts on Human Factors in Computing Systems, CHI EA 2013, pp. 1677–1682. ACM, New York (2013)
15. Lee, Y.J., Ghosh, J., Grauman, K.: Discovering important people and objects for egocentric video summarization. In: 2012 IEEE Conference on Computer Vision and Pattern Recognition (CVPR), pp. 1346–1353. IEEE (2012)
16. Lokoc, J., Bailer, W., Schoeffmann, K., Muenzer, B., Awad, G.: On influential trends in interactive video retrieval: video browser showdown 2015–2017. IEEE Trans. Multimed. **20**(12), 3361–3376 (2018)
17. Lokoč, J., Kovalčík, G., Souček, T.: Revisiting SIRET video retrieval tool. In: Schoeffmann, K., et al. (eds.) MMM 2018. LNCS, vol. 10705, pp. 419–424. Springer, Cham (2018). https://doi.org/10.1007/978-3-319-73600-6_44
18. Münzer, B., Leibetseder, A., Kletz, S., Primus, M.J., Schoeffmann, K.: lifeXplore at the lifelog search challenge 2018. In: ACM Workshop on The Lifelog Search Challenge, LSC 2018, pp. 3–8. ACM, New York (2018)
19. Schoeffmann, K., Münzer, B., Primus, J., Leibetseder, A.: The diveXplore system at the video browser showdown 2018 - final notes. CoRR abs/1804.01863 (2018)
20. Sellen, A.J., Whittaker, S.: Beyond total capture. Commun. ACM **53**(5), 70–77 (2010)
21. Sole, A.D.: Microsoft Computer Vision APIs Distilled: Getting Started with Cognitive Services. Apress, New York City (2017)

22. Song, S., Chandrasekhar, V., Cheung, N.-M., Narayan, S., Li, L., Lim, J.-H.: Activity recognition in egocentric life-logging videos. In: Jawahar, C.V., Shan, S. (eds.) ACCV 2014. LNCS, vol. 9010, pp. 445–458. Springer, Cham (2015). https://doi.org/10.1007/978-3-319-16634-6_33

23. Talavera, E., Dimiccoli, M., Bolaños, M., Aghaei, M., Radeva, P.: R-clustering for egocentric video segmentation. In: Paredes, R., Cardoso, J.S., Pardo, X.M. (eds.) IbPRIA 2015. LNCS, vol. 9117, pp. 327–336. Springer, Cham (2015). https://doi.org/10.1007/978-3-319-19390-8_37

24. Truong, T.-D., Dinh-Duy, T., Nguyen, V.-T., Tran, M.-T.: Lifelogging retrieval based on semantic concepts fusion. In: ACM Workshop on The Lifelog Search Challenge, LSC 2018, pp. 24–29. ACM, New York (2018)

25. Zhou, L., Hinbarji, Z., Dang-Nguyen, D.-T., Gurrin, C.: Lifer: an interactive lifelog retrieval system. In: ACM Workshop on The Lifelog Search Challenge, LSC 2018, pp. 9–14. ACM, New York (2018)

SEPHLA: Challenges and Opportunities Within Environment - Personal Health Archives

Tomohiro Sato, Minh-Son Dao$^{(\boxtimes)}$, Kota Kuribayashi, and Koji Zettsu

Big Data Analytics Laboratory, National Institute of Information
and Communications Technology,
4-2-1 Nukui-Kitamachi, Koganei, Tokyo 184-8795, Japan
{tosato,dao,kuribayashi,zettsu}@nict.go.jp

Abstract. It is well known that environment and human health have a close relationship. Many researchers have pointed out the high association between the condition of an environment (e.g. pollutant concentrations, weather variables) and the qualification of health (e.g. cardiorespiratory, psychophysiology) [1,10]. Meanwhile, environment information can be recorded accurately by sensors installed in stations, most of the health information comes from interviews, surveys, or records from medical organizations. The common approach for collecting and analyzing data to discover the association between environment and health outcomes is first isolating a predefined location then collecting all related data inside such a location. The size of this location can be scaled from local (e.g. city, province, country) to global (e.g. region, worldwide) scopes. Nevertheless, this approach cannot give a close-up perspective of an individual scale (i.e. the reaction of individual's health against his/her surrounding environment during his/her lifetime). To fulfill this gap, we create the SEPHLA: the surrounding-environment personal-health lifelog archive. This purpose of creating this archive is to create a dataset at the individual scale by collecting psychophysiological (e.g. perception, heart rate), pollutant concentrations (e.g. $PM_{2.5}$, NO_2, O_3), weather variables (e.g. temperature, humidity), and urban nature (e.g. GPS, images, comments) data via wearable sensors and smart-phones/lifelog-cameras attached to each person. We explore and exploit this archive for better understanding the impact of an environment on human health at the individual level. We also address challenges of organizing, extending, and searching SEPHLA archive.

Keywords: Lifelog · Environment · Air pollution · Urban nature
Personal health · Cardiorespiratory · Psychophysiology

1 Introduction

To address the challenge of understanding the impact of environmental risk factors on human health, many researches have been conducted. Although this

I. Kompatsiaris et al. (Eds.): MMM 2019, LNCS 11295, pp. 325–337, 2019.
https://doi.org/10.1007/978-3-030-05710-7_27

impact is extremely varied and complex in both severity and clinical significance, most of the researches agree that people who live in polluted areas tend to have worse health outcomes than those who live in clean areas [1].

Among environment factors, pollutant concentrations (e.g. fine particulate matter $PM_{2.5}$, Nitrogen dioxide NO_2, Ozone O_3, Sulfur dioxide SO_2), weather variables (e.g. temperature, humidity), and urban nature (e.g. GPS, images, comments) are popular factors that utilized to find associations with cardio-respiratory and psychological distress in health outcomes.

In [2], the influence of exposure to $PM_{2.5}$ on the development of adult's respiratory outcomes including asthma, sinusitis and chronic bronchitis is investigated in the USA from 2002 to 2005. The $PM_{2.5}$ data are collected from the United States Environmental Protection Agency (USEPA)[1], while the health outcomes are gathered from self-reported prevalence, National Health Interview Survey (NHIS)[2]. Two additional covariances are also recorded: (1) possible health-related covariance: sex, age, body mass index (BMI), smoking and exercise status, and (2) demographic covariance: race and ethnicity, education, and urbanicity. Along with the conclusion that increasing $PM_{2.5}$ may contribute to population sinusitis burdens, the authors discover that Non-Hispanic blacks may have more risks of asthma outcomes due to $PM_{2.5}$ than others.

In [3], the authors pay attention on the association of air pollution (e.g. Carbon monoxide CO, O_3 and PM_{10} collected from USEPA) and children's respiratory health. The research observes several years of early-life health treatments for each of nearly 700,000 children from 1997 to 1999 in California, USA. The conclusion of this research shows that there is a tight relation between CO and O_3 and children's contemporaneous respiratory treatments.

In [4], the association of traffic pollution and the incidence of cardio-respiratory outcomes in an adult cohort in London from 2005 to 2001 is investigated. In this research, NO_2 and $PM_{2.5}$ are considered as the traffic pollution risk factors. The cardio-respiratory outcomes (e.g. coronary heart disease, stroke, heart failure, chronic obstructive pulmonary diseases, pneumonia) are collected from clinical data via residential postcodes. Additional covariances of smoking and BMI are also gathered. The conclusion points out that the largest observed association is between traffic-related air pollution and heart failure.

In [5], low and middle-income countries in East Asia and Pacific regions (LMICs) are the objects of research. In these regions, the qualification of gaseous ambient air pollution and medical cares are considered worse than in high-income countries. Gaseous pollutants including NO_2, O_3, SO_2, and CO are collected along with meteorological trends. The cardio-respiratory outcomes are gathered via deaths and hospital admissions and emergency room visits plus data crawled from open sources such as PubMed[3], Web of Science, Embase, LILACs, Global Health, and ProQuest. The research points out that the greatest association observed is related to cardio-respiratory mortality. In the same research direction

---

[1] www.epa.gov.

[2] www.cdc.gov/nchs/nhis/index.htm.

[3] www.ncbi.nlm.nih.gov/pubmed/.

as described in [5], in [6], the authors discover the global association of air pollution and cardio-respiratory diseases over 28 countries. CO, SO_2, NO_2, O_3, $PM_{2.5}$, and PM_{10} are concerned as the major risk factors of air pollution that influence on cardiovascular and respiratory diseases whose data are collected via hospital admissions and mortality reports. Besides, additional variables like energy, transportation, and socioeconomic status may play the important role in the varying effect size of this association.

The effect of air pollution on psychological distress is also an interesting research topic. In [7], the authors discover that the increase of pollutant concentrations associates in reaction to visual stimuli and inability to concentrate. In this research, SO_2, NO_2, NO, $C_nH_m - CH_4$ and dust collected daily via stations installed in a city are concerned as the major factors of pollutant concentrations. The perception (i.e. ability to concentrate, reaction time) is self-rated daily. The urinary cortisol and catecholamines, blood-pressure and bodily complaints are measured weekly. The experience is carried out in Bavaria, Germany for 2 months.

In [8], the effect of air pollution on individual psychological distress is investigated in the USA from 1999 to 2011. $PM_{2.5}$ measured around the experimental locations are considered as the major risk factor of air pollution. These data are crawled from USEPA with the support of PSID's[4] supplemental Geospatial Match File. The output of this research is that $PM_{2.5}$ is significantly associated with increased psychological distress. The specific aspect of this research is that the data is considered at the individual level where demography, socio-economics, and health of individuals are taken into account as additional covariances.

All the methods mentioned above focus on understanding the association between environment and health outcomes in the long-term exposure manner. In [9], the authors pay attention on doing experiences in short-term exposure manner. The authors take into account SO_2, NO_2, PM_{10}, temperature, pressure, and humidity as environmental factors. The mortality caused by respiratory diseases are gathered by the death registration system in Hubei Provincial Center for Disease Control and Prevention.

Another impact of the environment on the health benefits is the urban nature. In [10], the authors point out the important role of urban nature in the healthy residents. Based on the fact that the major part of the human population lives in cities, the need of understanding the association of urban nature and mental health towards having a cost-effective tool to reduce health risks becomes the utmost requirement currently.

2 Motivation and Purposes

As we mentioned in Sect. 1, associations between the environmental factors and health conditions is one of the hot topics in the research field and also in the business field. $PM_{2.5}$, NO_2, O_3 and SO_2 are major air pollutants affecting our

---

[4] The Panel Study of Income Dynamic.

health. Temperature and humidity are used to evaluate the effect of weather variables on health outcomes. These data are mostly collected from metadata archives. Heart rate and related parameters are good indicator to monitor the health condition.

Quality of these data itself is essential for accuracy of data analysis. In most previous studies, environmental and health data separately collected were used, thus the coincidence between each other is also a key issue. The major approach to discover the association between environment and health outcomes is, first, isolating a predefined location, and then collecting all related data inside such a location in order to fulfill the differences in terms of time, place and situation, between the environment data and health data obtained. The size of this location can be scaled from local (e.g. city, province, country) to global (e.g. region, worldwide) scopes. These assumptions might be large error sources in the data analysis.

In this paper, we describe the data collecting campaign to make dataset of the environmental data and health data simultaneously collected. We introduced wearable sensors to obtain both data, thus the resolution of time and location is quite fine (i.e. the reaction of individual's health against his/her surrounding environment during his/her lifetime). The perception of individual participant was also obtained as annotation information. Section 3 describes the detail of the campaign and the archive. We explore and exploit this archive for better understanding the impact of an environment on human health in both spatial (e.g. individual and regional levels) and temporal (e.g short- and long-term exposure) dimensions. We also address the challenges of organizing, visualizing, extending, and searching the archive in Sect. 3.3.

3   The Campaign and the Archive

The DATATHON is the name of the campaign for collecting data from participants who live in the area we examine. The DATATHON comes from DATA and MaraTHON. The purpose of the campaign is to collect not only environment and personal health data but also a human reaction against urban nature. Moreover, the campaign, with the support of communications, gives the important message to the public towards getting people aware of the impacts of the environment on their health. Participants are asked to join the campaign for a certain number of days. During the campaign, each participant is requested to follow and do predefined routes and tasks, respectively. All data collected during the campaign are stored on our server to create the archive, namely SEPHLA - Surrounding-Environment Personal-Health Lifelog Archive. Following subsections will discuss in details the campaign and the archive.

3.1   Time, Locations, and Tasks

The DATATHON-2018 was performed in seven days: 10th, 11th, 24th, 25th, 31th March and 1st, 8th April 2018 in Fukuoka city, Japan. The number of participants of each day was 30, 14, 15, 27, 13, 14 and 20, respectively. Five routes were set in Fukuoka city, Japan (See Fig. 1). The length of each route varied from 4 to 5 km, and it took approximately 1.5–2.5 h to finish one route by walking along. Each route was designed to include several environmental features such as road, park, sightseeing area, coastal way, and woods. These routes were separated by spots which are considered as check-points where participants can stop and tag their comments. Tables 1, 2, 3, 4, 5 summarize spots' locations and environmental features of routes. Participants were separated into five groups and walked along these routes to collect environmental and personal data using wearable sensors and smartphones.

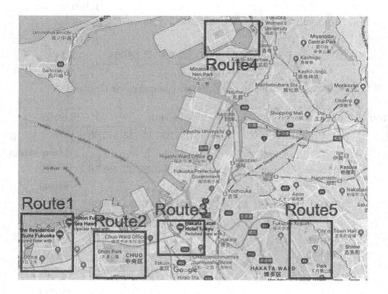

Fig. 1. Location of the five routes in Fukuoka City.

3.2 Sensors, Data, and Data Warehouse

Two wearable sensors are used for this campaign: (1) the atmospheric sensor, and (2) personal condition sensor. The former IoT sensor developed by NICT and Nagoya University collects the amount of $PM_{2.5}$ and weather variables (temperature and humidity). The latter, namely WHS-2, bought from Union Tool Co.[5] monitors heart rates and records 3-axis accelerometer values. Data collected from these sensors are stored in a data warehouse, namely Event Data Warehouse (EvWH), via small apps installed in participants' smartphones. At the EvWH, additional informations represented for the relax level of participants

---

[5] http://www.uniontool.co.jp/en/.

Table 1. Details of spots and features of Route 1

Route	Spot	Location	Feature
1	1 Fujisaki Sta.	130.34886, 33.58137	
			↓ Main street
	2 Nishijin Sta. PB	130.36003, 33.58397	
			↓ Path
	3 Fukuoka City Museum	130.35267, 33.58771	
			↓ Sightseeing area
	4 Momochi Bay 1	130.35126, 33.59451	
			↓ Bayside
	5 Momochi Bay 2	130.34459, 33.58782	
			↓ Street
	6 Momochi Park	130.34889, 33.58598	

Table 2. Details of spots and features of Route 2

Route	Spot	Location	Feature
2	1 Ropponmatsu Sta.	130.37724, 33.57766	
			↓ Main street
	2 Akasaka 3-chome Cross	130.38342, 33.58276	
			↓ Street
	3 Ohori Park Ent. 11	130.37599, 33.58299	
			↓ Park
	4 Kujira Park	130.37733, 33.58883	
			↓ Park
	5 Ohori Park Ent. 10	130.37458, 33.58380	
			↓ Street
	6 Ropponmatsu Park No. 2	130.37662, 33.57895	

are calculated by using heart rate data: (1) parasympathetic nerve activity is measured by the high-frequency component of a heart rate, and (2) sympathetic nerve activity is estimated by the ratio of low-frequency (LF) and high-frequency (HF) components of a heart rate [11]. These to sensors are equipped by all participants in all days of the campaign. Additionally, amounts of O_3 and NO_2 are monitored using commercialized portable sensors (Gasmaster model 2750, Kanomax Inc. and Personal Ozone Monitor, 2B Technologies Inc.). The amount of O_3 and NO_2 was observed in the two of five routes; Routes 1 and 3 on 10th, Routes 1 and 5 on 11th, Routes 1 and 2 on 24th, Routes 2 and 5 on 25th March, and Routes 1 and 4 on 1st April.

A smartphone is also utilized as another sensor for capturing perceptional and environmental data. In our context, the perception is considered as the

Table 3. Details of spots and features of Route 3

Route	Spot	Location	Feature
3	1 Kego Park	130.39948, 33.58822	
			↓ Shopping street
	2 Tenjinbashiguchi Cross	130.39836, 33.59230	
			↓ Underground arcade
	3 Tenchika Ent. East 12c	130.40191, 33.58738	
			↓ Main street
	4 Tenjin 1-chome Cross	130.40004, 33.59161	
			↓ Path
	5 Acros Fukuoka Garden Ent. 1	130.40206, 33.59092	
			↓ Garden
	6 Acros Fukuoka Garden Ent. 2	130.40328, 33.59119	
			↓ Park
	7 Tenjin Central Park	130.40336, 33.59011	
			↓ Path
	8 Daimaru department store	130.40058, 33.58919	

Table 4. Details of spots and features of Route 4

Route	Spot	Location	Feature
4	1 Kashii Bay North Park	130.42594, 33.66063	
			↓ Bayside path
	2 Kataosabashi Cross	130.43288, 33.65888	
			↓ Street
	3 Kashii Bay	130.43494, 33.66193	
			↓ Bayside path
	4 Aitaka Bridge	130.42796, 33.66458	
			↓ Street
	5 Island City Central Park 1	130.42374, 33.66387	
			↓ Park
	6 Island City Central Park 2	130.41950, 33.66395	

feeling of participants against their surrounding environment. We design five features for the perception data: crowdedness, ease of walking, fun, calmness, and quietness. Each feature has five levels from 1 (i.e. strongly disagree) to 5 (i.e. strongly agree) and can be scored by using an app installed on a smartphone. Participants are required to annotate their perception at each spot using their smartphone. Participants are also encouraged to take pictures whenever they feel the environment impacting on their perception. These data are transferred and stored in the EvWH as well. The data collected by sensors are summarized in Table 6.

Table 5. Details of spots and features of Route 5

Route	Spot	Location	Feature
5	1 Fukuoka Airport South Cross	130.45050, 33.59463	
			↓ Main street
	2 Cross	130.45682, 33.58311	
			↓ Path
	3 Otani Park	130.46068, 33.58273	
			↓ Mountain trail
	4 Maruo Observatory	130.46406, 33.58312	
			↓ Mountain trail
	5 Higashihirao Park Ent. 3	130.46029, 33.58941	
			↓ Street
	6 Shimousui-oimatu Park	130.45304, 33.59612	

Table 6. Data collected by sensors

ID	Sensor	Object	Data
1	Small IoT sensor	Pollutant concentrations weather variables	$PM_{2.5}$ Temperature, humidity
2	WHS-2	Physiology	Heart rate, three-axis acceleration, Relax level (LF/HF)
3	Smartphone (Physical)	Environment	Pictures, time, longitude, latitude
4	Smartphone (Semantic)	Perception	Crowdedness, ease of walking, fun, calmness, quietness, comments
5	Commercialized portable sensor	Pollutant concentrations	O_3 and NO_2

At the last day of the campaign, participants are asked to discuss to give evaluation rates for the air quality of all partitions of the route they participated, namely route's air quality (RAQ). A partition is determined as a part of a route limited by two consecutive spots. We define five-grade evaluation levels from very bad (1), bad (2), moderate (3), good (4), to very good (5) to support participants express their choices.

The air quality health index (AQHI) [12] estimated the relevant risk of air-pollutants on health outcomes is calculated using data of $PM_{2.5}$, O_3, NO_2, and sulfur dioxide (SO_2). The AQHI is developed based on the Poisson regression analysis of the air-pollutant measurements and the hospital admissions of respiratory and cardiovascular diseases. Since our sensors cannot measures SO_2, we use data provided by the Atmospheric Environmental Regional Observation System (AEROS) [13]. The AEROS which is operated by Japanese local governments provides hourly air pollutant data all over Japan for 24 h a day. The

O_3 and NO_2 data are also compensated from AEROS in case of no observation from the wearable sensors.

The discomfort index (DI) estimates the human comfort level due to the temperature and humidity condition [14]. We used the Japanese traditional DI given by Eq. 1.

$$DI = 0.81T + 0.01H * (0.99T - 14.3) + 46.3 \qquad (1)$$

where T and H represent temperature $[^0C]$ and relative humidity [%]. The DI value of 70 indicates the comfortable condition. Table 7 shows data that are annotated by participants and inferred by sensing data.

In order to guarantee the privacy, all data stored in EvWH are concerned as from anonymous; and all individual data are either deleted or masked.

Table 7. Data annotated by participants and inferred by sensing data

Parameter	Description	Inferred/annotated data
AQHI	Air quality health index	Inferred data
DI	Discomfort index	Inferred data
LF/HF	Level of relaxing	Inferred data
RQA	Route's air quality	Annotated data

3.3 Annotations and Visualizations

In order to visualize data, we create two infographics: (1) the radar chart, and (2) the air quality map. The former is to illustrate the perception, air quality health index, discomfort index, and level of relaxing. The latter is to reflect the participants' annotations that reflect the feeling of participants against the environment. The air quality map embedded.

Figure 2 shows the example of radar charts created by using data collected from Route 2 on 25th March. The Fig. 2(a) and (b) show data of the partitions limited by spots 1 and 2 (i.e. main street feature), and sports 4 and 5 (i.e. park feature), respectively. Observing these charts, we can see the similarity of environmental and physiological sensing data from two charts. In opposite, perception data have a significant difference. Obviously, the charts show that people feel more relaxed in the Park than on the Street.

Figure 3 illustrates the air quality map where the Route's Air Quality, pictures and comments taken and tagged by participants, and radar charts are integrated and displayed. This map semantically reflects the feeling (i.e. perception) of participants against the environment (i.e. urban nature, air pollution, and weather).

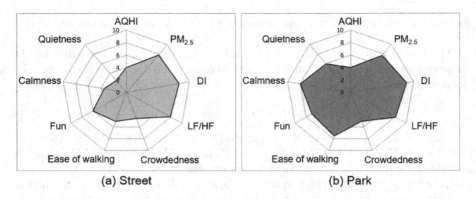

(a) Street   (b) Park

Fig. 2. The radar charts made by acquired data in the street (Spots 1 and 2) and in the park (Spots 4 and 5). The data acquired on 25th March was used.

The maps made by the participants are available on our website[6]. The data format is *geojson*, and the license is Creative Commons Attribution-ShareAlike 4.0 International (CC BY-SA 4.0).

4   Challenges and Opportunities

It indicates that our perception is controlled by factors those are not measurable by sensors. Quantification of our perception can be a new challenge. Image, sound and smell might be key components that affects to our feeling and emotion. Creating a model to predict our perception using such key components should be the next step of this research.

Currently, the SEPHLA archive contains enough data types for investigating the association between air pollution, urban nature, and personal health outcomes, especially psychic distress. Nevertheless, understanding such an association is not the only insight being gotten from SEPHLA. Through integration with other domains, archives, and sensors new opportunities are presented, namely:

– **Relaxing places recommendation:** Determining a good place and time for self-relaxing, enjoying a picnic, or practicing Zen can be a good application for urban people. Merging SEPHLA with lifelog data, personal photo album, and personal health monitoring to create an application that can recommend the best place and time for relaxing.
– **Healthy routes recommendation:** Lack of exercises could lead to the degradation of health. To encourage people to do outdoor exercises regularly, creating an application that can recommend a health route could be a good solution. Integrating SEPHLA with Google street view, personal photo album, social media resources can suggest healthy routes that can bring more

---

[6] http://datathon.jp/interactivemap/.

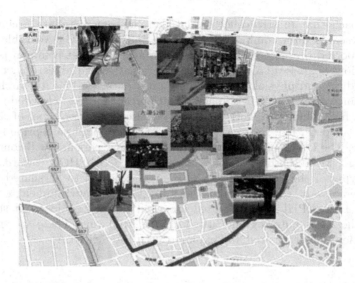

Fig. 3. Example of the air quality map made by the participants (map for Route 2). Colour of the line represents the level of air quality (Blue: Very Good, Green: Good, Yellow: Moderate, Brown: Bad, Red: Very Bad). (Color figure online)

relaxing and less air pollution for people. This application can also be utilized for not only exercising but also traveling.

- **Urban management assistants:** There is a strong evidence of the influence of urban nature to health benefits citizens [10]. Getting insights into SEPHLA can support the urban management towards improving urban nature for citizens' benefits.
- **Event Detection and Prediction:** With SEPHLA, researchers can build series of models that can help to predict and detect events such as health status (e.g. how about my heart rate if the air pollution and/or urban nature around me change?), air pollution degree (e.g. in a short-term exposure, along a walking route, how the air pollution fluctuates?), changes of perception (e.g. for next 30 min which perception a person feel when walking around a city?).

Although the potential of SEPHLA is enormous, there are challenges to be overcome such as privacy concerns, data security, data warehouse management, and effective and efficient search and indexing tools. Nevertheless, we believe that these challenges are not the obstacle that cannot be broken through. In fact, we have developed a real-time complex event discovery platform for managing SEPHLA [15]. Besides, comparing benefits of SEPHLA with its challenges, SEPHLA is worth to be built and spread to communities.

5   Conclusions

We introduce the DATATHON campaign and the SEPHLA archive to collect and store environment and health data coming from individuals. Differ the common approach that mostly collects related data from metadata archives, our approach records data coming directly from individuals via wearable sensors and self-reported prevalence. The archive contains the most common pollutant concentrations (e.g. PM2.5, NO2, SO2, O3), weather variables (e.g. temperature, humidity) and physiology (e.g. heart rate) data. Besides, the archive also stores urban nature (e.g. GPS, images) and perception (e.g. crowdedness, ease of walking, fun, calmness, quietness) data. We also create two types of charts for visualizing air pollution, relaxing levels, urban nature, and perception stored in the archive. The DATATHON is organized twice per years and will continue for several years. More sensors will be introduced in DATATHON towards enriching data types of the archive. The SEPHLA is expected to be shared publicly for those who want to understand the impact of the environment on health outcomes. The SEPHLA can be used for event detecting and event searching as well as health monitoring and urban nature evaluating. There are enormous opportunities to be exploited and explored with the SEPHLA.

References

1. Prüss-Üstün, A., Corvalán, C.: Preventing disease through healthy environments - towards an estimate of the environmental burden of disease. World Health Organ. (2006). ISBN 92 4 159382 2
2. Nachman, K.E., Parker, J.-D.: Exposures to fine particulate air pollution and respiratory outcomes in adults using two national datasets: a cross-sectional study. J. Environ. Health **11**, 25 (2012)
3. Beatty, T.K.-M., Shimshack, J.-P.: Air pollution and children's respiratory health: a cohort analysis. J. Environ. Econ. Manag. **67**(1), 39–57 (2014)
4. Carey, M., et al.: Traffic pollution and the incidence of cardiorespiratory outcomes in an adult cohort in London. J. Occup. Environ. Med. **73**, 849–856 (2016)
5. Newell, K., Kartsonaki, C., Lam, K.B.H., Kurmi, O.: Cardiorespiratory health effects of gaseous ambient air pollution exposure in low and middle income countries: a systematic review and meta-analysis. J. Environ. Health **17**(41), 1–14 (2018)
6. Requia, J.-W., Adams, D.-M., Arain, A., Papatheodorou, S., Koutrakis, P., Mahmoud, M.: Global association of air pollution and cardiorespiratory diseases: a systematic review, meta-analysis, and investigation of modifier variables. Syst. Rev. AJPH **108**(S2), 123–130 (2018)
7. Bullinger, M.: Psychological effects of air pollution on healthy residents: a time-series approach. J. Environ. Psychol. **9**, 103–118 (1989)
8. Sass, V., Kravitz-Wirtz, N., Karceski, M.-S., Hajat, A., Crowder, K., Takeuchi, D.: The effects of air pollution on individual psychological distress. J. Health Place **48**, 72–79 (2017)
9. Ren, M., et al.: The short-term effects of air pollutants on respiratory disease mortality in Wuhan, China: comparison of time-series and case-crossover analyses. Sci. Rep. **7**(40482), 1–9 (2017)
10. Shanahan, D.F., Fuller, R.A., Bush, R., Lin, B.B., Gaston, K.J.: The health benefits of urban nature: how much do we need? Bioscience **65**(5), 476–485 (2015)
11. Pagani, M., et al.: Power spectral analysis of heart rate and arterial pressure variabilities as a marker of sympatho-vagal interaction in man and conscious dog. Circ. Res. **59**, 178–193 (1986)

12. Wong, T.W., Tam, W.W.S., Yu, I.T.S., Lau, A.K.H., Pang, S.W., Wong, A.H.S.: Developing a risk-based air quality health index. Atmos. Environ. **76**, 52–58 (2013)
13. Nishi, A., Araki, K., Saito, K., Kawabata, K., Seko, H.: The consideration and application of the quality control method for the atmospheric environmental regional observation system (AEROS) meteorological observation data. Tenki (Bull. J. Meteorol. Soc. Jpn.) **62**(8), 627–639 (2015)
14. Thom, E.C.: The discomfort index. Weatherwise **12**, 57–60 (1959)
15. Dao, M.S., Pongpaichet, S., Jalali, L., Kim, K.S., Jain, R., Zettsu, K.: A real-time complex event discovery platform for cyber-physical-social system. In: ICMR 2014 (2014)

Athens Urban Soundscape (ATHUS): A Dataset for Urban Soundscape Quality Recognition

Theodoros Giannakopoulos[1,2]([✉]), Margarita Orfanidi[3], and Stavros Perantonis[2]

[1] Behavioral Signal Technologies Inc., Los Angeles, USA
tyiannak@gmail.com
[2] National Center for Scientific Research Demokritos, Athens, Greece
sper@iit.demokritos.gr
[3] National Technical University of Athens, Athens, Greece
orfanidi.margarita@gmail.com
http://tyiannak.github.io

Abstract. Soundscape can be regarded as the auditory landscape, conceived individually or at collaborative level. This paper presents ATHUS (ATHens Urban Soundscape), a dataset of audio recordings of ambient urban sounds, which has been annotated in terms of the corresponding perceived soundscape quality. To build our dataset, several users have recorded sounds using a simple smartphone application, which they also used to annotate the recordings, in terms of the perceived quality of the soundscape (i.e. level of "pleasantness"), in a range of 1 (unbearable) to 5 (optimal). The dataset has been made publicly available (in http://users.iit.demokritos.gr/~tyianak/soundscape) as an audio feature representation form, so that it can directly be used in a supervised machine learning pipeline without need for feature extraction. In addition, this paper presents and publicly provides (https://github.com/tyiannak/soundscape_quality) a baseline approach, which demonstrates how the dataset can be used to train a supervised model to predict soundscape quality levels. Experiments under various setups using this library have demonstrated that Support Vector Machine Regression outperforms SVM Classification for the particular task, which is something expected if we consider the gradual nature of the soundscape quality labels. The goal of this paper is to provide to machine learning engineers, working on audio analytics, a first step towards the automatic recognition of soundscape quality in urban spaces, which could lead to powerful assessment tools in the hands of policy makers with regards to noise pollution and sustainable urban living.

Keywords: Audio analysis · Soundscape quality
Audio classification · Regression · Open-source

This research was supported by the Greek State Scholarship Foundation (IKY).

I. Kompatsiaris et al. (Eds.): MMM 2019, LNCS 11295, pp. 338–348, 2019.
https://doi.org/10.1007/978-3-030-05710-7_28

1   Introduction

1.1   Motivation

The population size in urban areas during the last century has led to enormous changes in traffic flow, commercial and industrial activities and therefore a respective increase of noise pollution in the urban environments. This growing environmental issue has led to important life quality-related risks for billions of citizens worldwide. Therefore, sustainable urban planning and decision making needs to seriously take into consideration the task of mitigating environmental noise. Noise pollution in big cities is not simply correlated to high energy audio signals: in most of the cases noise pollution is characterized by low-frequency and continuous background sounds.

It is therefore not straightforward to automatically assess soundscape quality in urban spaces using simple rules and heuristics that are based on basic features such as sound volume and energy. More advanced techniques are required, that make use of deeper audio features and more sophisticated audio analytics techniques. Such techniques should be based on advanced signal processing and pattern recognition methodologies, such as supervised learning and regression. It is therefore obvious that well-defined datasets are required to train and evaluate such machine learning applications. This research effort aims to provide such a dataset of urban soundscape recordings with corresponding annotations with respect to the levels of "pleasantness" i.e. the perceived soundscape quality. In addition, we demonstrate how the dataset can be used to train and validate a signal analysis and machine learning pipeline. In the near future, fully automated soundscape quality estimators could run in the smartphones of volunteers and active citizens, gathering valuable knowledge regarding the quality of urban soundscapes. This would define an excellent paradigm of the "human-in-the-loop" factor for AI applications and in the context of a crowdsourcing rationale.

1.2   Related Work

Despite it's obvious impact, the work towards automated analysis of soundscape quality is relatively limited. In [1] 12 quality attributes have been adopted (e.g. soothing, pleasant, etc.) to characterize four types of urban residential areas, exposed to road-traffic noise, while some energy- related signal statistics have been demonstrated in terms of their correlation to the perceived soundscape quality. In [10], the authors used samples of ambient sounds in various urban situations in two French cities and passers-by have been asked to express their opinion about the respective soundscapes through questionnaires. This resulted in correlations between perceptual characteristics and simple signal features (e.g. the deviation of the Equivalent Continuous Level).

In addition, [12] presents statistical results based on a questionnaire- based survey and objective soundscape attributes related to recordings from 14 urban open public spaces across Europe. These results in general indicate statistical relationships between acoustic comfort evaluations and the (background) sound level. The authors also note that the acoustic comfort evaluation is greatly affected by the sound source type. For example introducing a pleasant sound can considerably improve the acoustic comfort, even when its sound level is rather high. However, no automatic sound analysis methodologies are adopted in order to model the particular nature of such sounds. [9] highlights how the use of the notion of soundscapes can help in conceiving ambient sound environments in urban areas.

In [8] binaural recording has been used to analyze 32 recordings of urban environments. Two psychoacoustic parameters, namely loudness and sharpness, along with the equivalent sound level (dBA) have been used as audio features. Correlations between these parameters and the perception of (un)pleasantness (manually provided 25 inhabitants) have been extracted. Highest correlations have been found for very unpleasant signals. The research work presented in [2] focused in reporting acoustic statistics related to five urban parks in the city of Milan. Features like the unweighted 1/3- octave spectrum center of gravity and the sound pressure level exceeded 50% of the time (LA50) have been adopted. [13] the authors propose using Neural Networks for predicting subjective evaluations of sound level and acoustic comfort, using high level measurements.

In [11] a wide set of audio features is used to represent the audio signal and then regression models are adopted to predict the soundscape affect, in the context of a *music* performance environment. A study concerning bioacoustic signals [4] performs an automated procedure of categorization that incorporates dynamic time-warping and an adaptive resonance theory neural network to result in biologically meaningful outcomes about the natural environment. In [6] instead of adopting heuristic rules and simple acoustic statistics, a fully automatic framework towards soundscape quality estimation has been presented. Towards this end, mid-term audio feature extraction has been adopted, along with Support Vector Machines Regression. Two methodologies were proposed in order to map the feature representations to the soundscape quality levels: (a) direct regression and (b) a two-stage regression that first estimates intermediate labels related to the context of the recording and then it uses a meta-regressor to map these labels to the final soundscape quality.

1.3   Contribution

The aforementioned research efforts indicate that there is a need for a common audio dataset which is annotated in terms of the corresponding soundscape quality. In this paper we present ATHens Urban Soundscape (ATHUS), a dataset of annotated sounds recorded in Athens, Greece and annotated in terms of the corresponding soundscape quality. Towards this end, almost 1000 recordings have been manually labelled in a range 1 (unbearable soundscape) to 5 (optimal soundscape). The dataset is provided publicly, in the form of audio feature representations (http://users.iit.demokritos.gr/~tyianak/soundscape), along with the respective ground-truth soundscape quality annotations.

In addition, a baseline audio analysis approach for automatic recognition of the soundscape quality is implemented and publicly provided in (https://github.com/tyiannak/soundscape_quality) for experimentation and performance comparison of future methods. In this way, this paper, apart from offering a well annotated dataset, demonstrates how basic feature extraction and classification/regression can be used to automatically assess the perceived soundscape quality.

2   Audio Data Collection and Annotation

2.1   Data Collection and Statistics

The audio data have been recorded in Athens, Greece, a metropolitan area of more than 4 million citizens, and one of the top ten metropolitan areas of Europe, in terms of overall population. The recordings have taken place in a period of almost 4 years, by 10 different humans using 13 different types of smartphone devices. Each recording was around 30 s of average duration. Detailed statistics regarding the original audio dataset are presented in Table 1.

Table 1. General dataset statistics

Total num of recordings	978
Min duration (sec)	11.4
Average duration (sec)	26.99
Max duration (sec)	78.83
Total duration (hours)	7.33
Number of unique devices	10
First day	2015-10-23
Last day	2018-05-30
Total annotation period (days)	950
Unique annotation days	92

Each recording has been manually annotated by the user that also performed the recording, using a simple Android application. The application is also available online (http://users.iit.demokritos.gr/~tyianak/soundscape/). Before starting the recording process, the application gets the geospatial coordinates using the smartphone's GPS sensor, while the user also provides general information regarding her age, gender and educational level (demographic data). Then, the recording process starts, and as soon as the user stops it, she finally provides the perceived soundscape quality, in the range of 1 (unbearable sounscape quality) to 5 (optimal soundscape quality). As a final step, the data and metadata are uploaded to a database.

Figure 2 shows the distributions of the geospatial coordinates of the recordings on maps with different zoom ratios. Figure 3 shows the histogram of the

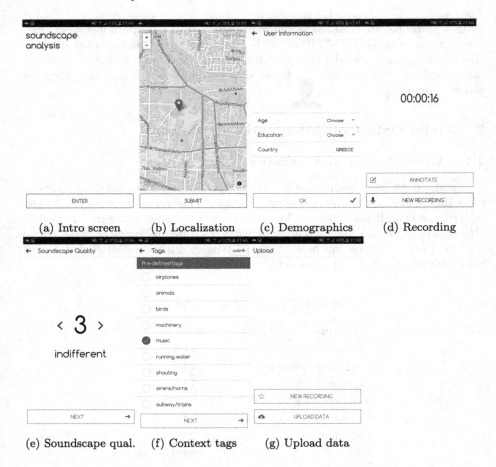

(a) Intro screen   (b) Localization   (c) Demographics   (d) Recording

(e) Soundscape qual.   (f) Context tags   (g) Upload data

Fig. 1. Screenshots of the annotation tool

soundscape quality values. Most of the values are concentrated around the "neutral" range, i.e. soundscape quality level is in the range 2 to 3. However, the task is not significantly imbalanced, since almost 30% of the annotations are distributed among extreme values (i.e. either 1 or 5) (Fig. 1).

2.2 Dataset Format

Each audio recording has been represented using either a sequence of short-term audio features or a spectrogram. In both cases, the *pyAudioAnalysis* library [5] has been used to extract the corresponding feature representations in either numpy binary files or PNG image files. In particular, two different feature representations have been provided:

- feature matrix: for each audio recording, the 34 short-term features available at *pyAudioAnalysis* library are extracted using, leading to a $34 \times N$ feature

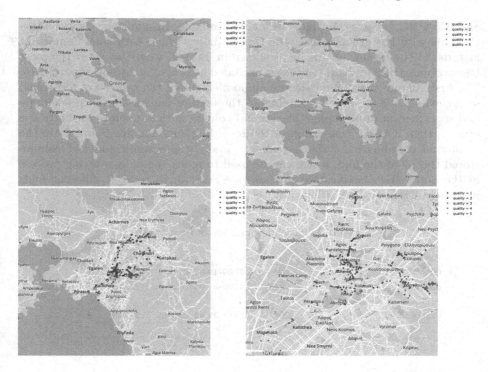

Fig. 2. Map distributions of the recordings of the dataset. Colors represent different annotated soundscape qualities (Color figure online)

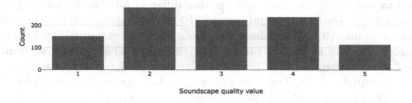

Fig. 3. Distribution of the soundscape quality values

matrix, where N is the number of short-term frames. A 50 ms window size has been adopted, with a 50% overlap, i.e. 25 ms window step. Each feature matrix is saved to a *numpy* binary file.

– spectrogram: with the same window size and step (50 ms frame size, 25 ms frame step), the *librosa* library [7] has been used to extract the spectrograms from each recording. The spectrograms have been saved to a PNG image file.

Therefore, each audio recording with a unique identifier $< ID >$ corresponds to a binary file $< ID > .npy$ where the short-term feature matrix is stored, and an image file $< ID > .npy$, where the respective spectrogram is stored. The dataset consists of 978 audio recordings in total, so 978 NPY feature matrix files and 978 PNG spectrogram files are made available. In addition, we provide a CSV file with the groundtruth soundscape quality along with some important metadata. The format of this file is shown in Table 2, where we show the most basic columns of metadata (the 1st is excluded as it is of no major importance). The first column corresponds to the audio filename of the respective recording, so for example 0000.wav corresponds to the feature matrix stored in 0000.npy and spectrogram in 0000.png. The second column is the annotated soundscape quality, then it is the timestamp of the recording and columns 5 and 6 are the geospatial coordinates of the recording. Finally, the seventh and last column stored the ID of the fold, which can be used to index the data splitting process in the automatic classification process (see Sect. 3). In total, 7 different folds have been defined on the whole dataset.

Table 2. Basic annotations and metadata

Audio name [2]	Soundscape [3]	Timespamp [4]	Geo 1 [5]	Geo 2 [6]	Fold [7]
0000.wav	4	2015-10-23T09-49-08	37.976	23.777	1
0001.wav	3	2015-10-23T09-54-04	37.976	23.769	1
...	...	...	...	...	...
0225.wav	2	2017-08-17T08-29-42	38.043	23.774	3
...	...	...	...	...	...

Apart from the individual annotations performed by the different human annotators, we have also performed an inter-annotator experiment, in the context of which we measured the agreement between different human annotators for the same recordings. Towards this end, we used 100 recordings that follow the overall class distribution. All 100 recordings have been manually annotated by 5 external annotators. These annotations proved that there is a 60% of exact agreement, for the 5-class classification task while the respective mean absolute error was found to be equal to 0.45. These set upper bounds of performance to the 5-class classification tasks presented in the experimental section.

3   Soundscape Recognition Baseline Method

3.1   Baseline Method

Along with the annotated dataset itself, a baseline approach that uses the short-term audio feature matrices to automatically recognize the soundscape quality of each recording, is also presented. The Python code for this method is also made publicly available at https://github.com/tyiannak/soundscape_quality. The baseline method performs the following steps: First, for each short-term feature sequence, i.e. for each row of the feature matrix of each recording, the delta sequences are computed, as an estimate of the derivative of the initial feature sequence. The deltas are computed using three different time differences, namely 1, 3 and 7 short-term windows. This yields in 3 total delta sequences for each initial feature sequence. Then for each feature sequence (and the corresponding three delta sequences), three long-term feature statistics are computed among the whole recording. These statistics are: the mean value, the standard deviation and the 25% and 75% percentiles. The aforementioned process leads to a final feature representation of 34 short-term features × 4 sequences (1 static and 3 delta) × 4 feature statistics, i.e. 544 dimensions that characterize the whole audio recording.

Using this 544-dimensional feature space, a Support Vector Machine model, with an RBF kernel is evaluated for different values of the C parameter, both as a regressor and a classifier. Note that evaluation is not performed using random permutations of the samples, but using the predefined fold IDs, also provided in the datasets, as described in Sect. 2. Using a random fold setup would be biased, as it would depend on annotations of the same user, possibly recorded during the same day and at the same place. The predefined folds have been carefully defined to avoid such biases. As explained above, SVMs have been used both in regression and classification model. In addition, since the initial dataset is slightly imbalanced (extreme values of soundscape quality are a bit less probable than values 2, 3 and 4), the SMOTE oversampling technique [3] has been used to make the dataset balanced.

3.2 Performance Results

The open source code that implements the baseline method described in Sect. 3.1, can be used to perform the 7-fold validation, using the predefined folds provided in the dataset. The experimentation process takes places for various values of the SVM C parameter. The performance measure used is the Mean Absolute Error (MAE). In addition, for comparison reasons, the MAE for the baseline random soundscape quality estimation is also computed. Finally, apart from the regression validation through the MAE performance measure, the script also extracts the confusion matrix for the classification task (i.e. if estimated soundscape qualities are rounded to the closest integers in the range 1 to 5). In that case, the average F1 measure and the overall classification accuracy are also reported. The implemented methodology described in Sect. 3.1, has the following parameters:

- SVM type: classification and regression
- Class balancing: without and with SMOTE oversampling

Therefore, in total the following 4 combinations of methods have been used: SVC, SVC+SM (SMOTE), SVR and SVR+SR. Note that classification F1 and accuracy measures are also computed for the SVR method, since in that case the estimated soundscape qualities are rounded to the nearest integer. The final results of the aforementioned techniques are summarized in Table 3. In additions, experiments have been carried out on two simpler versions of the soundscape quality tasks, using two different modes: first, the soundscape quality values

1 and 2, as well as classes 4 and 5 and second, soundscape qualities 2 and 4 have been excluded, so that we can demonstrate the ability of the classification/regression methods to discriminate between neutral and extreme audio soundscape quality classes (Table 4).

Table 3. Performance results for the 5-class soundscape quality task

Measure	Random	SVC	SVC+SM	SVR	SVR+SM
MAE	1.55	1.24	1.35	0.89	**0.88**
F1	7.3%	32.3%	37.5%	36.9%	**40.1%**
Acc	22.3%	37.4%	38.2%	41.9%	**42.3%**

Table 4. Performance results for the 3-class soundscape quality task (soundscape qualities 1 and 2 are grouped, as well as soundscape qualities 4 and 5

Measure	Random	SVC	SVC+SM	SVR	SVR+SM
MAE	0.78	0.74	0.66	0.49	**0.48**
F1	20.1%	50.3%	**57.0%**	52.1%	51.1%
Acc	43.1%	**62.7%**	61.0%	51.7%	50.2%

In almost all cases, it is clear that (a) regression outperforms classification and (b) upsampling using the SMOTE method also boosts the final performance of both the classifier and the regression methods. Finally, for the initial task (i.e. the 5-level soundscape quality task), we illustrate the overall confusion matrix, aggregated over all 7 folds in Fig. 4. It is obvious that extreme errors are of very low or even zero probability: for example only 2.5% of the "unbearable" (soundscape "1") recordings are misclassified as soundscape "4" and none as soundscape "5". In general, only 9.6% of the data are misclassified to a soundscape quality label whose distance from the ground truth label is at least 2 (e.g. soundscape 1 misclassified as either 3, 4 or 5, etc.) (Table 5).

Table 5. Performance results for the 3-class soundscape quality task (soundscape qualities 2 and 4 are excluded

Measure	Random	SVC	SVC+SM	SVR	SVR+SM
MAE	0.54	0.46	0.40	0.30	**0.29**
F1	21.0%	43.8%	65.9%	64.2%	**68.3%**
Acc	46.1%	56.0%	66.4%	67.2%	**69.8%**

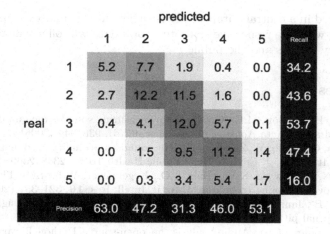

Fig. 4. Confusion matrix for the SVR + SMOTE method

4 Conclusions

In this paper we have presented ATHUS, an openly available dataset of audio recordings from urban soundscapes, annotated in terms of the respective soundscape quality. The dataset has been made publicly available (http://users.iit. demokritos.gr/~tyianak/soundscape), in the form of audio feature representations, along with a baseline audio analytics approach, implemented in Python and also openly provided at https://github.com/tyiannak/soundscape_quality, in order to demonstrate how the data can be used to automatically estimate soundscape quality. The baseline method provided with the dataset in this paper has demonstrated that, even with a baseline approach, soundscape quality can be predicted with almost 42% accuracy at an exact resolution of 5 possible gradations (where random selection achieves 22%), while "critical" errors, i.e. misclassifications with a distance between the real and the predicted soundscape quality level that are at equal or larger than 2, appear with a rate of just 10%.

The contribution of this paper lays in the fact that it is the first time such a dataset is made available, focusing on the particular task of soundscape quality estimation. This will help audio analysis researchers to evaluate their methods and build more sophisticated approaches towards the automatic assessment of soundscape quality. This will constitute a power tool in the hands of policy makers with regards to sustainable urban planning that focuses on the quality of urban landscapes and soundscapes.

The long-term vision of such an undertaking is a fully automated and crowd-sourcing pipeline for soundscape quality estimation. Such an approach will involve several users who will contribute their smartphones for both recording and automatic audio analysis. In such a way, volunteers will offer the computational power of their smartphones for a few seconds per week, and when being outdoors the quality of their surrounding soundscape would be estimated and aggregated in a central database. These aggregated soundscape quality estimates, along with the respective spatiotemporal data will offer valuable knowledge to policy makers and the public.

References

1. Berglund, B., Nilsson, M.E.: On a tool for measuring soundscape quality in urban residential areas. Acta Acust. United Acust. **92**(6), 938–944 (2006)
2. Brambilla, G., Gallo, V., Zambon, G.: The soundscape quality in some urban parks in Milan, Italy. Int. J. Environ. Res. Public Health **10**(6), 2348–2369 (2013)
3. Chawla, N.V., Bowyer, K.W., Hall, L.O., Kegelmeyer, W.P.: SMOTE: synthetic minority over-sampling technique. J. Artif. Intell. Res. **16**, 321–357 (2002)
4. Deecke, V.B., Janik, V.M.: Automated categorization of bioacoustic signals: avoiding perceptual pitfalls. J. Acoust. Soc. Am. **119**(1), 645–653 (2006)
5. Giannakopoulos, T.: pyAudioAnalysis: an open-source Python library for audio signal analysis. PloS one **10**(12), e0144610 (2015)
6. Giannakopoulos, T., Siantikos, G., Perantonis, S., Votsi, N.E., Pantis, J.: Automatic soundscape quality estimation using audio analysis. In: Proceedings of the 8th ACM International Conference on PErvasive Technologies Related to Assistive Environments, p. 19. ACM (2015)
7. McFee, B., et al.: LibROSA: audio and music signal analysis in Python. In: Proceedings of the 14th Python in Science Conference, pp. 18–25 (2015)
8. Morillas, J.B., Escobar, V.G., Vílchez-Gómez, R., Sierra, J.M., del Río, F.C.: Sound quality in urban environments and its relationship with some acoustics parameters. Acústica (2008)
9. Raimbault, M., Dubois, D.: Urban soundscapes: experiences and knowledge. Cities **22**(5), 339–350 (2005)
10. Raimbault, M., Lavandier, C., Bérengier, M.: Ambient sound assessment of urban environments: field studies in two French cities. Appl. Acoust. **64**(12), 1241–1256 (2003)
11. Thorogood, M., Pasquier, P.: Impress: a machine learning approach to soundscape affect classification for a music performance environment. In: NIME, pp. 256–260 (2013)
12. Yang, W., Kang, J.: Acoustic comfort evaluation in urban open public spaces. Appl. Acoust. **66**(2), 211–229 (2005)
13. Yu, L., Kang, J.: Modeling subjective evaluation of soundscape quality in urban open spaces: an artificial neural network approach. J. Acoust. Soc. Am. **126**(3), 1163–1174 (2009)

V3C – A Research Video Collection

Luca Rossetto[1(✉)], Heiko Schuldt[1], George Awad[2], and Asad A. Butt[2]

[1] Databases and Information Systems Research Group,
Department of Mathematics and Computer Science,
University of Basel, Basel, Switzerland
{luca.rossetto,heiko.schuldt}@unibas.ch
[2] Information Technology Laboratory, Information Access Division,
National Institute of Standards and Technology, Gaithersburg, MD, USA
{george.awad,asad.butt}@nist.gov

Abstract. With the widespread use of smartphones as recording devices
and the massive growth in bandwidth, the number and volume of video
collections has increased significantly in the last years. This poses novel
challenges to the management of these large-scale video data and especially to the analysis of and retrieval from such video collections. At the
same time, existing video datasets used for research and experimentation are either not large enough to represent current collections or do not
reflect the properties of video commonly found on the Internet in terms
of content, length, or resolution.

In this paper, we introduce the *Vimeo Creative Commons Collection*, in short V3C, a collection of 28'450 videos (with overall length
of about 3'800 h) published under creative commons license on Vimeo.
V3C comes with a shot segmentation for each video, together with the
resulting keyframes in original as well as reduced resolution and additional metadata. It is intended to be used from 2019 at the International
large-scale TREC Video Retrieval Evaluation campaign (TRECVid).

1 Introduction

Over recent years, video has become a significant portion of the overall data
which populates the web. This has been due to the fact that the production
and distribution of video has shifted from a complex and costly endeavor to
something accessible to everybody with a smart phone or similar device and a
connection to the internet. This growth of content enabled new possibilities in
various research areas which are able to make use of it. Despite the access to
such large amounts of data, there remains a need for standardized datasets for
computer vision and multimedia tasks. Multiple such datasets have been proposed over the years. A prominent example of a video dataset is the IACC [5]
which has been used for several years now for international evaluation campaigns such as TRECVid [2]. Other examples of datasets in the video context
include the YFCC100M [8] which, despite being sourced from the photo-sharing
platform Flickr[1], contains a considerable amount of video material, the Movie

---

[1] https://flickr.com/.

© Springer Nature Switzerland AG 2019
I. Kompatsiaris et al. (Eds.): MMM 2019, LNCS 11295, pp. 349–360, 2019.
https://doi.org/10.1007/978-3-030-05710-7_29

Memorability Database [4] which is comprised of memorable sequences from 100 Hollywood-quality movies or the YouTube-8M [1] dataset which in contrast, despite being sourced from YouTube[2], does not contain the original videos themselves. The content of all of these collections does, however, differ substantially from the type of web video commonly found 'in the wild' [7].

In this paper, we present the *Vimeo Creative Commons Collection* or *V3C* for short. It is composed of 28'450 videos collected from the video sharing platform Vimeo[3]. Apart from the videos themselves, the collection includes meta and shot-segmentation data for each video, together with the resulting keyframes in original as well as reduced resolution. The objective of V3C is to eventually complement or even replace existing collections in real-world video retrieval evaluation campaigns and thus to tailor the latter more to the type of video that can be found on the Internet.

The remainder of this paper is structured as follows: Sect. 2 gives an overview of the process of how the collection was assembled and Sect. 3 introduces the collection itself, its structure and some of its properties. Finally, Sect. 4 concludes.

2   Collection Process

The requirements for usable video sources from which to compile a collection were as follows:

- The platform must be freely accessible.
- It must host a large amount of diverse and contemporary video content.
- At least a portion of the content must be published under a creative commons[4] license and can therefore be redistributed in such a collection.

Two candidates for such collections are Vimeo and YouTube. Vimeo was chosen over YouTube because while YouTube offers its users the possibility to publish videos under a creative commons attribution license which would allow the reuse and redistribution of the video material, YouTube's *Terms of Service* [9] explicitly forbid the download of any video on the platform for any reason other than playback in the context of a video stream.

We utilized the Vimeo categorization system for video collection. Videos are placed in 16 broad categories, which are further divided into subcategories. Videos in each category were examined to determine if they satisfied the 'real world' requirements for the collection. Four top level categories were included in the collection, while 3 were excluded. For the remaining 9 categories, only some subcategories were included. The following are the 4 categories completely included in the collection: 'Personal', 'Documentary', 'Sports' and 'Travel'.

An overview of the excluded categories can be seen in Fig. 1. Categories that had very low visual diversity (such as 'Talks'), or did not represent real

---

[2] https://youtube.com/.
[3] https://vimeo.com/.
[4] https://creativecommons.org/.

world scenarios were removed. Categories (or subcategories) with a lot of animation/graphics, or non standard content with little or no describable activity were excluded from the collection. Videos from the selected categories were then filtered by duration and license.

The obtained list of candidate videos was downloaded from Vimeo using an open-source video download utility[5]. The download was performed sequentially in order to not cause unnecessary load on the side of the platform. All downloaded videos were subsequently checked to ensure they could be properly decoded by a commonly used video decoding utility[6].

The videos were segmented and analyzed using the open-source content-based video retrieval engine Cineast [6]. Videos with a distribution of segment lengths which were sufficiently different from the mean were flagged for manual inspection as this indicated either very low or very high visual diversity as in the cases of either mostly static frames or very noisy videos. During this step, videos were also checked to ensure that the collection does not contain exact duplicates.

Out of the remaining videos, three subsets with increasing size were randomly selected. Sequential numerical ids were assigned to the selected videos in such a way that the first id in the second part is one larger than the last id in the first part and so on, in order to facilitate situations in which multiple parts are to be used in conjunction.

3   The Vimeo Creative Commons Collection

The following provides an overview of the structure as well as various technical and semantic properties of the *Vimeo Creative Commons Collection*.

3.1   Collection Structure

The collection consists of 28'450 videos with a duration between 3 and 60 min each and a total combined duration of slightly above 3'800 h, divided into three partitions. Table 1 provides an overview of the three partitions. Similar to the IACC, the V3C also includes a *master shot reference* which segments every video into sequential non-overlapping parts, based on the visual content of the videos. For every one of these parts, a full resolution representative key-frame as well as a thumbnail image of reduced resolution is provided. Additionally, there are meta data files containing both technical as well as semantic information for every video which was also obtained from Vimeo.

Every video in the collection has been assigned a sequential numerical id. These ids are then used for all aspects of the collection. Figure 2 illustrates the directory structure which is used to organize the different aspects of the collection. This structure is identical for all three partitions. The *info* directory

---

[5] https://github.com/rg3/youtube-dl.
[6] https://ffmpeg.org/.

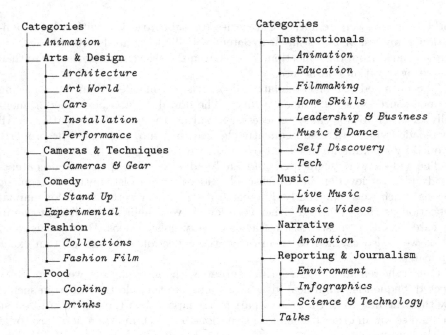

Fig. 1. Removed categories and subcategories are *emphasized*.

contains one json-file per video which holds metadata obtained from Vimeo. This metadata contains both semantic information – such as video title, description and associated tags – as well as technical information including video duration, resolution, license and upload date. The *msb* directory contains for each video a file in tab-separated format which lists the temporal start and end-positions for every automatically detected segment in a video. The *keyframes* and *thumbnails* directories each contain a subdirectory per video which hold one representative frame per video segment in a PNG format. The *keyframes* are kept in the original video resolution while the thumbnails are downscaled to a width of 200 pixels. Finally the *videos* directory contains a subdirectory per video, each of which containing the video itself as well as the video description and a file with technical information describing the download process.

Table 1. Overview of the partitions of the V3C

Partition	V3C1	V3C2	V3C3	Total
File size (videos)	1.3 TB	1.6 TB	1.8 TB	4.8 TB
File size (total)	2.4 TB	3.0 TB	3.3 TB	8.7 TB
Number of videos	7'475	9'760	11'215	28'450
Combined video duration	1'000 h, 23 min, 50 s	1'300 h, 52 min,48 s	1'500 h, 8 min, 57 s	3801 h, 25 min, 35 s
Mean video duration	8 min, 2 s	7 min, 59 s	8 min, 1 s	8 min, 1 s
Number of segments	1'082'659	1'425'454	1'635'580	4'143'693

3.2   Statistical Properties

The following presents an overview of the distribution of selected categories throughout the collection.

The age distribution of the videos of the entire collection as determined by the upload date of the individual video is illustrated in Fig. 3. It is shown in comparison to the distribution originally presented in [7] for a large sample of Vimeo in general. The trace representing the V3C is less clean than the one for the Vimeo dataset due to the large difference in number of data points. It can however still be seen that both traces have a similar overall shape, at least for the parts of the plot where there is data available for both. Other than the Vimeo dataset from [7], the collection of which was completed mid 2016, the V3C includes videos from as late as early 2018 which explains the difference in shape towards the right side of the plot.

The distribution of video duration and resolution is shown in Figs. 4 and 5 respectively, again in comparison to the larger Vimeo distributions. It can be seen that wherever there were no additional restrictions, the properties of the V3C follow those of the overall Vimeo dataset rather closely. At least in terms of these three properties, the V3C can therefore be considered reasonably representative of the type of web video generally found on Vimeo.

An overview of the languages detected by the same method as employed in [7], based on the title and description of the videos can be seen in Table 2. It shows the top-10 languages for either the V3C or the dataset from [7]. The column labeled '?' represents the instances where language detection did not yield any result. It can be seen that for the videos, the titles and descriptions of which were distinct enough for language detection, the distribution within the V3C is similar to the Vimeo dataset. No language analysis based on the audio data of the videos has been performed yet.

Table 3 shows the categories and the number of videos per collection part which have been assigned to a particular category on Vimeo. Every video can be assigned to multiple categories, the numbers shown in the table do therefore not sum to the total number of videos. Despite the categories having a structure which implies a hierarchy, a video can be assigned to both a category and sub-

Table 2. Overview of the detected languages in the video title and description of the V3C in percent

	?	en	de	fr	it	es	cy	pl	nl	pt	ko	ru
Vimeo	63.07	27.36	1.38	1.35	0.62	0.48	0.24	0.37	0.3	0.66	0.62	0.43
V3C	69.87	24.5	1.36	1.11	0.47	0.41	0.36	0.32	0.26	0.26	0	0
V3C1	68.52	25.34	1.65	1.23	0.54	0.64	0.31	0.29	0.28	0.25	0	0
V3C2	70.83	23.85	1.21	1.11	0.44	0.33	0.33	0.35	0.22	0.19	0	0
V3C3	69.94	24.63	1.3	1.04	0.45	0.33	0.41	0.32	0.29	0.26	0	0

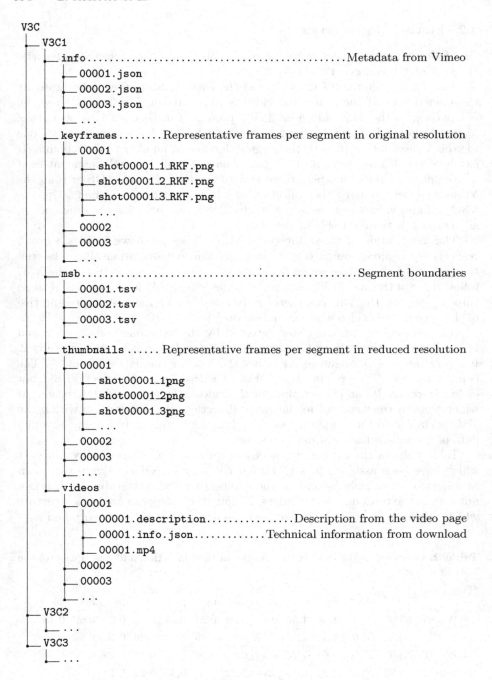

Fig. 2. Directory structure of the V3C

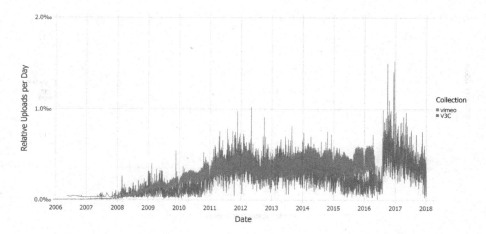

Fig. 3. Daily relative video uploads from the V3C and the Vimeo dataset

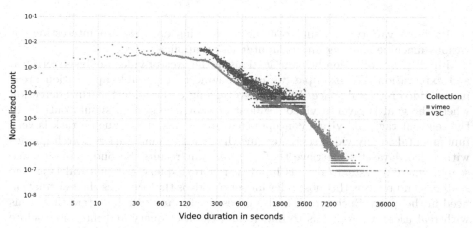

Fig. 4. Scatter plot showing the duration of videos from the V3C and the Vimeo dataset

category, but it does not have to. The large number of used categories shown in the table implies a wide range of content which can be found in the collection.

3.3 Possible Uses

Due to the large diversity of video content contained within the collection, it can be useful for video-related applications in multiple areas. The large number of different video resolutions – and to a lesser extent frame-rates – makes this dataset interesting for video transport and storage applications such as the development of novel encoding schemes, streaming mechanisms or error-correction techniques.

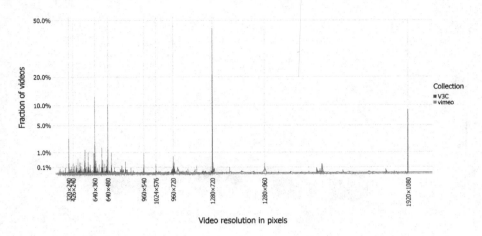

Fig. 5. Distribution of video resolutions in the V3C

Its large variety in visual content makes this dataset also interesting for various machine learning and computer vision applications.

Finally, the collection has applications in the area of video analysis, retrieval and exploration. For example, we can imagine four possible application areas in the video retrieval space. First, video tagging or high-level feature detection where the goal is given a video segment or shot, the system should output all the relevant tags and visual concepts that are in this video. Such a task is very fundamental to any video search engine that tries to match users search queries with video dataset to retrieve the most relevant results. Second, ad-hoc video search where a system takes as input a user text query as a natural language sentence and returns the most relevant set of videos that satisfies the information need in the query. Such a task is also necessary for any search system that deals with real users where it has to understand the user query and intention before retrieving the set of results that matches the text query. Third, trying to find a video or a video segment which one believes to have seen but the name of which one does not recall is often called "known item search". Queries are created based on some knowledge of the collection such that there is a high probability that there is only one video or video segment that satisfies the search. Fourth, the application of video captioning or description in recent years gained a lot of attention. Here the idea is how can a system describe a video segment in a textual form that contains all the important facets such as 'who', 'what', 'where', 'when' so essentially textual summary of the video. As the V3C collection includes a master shot boundary splitting a whole video into smaller shots, the video captioning task can be run on those small video shots as currently the state of the art can not handle longer videos and give a logical and human readable description for the whole video in textual form.

Table 3. Category assignment per video and collection part

Vimeo category	Number of videos		
	V3C1	V3C2	V3C3
/categories/art	660	891	1'010
/categories/art/homesandliving/videos	11	11	13
/categories/art/personaltechdesign/videos	15	17	14
/categories/cameratechniques	513	703	749
/categories/cameratechniques/drones/videos	156	191	204
/categories/cameratechniques/macroandslomo/videos	12	18	14
/categories/cameratechniques/timelapse/videos	161	252	281
/categories/comedy	252	315	388
/categories/comedy/comicnarrative/videos	74	69	86
/categories/documentary	1'396	1'787	2'086
/categories/documentary/artsandcraft/videos	54	82	99
/categories/documentary/cultureandtech/videos	78	124	117
/categories/documentary/nature/videos	155	191	191
/categories/documentary/people/videos	206	272	342
/categories/documentary/sportsdocumentary/videos	17	32	34
/categories/fashion	166	226	255
/categories/fashion/fashionprofiles/videos	8	5	12
/categories/food	87	131	145
/categories/food/profiles/videos	15	26	24
/categories/hd/canon/videos	894	1'122	1'328
/categories/hd/dslr/videos	438	528	660
/categories/hd/pockethd/videos	2	4	4
/categories/hd/red/videos	16	27	25
/categories/hd/slowmotion/videos	23	36	45
/categories/instructionals	283	389	402
/categories/instructionals/healthandfitness/videos	38	52	61
/categories/instructionals/martialarts/videos	8	11	20
/categories/instructionals/outdoorskills/videos	4	6	6
/categories/journalism	991	1'209	1'544
/categories/journalism/nonprofit/videos	67	80	116
/categories/journalism/politics/videos	131	155	182
/categories/journalism/startups/videos	8	12	18
/categories/journalism/videojournalism/videos	182	226	305
/categories/music	1'066	1'347	1'568
/categories/music/musicdocumentary/videos	50	52	77
/categories/narrative	2'114	2'614	3'014
/categories/narrative/comedicfilm/videos	66	90	111

(*continued*)

Table 3. (*continued*)

Vimeo category	Number of videos		
	V3C1	V3C2	V3C3
/categories/narrative/drama/videos	60	73	95
/categories/narrative/horror/videos	30	38	34
/categories/narrative/lyrical/videos	2	11	12
/categories/narrative/musical/videos	3	3	7
/categories/narrative/romance/videos	22	34	25
/categories/narrative/scifi/videos	19	14	17
/categories/nature-toplevel-modonly	0	0	1
/categories/personal	916	1'200	1'378
/categories/personal/cameo/videos	6	8	5
/categories/personal/stories/videos	158	221	246
/categories/productsandequipment/cameras/videos	13	25	27
/categories/productsandequipment/editingproducts/videos	49	74	86
/categories/productsandequipment/lighting/videos	12	13	25
/categories/productsandequipment/producttutorials/videos	13	9	10
/categories/sports	1'487	2'036	2'213
/categories/sports/bikes/videos	152	211	196
/categories/sports/everythingelse/videos	39	43	52
/categories/sports/outdoorsports/videos	392	522	604
/categories/sports/skate/videos	147	227	207
/categories/sports/sky/videos	84	132	172
/categories/sports/snow/videos	75	96	117
/categories/sports/surf/videos	76	104	110
/categories/technology	0	0	1
/categories/technology/installations/videos	3	8	9
/categories/technology/personaltech/videos	5	2	6
/categories/technology/software/videos	2	9	12
/categories/technology/techdocs/videos	16	21	18
/categories/travel	1'893	2'450	2'803
/categories/travel/africa/videos	22	15	24
/categories/travel/antarctica/videos	1	2	4
/categories/travel/asia/videos	55	82	73
/categories/travel/australasia/videos	7	12	10
/categories/travel/europe/videos	94	124	120
/categories/travel/northamerica/videos	44	53	56
/categories/travel/southamerica/videos	13	21	15
/categories/travel/space/videos	5	6	10
/categories/videoschool	1	0	0

3.4   Availability

We are planning to launch and make available this collection at the 2019 TRECVid video retrieval benchmark where different research groups participate in one or more tracks. In addition, the collection will be shared at the Interactive Video Browser Showdown (VBS) [3] which collaborates with TRECVid organizing the Video Ad-hoc Search track. The collection will be available to the benchmark participants as well as the public for download. After the annual benchmark cycle is concluded, we will also provide the ground truth judgments and queries/topics for the tasks that used the V3C collection so that research groups can reuse the dataset in their local experiments and reproduce results.

4   Conclusions

In this paper, we introduced the Vimeo Creative Commons Collection (V3C). It is comprised of roughly 3'800 h of creative commons video obtained from the web video platform Vimeo and is augmented with technical and semantic metadata as well as shot boundary information and accompanying keyframes. V3C is subdivided into three partitions with increasing length from roughly 1'000 h up to 1'500 h so that the collection can be used for at least three consecutive years in a video search benchmark with increasing complexity. Information on where to download the V3C collection and/or its partitions will be made available together with the publication of the video search benchmark challenges.

Acknowledgements. This work was partly supported by the Swiss National Science Foundation, project IMOTION (20CH21_151571).

Disclaimer: Certain commercial entities, equipment, or materials may be identified in this document in order to describe an experimental procedure or concept adequately. Such identification is not intended to imply recommendation or endorsement by the National Institute of Standards and Technology, nor is it intended to imply that the entities, materials, or equipment are necessarily the best available for the purpose.

References

1. Abu-El-Haija, S., et al.: Youtube-8m: a large-scale video classification benchmark. arXiv preprint arXiv:1609.08675 (2016)
2. Awad, G., et al.: Trecvid 2017: evaluating ad-hoc and instance video search, events detection, video captioning and hyperlinking. In: Proceedings of TRECVID 2017. NIST, USA (2017)
3. Cobârzan, C., et al.: Interactive video search tools: a detailed analysis of the video browser showdown 2015. Multimed. Tools Appl. **76**(4), 5539–5571 (2017)
4. Cohendet, R., Yadati, K., Duong, N.Q.K., Demarty, C.-H.: Annotating, understanding, and predicting long-term video memorability. In: Proceedings of the 2018 ACM on International Conference on Multimedia Retrieval, pp. 178–186. ACM (2018)
5. Over, P., Awad, G., Smeaton, A.F., Foley, C., Lanagan, J.: Creating a web-scale video collection for research. In: Proceedings of the 1st Workshop on Web-Scale Multimedia Corpus, pp. 25–32. ACM (2009)

6. Rossetto, L., Giangreco, I., Schuldt, H.: Cineast: a multi-feature sketch-based video retrieval engine. In: 2014 IEEE International Symposium on Multimedia (ISM), pp. 18–23. IEEE (2014)
7. Rossetto, L., Schuldt, H.: Web video in numbers - an analysis of web-video metadata. arXiv preprint arXiv:1707.01340 (2017)
8. Thomee, B., et al.: YFCC100M: the new data in multimedia research. Commun. ACM **59**(2), 64–73 (2016)
9. YouTube Terms of Service. https://www.youtube.com/static?template=terms (2018). Accessed 15 June 2018

Image Aesthetics Assessment Using Fully Convolutional Neural Networks

Konstantinos Apostolidis and Vasileios Mezaris[(✉)]

Information Technologies Institute/CERTH, 6th km Charilaou - Thermi Road,
Thermi, Thessaloniki, Greece
{kapost,bmezaris}@iti.gr

Abstract. This paper presents a new method for assessing the aesthetic quality of images. Based on the findings of previous works on this topic, we propose a method that addresses the shortcomings of existing ones, by: (a) Making possible to feed higher-resolution images in the network, by introducing a fully convolutional neural network as the classifier. (b) Maintaining the original aspect ratio of images in the input of the network, to avoid distortions caused by re-scaling. And (c) combining local and global features from the image for making the assessment of its aesthetic quality. The proposed method is shown to achieve state of the art results on a standard large-scale benchmark dataset.

Keywords: Image aesthetics · Deep learning
Fully convolutional neural networks

1 Introduction

Aesthetic quality assessment is an established task in the field of image processing and aims at computationally distinguishing high aesthetic quality photos from low aesthetic quality ones. Aesthetic quality assessment solutions can contribute to applications and tasks such as image re-ranking [31,35], search and retrieval of photos [27] and videos [14], image enhancement methods [1,9] and image collection summarization and preservation [26,31]. The automatic prediction of a photo's aesthetic value is a challenging problem because, among others, humans often assess the aesthetic quality based on their subjective criteria; thus, it is difficult to define a clear and subjective set of rules for automating this assessment.

In this paper, we present an automatic aesthetic assessment method based on a fully convolutional neural network that utilizes skip connections and a setup for minimizing the sizing distortions of the input image. The rest of the paper is organized as follows: in Sect. 2 we review the related work. In Sect. 3 we present the proposed method in detail. This is followed by reporting the experimental setup, results and comparisons in Sect. 4, and finally we draw conclusions and provide a brief future outlook in Sect. 5.

© Springer Nature Switzerland AG 2019
I. Kompatsiaris et al. (Eds.): MMM 2019, LNCS 11295, pp. 361–373, 2019.
https://doi.org/10.1007/978-3-030-05710-7_30

2 Related Work

The early attempts on image aesthetic quality assessment used handcrafted features, such as the methods of [24] and [22]. Both of these methods base their features on photographic rules that usually apply in aesthetically appealing photos. The method of [17] also uses handcrafted features but with a focus on efficiency.

Due to the success of deep convolutional neural networks (DCNN) on image classification [30,32] and transfer learning [5], more recent attempts are based on the use of DCNNs. To our knowledge, the first of such methods is [19]. In [19] a deep learning system is introduced (RAPID - RAting PIctorial aesthetics using Deep learning) that aims to incorporate heterogeneous inputs generated from the image, which include a global view and local views. The global view is represented by a normalized-to-square-size input, while local views are represented by small randomly-cropped square parts of the original high-resolution image. Additionally, the method of [19] utilizes certain style attributes of images (e.g. "color harmony", "good lighting", "object emphasis", "vivid color", etc.) to help improve the aesthetic quality categorization accuracy; however, generating these attribute annotations may result in high inference times. In a later work [20], the same authors employ the style and semantic attributes of images to further boost the aesthetic categorization performance. [21] claims that the constraint of the neural networks to take a fixed- and squared-size image as input (i.e. images need to be transformed via cropping, scaling, or padding) compromises the assessment of the aesthetic quality of the original images. To alleviate this, [21] presents a composition-preserving deep convolutional network method that directly learns aesthetic features from the original input images without any image transformations.

In [12] its authors argue that the two classes of high and low aesthetic qualities contain large intra-class differences, and propose a model to jointly learn meaningful photographic attributes and image content information that can help regularize the complicated photo aesthetic rating problem. To train their model, they assemble a new aesthetics and attributes database (AADB).

In [2] its authors investigate the use of a DCNN to predict image aesthetics by fine-tuning a canonical CNN architecture, originally trained to classify objects and scenes, casting the image aesthetic quality prediction as a regression problem. They also investigate whether image aesthetic quality is a global or local attribute, and the role played by bottom-up and top-down salient regions to the prediction of the global image aesthetics. In [11], its authors aiming once again to take both local and global features of images into consideration, propose a DCNN architecture named ILGNet, which combines both the Inception modules and a connected layer of both local and global features. The network contains one pre-treatment layer and three inception modules. Two intermediate layers of local features are connected to a layer of global features, resulting in a 1024-dimension layer. Finally, in [7], a complex framework for aesthetic quality assessment is introduced. Specifically, the authors design several rule-based aesthetic features, and also use content-based features extracted with the help of a DCNN. They claim that these two type of features are complementary to each other, and combine them using a Multi Kernel Learning method. To our knowledge, this method achieves the state of the art results on the popular AVA2 dataset.

Finally, we should note that there are several works that deal with the relation between users' preferences and the assessment of the aesthetic quality of photos, such as [3, 4, 29, 34]. However, this is out of the scope of our present work, since we are addressing the problem of user-independent prediction of image aesthetic quality similarly to [2, 7, 11, 12, 21, 24, 33] and many other works.

From the review of the related work, it can be easily asserted that after the introduction of DCNNs for aesthetic quality assessment the main effort has focused on two directions: (a) minimizing the sizing distortions of the input image; (b) combining local and global features to facilitate the aesthetics assessment. Inspired by there, we set three objectives: (a) using a fully convolutional neural network, to experiment with feeding higher-resolution images to the network (this is done in a way that weights can be copied from a pre-trained model, without needing to re-train the network from scratch); (b) introducing an approach for maintaining the aspect ratio of the input image; (c) introducing a skip connection in our network to combine the output from early layers to that of the later layers, thus introducing information from local features to the final decision of the network.

3   Proposed Method

A fully connected (FC) layer has nodes connected to all activations in the previous layer, hence, requires a fixed size of input data. It is worth noting that the only difference between an FC layer and a convolutional layer is that the neurons in the convolutional layer are connected only to a local region in the input. However, the neurons in both layers still compute dot products, so their functional form is identical.

Therefore, our first step is to convert the network to a fully convolutional network (FCN). To do so we must change the FC layers to convolutional layers (see Fig. 1a and b). For the purpose of this paper we use the VGG16 architecture [30] for simplicity - yet our method can be applied to any DCNN architecture with little modification. This architecture has three FC layers at the end of the network. We can convert each of these three FC layers to convolutional layers as follows:

- Replace the first FC layer that requires a $7 \times 7 \times 512$ tensor with a convolutional layer that uses filter size equal to 7, giving an output tensor of $1 \times 1 \times 4096$ dimension.
- Replace the second FC layer with a CONV layer that uses filter size equal to 1, giving an output tensor of $1 \times 1 \times 4096$ dimension;
- Replace the last FC layer similarly, with filter size equal to 1, giving the final output tensor of $1 \times 1 \times 2$ dimension since we want to fine-tune the network for the two-class aesthetic quality assessment problem.

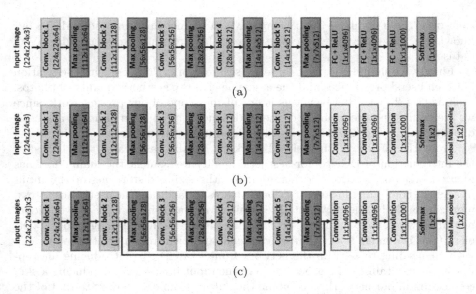

Fig. 1. Network models used in this work: (a) the original VGG16 network, trained for 1000 ImageNet classes, (b) the fully convolutional version of VGG16, for 2 classes (high aesthetic quality, low aesthetic quality), (c) the proposed fully convolutional VGG16, with an added skip connection (after the second convolutional block to the decision convolutional layers) and accepting a triplet of image croppings as input. In all the above model illustrations the following color-coding is used: yellow for convolutional layers, dark yellow for blocks of convolutional layers, green for fully connected layers, orange for softmax operations, blue for max pooling operations, light blue for global max pooling operations. (Color figure online)

This conversion allows us to "slide" the original convolutional network very efficiently across many spatial positions in a larger image, in a single forward pass, an advantage which is known in the literature; FCNs were first used in [23] to classify series of handwritten digits and more recently for semantic segmentation [18]. Additionally, each of these conversions could in practice involve manipulating (i.e. reshaping) the weight matrix in each FC layer into the weights of the convolutional layer filters. Therefore, we can easily copy the weights of a pre-trained VGG16 on ImageNet [13]. This in turn, allows for faster training times and does not require a large collection of training images, since the network is not trained from scratch.

One thing to note here is that since we "slide" the convolutional network in the image, the FCN produces many decisions, one for each spatial region analyzed. Therefore, to come up with a single decision and to be able to re-train the network we add on top of the FCN a global pooling operation layer for spatial data. This can be either a global max pooling layer or a global average pooling layer. In the experiments conducted in Sect. 4, we test both approaches.

Regarding our objective to maintain the original aspect ratio, there are various known approaches: (a) cropping the center part of the image (and discarding the cropped parts), (b) padding the image (adding blank borders) to make it of square size, (c) feeding the image in an FCN at its original size, (d) feeding multiple croppings of the image to ensure that the whole surface is scanned by the network (even though overlapping of the scanned regions may occur). The third of the above approaches can only be achieved if an FCN is utilized. In the case of the second option (padding) some literature works argue that introducing blank parts in the input image can greatly deteriorate the performance of the network. Thus, we examine one more variation in which the input image is fed as a padded and masked square image. To achieve this, we input to the network a binary mask (containing ones for the areas that exist in the original image and zeros for the added black areas). An element-wise multiplication takes place before the decision layers (namely, the convolutional layers that replaced the FC layers of the original model) to zero the filters output in the blank areas of the image. Another approach, in the spirit of performing multiple croppings (but not previously used for aesthetics assessment), is proposed in the present work. As shown in Fig. 2, three overlapping croppings of each input image are jointly fed into the network. All of the aforementioned approaches are evaluated in Sect. 4.

The notion of introducing skip connections in a neural network is known in the literature (in different application domains, such as biomedical image segmentation [8]). We should note here that this is different to connecting multiple layers in a network as in [16], or the way used in the Dense architecture of neural networks [10]: skip connections aim to combine the output from a single early layer with the decision made in the last layers. However, the choice of which early layer's output to use is not an easy one; the results of extensive experiments regarding the effect of using skip connections in DCNNs on classifying images in [15] show that this choice heavily depends on the specific application domain. Tests were reported in [15] on seven datasets of different nature (classification of gender, texture, recognition of digits and objects). Since the aesthetic quality assessment problem is probably more closely related to texture classification (compared to the other application domains examined in [15]) and based upon the observation reported in [15], we choose to introduce a skip connection from immediately after the second convolution block to the layer prior to decision layers (i.e. the convolutional layers that replaced the FC layers of the original model, see Fig. 1c).

4   Experimental Results

4.1   Dataset

The Aesthetic Visual Analysis (AVA) dataset [25] is a list of image ids from DPChallenge.com, which is a on-line photography social network. There are in total 255529 photos, each of which is rated by a large number of persons. The range of the scores used for the rating is 1–10. We choose to use the AVA dataset since it is the largest in the domain of aesthetic quality assessment. Two, widely

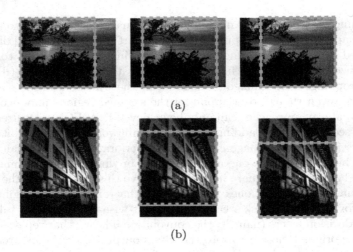

Fig. 2. Illustration of the proposed three croppings with respect to the original image (a) for images in landscape mode, (b) for images in portrait mode.

used, ways of splitting the AVA dataset into training and test portions are found in the literature:

- AVA1: The score of 5 is chosen as the threshold to distinguish the AVA images to high and low aesthetic quality. This way 74673 images are labeled as of high aesthetic quality and 180856 are labeled as of low aesthetic quality. The dataset is randomly split into the training set (totaling 234599 images) and testing set (19930 images) [12,25,33,34].
- AVA2: The images in the AVA dataset are sorted according to their mean aesthetic quality score. The top 10% images are labeled as of good aesthetic quality and the bottom 10% are labeled as of bad aesthetic quality. This way 51106 images are used from the dataset. These images are randomly divided into 2 equally-sized sets, which are the training and testing sets, respectively [6,7,12,14,24,25,33].

Similarly to most of the recent literature works, we choose to use the AVA2 dataset in the experiments conducted in the sequel, since the way that it is constructed ensures the reliability of the ground-truth aesthetic quality annotations.

4.2 Experimental Setup

As already mentioned we base our proposed FCN on the VGG16 [30] architecture for the sake of simplicity, yet our method can be applied to any DCNN architecture with limited modifications. For implementation, we used the Keras neural network API[1]. Our experimental setup regarding the tests conducted in

---

[1] https://keras.io/.

this section is as follows: we set the starting learning rate to 0.01; and used a callback function of Keras to reduce the learning rate if the validation accuracy is not increased for three consecutive epochs. The batch size was fixed to 8, unless noted otherwise. We set the number of training epochs to 40. The results reported here are the achieved accuracy by using the model after the 40th epoch. The code for converting VGG16 (as well as numerous other architectures) to an FCN, the implementation of skip connections and the methods tested for maintaining the original aspect ratio are made publicly available online[2]. All experiments were conducted on a PC with an i7-4770K CPU, 16 GB of RAM and a Nvidia GTX 1080 Ti GPU.

4.3   Results

We first conducted some preliminary experiments in order to test: (a) the relation of input image size to the accuracy. The performance of all tested setups was evaluated both in terms of detection accuracy and the time-efficiency (measuring the average inference time for a single image). Table 1 reports the results of each compared approach. The first column of this table cites the name of the used network. The second column reports the input image size. We performed experiments by resizing the AVA2 images to: (a) the size that the VGG16 model was originally trained for (224×224), (b) 1.5× this original VGG16 size, (c) 2× the original VGG16 size and (d) 3× the original VGG16 size, resulting to testing images finally resized to size 224×224, 336×336, 448×448 and 672×672 pixels, respectively. We also performed experiments where we fed the input image resizing its height to 336 pixels and accordingly adjusting its width in order to maintain its original aspect ratio (denoted as "$336 \times$ A.W" in the last four rows of Table 1). In the third column, we report the batch size used during the training phase. As already mentioned this was fixed to the value of 8 except for the experiments in the last four rows of Table 1, since in these specific setups images of different sizes cannot be fed into the network in a single batch. The fourth column reports whether we freeze any layers (i.e. not updating the weights of these layers) or not. The fifth column reports the type of global pooling applied at the end of the network (only when using the proposed FCN; not applicable when using the original VGG16). Finally in the last two columns we report the average inference time and the accuracy achieved in the AVA2 dataset. Examining Table 1, we observe that increasing the input image size does not necessarily improve the results. Specifically, increasing the input size from 224×224 to 336×336 achieved better accuracy in all cases. However, further increasing the input size from 336×336 to 448×448 or 672×672 consistently led to slight reduction of the performance of the network. In the cases where we adjusted the images' height to the fixed value of 336 pixels while maintaining the original aspect ratio, the network yielded very poor performance, mainly due to using a batch size equal to 1. Additionally, with respect to the time-efficiency, we

---

[2] Implementation of fully convolutional networks in Keras is available at https://github.com/bmezaris/fully_convolutional_networks.

observe that increasing the image size quadratically increases the inference time for a single image. The average inference time of 790 ms for the 672 × 672 size of input image is possibly prohibitively high for real-world applications, which is an additional reason to not use such large input sizes.

Table 1. Results of preliminary tests.

Setup used	Input size (h. × w.)	Batch size	Freeze	Global pooling	Infer time (avg ± dev.) (ms)	AVA2 accuracy (%)
VGG16	224 × 224	8	Yes	N/A	110 ± 5	84.03
VGG16	224 × 224	8	No	N/A	110 ± 5	85.04
FCN	224 × 224	8	Yes	Max	120 ± 5	84.57
FCN	224 × 224	8	Yes	Average	120 ± 5	84.96
FCN	224 × 224	8	No	Max	120 ± 5	86.20
FCN	224 × 224	8	No	Average	120 ± 5	85.06
FCN	336 × 336	8	Yes	Max	160 ± 5	88.35
FCN	336 × 336	8	Yes	Average	160 ± 5	88.26
FCN	336 × 336	8	No	Max	160 ± 5	**88.44**
FCN	336 × 336	8	No	Average	160 ± 5	88.21
FCN	448 × 448	8	Yes	Max	480 ± 5	87.65
FCN	448 × 448	8	Yes	Average	480 ± 5	87.35
FCN	448 × 448	8	No	Max	480 ± 5	88.01
FCN	448 × 448	8	No	Average	480 ± 5	86.91
FCN	672 × 672	8	Yes	Max	790 ± 5	86.03
FCN	672 × 672	8	Yes	Average	790 ± 5	85.66
FCN	672 × 672	8	No	Max	790 ± 5	87.52
FCN	672 × 672	8	No	Average	790 ± 5	87.07
FCN	336 × A.W.	1	Yes	Max	280 ± 100	66.02
FCN	336 × A.W.	1	Yes	Average	280 ± 100	61.28
FCN	336 × A.W.	1	No	Max	280 ± 100	73.02
FCN	336 × A.W.	1	No	Average	280 ± 100	71.17

Regarding the freezing of layers during the fine-tuning process we tested two approaches: (a) freezing the first layers up to the end of the second convolutional block of VGG16 (denoted as "Yes" in the fourth column of Table 1), and (b) not freezing any layer (denoted as "No" in the fourth column of Table 1). It is known in the literature [28] that the weights of the first network layers can remain frozen, i.e., they are copied from the pre-trained DCNN and kept unchanged, since these learn low-level image characteristics which are useful for most types of image classification. However, as can be asserted from Table 1, not freezing any layer consistently gives better accuracy. This can be explained from the fact that the problem of aesthetic quality assessment is quite different from image classification in ImageNet. Thus, it is better to let the network adjust the weights of all its layers.

Concerning the type of global pooling applied at the end of the network, we notice that using global max pooling in most cases yields better results. Therefore, for the next set of experiments: (a) we use the global max pooling operation as the last layer in the network, (b) we do not freeze any layer during the fine-tuning process, and (c) we input images of size 336×336 to the network.

Table 2. Results of tests regarding methods preserving the aspect ratio of the original images.

Setup used	Infer time (avg $\pm$ dev.) (ms)	AVA2 accuracy (%)
FCN	160 $\pm$ 5	88.44
FCN + padding	110 $\pm$ 5	86.08
FCN + cropping	110 $\pm$ 5	86.53
FCN + masking	120 $\pm$ 5	87.61
FCN + 3× croppings	150 $\pm$ 5	**89.94**

We proceed to conduct experiments to test different approaches for maintaining the original aspect ratio on the best performing setup of Table 1. The results are reported in Table 2 and the result of the best performing setup of Table 1 is copied in the first row of the new table. We notice that the first three approaches reported in Table 2 ("FCN + padding", "FCN + cropping", "FCN + masking") lead to lower the accuracy, compared to not maintaining the original aspect ratio (i.e. resizing images to 336×336 pixels). Contrary to this, the proposed last approach of Table 2 that uses three croppings of the original image to include all the surface of the image in the network exhibits increased accuracy, reaching 89.94%.

Table 3. Results of tests regarding the effect of adding a skip connection to the network.

Setup used	Infer time (avg $\pm$ dev.) (ms)	AVA2 accuracy (%)
FCN + masking	120 $\pm$ 5	87.61
FCN + 3× croppings	150 $\pm$ 5	89.74
FCN + masking + skip connection	120 $\pm$ 5	83.40
FCN + 3× croppings + skip connection	150 $\pm$ 5	**91.01**

Then we test the effect of adding a skip connection to the best performing setup of Table 2. The new results are reported in Table 3 and the results of the "FCN + masking" and "FCN + 3× croppings" setups from Table 2 are copied in the first two rows of the new table. We observe that introducing a skip connection improves the achieved accuracy in the case of "FCN + 3× croppings" setup. On the other hand, introducing the skip connection on the "masking" setup considerably reduces the accuracy, since the values of the filters that where excluded using the mask are re-introduced in the decision layer.

Finally, the "FCN + 3× croppings + skip connection", which is the method proposed in this work, is shown in Table 2 to achieve state of the art results, outperforming [7,11,24,33] that report accuracy scores of up to 90.76% on the AVA2 dataset. This is achieved even though the VGG16 architecture, that our network is based on, is not the most powerful deep network architecture, as documented by the literature on object/image annotation and other similar problems (Table 4).

Table 4. Comparison of the proposed method to methods of the literature.

Method	AVA2 accuracy (%)
Handcrafted features [24]	77.08
MSDLM [33]	84.88
ILGNet [11]	85.62
MKL_3 [7]	90.76
Proposed (FCN + 3× croppings + skip connection)	**91.01**

5   Conclusions

In this paper we presented a method for assessing the aesthetic quality of images. Drawing inspiration from the related literature we converted a deep convolutional neural network to a fully convolutional network, in order to be able to feed images of arbitrary size to the network. A variety of conducted experiments provided useful insight regarding the tuning of parameters of our proposed network. Additionally, we proposed an approach for maintaining the original aspect ratio of the input images. Finally, we introduced a skip connection in the network, to combine local and global information of the input image in the aesthetic quality assessment decision. Combining all the proposed techniques we achieve state of the art results as can be ascertained by our experiments and comparisons. In the future, we plan to examine the impact of these proposed techniques on different network architectures.

Acknowledgments. This work was supported by the EU's Horizon 2020 research and innovation programme under contracts H2020-687786 InVID and H2020-732665 EMMA.

References

1. Bhattacharya, S., Sukthankar, R., Shah, M.: A framework for photo-quality assessment and enhancement based on visual aesthetics. In: Proceedings of 18th ACM International Conference on Multimedia (MM), pp. 271–280. ACM (2010)
2. Bianco, S., Celona, L., Napoletano, P., Schettini, R.: Predicting image aesthetics with deep learning. In: Blanc-Talon, J., Distante, C., Philips, W., Popescu, D., Scheunders, P. (eds.) ACIVS 2016. LNCS, vol. 10016, pp. 117–125. Springer, Cham (2016). https://doi.org/10.1007/978-3-319-48680-2_11
3. Cui, C., Fang, H., Deng, X., Nie, X., Dai, H., Yin, Y.: Distribution-oriented aesthetics assessment for image search. In: Proceedings of 40th International SIGIR Conference on Research and Development in Information Retrieval, pp. 1013–1016. ACM (2017)
4. Deng, X., Cui, C., Fang, H., Nie, X., Yin, Y.: Personalized image aesthetics assessment. In: Proceedings of Conference on Information and Knowledge Management, pp. 2043–2046. ACM (2017)
5. Donahue, J., et al.: DeCAF: a deep convolutional activation feature for generic visual recognition. In: Proceedings of International Conference on Machine Learning (ICML), pp. 647–655 (2014)
6. Dong, Z., Shen, X., Li, H., Tian, X.: Photo quality assessment with DCNN that understands image well. In: He, X., Luo, S., Tao, D., Xu, C., Yang, J., Hasan, M.A. (eds.) MMM 2015. LNCS, vol. 8936, pp. 524–535. Springer, Cham (2015). https://doi.org/10.1007/978-3-319-14442-9_57
7. Dong, Z., Tian, X.: Multi-level photo quality assessment with multi-view features. Neurocomputing **168**, 308–319 (2015)
8. Drozdzal, M., Vorontsov, E., Chartrand, G., Kadoury, S., Pal, C.: The importance of skip connections in biomedical image segmentation. In: Carneiro, G., et al. (eds.) LABELS/DLMIA -2016. LNCS, vol. 10008, pp. 179–187. Springer, Cham (2016). https://doi.org/10.1007/978-3-319-46976-8_19
9. Guo, Y., Liu, M., Gu, T., Wang, W.: Improving photo composition elegantly: considering image similarity during composition optimization. In: Computer Graphics Forum, vol. 31, pp. 2193–2202. Wiley Online Library (2012)
10. Huang, G., Liu, Z., Van Der Maaten, L., Weinberger, K.Q.: Densely connected convolutional networks. In: Proceedings of Conference on Computer Vision and Pattern Recognition (CVPR), vol. 1, p. 3 (2017)
11. Jin, X., Chi, J., Peng, S., Tian, Y., Ye, C., Li, X.: Deep image aesthetics classification using inception modules and fine-tuning connected layer. In: Proceedings of IEEE 8th International Conference on Wireless Communications & Signal Processing (WCSP), pp. 1–6. IEEE (2016)
12. Kong, S., Shen, X., Lin, Z., Mech, R., Fowlkes, C.: Photo aesthetics ranking network with attributes and content adaptation. In: Leibe, B., Matas, J., Sebe, N., Welling, M. (eds.) ECCV 2016. LNCS, vol. 9905, pp. 662–679. Springer, Cham (2016). https://doi.org/10.1007/978-3-319-46448-0_40
13. Krizhevsky, A., Ilya, S., Hinton, G.: ImageNet classification with deep convolutional neural networks. In: Proceedings of Conference on Advances in Neural Information Processing Systems (NIPS), pp. 1097–1105. Curran Associates, Inc. (2012)
14. Lemarchand, F.: From computational aesthetic prediction for images to films and online videos. Avant **8**, 69–78 (2017)
15. Li, Y., Zhang, T., Liu, Z., Hu, H.: A concatenating framework of shortcut convolutional neural networks. arXiv preprint arXiv:1710.00974 (2017)

16. Liang, M., Hu, X., Zhang, B.: Convolutional neural networks with intra-layer recurrent connections for scene labeling. In: Proceedings of Conference on Advances in Neural Information Processing Systems (NIPS), Red Hook, NY Curran, pp. 937–945 (2015)

17. Lo, K.Y., Liu, K.H., Chen, C.S.: Assessment of photo aesthetics with efficiency. In: Proceedings of 21st International Conference on Pattern Recognition (ICPR), pp. 2186–2189. IEEE (2012)

18. Long, J., Shelhamer, E., Darrell, T.: Fully convolutional networks for semantic segmentation. In: Proceedings of Conference on Computer Vision and Pattern Recognition (CVPR), pp. 3431–3440. IEEE (2015)

19. Lu, X., Lin, Z., Jin, H., Yang, J., Wang, J.Z.: Rapid: rating pictorial aesthetics using deep learning. In: Proceedings of 22nd ACM Internatioanl Conference on Multimedia (MM), pp. 457–466. ACM (2014)

20. Lu, X., Lin, Z., Jin, H., Yang, J., Wang, J.Z.: Rating image aesthetics using deep learning. IEEE Trans. Multimedia **17**(11), 2021–2034 (2015)

21. Mai, L., Jin, H., Liu, F.: Composition-preserving deep photo aesthetics assessment. In: Proceedings of Conference on Computer Vision and Pattern Recognition (CVPR), pp. 497–506. IEEE (2016)

22. Marchesotti, L., Perronnin, F., Larlus, D., Csurka, G.: Assessing the aesthetic quality of photographs using generic image descriptors. In: Proceedings of IEEE International Conference on Computer Vision (ICCV), pp. 1784–1791. IEEE (2011)

23. Matan, O., Burges, C.J., LeCun, Y., Denker, J.S.: Multi-digit recognition using a space displacement neural network. In: Proceedings of Conference on Advances in Neural Information Processing Systems (NIPS), pp. 488–495 (1992)

24. Mavridaki, E., Mezaris, V.: A comprehensive aesthetic quality assessment method for natural images using basic rules of photography. In: Proceedings of IEEE International Conference on Image Processing (ICIP), pp. 887–891. IEEE (2015)

25. Murray, N., Marchesotti, L., Perronnin, F.: AVA: a large-scale database for aesthetic visual analysis. In: Proceedings of Conference on Computer Vision and Pattern Recognition (CVPR), pp. 2408–2415. IEEE (2012)

26. Nejdl, W., Niederee, C.: Photos to remember, photos to forget. IEEE Trans. MultiMedia (TMM) **22**(1), 6–11 (2015)

27. Obrador, P., Anguera, X., de Oliveira, R., Oliver, N.: The role of tags and image aesthetics in social image search. In: Proceedings of 1st SIGMM Workshop on Social Media, pp. 65–72. ACM (2009)

28. Pittaras, N., Markatopoulou, F., Mezaris, V., Patras, I.: Comparison of fine-tuning and extension strategies for deep convolutional neural networks. In: Amsaleg, L., Guðmundsson, G.Þ., Gurrin, C., Jónsson, B.Þ., Satoh, S. (eds.) MMM 2017. LNCS, vol. 10132, pp. 102–114. Springer, Cham (2017). https://doi.org/10.1007/978-3-319-51811-4_9

29. Ren, J., Shen, X., Lin, Z.L., Mech, R., Foran, D.J.: Personalized image aesthetics. In: Proceedings of IEEE International Conference on Computer Vision (ICCV), pp. 638–647. IEEE (2017)

30. Simonyan, K., Zisserman, A.: Very deep convolutional networks for large-scale image recognition. In: Proceedings of International Conference on Learning Representations (ICLR) (2015)

31. Su, H.H., Chen, T.W., Kao, C.C., Hsu, W.H., Chien, S.Y.: Preference-aware view recommendation system for scenic photos based on bag-of-aesthetics-preserving features. IEEE Trans. Multimedia (TMM) **14**(3), 833–843 (2012)

32. Szegedy, C., et al.: Going deeper with convolutions. In: Proceedings of Conference on Computer Vision and Pattern Recognition (CVPR), pp. 1–9. IEEE (2015)

33. Wang, W., Zhao, M., Wang, L., Huang, J., Cai, C., Xu, X.: A multi-scene deep learning model for image aesthetic evaluation. Sig. Process. Image Commun. **47**, 511–518 (2016)
34. Wang, Z., Liu, D., Chang, S., Dolcos, F., Beck, D., Huang, T.: Image aesthetics assessment using deep Chatterjee's machine. In: Proceedings of IEEE International Joint Conference on Neural Networks (IJCNN), pp. 941–948. IEEE (2017)
35. Yeh, C.H., Ho, Y.C., Barsky, B.A., Ouhyoung, M.: Personalized photograph ranking and selection system. In: Proceedings of 18th ACM International Conference on Multimedia (MM), pp. 211–220. ACM (2010)

Detecting Tampered Videos with Multimedia Forensics and Deep Learning

Markos Zampoglou[1]([✉]), Foteini Markatopoulou[1], Gregoire Mercier[2],
Despoina Touska[1], Evlampios Apostolidis[1,3], Symeon Papadopoulos[1],
Roger Cozien[2], Ioannis Patras[3], Vasileios Mezaris[1], and Ioannis Kompatsiaris[1]

[1] Centre for Research and Technology Hellas, Thermi-Thessaloniki, Greece
{markzampoglou,markatopoulou,apostolid,papadop,bmezaris,ikom}@iti.gr
[2] eXo maKina, Paris, France
{gregoire.mercier,roger.cozien}@exomakina.fr
[3] School of EECS, Queen Mary University of London, London, UK
I.Patras@qmul.ac.uk
https://mklab.iti.gr/, http://www.exomakina.fr

Abstract. User-Generated Content (UGC) has become an integral part
of the news reporting cycle. As a result, the need to verify videos collected
from social media and Web sources is becoming increasingly important
for news organisations. While video verification is attracting a lot of
attention, there has been limited effort so far in applying video forensics
to real-world data. In this work we present an approach for automatic
video manipulation detection inspired by manual verification approaches.
In a typical manual verification setting, video filter outputs are visually
interpreted by human experts. We use two such forensics filters designed
for manual verification, one based on Discrete Cosine Transform (DCT)
coefficients and a second based on video requantization errors, and combine them with Deep Convolutional Neural Networks (CNN) designed
for image classification. We compare the performance of the proposed
approach to other works from the state of the art, and discover that,
while competing approaches perform better when trained with videos
from the same dataset, one of the proposed filters demonstrates superior
performance in cross-dataset settings. We discuss the implications of our
work and the limitations of the current experimental setup, and propose
directions for future research in this area.

Keywords: Video forensics · Video tampering detection
Video verification · Video manipulation detection
User-generated video

1 Introduction

With the proliferation of multimedia capturing devices during the last decades,
the amount of video content produced by non-professionals has increased rapidly.

© Springer Nature Switzerland AG 2019
I. Kompatsiaris et al. (Eds.): MMM 2019, LNCS 11295, pp. 374–386, 2019.
https://doi.org/10.1007/978-3-030-05710-7_31

Respectable news agencies nowadays often need to rely on User-Generated Content (UGC) for news reporting. However, the videos shared by users may not be authentic. People may manipulate a video for various purposes, including propaganda or comedic effect, but such tampered videos pose a major challenge for news organizations, since publishing a tampered video as legitimate news could seriously hurt an organization's reputation. This creates an urgent need for tools that can assist professionals to identify and avoid tampered content.

Multimedia forensics aims to address this need by providing algorithms and systems that assist investigators with locating traces of tampering and extracting information on the history of a multimedia item. Research in automatic video verification has made important progress in the recent past; however, state-of-the-art solutions are not yet mature enough for use by journalists without specialized training. Currently, real-world video forensics mostly rely on expert verification, i.e. trained professionals visually examining the content under various image maps (or *filters*[1]) in order to spot inconsistencies.

In this work, we explore the potential of two such novel filters, originally designed for human visual inspection, in the context of automatic verification. The filter outputs are used to train a number of deep learning visual classifiers, in order to learn to discriminate between authentic and tampered videos. Besides evaluations on established experimental forensics datasets, we also evaluate them on a dataset of well-known tampered and untampered news-related videos from YouTube to assess their potential in real-world settings. Our findings highlight the potential of adapting manual forensics approaches for automatic video verification, as well as the importance of cross-dataset evaluations when aiming for real-world application. A third contribution of this work is a small dataset of tampered and untampered videos collected from Web and social media sources that is representative of real cases.

2   Related Work

Multimedia forensics has been an active research field for more than a decade. A number of algorithms (known as *active* forensics) work by embedding invisible watermarks on images which are disturbed in case of tampering. Alternatively, *passive* forensics aim to detect tampering without any prior knowledge [12]. Image forensics is an older field than video forensics, with a larger body of proposed algorithms and experimental datasets, and is slowly reaching maturity as certain algorithms or algorithm combinations are approaching sufficient accuracy for real-world application. Image tampering detection is often based on detecting local inconsistencies in JPEG compression information, or – especially in the cases of high-quality, low-compression images – detecting local inconsistencies in the high-frequency noise patterns left by the capturing device. A survey and evaluation of algorithms focused on image splicing can be found in [23].

---

[1] While not all maps are technically the result of filtering, the term *filters* is widely used in the market and will also be used here.

The progress in image forensics might lead to the conclusion that similar approaches could work for tampered video detection. If videos were simply sequences of frames, this might hold true. However, modern video compression is a much more complex process that often removes all traces such as camera error residues and single-frame compression traces [14]. Proposed video forensics approaches can be organized in three categories: double/multiple quantization detection, inter-frame forgery detection, and region tampering detection.

In the first case, systems attempt to detect if a video or parts of it have been quantized multiple times [16, 21]. A video posing as a camera-original User-Generated Content (UGC) but exhibiting traces of multiple quantizations may be suspicious. However, with respect to newsworthy UGC, such approaches are not particularly relevant since in the vast majority of cases videos are acquired from social media sources. As a result, both tampered and untampered videos typically undergo multiple strong requantizations and, without access to a purported camera original, they have little to offer in our task.

In the second category, algorithms aim to detect cases where frames have been inserted in a sequence, which has been consecutively requantized [20, 24]. Since newsworthy UGC generally consists of a single shot, such frame insertions are unlikely to pass unnoticed. Frame insertion detection may be useful for videos with fixed background (e.g. CCTV footage) or for edited videos where new shots are added afterwards, but the task is outside the scope of this work.

Finally, the third category concerns cases where parts of a video sequence (e.g. an object) have been inserted in the frames of another. This the most relevant scenario for UGC, and the focus of our work. Video region tampering detection algorithms share many common principles with image splicing detection algorithms. In both cases, the assumption is that there exists some invisible pattern in the item, caused by the capturing or the compression process, which is distinctive, detectable, and can be disturbed when foreign content is inserted. Some approaches are based solely on the spatial information extracted independently from frames. Among them, the most prominent ones use oriented gradients [17], the Discrete Cosine Transform (DCT) coefficients' histogram [6], or Zernike moments [2]. These work well as long as the video quality is high, but tend to fail at higher compression rates as the traces on which they are based are erased. Other region tampering detection strategies are based on the motion component of the video coding, modeling motion vector statistics [7, 19] or motion compensation error statistics [1]. These approaches work better with still background and slow moving objects, using motion to identify shapes/objects of interest in the video. However, these conditions are not often met by UGC.

Other strategies focus on temporal noise [9] or correlation behavior [8]. The noise estimation induces a predictable feature shape or background, which imposes an implicit hypothesis such as a limited global motion. The *Cobalt* filter we present in Sect. 3 adopts a similar strategy. The Motion Compensated Edge Artifact is another alternative to deal with the temporal behavior of residuals between I, P and B frames without requiring strong hypotheses on the motion or background contents. These periodic artifacts in the DCT coefficients may be extracted through a thresholding technique [15] or spectral analysis [3]. This approach is also used for inter-frame forgery detection under the assumption that the statistical representativeness of the tampered area should be high.

Recently, the introduction of deep learning approaches has led to improved performance and promising results for video manipulation detection. In [22], the inter-frame differences are calculated for the entire video, then a high-pass filter is applied to each difference output and the outputs are used to classify the entire video as tampered or untampered. High-pass filters have been used successfully in the past in conjunction with machine learning approaches with promising results in images [4]. In a similar manner, [13] presents a set of deep learning approaches for detecting face-swap videos created by Generative Adversarial Networks. Besides presenting a very large-scale dataset for training and evaluations, they show that a modified Xception network architecture can be used to detect forged videos on a per-frame basis.

In parallel to published academic work, a separate line of research is conducted by private companies, with a focus on the creation of filters for manual analysis by trained experts. These filters represent various aspects of video content, including pixel value relations, motion patterns, or compression parameters, and aim at highlighting inconsistencies in ways that can be spotted by a trained person. Given that tools based on such filters are currently in use by news organizations and state agencies for judiciary or security reasons, we decided to explore their potential for automatic video tampering detection, when using them in tandem with deep learning frameworks.

3   Methodology

The approach we explore is based on a two-step process: forensics-based feature extraction and classification. The feature extraction step is based on two novel filters, while the classification step is based on a modified version of the GoogLeNet and ResNet deep Convolutional Neural Networks (CNN).

3.1   Forensics-Based Filters

The filters we used in our experiments, originally designed to produce visible output maps that can be analyzed by humans, are named $Q4$ and *Cobalt*. The $Q4$ filter is used to analyze the decomposition of the image through the Discrete Cosine Transform (DCT). It is applied on each individual video frame, irrespective of whether they are I, P, or B frames. Each frame is split into $N \times N$ blocks (typically $N = 8$), and the two-dimensional DCT is applied to transform each image block into a block of the same size in which the coefficients are identified based on their frequency. The first coefficient $(0, 0)$ represents low frequency information, while higher coefficients represent higher frequencies. JPEG compression takes place in the YCbCr color spectrum, and we then use the Y channel (luminance) for further analysis.

If we transform all $N \times N$ blocks of a single image band with the DCT, we can build $N \times N$ (e.g. 64 for JPEG) different coefficient arrays, each one using a single coefficient from every block - for example, an image of the coefficients $(0, 0)$ of each block, and a different one using the coefficients $(0, 1)$. Each one of the $N \times N$ coefficient arrays has size equal to $1/N$ of the original image in each dimension. An artificially colorized RGB image may then be generated by selecting 3 of these arrays and assigning each to one of the three RGB color channels. This allows us to visualize three of the DCT coefficient arrays simultaneously, as well as the potential correlation between them. Combined together, the images from all frames can form a new video of the same length as the original video, which can then be used for analysis. The typical block size for DCT (e.g. in JPEG compression) is 8×8. However, analysis in 8×8 blocks yields too small coefficient arrays. Instead, 2×2 blocks are used so that the resulting output frame is only half the original size. A selection of coefficients $(0, 1)$, $(1, 0)$ and $(1, 1)$ generates the final output video map of the Q4 filter.

The second filter we use is the *Cobalt* filter. This compares the original video with a modified version of it, re-quantized using MPEG-4 at a different quality level (and a correspondingly different bit rate). If the initial video contains a (small) area that comes from another stream, this area may have undergone MPEG-4 quantization at a level which is different from the original one. This area may remain undetectable by any global strategy attempting to detect multiple quantization. The principle of the Cobalt filter is straightforward: We requantize the video and calculate the per-pixel values, creating an *Error Video*, i.e. a video depicting the differences. In theory, if we requantize using the exact same parameters that were used for the original video, there will be almost no error to be seen. As the difference with the original increases, so does the intensity of the error video. In designing Cobalt, a "compare-to-worst" strategy has been investigated, i.e. if a constant quality encoding is done, the comparison will be performed with the worst possible quality, and conversely, if a constant bit rate encoding is done, the comparison is performed with the worst possible bit rate. This induces a significantly contrasted video of errors when the quantization history of the initial video is not homogeneous.

3.2   Filter Output Classification

Both filters produce outputs in the form of RGB images. Following the idea that the filter maps were originally intended to be visually evaluated by a human expert, we decided to treat the problem as a visual classification task. This allows us to combine the maps with Convolutional Neural Networks pre-trained for image classification. Specifically, we take an instance of GoogLeNet [18] and an instance of ResNet [5], both pre-trained on the ImageNet classification task, and adapt them to the needs of our task. The image outputs from the filtering process are scaled to match the default input size of the CNNs, i.e. 224×224 pixels. In contrast to other forensics-based approaches, where rescaling might destroy sensitive traces, the filters we use are aimed for visual interpretation by humans, so - as in any other classification task - rescaling should not cause problems.

To improve classification performance, the networks are extended using the method of [11], according to which adding an extra Fully Connected (FC) layer prior to the final FC layer can improve performance when fine-tuning a pre-trained network. In this case, we added a 128-unit FC layer to both networks, and also replaced the final 1000-unit FC layer with a 2-unit layer, since instead of the 1000-class ImageNet classification task, here we are dealing with a binary (tampered/untampered) task. As the resulting networks are designed for image classification, we feed the filter outputs to each network one frame at a time, during both training and classification.

4 Experimental Study

4.1 Datasets and Experimental Setup

The datasets we used for our study came from two separate sources. One comprised the Development datasets provided by the NIST 2018 Media Forensics Challenge[2] for the *Video Manipulation Detection* task. There are two separate development datasets, named Dev1 and Dev2, the first consisting of 30 video pairs (i.e. 30 tampered videos and their 30 untampered sources), and the second of 86 video pairs, containing approximately 44K and 134K frames respectively. The task also included a large number of distractor videos, which were not included in our experiments. These two datasets, Dev1 and Dev2, are treated as independent sets, but since they originate from the same source, they likely exhibit similar features.

The second source of videos was the InVID Fake Video Corpus [10] (Fig. 1), developed over the course of the InVID project. The Fake Video Corpus (FVC) contains 110 real and 117 fake newsworthy videos from social media sources, which include not only videos that have been tampered but also videos that are contextually false (e.g. whose description on YouTube contains misinformation about what is shown). Out of that dataset, we selected 35 real videos that comprise single-shot, unedited videos, and 33 fake videos that include tampered UGC, but no explicit edit effects such as cuts or text overlay because these would be easy to detect compared to the single-shot untampered videos. This dataset contains 163K frames, equally split between tampered and untampered videos.

The temporal annotation of the datasets is incomplete, i.e. we do not always know where and when the tampering takes place, only that a video contains a tampered part. For our experiments, we treated all frames originating from untampered videos as untampered, and all frames originating from tampered videos as tampered. This is a weak assumption that will surely also lead to erroneous annotations. Based on manual inspection, we found that this assumption does hold true for the majority of videos, and thus we consider the quality of annotations adequate for the task.

---

[2] https://www.nist.gov/itl/iad/mig/media-forensics-challenge-2018.

Fig. 1. Indicative videos from the FVC dataset. Top (tampered videos): "Bear attacks cyclist", "Lava selfie", "Bear attacks snowboarder", "Eagle drops snake". Bottom (untampered videos): "Stockholm attack", "Hudson landing", "Istanbul attack" and "Giant aligator in golf field".

Experimental Setup. In order to evaluate the proposed approaches, the two filters, Q4 and Cobalt, were applied to all frames of the videos, and then each of the two networks was trained with each filter output independently on the task of distinguishing between tampered and untampered frames. For comparison, we also implemented the following video features from the state of the art:

- *rawKeyframes* [13]. The video is decoded into its frames and the raw keyframes (without any filtering process) are given as input to the deep network.
- *highPass frames* [4]. The video is decoded into its frames, each frame is filtered by a high-pass filter and the filtered frame is given as input to the deep network.
- *frameDifference* [22]. The video is decoded into its frames, the frame difference between two neighboring frames is calculated, the new filtered frame is also processed by a high-pass filter and the final filtered frame is given as input to the deep network.

The filter outputs are used to train the networks. During evaluation, for each video the arithmetic mean of the classification scores for all of its frames is calculated separately for each class (tampered, untampered). The video is classified as tampered if the average score for the tampered class is larger than the average score for the untampered class. Experiments were run both by training and evaluating on the same dataset (using 5-fold cross-validation) and by training and testing on different datasets to evaluate each algorithm's ability to generalize. In all cases, we used three performance measures: Accuracy, Mean Average Precision (MAP), and Mean Precision for the top-20 retrieved items (MP@20).

4.2 Within-Dataset Experiments

Preliminary evaluations of the proposed approach took the form of within-dataset evaluations, using five-fold cross-validation. We used the two datasets

Table 1. Within-dataset evaluations

Dataset	Filter-DCNN	Accuracy	MAP	MP@20
Dev1	cobalt-gnet	**0.6833**	0.7614	-
	cobalt-resnet	0.5833	0.6073	-
	q4-gnet	0.6500	**0.7856**	-
	q4-resnet	0.6333	0.7335	-
Dev2	cobalt-gnet	0.8791	**0.9568**	**0.8200**
	cobalt-resnet	0.7972	0.8633	0.7600
	q4-gnet	**0.8843**	0.9472	0.7900
	q4-resnet	0.8382	0.9433	0.7600
Dev1 + Dev2	cobalt-gnet	**0.8509**	0.9257	0.9100
	cobalt-resnet	0.8217	0.9069	0.8700
	q4-gnet	0.8408	**0.9369**	**0.9200**
	q4-resnet	0.8021	0.9155	0.8700

from the NIST Challenge (Dev1 and Dev2), as well as their union, for these runs. The results are presented in Table 1.

The results show that, for all filters and models, Dev1 is significantly more challenging. Accuracy for all cases ranges between 0.58 and 0.68, while the same measure for Dev2 ranges from 0.79 to 0.88. Mean Average Precision follows a similar pattern. It should be noted that the MP@20 measure does not apply to Dev1 cross-validation due to its small size (the test set would always contain less than 20 items).

Merging the two datasets gives us the largest cross-validation dataset set from which we can expect the most reliable results. In terms of Accuracy and MAP, for Dev1 + Dev2 the results are slightly worse than Dev2, and significantly better than Dev1. MP@20 is improved compared to Dev2 but this can be attributed to the relatively small size of Dev2. Overall, the results appear encouraging, reaching a Mean Average Precision of 0.94 for the Dev1 + Dev2 set. GoogLeNet seems to generally perform better than ResNet. In terms of performance, the two filters appear comparable, with Cobalt outperforming Q4 at some cases, and the inverse being true for others.

4.3   Cross-dataset Experiments

Using the same dataset or datasets from the same origin for training and testing is a common practice in evaluations in the field. However, as in all machine learning tasks, the machine learning algorithm may end up picking up features that are characteristic of the particular datasets. This means that the resulting model will be unsuitable for real-world application. Our main set of evaluations concerns the ability of the proposed algorithms to deal with cross-dataset classification, i.e. training the model on one dataset and testing it on another. We used three datasets: Dev1, Dev2, and FVC. We run three sets of experiments using a different dataset for training each time. One set was run using Dev1 as the training set, the second using Dev2, and the third using their combination. Dev1 and Dev2 originate from the same source, and thus, while different, may exhibit similar patterns. Thus, we would expect that training on Dev1 and evaluating on Dev2 or vice versa would be easier than evaluating on FVC.

Table 2. Cross-dataset evaluations (Train: Dev1)

Training	Testing	Filter-DCNN	Accuracy	MAP	MP@20
Dev1	Dev2	cobalt-gnet	0.6033	0.8246	0.9000
		cobalt-resnet	0.6364	0.8335	0.9000
		q4-gnet	0.5124	0.8262	0.9000
		q4-resnet	0.5041	0.8168	0.9000
		rawKeyframes-gnet [13]	0.5868	0.8457	0.8500
		rawKeyframes-resnet [13]	0.2893	0.6588	0.4000
		highPass-gnet [4]	0.5620	0.8134	0.8500
		highPass-resnet [4]	0.5537	0.7969	0.8000
		frameDifference-gnet [22]	0.6942	**0.8553**	**0.9000**
		frameDifference-resnet [22]	**0.7190**	0.8286	0.8500
	FVC	cobalt-gnet	0.4412	0.3996	0.3000
		cobalt-resnet	0.4706	0.5213	0.5000
		q4-gnet	0.58824	0.6697	0.6000
		q4-resnet	**0.6029**	**0.6947**	**0.7000**
		rawKeyframes-gnet [13]	0.5294	0.5221	0.5000
		rawKeyframes-resnet [13]	0.5147	0.4133	0.2500
		highPass-gnet [4]	0.5441	0.5365	0.5000
		highPass-resnet [4]	0.5000	0.5307	0.6000
		frameDifference-gnet [22]	0.5735	0.5162	0.4500
		frameDifference-resnet [22]	0.5441	0.4815	0.5000

The results are shown in Tables 2, 3, and 4. As expected, evaluations on the FVC dataset yield relatively lower performance than evaluations on Dev1 and Dev2. In terms of algorithm performance, a discernible pattern is that, while the state of the art seems to outperform the proposed approaches on similar datasets (i.e. training on Dev1 and testing on Dev2 or vice versa), the Q4 filter seems to outperform all other approaches when tested on FVC. Specifically, *frameDifference* from [22] clearly outperforms all competing approaches when cross-tested between Dev1 and Dev2. However, its performance drops significantly when evaluated on the FVC dataset, indicating an inability to generalize to different, – and in particular, real-world – cases. This is important, since in real-world application and especially in the news domain, the data will most likely resemble those

Table 3. Cross-dataset evaluations (Train: Dev2)

Training	Testing	Filter-DCNN	Accuracy	MAP	MP@20
Dev2	Dev1	cobalt-gnet	0.6167	0.6319	0.6500
		cobalt-resnet	0.5333	0.7216	0.6000
		q4-gnet	**0.6500**	0.7191	**0.7000**
		q4-resnet	0.5833	0.6351	0.6000
		rawKeyframes-gnet	**0.6500**	0.6936	0.6500
		rawKeyframes-resnet	0.6333	0.6984	0.6500
		highPass-gnet [4]	0.5667	0.6397	0.6500
		highPass-resnet [4]	**0.6500**	0.6920	**0.7000**
		frameDifference-gnet [22]	0.6167	**0.7572**	**0.7000**
		frameDifference-resnet [22]	**0.6500**	0.7189	**0.7000**
	FVC	cobalt-gnet	0.5588	0.5586	0.5500
		cobalt-resnet	0.5000	0.4669	0.4000
		q4-gnet	**0.6177**	**0.6558**	0.7000
		q4-resnet	0.5147	0.4525	0.4000
		rawKeyframes-gnet [13]	0.5147	0.6208	**0.7000**
		rawKeyframes-resnet [13]	0.5735	0.6314	0.6500
		highPass-gnet [4]	0.4706	0.5218	0.4500
		highPass-resnet [4]	0.5588	0.5596	0.6000
		frameDifference-gnet [22]	0.5000	0.5652	0.6000
		frameDifference-resnet [22]	0.5000	0.5702	0.6500

Table 4. Cross-dataset evaluations (Train: Dev1 + Dev2)

Training	Testing	Filter-DCNN	Accuracy	MAP	MP@20
Dev1 + Dev2	FVC	cobalt-gnet	0.4706	0.4577	0.4000
		cobalt-resnet	0.4853	0.4651	0.4500
		q4-gnet	**0.6471**	**0.7114**	**0.7000**
		q4-resnet	0.5882	0.6044	0.6500
		rawKeyframes-gnet	0.5882	0.5453	0.5000
		rawKeyframes-resnet	0.5441	0.5175	0.5500
		highPass-gnet	0.5294	0.5397	0.5500
		highPass-resnet	0.5441	0.5943	0.6000
		frameDifference-gnet	0.5441	0.5360	0.6000
		frameDifference-resnet	0.4706	0.5703	0.5500

of the FVC dataset (i.e. user-generated videos). It is unlikely that we will be able to collect enough videos to train a model so that it knows the characteristics of such videos beforehand.

The Q4 filter reaches a MAP of 0.71 when trained on the combination of the Dev1 and Dev2 datasets, and tested on the FVC dataset. This performance, while significantly higher than all alternatives, is far from sufficient for application in newsrooms. It is, however, indicative of the potential of the specific filter. Another observation concerns the choice of networks. While in most experiments there was no clear winner between GoogLeNet and ResNet, it seems that the former performs better on average, and consistently better or comparably to ResNet when tested on the FVC dataset.

5   Conclusions and Future Work

We presented our efforts in combining video forensics filters, originally designed to be visually examined by experts, with deep learning models for visual classification. We explored the potential of two forensics-based filters combined with two deep network architectures, and observed that, while for training and testing on similar videos the proposed approach performed comparably or worse than various state of the art filters, when evaluated on different datasets than the ones used for training, one of the proposed filters clearly outperformed all others. This is an encouraging result that may reveal the potential of such an approach towards automatic video verification, and especially for content originating from web and social media.

However, the current methodology has certain limitations that should be overcome in the future for the method to be usable in real settings. One is the problem of annotation. During our experiments, training and testing was run on a per-frame basis, in which all frames from tampered videos were treated as tampered, and all frames from untampered videos as untampered. This assumption is problematic, as a tampered video may also contain untampered frames. However, as we lack strong, frame-level annotation, all experiments were run using this weak assumption. For the same reason, the final classification of an entire video into "tampered" or "untampered" was done by majority voting. This may also distort results, as it is possible that only a few frames of a video have been tampered, and yet this video should be classified as tampered.

The limitations of the current evaluation mean that the results can only be treated as indicative. However, as the need for automatic video verification methods increases, and since the only solutions currently available on the market are filters designed for analysis by experts, the success of such filters using automatic visual classification methods is strongly encouraging. In the future, we aim to improve the accuracy of the approach in a number of ways. One is to improve the quality of the dataset by adding temporal annotations for tampered videos, in order to identify which frames are the tampered ones. Secondly, we intend to develop a larger collection of state-of-the-art implementations on video tampering detection, to allow for more comparisons. Finally, we will explore more nuanced alternatives to the current voting scheme where each video is classified as tampered if more than half the frames are classified as such.

Acknowledgements. This work is supported by the InVID project, which is funded by the European Commission's Horizon 2020 program under contract number 687786.

References

1. Chen, S., Tan, S., Li, B., Huang, J.: Automatic detection of object-based forgery in advanced video. IEEE Trans. on Circ. Syst. Video Technol. **26**(11), 2138–2151 (2016)
2. D'Amiano, L., Cozzolino, D., Poggi, G., Verdoliva, L.: Video forgery detection and localization based on 3D patchmatch. In: IEEE International Conference on Multimedia Expo Workshop (ICMEW) (2015)
3. Dong, Q., Yang, G., Zhu, N.: A MCEA based passive forensics scheme for detecting frame based video tampering. Digit. Investig. **9**, 151–159 (2012)
4. Fridrich, J., Kodovsky, J.: Rich models for steganalysis of digital images. IEEE Trans. Inf. Forensics Secur. **7**(3), 868–882 (2012)
5. He, K., Zhang, X., Ren, S., Sun, J.: Deep residual learning for image recognition. In: Proceedings of the IEEE Conference on Computer Vision and Pattern Recognition, pp. 770–778 (2016)
6. Labartino, D., Bianchi, T., Rosa, A.D., Fontani, M., Vazquez-Padin, D., Piva, A.: Localization of forgeries in MPEG-2 video through GOP size and DQ analysis. In: IEEE International Workshop on Multimedia and Signal Processing, pp. 494–499 (2013)
7. Li, L., Wang, X., Wang, G., Hu, G.: Detecting removed object from video with stationary background. In: Proceedings of the 11th International Conference on Digital Forensics and Watermarking (WDW), pp. 242–252 (2013)
8. Lin, C.S., Tsay, J.J.: A passive approach for effective detection and localization of region-level video forgery with spatio-temporal coherence analysis. Digit. Investig. **11**(2), 120–140 (2014)
9. Pandey, R., Singh, S., Shukla, K.: Passive copy-move forgery detection in videos. In: IEEE International Conference on Computer and Communications and Technology (ICCCT), pp. 301–306 (2014)
10. Papadopoulou, O., Zampoglou, M., Papadopoulos, S., Kompatsiaris, Y., Teyssou, D.: Invid Fake Video Corpus v2.0 (Version 2.0). Dataset on Zenodo (2018)
11. Pittaras, N., Markatopoulou, F., Mezaris, V., Patras, I.: Comparison of fine-tuning and extension strategies for deep convolutional neural networks. In: Amsaleg, L., Guðmundsson, G.Þ., Gurrin, C., Jónsson, B.Þ., Satoh, S. (eds.) MMM 2017. LNCS, vol. 10132, pp. 102–114. Springer, Cham (2017). https://doi.org/10.1007/978-3-319-51811-4_9
12. Piva, A.: An overview on image forensics. ISRN Sig. Process. **2013**, 22 p. (2013). Article ID 496701
13. Rössler, A., Cozzolino, D., Verdoliva, L., Riess, C., Thies, J., Nießner, M.: Face-Forensics: a large-scale video dataset for forgery detection in human faces. arXiv preprint arXiv:1803.09179 (2018)
14. Sitara, K., Mehtre, B.M.: Digital video tampering detection: an overview of passive techniques. Digit. Investig. **18**, 8–22 (2016)

15. Su, L., Huang, T., Yang, J.: A video forgery detection algorithm based on compressive sensing. Multimedia Tools Appl. **74**, 6641–6656 (2015)
16. Su, Y., Xu, J.: Detection of double compression in MPEG-2 videos. In: IEEE 2nd International Workshop on Intelligent Systems and Application (ISA) (2010)
17. Subramanyam, A., Emmanuel, S.: Video forgery detection using HOG features and compression properties. In: IEEE 14th International Workshop on Multimedia and Signal Processing (MMSP), pp. 89–94 (2012)
18. Szegedy, C., et al.: Going deeper with convolutions. In: Proceedings of the IEEE Conference on Computer Vision and Pattern Recognition, pp. 1–9 (2015)
19. Wang, W., Farid, H.: Exposing digital forgeries in interlaced and deinterlaced video. IEEE Trans. Inf. Forensics Secur. **2**(3), 438–449 (2007)
20. Wu, Y., Jiang, X., Sun, T., Wang, W.: Exposing video inter-frame forgery based on velocity field consistency. In: ICASSP (2014)
21. Xu, J., Su, Y., Liu, Q.: Detection of double MPEG-2 compression based on distribution of DCT coefficients. Int. J. Pattern Recogn. AI **27**(1), 1354001 (2013)
22. Yao, Y., Shi, Y., Weng, S., Guan, B.: Deep learning for detection of object-based forgery in advanced video. Symmetry **10**(1), 3 (2017)
23. Zampoglou, M., Papadopoulos, S., Kompatsiaris, Y.: Large-scale evaluation of splicing localization algorithms for web images. Multimedia Tools Appl. **76**(4), 4801–4834 (2017)
24. Zhang, Z., Hou, J., Ma, Q., Li, Z.: Efficient video frame insertion and deletion detection based on inconsistency of correlations between local binary pattern coded frames. Secur. Commun. Netw. **8**(2), 311–320 (2015)

Improving Robustness of Image Tampering Detection for Compression

Boubacar Diallo[✉], Thierry Urruty, Pascal Bourdon,
and Christine Fernandez-Maloigne

XLIM Research Institute (UMR CNRS 7252), University of Poitiers, Poitiers, France
{boubacar.diallo,thierry.urruty,pascal.bourdon,
christine.fernandez}@univ-poitiers.fr

Abstract. The task of verifying the originality and authenticity of images puts numerous constraints on tampering detection algorithms. Since most images are acquired on the internet, there is a significant probability that they have undergone transformations such as compression, noising, resizing and/or filtering, both before and after the possible alteration. Therefore, it is essential to improve the robustness of tampered image detection algorithms for such manipulations. As compression is the most common type of post-processing, we propose in our work a robust framework against this particular transformation. Our experiments on benchmark datasets show the contribution of our proposal for camera model identification and image tampering detection compared to recent literature approaches.

Keywords: Image forensics · Lossy compression
Camera model identification · Convolutional neural networks

1 Introduction

Nowadays, social networks have become affordable and powerful platforms for sharing, publishing any kind of images. Thus, with the advances of image editing techniques low-cost tampered or manipulated image generation processes have become widely available. Among these tampering techniques, copy-move, splicing and removal are the most common manipulations (see Fig. 1 for example).

- **Copy-move:** It copies and pastes of regions within the same image. This manipulation adds false information or hide information (covering it using other parts of the image).
- **Splicing:** It manipulates images by copying a region from one image and pasting it onto another. It can give the false impression that an additional element was present in a scene at the time that the photograph was captured.
- **Removal:** It eliminates regions from an authentic image followed by an inpainting technique that restores the image by filling holes using characteristics around the hole.

© Springer Nature Switzerland AG 2019
I. Kompatsiaris et al. (Eds.): MMM 2019, LNCS 11295, pp. 387–398, 2019.
https://doi.org/10.1007/978-3-030-05710-7_32

Even with careful inspection, non-expert users will have difficulties to recognize the tampered regions. Such images deliver misleading messages or even dangerous information causing important damage within the society.

Fig. 1. Examples of tampered images that have undergone different tampering techniques. From left to right are the examples showing manipulations of copy-move (*Adding missiles*), splicing (*Fake person*) and removal (*Missing person*).

Therefore, it is of primordial importance to develop forensic methods to validate the integrity of an image. For this reason, over the years, the forensic community has developed several techniques for image authenticity detection and integrity assessment [12,25]. Among the many investigated forensic issues, great attention has been devoted to camera model identification [17,18].

Indeed, detecting the model of an image source camera can be crucial for criminal investigations and legal proceedings. This information can be exploited for solving copyright infringement cases, as well as indicating the authors of illicit usages. Each camera model performs peculiar operations on image at acquisition time (e.g. different JPEG compression schemes, proprietary algorithms for Color Filter Array demosaicing, etc.). It leaves on each picture characteristic footprints which are exploited by the proposed approaches. Some authors in [22,29] have used co-occurrence statistics in different domains coupled to a variety of supervised classification techniques. Most existing techniques use local parametric models of an image or handcraft features to provide sufficient pixel statistics.

Combining forensic methodologies and recent advancements established by deep learning techniques in computer vision, some researchers [1,2,7,29] have proposed to learn camera identification features by using convolutional neural networks (CNN). The advantage of CNN is that they are capable of learning classification features directly from data, hence, they adaptively learn the cumulative traces induced by camera components.

While all of these methods have been very promising, CNN in their current form tend to learn only features related to image content. However, most images can experience unpredictable changes caused by content manipulations or geometric distortions such as lossy compression, noising, resizing and/or filtering, both before and after the possible alteration. It is therefore essential that tampered image detection algorithms take into account the robustness faced with these manipulations. In this paper, motivated by the fact that lossy compression is the most relevant type of image post-processing, we propose a robust framework which contributes in improving camera model identification and image tampering detection. Our experiments will first demonstrate the importance of taking lossy compression into account and then highlight the performance of our proposal.

The remainder of this article is structured as follows: we provide a brief overview of the state-of-the-art of image tampering detection methods using camera model identification in Sect. 2. Then, we present our general framework for camera model identification and image tampering detection in Sect. 3. Section 4 presents our exhaustive experiments. It first discusses the importance of lossy compression manipulation before highlighting the robustness of our proposal against such manipulation. Section 5 concludes our work and gives some perspectives of this work.

2 Related Work

2.1 Camera Model Identification

Forensic community researchers have developed "blindly" methods to determine an image camera model by identifying the fingerprints left when taking photographs [25]. Each camera model performs particular operations on image at acquisition pipeline time leaving characteristic fingerprints that can be exploited. These fingerprints are unique from one camera model to another and allow to study about the origin, processing history and authenticity of the captured images.

The first approaches developed used heuristically designed statistical metrics as features to measure and determine camera traces [17]. Then, other techniques use traces of specific physical components such as noise tracks left by camera sensors [28]. Other existing methods rely on the algorithmic components such as the unique implementation of JPEG compression [16] and traces left by demosaicing [10,11,26]. Given the difficulty of properly modelling typical operations of the image acquisition pipeline, other camera model identification methods exploit features mainly capturing statistical image properties paired with machine learning classifiers. A technique based on local binary patterns is proposed in [31]. Other researchers [22,29] exploit the pixel co-occurrence statistics with a variety of supervised classification techniques. These methods guarantee very accurate results, especially on full-resolution images that provide sufficient pixel statistics. All these existing techniques are often designed by local parametric models of image data [10,26] or use hand-crafted features [23].

However, recent works in research forensics suggest that learning camera features can be accomplished by using convolutional neural networks (CNN)

[1, 2, 7, 29]. This was made possible by recent advancements established by deep learning techniques in computer vision [6, 20]. They showed the possibility to improve the accuracy for detection and classification tasks by training on a great amount of data in order to learn characteristic features directly from the data itself.

2.2 Convolutional Neural Networks

Recent advances in deep learning have led to better performance because of the ability to learn extremely powerful image features with convolutional neural networks (CNN). In the late 1980s, CNN were first proposed by LeCun et al. [21] with the recognition of handwritten letters as an extended version of neural networks (NN). In 2012, with the availability of high-performance computing systems, such as GPUs or large-scale distributed clusters, CNN have become a widely used research tool. Thus, AlexNet [19], GoogLeNet [27] and ResNet [14] for example have become very popular CNN architectures because of impressive accuracy improvements for image classification and localization tasks.

In the last few years, many researchers showed a growing interest in image manipulation detection by applying different computer vision and deep-learning algorithms [1, 5, 7, 8, 23, 29]. In 2016, Bayar et al. [3] used the CNN and developed a new form of convolutional layer that is specifically designed to learn the manipulated features from an image. In this work, CNN are trained to detect multiple manipulations (Median filtering, Gaussian blurring, Additive white Gaussian noise, resizing) applied to a set of unaltered images. In [9], it is shown that both CNN and Long short-term memory (LSTM) based networks are effective in exploiting re-sampling features to detect tampered regions. The robustness against post-processing is not evaluated and it proposes in the future to detect image forgeries. The work in [4] examines the influence of several important CNN design choices for forensic applications, such as the use of a constrained convolutional layer or fixed high-pass filter at the beginning of the CNN. In [7, 8], two techniques are combined for image tampering detection and localisation, leveraging characteristic footprints left on images by different camera models. Firstly, it exploits a convolutional neural network (CNN) to extract characteristic camera model features from image patches. These features are then analysed by means of iterative clustering techniques in order to detect whether an image has been forged, and localise the affected region. Other methods are bound to specific problems as detecting specific tampering cues such as double-JPEG compression [1, 2], re-sampling and contrast enhancement [30]. A deep learning approach to identify facial retouching was also proposed by [24]. Recently, Huh et al. [15] propose a learning algorithm for detecting visual image manipulations that is trained only using a large dataset of real photographs. This model has been applied to the task of detecting and localising image splices.

While all of these methods have been very promising, CNN in their current form tend to learn only features related to image content. However, most images can experience unpredictable changes caused by content manipulations or geometric distortions such as compression, noising, and resizing. So it is essential that the tampered image detection algorithms need to take into account the robustness faced with these manipulations.

3 Proposed Method

In this section, we present our global framework which procures a robust solution for camera model identification and tampering image detection. The motivation of our work comes from the fact that most images are acquired on the internet. Among them, there is a significant proportion that has undergone some transformations such as lossy compression, noising, resizing and/or filtering, both before and after a possible alteration. It is therefore essential that tampered image detection algorithms strong robustness faced with these different manipulations. As compression is the most common and relevant type of post-processing when people share pictures on the internet, our experiments focus on this manipulation.

This work is divided in two parts as shown on Fig. 2. In the first one, we detail our deep learning approach to identify camera models. The following part details how it is included in a global framework to obtain robustness against compression for tampering image detection.

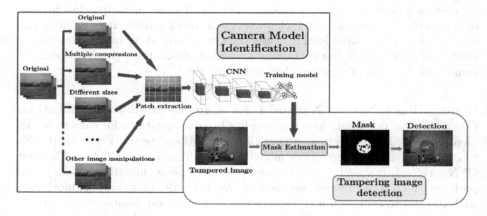

Fig. 2. The pipeline of our framework including the camera model identification learning phase and the tampering image detection method

3.1 Camera Model Identification

In this part, we will focus on camera model identification which is the main contribution of this paper (left part of Fig. 2). The possibility of detecting which camera model has been used to shoot a specific picture is of importance for many forensic tasks as criminal investigations and trials. In the case a deeper source identification (e.g. use of footprints left on images for tampering detection and localization), camera model identification (CMI) can be considered an important preliminary step. The most effective methods for this task are based on deep learning approaches. They extract distinctive features from the images of interest and use them to train a classifier. This approach requires a dataset of labelled images. In the next subsections, we detail each component of our framework presented on Fig. 2.

Image Transformations: The first and most important step for a deep learning strategy framework is the quality of the input data with respect to the desired application. As the objective is to detect image tampering on images shared on the internet, the trained CNN model needs to be fed with images that undergo similar transformations as any user could achieve such as lossy compression, noising, resizing and/or filtering. Thus, all original images have to be duplicated with transformed versions of itself. Experiments will show this step is of great importance to obtain good performance.

Patches Extraction: As state-of-the-art methods [4,8] for camera model classification gives promising results with small image patches, we also divide our image in small patches (64×64 pixels) as the second step of our robust framework for camera model identification. Indeed, the use of small image patches instead of full-resolution images better characterizes camera models in a reduced-size space. In order to avoid selecting overly dark or saturated regions, a threshold is used to exclude all patches containing saturated pixels. Each patch inherits the camera model label of its image before feeding the CNN.

Convolutional Neural Networks for Camera Model Identification: Given its great potential, deep learning has become inevitable for camera model identification. In this section, we exploit convolutional neural networks (CNN) to extract characteristic camera model features from image patches. The first CNN architecture specifically dedicated to camera model identification has been proposed in [7]. In this work, we use a similar network. This choice is motivated with the aim to achieve a high camera model attribution accuracy with a fairly small network architecture. Note that modifying the used CNN is not in the scope of this paper.

The used network contains 11 layers namely 4 convolutional layers, 3 max-pooling layers, 2 fully-connected layers, 1 ReLU layer and 1 Softmax layer. Image patches are fed into the CNN through an input layer, also known as the data layer. The structure of the CNN architecture is described in Table 1:

Training: The training architecture is characterized by 340,462 parameters, learned through Stochastic Gradient Descent on batches of 128 patches. Momentum is fixed to 0.9, weights decay is set to $7.5.10^{-3}$ while the learning rate is initialized to 0.015 and halves every 10 epochs. As trained CNN model M, we

Table 1. Structure of the CNN architecture [7]. N is the number of training classes

Layer	Input size	Kernel size	Stride	Num. filters	Output size
Conv1	$64 \times 64 \times 3$	4×4	1	32	$63 \times 63 \times 32$
Max-Pool1	$63 \times 63 \times 32$	-	2	-	$32 \times 32 \times 32$
Conv2	$32 \times 32 \times 32$	5×5	1	48	$28 \times 28 \times 48$
Max-Pool2	$28 \times 28 \times 48$	-	2	-	$14 \times 14 \times 48$
Conv3	$14 \times 14 \times 48$	5×5	1	64	$10 \times 10 \times 64$
Max-Pool3	$10 \times 10 \times 64$	-	2	-	$5 \times 5 \times 64$
Conv4	$5 \times 5 \times 64$	5×5	1	128	$1 \times 1 \times 128$
Fully1 (ReLU)	$1 \times 1 \times 128$	-	-	128	128
Fully2 (Softmax)	128	-	-	N	N

select the one that provides the smallest loss on validation patches within the first 50 training epochs.

Classification: The problem of camera model identification consists in detecting a model L (within a set of known camera models) used to shoot an image I. When a new image I is under analysis, the camera model is estimated as follows: a set of K patches is obtained from image I as described above. The last layer (Softmax) assigns a label to each patch. The predicted model for image I is obtained through majority voting on existing labels.

3.2 Tampering Image Detection

Here, we briefly present the method for image forgery detection and localization in case of images generated through composition of pictures shot with different camera models. In this scenario, we draw inspiration from [8] by considering that pristine images are pictures directly obtained from a camera. Conversely, forged images are those created by taking patches of a pristine image, and pasting them on images with different camera models. Under these assumptions, the proposed method is devised to estimate whether the totality of image patches comes from a single camera (i.e. the image is pristine), or some portions of the image are not coherent with the rest of the picture in terms of camera attribution (i.e. the image is forged). If this is the case, a localization of the forged region is also done.

The proposed method is described on the right part of Fig. 2. A tampered image I is first divided into non-overlapping patches. Each patch P is fed as input to a pretrained CNN to extract a feature vector f of N_{cams} elements corresponding to a number of cameras. This information is given as input to the clustering algorithm that estimates a tampering mask. The final output M is a binary mask, where black parts indicate patches belonging to the pristine region and white ones indicate forged patches. If no (or just a few) forged pixels are detected, the image is considered as pristine.

4   Experiments

In this section, we present our exhaustive experiment results. After detailing the experiment setup including chosen datasets and evaluation criteria, we propose a preliminary study highlighting the importance of compression as image manipulation technique. Then, we detail the performance of our framework for camera model identification and tampering image detection.

4.1   Experiment Setup

Test Datasets: Dresden dataset [13] is a publicly available dataset suitable for image source attribution problems. Dresden contains more than $13,000$ images of 18 different camera models. Note that we selected only natural JPEG photos from camera models with more than one instance. This dataset is split into a training, validation, and evaluation sets, denoted DT, DV and DE respectively.

To evaluate tampering detection algorithm, we use the image sets proposed in [8]. These two separate sets of altered data represent a set of "known" data from DE images and an "unknown" dataset which contains images from another 8 camera models not included in the CNN training phase. The objective of using those sets is to study the differences in performance when using "known" and "unknown" cameras. Both sets contain 500 pristine images and 500 tampered images generated following the process given in [8].

Finally, to evaluate the influence of compression, all images from the chosen datasets are compressed with different factor qualities (FQ): 90%, 80% and 70%. The trained CNN with those FQ are named CNN90, CNN80, CNN70 and CNNm respectively for 90%, 80%, 70% and mixed compressed data.

Evaluation Criteria: To evaluate the camera model identification performance, we use the average accuracy obtained with a majority voting. We evaluate detection performance on both "known" and "unknown" datasets in terms of accuracy, receiver operating characteristic (ROC) curves and Area Under the ROC Curve (AUC). These statistics are commonly known and used, they identify clearly the difference between the performance of studied approaches.

4.2   Influence of Compression on CMI

In this section we propose our preliminary study that highlights the importance of manipulation process on the CMI accuracy of our framework denoted CNNm compared to the one proposed by Bondi et al. [8].

To make this robustness assessment, we consider the original images of the Dresden Test dataset (DT) using a JPEG compression with quality factor values ranging from 70 to 100 with a step of 10. Table 2 shows the influence of the

Table 2. Influence of JPEG compression on camera model identification

Accuracy	Original	QF: 90%	QF: 80%	QF: 70%
Bondi et al. [7]	**0.91**	0.19	0.12	0.12
CNNm	0.82	**0.80**	**0.75**	**0.72**

JPEG compression on the CMI accuracy. As one may observe, the performance of Bondi's approach is superior to ours on Original images. However, their framework decreases dramatically even with a close quality factor ($QF = 90\%$) which is not the case for our proposal.

This result shows us that the CNN trained only on "Original" image for camera model identification is not robust to compression. The reason behind this is that JPEG compression mitigates similar anomalies between block pairs, destroying clues for patch-based approaches such as CNNs. Indeed, it is well-known that JPEG compression is a lossy operation. Because of the rounding errors, it can not only change the original values of pixels, but also leads to information loss.

Figure 3 confirms the fact that a CNN trained model on a specific compression quality factor gives higher accuracy only for this quality factor. However, our framework gives performing results on average of all mixed compressed test images. This results also proves the fact that under a certain quality factor threshold, results will worsen. However, under this threshold, the image quality is too poor to be of any use.

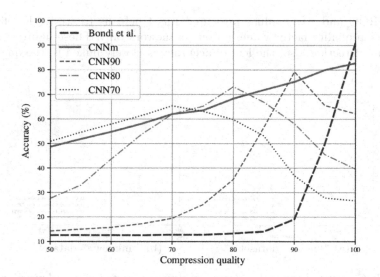

Fig. 3. Accuracy comparison curves of camera model identification

4.3   Image Tampering Detection

To confirm the first results, we study the influence of the JPEG compression on tampering detection algorithm. Similarly, the "Original" sets are also compressed with quality factors of 90%, 80% and 70%.

Table 3 shows detection performance on both "known" and "unknown" datasets. Once again, we observe similar observations. Our framework is close to Bondi et al.'s framework for uncompressed ("Original") images. However, our performance outperforms for any other compression quality factor. This result was predictable as the detection is based on the CNN trained for CMI.

Table 3. Tampering detection results with compressed images

Dataset	Compression	Accuracy		TPR	
		Bondi [8]	CNNm	Bondi [8]	CNNm
Known	*Original*	**0.84**	0.77	**0.9**	0.83
	90%	0.56	**0.72**	0.47	**0.68**
	80%	0.52	**0.65**	0.24	**0.48**
	70%	0.52	**0.61**	0.15	**0.38**
Unknown	*Original*	**0.79**	0.7	**0.84**	0.68
	90%	0.56	**0.63**	0.38	**0.46**
	80%	0.52	**0.57**	0.17	**0.30**
	70%	0.51	**0.56**	0.11	**0.26**

The ROC and AUC values presented Fig. 4 help us to study the effect of compression quality factor values on our framework only. Those figures that for tampering detection also, the loss of accuracy is closely linked to the quality of an image.

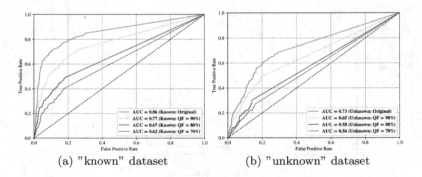

(a) "known" dataset   (b) "unknown" dataset

Fig. 4. ROC curves of tampering detection algorithm tested on (a) "known" and (b) "unknown" datasets with different compression values (90% and 80%)

5   Conclusion

In this paper, we propose a deep learning framework robust for camera identification model and tampering image detection. It includes any kind of manipulations that are commonly used by any user sharing images. We test our framework on the compression quality factor manipulation and show that our approach globally outperforms existing literature approaches. Our study emphasizes the fact that discriminant features from compressed images are harder to retrieve. Our future work will take this aspect into account to guarantee similar performance or very compressed data. We will also investigate neural network activation nodes to better understand the artifacts that help identifying camera models.

References

1. Amerini, I., Uricchio, T., Ballan, L., Caldelli, R.: Localization of jpeg double compression through multi-domain convolutional neural networks. In: Proceedings of IEEE CVPR Workshop on Media Forensics, vol. 3 (2017)
2. Barni, M., et al.: Aligned and non-aligned double JPEG detection using convolutional neural networks. J. Vis. Commun. Image Represent. **49**, 153–163 (2017)
3. Bayar, B., Stamm, M.C.: A deep learning approach to universal image manipulation detection using a new convolutional layer. In: Proceedings of the 4th ACM Workshop on Information Hiding and Multimedia Security, pp. 5–10. ACM (2016)
4. Bayar, B., Stamm, M.C.: Design principles of convolutional neural networks for multimedia forensics. Electron. Imaging **2017**(7), 77–86 (2017)
5. Bayar, B., Stamm, M.C.: Towards open set camera model identification using a deep learning framework. In: The 2018 IEEE International Conference on Acoustics, Speech and Signal Processing (ICASSP). IEEE (2018)
6. Bengio, Y., et al.: Learning deep architectures for AI. Found. Trends® Mach. Learn. **2**(1), 1–127 (2009)
7. Bondi, L., Baroffio, L., Güera, D., Bestagini, P., Delp, E.J., Tubaro, S.: First steps toward camera model identification with convolutional neural networks. IEEE Sig. Process. Lett. **24**(3), 259–263 (2017)
8. Bondi, L., Lameri, S., Güera, D., Bestagini, P., Delp, E.J., Tubaro, S.: Tampering detection and localization through clustering of camera-based CNN features. In: Proceedings of the IEEE Conference on Computer Vision and Pattern Recognition Workshops, pp. 1855–1864 (2017)
9. Bunk, J., et al.: Detection and localization of image forgeries using resampling features and deep learning. In: 2017 IEEE Conference on Computer Vision and Pattern Recognition Workshops (CVPRW), pp. 1881–1889. IEEE (2017)
10. Cao, H., Kot, A.C.: Accurate detection of demosaicing regularity for digital image forensics. IEEE Trans. Inf. Forensics Secur. **4**(4), 899–910 (2009)
11. Chen, C., Zhao, X., Stamm, M.C.: Detecting anti-forensic attacks on demosaicing-based camera model identification. In: 2017 IEEE International Conference on Image Processing (ICIP), pp. 1512–1516. IEEE (2017)
12. Farid, H.: Photo Forensics. MIT Press, Cambridge (2016)
13. Gloe, T., Böhme, R.: The 'Dresden image Database' for benchmarking digital image forensics. In: Proceedings of the 2010 ACM Symposium on Applied Computing, pp. 1584–1590. ACM (2010)

14. He, K., Zhang, X., Ren, S., Sun, J.: Deep residual learning for image recognition. In: Proceedings of the IEEE Conference on Computer Vision and Pattern Recognition, pp. 770–778 (2016)
15. Huh, M., Liu, A., Owens, A., Efros, A.A.: Fighting fake news: image splice detection via learned self-consistency. arXiv preprint arXiv:1805.04096 (2018)
16. Kee, E., Johnson, M.K., Farid, H.: Digital image authentication from JPEG headers. IEEE Trans. Inf. Forensics Secur. **6**(3–2), 1066–1075 (2011)
17. Kharrazi, M., Sencar, H.T., Memon, N.: Blind source camera identification. In: 2004 International Conference on Image Processing, ICIP 2004, vol. 1, pp. 709–712. IEEE (2004)
18. Kirchner, M., Gloe, T.: Forensic camera model identification. In: Handbook of Digital Forensics of Multimedia Data and Devices, pp. 329–374 (2015)
19. Krizhevsky, A., Sutskever, I., Hinton, G.E.: ImageNet classification with deep convolutional neural networks. In: Advances in Neural Information Processing Systems, pp. 1097–1105 (2012)
20. LeCun, Y., Bengio, Y., Hinton, G.: Deep learning. Nature **521**(7553), 436 (2015)
21. LeCun, Y., et al.: Backpropagation applied to handwritten zip code recognition. Neural Comput. **1**(4), 541–551 (1989)
22. Marra, F., Poggi, G., Sansone, C., Verdoliva, L.: Evaluation of residual-based local features for camera model identification. In: Murino, V., Puppo, E., Sona, D., Cristani, M., Sansone, C. (eds.) ICIAP 2015. LNCS, vol. 9281, pp. 11–18. Springer, Cham (2015). https://doi.org/10.1007/978-3-319-23222-5_2
23. Marra, F., Poggi, G., Sansone, C., Verdoliva, L.: A study of co-occurrence based local features for camera model identification. Multimedia Tools Appl. **76**(4), 4765–4781 (2017)
24. Rössler, A., Cozzolino, D., Verdoliva, L., Riess, C., Thies, J., Nießner, M.: FaceForensics: a large-scale video dataset for forgery detection in human faces. arXiv preprint arXiv:1803.09179 (2018)
25. Stamm, M.C., Wu, M., Liu, K.R.: Information forensics: an overview of the first decade. IEEE Access **1**, 167–200 (2013)
26. Swaminathan, A., Wu, M., Liu, K.R.: Nonintrusive component forensics of visual sensors using output images. IEEE Trans. Inf. Forensics Secur. **2**(1), 91–106 (2007)
27. Szegedy, C., et al.: Going deeper with convolutions. In: Proceedings of the IEEE Conference on Computer Vision and Pattern Recognition, pp. 1–9 (2015)
28. Thai, T.H., Cogranne, R., Retraint, F.: Camera model identification based on the heteroscedastic noise model. IEEE Trans. Image Process. **23**(1), 250–263 (2014)
29. Tuama, A., Comby, F., Chaumont, M.: Camera model identification with the use of deep convolutional neural networks. In: 2016 IEEE International Workshop on Information Forensics and Security (WIFS), pp. 1–6. IEEE (2016)
30. Wen, L., Qi, H., Lyu, S.: Contrast enhancement estimation for digital image forensics. ACM Trans. Multimedia Comput. Commun. Appl. (TOMM) **14**(2), 49 (2018)
31. Xu, G., Shi, Y.Q.: Camera model identification using local binary patterns. In: 2012 IEEE International Conference on Multimedia and Expo (ICME), pp. 392–397. IEEE (2012)

Audiovisual Annotation Procedure for Multi-view Field Recordings

Patrice Guyot[(✉)], Thierry Malon, Geoffrey Roman-Jimenez, Sylvie Chambon,
Vincent Charvillat, Alain Crouzil, André Péninou, Julien Pinquier,
Florence Sèdes, and Christine Sénac

IRIT, Université de Toulouse, CNRS, Toulouse, France
{patrice.guyot,thierry.malon,geoffrey.roman-jimenez,
sylvie.chambon,vincent.charvillat,alain.crouzil,andre.peninou,
julien.pinquier,florence.sedes,christine.senac}@irit.fr

Abstract. Audio and video parts of an audiovisual document interact to produce an audiovisual, or multi-modal, perception. Yet, automatic analysis on these documents are usually based on separate audio and video annotations. Regarding the audiovisual content, these annotations could be incomplete, or not relevant. Besides, the expanding possibilities of creating audiovisual documents lead to consider different kinds of contents, including videos filmed in uncontrolled conditions (i.e. fields recordings), or scenes filmed from different points of view (multi-view). In this paper we propose an original procedure to produce manual annotations in different contexts, including multi-modal and multi-view documents. This procedure, based on using both audio and video annotations, ensures consistency considering audio or video only, and provides additionally audiovisual information at a richer level. Finally, different applications are made possible when considering such annotated data. In particular, we present an example application in a network of recordings in which our annotations allow multi-source retrieval using mono or multi-modal queries.

Keywords: Audiovisual · Annotation · Multi-view · Multi-modal
Field recording · Multimedia · Ground truth

1 Introduction

Production of audiovisual documents is a fast-growing phenomenon which is founded on an increasing number of recording devices, for instance smartphones. In comparison to the data conceived in a controlled domain (e.g. TV, radio, music studio, motion capture studio, etc.), many recordings are generally produced in an uncontrolled context. They will be further referred to as *field recordings*.

Moreover, different audiovisual documents may correspond to the same scene, for instance a public event that is filmed by different points of view. These multi-view scenes contain lots of information and provide new opportunities for high-level automatic queries.

© Springer Nature Switzerland AG 2019
I. Kompatsiaris et al. (Eds.): MMM 2019, LNCS 11295, pp. 399–410, 2019.
https://doi.org/10.1007/978-3-030-05710-7_33

In the context of automatic analysis, the aim of the different tasks (e.g. detection, classification) is to reduce the quantity of information embedded in audiovisual documents towards some particular semantic concept. For example, a video with a car in the foreground contains lots of information (type of car, ground, objects in the background, weather, localization, etc.) that could be reduced to the concepts *car* or *nice weather*.

In order to produce a model and to evaluate the performances of the algorithms on a set of data, researchers generally build a manual annotation that expresses this semantic information. The result of such manual annotation is generally called *ground truth*. As it usually refers to information provided by direct observation, it requires researchers to develop objective criteria. The ground truth depends on the definition of a space in which the data are projected in the most appropriate manner within a specific context. This task is not always straightforward: for instance, in the context of Music Information Retrieval, the evaluation of *musical artist similarity* requires the development of an objective measurement, meanwhile artist similarity relies on an elusive concept [5]. Thus, it appears that the term *ground truth* is sometimes misleading because it does not reflect an objective *truth* [1]. In that respect, we will use the term *reference* which seems more accurate to designate the manual annotations.

Audiovisual documents are in essence based on two modalities: audio and video. Yet in the context of audiovisual documents, the annotations are generally mono-modal (audio or video), while the perception of an audiovisual content is multi-modal and thus leads to a richer interpretation. Moreover, the different modalities influence each other, making the mono-modality annotation difficult in a multi-modality context.

This paper addresses the issue of producing multi-modal annotations in an audiovisual context. We propose a low-cost procedure to manually annotate multi-view field recordings. This paper is organized as follows. We first present the relative works about annotation and perception of audiovisual contents. Section 3 presents a specific procedure to solve the multi-modal issues of audiovisual annotations. This procedure is usable in mono or multi-view contexts. Finally, different applications of this procedure are described in Sect. 4.

2   Related Works

2.1   Audio and Video Ground Truth: From Precise to Weak Annotations

The challenge of multimedia modeling, developed intensively during the 2000s, has produced multiple campaigns for information retrieval, for instance with video [20] or audio events [15]. In this framework, vast amount of data have been manually annotated. These annotations are usually precise and time consuming. For example, audio events, such as speaker turns in case of speaker diarisation, or music notes in the case of Music Information Retrieval, are usually annotated at a millisecond scale [3]. Moreover, as these annotations are hardly objective, an agreement between annotators is usually needed [21]. For these different tasks of annotation, different softwares have been proposed (see [19] for a comparison).

Lately, Deep Learning based approaches [9] outperform the state of the art in many domains. However, they require a large amount of data. Because a precise annotation of these data is almost impossible, recent datasets include only *weak annotations*. These weak annotations really differ from a precisely annotated ground truth, as they may be incomplete, not relevant and heterogeneous. For example, the Audioset dataset [6] provides a large set of audio data extracted from videos, but the annotations were tagged by YouTube users on the audiovisual content. In the area of vision, the AVA dataset [7] provides precise spatio-temporal annotations of persons conducting actions, but the sound of the video is not taken into account.

Finally, most of the research works are usually mono-modal based (only audio or video stream). The issue of merging audio and visual information to richer concepts is rarely addressed by the different scientific communities. In that scope, the softwares used for manual annotations seem to deal with multi-modality as a juxtaposition of mono-modal annotations.

2.2   Multi-modal and Multi-view

The modeling of multi-modal (or cross-modal) inputs is very challenging, for example when studying discourses containing speech and non-linguistic signs [8]. Some applications rely on a precise interaction between image and sound. For instance, the detection of talking heads has been addressed [11]. In this context, various works deal with the fusion of audio and video modalities, for example with early, intermediate or late fusion [18]. Besides, other applications deal with other modalities, for instance image and texts [17].

The issue of annotating a multi-modal dataset in the case of audiovisual content is clearly addressed in [10]. Whereas this study aims at automatically detecting overt aggression in public places, the authors state that "problems with automatically processing multi-modal data start already from the annotation level". The complexity of the interactions between modalities forced the authors to produce three different types of annotations: audio, video, and multi-modal. The combination of these three annotations increase the performances of an automatic detector based on a machine learning approach. However, the processing of these annotations is time-consuming and sensitive. Firstly, this procedure necessitates at least three different kinds of playbacks (audio, video and audiovisual) to perform the annotation. Secondly, in order to process independent annotations with limited influence among modalities, three different annotators at least are required.

Furthermore, increasing amounts of scenes are filmed simultaneously from different points of view. In particular, in the context of video surveillance, different cameras are usually used [22]. The framework of Motion Capture also provides interesting databases that include different views [16]. The reflective markers placed on a human body allow the recording of the absolute position of each part of the body, which can be directly used as a reference. However, these applications usually remain in the field of laboratory studies and are hard to deploy in a real-life context.

The context of field recordings is generally more challenging [2] due to the number of overlapping events and objects. Considering audio, many events overlap and produce a mixture. Moreover, the movement of the audio sources (for instance a passing car) makes it difficult to position the starting and ending boundaries of the events. Same kind of difficulties arise considering images, with occlusion, superposition, illumination and size of objects.

Different works review datasets from the perspective of multi-modal and multi-view features [12,13,16]. However, as observed in [13], these datasets are often limited by different criteria including presence of audio, realism for real life applications, and number of overlapping and disjoint views.

2.3   Audio-Vision

The relationship between sound and image has been investigated for a long time, in particular in the context of cinema. A reference book [4] details the different possibilities of using sounds in videos.

Focusing on the area where the action takes place, the first distinction has to be drawn between sounds of the scene that could be heard by the film's characters, and sounds that could not. The first category is called *diegetic* sounds. The second category consists of non-diegetic sounds that are added in a post-production step, for example in the case of voice-over. More precisely, the diegetic sound source can be on-screen or off-screen. Furthermore, the source of the sound can be at times visualized in the image. Otherwise, if the sound source is not visible, the sound is called *acousmatic*. Figure 1 summarizes these different interactions.

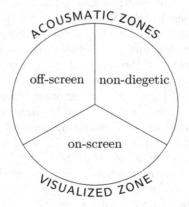

Fig. 1. The audiovisual scene (adapted from [4]).

In a multi-view sequence, the source of a sound may be either visualized or off-screen according to the different points of view. If the source of a sound is ambiguous or not visible in the current video, a different viewpoint may disclose it. We speak about *causal identification* when the source of a sound can be identified, whether it is visible or not in the current viewpoint.

As these different types of interaction are precisely depicted in a movie script, they are quite unusual in research papers. To our knowledge, research datasets do not provide information about on-screen and off-screen sounds. However, it seems that these different types of interaction have an influence on the perception and the understanding of the audiovisual content.

Finally, the audio and video parts interact in different ways to create an audiovisual perception. One of the clearest examples of the influence between audio and video lies in the McGurk effect [14], that demonstrates an interaction between hearing and vision in speech perception. Its most known implementation consists of a video of a human face saying a pseudo-word (*ga-ga*) with a voice over saying another one (*ba-ba*), leading to the perception of a third one (*da-da*). When annotating, this kind of phenomenon could occur in the same way and would lead to three different annotations (audio, video and audiovisual).

3   Audio/visual Annotation

3.1   Problematic

Audio and video annotations are usually based on different paradigms, but are both based on predefined categories to annotate, such as *car* or *speech*. Audio annotations usually consist in determining the start and the end of audio events and tag each event with a category (*engine noise, speech, horn sound*, etc.). Considering video, a usual procedure of annotation is to set a bounding box on each object of interest in each frame of the video and tag each object with some categories (*car, person, clothes*, etc.).

Procedures of annotation usually consider the audio and video streams as if they were disconnected and each media is annotated separately. In that process, a valuable information may be lost. In this article, we argue that the whole information embedded in an audiovisual content is greater than the sum of its audio and video parts. For example, if we separately annotate *speech* events (audio only) and *person* objects (video only), we cannot deduce if a visible person is the speaker or not.

In that context, some issues are clearly observable with the Audioset dataset (see Sect. 2.1). Most of the tags seem to have been set according to the video part, which usually dominates the audiovisual content. As a consequence, a video of a cat annotated as *cat* will also be annotated *cat* in the audio annotation, even if the cat remains silent in the video. To address these issues, we intend to merge the audio and video modalities into audiovisual objects. Practically, we aim to create an audiovisual object based on a moving bounding box and a corresponding audio event. Surprisingly, this task proved to be very difficult and many issues appeared and are detailed below.

A first challenge is about matching and merging one visual object and one audio event. First of all, we have considered a systematic fusion of events from the two modalities considering that this fusion could match segments from audio and video streams in the case of temporal overlapping. Unfortunately, this matching may introduce some wrong annotations when the audio annotation corresponds to an off-screen source. For example, Fig. 2 shows a car at the foreground. At the same moment the sound track is overpowered by an off-screen motorbike.

Fig. 2. Image bounding boxes around the cars. If a passing car is clearly visible at the foreground, a motorbike behind the camera overpowers the corresponding soundtrack.

A second challenge lies in the case of defining several annotations with temporal overlapping. The context of field recordings induces an audio mixture. Depending on his expertise, a human annotator may not be able to set precisely the starting and ending boundaries of the different audio events of this mixture. In this case, the matching between a specific audio event and the potential corresponding visual object can be impossible. In the same way, considering visual annotations, when annotating a group of objects, the annotator might be unable to draw bounding boxes around each element. Depending on the scale of the image or the mixing of objects in the image, the annotator may annotate each element separately, the entire group as a single object, or a mixture of single elements and rest of the group.

In this context, the issue consists of matching several audio and visual annotations with ensuring their relevancy. When many visual objects may have produced some sound events, the separation of the sound sources in the audio signal may be impossible. Let us consider the Fig. 3 that represents audio segments (time boundaries) and video annotations. In that scene, the passing of two consecutive vehicles have been auditory annotated as a single audio event. The solution for creating an audiovisual object from these annotations relies on the segmentation of the audio event in two parts to create two audiovisual objects. We have tested many possibilities to obtain the boundaries of the audio events but none of them was satisfying whatever the situation.

In a more sophisticated way, we could directly build audio, video and audiovisual annotations from the audiovisual stream. However, the completion of this task is not straightforward. Indeed, the influence of the audiovisual content may influence the annotation of the mono-modal streams. For instance, an annotator would more likely create an audio event for a moving car than for a stopped one, even if they both produce a motor noise.

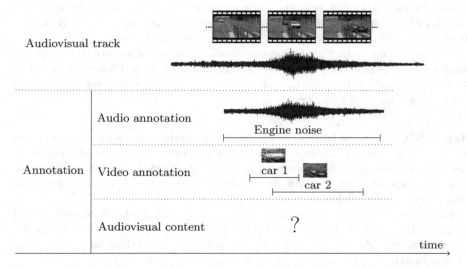

Fig. 3. Audiovisual annotation of the passing of two cars. In the audio modality, the passage of cars is heard as a unique lengthy sound. On the contrary, the video annotation clearly exhibits two different vehicles. Consequently, the automatic fusion of these two modalities to create audiovisual object(s) is very difficult to define.

3.2 Procedure of Annotation

We present here a procedure to obtain audio and visual annotations, as well as audiovisual information. It aims at satisfying the following goals:

- AUDIOVISUAL ADDED VALUE: the annotations must embed multi-modal information that allows a better understanding of the scene and an added value in comparison of the whole set of mono-modal annotations.
- MONO-MODAL USED: the audio and visual annotations must be usable in a mono-modal context. Therefore, additional information from other modality are not to be considered when creating mono-modal annotations.
- LOW ADDITIONAL COST: the audiovisual annotation must be objective and straightforward, and must not generate a heavy additional cost.

To address these different constraints, we propose the following two-steps protocol, which is designed to be processed manually.

Step 1: Mono-Modal Annotations. In this step, the audio and video annotations are processed separately. Optimally, the annotations have to be processed by different persons, without access to the other modality. For example, the annotator of the audio stream works only with audio. These two annotations can be processed in parallel.

For each modality, a unique identifier is set for each object in the scenes. The objects visible at different moments of the video (or on different videos in a multi-view context) must bear the same identifier. Similarly, the same identifier is set for each annotation of the same audio event in the case of a clearly unique event, for example a big explosion recorded by various devices.

At the end, an audio annotation contains description of audio events that are made up of *time boundaries*, *categories* and *identifier*. Visual annotations allow the description of objects on the basis of *time*, *spatial coordinates of bounding boxes*, *categories*, and *identifier*.

Step 2: Multi-modal Links. In a second step, audio and visual modalities are linked with each other. Links between audio and video identifiers are created in case of causal identification (see Sect. 2.3). In a multi-view case, an audio event could be associated with an off-screen object that is visible on another view. This process is detailed in next section.

In this step, the mono-modal annotations (audio or video) cannot be modified regarding the other modality, even if they appear to be wrong in the multi-modal context (see the McGurk effect in Sect. 2.3). These annotations were valid from a mono-modal annotation point of view and remain as they stand.

3.3   Implementation of Multi-modal Links

Considering the mono-modal annotations, we focus on audio and video annotations that temporally overlap. These annotations may refer to the same audio-visual document, or to different documents in the multi-view case.

Each of the audio annotations is considered in terms of sound source. If a causal identification is possible (see Sect. 2.3), we link audio to video annotations. A link means that audio annotations are enriched with the list of the linked visual objects considered as the source of the audio event. When an audio annotation is linked to several visual objects, the sources of the audio event can be all of the objects or some of them indifferently.

Table 1 summarizes the different annotation links between audio and video. Note that we only link audio event to video object (not video object to audio event) because of the unbalanced relationship between audio and video.

We detail below some concrete examples of links between audio and video annotations. In these examples, we focus on vehicles. However, as our procedure is generic, it can be applied on different kinds of events and objects.

Passing Vehicle: the audio and video events are linked if they undoubtedly originate from the same vehicle. If any doubt exists, for instance if the source of

Table 1. Annotation link procedure depending on the presence of audio and video annotations and the possibility of causal identification. A corresponds to an annotation of a single audio event (e.g. engine noise, speech, etc.). V corresponds to an annotation of a single visual object (e.g. car, person, etc.). $\{A_i\}$ corresponds to a set of audio annotations. $\{V_j\}$ corresponds to a set of video annotations. A link between annotations is denoted by $\rightarrow$.

	(1)	(2)	(3)		(4)		(5)		(6)	
Audio annotation	$\{A_i\}$	$\{\emptyset\}$	A		A		$\{A_i\}$		$\{A_i\}$	
Video annotation	$\{\emptyset\}$	$\{V_j\}$	V		$\{V_j\}$		V		$\{V_j\}$	
Causal identification	No	No	No	Yes	No	Yes	No	Yes	No	Yes
Annotation link	—	—	—	$A \rightarrow V$	—	$A \rightarrow \{V_j\}$	—	$\{A_i \rightarrow V\}$	—	$\{A_i \rightarrow \{V_j\}\}$

the audio event could be another vehicle that is not visible, the events are not linked (see Table 1 column 3 and Fig. 2).

Slammed Door: if a sound event occurs from the interaction of several visually annotated objects, we link the audio event to the each visual objects (see Table 1 column 4). For instance, in case of the closure of a car door with annotations for two objects (car and person), the audio event slammed door is linked to each of the two objects.

Passing Vehicle and Horn: in the case of multiple audio events that obviously originate from the same visual object, we link all audio events to the object (see Table 1 column 5). Thus, if an object *car* has been annotated visually and two audio events *engine* and *horn* are produced by the car, then the two audio events are linked to the visual object.

Passing of Multiple Vehicles: in the case of multiple vehicles passing with a different number of audio events (see Fig. 3), we link the audio events to all visual objects (see Table 1 column 6). However, if the audio source is not obvious (for instance a car horn when different vehicles are present), we do not link the audio event to any visual object.

4   Applications

We present hereafter different applications that are made possible by our procedure of annotation. In the case of mono-modal request, the annotated corpus can be used for different purposes. The audio annotations can be used in audio detection tasks (see [15] for examples). Similarly, the video annotations provide a framework for objects detection (see [20] for example). Using the bounding

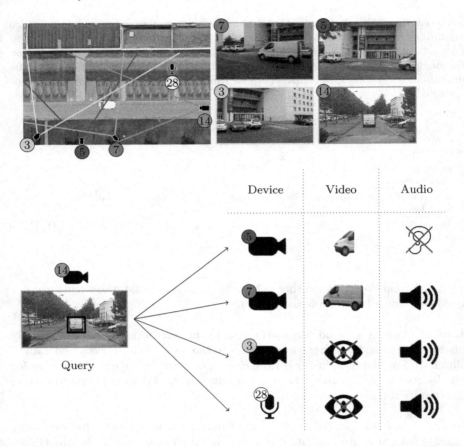

Fig. 4. Within a network of recording devices, our multi-modal annotation procedure allows to retrieve either visual objects only (camera 5), multi-modal objects (camera 7), or audio events only (camera 3, microphone 28) from audio or video queries. Note that camera 3 records audio and video, but the audible object is off-screen.

boxes drawn on each object, object re-identification based on image appearance can be driven.

In a context of surveillance with a network of recording devices (cameras recording video, microphones recording audio, smart-phones recording both video and audio...), our annotations allow users to perform different kinds of requests. Figure 4 illustrates this application in the context of the ToCaDa dataset [13]. Several devices are set around a scene: devices 3 and 7 record both audio and video, whereas devices 5 and 14 only record video stream. Finally, microphone 28 only records audio. From an audiovisual document, we may perform queries that can be either video only (for example by clicking the bounding box containing the vehicle on the video from camera 14) or audio only (for example by clicking on the represented audio event from the same video) in order to retrieve the object ID. All the audio events and video objects associated to the same ID are returned as results. These results can either be audio, visual, or audiovisual.

In a more complex application, this framework also allows multi-modal queries that aim to retrieve audiovisual objects, for example a vehicle with distinct sound and appearance.

5   Conclusion

In this paper, we propose a simple procedure to produce audiovisual annotations in different contexts such as multi-view dataset. Our approach aims to produce audio, visual, and audiovisual information. It is based on separate annotations on the audio and video modalities, followed by an audiovisual matching. In this way, an audiovisual annotation is produced, as well as audio and video annotations that remain relevant in a mono-modal context.

This procedure is simple. With respect to mono-modal annotations, our method does not extend the time of processing significantly. It can be deployed at a large scale, but, unlike *weak annotations*, maximizes the relevance of the annotation. Moreover, in the context of multi-view annotations, the required uniqueness of annotation identifiers allows for creating possibly relevant annotations not only with on-screen objects but also with off-screen objects. Finally, the resulting annotations produce a valuable approximation of what should be a *ground truth*.

References

1. Aroyo, L., Welty, C.: Truth is a lie: crowd truth and the seven myths of human annotation. AI Mag. **36**(1), 15–24 (2015)
2. Auer, E., et al.: Automatic annotation of media field recordings. In: ECAI 2010 Workshop on Language Technology for Cultural Heritage, Social Sciences, and Humanities (LaTeCH 2010), pp. 31–34. University de Lisbon (2010)
3. Bird, S., Liberman, M.: A formal framework for linguistic annotation. Speech Commun. **33**(1–2), 23–60 (2001)
4. Chion, M.: Audio-Vision: Sound on Screen. Columbia University Press, New York (1994)
5. Ellis, D.P., Whitman, B., Berenzweig, A., Lawrence, S.: The quest for ground truth in musical artist similarity. In: ISMIR, Paris, France (2002)
6. Gemmeke, J.F., et al.: Audio set: an ontology and human-labeled dataset for audio events. In: 2017 IEEE International Conference on Acoustics, Speech and Signal Processing (ICASSP), pp. 776–780. IEEE (2017)
7. Gu, C., et al.: AVA: a video dataset of spatio-temporally localized atomic visual actions. CoRR abs/1705.08421 (2017)
8. Iedema, R.: Multimodality, resemiotization: extending the analysis of discourse as multi-semiotic practice. Vis. Commun. **2**(1), 29–57 (2003)
9. LeCun, Y., Bengio, Y., Hinton, G.: Deep learning. Nature **521**(7553), 436 (2015)

10. Lefter, I., Rothkrantz, L.J.M., Burghouts, G., Yang, Z., Wiggers, P.: Addressing multimodality in overt aggression detection. In: Habernal, I., Matoušek, V. (eds.) TSD 2011. LNCS (LNAI), vol. 6836, pp. 25–32. Springer, Heidelberg (2011). https://doi.org/10.1007/978-3-642-23538-2_4

11. Li, D., Dimitrova, N., Li, M., Sethi, I.K.: Multimedia content processing through cross-modal association. In: Proceedings of the Eleventh ACM International Conference on Multimedia, pp. 604–611. ACM (2003)

12. Liu, A.A., Xu, N., Nie, W.Z., Su, Y.T., Wong, Y., Kankanhalli, M.: Benchmarking a multimodal and multiview and interactive dataset for human action recognition. IEEE Trans. Cybern. **47**(7), 1781–1794 (2017)

13. Malon, T., et al.: Toulouse campus surveillance dataset: scenarios, soundtracks, synchronized videos with overlapping and disjoint views (regular paper). In: ACM Multimedia Systems Conference (MMSys), Amsterdam, 12 June 2018–15 June 2018. ACM Multimedia Systems, June 2018

14. McGurk, H., MacDonald, J.: Hearing lips and seeing voices. Nature **264**(5588), 746 (1976)

15. Mesaros, A., et al.: DCASE 2017 challenge setup: tasks, datasets and baseline system. In: DCASE 2017-Workshop on Detection and Classification of Acoustic Scenes and Events (2017)

16. Ofli, F., Chaudhry, R., Kurillo, G., Vidal, R., Bajcsy, R.: Berkeley MHAD: a comprehensive multimodal human action database. In: 2013 IEEE Workshop on Applications of Computer Vision (WACV), pp. 53–60. IEEE (2013)

17. Pereira, J.C., et al.: On the role of correlation and abstraction in cross-modal multimedia retrieval. IEEE Trans. Pattern Anal. Mach. Intell. **36**(3), 521–535 (2014)

18. Pinquier, J., et al.: Strategies for multiple feature fusion with hierarchical hmm: application to activity recognition from wearable audiovisual sensors. In: 2012 21st International Conference on Pattern Recognition (ICPR), pp. 3192–3195. IEEE (2012)

19. Rohlfing, K., et al.: Comparison of multimodal annotation tools-workshop report. Gesprächforschung-Online-Zeitschrift zur Verbalen Interaktion **7**, 99–123 (2006)

20. Russakovsky, O., et al.: ImageNet Large scale visual recognition challenge. Int. J. Comput. Vis. (IJCV) **115**(3), 211–252 (2015)

21. Turnbull, D., Barrington, L., Torres, D., Lanckriet, G.: Semantic annotation and retrieval of music and sound effects. IEEE Trans. Audio Speech Lang. Process. **16**(2), 467–476 (2008)

22. Wang, X.: Intelligent multi-camera video surveillance: a review. Pattern Recogn. Lett. **34**(1), 3–19 (2013)

A Robust Multi-Athlete Tracking Algorithm by Exploiting Discriminant Features and Long-Term Dependencies

Nan Ran[1], Longteng Kong[1], Yunhong Wang[1], and Qingjie Liu[1,2(✉)]

[1] The State Key Laboratory of Virtual Reality Technology and Systems,
Beihang University, Beijing 100191, China
{nknanran,konglongteng,yhwang,qingjie.liu}@buaa.edu.cn
[2] Beijing Key Laboratory of Digital Media,
School of Computer Science and Engineering,
Beihang University, Beijing 100191, China

Abstract. This paper addresses multiple athletes tracking problem. Athletes tracking is the key to whether sports video analysis can be more effective and practical or not. One great challenge faced by multi-athlete tracking is that athletes, especially the athletes in the same team, share very similar appearance, thus, most existing MOT approaches are hardly applicable in this task. To address this problem, we put forward a novel triple-stream network which could capture long-term dependencies by exploiting pose information to better distinguish different athletes. The method is motivated by the fact that poses of athletes are distinct from each other in a period of time because they play different roles in the team thus could be used as a strong feature to match the correct athletes. We design our Multi-Athlete Tracking (MAT) model on top of the online tracking-by-detection paradigm whereby bounding boxes from the output of a detector are connected across video frames, and improve it from two aspects. Firstly, we propose a Pose-based Triple Stream Networks (PTSN) based on Long Short-Term Memory (LSTM) networks, which are capable of modeling and capturing more subtle differences between athletes. Secondly, based on PTSN, we propose a multi-athlete tracking algorithm that is robust to noisy detection and occlusion. We demonstrate the effectiveness of our method on a collection of volleyball videos by comparing it with recent advanced multi-object trackers.

Keywords: Sports video analysis · Multi-Athlete Tracking (MAT)
Long Short-Term Memory (LSTM) networks

1 Introduction

In recent years, sports video analysis has received increasing attention in academia and industry due to its scientific challenges and promising applications.

N. Ran and L. Kong—Authors contributed equally.

© Springer Nature Switzerland AG 2019
I. Kompatsiaris et al. (Eds.): MMM 2019, LNCS 11295, pp. 411–423, 2019.
https://doi.org/10.1007/978-3-030-05710-7_34

It covers a variety of application scenarios or research directions, including automatic game commentary, tactical analysis, player statistics, etc. Among these directions, athletes tracking is very basic and critical for sports video analysis. Several efforts have been made to address this issue. For instance, Mauthner [15] and Gomez [5] used particle filters to predict positions and velocities of players in beach volleyball games. They separate foreground and background to make athlete modeling easier, but cues in background may lose potentially useful in improving the stability and accuracy of trackers. Liu et al. [13] tracked players in basketball and hockey game videos from the view of tactics analysis. They try to predict all the possible move directions of players, but it may incur failure due to infinite possibilities. Lu et al. [14] employed object proposal scheme for scale refinement and introduced a candidate obstruction based strategy to track athletes in sports videos. However, it is not suitable for multi-athlete tracking.

There exists a number of approaches attempting to address Multi-Object Tracking (MOT) problem. Before deep learning achieves breakthrough progress, some traditional methods [9,20,21] used hand-crafted features to represent similarities, and tried to capture similar features between adjacent frames. Recently, Yu et al. [23] took advantage of high-performance detection and representative feature of CNNs, and achieved significantly better results on MOTChallenge [11,16] in both online and offline mode; Leal-Taixé et al. [10] defined a new CNN-based structure for people appearance representation to build effective relations between detections. Sadeghian et al. [19] presented a structure Recurrent Neural Networks (RNN) based network architecture that reasons jointly on multiple cues over a temporal window. However, in real sports scenes, there exists some specific difficulties, e.g. camera moving, occlusion and similar appearance properties such as clothing, height, body size. Specifically, in a volleyball game, athletes, especially the athletes in the same team wear same team jersey and with similar height and body size. Previous MOT tracking methods [3,7,8,19] mainly focus on appearance similarity, which has low resolving ability between athletes in the same team. As a result, introducing general-pupose MOT methods are hardly applicable to these scenes. Observing that even they have very similar appearance, the poses of them are distinct from each other within a period of time. This brings us idea that pose information may help to improve the performance of multi-athlete tracking. Motivated by this observation, we propose our multi-athlete tracking framework.

Like most popular multiple targets tracking methods, we follow the online tracking-by-detection paradigm, which can be defined as a process of utilizing a tracker to connect bounding boxes from the output of a detector across video frames to get the trajectories of targets, and improve it in terms of two aspects, i.e. similarity networks as well as tracking algorithm. Firstly, we design a triple-stream network by integrating pose information into three clues: appearance, motion and interaction. The network models pose-based composite features and could capture more subtle differences between athletes. Secondly, we design a multi-athlete tracking algorithm by incorporating propagation of bounding box, making it robust to noisy detection and occlusion. We demonstrate the effectiveness of our method by comparing it with recently proposed advanced multi-object trackers. Our method outperforms them on a collection of videos of volleyball games.

2   Multi-Athlete Tracking Framework

MAT is a special case of MOT. Similarly, It can be defined as detecting multiple athletes at each frame of a given sport video and matching their identities across different frames to generate a set of athletes trajectories (we call them tracklets) over times.

In order to complete this task, we employ the online tracking-by-detection paradigm. Specifically, we use a series of bounding boxes generated by the object detector Faster R-CNN [18] in each frame as inputs to the tracker. Whenever a new bounding box comes, a similarity network is applied to calculate the similarity scores between the tracked athletes and the candidate bounding box. If the similarity score is high enough, the new bounding box will be connected to the tracklet to form a new tracklet. When all candidate frames have been entered, all formed tracklets will be treated as tracker outputs.

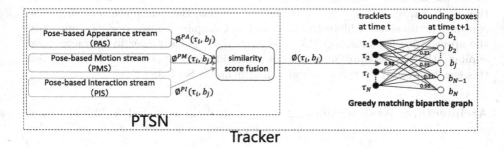

Fig. 1. Our multi-athlete tracking framework.

Our framework, as shown in Fig. 1, consists of the PTSN and the tracking algorithm. PSTN captures long-term dependencies by emphasizing pose similarity, making the tracker more robust to noisy detection and occlusions. Details of our proposed PTSN will be described in Sects. 2.1, 2.2, 2.3 and 2.4. Section 2.5 gives details of the designed multi-athlete tracking algorithm.

2.1   Overall Architecture of PTSN

The overall architecture of PTSN is shown in left-side of Fig. 1. It is comprised of three streams, including Pose-based Appearance Stream (PAS), Pose-based Motion Stream (PMS) and Posed-based Interaction Stream (PIS). Each of them generates similarity score $\phi^{PA}(\tau_i, b_j)$, $\phi^{PM}(\tau_i, b_j)$ and $\phi^{PI}(\tau_i, b_j)$ respectively and are fused through the average strategy into a final similarity score $\phi(\tau_i, b_j)$.

The score will be used to connect the tracklet τ_i and the detection b_j in a bipartite graph by gready match algorithm, as shown in right-side of Fig. 1. The details of the three streams of PTSN will be explained in the following three subsections.

It is particularly worth mentioning that pose feature is incorporated as an important clue in three streams, which will significantly enhances the ability of the network to distinguish similar athletes because of its ability in characterizing unique status of athletes under complex sports scenes. Moreover, by using LSTM as the main structure, our networks have the ability to encode long-term dependencies in the observed sequence. Unlike popular graph tracking based methods [1,9,20], whose similarity scores are only calculated in the previous frame of observation, our method calculates similarity score by inferring from the variable length observation sequences. This makes our network use more abundant information to determine similarity relationships.

2.2 Pose-Based Appearance Stream (PAS)

The main purpose of PAS is to combine pose and appearance feature of athletes to capture those more subtle differences between a tracked tracklet and a candidate bounding box. In other words, it can be viewed as a binary classification problem, with the goal of recognizing whether the candidate bounding box containing the same athlete to the tracklet. Compared with models using only the appearance features, our PAS has more distinguish power in characterizing similar athletes by combining pose information and appearance features, and this can be proved by the ablation experiments in Sect. 3.

Architecture: As shown in Fig. 2, our PAS is designed based on LSTM with a softmax layer as output. It accepts concatenation vectors $(\phi_1^{pa}, \phi_2^{pa}, ..., \phi_t^{pa}, \phi_{t+1}^{pa})$

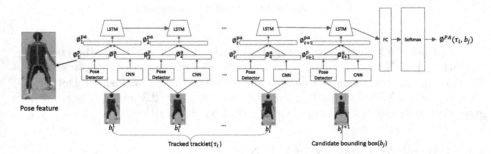

Fig. 2. Architecture of PAS. The inputs are τ_i and b_j. τ_i is tracklet of ith athlete, composed of his bounding boxes from time 1 to t, and b_j is a candidate detection at time $t + 1$. The concatenated features (*i.e.* pose features and appearance features) are fed into an LSTM followed by a softmax layer to generate the similarity score $\phi^{PA}(\tau_i, b_j)$.

which consist of pose features $(\phi_1^p, \phi_2^p, ..., \phi_t^p, \phi_{t+1}^p)$ from pose detector and appearance features $(\phi_1^a, \phi_2^a, ..., \phi_t^a, \phi_{t+1}^a)$ from CNN as input. Let $(b_i^1, b_i^2, ..., b_i^t)$ be a set of bounding boxes of tracked athlete's trajectory at timesteps $1, \ldots, t$, denoted by tracklet τ_i. Let b_j^{t+1} be the candidate bounding box at timestep t+1. The pose detector and CNN accept the image content within bounding boxes as input and produce a H-dimensional feature vector ϕ^p and ϕ^a respectively. These two H-dimensional feature vectors are concated to a 2H-dimensional feature vector ϕ^{pa}, and then it will be sent to the LSTM. The last hidden layer vector of LSTM is inputed to a softmax layer to derive a similarity score $\phi^{PA}(\tau_i, b_j)$ that measures the degree of similarity between b_j^{t+1} and $(b_i^1, b_i^2, ..., b_i^t)$. After the similarity score fusion and the greedy matching, we will decide whether to add b_j to τ_i or not, according to the score $\phi(\tau_i, b_j)$.

Note that we use last layer of AlphaPose [4] as pose feature and the first FC layer of ResNet [6] as appearance feature. Moreover, we pretrain ResNet-101 on Volly dataset, in order to capture the feature of the player rather than any general objects. We remove all existing FC layers and add an additional FC layer with fixed size output to obtain H-dimension feature.

2.3 Pose-Based Motion Stream (PMS)

The PMS is the second stream of PTSN, which exploits motion information of each joint of the athlete to capture significant difference between different athletes, thus computing the similarity score between a tracked tracklet and a candidate bounding box. The velocities of different players differ significantly, which make it easier to track the same athlete between two adjacent frames. Compared with representing velocity of an athlete by movement of the center of his/her bounding box, our PMS obtain velocity of each joint to describe motion

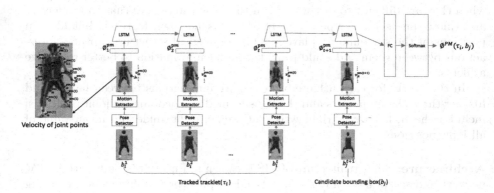

Fig. 3. Architecture of PMS. The inputs are τ and b_j. τ is tracklet of ith athlete, composed of his bounding boxes from time 1 to t, and b_j is a candidate detection at time $t + 1$. The motion features are fed into an LSTM followed by a softmax layer to generate the similarity score $\phi^{PM}(\tau_i, b_j)$. Velocity definition of body joints can be seen in left-side.

information of an athlete, resulting in increased robustness in discriminating athletes.

Architecture: As shown in Fig. 3, similar to PAS, the PMS is a structure based on LSTM with a softmax layer, that accepts the velocity features vectors $(\phi_1^{pm}, \phi_2^{pm}, ..., \phi_t^{pm}, \phi_{t+1}^{pm})$ from the motion extractor. Let $V_{ik}^{pm(t)}$ denotes the kth joint velocity of the ith athlete at the timestep t, which can be defined as:

$$V_{ik}^{pm(t)} = (V_{ik(x)}^{pm(t)}, V_{ik(y)}^{pm(t)}) = (X_{ik}^{pm(t-1)} - X_{ik}^{pm(t)}, Y_{ik}^{pm(t-1)} - Y_{ik}^{pm(t)}) \quad (1)$$

where $(X_{ik}^{pm(t)}, Y_{ik}^{pm(t)})$ are the 2D coordinates of ith athlete on the kth joint at timestep t on image. Velocities of sixteen joints derived from AlphaPose [4] can be seen from the left side of Fig. 3.

Let $(b_i^1, b_i^2, ..., b_i^t)$ be a set of bounding boxes of tracked athlete's trajectory at timesteps 1, . . . , t, denoted by tracklet τ_i. Let b_j^{t+1} be the candidate bounding box at timestep t + 1. The pose detector under motion extractor accept the raw content within each bounding box of athlete above and pass it through their layers until they finally produce a H-dimensional vector as input of LSTM. The last hidden layer vector of LSTM is inputed to a softmax layer to derive a similarity score $\phi^{PM}(\tau_i, b_j)$ that measures the degree of similarity between b_j and $(b_i^1, b_i^2, ..., b_i^t)$. After the similarity score fusion and the greedy matching, we will decide whether to add b_j to τ_i or not, according to the score $\phi(\tau_i, b_j)$.

2.4   Pose-Based Interaction Stream (PIS)

The third stream is PTSN. It represent interaction information between a specific athlete and players around him/her by computing similarity scores between a tracked box and candidates to form an Interaction Grid (IG). This is based on the fact that context features provide additional information to identify objects when they are difficult to distinguish. In this case, we believe that to re-identify an athlete, one should depend not only on his/her own features, but also on positions of the surrounding players. This topological structure captures interactions between them and could provide context information to better recognize athletes.

In this work, for each athlete, we compute interactions between he/her and his/her three closest players and the IG is formed by encoding six joint positions, including head, left wrist, right wrist, left ankle, right ankle and mean value of all joint positions.

Architecture: The architecture of PIS is shown in Fig. 4. It is built with LSTM network and accept a set of IGs as input and output a probability value indicating whether these IGs represent the same athlete. For instance, for the i-th athlete, we can obtain his/her IGs from the previous t frames: $(IG_i^1, IG_i^2, ..., IG_i^t)$. IG_i^t is calculated as follows:

$$IG_i^t(m, n) = \sum_{j \in \mathcal{N}_i, k \in \mathcal{P}_j} \mathbf{1}_{mn}[x_t^{jk} - x_t^i, y_t^{jk} - y_t^i] \quad (2)$$

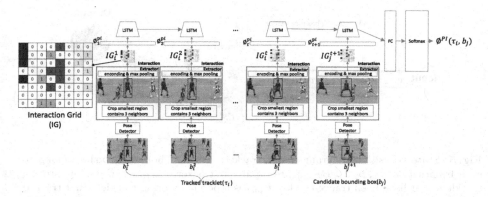

Fig. 4. The detail architecture of PIS. A pose detector is applied to obtain pose information of an athlete from previous t frames. The interaction grids of this athlete are calculated between his/her closest 3 neighbors at each frame. Then we apply a LSTM to encode interaction information for this athlete and compare it with candidate boxes b_j generated by the detector at timestep $t + 1$. Finally, the LSTM output a similarity score $\phi^{PI}(\tau_i, b_j)$ indicating probability of the candidate boxes containing the same athlete.

where $\mathbf{1}_{mn}[x, y]$ is an indicator function to check if the athlete's joint at (x, y) is in the (m, n) cell of the grid. $\mathcal{N}_i$ is the set of neighbors of the athlete i, $|\mathcal{N}_i| = 3$. $\mathcal{P}_j$ is the set of joints of neighbor j. At timestep $t + 1$, the Faster R-CNN generates a set of candidate bounding boxes $\{b_j^{t+1}\}$ potentially containing athletes. Similarly, we can obtain $\{IG_j^{t+1}\}$ for each box. As discussed above, the previous $(IG_i^1, IG_i^2, ..., IG_i^t)$ indicate the same athlete, we intend to find the same athlete from the candidate boxes by calculating the similarly scores between them. And for each candidate box b_j^{t+1} a similarly score $\phi^{PI}(\tau_i, b_j)$ can be obtained by PIS.

2.5   The Proposed Multi-Athlete Tracking Algorithm

After obtaining similarity scores described in Subsects. 2.2, 2.3 and 2.4, we use a simple average strategy to produce the final fusion score. In the following, we design a multi-athlete tracking algorithm based on the PTSN which has strong distinguish ability in recognizing similar athletes, making the tracker robust to noisy and occlusion. The tracking algorithm is shown in Algorithm 1. State transition diagram of our tracker is shown in Fig. 5. First of all, a set of bounding boxes belong to each frames $\{B^0, B^1, B^2, ..., B^{T-1}\}$ is inputted to our tracker, then filtered via Non-Maximum Suppression (NMS) operation. High score bounding boxes are selected to next step (as *a1* operation). On the contrary, low score bounding box is directly sent to die tracklets container (C_{die}), ending its life cycle (as *a2* operation). For each high score bounding box b_j, it is sent to PTSN together with each tracked tracklet τ_i belong to active tracklets container (C_{active}, consist of tracked tracklets $\{\tau_1, \tau_2, ..., \tau_i, ..., \tau_n\}$ in previous

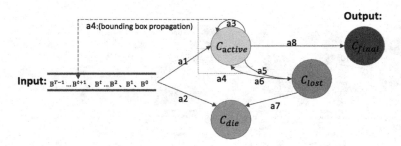

Fig. 5. State transition diagram of our tracker. A set of bounding boxes belong to each frames $\{B_0, B_1, B_2, ..., B_{T-1}\}$ are input our tracker. C_{active} is a pooling storing tracklets that have been tracked so far. C_{lost} is a pooling storing tracklets that tracked but lost. C_{die} is a pooling storing tracklets judged to be illegal. C_{final} is a pooling storing legal output tracklets. The transfer actions $\{a1, a2, ..., a8\}$ between them will be explained in detail below, and there will be corresponding annotation in the Algorithm 1.

frames) to decide whether to add b_j to τ_i or not. If succeed (similarity score over σ_{PTSN}), they will form new τ_i and update old τ_i in C_{active} (as $a3$ operation), then bounding box propagation operation will be done to predict next bounding box of τ_i in the following frame, according to velocity of τ_i (as $a4$ operation). If they fail, both b_j and old τ_i will be sent to next step (as $a5$ operation). We refer those old τ_i to missing tracklet. For the remaining detections, we compare with tracklets in C_{die} for targets recovery. The process will be done for every b_j. If they match successfully (smilarity score over σ_{PTSN}), they will be sent to T_{active} again (as $a6$ operation), and then bounding box propagation operation will be done to predict next bounding box of τ_i in the following frame, according to velocity of τ_i (as $a4$ operation). If they fail and the waiting time has exceeded the hyper-parameter $\delta_{waiting}$, they will be sent to C_{die}, ending its life cycle (as $a7$ operation). After that, still remaining bounding box will form a new tracklet and wait for a match in C_{lost}. When bounding boxes of the last frame B_{T-1} is executed, all tracklet of C_{active} will be copied to C_{final} as output of our tracker as long as they are longer than λ_{min} (as $a8$ operation). More detailed algorithm steps are strictly illustrated in Algorithm 1.

3   Experiment

To evaluate the proposed method, we conduct extensive experiments on the Volleyball(Voll) dataset. The database, implementation details, evaluation index, and results are described in the following.

Database. The public benchmark for sports video is very limited compared to that for general Multi-Target Tracking. In this study, we use a dataset collected from YouTube. The dataset contains 27 video clips of volleyball games, the size of

Algorithm 1. A multi-athlete tracking algorithm

Inputs:
$B = \{B^0, B^1, B^2, ..., B^{T-1}\} = \{\{b_0, b_1, ..., b_{N-1}\}^0, ..., \{b_0, b_1, ..., b_{N-1}\}^{T-1}\}$
Outputs:
C_{final}
1: Initial: $C_{active} = B^1$, $C_{lost} = \phi$, $C_{die} = \phi$, $C_{final} = \phi$
2: **for** $t = 2$ to $T - 1$ **do**
3:     $Bt = \text{NMS}(B^t)$
4:     **for** $\tau_i \in C_{active}$ **do**
5:         $b_{best} = b_j$, where $\max(\text{PTSN}(\tau_i, b_j))$, $b_j \in B^t$
6:         **if** $\text{PTSN}(\tau_i, b_j) \geq \sigma_{PTSN}$ **then**
7:             add b_{best} to τ_i and remove b_{best} from B^t
8:             predict b_p from τ_i and add b_p to B^{t+1}
9:         **else**
10:             move τ_i to C_{lost}
11:         **end if**
12:     **end for**
13:     **for** $\tau_i \in C_{lost}$ **do**
14:         $b_{best} = b_j$ where $\max(\text{PTSN}(\tau_i, b_j))$, $b_j \in B^t$
15:         **if** $\text{PTSN}(\tau_i, b_j) \geq \sigma_{PTSN}$ **then**
16:             add b_{best} to τ_i; remove b_{best} from B^t and move τ_i to C_{active}
17:             predict b_p from τ_i and add b_p to B^{t+1}
18:         **else**
19:             **if** $time_{waiting}(\tau_i) \geq \delta_{waiting}$ **then**
20:                 move τ_i to C_{die}
21:             **end if**
22:         **end if**
23:         **for** $b_j \in B^t$ **do**
24:             start a new tracklet with b_j and insert it into C_{lost}
25:         **end for**
26:     **end for**
27: **end for**
28: **for** $\tau_i \in C_{active}$ **do**
29:     **if** $len(\tau_i) \geq \lambda_{min}$ **then**
30:         add τ_i to C_{final}
31:     **end if**
32: **end for**

which is comparable to that of MOTChanllenge [11, 16]. Each video is captured from a game by a camera equipped at the end line of competition terrain, and there hence exist variations in background, illumination, body shape and clothing. The locations of players are manually labeled at each frame as groundtruth. In our experiments, 14 video clips are used for tuning the parameters of the model, and the others for testing.

Implementation Details. In our experiments, we set H (size of input vectors to LSTM) as 32 for all the tree streams, but the source of the input vector are different. 64-dimensional input vector of PAS ϕ_t^{pa} consists of 32-dimensional ϕ_t^p from the pose detector and 32-dimensional ϕ_t^{pa} from the ResNet; 32-dimensional input vector of PMS ϕ_t^{pm} comes from result processed by motion extractor; 64-dimensional input vector of PIS ϕ_t^{pi} is from expanding 8×8 Interaction Grid by column. The network hyper-parameters are chosen by cross validation and our framework is trained with Adam optimizer. Size of LSTM Hidden layer vector is

128. We train our PSTN with a mini-batch of 64, and initially set learning rate as 0.002 and decrease it by a factor of 0.1 in every 10 epochs. The PSTN was trained for 50 epochs.

Evaluation Indexes. To evaluate performance of multiple athletes tracking algorithms, we use metrics widely used in MOT [16]. Among them, Multiple Object Tracking Accuracy (MOTA) and Multiple Object Tracking Precision (MOTP) are two popular ones. According to [2], MOTA gives a very intuitive measure of the tracker's performance at detecting objects and keeping their trajectories. MOTP shows the ability of a tracker to estimate precise object positions. In addition, there are some indicators that we use to measure the quality of the method. Mostly Tracked targets (MT) can be defined as the ratio of ground-truth trajectories that are covered by a track predictions for at least 80% of their respective life span; Mostly Lost targets (ML) can be defined as the ratio of ground-truth trajectories that are covered by a track hypothesis for at most 20% of their respective life span; FP can be define as the total number of false positive and FN can be defined as the total number of false negatives (missed targets). IDS is defined as total number of identity switches [12].

Results Analysis. We explore the contributions of different components in PTSN to the performance of tracking on the test set. Table 1 shows the results. Clearly, combining all the three streams obtains the best results. Incorporating pose information (PAS) gains about 8% improvement compared with using only

Table 1. Oblation study of the PSTN. The results improve significantly as more information is added into the network. We can also clearly see that pose information is effective in strengthening tracker.

Tracker	MOTA↑	MOTP↑	MT↑	ML↓	FP↓	FN↓	IDS↓
AS	71.3	62.5	44.71%	19.43%	954	2,191	578
PAS	79.5	68.2	47.65%	16.03%	502	1,488	394
PAS + PMS	80.9	71.0	49.18%	15.31%	438	1,391	353
PAS + PMS + PIS	**84.1**	**76.3**	**52.1%**	**13.5%**	**325**	**1,105**	**286**

Table 2. Comparison with state-of-the-art trackers on the test dataset.

Tracker	MOTA↑	MOTP↑	MT↑	ML↓	FP↓	FN↓	IDS↓
MHT_DAM [8]	58.9	49.3	28.38%	35.07%	1,864	4,018	1,694
CEM [17]	62.3	55.1	39.79%	26.45%	1,342	2,976	1,052
RMOT [22]	60.1	52.5	38.01%	27.53%	1,573	3,271	1,218
MDPNN [19]	72.7	64.0	45.55%	18.03%	860	2,182	545
Ours	**84.1**	**76.3**	**52.1%**	**13.5%**	**325**	**1,105**	**286**

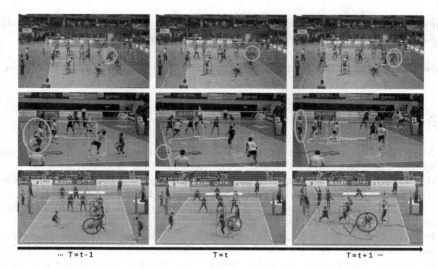

Fig. 6. Tracking results on the test sequences of the Voll dataset. (Color figure online)

appearance (AS) in terms of MOTA, indicating that pose information does help to improve tracking performance. Comparisons with four recently proposed multiple object tracking methods are summarized in Table 2. It can be observed that the proposed approach clearly outperforms the state-of-the-art ones, including MHT_DAM [8], CEM [17], RMOT [22] and MDPNN [19], on multiple metrics such as the MOTA, MT, and ML. It indicates the effectiveness of the PTSN as well as our proposed tracking algorithm for multi-athlete tracking in sports videos. By using long term dependencies of multiple clues, our method can largely recover back to the right target after an occlusion. Figure 6 illustrates some success and failure examples. We can see that in the first two rows, the athletes in green circles are occluded by the front ones, hence lost tracking states. But when the targets re-appear, our method re-match them with the correct identities. Our method is likely to fail in more difficult situation. For instance, the athlete in red circle in Fig. 6 is assigned with a new identity due to the large action changes and the long time occlusion.

4   Conclusion

In this paper, we propose a high similarity distinguishable method to track multiple athletes in sports videos. It is based on the online tracking-by-detection paradigm, and we mainly improve it from two aspects. First of all, we incorporate pose feature into three main clues, appearance, motion and interaction, finally forming PTSN with LSTM networks as the main structure. Then, we design a multi-athlete tracking algorithm that is robust to noisy detection and occlusion, since it incorporates the idea of bounding box propagation. The proposed method is evaluated on the Voll dataset, and the comparison with state-of-the-art trackers clearly demonstrates its advantage for this task.

Acknowledgments. This work was supported by the National Natural Science Foundation of China (61573045).

References

1. Adam, A., Rivlin, E., Shimshoni, I.: Robust fragments-based tracking using the integral histogram. In: CVPR, vol. 1, pp. 798–805. IEEE (2006)
2. Bernardin, K., Stiefelhagen, R.: Evaluating multiple object tracking performance: the CLEAR MOT metrics. J. Image Video Process. 1 (2008)
3. Dicle, C., Camps, O.I., Sznaier, M.: The way they move: tracking multiple targets with similar appearance. In: ICCV, pp. 2304–2311. IEEE (2013)
4. Fang, H., Xie, S., Tai, Y.W., Lu, C.: RMPE: regional multi-person pose estimation. In: ICCV, vol. 2 (2017)
5. Gomez, G., López, P.H., Link, D., Eskofier, B.: Tracking of ball and players in beach volleyball videos. PLoS ONE **9**, e111730 (2014)
6. He, K., Zhang, X., Ren, S., Sun, J.: Deep residual learning for image recognition. In: CVPR, pp. 770–778 (2016)
7. Henschel, R., Leal-Taixé, L., Cremers, D., Rosenhahn, B.: Improvements to Frank-Wolfe optimization for multi-detector multi-object tracking. CoRR (2017)
8. Kim, C., Li, F., Ciptadi, A., Rehg, J.M.: Multiple hypothesis tracking revisited. In: ICCV, pp. 4696–4704. IEEE (2015)
9. Kuo, C.H., Nevatia, R.: How does person identity recognition help multi-person tracking? In: CVPR, pp. 1217–1224. IEEE (2011)
10. Leal-Taixe, L., Canton-Ferrer, C., Schindler, K.: Learning by tracking: siamese CNN for robust target association. In: CVPR Workshop. IEEE, June 2016
11. Leal-Taixé, L., Milan, A., Reid, I., Roth, S., Schindler, K.: Motchallenge 2015: towards a benchmark for multi-target tracking. arXiv preprint arXiv:1504.01942 (2015)
12. Li, Y., Huang, C., Nevatia, R.: Learning to associate: hybridboosted multi-target tracker for crowded scene. In: CVPR (2009)
13. Liu, J., Carr, P., Collins, R.T., Liu, Y.: Tracking sports players with context-conditioned motion models. In: CVPR, pp. 1830–1837 (2013)
14. Lu, J., Huang, D., Wang, Y., Kong, L.: Scaling and occlusion robust athlete tracking in sports videos. In: 2016 IEEE International Conference on Acoustics, Speech and Signal Processing (ICASSP), pp. 1526–1530. IEEE (2016)
15. Mauthner, T., Koch, C., Tilp, M., Bischof, H.: Visual tracking of athletes in beach volleyball using a single camera. Int. J. Comput. Sci. Sport **6**(2), 21–34 (2007)
16. Milan, A., Leal-Taixé, L., Reid, I., Roth, S., Schindler, K.: MOT16: a benchmark for multi-object tracking. arXiv preprint arXiv:1603.00831 (2016)
17. Perazzi, F., Pont-Tuset, J., McWilliams, B., Van Gool, L., Gross, M., Sorkine-Hornung, A.: A benchmark dataset and evaluation methodology for video object segmentation. In: CVPR, pp. 724–732 (2016)
18. Ren, S., He, K., Girshick, R., Sun, J.: Faster R-CNN: towards real-time object detection with region proposal networks. In: NIPS, pp. 91–99. MIT Press (2015)
19. Sadeghian, A., Alahi, A., Savarese, S.: Tracking the untrackable: learning to track multiple cues with long-term dependencies. In: ICCV (2017)

20. Shu, G., Dehghan, A., Oreifej, O., Hand, E., Shah, M.: Part-based multiple-person tracking with partial occlusion handling. In: CVPR, pp. 1815–1821. IEEE (2012)
21. Yamaguchi, K., Berg, A.C., Ortiz, L.E., Berg, T.L.: Who are you with and where are you going? In: CVPR, pp. 1345–1352. IEEE (2011)
22. Yoon, J.H., Yang, M.H., Lim, J., Yoon, K.J.: Bayesian multi-object tracking using motion context from multiple objects. In: 2015 IEEE Winter Conference on Applications of Computer Vision (WACV), pp. 33–40. IEEE (2015)
23. Yu, F., Li, W., Li, Q., Liu, Y., Shi, X., Yan, J.: POI: multiple object tracking with high performance detection and appearance feature. In: Hua, G., Jégou, H. (eds.) ECCV 2016. LNCS, vol. 9914, pp. 36–42. Springer, Cham (2016). https://doi.org/10.1007/978-3-319-48881-3_3

Early Identification of Oil Spills in Satellite Images Using Deep CNNs

Marios Krestenitis$^{(\boxtimes)}$, Georgios Orfanidis, Konstantinos Ioannidis$^{(\boxtimes)}$, Konstantinos Avgerinakis, Stefanos Vrochidis, and Ioannis Kompatsiaris

Centre for Research and Technology Hellas, Information Techologies Institute, Thessaloniki, Greece
{mikrestenitis,g.orfanidis,kioannid,koafgeri,stefanos,ikom}@iti.gr

Abstract. Oil spill pollution comprises a significant threat of the oceanic and coastal ecosystems. A continuous monitoring framework with automatic detection capabilities could be valuable as an early warning system so as to minimize the response time of the authorities and prevent any environmental disaster. The usage of Synthetic Aperture Radar (SAR) data acquired from satellites have received a considerable attention in remote sensing and image analysis applications for disaster management, due to the wide area coverage and the all-weather capabilities. Over the past few years, multiple solutions have been proposed to identify oil spills over the sea surface by processing SAR images. In addition, deep convolutional neural networks (DCNN) have shown remarkable results in a wide variety of image analysis applications and could be deployed to overcome the performance of previously proposed methods. This paper describes the development of an image analysis approach utilizing the benefits of a deep CNN combined with SAR imagery to establish an early warning system for oil spill pollution identification. SAR images are semantically segmented into multiple areas of interest including oil spill, look-alikes, land areas, sea surface and ships. The model was trained and tested using multiple SAR images, acquired from the Copernicus Open Access Hub and manually annotated. The dataset is a result of Sentinel-1 missions and EMSA records for relative pollution events. The conducted experiments demonstrate that the deployed DCNN model can accurately discriminate oil spills from other instances providing the relevant authorities a valuable tool to manage the upcoming disaster effectively.

Keywords: Oil spill identification · SAR image analysis
Deep convolutional neural networks · Disaster management

1 Introduction

Oil slicks have a significant impact to the ocean and coastal environments as well as to maritime commerce and activities. Early measurement is crucial in such cases to manage the disaster and prevent further environmental damage. Toward this direction, various algorithms and approaches have been presented

© Springer Nature Switzerland AG 2019
I. Kompatsiaris et al. (Eds.): MMM 2019, LNCS 11295, pp. 424–435, 2019.
https://doi.org/10.1007/978-3-030-05710-7_35

to identify automatically oil polluted areas over the sea surface. Most of these methods process satellite data and apply various remote sensing principles.

Considering the main objective of an early warning system, the accurate identification of oil slicks could assist the relevant authorities to have a more complete overview of the event. A wider dispersion of oil slicks on sea surfaces will result to major environmental problems not only to the maritime environment but also in coastal territories if its detection time is significantly large. Reversing the posed problem, a framework that provides a better understanding of the oil polluted areas and how its dispersion involves will decrease the response time and thus, manage the disaster more efficient. An all-weather solution will enhance even more the reliability of the system for such situations. Thus, proper satellite image analysis can potentially provide such solutions towards the required early disaster management.

Aiming at identifying oil spills by analyzing visual representations, the proposed model processes SAR images due to their independence regarding the weather conditions and the acquisition time. The method deploys a DCNN and semantically segments the regions of the input image into instances of interests (oil-spills, ships, land etc.). Due to the nature of the architecture, the model essentially learns the physics behind the oil spills, like size and shape, and so, it can accurately classify the required image regions.

The rest of the paper is organized as follows. In Sect. 2, relevant works dealing with the oil spills identification problem are analyzed while in Sect. 3, the proposed model is outlined. Section 4 presents the corresponding experimental results and finally, conclusion are drawn in Sect. 5.

2   Related Work

Incentive algorithms were focused on the utilization of images in the visible spectrum. Numerous approaches were proposed such as exploiting polarized lenses [14] and hyper-spectral imaging [5]. Researches proved that in visible spectrum oil slicks and water cannot be sufficiently distinguished while further limitations are inserted due to weather and luminosity conditions. Nevertheless, the field is considered still active due to the advancements of sensing technologies. To surpass optical sensor constraints, microwave sensors including radars were utilized. For early pollution detection, the acquired data rely on specialized sensors, namely Synthetic Aperture Radar (SAR), where successive pulses of radio waves are transmitted from some altitude and their reflection is recorded to produce a representation of the scene. SAR imagery was primarily used in [12] due to its invariance in lighting conditions and the occlusion caused by the existence of clouds or fog [3].

"Bright" SAR image regions, known as sea clutters, are produced by capillary waves which, under the existence of oil spills, are depressed and depicted as dark formations. However wind slicks, wave shadows behind land, algae blooms, and so forth. [3] can result to similar formations minimizing the effectiveness of the oil spill detector. The most common procedure of similar detections includes four discrete phases [18]. The first two phases include the detection of the dark formations in SAR images and the corresponding feature extraction, respectively. The features are compared with some predefined values in the third phase and finally, a decision making model classifies each formation. Several disadvantages accompany this method, originating from the restriction of extracting a set of features, the absence of a solid agreement over their nature and the lack of research over their effectiveness.

The majority of such detectors involve a two-class classification procedure, where one class corresponds to oil spills and a second, more abstract class that corresponds to dark formations of all similar phenomena [3]. The second class is usually considered as a group of subclasses like current shear, internal waves and so on. The characterization of the "dark spots" is highly affected by adjacent contextual information, like the presence of similar formations, ship routes etc. Considering the high resolution of the satellite SAR sensors, the acquired images may include not only maritime areas but coastal territories, also. Since SAR sensors operates under microwave frequencies, metallic objects are depicted as bright spots due to the beam reflectance. This explicit discrimination results to a fixed number of classes which comprises the main set in most relevant approaches. For example, decision trees were utilized in [18] to classify the extracted geometrical and textual features and so, oil spills could be discriminated from lookalikes. In addition, an object-oriented approach was used in [10] to radar image analysis and improve manual classification at the scale of entire water bodies. Conventional neural networks were also utilized to identify such environmental disasters [16] focusing on classifying the entire input image with one single label. Finally, a deep CNN model was used in [13] to discriminate oil spills with lookalikes nonetheless, the analysis was limited to a binary classification process.

Aiming at mitigating the limitations imposed by the relevant approaches, the proposed method utilizes a DCNN to segment semantically the processed SAR images instead of labeling local patches or marking the entire images. The classification result is applied at a pixel level and thus, the final image representation includes a map with all pixels annotated. In addition, most of the relevant methods prerequisite the extraction of some features that can describe the characteristics of the oils spills. Due to the sequential convolutional layers of the model, the requirement of computing initially a set of features to be classified as other relevant methods is not valid. Moreover, in relevance to similar DCNN-based methods [13], the presented scheme comprises a multi-scale architecture with four parallel DCNN branches resulting to more accurate classifications. Finally, the model was trained to identify more instances including land territories which eventually could increase the situational awareness of the operational personnel to manage more effectively the pollution disaster.

3   Methodology

The presented oil slick detector intends to segment semantically the input images and highlight the identified instances unlike the single labeling of the entire

SAR image. Oil dispersion creates a wide range of irregular shapes that may also coincide with vessels or look alike objects. Thus, semantic segmentation could consist the most appropriate approach compared to other alternatives like defining multiple labels in input image [19] or bounding boxes over detected objects [9]. The presented method can analyze images containing multi-class objects without the need of breaking the image into multiple patches to label the identified instances.

The CNN model relies on the DeepLab model [1], which is reported to achieve high performances in various multi-class segmentation problems [7,15]. Following the DeepLab architecture, the presented oil slick detector consists of four DCNN branches to perform image semantic segmentation while convolution is applied with upsampled filters [8], originally introduced in [4]. Atrous convolution in combination with an Atrous Spatial Pyramid Pooling (ASPP) is deployed to provide parallel filters of different rate and meet the requirements for dense and wide *field-of-view* filters. Finally, bilinear interpolation is utilized to increase the resolution of the extracted feature maps and restore the initial resolution of the input image. In Fig. 1, a higher level representation of the overall procedure is presented.

The initially proposed model employs a fully convolutional architecture based on ResNet-101 model and pre-trained on MS-COCO dataset [11], which resulted to the highest performance in image semantic segmentation. Nonetheless, the repetition of max-pool blocks and strides through the network deteriorates the feature maps' resolution and increases the computational time requirements. To eliminate such constraints, atrous convolution was employed to control the feature maps' resolution over the network's layers.

As an example, in case of a 1-D input signal $x[i]$ atrous convolution with a filter $w[k]$ of length K, gives the output signal $y[i]$ as following:

$$y[i] = \sum_{k=1}^{K} x[i + r \cdot k]w[k], \tag{1}$$

where parameter r defines the stride with which signal $x[i]$ is sampled. Regular convolution can be considered a special case of (1) where $r = 1$.

DCNNs can identify similar objects of multiple scales and rotation due to the training procedure in similar representations. However, further robustness to scale variability is required for oil spill identification due to the orbit of the satellite. Scene and object representation in such images can display wide variety due to difference of the operational altitude. Moreover, oil spills present

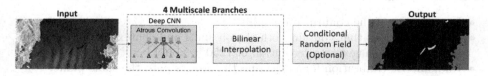

Fig. 1. High-level representation of the presented model.

extreme diversity in shape and size due to the physics of dispersion. The model deploys atrous spatial pyramid pooling for managing the scale variability and was inspired from the corresponding R-CNN technique in [6]. As a result, the classification efficiency of the multi-scale regions is achieved by resampling the feature maps at a set of different rates and further processing them before fusing for the final output. At the final process stage, bilinear interpolation is utilized for the extracted feature maps to regain the initial resolution of the input image. To further enhance the scaling robustness, the model was extended with a multi-scale process to resolve the scale variability issue.

More specifically, four parallel DCNN branches that share the same parameters are used and extract separate score maps from the original image, two rescaled versions and a fused version of all of them. The four branches are combined in one by taking the maximum score across them at each position. It should be also noted that the impact on detector's performance of final CRF layer of the DeepLab model was also examined through the experiments. However, it was exclude it from the finalized model's architecture since it is mainly useful to refine the segmentation results, which in our case did not improve segmentation accuracy rates. For the oil spill detection, objects and regions in SAR imagery present ambiguous shape outlines, resulting in minor improvements of the segmentation accuracy when CRF module is employed, while a computational overhead is added.

4   Experimental Results

4.1   Dataset Description

One key challenge that the researchers has to confront in classification models is the absence of a public dataset which may be utilized for benchmarking. In previous works [2, 10, 18] the required datasets were developed manually making relevant works almost non comparable. This constraint motivated us to develop a new dataset by collecting satellite SAR images of oil polluted areas via the European Space Agency (ESA) database, the Copernicus Open Access Hub[1]. To ensure the validity of the data and the inclusion of oils spills in the images, the European Maritime Safety Agency (EMSA) provided the confirmed oil spill events through the CleanSeaNet service along with their geographic coordinates. By this approach, we guaranteed that the dark spots depicted in the SAR images correspond to oil spills.

After downloading the appropriate records, a set of preprocessing stages were conducted so that the products could be processed as common images:

- Localization of the confirmed oil spills.
- Cropped regions that contain both the oil spills and contextual information. Rescaling the images to a resolution of 1250 × 650.
- Radiometric calibration for projecting the images onto the same plane.

---

[1] https://scihub.copernicus.eu/.

- Speckle noise suppression with a 7×7 median filter.
- Linear transformation from db to real luminosity values.

A sufficient number of SAR images were processed with the above procedure each of which may include instances of interest such as oil spills, look-alikes, ships and coastal territories. The representations were manually annotated based on the EMSA records accompanied with human identification. During the annotation process, every region was semantically marked with a specific colorization, producing a ground truth mask for every image. A training and a testing set consisting of 771 and 110 images,respectively, were created by randomly sampling the annotated images. Finally, it must be highlighted that the database is extended constantly and could be accessed by the community after receiving the proper confirmations by the relevant authorities.

4.2   Results

For the conducted experiments, three foreground classes were defined i.e. oil spills, look-alikes and ships as well as two classes for the background pixels corresponding to land and sea areas. The overall performance was measured in terms of pixel intersection-over-union (IoU) for every class and averaged for all classes (mIoU). Since the dataset will be meant for future methods benchmarking, a predefined training and testing set should be established. Thus, we decided not to cross-validate the dataset in order to produce comparable results with future proposed methods, following the approach of models benchmarking as in [1], where the model is evaluated in 4 benchmarking datasets. Furthermore, considering the stochastic nature of oil spills shape and size,representative training and testing sets can be produced by single splitting the dataset. Thus, cross-validation would add an exhaustive computational overhead.

Our initial experiments were conducted using the aforementioned dataset and by deploying a simple DCNN network [1] without any multi-scale approach implemented. The selected batch size is equal to 16 image patches while every batch fed into the model is considered as one step of the training process. The corresponding results are provided in Table 1. Based on the numerical results, it can be concluded that the background areas can be detected with high accuracy when the steps are increased, while oil spills and look-alikes drop bellow 50%. The latter is justifiable since the model cannot generalize without multi-scale analysis and thus, the dominant classes overfit the remaining classes. One interesting result is that "look-alike" class achieves its highest accuracy with 5K steps and drops gradually when they are increased, contrary to the oil spill accuracy. This behavior occurs because the pixels of both classes are usually misclassified. Comparing the results of the basic DCNN model with the results of the CRF expanded model (DCNN-CRF), no significant improvement was achieved since the mask does not contain substantial background noise due to the speckle filtering preprocessing stage.

The second set of our experiments included the testing of a multi-scale DCNN scheme to deal with the semantic segmentation of the SAR images. Due to the

Table 1. Segmentation results of simple model using mIoU/IoU.

Intersection-over-union (IoU)				
Steps	Sea surface	Oil spill	Look-alike	Land	mIoU
DCNN					
5k	93.4%	14.9%	**39.8%**	70.3%	54.6%
10k	93.3%	19.8%	36.5%	70.9%	55.1%
15k	93.1%	20.6%	36.5%	67.9%	54.5%
20k	**93.8%**	**21.4%**	35.8%	**75.1%**	**56.5%**
DCNN-CRF					
5k	93.7%	10.8%	**40.9%**	72.0%	54.4%
10k	93.5%	12.6%	36.7%	72.2%	53.8%
15k	93.2%	13.9%	36.2%	69.0%	53.1%
20k	**94.2%**	**15.4%**	36.9%	**77.5%**	**56.0%**

Table 2. Segmentation results of multiscale model using mIoU/IoU.

Intersection-over-union (IoU)				
Steps	Sea surface	Oil spill	Look-alike	Land	mIoU
Multi-scale DCNN					
15k	95.3%	43.4%	34.0%	85.1%	64.49%
20k	95.1%	47.6%	33.2%	85.8%	65.49%
25k	95.5%	40.3%	**53.5%**	82.5%	68.0%
30k	**96.0%**	**48.0%**	50.9%	**89.9%**	**71.2%**
35k	95.6%	42.3%	45.0%	87.3%	67.6%
Multi-scale DCNN-CRF					
15k	95.19%	37.0%	30.3%	89.8%	63.1%
20k	95.1%	38.1%	30.3%	89.8%	63.3%
25k	95.6%	30.6%	**53.3%**	84.7%	66.1%
30k	**96.0%**	**39.6%**	50.2%	**92.9%**	**69.7%**
35k	95.7%	34.1%	44.2%	90.8%	66.2%

computational overhead of the four parrallel DCNN branches the initial batch size (16) was reduced in this case to 2 image patches per training step. The results are presented in Table 2, where multi-scale DCNN and DCNN-CRF were evaluated. Regarding the CRF addition, the module did not improve significantly the performance of the model as observed also in the case of a single DCNN branch. In addition, the segmentation rates were increased according to the training steps, resulting to state-of-the-art outcomes when comparing to Table 1. Similar to the results of the first set of experiments, the background classes were identified more accurate than the foreground but, in comparison with the simple

Table 3. Segmentation results of simple model using mIoU/IoU.

Intersection-over-union (IoU)						
Steps	Sea surface	Oil spill	Look-alike	Ship	Land	mIoU
10k	93.0%	19.5%	**36.5%**	**12.7%**	67.5%	45.9%
20k	**93.6%**	**21.0%**	35.8%	11.5%	**72.0%**	**46.8%**

Table 4. Segmentation results of multiscale model using mIoU/IoU

Intersection-over-union (IoU)						
Steps	Sea surface	Oil spill	Look-alike	Ship	Land	mIoU
10k	95.6%	49.7%	**54.9%**	15.7%	86.9%	**60.6%**
20k	95.4%	50.1%	45.8%	20.1%	78.4%	58.0%
30k	95.1%	**50.3%**	35.4%	22.4%	87.5%	58.1%
40k	**95.8%**	38.1%	48.2%	**25.4%**	**88.8%**	59.3%

model, the accuracy rates were improved for the foreground regions, as well. This result occurs due to the lesser number of the foreground ground truth pixels in comparison with the corresponding background pixel. Nonetheless, a more efficient sampling approach could improve the results.

Additional experiments were performed to examine the model's segmentation capability in an extended version of our dataset, where ships and vessels were separately identified and thus, a new class was inserted. The extracted results are presented in Tables 3 and 4 for the simple and the multi-scale analysis, respectively. Results proved once again the advantage of the multi-scale technique over the simple DCNN. The corresponding results display a minor decrement in comparison with the four classes case nonetheless, as far it concerns the oil spill detection, the model can still identify accurately the polluted territories. On the contrary, ship localization rates are considered low, as expected, since the corresponding image regions are too narrow/small and therefore, difficult to be sufficiently identified. Moreover, the number of the ship samples was insufficient for the training process since the main objective was to identify the polluted areas and not directly their potential source. In order to have a more generic model that could deal pollution related tasks in general, the database will be augmented with further samples of objects of interest.

The results of both techniques can be visually compared in Fig. 2 for 4 and 5 classes (*simple* refers to one branch [13] while *msc* corresponds to the four branches approach). Analyzing the two figures, we can conclude that the proposed multi-scale DCNN outperforms the simple DCNN when oil spills and look-alikes are concerned. Both techniques perform high segmentation rates for background pixels, i.e. sea surface and land area, leading over 90% and 80%, respectively. Similarly, the foreground regions are identified equally sufficient, regardless the complexity of the task (oil spills and ship localization).

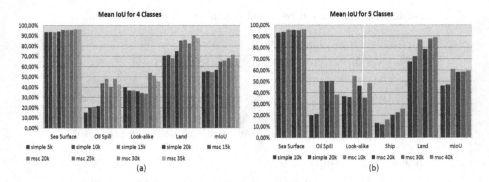

Fig. 2. Mean IoUs of (a) 4 classes and (b) 5 classes.

For comparisons, we additionally utilized the segmentation accuracy of the highest performance model in the four classes problem, so as it could be compared with simple models of image classification. Therefore, a determined amount of overlapping patches were cropped from each pair of ground truth and predicted masks. In order to arise a credible dataset, the following restrictions were introduced:

1. Apart from sea surface class, each patch should contain at least a minimum amount of pixels classified in one of the rest three classes. A threshold of 2% was selected implying that the class containing the most pixels should contain at least 2% of the amount of pixels of the sea surface class.
2. An image patch is labeled only if one of the three classes dominates. So, a threshold was defined equal to 50%, meaning that the dominant class should contain at least 50% of the amount of the pixels of a non dominant class.
3. If a patch does not satisfy the aforementioned rules, it is excluded from the accuracy estimation.

Classification results for image patches are presented in Table 5. Since calculated accuracy is dependent of the amount of patches extracted from every image, two different values for the horizontal-vertical ratio of patch size were examined. It should be noted that the results included in the tables are somehow dissimilar since, for the second metric, a single label is evaluated for every patch.

A possible comparison with relevant approaches would be somehow iniquitous due to the lack of a common image dataset as a base. Moreover, most of other relevant approaches attempt to solve a binary classification problem (oil spills and look-alikes), in contrast with the proposed method, excluding other information that may be valuable in disaster management. In addition, our algorithm annotates each pixel with one valid state where other methods designate image regions and so, accuracy is determined in a completely different basis. Thus, comparing classification approaches for different posed problems is somehow invalid. Nonetheless, some results of comparison are provided. The method

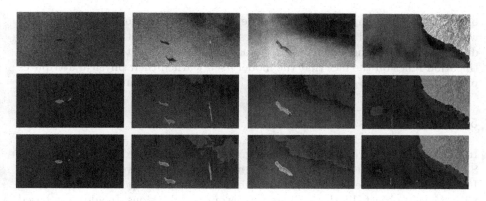

Fig. 3. Example of 4 testing images (from top to bottom): SAR images, ground truth masks and resulted detection masks overlaid over SAR images. (Color figure online)

in [16] which exploits a neural network resulted a 91.6% and 98.3% accuracy for oil spills and look-alikes (without considering the ship instances), respectively. Highest accuracy was achieved by the method in [18] which deployed a decision tree forest and achieved an accuracy equal to 85.0%. Finally, the probabilistic based method in [17] achieved accuracy equal to 78% and 99% for oil spill and look-alikes classes, respectively. Without the constraint of extracting features, initial results of the proposed approach are comparable to those of state-of-the-art methods and with the merit of semantically annotated regions.

Table 5. Segmentation accuracy results.

Image patch classification accuracy results			
Number of patches: 3,3			
Overall	Oil spill	Look-alike	Land
85.2%	89.1%	69.2%	97.4%
Number of patches: 5,3			
Overall	Oil spill	Look-alike	Land
84.1%	91.0%	67.6%	93.8%

For representation and qualitative purposes, Fig. 3 includes some examples of semantically annotated images in order to demonstrate the accuracy of the model and the distinctiveness of the problem. The cyan colored pixels denote the identified oil spill regions while the red marked pixels corresponds to look-alike areas. In addition, green marked territories resembles the coastal regions while black colored corresponds to the sea surface. Finally, the detected vessels are marked with brown color and cover the smallest image regions in the representations. Oil spills are very similar to look-alikes as both are represented by black masses and so, they can easily be misclassified. Nonetheless, the model was properly trained to discriminate these instances due to the differences they display as natural phenomena (size, shape etc.). Eventually, their accurate identification relies on the fact that the model itself learned their physical attributes providing a valuable discrimination for the disaster management authorities.

5 Conclusions

In this paper, a novel approach was proposed for oil spill detection based on SAR image analysis aiming at a disaster management framework at early stages. Robust DCNN models can automate the detection of the polluted areas along with relevant objects like look-alikes, vessels or coastal regions. In addition, based on the performed analysis, initial results indicate that such models can provide an accurate estimation about the upcoming disaster targeting the best situation awareness of the relevant authorities. Thus, such models can be integrated to wider frameworks for disaster and crisis management. The extracted results are comparable to the state-of-the-art results, nonetheless, for general classification problems. More specific for the oil spill detection problem, the adaptation of relevant and more accurate deep learning methods may lead to further improvement of the identification accuracy. Larger training sets with sufficient samples and images acquired with improved SAR sensors could substantially improve the accuracy values, also. Current work can be extended to manage similar environmental disasters like floods. Thus, relevant image samples will be required to enhance the current database in order to refine and retrain the model.

Acknowledgments. This work was supported by ROBORDER and EOPEN projects funded by the European Commission under grant agreements No 740593 and No 776019, respectively.

References

1. Chen, L.C., Papandreou, G., Kokkinos, I., Murphy, K., Yuille, A.L.: DeepLab: semantic image segmentation with deep convolutional nets, atrous convolution, and fully connected CRFs. arXiv preprint arXiv:1606.00915 (2016)
2. Cococcioni, M., Corucci, L., Masini, A., Nardelli, F.: SVME: an ensemble of support vector machines for detecting oil spills from full resolution MODIS images. Ocean Dyn. **62**(3), 449–467 (2012)
3. Fingas, M., Brown, C.: Review of oil spill remote sensing. Mar. Pollut. Bull. **83**(1), 9–23 (2014)
4. Giusti, A., Ciresan, D.C., Masci, J., Gambardella, L.M., Schmidhuber, J.: Fast image scanning with deep max-pooling convolutional neural networks. In: 2013 20th IEEE International Conference on Image Processing (ICIP), pp. 4034–4038. IEEE (2013)
5. Gonzalez, C., Sánchez, S., Paz, A., Resano, J., Mozos, D., Plaza, A.: Use of FPGA or GPU-based architectures for remotely sensed hyperspectral image processing. Integr. VLSI J. **46**(2), 89–103 (2013)

6. He, K., Zhang, X., Ren, S., Sun, J.: Spatial pyramid pooling in deep convolutional networks for visual recognition. In: Fleet, D., Pajdla, T., Schiele, B., Tuytelaars, T. (eds.) ECCV 2014. LNCS, vol. 8691, pp. 346–361. Springer, Cham (2014). https://doi.org/10.1007/978-3-319-10578-9_23

7. He, K., Zhang, X., Ren, S., Sun, J.: Deep residual learning for image recognition. In: Proceedings of the IEEE Conference on Computer Vision and Pattern Recognition, pp. 770–778 (2016)

8. Holschneider, M., Kronland-Martinet, R., Morlet, J., Tchamitchian, P.: A real-time algorithm for signal analysis with the help of the wavelet transform. In: Combes, J.M., Grossmann, A., Tchamitchian, P. (eds.) Wavelets, pp. 286–297. Springer, Heidelberg (1990). https://doi.org/10.1007/978-3-642-75988-8_28

9. Karpathy, A., Fei-Fei, L.: Deep visual-semantic alignments for generating image descriptions. In: Proceedings of the IEEE Conference on Computer Vision and Pattern Recognition, pp. 3128–3137 (2015)

10. Konik, M., Bradtke, K.: Object-oriented approach to oil spill detection using envisat ASAR images. ISPRS J. Photogram. Remote Sens. **118**, 37–52 (2016)

11. Lin, T.-Y., et al.: Microsoft COCO: common objects in context. In: Fleet, D., Pajdla, T., Schiele, B., Tuytelaars, T. (eds.) ECCV 2014. LNCS, vol. 8693, pp. 740–755. Springer, Cham (2014). https://doi.org/10.1007/978-3-319-10602-1_48

12. Mastin, G.A., Manson, J., Bradley, J., Axline, R., Hover, G.: A comparative evaluation of SAR and SLAR. Technical report, Sandia National Labs., Albuquerque, NM (United States) (1993)

13. Orfanidis, G., Ioannidis, K., Avgerinakis, K., Vrochidis, S., Kompatsiaris, I.: A deep neural network for oil spill semantic segmentation in SAR images. In: Accepted for presentation in IEEE International Conference on Image Processing. IEEE (2018)

14. Shen, H.Y., Zhou, P.C., Feng, S.R.: Research on multi-angle near infrared spectral-polarimetric characteristic for polluted water by spilled oil. In: International Symposium on Photoelectronic Detection and Imaging 2011: Advances in Infrared Imaging and Applications, vol. 8193, p. 81930M. International Society for Optics and Photonics (2011)

15. Simonyan, K., Zisserman, A.: Very deep convolutional networks for large-scale image recognition. arXiv preprint arXiv:1409.1556 (2014)

16. Singha, S., Bellerby, T.J., Trieschmann, O.: Satellite oil spill detection using artificial neural networks. IEEE J. Sel. Top. Appl. Earth Obs. Remote Sens. **6**(6), 2355–2363 (2013)

17. Solberg, A.H., Brekke, C., Husoy, P.O.: Oil spill detection in radarsat and envisat SAR images. IEEE Trans. Geosci. Remote Sens. **45**(3), 746–755 (2007)

18. Topouzelis, K., Psyllos, A.: Oil spill feature selection and classification using decision tree forest on SAR image data. ISPRS J. Photogram. Remote Sens. **68**, 135–143 (2012)

19. Vinyals, O., Toshev, A., Bengio, S., Erhan, D.: Show and tell: a neural image caption generator. In: 2015 IEEE Conference on Computer Vision and Pattern Recognition (CVPR), pp. 3156–3164. IEEE (2015)

Point Cloud Colorization Based on Densely Annotated 3D Shape Dataset

Xu Cao and Katashi Nagao[✉]

Department of Intelligent Systems, Graduate School of Informatics,
Nagoya University, Nagoya, Japan
sou@nagao.nuie.nagoya-u.ac.jp, nagao@i.nagoya-u.ac.jp

Abstract. This paper introduces DensePoint, a densely sampled and annotated point cloud dataset containing over 10,000 single objects across 16 categories, by merging different kind of information from two existing datasets. Each point cloud in DensePoint contains 40,000 points, and each point is associated with two sorts of information: RGB value and part annotation. In addition, we propose a method for point cloud colorization by utilizing Generative Adversarial Networks (GANs). The network makes it possible to generate colours for point clouds of single objects by only giving the point cloud itself. Experiments on DensePoint show that there exist clear boundaries in point clouds between different parts of an object, suggesting that the proposed network is able to generate reasonably good colours. Our dataset is publicly available on the project page (http://rwdc.nagao.nuie.nagoya-u.ac.jp/DensePoint).

Keywords: Point cloud dataset · Colorization
Generative adversarial networks

1 Introduction

Today, there are multiple devices and applications that have introduced 3D objects and scenes in different areas, such as architecture, engineering, and construction. 3D digitization of the real world is becoming essential for developing a variety of applications such as autonomous driving, robotics, and augmented/virtual reality. Medical and cultural fields, and many others, have benefitted from 3D digitization; examples include prosthesis construction adapted to the anthropometry of each patient or making virtual tours through historic buildings.

A point cloud, which is a 3D representation of real-world objects, consists of a set of points with XYZ-coordinates. A point cloud can be obtained by range-sensing devices such as LiDAR (light detection and ranging). LiDAR has a 360-degree field of view but can only provide sparse depth information. In the case of indoor scene capture, a LiDAR-based 3D scanner solved this problem by vertically rotating LiDAR to acquire sparse point clouds from different orientations and merging them into a dense point cloud. However, the point clouds obtained by LiDAR do not have colour information, making it hard to utilize them in some applications. This does not necessarily mean we need to complete point clouds with accurate colour information. In Nagao et al.'s study [12], an indoor scene is represented as a coloured point cloud and

I. Kompatsiaris et al. (Eds.): MMM 2019, LNCS 11295, pp. 436–446, 2019.
https://doi.org/10.1007/978-3-030-05710-7_36

imported into a virtual reality application such as a simulation of a disaster experience. In the case of virtual reality, there is no need for the colours of objects to be exactly the same as those of the real world.

We also require object part information, such as head and body information, because it is impossible to properly transform objects (e.g., disassemble them due to the impact of, for example, an earthquake) in simulation without object part information.

To handle the problems of object colorization and part segmentation, first of all, we constructed DensePoint, which is a dataset that contains the shape, colour, and part information of the object by using a 3D point cloud. DensePoint is an extension of the information in the ShapeNet [2] and ShapeNetPart [25] published datasets.

In this paper, we tackle an automatic point cloud colorization problem as the first application of the DensePoint dataset. That is, given a point cloud without colour information, our goal is to generate a reasonably good colorized point cloud. We take inspiration from pix2pix [8], in which images from one domain are translated into another domain, resulting in interesting applications such as monochrome image colorization. To the best of our knowledge, the point cloud colorization task has not been challenged yet. We think the reasons are the lack of a coloured point cloud dataset and the intractable properties of point clouds. As mentioned earlier, we first constructed a richly annotated point cloud dataset and then adopted recent advances of Generative Adversarial Networks (GANs) to handle the point cloud colorization problem.

2 Related Work

2.1 3D Shape Repository

A key factor of the success of data-driven algorithms is large-scale and well-annotated datasets. Early efforts in constructing 3D model datasets either do not pay attention to the numbers of models [3] or do not focus on annotating the model [17]. Wu et al.'s study [22] demonstrated the benefit of a large 3D dataset in training convolutional neural networks for 3D object classification tasks, and the dataset named ModelNet has been one benchmark for 3D object classification. The emergence of the large-scale 3D shape repository ShapeNet [2] has facilitated researches in computer graphics, computer vision, and many other fields. ShapeNet provides over 55k single clean mesh models of multiple categories collected from public online sources and other datasets and organizes these models under WordNet taxonomy. Several studies contribute augmentations to the original ShapeNet. ShapeNetPart [25] adds part annotations to 3D shapes of ShapeNet while ObjectNet3D [23] aligns objects in images with 3D shape instances and their pose estimations. In Shao et al.'s study [16], the physical attributes of real-world objects, such as weights and dimensions, are collected from the Internet and then assigned to 3D shapes.

2.2   Deep Learning for Point Clouds

Because of the unstructured data format, it is hard for point cloud classification to benefit from the advances of convolutional operation, which has become a standard approach in image classification, segmentation, or object detection tasks. PointNet [14] was the first neural network to address point cloud classification and segmentation by applying point-wise convolution and using a symmetric function to aggregate feature-wise information. PointNet++ [15] improved on PointNet by capturing local structure in a hierarchical way. Other point cloud classification attempts focus on modifying convolutional operation to adapt it to the special format of point clouds [9, 20].

2.3   Generative Adversarial Nets for 3D Shape Synthesis

With recent advances of Generative Adversarial Networks [6, 7], many studies contribute to 3D shape generation and completion in a data-driven approach. 3D-GAN [21] and 3D-IWGAN [18] generate volumetric objects by learning a probabilistic mapping from latent space to volumetric object space. 3D shape reconstruction is another task in which a complete 3D object is reconstructed from a partial observation or data in a different modality, such as partial depth view [24], image [18, 21], or multi-view sketches [11]. Even a complete indoor scene can be reconstructed from partial observations, such as an incomplete 3D scan [4] or a single depth view [19]. While these studies focus on volumetric representations of 3D objects, recent studies have also addressed the problem of generating a 3D object in the form of point clouds [5, 10, 13].

3   Point Cloud Dataset Construction

In this section, we describe our procedure for constructing a dataset containing densely sampled point clouds with each point associated with RGB colour and a part label.

3.1   Data Source

We use ShapeNet [2] and ShapeNetPart [25] as our data source, of which the former provides over 50,000 mesh models across 55 categories and the latter comprise over 30,000 per-point labelled point clouds from 16 categories. As ShapeNetPart is an extension of ShapeNet, both datasets contain the same 3D objects yet in a different modality. We focus on the intersection of the two datasets, a set of over 10,000 3D models, and combine the information of 3D models in different modalities.

3.2   Point Cloud Sampling and Alignment

We first uniformly sample points from the surface of mesh objects that have texture in ShapeNet [1]. For each mesh, we densely sample 40,000 points (Fig. 1).

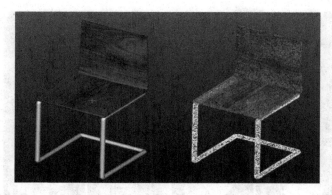

Fig. 1. Sampled point cloud visualization. Left: mesh object of chair from ShapeNet. Right: corresponding sampled point cloud.

The alignment process (Fig. 2) consists of 4 separate steps. First, the coloured point clouds are rotated such that the orientations of the point cloud pairs are the same. Second, the centres of the bounding boxes are matched so that the offset of the point cloud pairs disappears. Third, the scales of the point cloud pairs are adjusted to make sure they are the same size. Finally, for point clouds pairs that don't align well, we manually adjust them.

To evaluate the degree of alignment between the point cloud pairs, we utilize the one-sided Hausdorff distance. The one-sided Hausdorff distance between a set of points A and another set of points B is the smallest distance such that for every point of A, there must exist at least one point of B within the distance. Formally, the distance is defined as:

$$d(A, B) = max_{a \in A}\{min_{b \in B}\{\| a - b \|_2\}\}$$

where a and b represent a single point of A and B, respectively. In our case, a and b are vectors of 3 elements representing x, y, and z coordinates in Euclidean space.

After each step, we compute the one-sided Hausdorff distance for all point cloud pairs and then compute the average distance for each category (Fig. 3). We found that for all 16 categories, the average one-sided Hausdorff distance decreases as the point cloud pairs are progressively processed, which verifies the effectiveness of the process.

Finally, we use the one-sided Hausdorff distance to check whether abnormal operation happened in previous steps by computing the one-sided Hausdorff distance between the point cloud pairs after each step. Ideally, the distance should keep decreasing as the alignment process is going on since each step makes the point cloud pairs more similar. We consider point cloud pairs where the distance does not decrease during the process as abnormal point cloud pairs and manually check and adjust the point cloud pairs.

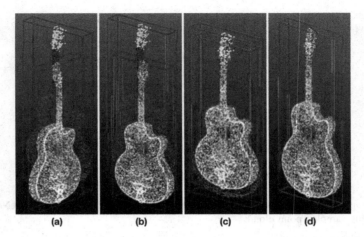

Fig. 2. Illustration of alignment process of a point cloud pair. Denser one is sampled from mesh model of ShapeNet, and its colour represents RGB value, while sparser one is from ShapeNetPart, and different colour of points means different parts of object. (a) Original point cloud pair. Note that neither orientation nor scale is same although they originate from same mesh object. (b) After rotation, orientation of point cloud pair became same. (c) Centres of bounding boxes is matched. (d) Scale of point cloud pair is adjusted to be same.

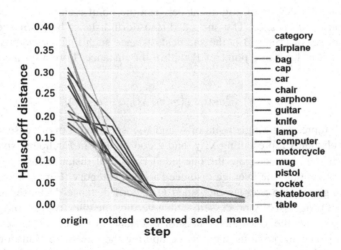

Fig. 3. Change of average one-sided Hausdorff distance for all 16 categories. X-axis represents different processing steps, and Y-axis represents one-sided Hausdorff distance. Point cloud pairs from all categories achieve low Hausdorff distance at the end of our proposed procedure.

3.3 Label Annotation Transfer

After each point cloud pair is aligned, the problem becomes how to transfer label annotation from the sparse point cloud to the dense point cloud. A prior observation is that points with the same part label are spatially close and clustered, which means there is a high probability for a point to have the same label as those around it. Therefore, we adopt the K-nearest neighbours algorithm for point-wise classification, in which the training data is the points from the point cloud with label annotation, and the test data is the points without label annotation. We train each classifier for every point cloud pair, resulting in over 10,000 classifiers. To find out the best classifier, we consider the combination of two hyperparameters. The first one is K, which is the number of nearest points in the training data to be searched for. The second one is the weight strategy associated with the K-nearest points when voting for the test point label. We search for K from 1 to 17 with a step of 2 and chose two different weight strategies, whether the weights are all the same as the weight of 1 or are inverse to the distance from the query point to the nearest point.

This search strategy results in 18 hyperparameter settings. To decide the best classifier among the 18 settings, we adopt 10-fold cross-validation, which is a standard technique to evaluate trained classifiers. In Table 1, we report the average best validation accuracy of point clouds in each category, from which we can see that all classifiers achieve over 95 percent prediction accuracy. After the best classifiers are decided, we deploy them on test point clouds.

Table 1. KNN average best validation accuracy for each category

Category	Guitar	Knife	Pistol	Lamp	Chair	Table	Mug	Car
Accuracy	98.8	98.9	98.7	99.2	97.6	98.7	99.5	95.5
Category	Bag	Cap	Earphone	Laptop	Skateboard	Rocket	Motorbike	Plane
Accuracy	99.4	98.8	98.7	98.7	98.7	97.4	96.0	96.1

3.4 Dataset Statistics

The detailed statistics of the dataset are summarized in Table 2. We demonstrate examples of each category from our dataset in Fig. 4.

Table 2. DensePoint Dataset Statistics

Category	Guitar	Knife	Pistol	Lamp	Chair	Table	Mug	Car
No. of instances	611	266	166	790	1998	3860	66	402
No. of part labels	3	2	3	4	4	3	2	4
Category	Bag	Cap	Earphone	Laptop	Skateboard	Rocket	Motorbike	Plane
No. of instances	57	31	36	338	127	29	159	1492
No. of part labels	2	2	3	2	3	3	6	4

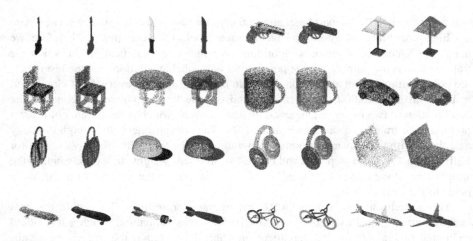

Fig. 4. One example of each category from our DensePoint dataset. Each point cloud contains 40,000 points. Left image of each pair is represented by RGB value, and right image is same point cloud represented by part label.

4   Point Cloud Colorization

In this section, we explain the architecture of the network, the experiment and the result of point cloud colorization.

4.1   Network Architecture

We utilize the adversarial scheme of pix2pix [8] and repurpose PointNet [14] segmentation network to colour regression. The architecture of our proposed network is illustrated in Fig. 5. It comprises two neural networks, named generator and discriminator. For the generator architecture, we modify the segmentation version of PointNet, which applies a convolutional operation point by point and then summarizes global information into a vector feature by feature. To accomplish point-wise classification, the global information vector is copied and concatenated with each point-wise feature vector from previous intermediate layer outputs. The activation function of the final layer is a Tanh non-linearity, thus alternating its function from point cloud segmentation to colour regression. For the discriminator architecture, we modify the classification version of PointNet by setting the number of neurons of the output layer to 1, which outputs the probability of the input coloured point cloud being real.

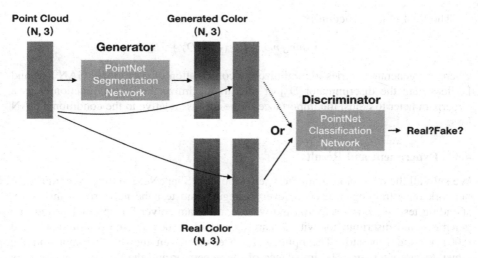

Fig. 5. Our generative adversarial network's architecture. Generator, modified from PointNet segmentation network, predicts point-wise colour for N x 3 input point clouds. The predicted colour concatenated with the point cloud, along with the ground truth coloured point cloud, is fed into the discriminator.

4.2   Objective Function

The goal of the generator is to generate realistic point-wise colours for point clouds that are difficult for the discriminator to distinguish from the real coloured point clouds, while the goal of the discriminator is to enhance its own ability to distinguish real colours from generated or fake colours. The optimal situation would be a Nash equilibrium in which neither the generator could fool the discriminator by providing realistic samples nor could the discriminator distinguish real samples from fake samples.

Following pix2pix [8], we utilize a combination of conditional GAN loss and L1 loss, in which conditional GAN loss is defined as:

$$L_{cGAN}(G,D) = \mathbb{E}_{x,y}[log(x,y)] + \mathbb{E}_{x,z}[log(1 - D(x, G(x,z)))],$$

and L1 loss is defined as:

$$L_{l_1}(G) = \mathbb{E}_{x,y,z}[\| y - G(x,z) \|_1],$$

where in our case x is the input N x 3 tensor representing a point cloud, and y is the output N x 3 tensor of generator representing point-wise RGB colour. Note that in traditional GANs, z is a random vector input to the generator, which ensures the variation of the output. In our case, we keep the dropout layer at test time so that there is variation of the generated colour for the point clouds.

The final object function is:

$$G^* = \arg min_G max_D L_{cGAN}(G, D) + \lambda L_{l_1}(G),$$

where the generator G tries to minimize the combination of conditional GAN loss and L1 loss, and the discriminator D just tries to maximize the object function. λ is a hyperparameter to adjust the importance of the L1 loss relative to the conditional GAN loss.

4.3   Experiment and Results

We split all the data into training/test sets following ShapeNet's setting. We train each network on a training dataset for every category and test the network on the corresponding test set. λ is set to 10, and we use an Adam solver for optimizing both the generator and discriminator with a learning rate of 0.0001 for the discriminator and 0.001 for the generator. The optimization steps between the discriminator and the generator are alternate. The imbalance of the generator and the discriminator usually leads to a vanishing gradient and training failure, we adopt a simple strategy to alleviate the problem. Whenever the probability of the discriminator judging the real coloured point cloud to be real is higher than 0.7, we skip training the discriminator this round and jump forward to train the generator until the probability is lower than 0.7. The batch size is 8, and we train our networks for 200 epochs.

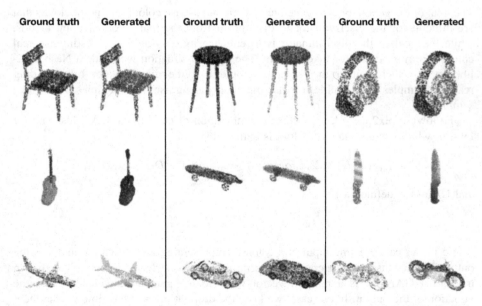

Fig. 6. Colorization results on test dataset. Left image in pair is ground-truth coloured point cloud while right image in pair is colorized point cloud. Note that during whole training and test process, we did not give network any information about object parts, but there exist clear boundaries between different parts of a single object.

We demonstrate our test results in Fig. 6. We found that our proposed network is able to generate reasonably good and beautiful colours for point clouds. Another surprising finding is that the network tends to learn to colorize different parts with different colour patterns by itself even though we did not explicitly provide any information related to the object parts. We observe this phenomenon in almost every category, suggesting that it is not just sampling error and is worth studying further.

5   Conclusion and Future Work

In this study, we introduce DensePoint, a point cloud dataset comprising over 10,000 single objects across 16 categories, with each point associated with an RGB value and a part label. We also proposed a GAN-based neural network for point cloud colorization task, in which only the point cloud is fed into the network. Clear boundaries between different parts in colourized point clouds indicate that our network is able to generate reasonably good colours for a single object point cloud even if we do not give the network part label information.

Future work includes refining the quality of the label annotations of points as we observe the fact that around the boundary of two sets of points from different parts, there exist some vague and wrong annotations. Another area of future work is exploring the tasks that could be accomplished by utilizing this dataset, such as predicting point-wise part labels while generating the colour for the point clouds at the same time.

References

1. CloudCompare. http://www.cloudcompare.org
2. Chang, A.X., et al.: ShapeNet: an information-rich 3D model repository. Technical report arXiv: 1512.03012 [cs.GR] (2015)
3. Chen, X., Golovinskiy, A., Funkhouser, T.: A benchmark for 3D mesh segmentation. ACM Trans. Graph. **28**(3), 73 (2009). (Proc. SIGGRAPH)
4. Dai, A., Ritchie, D., Bokeloh, M., Reed, S., Sturm, J. and Nießner, M.: ScanComplete: large-scale scene completion and semantic segmentation for 3D scans. In: Proceedings of Computer Vision and Pattern Recognition (CVPR). IEEE (2018)
5. Fan, H., Su, H., Guibas, L.J.: A point set generation network for 3D object reconstruction from a single image. In: Proceedings of 2017 IEEE Conference on Computer Vision and Pattern Recognition, CVPR 2017, pp. 2463–2471 (2017)
6. Goodfellow, I., et al.: Generative adversarial nets. In: Ghahramani, Z., Welling, M., Cortes, C., Lawrence, N.D., Weinberger, K.Q. (eds.) Advances in Neural Information Processing Systems, vol. 27, pp. 2672–2680 (2014)
7. Gulrajani, I., Ahmed, F., Arjovsky, M., Dumoulin, V., Courville, A.C.: Improved training of Wasserstein gans. In: Guyon, I., et al. (eds.) Advances in Neural Information Processing Systems, vol. 30, pp. 5767–5777. Curran Associates, Inc. (2017)
8. Isola, P., Zhu, J.Y., Zhou, T., Efros, A.A.: Image-to-image translation with conditional adversarial networks. In: CVPR (2017)
9. Klokov, R., Lempitsky, V.: Escape from cells: deep kd-networks for the recognition of 3D point cloud models. In: Proceedings of the IEEE International Conference on Computer Vision (ICCV) (2017)

10. Lin, C.H., Kong, C., Lucey, S.: Learning efficient point cloud generation for dense 3D object reconstruction. In: Proceedings of AAAI Conference on Artificial Intelligence (AAAI) (2018)
11. Lun, Z., Gadelha, M., Kalogerakis, E., Maji, S., Wang, R.: 3D shape reconstruction from sketches via multi-view convolutional networks. In: Proceedings of 2017 International Conference on 3D Vision (3DV) (2017)
12. Nagao, K., Miyakawa, Y.: Building scale VR: sutomatically creating indoor 3D maps and its application to simulation of disaster situations. In: Proceedings of Future Technologies Conference (FTC) (2017)
13. Panos, A., Olga, D., Ioannis, M., Leonidas, G.: Learning representations and generative models for 3D point clouds In: Proceedings of International Conference on Learning Representations (ICLR) (2018)
14. Qi, C.R., Su, H., Mo, K., Guibas, L.J.: PointNet: deep learning on point sets for 3D classification and segmentation. In: Proceedings of Computer Vision and Pattern Recognition (CVPR). IEEE (2017)
15. Qi, C.R., Yi, L., Su, H., Guibas, L.J.: PointNet++: deep hierarchical feature learning on point sets in a metric space. arXiv preprint arXiv: 1706.02413 (2017)
16. Shao, L., Chang, A.X., Su, H., Savva, M., Guibas, L.J.: Cross-modal attribute transfer for rescaling 3D models. In: Proceedings of 2017 International Conference on 3D Vision (3DV), pp. 640–648 (2017)
17. Shilane, P., Min, P., Kazhdan, M., Funkhouser, T.: The Princeton shape benchmark. In: Shape Modeling International (2004)
18. Smith, E.J., Meger, D.: Improved adversarial systems for 3D object generation and reconstruction. In: Levine, S., Vanhoucke, V., Goldberg, K. (eds.) Proceedings of the 1st Annual Conference on Robot Learning. Proceedings of Machine Learning Research, vol. 78, pp. 87–96. PMLR (2017)
19. Song, S., Yu, F., Zeng, A., Chang, A.X., Savva, M., Funkhouser, T.: Semantic scene completion from a single depth image. In: Proceedings of the 30th IEEE Conference on Computer Vision and Pattern Recognition (2017)
20. Su, H., et al.: SPLATNet: sparse lattice networks for point cloud processing. In: Proceedings of the IEEE Conference on Computer Vision and Pattern Recognition, pp. 2530–2539 (2018)
21. Wu, J., Zhang, C., Xue, T., Freeman, W.T., Tenenbaum, J.B.: Learning a probabilistic latent space of object shapes via 3D generative-adversarial modeling. In: Advances in Neural Information Processing Systems, pp. 82–90 (2016)
22. Wu, Z., et al.: 3D ShapeNets: a deep representation for volumetric shapes. In: Proceedings of the IEEE Conference on Computer Vision and Pattern Recognition (CVPR) (2015)
23. Xiang, Y., et al.: ObjectNet3D: a large scale database for 3D object recognition. In: Proceedings of European Conference Computer Vision (ECCV) (2016)
24. Yang, B., Wen, H., Wang, S., Clark, R., Markham, A., Trigoni, N.: 3D object reconstruction from a single depth view with adversarial learning. In: Proceedings of International Conference on Computer Vision Workshops (ICCVW) (2017)
25. Yi, L., et al.: A scalable active framework for region annotation in 3D shape collections. In: Proceedings of SIGGRAPH Asia (2016)

evolve2vec: Learning Network Representations Using Temporal Unfolding

Nikolaos Bastas, Theodoros Semertzidis[✉], Apostolos Axenopoulos, and Petros Daras

Centre for Research and Technology, Hellas (CERTH), 57001 Thessaloniki, Greece
{nimpasta,theosem,axenop,daras}@iti.gr

Abstract. In the past few years, various methods have been developed that attempt to embed graph nodes (e.g. users that interact through a social platform) onto low-dimensional vector spaces, exploiting the relationships (commonly displayed as edges) among them. The extracted vector representations of the graph nodes are then used to effectively solve machine learning tasks such as node classification or link prediction. These methods, however, focus on the static properties of the underlying networks, neglecting the temporal unfolding of those relationships. This affects the quality of representations, since the edges don't encode the response times (i.e. speed) of the users' (i.e. nodes) interactions. To overcome this limitation, we propose an unsupervised method that relies on temporal random walks unfolding at the same timescale as the evolution of the underlying dataset. We demonstrate its superiority against state-of-the-art techniques on the tasks of hidden link prediction and future link forecast. Moreover, by interpolating between the fully static and fully temporal setting, we show that the incorporation of topological information of past interactions can further increase our method efficiency.

Keywords: Temporal random walks · Representation learning
Link prediction · Link forecast

1 Introduction

In many real world applications, such as social media and other communication platforms, it is convenient to represent entities as nodes and their interactions as links within a network. In recent years, there has been an increasing research interest towards embedding those entities in low dimensional vector spaces, preserving their structural proximity. This approach is called network representation learning and was first introduced in [13] with DeepWalk. The basic idea was to use truncated random walks on static graphs and sample sequences of entities that enclose topological information. Then, these samples were fed into the skip-gram model [10] to produce low dimensional vector representations for

© Springer Nature Switzerland AG 2019
I. Kompatsiaris et al. (Eds.): MMM 2019, LNCS 11295, pp. 447–458, 2019.
https://doi.org/10.1007/978-3-030-05710-7_37

each entity while maintaining their proximity in the new space. Since then, various techniques have been proposed using either random walks [5] or structural properties [15] of the interaction graph.

These methods, however, assume that interactions remain unchanged; this is an unrealistic setting, as all natural and human-related phenomena evolve in time. For example, suppose that the following set of interactions occurs: (A, B, t_1), (A, C, t_2), (D, E, t_3) and (A, D, t_4), where A, B, C, D and E are users and t_i the respective timestamps. In the static representation, the path $A \rightarrow D \rightarrow E$ exists; however, in the temporal case, this cannot happen. Thus, the structural proximity expected in the former case is an artifact of the aggregation process.

A few works have been published dealing with these considerations. In [4], deep autoencoders combined with a heuristic technique for adapting to newly observed interactions are used while in [17], a proximity score is assigned to each pair of graph nodes belonging to a randomly traversed path, incorporated as a weighting factor during the embedding process. Finally, in [12], the authors create the ego-network of each node, using present and past links within a time window and run truncated random walks in the same vein as [13].

In this paper, we propose evolve2vec, an unsupervised method that exploits temporal random walks in order to incorporate structural as well as temporal proximity to generate vector representations. Its main features are the following:

- Sufficient and balanced temporal information integration due to the sampling process.
- No assumptions regarding the structure of the dataset.
- Causality preservation by using random walks that respect the directionality of the interactions.
- Flexibility, by interpolating between a fully static and a fully dynamic setting.
- Parallelizable, which allow for scalability.
- Superiority against state-of-the-art methods for the tasks of hidden link prediction and future link forecast.

The remainder of the paper is organized as follows: the related work in representation learning is outlined in Sect. 2 and the proposed method is illustrated in Sect. 3. The experimental setup, datasets and baselines are presented in Sect. 4, while the results are discussed in Sect. 5. Conclusions and future directions are provided in Sect. 6.

2   Related Work

Network Representation Learning (NRL) has received a lot of attention in recent years. It refers to a collection of methods that aim at efficiently compressing any information related to different entities (e.g. nodes in a graph) or groups of them (e.g. subgraphs, communities or whole graphs) in a lower dimensional space, in order to facilitate the application of machine learning tasks, such as link prediction and node classification. The basic difference from other representation learning methods is that NRL incorporates the established relations between the entities during the learning process.

The main objective of NRL methods is to produce vector representations that preserve the structural (and/or other type of) similarity between the entities. Various approaches have been developed exploiting random walks [5,13] or topology [15,16] on static graphs. A comprehensive review for static graph embedding is given in [2].

While the previous methods have produced remarkable results on various tasks, they disregard the temporal evolution of real-world networks. A way to overcome such a problem was proposed in [6], where the authors first obtain vector representations in different snapshots and then perform proper rotations to align them.

Recently, a method based on deep autoencoders is adapted to the case of evolving networks [4]. Given a sequence of graph snapshots $\mathcal{G} = \{G_1, G_2, \ldots, G_m\}$ the autoencoder learns how to reconstruct each graph G_i by preserving the first and second order proximity of the graph nodes. After learning the representation for the nodes in G_i, it moves to the next snapshot G_{i+1}, using as initial values the obtained node embeddings in G_i. In order to overcome limitations concerning the introduction of new nodes, the authors propose an adaptive mechanism to decide whether more encoder and decoder layers should be added. The method has shown potential in uncovering hidden relations.

Another attempt towards this direction is the method proposed in [17]. First, for each node in the graph and up to a predefined coverage limit, a randomly traversed path is sampled. For each pair of nodes within these paths, a proximity score is calculated and used as a weighting factor in a logistic regression process. The proximity score is controlled by a damping parameter. The paths are updated during the evolution of the network if an interaction occurs. This method is applied on large-scale dynamic graphs for the link forecasting task.

In [12], the authors propose the following approach: suppose that the data is represented as a set of graph snapshots $\mathcal{G} = \{G_t, G_{t-1}, \ldots, G_{t-\tau}\}$ where t is the current timestamp and τ the length of a time window. For each graph node in the current snapshot G_t, denoted as u_t, a new graph is created that contains G_t and all the neighbors of u in the previous snapshots down to $t - \tau$. All past appearances of u are considered as different instances. Starting from node u_t, a set of random walks is generated on the resulting graph in the same way as in [13]. The sequences of graph nodes produced in this manner are fed in a skip-gram model [10] to obtain the embeddings. The results are used for trajectory classification. Although [12] shares a similar idea with our method, the main difference is that it relies on a static representation and does not take into account the temporal patterns.

3   Proposed Method

Consider a collection of timestamped ordered sequences of the form (u, v, t), where u and v are the interacting entities at time t. For convenience, suppose that these entities are social media users and their interactions are messages exchanged at the specific timestamps[1]. A schematic illustration is provided in Fig. 1.

We are interested in representing the users in a way that the topological as well as the temporal properties of the interactions are preserved. We expect that past interactions (e.g. before a timestamp T_s) contribute mainly to the topology of the network, while the more recent interactions are more important to encode the temporal information. We also preserve the directionality of the interactions.

In this respect, we split the time range $[T_0, T_{max}]$ into two parts: the static part $[T_0, T_s]$ (Fig. 1 bottom, left), which contains only topological information and the temporal part $(T_s, T_{max}]$ (Fig. 1 bottom, right), which refers to the recent past and is expected to preserve the temporal properties. By changing T_s in the range of $[T_0, T_{max}]$, we can interpolate between a fully static ($T_s = T_{max}$) and a fully temporal approach ($T_s = T_0$).

In each part, we launch random walks, starting from users that have at least one outgoing interaction. For example, in Fig. 1 (bottom, left), which stands for the static part, these starting points are users A,B,C and E. In the temporal part, such a user may appear in more than one snapshots and this should be taken into account. For example, user C appears in the first, second and fourth snapshot (Fig. 1 (bottom, right)) from left to right. Thus, in this case, we have to find all possible appearances L of such users within $(T_s, T_{max}]$ and randomly choose M of them. In the case where $L < M$, we set $M = L$.

In the static part, starting from those users, we initiate c realizations of directed random walks of length r. For example, if A is the initial point, then the possible random walk trajectories are: $A \rightarrow C \rightarrow F$ or $A \rightarrow D$. If the user has no outgoing connections to others, the walker gets trapped and remains there until it reaches r steps.

For the temporal part, we follow [14]. More precisely, if a walker resides on a user and there is an outgoing edge in a given snapshot, then it moves to the new user, otherwise it stays in the current one until there is an outgoing edge. Following Fig. 1 (bottom, right), if a walker starts from user C in the first snapshot, then its trajectory should be $C \rightarrow A \rightarrow A \rightarrow B \rightarrow B \rightarrow D$. At the last user, it stays for $r - l + 1$ steps, where l is the length of the trajectory. Note that if the starting point is user C in the second snapshot, then the trajectory is $C \rightarrow E$ and the walker remain at E until the end.

When the random walks have finished, we end up with a set of sequences $\mathcal{RW}$ of the form $\{u_1, u_2, \ldots, u_{r+1}\}$ which is comprised of static and temporal random walks. Then, following [13], we feed them as a corpus in the the skip-gram model [10]. In this way, we obtain user representations that have incorporated user co-occurence within a window w_{w2v}, which are the result of a mixed effect of topology and temporal evolution.

---

[1] However, many other processes can be represented as an ordered sequence.

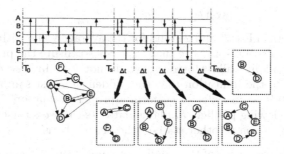

Fig. 1. A typical example of temporal interactions. Upper part: evolution of interactions denoted with arrows between entities A-F. Lower part, left: directed static
network constructed by aggregating all the interactions present in the time interval
$[T_0, T_s]$. Right: temporal snapshots using resolution Δt.

4   Experimental Setup

We evaluate our approach with respect to the tasks of hidden link prediction
and future link forecasting. There is a subtle difference between these (seemingly
similar) tasks: in hidden link prediction, the representations are acquired using
all the data except for a portion p, which is used as a test set. In this respect,
we have indirectly incorporated topological and temporal information during
the embedding process that may characterize hidden interactions. In the case
of future link forecasting, we use data not seen before (in terms of topology or
dynamics), while we use all the available past data to produce representations.

The experiments were implemented on a Ubuntu 14.04 LTS system using a
single Intel(R) Core(TM) i5-2500K at 3.30 GHz and a 16 GB RAM. We have
used a maximum of 8 cores, to be consistent with [17]. The parameter values
used for the embeddings are: $r = 10$, $c = 10$, $M = 10$, $w_{w2v} = 3$ and $d = 128$.
Next, we explain in more detail the tasks, datasets, metrics and baselines used
in the experiments.

4.1   Hidden Link Prediction

We follow the setup proposed in [4]. Given a sequence of snapshots
$\{G_1, G_2, \ldots, G_t\}$, we remove at random 15% of the links in G_t. We ensure that
the removed links have not appeared in previous snapshots. In this respect, the
dataset is split into two parts: the sequence $\{G_1, G_2, \ldots, G_t \setminus G_{rem}\}$ which will
be used for training evolve2vec and the testing part G_{rem} for the validation of
the embedding accuracy, as displayed in [16]. We repeat this process five times
and report the results.

More precisely, at each time step t and run i, we define the mean average
precision $MAP(t; i)$, as presented in [4, 16] and calculate the following quantities:

$$MAP(t) = \langle MAP(t; i)\rangle_i \tag{1}$$

$$MAP_{avg} = \langle MAP(t) \rangle_{t=t_{min}}^{T} \tag{2}$$

where the brackets in Eqs. 1 and 2 stand for the average value with respect to the index denoted as a subscript. Note that $t_{min} > r$ to ensure the proper unfolding of a temporal random walk. Moreover, we do not take into account self-links. Finally, we impose the limitation that the hidden link test sample should have more than $l = 10$ links in order to perform a proper evaluation.

We use the following publicly available datasets to assess the efficiency of our approach in comparison to other state-of-the art methods:

- ENRON [8]. It comprises of the email communication between Enron employees, spanning a period between January 1999 and July 2002. We follow [4], using a week resolution, starting from January 1999.
- HEP-TH [3]. It consists of the abstracts of papers on the topic of High Energy Physics Theory conference, starting from January 1993 until April 2003. As in [4], we take the first five years and construct a series of 70 graphs, which display the evolution of collaboration between the authors.

The statistics of the datasets are summarized in Table 1.

Table 1. Summary statistics of the datasets used in the experiments.

Dataset	$|V|$	$|E|_{temp}$	$|E|_{aggr}$	$|T|$	$\frac{|E|_{temp}}{|T|}$	Resolution
ENRON	184	125, 409	3, 129	22, 633	5.54	Week
HEP-TH	22, 908	2, 673, 133	2, 444, 798	219	12,206	Month
DIGG	279, 630	1, 731, 653	1, 731, 653	1, 644, 370	1.05	1-min
YOUTUBE	3, 223, 585	9, 375, 374	9, 375, 374	203	46,184	Dataset's resolution

In order to assess the effectiveness of our method, we compare our results against those illustrated in [4] and concern the following baselines:

- SDNE [16]: It applies deep autoencoders to exploit non - linearities and the first and second order proximity of the static graph. It is applied on each snapshot to produce node embeddings.
- Graph Factorization [1]: A distributed Graph Factorization (GF) method for large-scale datasets, used in [4] to sequentially produce node embeddings which are used to initialize the next step. It is denoted as GF_{init}.
- An alignment process [6], for the embeddings produced from GF and SDNE on each snapshot. Using the same notation as in [4], we indicate these approaches as GF_{align} and $SDNE_{align}$.
- DynGEM [4]: It is described in Sect. 2.

4.2   Future Link Forecasting

In the case of link forecasting, we follow the experimental setup proposed in [17], by calculating the ROC-AUC values as indicated in [9]. More specifically, if n'

is the number of times an unobserved link has a higher similarity score than a non-existing link picked at random and n'' are the times that are equal, then the AUC score is given by:

$$AUC = \frac{n' + 0.5 \cdot n''}{n} \qquad (3)$$

with n the total number of comparisons. The similarity scores are calculated using the operators proposed in [5], which are listed in Table 2. We denote as evolve2vec(H) the combination of evolve2vec with Hadamard, evolve2vec(L1) the combination with the Weighted-L1 and evolve2vec(L2) with the Weighted-L2 operators, respectively. We perform five different runs and average over the obtained values of Eq. 3.

Table 2. Definitions of the binary operators [5]. $f()$ is the mapping function, u, v are the entities to be mapped and i the index of the embedding vector.

Operator	Hadamard	Weighted-L1	Weighted-L2
Definition	$f_i(u) \cdot f_i(v)$	$|f_i(u) - f_i(v)|$	$|f_i(u) - f_i(v)|^2$

We use the following publicly available datasets to evaluate the performance of our method:

- YOUTUBE [11]: It is an undirected social network of YouTube users collected during the years 2006–2007. We keep the temporal resolution of the dataset collection process.
- DIGG [7]: It is a directed social network collected in 2009. We define a 1-min resolution over the existing data.

Summary statistics of the previous datasets are provided in Table 1. We split them as indicated in [17]. In this setting, T0x refers to the training part and T(x+1) to the link forecasting part.

In this task, we are interested in two aspects: (a) what will be the performance if we learn node representations based on both static and temporal random walks and (b) how the performance of node representation changes as we are moving away from the last timestamp of the training dataset. In the case of YOUTUBE, we set T_s to a fixed non-zero value to answer both questions, while in DIGG, we interpolate between $T_s = 0$ and $T_s = T_{max}$, to obtain a more comprehensive picture of those effects. The parameters for the embedding are given in Sect. 4, while the T_s values are denoted in Sect. 5.

We compare our method to the results obtained in [17] for the following methods:

- DeepWalk [13]: It uses truncated random walks to sample sequences of adjacent nodes in a graph. These are fed in a skip-gram model [10] to produce the node embeddings.

– LINE [15]: It is based on minimizing the reconstruction error of the graph
by preserving the structural proximity between nodes. It uses either the
first-order (LINE(1^{rst}), the second-order proximity (LINE(2nd) or both
(LINE($1^{rst} + 2^{nd}$) to embed the nodes in a d dimensional vector space.
– DNPS [17]: It is described in Sect. 2.

5   Results and Discussion

As presented in Sect. 4, we are interested in the efficiency of evolve2vec in (a)
predicting hidden relations between entities within already seen (but incomplete)
datasets as well as (b) to forecast interactions in the future. In the following, we
present our findings against those reported in [4] for link prediction and [17] for
link forecast, using the same settings and baselines, as in the reference papers,
respectively.

5.1   Hidden Link Prediction

In Table 3, we illustrate the average MAP values reported for ENRON and HEP-
TH datasets in [4] against those obtained using evolve2vec.

In both datasets, we observe that our method is better than the baselines.
This difference is more pronounced in ENRON dataset. The results indicate that
evolve2vec can effectively identify hidden links.

Table 3. Average MAP for hidden link prediction for the ENRON and HEP-TH
datasets.

Method	evolve2vec	DynGEM	GF_{align}	GF_{init}	$SDNE_{align}$	SDNE
ENRON	**0.32**	0.084	0.021	0.017	0.06	0.081
HEP-TH	**0.31**	0.26	0.04	0.042	0.17	0.1

5.2   Link Forecasting

We start with the results obtained for YOUTUBE dataset. In Fig. 2, we plot
the AUC values for each test dataset T(x+1). evolve2vec(H) behaves better
than the rest of the baselines between T2 and T5, while evolve2vec(L1) and
evolve2vec(L2) perform poorly for the same range. This is also manifested in
the gain/loss of each operator with respect to DNPS. Specifically, evolve2vec(H)
exhibits a gain between a minimum of 0.19% for T2 and a maximum of 1.5% at
T4. evolve2vec(L1) and evolve2vec(L2) are inferior compared to DNPS, with a
maximum loss of 3% at T2 and a minimum of 0.5% at T5.

However, as we incorporate more of the YOUTUBE dataset, evolve2vec(L1) and evolve2vec(L2) approach both evolve2vec(H) and DNPS values and surpasses them for $x + 1 \geq 6$. In terms of gain/loss for the range T6-T9, evolve2vec(L1) and evolve2vec(L2) are superior by $1 - 3.5\%$ compared to DNPS.

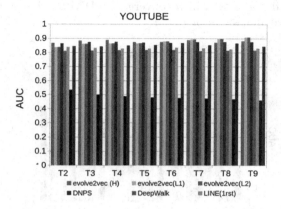

Fig. 2. Plot of AUC for future link forecast for consecutive T(x+1) sets. For each T(x+1) and left to right: evolve2vec(H), evolve2vec(L1), evolve2vec(L2), DNPS, Deep-Walk, LINE(1rst), LINE(2nd), LINE(1rst+2nd). The evaluation is performed using all the data within T(x+1) sets.

In Fig. 3, we plot the evolution of the AUC with respect to the dataset resolution for T3 and T9 respectively. In Fig. 3(a), we observe that for time stamps close to the end of the training set, all operators are higher than the DNPS value. As we move to the end of T3, evolve2vec(L1) and evolve2vec(L2) converge to DNPS and at $t = 81$, they become inferior. evolve2vec(H) remains the best for all the time range, even though with considerable losses.

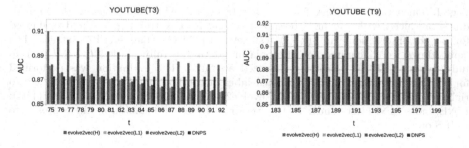

Fig. 3. Plot of AUC for future link forecast and increasing time stamps t, considering all the interactions up to t, for (a) T3 and (b) T9. For each t and from left to right: evolve2vec(H), evolve2vec(L1), evolve2vec(L2) and DNPS.

In Fig. 3(b) (T9), all the operators are better than DNPS for the whole range of time. The evolution pattern, however, is different from that in Fig. 3(a). At the beginning, we observe an initial increase in the performance, reaching a maximum at a time point that is different between Hadamard ($t = 185$) and Weighted-L1 and L2 operators ($t = 188$), followed by a smooth decrease. Except for the Hadamard operator, which converges to DNPS value as t increases, the other operators remain superior by far.

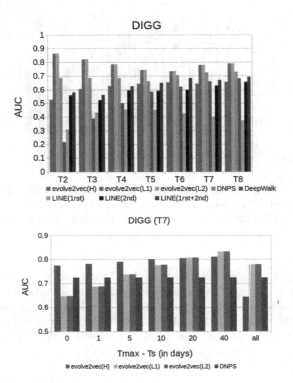

Fig. 4. Future link forecast for DIGG dataset. (a) AUC values using the embeddings produced with the fully temporal setting in T0x training sets and evaluated for all the interactions in T(x+1) test sets. (b) AUC values for T7 test set. The embeddings were acquired by interpolating from the fully static ($T_s = T_{max}$) to fully dynamic ($T_s = 0$) setting (denoted as "all"). The evaluation was performed for all the interactions in T7. For each label in the horizontal axis and from left to right: evolve2vec(H), evolve2vec(L1), evolve2vec(L2), DNPS, DeepWalk, LINE(1rst), LINE(2nd), LINE(1rst+2nd). In (b) we omit the other techniques and compare to DNPS only.

In Fig. 4, we continue our investigation with the DIGG dataset. In Fig. 4(a), we observe that for all T(x+1), the AUC values obtained for evolve2vec(L1) evolve2vec(L2) are superior compared to DNPS and the rest of the baselines while the evolve2vec(H) operator performs poorly.

To illustrate the effect of mixed spatial and temporal random walks on the prediction efficiency, we plot in Fig. 4(b) the AUC for T7 set, using the hybrid random walk approach, moving from a fully static $(T_{max} - T_s = 0)$ to fully temporal $(T_s = 0)$ setting. We keep only the DNPS baseline as the rest of them are inferior. We observe that for the fully static case, the evolve2vec(H) operator behaves considerable better than evolve2vec(L1), evolve2vec(L2) and DNPS. However, as we incorporate more temporal information, we observe that the three operators increase in terms of AUC and converge to each other, while for $T_{max} - T_s = 5$ (in days) all behave better than DNPS. The performance reaches a maximum at $T_{max} - T_s = 40$ days and then it drops. Considering the full range as time varying, evolve2vec (L1) and evolve2vec(L2) continue to be better than DNPS, while evolve2vec(H) is the last.

In summary, the results indicate that evolve2vec combined with the operators listed in Table 1 can provide state-of-the-art results in future link forecast. Moreover, the hybrid approach significantly improves the performance, while there seems to be a optimal T_s which is expected to be dataset-dependent.

6   Conclusions

Learning informative representations of various entities and employing them into machine learning tasks has demonstrated its high potential in the past years. The incorporation of the connectivity patterns between those entities has provided a more efficient way in capturing the wealth of relations developed and, in this respect, obtaining representations closer to reality.

This new area, called network representation learning, has mainly focused on the static properties of the interactions, neglecting their temporal evolution. While there has been a great success in various tasks such as classification and prediction, the integration of more realistic features is expected to benefit them.

Towards this goal, we have developed a novel method that incorporates temporal random walks to represent entities in a low dimensional vector space and interpolates between a fully static and fully temporal setting. We have applied it to the hidden link prediction and future link forecast tasks and compared it against state-of-the-art methods. The results indicate the superiority of our approach in both of them and its high efficiency in short and long term prediction. Moreover, the Weighted-L1 and Weighted-L2 operators leads to better results than Hadamard in future link forecast and should be preferred.

Several improvements can be incorporated in evolve2vec, such as the sampling of the starting points for the temporal random walks, the variable length intervals for data aggregation or the inductive learning through more general representations (e.g. communities) and their temporal evolution. These are left for future research.

Acknowledgments. The work presented in this paper was supported by the European Commission under contract H2020-700381 ASGARD.

References

1. Ahmed, A., Shervashidze, N., Narayanamurthy, S., Josifovski, V., Smola, A.J.: Distributed large-scale natural graph factorization. In: Proceedings of the 22nd International Conference on World Wide Web. WWW 2013, pp. 37–48. ACM, New York (2013)
2. Cai, H., Zheng, V.W., Chang, K.C.C.: A comprehensive survey of graph embedding: problems, techniques and applications. arXiv:1709.07604 [cs.AI] (2018)
3. Gehrke, J., Ginsparg, P., Kleinberg, J.: Overview of the 2003 KDD cup. SIGKDD Explor. Newsl. **5**(2), 149–151 (2003)
4. Goyal, P., Kamra, N., He, X., Liu, Y.: DynGEM: deep embedding method for dynamic graphs (2017). http://www-scf.usc.edu/~nkamra/pdf/dyngem.pdf
5. Grover, A., Leskovec, J.: Node2vec: scalable feature learning for networks. In: Proceedings of the 22nd ACM SIGKDD International Conference on Knowledge Discovery and Data Mining, pp. 855–864. ACM, New York (2016)
6. Hamilton, W.L., Leskovec, J., Jurafsky, D.: Diachronic word embeddings reveal statistical laws of semantic change. arXiv:1605.09096 [cs.CL] (2016)
7. Hogg, T., Lerman, K.: Social dynamics of Digg. EPJ Data Sci. **1**(1), 5 (2012). https://doi.org/10.1140/epjds5
8. Klimt, B., Yang, Y.: The enron corpus: a new dataset for email classification research. In: Boulicaut, J.-F., Esposito, F., Giannotti, F., Pedreschi, D. (eds.) ECML 2004. LNCS (LNAI), vol. 3201, pp. 217–226. Springer, Heidelberg (2004). https://doi.org/10.1007/978-3-540-30115-8_22
9. Lü, L., Zhou, T.: Link prediction in complex networks: a survey. Physica A: Stati. Mech. Appl. **390**(6), 1150–1170 (2011)
10. Mikolov, T., Chen, K., Corrado, G., Dean, J.: Efficient estimation of word representations in vector space. arxiv:1301.3781 [cs.CL] (2013)
11. Mislove, A.E.: Online social networks: measurement, analysis, and applications to distributed information systems. Ph.D. thesis, Rice University (2009)
12. Pandhre, S., Mittal, H., Gupta, M., Balasubramanian, V.N.: STwalk: learning trajectory representations in temporal graphs. arXiv:1711.04150 [cs.SI] (2018)
13. Perozzi, B., Al-Rfou, R., Skiena, S.: DeepWalk: online learning of social representations. In: Proceedings of the 20th ACM SIGKDD International Conference on Knowledge Discovery and Data Mining, pp. 701–710. ACM, New York (2014)
14. Starnini, M., Baronchelli, A., Barrat, A., Pastor-Satorras, R.: Random walks on temporal networks. Phys. Rev. E **85**, 056115 (2012)
15. Tang, J., Qu, M., Wang, M., Zhang, M., Yan, J., Mei, Q.: LINE: large-scale information network embedding. In: Proceedings of the 24th International Conference on World Wide Web. WWW 2015, pp. 1067–1077 (2015)
16. Wang, D., Cui, P., Zhu, W.: Structural deep network embedding. In: Proceedings of the 22Nd ACM SIGKDD International Conference on Knowledge Discovery and Data Mining. KDD 2016, pp. 1225–1234. ACM, New York (2016)
17. Zhiyuli, A., Liang, X., Xu, Z.: Learning distributed representations for large-scale dynamic social networks. In: IEEE INFOCOM 2017 - IEEE Conference on Computer Communications, pp. 1–9, May 2017

The Impact of Packet Loss and Google Congestion Control on QoE for WebRTC-Based Mobile Multiparty Audiovisual Telemeetings

Dunja Vucic[1(✉)] and Lea Skorin-Kapov[2]

[1] Ericsson Nikola Tesla d.d., Krapinska 45, Zagreb, Croatia
dunja.vucic@ericsson.com
[2] Faculty of Electrical Engineering and Computing, University of Zagreb, Unska 3, Zagreb, Croatia
lea.skorin-kapov@fer.hr

Abstract. While previous expensive and complex desktop video conferencing solutions had a restricted reach, the emergence of the WebRTC (Web Real-Time Communication) open framework has provided an opportunity to redefine the video conferencing communication landscape. In particular, technological advances in terms of high resolution displays, cameras, and high speed wireless access networks have set the ground for emerging multiparty video telemeeting solutions realized via mobile devices. However, deploying multiparty video communication solutions on smart phones calls for the need to optimize video encoding parameters due to limited device processing power and dynamic wireless network conditions. In this paper, we report on a subjective user study involving 30 participants taking part in three-party audiovisual telemeetings on mobile devices. We conduct an experimental investigation of the Google Congestion Control (GCC) Algorithm in light of packet loss and under various video codec configurations, with the aim being to observe the impact on end user Quality of Experience (QoE). Results provide insights related to QoE-driven video encoding adaptation (in terms of bit rate, resolution, and frame rate), and show that in certain cases, adaptation invoked by GCC leads to video interruption. In majority of other cases, we observed that it took approximately 25 s for the video stream to recover to an acceptable quality level after the temporary occurrence of network packet loss.

Keywords: QoE · Audiovisual telemeeting · Multiparty · Mobile GCC

1 Introduction

In the context of mobile networks, characterized by variable network resource availability, challenges arise with respect to meeting the Quality of Experience

© Springer Nature Switzerland AG 2019
I. Kompatsiaris et al. (Eds.): MMM 2019, LNCS 11295, pp. 459–470, 2019.
https://doi.org/10.1007/978-3-030-05710-7_38

(QoE) requirements of conversational real-time, media rich, and multi-user services. With the move towards 4G, and subsequently 5G networks, the aim will be to meet the requirements of low latency and high-volume service scenarios. In addition to network requirements, mobile multiparty video conferencing and telemeeting services impose strict requirements in terms of end user device processing capabilities, with the need for real-time encoding and decoding of multiple media streams. The term *telemeeting* is commonly used to encompass more flexible and interactive communication scenarios than those typically considered in the scope of a conventional business video conference, such as a private meeting in a leisure context [1].

Multiparty video call optimization is thus a challenging task due to dynamic wireless networks, heterogeneous mobile devices, and contexts. To optimize service performance, in particular from a QoE point of view, there is a need for dynamic service adaptation and optimization mechanisms in light of varying resource availability [2]. Given the mobile device context and corresponding screen sizes, the question is which video quality levels are necessary to achieve acceptable QoE, thus avoiding the delivering of quality levels beyond those that contribute to QoE improvement. Video encoding adaptation strategies may be deployed to downsize traffic by adapting parameters such as bitrate, resolution, and frame rate, so as to optimize end user QoE under variable system and network conditions.

With video conferencing/telemeeting services typically designed to use UDP rather than TCP, the deployment of congestions control mechanisms is left to the application layer [3]. As such, the Google Congestion Control (GCC) algorithm has been specifically designed to work with RTP/RTCP protocols and target real-time streams such as telephony and video conferencing. In particular, the delay gradient is used to infer congestion. Based on packet loss, delay, and bandwidth estimations, the algorithm dynamically adjusts the data rate of streams by invoking stream adaptation, including bitrate, resolution, and frame rate adaptation [4].

In this paper, we conduct an empirical study to explore how GCC handles network packet loss under different video resolutions, bit rates, and frame rate constraints. We report on a subjective user study involving 30 participants aimed to investigate how this adaptation influences QoE in the context of three-party mobile audiovisual telemeetings realized via the WebRTC paradigm. Results show that in certain cases, adaptation invoked by GCC leads to video interruption. In other cases, it took approximately 25 s for the video stream to recover to preconfigured video encoding parameters after the temporary occurrence of network packet loss. Subjective results indicate that quality degradations resulting from packet loss and GCC activation are often lower in cases when the video codec is configured to deliver streams at lower quality levels.

2   Background and Related Work

WebRTC and GCC. Today, various solutions and configurations exist for enabling audiovisual communications. One of the main driving forces has been the evolution of the technologies and APIs related to the WebRTC standards, enabling browser-to-browser real-time communication with built-in real-time audio and video functions without requiring any plugins [5]. The basic WebRTC architecture includes a server and at least two peers. Each peer loads the application in their local environment (browser). The application uses the WebRTC API to communicate with the local context. To enable WebRTC applications to load quicker and run smoother, the GCC algorithm was proposed within the RMCAT IETF WG to dynamically invoke stream adaptation [4]. The GCC algorithm includes two control elements: a *delay-based* controller on the receiver side, and a *loss-based* controller on the sender side (which complements the delay-based controller if losses are detected). The congestion controller on the sender side bases decisions on measured round-trip time, packet loss, and available bandwidth estimates [6]. In short, if 2–10% of the packets have been lost since the previous report from the receiver, the sender rate will be kept unchanged. If more than 10% of the packets have been lost the rate will be decreased. If less than 2% of the packets have been lost, then the rate will be increased [4].

Performance and Quality Assessment. Terms necessary for subjective quality assessment of multiparty telemeeting services are defined in ITU-T Recommendation P.1301 [7]. A comprehensive study of QoE for multiparty conferencing and telemeeting systems providing methods and conceptual models for perceptual assessment and prediction, emphasizing communication complexity and involvement, is given in [1]. While a wide range of user and context factors impact QoE (out of scope for this work), system influence factors include packet loss, delay, jitter, and bandwidth limitations. In [8], Schimtt et al. conducted subjective assessment studies with a four-way desktop video conferencing system, and investigated the impact of bit rate and packet-loss on overall quality, audio quality, and video quality under different Internet access technologies (broadband, DSL, and mobile). Schimtt et al. studied the patterns of user characteristics and interactions to identify two types of users: those that notice degradations in video quality and identify these as reflecting strongly on subjective ratings for audio quality; and users for whom video quality degradation has a low impact on audio quality [9]. In their subsequent work [10], the authors investigated how impaired video quality, caused by lower encoding bit rates or packet loss, influenced user interactions. Authors conducted experiments over a video conferencing system and groups of four people with the goal being to jointly build a Lego model. Obtained results showed that interaction was impacted by the lowest quality. Lack of details in the video forced participants to verbally express missing details.

In [11], Jansen et al. provide an extensive investigation of the effects of latency, packet loss, and bandwidth on the performance of WebRTC-based video conferencing by emulating various environments. They detect that in case of inserted packet loss, it takes around 30 s to reach the maximum bit rate when packet loss is removed. The authors also evaluate the performance of WebRTC on mobile devices and show the impact of limited computational capacity on call quality. Previous experiments focusing on mobile video call quality, and conducted over Wi-Fi, showed sensitivity to bursty packet losses and long packet delays [12].

In multiparty video-mediated conversations, research results suggest that conversations with a one-way delay between one and two seconds are no longer possible without additional explicit organizing mechanisms [13]. Xu et al. [14] investigated how to increase mouth-to-ear delay within just noticeable differences, to conceal its losses, but without perceptible reductions in terms of interactivity.

Previous studies have clearly shown that a wide variety of subjective and objective parameters influence the QoE of multiparty video conferencing/telemeeting scenarios. Numerous combinations and interplays of impact factors make it challenging to distinguish, define, and measure critical conditions. In this paper, we aim to provide insights into the performance of mobile multiparty telemeetings under severe packet loss.

3   Experimental Design

Experiments were conducted involving interactive three-party audiovisual conversations in a natural environment and leisure context over a Wi-Fi network with symmetric device conditions so as to eliminate the impact of different devices. Experiments were carried out in a controlled environment and used to collect subjective end user assessments, rating the impact of packet loss on perceived quality. Moreover, WebRTC call-related statistics were collected for the purpose of performance analysis.

3.1   Methodology

The three-party video telemeeting was set up using a WebRTC application running on the *Licode*[1] open source media server installed in a local network, to avoid impairments caused by a commercial network, enabling us to preconfigure application parameters: bit rate, fame rate, and video resolution (Fig. 1).

These default settings were then dynamically adapted based on activation of the GCC algorithm in response to inserted loss. The Licode media server was installed on a laptop with Intel Core i5 Processor, 2.6 GHz, 8 GB RAM and Ubuntu 14.04. Experiments were conducted in a natural home environment, with all three participants taking part in the call using mobile phones Samsung Galaxy S6 with quad-core CPU, Mali-T760MP8 GPU, 3 GB of RAM, 5.1" display size, 1440 × 2560 px display resolution, Android ver.6.0.1 and Chrome 55.0.2883.91 (Fig. 2).

We note that the participants were physically located in three separate rooms and could not see/hear each other outside of the established call. The rooms had the following dimensions LxWxH (cm): room 1 - 385 × 327 × 260, room 2 - 385 × 250 × 260, room 3 - 385 × 320 × 260.

---

[1] http://lynckia.com/licode/.

Fig. 1. Testbed set-up over a LAN

Fig. 2. Example three-party video conversation in the Chrome browser. The upper right window portrays the local self-recording video.

Packet loss was artificially generated in the experiments using the Albedo *Net.Storm*[2] network emulator, which enabled Ethernet frame loss insertion. Net.Storm is a hardware-based emulator with the capability to emulate different degradations or impairments in Ethernet/IP networks. We used the function *frame periodic burst* to drop frame bursts, with a configurable number of frames that make up each loss burst and the separation between loss bursts. Loss bursts were periodically inserted, with burst length of 10 frames, and burst separation of 5 frames between consecutive loss bursts. We initiated packet loss starting after the first minute of each test conversation, and lasting for 10 s, after which the impairment was turned off. We specifically designed experiments with longer-term and significant burst behavior, to explore to which extent the GCC algorithm lowers video quality, and how this degradation will be perceived by participants. The test schedule consisted of participants rating 8 test conditions with different combinations of video resolutions (480×320 and 640×480), bit

---

[2] http://www.albedotelecom.com/pages/fieldtools/src/netstorm.php.

rates (300 kbps and 600 kbps) and frame rates (15 fps and 20 fps), each lasting 3 min (Table 1). With 15 participant groups, overall 120 tests were performed.

Table 1. Test schedule

Experiment	Video resolution	Frame rate	Bit rate
Test case 1 (TC1)	480 × 320	15 fps	300 kbps
Test case 2 (TC2)	480 × 320	15 fps	600 kbps
Test case 3 (TC3)	480 × 320	20 fps	300 kbps
Test case 4 (TC4)	480 × 320	20 fps	600 kbps
Test case 5 (TC5)	640 × 480	15 fps	300 kbps
Test case 6 (TC6)	640 × 480	15 fps	600 kbps
Test case 7 (TC7)	640 × 480	20 fps	300 kbps
Test case 8 (TC8)	640 × 480	20 fps	600 kbps

A preliminary test was carried out to introduce participants with the test procedure and assessment questionnaire, but results were not taken into account. After each 3 min session was finished, participants were asked to rate audio quality, visual quality, AV synchronization, and overall quality using a paper questionnaire and the five point ACR (Absolute Category Rating) scale: 1 "Bad", 2 "Poor", 3 "Fair", 4 "Good", 5 "Excellent". We decided to split audiovisual quality to audio and video quality because packet loss may have significant influence on the video quality, while still providing acceptable audio quality.

3.2 Participants

Thirty participants took part in the study, 16 male and 14 female subjects, with an average age of 40 years (min 33, max 49). Participants were divided into 15 fixed groups, with one fixed user added to each group as a third participant, to monitor the service and help keep the conversation flowing (this fixed third participant did not provide any subjective ratings). All participants were employed, 9 of them with high school education and 21 with a University degree. Participants reported having previous experience with the following video conversation applications (numbers indicate no. of participants): Skype (23), Viber (15), WhatsApp (13), Google hangouts (4), Facebook (1). The Croatian language was chosen to represent a natural interactive free conversation, without any specific preassigned tasks. The selected subjects were not experts in audiovisual communications. Sixteen subjects have previously participated in subjective assessment. Subjects were volunteers, all with normal hearing, and 16 of them have corrected vision.

4   Results

Analysis of Subjective Quality Ratings. We discuss the influence of packet loss on perceived quality for different test conditions (results shown in Table 2). The average packet loss values for incoming traffic ranged from 2.28% in test case 1 to 3.82% in test case 7, and for outgoing traffic for all test cases ranged between 0.46% to 1.59%. We found that all test conditions provided on average at least "Fair" audio, video, and overall quality, as well as AV synchronization. TC1 provided the highest average rating for audio quality (3.47) with the following Licode settings for all flows: 320 × 480 resolution, 15 fps, and 300 kbps encoding bit rate. The highest synchronization (3.63) and overall quality ratings (3.6) were provided by TC6. TC8 received the highest mean rating for video quality (3.63).

Table 2. Highest MOS values

Test conditions	Evaluated	MOS ratings
Test case 1 480 × 320, 15 fps, 300 kbps	Audio quality	3.47
Test case 8 640 × 480, 20 fps, 600 kbps	Video quality	3.63
Test case 6 640 × 480, 15 fps, 600 kbps	AV synchronization	3.63
Test case 6 640 × 480, 15 fps, 600 kbps	Overall quality	3.6

To provide better insights into rating distributions, Fig. 3 shows the percentage of participants providing each rating score for audio quality, video quality, AV synchronization and overall quality for each test condition.

TC5 (resolution 640 × 480, 15 fps, bit rate 300 kbps) had the smallest difference between all tested ratings. In test cases 480 × 320, 15 fps, 300 kbps; 480 × 320, 20 fps, 600 kbps; and 640 × 480, 15 fps, 600 kbps, more than 50% of participants rated audio quality as "Good" or higher, and more than 60% of participants rated AV synchronization as "Good" or higher. In test case 640 × 480, 20 fps, 600 kbps, more than 56% of participants rated video quality as "Good" or "Excellent". In case of overall quality and test case 640 × 480, 15 fps, 600 kbps, more than 63% of participants rated it as "Good" or higher. Only in the TC1 with 480 × 320, 15 fps, 300 kbps, the rating "Bad" was never given. TC2 at 480 × 320, 15 fps, 600 kbps had the highest overall number of bad ratings combining all rated variables. On the other hand, TC8 at 640 × 480, 20 fps, 600 kbps had the highest overall number of "Excellent" ratings combining all rated variables. The percentage of dissatisfied participants who consider overall quality of the test condition either "Poor" or "Bad" is highest in TC4 at 480 × 320, 20 fps, 600 kbps, with a share of 26.67%.

We used a one-way ANOVA to check for significant differences between audio quality, video quality, AV synchronization and overall quality for each test condition. Results given in Table 3 show that no significant difference exist between MOS scores.

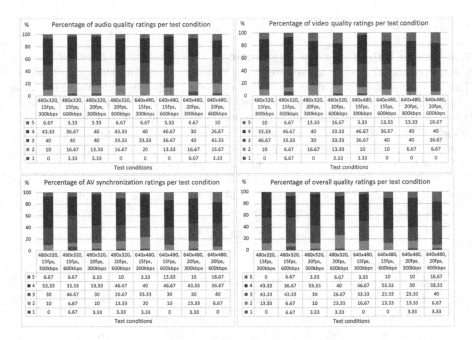

Fig. 3. Distribution of ratings per test condition for audio quality, video quality, AV synchronization and overall quality.

To find out if there is significant difference between test conditions per each evaluated variable (audio quality, video quality, overall quality and AV synchronization), we again used one-way ANOVA and confirmed that there is no significant difference between test conditions.

Implication of Results: insights showing that no significant differences in terms of subjective ratings exist between test conditions, can be utilized by future service adaptation strategies in terms of setting thresholds for video encoding parameters. Bandwidth consumption may thus be reduced with nearly no loss in terms of perceived quality, and thus aid in avoiding the onset of congestion-related disturbances.

Impact of Inserted Packet Loss on Performance. In each test session participants reported service impairments. In response to inserted packet loss, Chrome tries to reduce the resolution, frame rate and bit rate. As a result, actual sent values start to differ from those initially configured. Ten seconds of inserted bursty packet loss caused 25 to 50 s of video conversation with lower quality, after which the service managed to restore values preconfigured by the media server. In some cases, the service never restored to the initial settings, but continued running on the reduced ones.

Subjects reported video loss of one participant after inserted packet loss in all test cases except TC1 (300 kps, 480×320, 15 fps) and TC8 (600 kps, 640×480,

Table 3. ANOVA results for audio quality, video quality, AV synchronization and overall quality per each test condition

Test case	SS	df	MS	F	P-value	F crit
480 × 320 15 fps 300 kbps	1.09	3.00	0.36	0.62	0.61	2.68
480 × 320 15 fps 600 kbps	0.63	3.00	0.21	0.24	0.87	2.68
480 × 320 20 fps 300 kbps	0.89	3.00	0.30	0.38	0.77	2.68
480 × 320 20 fps 600 kbps	1.09	3.00	0.36	0.39	0.76	2.68
640 × 480 15 fps 300 kbps	0.57	3.00	0.19	0.25	0.86	2.68
640 × 480 15 fps 600 kbps	0.96	3.00	0.32	0.46	0.71	2.68
640 × 480 20 fps 300 kbps	3.63	3.00	1.21	1.36	0.26	2.68
640 × 480 20 fps 600 kbps	3.50	3.00	1.17	1.40	0.25	2.68

20 fps). Complete video loss of one participant occurred in 8% of all sessions, with the video remaining lost until the end of the session. We note that this effect has also been observed and reported in previous work [15], where WebRTC is trying to adapt to the loss of link capacity but remains unrecovered after the network conditions were restored.

The highest MOS rating (3.54) for all rated quality dimensions was observed for TC6, where video loss occurred two times. TC2 (480 × 320, 15 fps, 600 kbps) had one video loss occurrence and obtained the lowest MOS score of 3.29. While video loss had a significant impact on certain participants, for other participants it did not contribute to the quality perception at all. For example, in test group 8, Fig. 4 portrays outgoing and incoming bitrates for TC2 (480 × 320, 15 fps, 600 kbps). What we observe is that quality degradation lasted for approximately 35 s. The video bitrate of one incoming participant stream dropped to zero in the 100th second, and failed to recover for the remainder of the session. One participant in this case rated audio quality with "Poor" and video quality, AV synchronization and overall quality with "Bad". Another participant from the same group rated audio quality with "Good" and video quality, AV synchronization and overall quality with "Fair".

What we can conclude is that in a leisure context, temporary lose of a video stream does not have such a significant impact on QoE, as long as there is limited audio degradation.

To obtain WebRTC statistics for each call, we used the *webrtc-internals* tool, implemented within the Chrome browser [16,17]. Overall test statistics obtained from webrtc-internals data across all test sessions are given in Table 4. The lowest recorded resolution was 240 × 160, with frame rate 1 fps, and bit rate 15 kbps. In some cases, bit rates with values around 30kbps lasted for approximately 30 s, which is a significant period in the context of 3 min-long conversations. On average, TC1 managed to maintain preconfigured video encoding values for the longest time during the session. The default resolution of 480 × 320 occurred during the conversation in 76.33% of session time. The default frame rate of

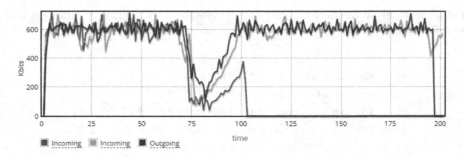

Fig. 4. Outgoing and incoming video bitrate for test case 2 480 × 320, 15 fps, 600 kbps

Table 4. WebRTC internals collected and analyzed data of mean values per test condition.

Test case	15 fps 300 kbps	15 fps 600 kbps	20 fps 300 kbps	20 fps 600 kbps
Obtained resolution 480 × 320 default	76.33%	76.22%	73.06%	73.95%
Obtained resolution 360 × 240	13.83%	13.01%	13.11%	16.52%
Obtained resolution 240 × 160	9.84%	10.54%	13.65%	9.31%
1–6 fps	1.77%	0.46%	0.18%	0.5%
6–13 fps	4.25%	3.87%	1.32%	1.87%
≥13 fps	93.74%	82.48%	92.27%	89.66%
Default frame rate	73.61%	63.62%	50.22%	49.73%
AVG # of packets lost	370.79	354.37	305.23	346.01
AVG # of packets received	9778.44	11660.53	8713.48	11573.91
AVG # of packets received per second	41.06	52.87	42.5	52.88
Test case	15 fps 300 kbps	15 fps 600 kbps	20 fps 300 kbps	20 fps 600 kbps
Obtained resolution 640 × 480 default	32.05%	21.77%	48.05%	29.23%
Obtained resolution 480 × 360	47.45%	74.09%	26.21%	65.49%
Obtained resolution 320 × 240	17.01%	2.48%	24.95%	3.58%
Obtained resolution 240 × 180	1.26%	1.66%	0.78%	1.68%
1–6 fps	0.77%	0.83%	0.4%	0.66%
6–13 fps	3.24%	3.51%	1.6%	1.61%
≥13 fps	89.81%	89.24%	95.27%	93.86%
Default frame rate	67.95%	69.05%	46.37%	48.67%
AVG # of packets lost	290.8	353.41	332.87	415.26
AVG # of packets received	8774.36	11720.99	9825.01	12010.96
AVG # of packets received per second	42.6	54.68	44.88	55.62

15 fps was observed in 73.61% of overall session time. TC6 maintained a default resolution of 640 × 480 for only 21.77% of session time. In TC7, the default frame rate of 20 fps showed up with the lowest frequency in 46.37% of session time.

For test cases with resolution 480 × 320, the average number of lost packets ranged from 305.23 to 370.79, and for resolution 640 × 480 between 290.8 and 415.26. The average number of packets received per second was lowest in TC1, while the highest received rates were achieved in TC6. Considering video resolution, frame rate, and bit rate results showed that the quality degradation caused by packet loss is smaller for 480×320 resolution than 640×480. GCC activation lowered the frame rates as well, but for both preconfigured values 15 and 20 fps, rates higher than 13 fps, which should be enough for relatively still content (such as normal conversation via a small smartphone screen), occurred in at least 82.48% of the session.

The GCC algorithm attempts to adjust the video quality to match the available resources so that the video service flows smoothly for each participant in the session. However, our empirical results show that in some cases, adaptations are too extreme, and the service is not capable of recovering entirely after disturbances are finished. Video quality reduction should be applied, but it raises the question as to what extent parameters should be adjusted so as to maintain acceptable QoE.

5   Conclusion

The goal of this paper has been to investigate the impact of packet loss and the invoked GCC algorithm on QoE in the case of mobile multiparty audiovisual telemeetings. Subjective studies were conducted for test scenarios differing in default video codec configuration settings. Results showed that no significant differences in subjective ratings exist between test conditions. A possible reason why subjects did not significantly notice video quality degradation or enhancement between test conditions is the smartphone display size, with a rather small video container for displaying each stream. Further data analysis indicates that quality reduction caused by temporarily inserted packet loss and the GCC algorithm is lower and lasts for a shorter time period in cases when sessions were configured with lower default video quality (in terms of resolution, fps, bitrate) as compared to sessions originally configured to stream higher video quality.

Performance measurements showed that packet loss caused severe disturbances, in some cases even the reduction of video bitrate to nearly zero. The impact of a "lost" video stream on overall QoE was found to differ greatly among participants, which can be attributed to differences in end user expectations. As long as the audio quality remained satisfactory, most participants provided high quality scores. Considering that audio was not lost in any sessions, we can conclude that in a leisure conversational context, where participants are also acquaintances, temporary video loss may not present a strong negative impact. Future studies will further investigate the impact of various video codec settings and network impairments on QoE. Moreover, we aim to measure and quantify the impact of different bit rate, resolution, and frame rate settings on objective video metrics such as blurriness and blockiness in mobile telemeeting scenarios.

References

1. Skowronek, J.: Quality of experience of multiparty conferencing and telemeeting systems. Ph.D. thesis, Technical University of Berlin (2017)

2. Vučić, D., Skorin-Kapov, L., Sužnjević, M.: The impact of bandwidth limitations and video resolution size on QoE for WebRTC-based mobile multi-party video conferencing. In: Proceedings of the 5th ISCA/DEGA Workshop on Perceptual Quality of Systems, PQS, Berlin (2016)
3. Carlucci, G., et al.: Congestion control for web real-time communication. IEEE/ACM Trans. Networking (TON) 25(5), 2629–2642 (2017)
4. Holmer, S., Lundin, H., Carlucci, G., De Cicco, L., Mascolo, S.: A google congestion control algorithm for real-time communication, IETF draft (2016)
5. Alvestrand, H.: Overview: real time protocols for browser-based applications (2013)
6. Carlucci, G., De Cicco, L., Holmer, S., Mascolo, S.: Analysis and design of the google congestion control for web real-time communication (WebRTC). In: Proceedings of the 7th International Conference on Multimedia Systems, p. 13. ACM (2016)
7. ITU-T. Recommendation P.1301: Subjective quality evaluation of audio and audiovisual telemeetings. International Standard. International Telecommunication Union, Geneva, Switzerland (2017)
8. Schmitt, M., Redi, J., Cesar, P., Bulterman, D.: 1Mbps is enough: video quality and individual idiosyncrasies in multiparty HD video-conferencing. In: Eighth International Conference on Quality of Multimedia Experience (QoMEX), pp. 1–6. IEEE (2016)
9. Schmitt, M., Redi, J., Cesar, P.: Towards context-aware interactive Quality of Experience evaluation for audiovisual multiparty conferencing. In: Proceedings of the 5th PQS, Berlin, pp. 64–68 (2016)
10. Schmitt, M., Redi, J., Bulterman, D., Cesar, P.S.: Towards individual QoE for multiparty videoconferencing. IEEE Trans. Multimedia 20(7), 1781–1795 (2018)
11. Jansen, B., Goodwin, T., Gupta, V., Kuipers, F., Zussman, G.: Performance evaluation of WebRTC-based video conferencing. ACM SIGMETRICS Perform. Eval. Rev. 45(2), 56–68 (2018)
12. Yu, C., Xu, Y., Liu, B., Liu, Y.: "Can you SEE me now?" A measurement study of mobile video calls. In: 2014 Proceedings of IEEE, INFOCOM, pp. 1456–1464 (2014)
13. Schmitt, M., Gunkel, S., Cesar, P., Bulterman, D.: The influence of interactivity patterns on the Quality of Experience in multi-party video-mediated conversations under symmetric delay conditions. In: Proceedings of the 3rd International Workshop on Socially-aware Multimedia, pp. 13–16 (2014)
14. Xu, J., Wah, B.W.: Exploiting just-noticeable difference of delays for improving quality of experience in video conferencing. In: Proceedings of the 4th ACM Multimedia Systems Conference, pp. 238–248. ACM (2013)
15. Fouladi, S., Emmons, J., Orbay, E., Wu, C., Wahby, R.S., Winstein, K.: Salsify: low-latency network video through tighter integration between a video codec and a transport protocol. In: 15th (USENIX) Symposium on Networked Systems Design and Implementation (2018)
16. Ammar, D., De Moor, K., Xie, M., Fiedler, M., Heegaard, P.: Video QoE killer and performance statistics in WebRTC-based video communication. In: Sixth International Conference on Communications and Electronics (ICCE), pp. 429–436. IEEE (2016)
17. De Moor, K., Arndt, S., Ammar, D., Voigt-Antons, J.N., Perkis, A., Heegaard, P.E.: Exploring diverse measures for evaluating QoE in the context of WebRTC. In: 2017 Ninth International Conference on Quality of Multimedia Experience (QoMEX), pp. 1–3. IEEE (2017)

Hierarchical Temporal Pooling for Efficient Online Action Recognition

Can Zhang[1], Yuexian Zou[1,2(✉)], and Guang Chen[1]

[1] ADSPLAB, School of ECE, Peking University, Shenzhen, China
zouyx@pkusz.edu.cn
[2] Peng Cheng Laboratory, Shenzhen, China

Abstract. Action recognition in videos is a difficult and challenging task. Recent developed deep learning-based action recognition methods have achieved the state-of-the-art performance on several action recognition benchmarks. However, it is noted that these methods are inefficient since they are of large model size and require long runtime which restrict their practical applications. In this study, we focus on improving the accuracy and efficiency of action recognition following the two-stream ConvNets by investigating the effective video-level representations. Our motivation stems from the observation that redundant information widely exists in adjacent frames in the videos and humans do not recognize actions based on frame-level features. Therefore, to extract the effective video-level features, a Hierarchical Temporal Pooling (HTP) module is proposed and a two-stream action recognition network termed as HTP-Net (Two-stream) is developed, which is carefully designed to obtain effective video-level representations by hierarchically incorporating the temporal motion and spatial appearance features. It is worth noting that all two-stream action recognition methods using optical flow as one of the inputs are computationally inefficient since calculating optical flow is time-consuming. To improve the efficiency, in our study, we do not consider using optical flow but consider only raw RGB as input to our HTP-Net termed as HTP-Net (RGB) for a clear and concise presentation. Extensive experiments have been conducted on two benchmarks: UCF101 and HMDB51. Experimental results demonstrate that HTP-Net (Two-stream) achieves the state-of-the-art performance and HTP-Net (RGB) offers competitive action recognition accuracy but is approximately 1-2 orders of magnitude faster than other state-of-the-art single stream action recognition methods. Specifically, our HTP-Net (RGB) runs at 42 videos per second (vps) and 672 frames per second (fps) on an NVIDIA Titan X GPU, which enables real-time action recognition and is of great value in practical applications.

Keywords: Action recognition · Hierarchical Temporal Pooling
Real-time

1 Introduction

Recently, action recognition in videos has already become a challenging and fundamental problem in computer vision research area, which has potential applications in many areas like intelligent life assistance and video surveillance analysis. Research

© Springer Nature Switzerland AG 2019
I. Kompatsiaris et al. (Eds.): MMM 2019, LNCS 11295, pp. 471–482, 2019.
https://doi.org/10.1007/978-3-030-05710-7_39

shows that Convolutional Neural Networks (CNNs) are the most important key players in image and video processing. The representatives include AlexNet [1], VGG [2], ResNet [3], and GoogleNet [4]. So far, extracting credible spatio-temporal features with CNNs is still an active research topic.

CNN-based architectures for action recognition can be divided into two major categories: (1) *Two-stream ConvNets*: This method decomposes the input video into spatial and temporal streams, which learns appearance and motion features respectively. Each stream is trained separately, and various fusion strategies like consensus pooling [5], 3D pooling [6], or trajectory-constrained pooling [7] are applied to fuse the outputs at the end, aiming to learn spatio-temporal features. Under this framework, Simonyan *et al.* devised two-stream ConvNets [6] by processing RGB images in spatial stream and stacked optical flow in temporal stream separately. Wang *et al.* proposed Temporal Segment Network (TSN) [5] to make the two-stream ConvNets go deeper and explore the cross-modality pre-training. TSN greatly outperforms previous traditional methods like improved Dense Trajectories (iDT) [8]. (2) *3D ConvNets*: This method applies on long-term input video frames and can aggregate not only the spatial appearance information in each frame but also the temporal transformation across neighboring frames. 3D ConvNets using convolutions in time dimension were firstly introduced by Baccouche *et al.* [9] and Ji *et al.* [10]. Later, Tran *et al.* applied 3D ConvNets [11] on large-scale datasets and further integrated deep ResNet with 3D convolutions, which is called Res3D [12].

Although two-stream ConvNets and 3D ConvNets have achieved great success for recognizing actions in unconstrained scenes, their results are far from meeting the needs of practical applications. From the perspective of accuracy, two-stream ConvNets are generally superior to 3D ConvNets because the ultra-deep networks and pretrained models from large-scale image classification task can be easily applied. Nevertheless, calculating optical flow in advance and training two separate streams are time-consuming. To address this problem, 3D ConvNets encode the spatio-temporal information by extending the convolutions and pooling operations from 2D to 3D. However, the training process of 3D ConvNets is more computationally expensive and the model size is larger compared with two-stream ConvNets. For example, the model size of the 33-layer 2D BN-Inception [13] is 39 MB while the model size of the widely used 11-layer 3D ConvNets (C3D) is 321 MB which is 8 times larger. This "fatal flaw" can't be ignored for efficiency concern.

Our objective in this paper is to improve the efficiency of action recognition by devising the Hierarchical Temporal Pooling (HTP) module into two-stream ConvNets, which leads to an extremely efficient action recognition network termed as HTP-Net (Two-stream). Empirically, calculating optical flow is time-consuming for two-stream ConvNets. So following the common practice, we only evaluate the efficiency of our HTP-Net with raw RGB frames as input, namely HTP-Net (RGB). Through the experiments conducted on two benchmarks, we demonstrated that HTP-Net (Two-stream) achieves the state-of-the-art performance and HTP-Net (RGB) offers competitive action recognition accuracy but is approximately 1-2 orders of magnitude faster than other state-of-the-art single stream action recognition methods, which perfectly fits the real-time action recognition applications.

2 Proposed HTP-Net

2.1 Overall Architecture

The network architecture of our proposed HTP-Net is shown in Fig. 1.

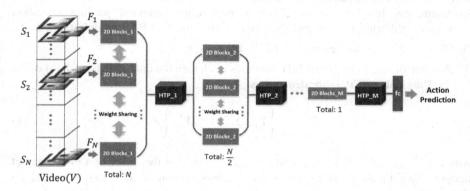

Fig. 1. The architecture of HTP-Net. The entire video is split into N subsections with equal length, denoted as $S_1, \ldots, S_N$. One frame is randomly sampled in each subsection. These sampled frames are processed by the clusters of 2D blocks (in blue color) and 3D HTP modules (in green color). 2D blocks are applied to yield spatial appearance representations and 3D HTP module is used to merge the temporal motion and spatial appearance information simultaneously. (Color figure online)

Sampling Strategy. Given an input video V consisting of variable numbers of frames. Considering the redundancy existing in consecutive frames and the limitation of memory size, we split the entire video into N subsections $\{S_1, S_2, \cdots, S_N\}$ of equal duration. For each subsection, one frame is randomly chosen, the selected N-frames are denoted as $F_i(i = 1, 2, \ldots, N)$. This sampling strategy is proved to be effective by many state-of-the-art methods [5, 14–16], which not only allows the whole video to be processed with reasonable computational cost, but also brings appearance diversity due to the stochastic selection method.

Network Architecture. As shown in Fig. 1, the green 3D HTP modules are sandwiched between the clusters of blue 2D blocks (weight sharing). The 2D blocks in different layers represent the different parts of the 2D ConvNet. For instance, we divide the BN-Inception architecture [13] into five parts (partition points are in conv2, inception-3c, inception-4e and inception-5b layers). The detailed explanations are given in Sect. 3.1. In Fig. 1, the first column of 2D blocks is denoted as "2D blocks_1" which indicates the first part of BN-Inception architecture (until conv2 layer), and so on. Our proposed HTP module is used to merge the temporal motion and spatial appearance information simultaneously. In our design, temporal downsampling is performed at each HTP module with 3D pooling operation, and hence no additional parameters are required, making the size of our model becomes rather small.

As mentioned above, N frames $\{F_1, F_2, \cdots, F_N\}$ are randomly extracted from the video, each of these frames is fed into the 2D blocks respectively, and the 2D blocks compute the appearance features containing spatial information for each frame independently. Feature maps obtained from the "2D blocks_1" can be denoted as $\left\{X_1^{(1)}, X_2^{(1)}, \cdots, X_N^{(1)}\right\}$. Before and after 3D pooling, the feature vectors are permuted in HTP modules. The permutation details are elaborated in Sect. 2.2. In HTP module, the spatiotemporal features are acquired by performing temporal pooling operation between neighboring frames, and the features after the first HTP module (denoted as "HTP_1" in Fig. 1) are denoted as $\left\{Y_1^{(1)}, Y_2^{(1)}, \cdots, Y_{\frac{N}{2}}^{(1)}\right\}$.

Assume the total number of HTP modules is M, then the output features $\mathcal{F}(j)$ of the j-th HTP module (HTP_j) are denoted as:

$$\mathcal{F}(j) = \left\{Y_1^{(j)}, Y_2^{(j)}, \cdots, Y_{\frac{N}{2^j}}^{(j)}\right\} \tag{1}$$

where $Y_i^{(j)} \in \mathbb{R}^d$, $i = 1, 2, \ldots, \frac{N}{2^j}$ and $j = 1, 2, \ldots, M$, d is the dimension of the output features. To get a video-level spatiotemporal representation, let $M = \log_2 N$, so that the last HTP module (HTP_M) only outputs a single feature $Y_1^{(M)}$, which contains adequate information for video feature learning, we will show the superior performance later in Sect. 3.

The proposed network architecture in this paper is interpretable and efficient, and it is evident that the HTP-Net can be easily trained end-to-end. Instead of predicting action classes by aggregating numerous frame-level predictions, our approach only processes N frames to get video-level features at runtime, which makes it capable of inferring the action happens in the video at the first sight, without "hesitation".

2.2 Proposed HTP Module

Recently, for image classification task, the rise of 2D ConvNets convincingly demonstrates high performance of capturing useful static information especially in spatial domain. The motivation of our HTP module is to utilize the 2D ConvNets to encode appearance effectively in individual frames, and integrate temporal correlation into spatial representation by performing 3D pooling on time domain.

As shown in Fig. 2, the HTP module contains two operations: *dimension permutation* and *3D temporal pooling*. Note that "*dimension permutation*" can be divided into "temporal stacking" and "spatial stacking". Details are elaborated below.

Dimension Permutation. 2D ConvNets process 3D tensors of size $C \times W \times H$, where C denotes the channel number, W and H denote the width and height in space dimension respectively, which means the temporal relation within the video frames is ignored and N frames are treated similarly to channels. While 3D ConvNets operate 4D tensors of size $C \times T \times W \times H$, where T is the time span. Therefore, dimension permutation is essential as the 2D and 3D operations exist alternately in our HTP-net, including temporal stacking and spatial stacking.

Temporal Stacking aims to provide correct input volumes for 3D pooling by stacking the feature maps in time order, so the tensors' dimensions are transformed from 3D to 4D. Figure 2 shows the details of the first HTP module as an example. Specifically, the "2D Blocks_1" (weight sharing) receive N frames as input and produce N feature representations, and each of the representations can be expressed as volumes $X_i \in \mathbb{R}^{K \times W \times H}(i = 1, 2, \ldots, N)$, where K denotes the number of convolutional filters applied in the end of the blocks. X_i consists of K feature maps of equal size $P_j^{(i)} \in \mathbb{R}^{W \times H}(j = 1, 2, \ldots, K)$, so each feature vector obtained from the 2D blocks can be represented as:

$$X_i = \left\{ P_1^{(i)}, P_2^{(i)}, \ldots, P_K^{(i)} \right\} \tag{2}$$

Feature map $P_j^{(i)}$ is the basic unit during permutation procedure. Feature maps with the same j index will be stacked by ascending order of the i index. In other words, every feature map in the original volume $X_i(i = 1, 2, \ldots, N)$ will be evenly assigned to K permuted volumes X_m', where $X_m' \in \mathbb{R}^{N \times W \times H}(m = 1, 2, \ldots, K)$.

For example, the first permuted volume X_1' contains a total number of N feature maps $P_1^{(i)}(i = 1, 2, \ldots, N)$ with the same j index (in this case $j = 1$), and each feature map is sorted chronologically. Hence after permutation, $X_1' = \left[P_1^{(1)}, P_1^{(2)}, \ldots, P_1^{(N)} \right]$. Therefore, all the permuted features can be derived as follows:

$$X_m' = \left\{ P_m^{(1)}, P_m^{(2)}, \ldots, P_m^{(N)} \right\} \tag{3}$$

In conclusion, the input volumes of the HTP module are N 3D tensors of size $K \times W \times H$, which cannot be directly processed by 3D pooling due to dimension mismatch. After temporal stacking, the extracted frames number N, which represents the time span of the input video, will be transposed to time dimension. Specifically, N 3D tensors of size $K \times W \times H$ will be correctly permuted to a 4D tensor of size $K \times N \times W \times H$. So far, 3D pooling can deal with the 4D tensor properly.

Spatial Stacking aims to provide correct input volumes for the following 2D blocks by stacking the feature maps in spatial order, so the tensors' dimensions are transformed from 4D to 3D. To some extent, spatial stacking is the inverse transformation of the temporal stacking. Note that temporal downsampling is performed at HTP module, so the time span changes from N to N' (in this case $N' = \frac{N}{2}$). Similarly, the pooled features can be expressed as volumes $Y_m' \in \mathbb{R}^{N' \times W \times H}(m = 1, 2, \ldots, K)$:

$$Y_m' = \left\{ Q_m^{(1)}, Q_m^{(2)}, \ldots, Q_m^{(N')} \right\} \tag{4}$$

where each $Q_j^{(i')} \in \mathbb{R}^{W \times H}(i' = 1, 2, \ldots, N'; j = 1, 2, \ldots, K)$ represents the obtained feature map after pooling. To be further processed by the upcoming 2D blocks, it's important that the feature maps should be re-stacked spatially. Similar to the pattern of temporal stacking, feature maps with the same i' index will be stacked by ascending order of the j index, indicated below:

$$Y_{i'} = \left\{ Q_1^{(i')}, Q_2^{(i')}, \ldots, Q_K^{(i')} \right\} \tag{5}$$

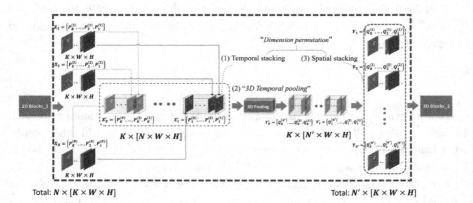

Fig. 2. Details of our HTP module. The HTP module contains two operations: *dimension permutation* and *3D temporal pooling*. Note that "*dimension permutation*" includes "temporal stacking" and "spatial stacking". Before and after *3D temporal pooling*, the series of feature maps are permuted in HTP modules. According to the time order, the process can also be summarized as three steps: (1) temporal stacking; (2) 3D temporal pooling; (3) spatial stacking.

After spatial stacking, the feature volumes are restored to N' tensors of size $K \times W \times H$, so that the following 2D ConvNets can operate the tensors correctly.

3D Temporal Pooling. Based on the observations that: (1) redundant information exists widely in consecutive sampled frames; (2) 2D convolution has the ability of encoding spatial information effectively in individual frames. We find that it's essential to pool across time dimension to merge the temporal and spatial information simultaneously. As mentioned above, given the input feature maps $P_j^{(i)}$ ($i = 1, 2, \ldots, N; j = 1, 2, \ldots, K$), the obtained feature maps after 3D pooling operation are $Q_j^{(i')}$ ($i' = 1, 2, \ldots, N'; j = 1, 2, \ldots, K$). In each HTP module, let j equals a specific value j_0, the response of each pooling layer is obtained by a function:

$$\mathcal{H} : \left\{ P_{j_0}^{(m)}, P_{j_0}^{(m+1)}, \ldots, P_{j_0}^{(n)} \right\} \rightarrow Q_{j_0}^{(m \rightarrow n)} \tag{6}$$

where $m, n \in \{1, 2, \ldots, N\}$, and $m < n$. Obviously, we can use different pooling functions. For presentation clarity, some commonly used pooling functions $\mathcal{H}$ are given below.

- Average pooling:

$$Q_{j_0}^{(m \to n)} = \left(P_{j_0}^{(m)} \oplus P_{j_0}^{(m+1)} \oplus \ldots \oplus P_{j_0}^{(n)} \right) / (n - m + 1) \qquad (7)$$

- Max pooling:

$$Q_{j_0}^{(m \to n)} = max \left\{ P_{j_0}^{(m)}, P_{j_0}^{(m+1)}, \ldots, P_{j_0}^{(n)} \right\} \qquad (8)$$

3 Experiments and Analysis

3.1 Experimental Settings

Network Architecture Details. In consideration of the trade-off between accuracy and efficiency, we choose BN-Inception as the backbone network. As common practice, here we choose the number of sampled frames $N = 16$. In order to only obtain a single video-level feature after the last HTP module (HTP_M), the total layer number M should be 4 ($M = \log_2 N = 4$). The architecture details are shown in Table 1.

Table 1. HTP-Net architecture details. This network receives an input size of $16 \times 224 \times 224$ to keep a balance between memory capacity and runtime efficiency. Temporal downsampling is performed in each "HTP_x" module. The 2D patch size corresponds to $W \times H$, while the 3D counterpart represents $T \times W \times H$. The 4D output size corresponds to $C \times T \times W \times H$.

Layer name	Patch size/stride	Output size	Layer name	Patch size/stride	Output size
conv1	7×7/2	64×16×112×112	inception (4b)		576×4×14×14
2D max pool1	3×3/2	64×16×56×56	inception (4c)		608×4×14×14
conv2	3×3/1	192×16×56×56	inception (4d)		608×4×14×14
HTP_1	2×3×3/2×2×2	192×8×28×28	inception (4e)	stride 2	1056×4×7×7
inception (3a)		256×8×28×28	HTP_3	2×1×1/2×1×1	1056×2×7×7
inception (3b)		320×8×28×28	inception (5a)		1024×2×7×7
inception (3c)	stride 2	576×8×14×14	inception (5b)		1024×2×7×7
HTP_2	2×1×1/2×1×1	576×4×14×14	HTP_4	2×1×1/2×1×1	1024×1×7×7
inception (4a)		576×4×14×14	2D avg pool, dropout, "#class"-d fc, softmax		

Note that the patch size and stride of "HTP_1" module differ from other "HTP_x" modules. Considering the spatial downsampling is performed in the original 2D BN-Inception network, the spatial and temporal downsampling need to be combined.

Datasets. We evaluate the performance of HTP-Net on the most commonly well-known action recognition benchmarks: UCF101 [17] and HMDB51 [18]. The UCF101 dataset includes 13,320 video clips with 101 action classes. The video sequences in HMDB51 dataset are extracted from various sources, including movies and online videos. This dataset contains 6,766 videos with 51 actions. In our experiments, we follow the official evaluation scheme that three standard training and testing splits are evaluated separately and the mean average accuracy over these three splits are calculated as the final result.

Implementation Details. 16 frames are randomly selected from each equally divided subsections, and this sampling strategy ensures the whole video to be processed with reasonable computational cost and brings appearances diversity due to the random selection scheme. We use mini-batch SGD optimization method and utilize dropout in each fully connected layer to train our HTP-Net. The learning rate is initialized as 0.001 and reduces by a factor of 10 when the validation error saturates. The HTP-Net is trained with batch size of 32, momentum of 0.9 and dropout ratio of 0.8. Data augmentation techniques introduced in [2, 5] are applied to produce appearance diversity as well as prevent serious over-fitting problem. Specifically, the size of input frames are fixed as 340 × 256, then we employ scale jittering with horizontal flipping and corner cropping. These cropped regions will be resized to 224 × 224 before being fed into the network.

3.2 Benchmark Comparison

After detailed elaboration of HTP-Net architectures and experimental settings, final benchmark experiments are conducted on UCF101 and HMDB51 datasets over three standard splits for further evaluating the performance of our proposed HTP-Net. Here three setups are considered: (1) only RGB images as input; (2) only stacked optical flow images as input; (3) two-stream fusion strategy using RGB and optical flow images simultaneously, which lead to three different networks. These three networks are denoted as HTP-Net (RGB), HTP-Net (Optical Flow) and HTP-Net (Two-stream) respectively for clear and concise presentation. The accuracy results on each testing splits are summarized in Table 2. As shown in the last row of Table 2, for UCF101 dataset, the average accuracies of HTP-Net (RGB), HTP-Net (Optical Flow) and HTP-Net (Two-stream) are 90.2%, 93.0% and 96.2%, respectively. As for HMDB51 dataset, the average accuracies are 62.9%, 74.7% and 77.6%, respectively. Obviously, HTP-Net (Two-stream) outperforms other two networks and optical flow information does help in improving action recognition accuracy.

In the following, we conduct experiment to compare the average accuracy of HTP-Net (Two-stream) with several state-of-the-art methods on UCF101 and HMDB51 benchmarks. In this experiment, the comparison methods include traditional methods [8], baseline networks [5–7, 11] and recent mainstream approaches [14–16, 19, 20]. The results are reported in Table 3. As shown in Table 3, HTP-Net (Two-stream)

Table 2. The accuracy performance on UCF101 and HMDB51.

#	UCF101 Accuracy (%)			HMDB51 Accuracy (%)		
	HTP-Net (RGB)	HTP-Net (optical flow)	HTP-Net (two-stream)	HTP-Net (RGB)	HTP-Net (optical flow)	HTP-Net (two-stream)
Split1	90.0	91.5	95.7	63.9	74.9	79.2
Split2	90.8	93.7	96.8	62.3	73.9	76.0
Split3	89.7	93.7	96.0	62.6	75.4	77.5
Average	90.2	93.0	**96.2**	62.9	74.7	**77.6**

Table 3. Accuracy comparison with state-of-the-art methods.

Method	Backbone Network	UCF101 (%)	HMDB51 (%)
IDT [8]	–	85.9	57.2
Two-stream [6]	VGG-M	88.0	59.4
TDD [7]	VGG-M	90.3	63.2
C3D [11]	ResNet-18	85.2	–
TSN [5]	BN-Inception	94.2	70.7
DOVF [15]	BN-Inception	94.9	71.7
ActionVLAD [19]	VGG-16	92.7	66.9
TLE [20]	BN-Inception	95.6	71.1
ECO_{En-RGB} [14]	BN-Inception	94.8	72.4
DTPP [16]	BN-Inception	95.8	74.8
HTP-Net (two-stream)	BN-Inception	**96.2***	**77.6***

* indicates the best results.

obtains superior results, which outperforms previous best approach by 0.4% on UCF101 and 2.8% on HMDB51.

3.3 Efficiency Comparison

Without doubt, calculating optical flow is time-consuming. So training a two-stream ConvNets using stacked optical flow images as input ask for more computational cost. Hence, in consideration of real-time action recognition, using optical flow is not a good choice. As a common practice so far for action recognition task, the efficiency comparison is conducted by using raw RGB input only. In this subsection, we only evaluate the efficiency performance of our HTP-Net (RGB). All experiments are running on an NVIDIA Titan X GPU.

Table 4. Efficiency comparison with five state-of-the-art methods with NVIDIA Titan X GPU on UCF101 and HMDB51 datasets (only using RGB images as input). Note that I/O time is not considered for the reported speed.

Method	Speed (vps/fps)	Model size (MB)	UCF101 (%)	HMDB51 (%)
Res3D [12]	1.1/-	144	85.8	54.9
ARTNet [21]	1.8/-	151	**93.5***	67.6
TSN [5]	12.6/-	**39.7***	87.7	51.0
ECO$_{16F}$ [14]	24.5/392.0	>128	92.8	**68.5***
ECO$_{Lite-16F}$ [14]	35.3/564.8	128	91.6	68.2
HTP-Net (RGB)	**42*/672***	**39.7***	90.2	62.9

* indicates the best results.

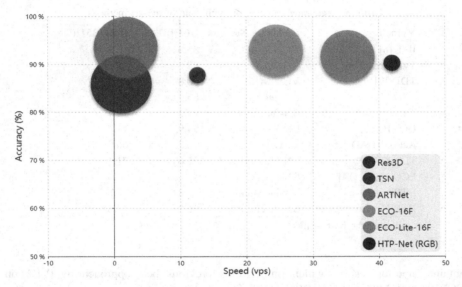

Fig. 3. Efficiency comparison on UCF101 (over three splits) for HTP-Net (RGB) and other state-of-the-art methods. The bubble size and the model size are positive correlation. Our approach HTP-Net (RGB) (red bubble) is a trade-off among the three evaluation metrics: speed, model size and accuracy. (Color figure online)

Here, three evaluation metrics are used: speed, model size and accuracy. And two speed measurement metrics are reported: videos per second (vps) and frames per second (fps). The results are summarized in Table 4. For visualization purpose, a bubble chart is displayed in Fig. 3.

From Table 4, for the running speed, it is encouraged to see that our HTP-Net (RGB) outperforms TSN (2D CNN), Res3D (3D CNN) and ECO (2D-3D combined CNN) by 29.4vps, 40.9vps and 6.7vps, respectively. These results indirectly illustrate the ability of our HTP-net (RGB) to efficiently encode the spatio-temporal information of videos. Besides, as expected, the model size of our HTP-Net (RGB) is comparable with that of TSN but much smaller than other methods. Specifically, our HTP-Net (RGB) only occupies 39.7 MB storage, while other methods (except TSN) even reaches 151 MB which is 3-4 times larger. It is clear that our HTP-Net (RGB) benefits from the less parameters in 2D ConvNets and the ability of modeling spatio-temporal information effectively by 3D pooling. However, from the last two columns in Table 4, we can see that the action recognition accuracy of our HTP-Net (RGB) is higher than that of Res3D and TSN but lower than that of ARTNet and ECO which utilize more complex networks. Moreover, from the results shown in Table 2, it can be concluded that optical flow modality is still able to provide supplementary information for action recognition. In the future, we intend to further improve our HTP-Net (RGB) to narrow the accuracy gap between single stream and two-stream inputs.

As shown in Fig. 3, the small red bubble in the upper right corner represents HTP-Net (RGB), which clearly shows that our devised HTP-Net (RGB) is a computationally efficient light model with competitive action recognition accuracy.

4 Conclusion

In this paper, a delicate Hierarchical Temporal Pooling (HTP) is proposed, which is a light-weighted module for merging the temporal motion and spatial appearance information simultaneously. With the two-stream ConvNets, an efficient action recognition network termed as HTP-Net is developed, which is able to obtain the effective video-level representations. As demonstrated on UCF101 and HMDB51 datasets, it is encouraged to see that our HTP-Net (Two-stream) has brought the state-of-the-art results to a new level, and HTP-Net (RGB) processes videos much faster with smaller model size. Specifically, our model with HTP-Net (RGB) runs at 42 videos per second (vps) and 672 frames per second (fps) on an NVIDIA Titan X GPU with competitive action recognition accuracy, which is able to perform real-time action recognition and is of great value in practical applications.

In the future, we will work on improving the action recognition accuracy of our HTP-Net (RGB) while maintaining its outstanding properties in terms of light model and computational efficiency.

Acknowledgment. This paper was partially supported by the Shenzhen Science & Technology Fundamental Research Program (No: JCYJ20160330095814461) & Shenzhen Key Laboratory for Intelligent Multimedia and Virtual Reality (ZDSYS201703031405467). Special Acknowledgements are given to Aoto-PKUSZ Joint Research Center of Artificial Intelligence on Scene Cognition & Technology Innovation for its support.

References

1. Krizhevsky, A., Sutskever, I., Hinton, G.E.: ImageNet classification with deep convolutional neural networks. In: Advances in Neural Information Processing Systems, pp. 1097–1105 (2012)
2. Simonyan, K., Zisserman, A.: Very deep convolutional networks for large-scale image recognition. arXiv preprint arXiv:1409.1556 (2014)

3. He, K., Zhang, X., Ren, S., Sun, J.: Deep residual learning for image recognition. In: Proceedings of the IEEE Conference on Computer Vision and Pattern Recognition, pp. 770–778 (2016)
4. Szegedy, C., et al.: Going deeper with convolutions. In: Proceedings of the IEEE Conference on Computer Vision and Pattern Recognition, pp. 1–9 (2015)
5. Wang, L., et al.: Temporal segment networks: towards good practices for deep action recognition. In: Leibe, B., Matas, J., Sebe, N., Welling, M. (eds.) ECCV 2016. LNCS, vol. 9912, pp. 20–36. Springer, Cham (2016). https://doi.org/10.1007/978-3-319-46484-8_2
6. Simonyan, K., Zisserman, A.: Two-stream convolutional networks for action recognition in videos. In: Advances in Neural Information Processing Systems, pp. 568–576 (2014)
7. Wang, L., Qiao, Y., Tang, X.: Action recognition with trajectory-pooled deep-convolutional descriptors. In: Proceedings of the IEEE Conference on Computer Vision and Pattern Recognition, pp. 4305–4314 (2015)
8. Wang, H., Schmid, C.: Action recognition with improved trajectories. In: Proceedings of the IEEE International Conference on Computer Vision, pp. 3551–3558 (2013)
9. Baccouche, M., Mamalet, F., Wolf, C., Garcia, C., Baskurt, A.: Sequential deep learning for human action recognition. In: Salah, A.A., Lepri, B. (eds.) HBU 2011. LNCS, vol. 7065, pp. 29–39. Springer, Heidelberg (2011). https://doi.org/10.1007/978-3-642-25446-8_4
10. Ji, S., Xu, W., Yang, M., Yu, K.: 3D convolutional neural networks for human action recognition. IEEE Trans. Pattern Anal. Mach. Intell. **35**, 221–231 (2013)
11. Tran, D., Bourdev, L., Fergus, R., Torresani, L., Paluri, M.: Learning spatiotemporal features with 3D convolutional networks. In: 2015 IEEE International Conference on Computer Vision (ICCV), pp. 4489–4497. IEEE (2015)
12. Tran, D., Ray, J., Shou, Z., Chang, S.-F., Paluri, M.: ConvNet architecture search for spatiotemporal feature learning. arXiv preprint arXiv:1708.05038 (2017)
13. Ioffe, S., Szegedy, C.: Batch normalization: accelerating deep network training by reducing internal covariate shift. arXiv preprint arXiv:1502.03167 (2015)
14. Zolfaghari, M., Singh, K., Brox, T.: ECO: efficient convolutional network for online video understanding. arXiv preprint arXiv:1804.09066 (2018)
15. Lan, Z., Zhu, Y., Hauptmann, A.G., Newsam, S.: Deep local video feature for action recognition. In: 2017 IEEE Conference on Computer Vision and Pattern Recognition Workshops (CVPRW), pp. 1219–1225. IEEE (2017)
16. Zhu, J., Zou, W., Zhu, Z.: End-to-end video-level representation learning for action recognition. arXiv preprint arXiv:1711.04161 (2017)
17. Soomro, K., Zamir, A.R., Shah, M.: UCF101: a dataset of 101 human actions classes from videos in the wild. arXiv preprint arXiv:1212.0402 (2012)
18. Kuehne, H., Jhuang, H., Garrote, E., Poggio, T., Serre, T.: HMDB: a large video database for human motion recognition. In: 2011 IEEE International Conference on Computer Vision (ICCV), pp. 2556–2563. IEEE (2011)
19. Girdhar, R., Ramanan, D., Gupta, A., Sivic, J., Russell, B.: ActionVLAD: learning spatio-temporal aggregation for action classification. In: CVPR, p. 3 (2017)
20. Diba, A., Sharma, V., Van Gool, L.: Deep temporal linear encoding networks. In: Proceedings of the IEEE Conference on Computer Vision and Pattern Recognition (2017)
21. Wang, L., Li, W., Li, W., Van Gool, L.: Appearance-and-relation networks for video classification. arXiv preprint arXiv:1711.09125 (2017)

Generative Adversarial Networks with Enhanced Symmetric Residual Units for Single Image Super-Resolution

Xianyu Wu[1], Xiaojie Li[1(✉)], Jia He[1], Xi Wu[1], and Imran Mumtaz[2]

[1] Chengdu University of Information Technology, Chengdu, China
lixj@cuit.edu.cn
[2] University of Agriculture Faisalabad, Faisalabad, Pakistan

Abstract. In this paper, we propose a new generative adversarial network (GAN) with enhanced symmetric residual units for single image super-resolution (ERGAN). ERGAN consists of a generator network and a discriminator network. The former can maximally reconstruct a super-resolution image similar to the original image. This lead to the discriminator network cannot distinguish the image from the training data or the generated sample. Combining residual units used in the generator network, ERGAN can retain the high-frequency features and alleviate the difficulty training in deep networks. Moreover, we constructed the symmetric skip-connections in residual units. This reused features generated from the low-level, and learned more high-frequency content. Moreover, ERGAN reconstructed the super-resolution image by four times the length and width of the original image and exhibited better visual characteristics. Experimental results on extensive benchmark evaluation showed that ERGAN significantly outperformed state-of-the-art approaches in terms of accuracy and vision.

Keywords: Super-resolution · GAN · Residual units
Symmetric skip-connection

1 Introduction

Super-resolution (SR) technology is used to reconstruct a high-resolution (HR) image from a low-resolution (LR) image or sequence of images. Current image super-resolution methods can be classified into three main categories: interpolation-based [11], reconstructed-based [10], and learning-based [15]. Although many learning-based restoration methods that do not use non-neural networks have been developed, they are not as effective as the deep learning-based super-resolution technology [17].

Deep learning has recently yielded a n umber of training methods to reconstruct super-resolution images. Many relevant approaches have been proposed in the literature [2,6,7,9]. SRCNN, proposed by Dong, Chen, He et al. [2], is the first deep neural network method to surpass traditional methods. However, the

© Springer Nature Switzerland AG 2019
I. Kompatsiaris et al. (Eds.): MMM 2019, LNCS 11295, pp. 483–494, 2019.
https://doi.org/10.1007/978-3-030-05710-7_40

SRCNN network is unstable and difficult to train. Moreover, the image obtained by minimizing the mean squared error (MSE) is too smooth, which also significantly reduces the peak signal-to-noise ratio (PSNR). MDSR, proposed by [9], removes unnecessary modules (e.g, Batch Normalization) in the traditional residual network, and creates a multi-scale deep super-resolution system and training method. The LapSRN image super-resolution structure was proposed based on the Laplacian Pyramid [6]. Each level of the pyramid takes a feature map of the rough resolution as input and uses deconvolution to obtain finer feature maps. Moreover, a robust Charbonnier loss function is used to train the network and obtain a better super-resolution effect. The latest method, SRGAN, proposed by Ledig et al. [7], is composed of two parts: Generator G and Discriminator D. G is used to generate super-resolution images that are close to natural images. D can distinguish the image from the generator network or the training data.

Furthermore, the classical generative adversarial network (GAN) was proposed by Goodfellow et al. [4]. It is composed of two parts: a generator G and a discriminator D. G can be used to generate images $G(z)$ close in quality to the original images. D can distinguish the generated image from the generator network or the training data X. The process of optimization of GAN is a min-max problem in game theory. We know that the goal of the generator is to learn the distributed P_g on the training data X. Therefore, the input to the generator is a random vector z satisfies a uniform or a Gaussian distribution $P_z(z)$, then input z is mapped to the data space $G(z; \theta_g)$. On the contrary, the discriminator network can be used as a function that maps image data to a probability that the given image is from the real data distribution P_g, rather than the generator distribution. The objective function of the GAN can be described as follows:

$$\min_{D} \max_{G} f(D, G) = E_{x \sim p_{data}(x)}[log D(x)]$$
$$+ E_{z \sim p_z(z)}[log(1 - D(G(z)))] \tag{1}$$

Studies from Radfold et al. [12], Fergus et al. [3] have used the GAN in image generation applications. In contrast to supervised GAN methods, the DCGAN is an unsupervised learning method and an improvement over them [12]. The main improvement is in the network structure. Compared with traditional GAN, the generator network creates maps between random vectors to the generated images. The Perceptual GAN (PGAN) [8] allows G to convert a small object into a large object one. The PGAN discovers the structural association between objects of different scales, and improves the representation of small objects by rendering them similar to large objects.

In this paper, we propose a new Generative Adversarial Network (ERGAN) with Enhanced symmetric Residual units for single image super-resolution. It is composed of two parts: G and D. To generate super-resolution images that are similar to the original images, residual units and symmetric skip-connections are used in G. Residual units can retain the feature details; thus, our model can learn more content. It can also alleviate the difficulty of training in deep networks.

Moreover, the symmetric skip-connections used between residual units can reuse features generated from the low-level and learn more high-frequency content. The proposed network can reconstruct the super-resolution image by four times the length and width of the original image. Experimental results show that our model can generate images that are similar to the original images (Fig. 1).

(a) Original   (b) ERGAN (proposed)

Fig. 1. ×4 super-resolution result of our method on DIV2K is close to the original image, and we cropped a small pane arbitrarily in our results and corresponding HR image, the visual effect is almost indistinguishable.

2   GAN with Enhanced Symmetric Residual Units (ERGAN)

Inspired by the original GAN, the proposed ERGAN method is composed of Generator G and Discriminator D. Unlike the traditional GAN, it generates high-quality images by generating random noise z. Our goal is to obtain a super-resolution image from a low-resolution image through the generator network. Instead of the random vector z, we construct it as a low-resolution image (denoted by I^{LR}) from the original high-resolution image following 4-fold downscaling, following which it is used as the input of the generator network.

2.1   Architecture Network

The structure of a model of our network is shown in Fig. 2. The generator network is composed of residual units and symmetric skip-connections employing 64 feature maps, the convolution kernel size is 3×3, the step length S is 1, the activation function uses ReLU, and complement zero is set to SAME. This is followed by the first convolution layer with a residual unit. Each residual

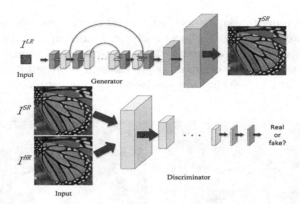

Fig. 2. The proposed ERGAN architecture network. Our framework consists of a generator G (top) and a discriminator D (below). Blue block represents convolution layer, green block represents residual unit, yellow block represents two times magnification subpixel layer. Orange arrows indicate symmetric skip-connections between residual units. Grey represents Flatten layer, red represents Dense layer. (Color figure online)

unit consists of the conv-BN-ReLU-conv-BN layer (see Fig. 3). In the overlapping convolution following each residual unit, multi symmetric skip-connections are added to the model. Two sub-pixel convolutions are then added to obtain the length and width of output image magnified four times. The discriminator network also uses multiple convolutions and the LeakyReLU as the activation function, but no longer adds a skip-connection. At the end of the convolution, the tensor is stretched into a vector using a flatten layer and dense layer. We choose loss function L_1, consider the network that contains the residual units and symmetric skip-connections in the generator network, and enter a low-resolution image into the generator network.

Residual Units: Increasing the depth of the network can significantly improve its performance, whereas after a very deep layer, the important details in the image may be lost. Inspired by DRRN [16], we use multi-layer residual units to solve this problem, so that the details of images are preserved after passing through the network layer. A residual unit is shown in Fig. 3, it is formulated as Eq. (2):

$$R^b = F(R^{b-1}, W) + R^{b-1}, \qquad (2)$$

where b is the number of residual units in the network and $b = 1, 2, \cdots, n$, $R^{(b-1)}$ and R^b are the input and output of the $b - th$ residual unit, respectively, and F denotes the residual function. From Fig. 2, we can see that the first layer is a convolution layer, followed by a residual unit.

Symmetric Skip-Connections: In the proposed model, all residual units use symmetric skip-connection. The image features of the front layer is connected

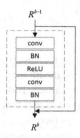

Fig. 3. Residual unit.

to the output of the symmetric residual unit as the input of the next convolution layer, which learn more high-frequency content. Like U-Net [13], the high-frequency features generated from low-level as input so that the network can propagate information to higher level layers.

2.2 Loss Function

The pixel based MSE function is a very popular loss function in image generation. It is beneficial to yeild a very high PSNR, which is a widely used evaluation criterion for image super-resolution reconstruction. However, it loses high-frequency content, which causes the reconstruction image to have an overly smooth textures. VGG loss, proposed in [14], can solve this problem. It extracts high-level features from the ImageNet pretrained VGG network [1], and the direct high-level feature mean squared error of the image is obtained. To optimize the G and D networks, the following D_{loss} and G_{loss} are used:

$$
\begin{aligned}
D_{loss} = {} & E_{I^{HR} \sim p_{train}(I^{HR})} \left[D(I^{HR}) + a \right] \\
& + E_{I^{LR} \sim p_G(I^{LR})} \left[D(G(I^{LR}) + b) \right],
\end{aligned}
\tag{3}
$$

where a and b are constant, I^{HR} denotes the high-resolution image and I^{LR} denotes the low-resolution image, $D(I^{HR})$ represents the training data input into the discriminator network, picture $G(I^{LR})$ is generated by G, and $(D(G(I^{LR}))$ indicates the probability that $G(I^{LR})$ is from the training data or the generator network.

$$
G_{loss} = G_{adv} + G_{MSE} + G_{VGG},
\tag{4}
$$

where

$$
G_{adv} = E_{I^{LR} \sim p_G(I^{LR})}(D(G(I^{LR})) + c),
\tag{5}
$$

$$
G_{MSE} = \sum_{x=1} \sum_{y=1} \left| I_{x,y}^{HR} - G_{our}(I_{x,y}^{LR}) \right|,
\tag{6}
$$

$$G_{VGG} = \sum_{x=1}\sum_{y=1} \left| I_{x,y}^{HR} - G_{vgg}(I_{x,y}^{LR}) \right|, \tag{7}$$

where c is a constant. G_{MSE} represents the pixel-based MSE and G_{VGG} represents the high-level feature mean squared error. Generally, D_{loss} and G_{adv} are considered as adversarial losses. Adversarial losses can maximize the probability of successfully determining a given image from the training data or the generated samples. For the generator network, adversarial loss wants to learn the real images and deceive the discriminator network to generate super-resolution images that are similar to them. To better deceive the discriminator network such that the generator network generates images that are similar to the original images, we set $a = -1, b = 0$, and $c = -1$.

2.3   Factors Affecting Network Performance

We reinforce the factors that can determine the performance of our network, including the number of residual units b and symmetric skip-connections, and the loss function. Our ERGAN are with 16 residual units and symmetric skip-connections in the generator network, the loss function with L_1 norm. More relevant comparisons regarding them are designed, several strategies with which we have experimented are:

1. ERGAN with 4 residual units for the generator network (denoted by g_{rb}^4).
2. ERGAN with 8 residual units for the generator network (denoted by g_{rb}^8).
3. ERGAN without symmetric skip-connections for the generator network (denoted by g_{-sc}).
4. ERGAN use loss function with L_2 norm (denoted by g^2).

3   Experiments and Discussion

3.1   Datasets and Data Preprocessing

Datasets: The training dataset used in our experiment was DIV2K which is one of the popular high-quality image dataset in super-resolution task. The DIV2K dataset includes 800 training images, 100 validation images, and 100 test images. We compared the performance on the standard benchmark datasets: Set5, Set14, BSD100, and Urban100.

Experimental Setup: In order to get more datasets, we only need to make minor adjustments to the existing training datasets (i.e., data argmentation). We turned the training datasets into flipped, rotated and translated, and finally we got more datasets with augmented versions. For training, we used the 384×384 sub-images captured from the training images, and 96×96 I^{LR} RGB images obtained with a 4 times downscaling as the input of the generator network. Our model used the Adam Optimizer by setting $\beta_1 = 0.9$. We set $batchsize = 16$ as

Table 1. Quantitative evaluation of state-of-the-art super-resolution methods: average PSNR and SSIM for 4 upscaling on Set5, Set14, BSD100 and Urban100. Bold indicates the best performance.

PSNR/SSIM	Set5	Set14	BSD100	Urban100
Bicubic	28.42/0.8104	26.00/0.7027	25.96/0.6675	23.14/0.6577
A+	30.28/0.8603	27.32/0.7491	26.82/0.7087	24.32/0.7183
SRCNN	30.48/0.8628	27.49/0.7503	26.90/0.7101	24.52/0.7221
SelfExSR	30.31/0.8619	27.40/0.7518	26.84/0.7106	24.79/0.7374
ERGAN	**31.06/0.8802**	**27.72/0.7673**	**27.14/0.7223**	**25.17/0.7493**

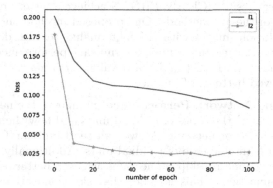

Fig. 4. Similar to the network structure of ERGAN, we considered the convergence of ERGAN with different loss functions. The blue solid line and orange dotted line represent the convergence curves of G in the ERGAN with the L_1 and L_2 loss functions, respectively, in the first 100 epochs. (Color figure online)

the cardinality of each instance of training. We initialized the learning rate with $1e-4$, and adjusted it automatically every 500 epoch.

We used the MATLAB to evaluate the results, which showed that our model achieved better PNSR and structural similarity index (SSIM) values, and a single low-resolution image reconstructed 4 times upscaling to obtain a super-resolution image. We also evaluated several factors that determine the performance of our network, including the number of residual units, symmetric skip-connections and the loss function. For each configuration, our experiments were implemented in Python by using TensorLayer and based on 16 residual units. We trained the networks on an NVIDIA Tesla M40 GPU. It took three days to train our model.

3.2   Evaluations on the Testing Dataset

Comparison with State-of-the-Art Models: In this section, we compare our approach with the state-of-art methods including Bicubic, A+ [17], SRCNN [2], SelfExSR [5]. Quantitative evaluations are summarized in Table 1 PSNR and

SSIM values on four benchmark datasets. Table 1 shows quantitative comparisons for ×4 super-resolution. We can clearly see that the performance of our model was better than that of state-of-art methods.

In Tables 2, we show visual comparisons on BSD100 and Urban100 for ×4 super-resolution. We note that a small pane was considered arbitrarily in the high-resolution image, and we magnified the small pane as a sub-image. We can clearly compare the differences between the corresponding sub-images in Bicubic, A+ [17], SRCNN [2], SelfExSR [5], ERGAN, and high-resolution (HR). The super-resolution images that we reconstructed using ERGAN retained more detail texture than other methods. As we can see, the sub-images in both super-resolution images observed in ERGAN recovered shape lines, whereas other methods had blurry results. Clearly, ERGAN achieved better performance compared with state-of-the-art methods. Our proposed method successfully reconstruct super-resolution images with the high-quality texture details and edges like high-resolution images and exhibit a significant performance. Regardless of whether we consider the PSNR and SSIM values or human visual perception, our method achieved better performance.

Factors Affecting Network Performance: Similar to the network structure of ERGAN, we redefine the series of residual units and how the number of units affect the performance of network. As we can see from the Table 3, PSNR is also increasing with the increase of residual units. Additionally, using the same loss function with symmetric skip-connections achieved better performance than removing skip-connections. This is proof that skip-connections can reuse the high-frequency features generated from the front layers and learn more high-frequency information.

We also considered the convergence of G in ERGAN with different loss functions. From Tables 3, we found that using L_1 in the same residual units achieved a higher PSNR value than using L_2. In ERGAN with the L_2 loss function, we can also obtained a satisfactory results. Simultaneously, we also observed that under the first 100 epochs in Fig. 4, L_2 converged faster than L_1. However, to generate super-resolution images that were similar to the original images, we eventually adopted L_1.

We further evaluated several factors that can determine the performance of our network and get the super-resolution images on DIV2K dataset. Figure 6 show the visual effect of our relevant comparisons, The first row of images is the result of ×4 super resolution. We can see that the result of g_{rb}^4 was too blur, the g_{rb}^8 have some strange grids and lines can be obtained when processing straight edges, and the g_{-sc} result was lack some texture details and look unnatural. Our proposed ERGAN method was close to the original image. The ERGAN generated more realistic textures and higher-frequency content than other related methods we proposed.

Comparison with SRGAN: We compare our approach with SRGAN on the same training dataset for ×4 super-resolution. From Fig. 5, the outputs ×4 of super-resolution reconstruction on several benchmark datasets are listed in Fig. 5. We can clearly compare the differences among the sub-images generated

Table 2. Visual comparison on BSD100 and Urban100 with ×4 super-resolution. Our method shows a sharper visual result than state-of-the-art methods.

Table 3. Average PSNR and SSIM for 4 upscaling on Set5, Set14, BSD100, Urban100 and DIV2K datasets. The best performance is indicated in bold.

PSNR/SSIM	Set5	Set14	BSD100	Urban100	DIV2K
g_{rb}^4	30.58/0.8704	26.87/0.6973	26.25/0.6703	24.73/0.7102	27.49/0.8616
g_{rb}^8	30.86/0.8727	27.05/0.7098	26.30/0.6939	25.07/0.7165	27.58/0.8662
g_{-sc}	29.69/0.8443	27.15/0.7117	26.37/0.6952	24.48/0.7119	27.63/0.8405
g^2	30.35/0.8633	27.46/0.7516	26.79/0.7118	25.08/0.7429	27.66/0.8720
ERGAN	**31.06/0.8802**	**27.72/0.7673**	**27.14/0.7223**	**25.17/0.7493**	**28.07/0.8834**

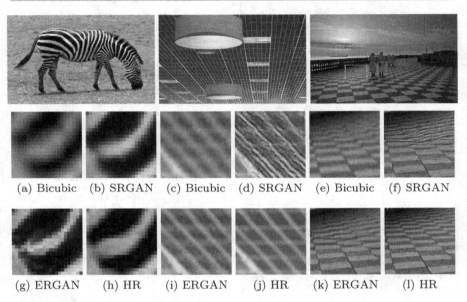

(a) Bicubic   (b) SRGAN   (c) Bicubic   (d) SRGAN   (e) Bicubic   (f) SRGAN

(g) ERGAN   (h) HR   (i) ERGAN   (j) HR   (k) ERGAN   (l) HR

Fig. 5. Visual comparison on DIV2K dataset for × 4 super-resolution. Our method ERGAN shows a better visual result than SRGAN.

(a) g_{rb}^4 (28.25/0.8859)   (b) g_{rb}^8 (30.41/0.8936)   (c) g_{-sc} (30.97/0.9007)   (d) ERGAN (31.27/0.9023)   (e) HR (PSNR/SSIM)

Fig. 6. Visual results (a)–(d) obtained from the related methods we proposed on DIV2K dataset.

by Bicubic, SRGAN, ERGAN, and HR. The SRGAN method for ×4 super-resolution had unnatural textures in local reconstruction (e.g., ceiling and floors). We also see that the super-resolution images generated by our ERGAN were better.

4   Conclusion

In this paper, we proposed a new generative adversarial network with enhanced symmetric residual units for single image super-resolution. Residual learning and symmetric skip-connections were adopted for the generator and a L_1 loss function was used to train our model. The symmetric skip-connections can reuse features generated from the low-level, and learned more high-frequency content. The proposed method can reconstructed image super-resolution by four times the length and width of the original image, and exhibited better visual performance. Experimental results illustrated that our method significantly outperformed state-of-the-art approaches in terms of accuracy and vision. In the future, to accurately and effectively reconstruct a super-resolution image from low-resolution images, we will research multi-scale image super-resolution reconstruction by reducing model size and training time.

Acknowledgment. This work was supported by the National Natural Science Foundation of China (Grant Nos. 61602066) and by the Project Supported by the Scientific Research Foundation of the Education Department of Sichuan Province(17ZA0063 and 2017JQ0030) and the Scientific Research Foundation (KYTZ201608) of CUIT, and partially supported by Sichuan International Science and Technology Cooperation and Exchange Research Program (2016HH0018), and Sichuan Science and Technology Program (2018GZ0184).

References

1. Bruna, J., Sprechmann, P., Lecun, Y.: Super-resolution with deep convolutional sufficient statistics. Comput. Sci. (2015)
2. Dong, C., Chen, C.L., He, K., Tang, X.: Image super-resolution using deep convolutional networks. IEEE Trans. Pattern Anal. Mach. Intell. **38**(2), 295–307 (2016)
3. Denton, E., Chintala, S., Szlam, A., Fergus, R.: Deep generative image modelsusing a Laplacian pyramid of adversarial networks. In: International Conference on Neural Information Processing Systems, pp. 1486–1494 (2015)
4. Goodfellow, I.J., et al.: Generative adversarial nets. In: International Conference on Neural Information Processing Systems, pp. 2672–2680 (2014)
5. Huang, J.B., Singh, A., Ahuja, N.: Single image super-resolution from transformed self-exemplars. In: Computer Vision and Pattern Recognition, pp. 5197–5206 (2015)
6. Lai, W.S., Huang, J.B., Ahuja, N., Yang, M.H.: Deep Laplacian pyramid networks for fast and accurate super-resolution. In: IEEE Conference on Computer Vision and Pattern Recognition, pp. 5835–5843 (2017)

7. Ledig, C., et al.: Photo-realistic single image super-resolution using a generative adversarial network. In: Computer Vision and Pattern Recognition, pp. 105–114 (2017)

8. Li, J., Liang, X., Wei, Y., Xu, T., Feng, J., Yan, S.: Perceptual generative adversarial networks for small object detection. In: Computer Vision and Pattern Recognition, pp. 1951–1959 (2017)

9. Lim, B., Son, S., Kim, H., Nah, S., Lee, K.M.: Enhanced deep residual networks for single image super-resolution. In: Computer Vision and Pattern Recognition Workshops, pp. 1132–1140 (2017)

10. Lin, Z., Shum, H.Y.: On the fundamental limits of reconstruction-based super-resolution algorithms. In: Proceedings of the 2001 IEEE Computer Society Conference on Computer Vision and Pattern Recognition, CVPR 2001, vol. 1, pp. I-1171-I-1176 (2001)

11. Nuno-Maganda, M.A., Arias-Estrada, M.O.: Real-time FPGA-based architecture for bicubic interpolation: an application for digital image scaling. In: International Conference on Reconfigurable Computing and FPGAs, p. 1 (2005)

12. Radford, A., Metz, L., Chintala, S.: Unsupervised representation learning with deep convolutional generative adversarial networks. Comput. Sci. (2015)

13. Ronneberger, O., Fischer, P., Brox, T.: U-net: convolutional networks for biomedical image segmentation. In: Navab, N., Hornegger, J., Wells, W.M., Frangi, A.F. (eds.) MICCAI 2015. LNCS, vol. 9351, pp. 234–241. Springer, Cham (2015). https://doi.org/10.1007/978-3-319-24574-4_28

14. Simonyan, K., Zisserman, A.: Very deep convolutional networks for large-scale image recognition. Comput. Sci. (2014)

15. Song, H., Huang, B., Liu, Q., Zhang, K.: Improving the spatial resolution of landsat TM/ETM+ through fusion with SPOT5 images via learning-based super-resolution. IEEE Trans. Geosci. Remote Sens. **53**(3), 1195–1204 (2014)

16. Tai, Y., Yang, J., Liu, X.: Image super-resolution via deep recursive residual network. In: IEEE Conference on Computer Vision and Pattern Recognition, pp. 2790–2798 (2017)

17. Timofte, R., De Smet, V., Van Gool, L.: A+: adjusted anchored neighborhood regression for fast super-resolution. In: Cremers, D., Reid, I., Saito, H., Yang, M.-H. (eds.) ACCV 2014. LNCS, vol. 9006, pp. 111–126. Springer, Cham (2015). https://doi.org/10.1007/978-3-319-16817-3_8

3D ResNets for 3D Object Classification

Anastasia Ioannidou, Elisavet Chatzilari$^{(\boxtimes)}$, Spiros Nikolopoulos,
and Ioannis Kompatsiaris

Information Technologies Institute, Centre for Research and Technology Hellas,
57001 Thermi, Greece
anastacia.ioannidou@gmail.com, {ehatzi,nikolopo,ikom}@iti.gr
http://mklab.iti.gr/

Abstract. During the last few years, deeper and deeper networks have
been constantly proposed for addressing computer vision tasks. Residual Networks (ResNets) are the latest advancement in the field of deep
learning that led to remarkable results in several image recognition and
detection tasks. In this work, we modify two variants of the original
ResNets, i.e. Wide Residual Networks (WRNs) and Residual of Residual
Networks (RoRs), to work on 3D data and investigate for the first time, to
our knowledge, their performance in the task of 3D object classification.
We use a dataset containing volumetric representations of 3D models so
as to fully exploit the underlying 3D information and present evidence
that '3D ResNets' constitute a valuable tool for classifying objects on 3D
data as well.

Keywords: 3D object classification · 3D object recognition
Deep learning · Residual networks

1 Introduction

During the last few years, Deep Neural Networks (DNNs) have achieved state-
of-the-art performance in almost every computer vision task. Initially, they were
successfully adopted to applications such as speech recognition, object tracking
and image classification, but today they are also used to tackle more complicated
problems, e.g. video classification, 3D segmentation and 3D object recognition.
Convolutional Neural Networks (CNNs), in particular, have shown excellent performance in scenarios involving large datasets. A detailed review on CNNs and
their various applications can be found in [4]. As expected, CNNs' outstanding performance later attracted the attention of researchers working towards 3D
data analysis and understanding as well.

Experimental results indicate that deeper networks provide more representa-
tional power and higher accuracy. One of the latest trends in designing efficient
deep networks is adding residual connections. Residual Networks (ResNets) were
initially introduced in [6] and later extended in [7] achieving remarkable performance on the tasks of image classification, segmentation, object detection and

© Springer Nature Switzerland AG 2019
I. Kompatsiaris et al. (Eds.): MMM 2019, LNCS 11295, pp. 495–506, 2019.
https://doi.org/10.1007/978-3-030-05710-7_41

localization. ResNets address one of the biggest DNNs' challenges, i.e. exploding/vanishing gradients, by adding shortcut (or skip) connections to the network that allow to better update the weights in the early layers of a deep network. This development allowed the training of very deep networks (up to 1 K layers [7]) that led to performances even beyond the human-level ones [5]. The basic residual block is shown in Fig. 1. As it can be seen, input x passes through two stacked weight layers (i.e. convolutional layers) and the output is added to the initial input which skips the stacked layers through the employed identity function. In the original version of ResNets, after each convolutional layer, Batch Normalization (BN) [11] and the ReLU activation function were applied. In the improved version of ResNets (Pre-ResNets), though, it was shown that pre-activation, i.e. applying BN and ReLU before the convolution layer, led to better results.

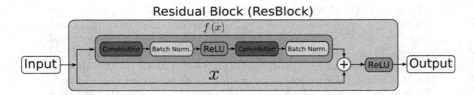

Fig. 1. Original residual block (image from [9])

Concurrently with ResNets, Highway Networks [20] were proposed employing shortcut connections as well, but with gating functions whose weights needed to be learned. Recently, several variations of the original ResNets have also been proposed. In [9], a novel training algorithm that allows training deep residual networks with Stochastic Depth (SD) was introduced. The authors explored the scenario of randomly removing layers during the training phase while exploiting full network depth at test time. Experimental results showed that stochastic depth can lead to reduced training time and test error. "ResNet in ResNet" (RiR) [22] presented an extension of the standard resnet blocks by adding more convolutional layers. The new RiR block has two stacked layers each of which is composed of two parallel streams, a residual and a non-residual one. Improved results were reported on CIFAR-10 and CIFAR-100 datasets. The authors of Wide Residual Networks (WRNs) [25] proposed the widening of ResNet blocks by adding more feature planes in the convolutional layers and argued that'wide' networks are faster to train and perform better than 'thin' ResNet models with approximately the same number of parameters. Residual Networks of Residual Networks (RoRs) [26] from the other side is a novel architecture that introduces level-wise shortcut connections that can also be incorporated to other residual networks for increasing their performance. RoRs achieved state-of-the-art results with the most popular image datasets used for classification. Long Short-Term Memory (LSTM) networks are variants of Recurrent Neural Networks (RNNs) proposed for tackling the problem of vanishing gradients in recurrent networks.

Interestingly, the authors of [16] proposed an architecture, referred to as Convolutional Residual Memory Networks (CRMNs), where a LSTM is placed on top of a ResNet leading to promising results.

Despite their success though, residual networks have not been tested yet in tasks utilizing 3D data. In this work, we modify two recently proposed variations of residual networks, namely (1) Wide Residual Networks (WRNs) [25] and (2) Residual of Residual Networks (RoRs) i.e. Multilevel Residual Networks [26], and use them to perform 3D object classification. We test the adapted architectures on one of the most popular 3D datasets, i.e. Princeton's ModelNet [24] consisting of 3D CAD models from common object categories, and present comparable experimental results with the state-of-the-art.

The remainder of the paper is organized as follows. Section 2 briefly reviews the DNN-based state-of-the-art works for 3D object classification. Section 3 presents the residual architectures studied in this work, while Sect. 4 describes all experimental details and results. Finally, Sect. 5 discusses conclusions and future work.

2   Related Work

Due to increased availability of 3D data, a need for efficient and reliable 3D object recognition and classification methods has emerged. The popular DNNs are primarily designed to work with 1D and/or 2D data, hence their adaptation to the 3D case is not trivial. A review on how 3D data can be employed in DNNs can be found in [10].

Towards 3D object classification, several works addressing the task using a deep architecture are already available. One of the first approaches is 3D ShapeNets [24], i.e. a Convolutional Deep Belief Network (CDBN) with five layers accepting as input binary 3D voxel grids. Along with the proposed network, the authors of this work released a large-scale 3D dataset with CAD models from 662 unique categories, named *ModelNet*, that is used in the experimental evaluation of almost every related method ever since. A voxelized representation of the 3D data is also used in [15]. A CNN with two convolutional, one pooling and one fully-connected layer is employed in this work leading to better classification results compared to 3D ShapeNets. Also working on the voxelized 3D point cloud, in [18], the authors propose a convolutional network (ORION) that not only produces the labels of the 3D objects, but also their pose. The authors of [14] proposed the Kd-Nets, working directly on the unstructured point clouds without requiring that the point clouds are voxelized. This is accomplished since there are no convolutional layers in their architecture and as a result they avoid any problems that might occur during the voxelization due to poor scaling.

Approaches where multiple views of the 3D objects are provided to the network can be found in [12,21]. Multi-View CNN (MVCNN) [21] learns to combine any number of input views of an object without any particular order through a view pooling layer. Setups with 12 and 80 views were tested increasing the classification accuracy significantly compared to other DNNs like [24]. Qi et al. [17] managed to introduce improvements to MVCNN's performance by using enhanced data augmentation and multi-resolution 3D filtering in order to exploit information from multiple scales. Multiple views organized in pairs were used in [12]. The authors employed a known CNN, that is VGG-M [2], and concatenated the outputs of the convolutional layers from the two images before providing them to the first fully-connected layer. The introduced model surpassed the performance of voxel-based 3D ShapeNets [24] and the MVCNN approach of Su et al. [21] on the ModelNet dataset.

Recently, ensemble architectures have become popular. A work that attempts to combine the advantages of different modalities of the 3D models can be found in [8]. Two volumetric neural networks were combined with a multi-view network after the final fully-connected layer. A linear combination of class scores was then taken with the predicted class being the one with the highest score. An ensemble of 6 volumetric models was proposed in [1] achieving the current state-of-the-art classification accuracy on both ModelNet10 (i.e. 97.14%) and ModelNet40 (i.e. 95.54%) datasets. The final result was computed by summing the predictions from all 6 models. The proposed architecture led to excellent performance, however, is significantly more complex compared to most existing networks from the relevant literature requiring 6 days of training on a Titan X.

Despite the existing significant works on 3D object classification, computational cost is still a bottleneck, especially when working on pure 3D representations. Networks including sophisticated modules or ensembles of large topologies require increased training time and hardware resources that are not always available. In this work, we extend two of the most recent variants of residual networks in 2D-image classification, adapt them to the 3D domain keeping complexity in mind and investigate the efficiency of these '3D ResNets' on classifying volumetric 3D shapes.

3   3D Classification with Residual Networks

The authors of [25] have recently investigated several architectures of ResNet blocks and ended up proposing 'widening' by adding more feature planes in the convolutional layers. More specifically, WRNs consist of an initial convolutional layer followed by 3 groups of residual blocks. Additionally, an average pooling layer and a classifier completes the architecture, while dropout [19] was used for regularization. Experimental evaluation showed that widening boosts the performance compared to that of 'thin' ResNet models with approximately the same number of parameters and at the same time, accelerates training mostly due to the strong parallelization that can be applied in the convolutional layers.

In [26], level-wise shortcut connections were introduced to enhance the performance of ResNets. 'Residual Networks of Residual Networks' (RoRs) is a novel architecture with 3 shortcut levels (i.e. root, middle and final level) that allow information to flow directly from the upper layers to lower layers. Except for their original RoR architecture, the authors also incorporated the RoR concept to other residual networks, in particular Pre-ResNets and WRNs (denoted as Pre-RoR-3 and RoR-3-WRN respectively in [26]). Extensive experiments on the most popular image datasets used for classification indicated that RoRs can improve performance without bringing additional computational cost.

In this paper, our goal is to study the performance of residual networks on the task of 3D object classification. Towards this direction, we explored several variations of the original ResNets and trained a variety of models with different network and training parameters in order to get insights and identify best strategies. We tested networks of varying depth and width and explored suitable values for the learning rate, dropout, weight decay and activation functions. Except from the classification accuracy, the computational cost was also taken into account during our experimentation. We focused on networks with a relatively small number of parameters (up to 2.5 M) requiring a reasonable time to train.

Starting from *Wide Residual Networks*, we initially explored different values for the width (denoted with k) and the number of convolutional layers denoted with n. The depth of the network denoted with N is computed as $N = (n - 4)/6$. Due to memory limitations, we were able to train networks with $k = 2$, i.e. networks that are two times wider than the original ResNets. With respect to the number of convolutional layers, we tested values between 10 and 22, therefore N was in the range [1...3]. In addition, the notation WRN-n-k is used to describe a wide residual network with n convolutional layers and width k. The adapted WRN structure incorporates 3D convolutions and is depicted in Table 1. Regarding multilevel residual networks, we tested in our experiments Pre-RoR and RoR-WRN with 16 convolutional layers, i.e. N = 2, k = 1 (for Pre-RoR) and k = 2 (for WRNs), on ModelNet10. The multilevel structure is demonstrated in Fig. 2.

Table 1. Structure of adapted WRNs for 3D object classification

Group	Output size	[3D filter size, #filters]	
conv1	$32 \times 32 \times 32$	$[3 \times 3 \times 3, 16]$	
conv2	$32 \times 32 \times 32$	$[3 \times 3 \times 3, 16 \times k]$	$\Big\} \times N$
		$[3 \times 3 \times 3, 16 \times k]$	
conv3	$16 \times 16 \times 16$	$[3 \times 3 \times 3, 32 \times k]$	$\Big\} \times N$
		$[3 \times 3 \times 3, 32 \times k]$	
conv4	$8 \times 8 \times 8$	$[3 \times 3 \times 3, 64 \times k]$	$\Big\} \times N$
		$[3 \times 3 \times 3, 64 \times k]$	
avg-pool	$1 \times 1 \times 1$	$[8 \times 8 \times 8]$	

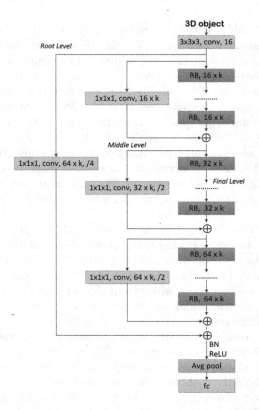

Fig. 2. Adapted Pre-RoR-3 (if k = 1) and RoR-3-WRN (if k > 1) architectures

4   Experimental Results

4.1   Dataset and Implementation

ModelNet is a large 3D dataset containing more than 120K CAD models of objects from 662 categories. The dataset was released in 2015, and thereafter its two publicly available subsets, i.e. ModelNet10 and ModelNet40, are commonly used in works related to 3D object recognition and classification. To perform our experimental evaluation, we employ ModelNet10 that consists of 4899 models (3991 for training and 908 for testing) each manually aligned by the authors of the dataset. Binary voxelized versions of the 3D models are provided to our network. The resolution of the occupancy grid affects the classification accuracy, since it determines in which extent the 3D object's details will be apparent, as depicted in Fig. 3. Obviously, a larger volume size leads to a better representation but also to an increased computational cost, hence a compromise needs to be made. In this work, the employed grid size is $32 \times 32 \times 32$. As a pre-processing step, the voxels were transformed from $\{0, 1\}$ to $\{-1, 1\}$. In addition, the dataset is augmented by 12 copies (i.e. rotations around the z axis) of each model. Inspired

Table 2. Classification results on ModelNet10 using wide residual networks & residual of residual networks

Network	#params	Train accuracy	Test accuracy
WRN-16-2-modified	∼0.5M	98.70%	92.18%
WRN-22-2-modified	∼0.7M	99.57%	92.95%
Pre-RoR (N = 2, k = 1)	∼0.5M	99.8%	92.84%
RoR-WRN-16-2	∼2M	99.8%	94.00%

by [15], one randomly mirrored and shifted instance of each object is also added in the dataset. An indicative 3D object and its 12 voxelized rotations are depicted in Fig. 4.

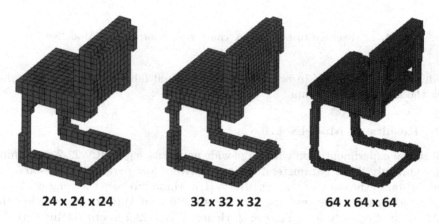

24 x 24 x 24   **32 x 32 x 32**   **64 x 64 x 64**

Fig. 3. 3D object from ModelNet voxelized in 3 different resolutions

All of our experiments were conducted on a Linux machine with 128GB RAM and a NVIDIA GeForce GTX 1070 GPU. The deep learning framework that was used was Keras [3] running on top of Theano [23].

4.2 Training

During training, we split the original training set randomly into a 'train' set, containing 75% of the 3D models, and a 'validation' set, containing the remaining 25% of models. The tested networks were trained from scratch using Adam optimizer [13] for fast convergence. We used fixed learning rates, such as 0.001 or 0.0001, since larger values reduced the performance. Categorical cross-entropy was used as the objective. All convolutional layers were initialized with the method of [5]. During training, every copy of a 3D model was considered as a separate train sample. At inference time, the predictions of all copies of a 3D

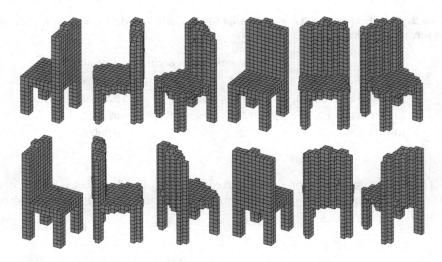

Fig. 4. 12 voxelized rotations of a 'chair' train sample from ModelNet10

model were summed up in order to make the final label assignment to it, i.e.
pick the argmax on the sum.

4.3   Results on ModelNet10

Our initial experimentation with large wide networks, e.g. WRN-22-2 containing
approximately 3.2M parameters, led to relatively low performance (∼90%) in
comparison to the state-of-the-art (97.1% [1]). Aiming to keep the computational
cost as low as possible, we changed the structure of WRNs by removing the
final group of convolutions, i.e. *conv4*. Hence, WRN-22-2 in our setting actually
contains 15 convolutional layers and not 22 as the original WRN would have. We
denote these networks as *WRN-n-k-modified*. Additionally, inspired by works like
[15], we investigated using Leaky ReLU as the activation function in the trained
networks instead of the original ReLU and found this to lead to a slight boost
of approximately 0.5% in the classification accuracy. In these experiments, a
dropout keep rate of 0.7 was used, while batch size was set to 32. Moreover,
L2 regularization to the weights by a factor of 0.0001 was applied. Some of the
results we obtained with WRNs after training for 50 epochs are provided in
Table 2. As shown, an accuracy of over 92% can be yielded by a 'wide' network
of less than 500 K parameters. In contrast, VoxNet [15], for example, achieves the
same accuracy with a network containing twice the parameters. By adding more
(convolutional) layers leading to a network of approximately 700 K parameters,
a slight improvement in performance is observed (0.77%).

For training Pre-RoRs, no dropout or regularization of the weights was
applied. Additionally, ReLU was used as the activation function as originally
proposed by the authors. The classification results for ModelNet10 are included
in Table 2. It can be seen that a Residual of Residual Network of approximately

500 K parameters leads to better performance in comparison to a Wide network with the same number of parameters. In addition, a 'wide' Residual of Residual Network containing around 2M parameters achieves an accuracy of 94%.

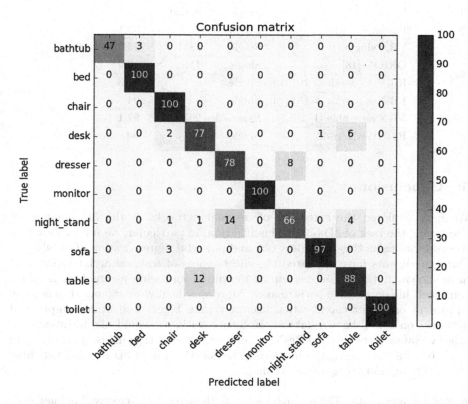

Fig. 5. Confusion matrix of our best performing model on ModelNet10

In Table 3, recent classification results on ModelNet10 from relevant works are reported. As it can be seen, the state-of-the-art performance on this dataset is 97.1% achieved with an ensemble of 6 networks, though, containing 90M parameters. The next best performing networks have an accuracy in the range of 93.3%-94% achieved from networks containing several million parameters. Our best model, i.e. RoR-WRN-16-2 with only 2M parameters, after approximately 18 hours of training achieves a classification accuracy equal to the best performance reported so far from a single model architecture. In contrast, the equally performing Kd-Net with depth 15 (94%), requires 5 days to train on the faster Titan GPU, while its slimmer version (depth 10) performing 93.3% requires 16 hours. In Fig. 5, the confusion matrix of this model on ModelNet10 is depicted. As it can be seen, most of the misclassified 3D models were assigned a label of a similar category compared to the ground truth.

Table 3. Classification accuracy (%) on ModelNet10 of our best performing model in comparison with other models from the literature

Model	Type	# params	ModelNet10
VoxNet [15]	Single	0.92M	92
FusionNet [8]	Ensemble	118M	93.1
VRN single [1]	Single	18M	93.6
ORION [18]	Single	4M	93.9
Kd-Net (depth = 10) [14]	Single	-	93.3
Kd-Net (depth = 15) [14]	Single	-	94
VRN ensemble [1]	Ensemble	90M	97.1
RoR-WRN-16-2	Single	2M	**94**

5   Conclusions

We have explored the extension of residual networks in the 3D domain for addressing the task of 3D object classification. In particular, we used volumetric representations as they provide a rich and powerful representation of 3D shapes. Our experiments have validated the effectiveness of residual architectures and have shown that the combination of multilevel and wide residual connections can result in competitive performance. More specifically, we managed to achieve equivalent or better classification accuracy than bigger and more complicated networks on a well-known dataset. In future work, we would like to investigate other variants of the original ResNets and test different training configurations in order to gain more insights considering the effectiveness of 3D residual networks on classifying and recognizing 3D shapes.

Acknowledgements. The research leading to these results has received funding from the European Union H2020 Horizon Programme (2014–2020) under grant agreement 665066, project DigiArt (The Internet Of Historical Things And Building New 3D Cultural Worlds).

References

1. Brock, A., Lim, T., Ritchie, J., Weston, N.: Generative and discriminative voxel modeling with convolutional neural networks. CoRR abs/1608.04236 (2016). http://arxiv.org/abs/1608.04236
2. Chatfield, K., Simonyan, K., Vedaldi, A., Zisserman, A.: Return of the devil in the details: delving deep into convolutional nets. In: British Machine Vision Conference (BMVC) (2014)
3. Chollet, F., et al.: Keras (2015). https://github.com/fchollet/keras
4. Gu, J., et al.: Recent advances in convolutional neural networks. Pattern Recognit. **77**, 354–377 (2018). https://doi.org/10.1016/j.patcog.2017.10.013

5. He, K., Zhang, X., Ren, S., Sun, J.: Delving deep into rectifiers: surpassing human-level performance on ImageNet classification. In: IEEE International Conference on Computer Vision ICCV, pp. 1026–1034 (2015)
6. He, K., Zhang, X., Ren, S., Sun, J.: Deep residual learning for image recognition. In: IEEE Conference on Computer Vision and Pattern Recognition (CVPR), pp. 770–778 (2016)
7. He, K., Zhang, X., Ren, S., Sun, J.: Identity mappings in deep residual networks. In: Leibe, B., Matas, J., Sebe, N., Welling, M. (eds.) ECCV 2016. LNCS, vol. 9908, pp. 630–645. Springer, Cham (2016). https://doi.org/10.1007/978-3-319-46493-0_38
8. Hegde, V., Zadeh, R.: FusionNet: 3D object classification using multiple data representations. CoRR abs/1607.05695 (2016).http://arxiv.org/abs/1607.05695
9. Huang, G., Sun, Y., Liu, Z., Sedra, D., Weinberger, K.Q.: Deep networks with stochastic depth. In: Leibe, B., Matas, J., Sebe, N., Welling, M. (eds.) ECCV 2016. LNCS, vol. 9908, pp. 646–661. Springer, Cham (2016). https://doi.org/10.1007/978-3-319-46493-0_39
10. Ioannidou, A., Chatzilari, E., Nikolopoulos, S., Kompatsiaris, I.: Deep learning advances in computer vision with 3D data: a survey. ACM Comput. Surv. 50(2), 201–2038 (2017). https://doi.org/10.1145/3042064
11. Ioffe, S., Szegedy, C.: Batch normalization: accelerating deep network trainingby reducing internal covariate shift. In: Proceedings of the 32nd International Conference on Machine Learning (ICML), pp. 448–456 (2015).http://jmlr.org/proceedings/papers/v37/ioffe15.html
12. Johns, E., Leutenegger, S., Davison, A.: Pairwise decomposition of image sequences for active multi-view recognition. In: IEEE Conference on Computer Vision and Pattern Recognition (CVPR), pp. 3813–3822 (2016)
13. Kingma, D., Ba, J.: Adam: a method for stochastic optimization. CoRR abs/1412.6980 (2014). http://arxiv.org/abs/1412.6980
14. Klokov, R., Lempitsky, V.: Escape from cells: deep Kd-networks for the recognition of 3D point cloud models. CoRR abs/1704.01222 (2017). http://arxiv.org/abs/1704.01222
15. Maturana, D., Scherer, S.: VoxNet: a 3D convolutional neural network forreal-time object recognition. In: IEEE/RSJ International Conference on Intelligent Robots and Systems (IROS), pp. 922–928 (2015)
16. Moniz, J., Pal, C.: Convolutional residual memory networks. CoRR abs/1606.05262 (2016). http://arxiv.org/abs/1606.05262
17. Qi, C., Su, H., Nießner, M., Dai, A., Yan, M., Guibas, L.: Volumetric and multi-view CNNs for object classification on 3D data. CoRR abs/1604.03265 (2016). http://arxiv.org/abs/1604.03265
18. Sedaghat, N., Zolfaghari, M., Brox, T.: Orientation-boosted voxel nets for 3D object recognition. CoRR abs/1604.03351 (2016). http://arxiv.org/abs/1604.03351
19. Srivastava, N., Hinton, G., Krizhevsky, A., Sutskever, I., Salakhutdinov, R.: Dropout: a simple way to prevent neural networks from overfitting. J. Mach. Learn. Res. 15, 1929–1958 (2014)
20. Srivastava, R., Greff, K., Schmidhuber, J.: Highway networks. CoRR abs/1505.00387 (2015). http://arxiv.org/abs/1505.00387
21. Su, H., Maji, S., Kalogerakis, E., Learned-Miller, E.: Multi-view convolutional neural networks for 3D shape recognition. In: Proceedings of the IEEE International Conference on Computer Vision (ICCV), pp. 945–953 (2015)
22. Targ, S., Almeida, D., Lyman, K.: Resnet in resnet: generalizing residual architectures. CoRR abs/1603.08029 (2016).http://arxiv.org/abs/1603.08029

23. Theano Development Team: Theano: A Python framework for fast computation of mathematical expressions. arXiv e-prints abs/1605.02688, May 2016. http://arxiv.org/abs/1605.02688
24. Wu, Z., et al.: 3D ShapeNets: a deep representation for volumetric shapes. In: IEEE Conference on Computer Vision and Pattern Recognition (CVPR), June 2015
25. Zagoruyko, S., Komodakis, N.: Wide residual networks. In: BMVC (2016)
26. Zhang, K., Sun, M., Han, X., Yuan, X., Guo, L., Liu, T.: Residual networks of residual networks: multilevel residual networks. IEEE Trans. Circ. Syst. Video Technol. **PP**(99), 1 (2017)

Four Models for Automatic Recognition of Left and Right Eye in Fundus Images

Xin Lai[1,2], Xirong Li[1], Rui Qian[1], Dayong Ding[2], Jun Wu[3], and Jieping Xu[1(✉)]

[1] Key Lab of DEKE, Remin University of China, Beijing 100872, China
xjieping@ruc.edu.cn
[2] Vistel AI Lab, Beijing 100872, China
[3] Northwestern Polytechnical University, Xi'an 710072, China

Abstract. Fundus image analysis is crucial for eye condition screening and diagnosis and consequently personalized health management in a long term. This paper targets at left and right eye recognition, a basic module for fundus image analysis. We study how to automatically assign left-eye/right-eye labels to fundus images of posterior pole. For this under-explored task, four models are developed. Two of them are based on optic disc localization, using extremely simple max intensity and more advanced Faster R-CNN, respectively. The other two models require no localization, but perform holistic image classification using classical Local Binary Patterns (LBP) features and fine-tuned ResNet-18, respectively. The four models are tested on a real-world set of 1,633 fundus images from 834 subjects. Fine-tuned ResNet-18 has the highest accuracy of 0.9847. Interestingly, the LBP based model, with the trick of left-right contrastive classification, performs closely to the deep model, with an accuracy of 0.9718.

Keywords: Medical image analysis · Fundus images
Left and right eye recognition · Optic disc localization
Left-right contrastive classification · Deep learning

1 Introduction

Medical image analysis, either content-based or using multiple modalities, is crucial for both instant computer-aided diagnosis and longer-term personal health management. Among different types of medical images, fundus images are of unique importance for two reasons. First, fundus photography, imaging the retina of an eye including retinal vasculature, optic disc, and macula, provides an effective measure for ophthalmologists to evaluate conditions such as diabetic retinopathy, age-related macular degeneration, and glaucoma. These disorders are known to be sight threatening and even result in vision loss. Second, fundus photography is noninvasive, and the invention of non-mydriatic fundus cameras makes it even more patient-friendly and thus well suited for routinely health screening. This paper contributes to fundus image analysis. Different from current works that focus on diagnosis related tasks [3,8], we aim for *left and right*

© Springer Nature Switzerland AG 2019
I. Kompatsiaris et al. (Eds.): MMM 2019, LNCS 11295, pp. 507–517, 2019.
https://doi.org/10.1007/978-3-030-05710-7_42

eye recognition, *i.e.,* automatically determining if a specific fundus image is from a left or a right eye.

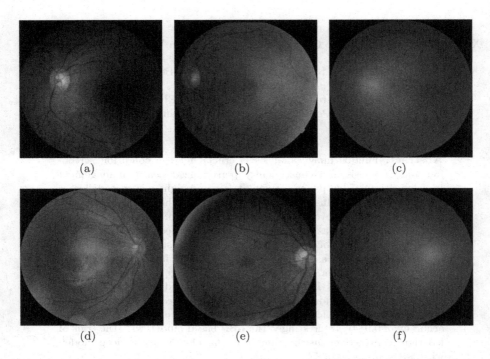

(a)   (b)   (c)

(d)   (e)   (f)

Fig. 1. Examples of fundus images, with the first row showing images taken from left eyes and the second row showing images from right eyes. These images capture the posterior pole, *i.e.,* the retina between the optic disc and the macula. The two artificial images in the last column are generated by averaging many left-eye and right-eye images, respectively.

The left-eye and right-eye labels are basic contextual information that needs to be associated with a specific fundus image. The labels are necessary because the conditions of a subject's two eyes are not necessarily correlated. Diagnosis and health monitoring have to be performed and documented per eye. Besides, the labels are important for other applications such as fundus based person verification [6], where pairs of images to be compared have to be both left-eye or both right-eye. At present, this labeling task is manually accomplished, mainly by fundus camera operators.

Despite its importance, left and right eye recognition appears to be largely unexplored. Few efforts have been made [14,15], both trying to leverage the location of the optic disc. The optic disc is the entry point for the major blood vessels that supply the retina [2]. Its area, roughly shaped as an ellipse, is typically the brightest in a fundus image, see Fig. 1. Tan *et al.* [14] develop their left and right eye recognition based on optic disc localization and vessel segmentation. In particular, they first identify a region of interest (ROI) based on pixel intensities. Vessels within this ROI are segmented. A given image is classified as left-eye, if the left half of the ROI has less vessel pixels than the right half. They report a classification accuracy of 0.923 on a set of 194 fundus images. Later in [15], the same team improves over [14] by training an SVM classifiers based on segmentation-based features, reporting an accuracy of 0.941 on a set of 102 fundus images. Similar to the two pioneering works we also exploit the optic disc. Our major novelties are that we develop new models that require no optic disc localization, nor vessel segmentation, see Table 1. Moreover we investigate deep learning techniques that have not been considered for this task.

Table 1. Major characteristics of the two existing and four proposed models for left and right eye recognition in fundus images.

Model	Optic disk localization?	Vessel segmentation?	Learning based?	Deep learning?
Tan *et al.* [14]	✓	✓	✗	✗
Tan *et al.* [15]	✓	✓	✓	✗
This work:				
ODL-MI	✓	✗	✗	✗
ODL-CNN	✓	✗	✓	✓
LRCC	✗	✗	✓	✗
FT-CNN	✗	✗	✓	✓

In ophthalmology, the posterior pole refers to the retina between the optic disc and the macula [1]. These two areas are crucial for examination and diagnosis. Hence, fundus images of posterior pole are most commonly used in practice. In such images, the optic disc is typically observed at the left half of a left-eye image, and at the right half of a right-eye image. This phenomenon is demonstrated by averaging left-eye images and right-eye images, respectively, see the last column of Fig. 1. The above observation leads to the following questions: *Is precise localization of the optic disc necessary? Can the problem of left and right eye recognition be effectively solved by determining at which half the optic disc appears?*

For answering these two questions, this paper makes contributions as follows:

1. We propose two types of models, according to their dependency on optic disc localization. For both types, we look into traditional image processing techniques and present-day deep learning techniques. The combination leads to four distinct models.
2. We show that with a proper design, the proposed non-deep learning model is nearly comparable to the ResNet-18 based model, yet is computationally light with no need of GPU for training and execution.
3. Experiments on a test set of 1,633 fundus images from 834 subjects, which are over 10 times larger than those reported in the literature, show the state-of-the-art performance of the proposed models.

The rest of the paper is organized as follows. The proposed models are described in Sect. 2, followed by experiments in Sect. 3. We conclude the paper in Sect. 4.

2 Four Models for Left and Right Eye Recognition

2.1 Problem Statement

Given a fundus image of posterior pole, the problem of left and right eye recognition is to automatically determine whether the fundus image was taken from the left or right eye of a specific person. A binary classification model is thus required. Without loss of generality, we consider fundus images from left eyes as positive instances. Accordingly, fundus images from right eyes are treated as negatives. Let x be a fundus image, and x_l and x_r denoting the left and right half of the image, respectively. Let y be a binary variable, where $y = 1$ indicates left eye and 0 otherwise. We use $p(y = 1|x) \in [0, 1]$ to denote a model that produces a probabilistic output of being left eye, and $h(x) \in \{0, 1\}$ as a model that gives a hard classification.

Next, we propose four models, where the first two models count on optic disc localization, while the last two models require no localization. Figure 2 conceptually illustrate the proposed models.

2.2 Model I. Optic Disc Localization by Max-Intensity (ODL-MI)

As noted in Sect. 1, the location of the optic disc is a strong cue for left and right eye recognition. In the meanwhile, the optic disc tends to be the brightest area in a normal fundus image. To exploit this priori knowledge, we propose a naive model which looks for the brightest region, i.e., the region with the maximum intensity. Hence, we term this model *Optic Disc Localization by Max-Intensity*, abbreviated as ODL-MI.

Given a color fundus image x, ODL-MI first converts x to gray-scale. The image is then uniformly divided into $s \times s$ regions, with s empirically set to 10. The intensity of each region is obtained by averaging the intensity of all pixels within the region. Accordingly, the region with the maximum intensity is localized, *i.e.,*

$$i^*, j^* = \operatorname*{argmax}_{i,j \in \{1,\dots,s\}} Intensity(x, i, j), \tag{1}$$

where $Intensity(x, i, j)$ returns the averaged intensity of the region indexed by i and j. If the center of this region falls in x_l, the image will be classified as left eye. We formalize the above classification process as

$$h_{ODL-MI}(x) = \begin{cases} 1, & \text{if the center of region } (i^*, j^*) \text{ falls in } x_l \\ 0, & \text{otherwise.} \end{cases} \tag{2}$$

The effectiveness of this fully intensity-driven model depends on image quality. For varied reasons including bad photography and bad eye conditions, some part of a fundus image might appear to be more brighter than the optic disc, see Fig. 1(e). So we consider learning-based optic disc localization as follows.

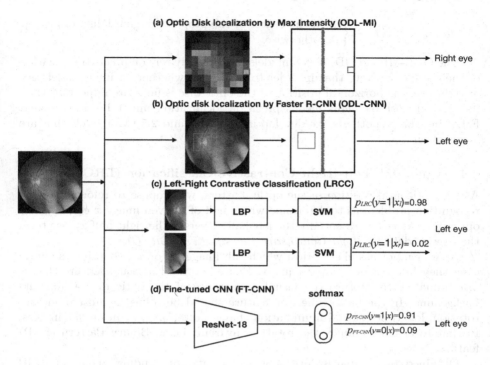

Fig. 2. A conceptual diagram of the four proposed models for left and right eye recognition. The first two models, *i.e.,* ODL-MI and ODL-CNN, are based on optic disc localization, while the LRCC and FT-CNN models are *localization free*, resolving the recognition problem by holistic classification. Note that For LRCC, the two sub images, corresponding to the left and right half of the input image, go through the same LBP feature extraction module and the same SVM classification module.

2.3 Model II: Optic Disc Localization by CNN (ODL-CNN)

In this model, we improve the optic disc localization component of ODL-MI, by substituting an object detection CNN for the intensity-based rule. Notice that for left and right eye recognition, knowing the precise boundary of the optic disc is unnecessary. A bounding box centered around the optic disc is adequate. In that regard, we adopt Faster R-CNN [12], a well-performed CNN for object detection and localization. In particular, we use Faster R-CNN we trained for the task of joint segmentation of the optic disc and the optic cup in fundus images. Given a test image, the network proposes 300 candidate regions of interest. The proposed regions are then fed into the classification block of Faster R-CNN. Consequently, each region is predicted with a probability of covering the optic disc region. After non-maximum suppression, the best region is selected as the final proposal. We consider the center of this region as the coordinate of the optic disc. Subsequently, a similar decision rule as described in Sect. 2.2 is applied, *i.e.,*

$$h_{ODL-CNN}(x) = \begin{cases} 1, & \text{if the center of the proposed region falls in } x_l \\ 0, & \text{otherwise.} \end{cases} \quad (3)$$

The ODL-MI and ODL-CNN models both heavily rely on precise localization of the optic disc. Note that in order to determine whether an image is left-eye or right eye, the horizontal position of the optic disc is far more important than its vertical position. This means precision localization might be unnecessary. Following this hypothesis, we develop in Sects. 2.4 and 2.5 two models that are localization free.

2.4   Model III. Left-Right Contrastive Classification (LRCC)

As the horizontal position of the optic matters, we propose to reformulate the recognition problem as to determine which half of a given image x contains the optic disc. As this is essentially the left half x_l versus the right half x_r, we term the new model *Left-Right Contrastive Classification (LRCC)*.

As we cannot assume a priori which sub image, x_l or x_r, contains the optic disc, they have to be treated equally. Hence, we need a visual feature that is discriminative to capture the visual appearance of the optic disc against its background. In the meanwhile, the feature should be robust against moderate rotation, low contrast and illumination changes often present in fundus images. In that regard, we employ the rotation-invariant Local Binary Pattern (LBP) feature [7].

Obtained by comparing every pixel with its surrounding pixels, an LBP descriptor can recognize bright and dark spots and edges of curvature at a given scale [7]. Specifically, for each pixel in an image, a circle of radius R centered on this pixel is first formed. Every pixel on the circle is compared against the central pixel, with the comparison result encoded as 1 if larger and 0 otherwise. This results in a binary pattern of length $8 \times R$. Note that, the pattern changes with respect to the choice of the starting point and the rotation of the image. The rotation-invariant LBP cancels out such changes by circling the pattern end to end, and categorizing it into a fixed set of classes based on the number of bitwise 0/1 changes in the circle. In this work the radius R is empirically set to 3, resulting in a 25-dimensional LBP feature per sub image. The feature has been l_1 normalized in advance to the subsequent supervised learning.

To train the LRCC model, we construct training instances at follows. For a left-eye image, its left sub image is used as a positive instance with its right sub image as negative. While for a right-eye image, its left sub image will be treated as a negative instance. In this context, $p_{LRCC}(y = 1|x_l)$ and $p_{LRCC}(y = 1|x_r)$ indicate the probability of the optic disc occurring in the left half and the right half, respectively. We train a linear SVM to produce the two probabilities. Accordingly, the LRCC model is expressed as

$$h_{LRCC}(x) = \begin{cases} 1, & p_{LRCC}(y = 1|x_l) > p_{LRCC}(y = 1|x_r) \\ 0, & \text{otherwise.} \end{cases} \quad (4)$$

Note that the left-right contrastive strategy allows LRCC to get rid of thresholding.

2.5   Model IV. Classification by Fine-Tuned CNN (FT-CNN)

We aim to build a deep CNN model that directly categorizes an input image into either left or right eye. Note that the relatively limited availability of our training data makes it difficult to effectively learn a new CNN from scratch. We therefore turn to fine tuning [11,17]. The main idea of this training strategy is to initialize the new CNN with its counterpart pre-trained on the large-scale ImageNet dataset.

In this work we adapt a ResNet-18 network [4], which strikes a good balance between classification accuracy and GPU footprint. The network has been pre-trained predict 1,000 visual objects defined in the ImageNet Large Scale Visual Recognition Challenge [13]. For our binary classification task, we replace the task layer, *i.e.*, the last fully connected layer, of ResNet-18 by a new fully connected layer consisting of two neurons. Accordingly, our CNN-based model is expressed as

$$p_{cnn}(y|x) := softmax(\text{ResNet-18}(x)), \tag{5}$$

where *softmax* indicates a softmax layer converting the output of ResNet-18 network into probabilist output. Accordingly, FT-CNN makes a decision as

$$h_{FT-CNN}(x) = \underset{\hat{y} \in \{0,1\}}{\mathrm{argmax}}\, p_{cnn}(y = \hat{y}|x). \tag{6}$$

The model is re-trained to minimize the cross entropy loss by stochastic gradient descent with a momentum of 0.9. The learning rate is initially set to 0.001, and decays every 7 epochs. The number of epochs is 150 in total. The model scoring the best validation accuracy is retained.

3   Experiments

3.1   Experimental Setup

Datasets. We use the public Kaggle fundus image dataset [5] as our training data. While originally developed for diabetic retinopathy detection, the left and right eye information of the Kaggle images can be extracted from their filenames. Nevertheless, we observe incorrect labels, *e.g.*, images with their filename indicating left eye might actually be right eye, and vice versa. We improve label quality by manually verifying and correcting the original annotations. To make manual labeling affordable, we took a random subset of around 12 K images. During the labeling process, images that cannot be categorized, *e.g.*, those with optic discs invisible, were removed. This results in a set of 11,126 images, 60% of which is used for training and the remaining 40% is used as an validation set for optimizing hyper parameters. We constructed a test set of 1,633 images collected through eye screening programmes performed in local sites. Therefore, the test set is completely independent of our training and validation sets. The

Table 2. Basic statistics of datasets used in our experiments. We use a random subset of the Kaggle DR dataset [5] for training and validation, and an independent set of 1,633 fundus images for testing.

	Training set	Validation set	Test set
Left-eye images	3,286	2,194	778
Right-eye images	3,369	2,277	845
Total	6,655	4,471	1,633

test images come from 834 subjects, with 474 females and 360 males. Table 2 presents basic statistics of the three datasets.

Preprocessing. Note that a fundus image is captured under a specific spatial extend of a circular field-of-view, visually indicated by a round mask. As there is no relevant information outside the mask, each image has been automatically cropped as follows. We use a square bounding box tangent to the round mask, so that the cropped image is a square one containing only the field-of-view. The bounding box is estimated by fitting a circle from candidate points detected on the boundary of the mask.

Implementations. We use the scikit-image toolbox [16] to extract the LBP features, and scikit-learn [10] to train the SVM models. The penalty parameter C is selected to maximize the model accuracy on the validation set. For deep learning we use PyTorch [9].

Evaluation Criterion. As the two classes are more or less balanced, we report accuracy, *i.e.*, the rate of test images correctly predicted.

3.2 Results

Table 3 summarizes the performance of the four models on the test set. FT-CNN, with an accuracy of 0.9847, performs the best. It is followed by ODL-CNN (0.9767), LRCC (0.9718) and ODL-MI (0.9314).

Misclassification by ODL-MI is mainly due to its incorrect localization of the optic disc, see examples #7 and #11 in Table 4. For ODL-CNN, it performs

Table 3. Performance of the four proposed models on the test set, sorted in ascending order according to their recognition accuracy. The notation $X \rightarrow Y$ means X is predicated as Y. Fine-tuned CNN (FT-CNN) is the best.

Proposed model	Correct prediction		Incorrect prediction		Accuracy
	$Left \rightarrow Left$	$Right \rightarrow Right$	$Left \rightarrow Right$	$Right \rightarrow Left$	
ODL-MI	733	788	55	57	0.9314
LRCC	772	815	16	30	0.9718
ODL-CNN	783	812	5	33	0.9767
FT-CNN	786	822	2	23	**0.9847**

Table 4. Some results of left and right eye recognition produced by the four models, with correct and incorrect prediction marked by ✓and ✗. Optic disk regions found by ODL-MI and ODL-CNN are highlighted by the small blue and larger purple squares, respectively. Best viewed in color.

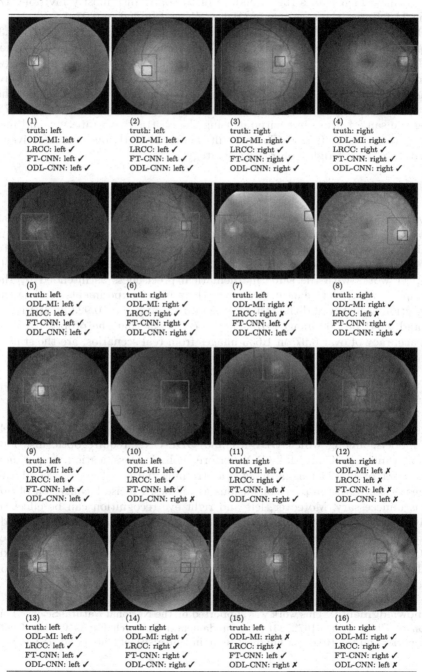

(1)	(2)	(3)	(4)
truth: left	truth: left	truth: right	truth: right
ODL-MI: left ✓	ODL-MI: left ✓	ODL-MI: right ✓	ODL-MI: right ✓
LRCC: left ✓	LRCC: left ✓	LRCC: right ✓	LRCC: right ✓
FT-CNN: left ✓	FT-CNN: left ✓	FT-CNN: right ✓	FT-CNN: right ✓
ODL-CNN: left ✓	ODL-CNN: left ✓	ODL-CNN: right ✓	ODL-CNN: right ✓

(5)	(6)	(7)	(8)
truth: left	truth: right	truth: left	truth: right
ODL-MI: left ✓	ODL-MI: right ✓	ODL-MI: right ✗	ODL-MI: right ✓
LRCC: left ✓	LRCC: right ✓	LRCC: left ✓	LRCC: left ✗
FT-CNN: left ✓	FT-CNN: right ✓	FT-CNN: left ✓	FT-CNN: right ✓
ODL-CNN: left ✓	ODL-CNN: right ✓	ODL-CNN: left ✓	ODL-CNN: right ✓

(9)	(10)	(11)	(12)
truth: left	truth: left	truth: right	truth: right
ODL-MI: left ✓	ODL-MI: left ✓	ODL-MI: left ✗	ODL-MI: left ✗
LRCC: left ✓	LRCC: left ✓	LRCC: right ✓	LRCC: left ✗
FT-CNN: left ✓	FT-CNN: left ✓	FT-CNN: left ✗	FT-CNN: left ✗
ODL-CNN: left ✓	ODL-CNN: right ✗	ODL-CNN: right ✓	ODL-CNN: left ✗

(13)	(14)	(15)	(16)
truth: left	truth: right	truth: left	truth: right
ODL-MI: left ✓	ODL-MI: right ✓	ODL-MI: right ✗	ODL-MI: right ✓
LRCC: left ✓	LRCC: right ✓	LRCC: right ✗	LRCC: right ✓
FT-CNN: left ✓	FT-CNN: right ✓	FT-CNN: left ✓	FT-CNN: right ✓
ODL-CNN: left ✓	ODL-CNN: right ✓	ODL-CNN: right ✗	ODL-CNN: left ✗

quite well when the optic disc can be located, scoring an accuracy of 0.9851. However, for 24 test images, ODL-CNN gives no object proposal. Consider the test image #16 in Table 4 for instance. This image shows the symptom of optic disc edema, which makes the boundary of the optic disc mostly invisible. Due to the 24 failures, the accuracy of ODL-CNN is dropped to 0.9767.

Despite its simplicity, LRCC works quite well, with a relative loss of 1.3% compared to FT-CNN. Moreover, LRCC is computationally light, with no need of GPU resources for training and execution. The left-right contrastive strategy is found to be effective. Simply using the 8-dimensional intensity histogram gives an accuracy of 0.9357. Using LBP alone gives an accuracy of 0.9706. Their concatenation brings in a marginal improvement, reaching an accuracy of 0.9718. Using the same feature but without using the contrastive strategy would make the accuracy drop to 0.5266. These results allow us to attribute the effectiveness of LRCC to its left-right contrastive strategy.

3.3 Discussion

As we mentioned in Sect. 1, [14] and [15] are the two initial attempts for left and right eye recognition in fundus images. However, both their code and data are not publicly accessible. Moreover, their models involve a number of hyper parameters that are not clearly documented. Consequently, it is difficult to replicate the two peer works with the same mathematical preciseness as intended by their developers. We therefore do not compare them in our experiments. Taking their recognition accuracy and the test set size into account, *i.e.*, 0.923 on 194 images [14] and 0.941 on 102 images [15], we are confident that the proposed models, with accuracy of over 0.97 on 1,633 images from real scenarios, are the state-of-the-art.

4   Conclusions

For automatic recognition of left and right eye in fundus images, we develop four models, among which ODL-MI and ODL-CNN require optic disc localization, while LRCC and FT-CNN perform holistic classification. Experiments using a set of 11,126 Kaggle images as training data and a new set of 1,633 images as test data support conclusions as follows. Precise localization of optic disc is unnecessary. Moreover, left and right eye recognition can be effectively resolved by determining which half of a fundus image contains the optic disc using the LRCC model. For the state-of-the-art performance, we recommend FT-CNN, which obtains an accuracy of 0.9847 on our test set. When striking a balance between recognition accuracy and computational resource, we recommend LRCC, which has an accuracy of 0.9718.

Acknowledgments. This work was supported by the National Natural Science Foundation of China (No. 61672523), the Fundamental Research Funds for the Central Universities and the Research Funds of Renmin University of China (No. 18XNLG19).

References

1. Cassin, B., Solomon, S.: Dictionary of Eye Terminology. Triad Publishing Company, Gainesville (1990)
2. Gamm, D.M., Albert, D.M.: Blind spot (2011). https://www.britannica.com/science/blind-spot. Accessed 30 July 2018
3. Gargeya, R., Leng, T.: Automated identification of diabetic retinopathy using deep learning. Ophthalmology **124**(7), 962–969 (2017)
4. He, K., Zhang, X., Ren, S., Sun, J.: Deep residual learning for image recognition. In: Proceedings of the CVPR (2016)
5. Kaggle: Diabetic retinopathy detection (2015). https://www.kaggle.com/c/diabetic-retinopathy-detection
6. Oinonen, H., Forsvik, H., Ruusuvuori, P., Yli-Harja, O., Voipio, V., Huttunen, H.: Identity verification based on vessel matching from fundus images. In: Proceedings of the ICIP (2010)
7. Ojala, T., PietikaEinen, M., MaEenpaEaE, T.: Multiresolution gray-scale and rotation invariant texture classification with local binary patterns. T-PAMI **24**(7), 971–987 (2002)
8. Orlando, J., Prokofyeva, E., del Fresno, M., Blaschko, M.: Convolutional neural network transfer for automated glaucoma identification. In: Proceedings of the ISMIPA (2017)
9. Paszke, A., et al.: Automatic differentiation in PyTorch. In: NIPS-W (2017)
10. Pedregosa, F., et al.: Scikit-learn: machine learning in Python. JMLR **12**, 2825–2830 (2011)
11. Pittaras, N., Markatopoulou, F., Mezaris, V., Patras, I.: Comparison of fine-tuning and extension strategies for deep convolutional neural networks. In: Proceedings of the MMM (2017)
12. Ren, S., He, K., Girshick, R., Sun, J.: Faster R-CNN: towards real-time object detection with region proposal networks. T-PAMI **39**, 1137–1149 (2017)
13. Russakovsky, O., et al.: ImageNet large scale visual recognition challenge. IJCV **115**(3), 211–252 (2015)
14. Tan, N.M., et al.: Automatic detection of left and right eye in retinal fundus images. In: Lim, C.T., Goh, J.C.H. (eds.) ICBME 2009, vol. 23, pp. 610–614. Springer, Heidelberg (2009). https://doi.org/10.1007/978-3-540-92841-6_150
15. Tan, N.M., et al.: Classification of left and right eye retinal images. In: Proceedings of the SPIE (2010)
16. van der Walt, S., et al.: the scikit-image contributors: scikit-Image: image processing in Python. PeerJ **2**, e453 (2014)
17. Wei, Q., Li, X., Wang, H., Ding, D., Yu, W., Chen, Y.: Laser scar detection in fundus images using convolutional neural networks. In: Proceedings of the ACCV (2018)

On the Unsolved Problem of Shot Boundary Detection for Music Videos

Alexander Schindler[1]($\boxtimes$) and Andreas Rauber[2]

[1] Center for Digital Safety and Security,
AIT Austrian Institute of Technology GmbH, 1210 Vienna, Austria
`alexander.schindler@ait.ac.at`
`http://ait.ac.at`
[2] Institute of Information Systems Engineering, Vienna University of Technology,
1040 Vienna, Austria
`rauber@ifs.tuwien.ac.at`
`http://www.ifs.tuwien.ac.at`

Abstract. This paper discusses open problems of detecting shot boundaries for music videos. The number of shots per second and the type of transition are considered to be a discriminating feature for music videos and a potential multi-modal music feature. By providing an extensive list of effects and transition types that are rare in cinematic productions but common in music videos, we emphasize the artistic use of transitions in music videos. By the use of examples we discuss in detail the shortcomings of state-of-the-art approaches and provide suggestions to address these issues.

Keywords: Music Information Retrieval · Music videos
Shot boundary detection

1 Introduction

Music videos have recently started to gain attention in the field of Music Information Retrieval (MIR). Various MIR tasks are approached from an audio-visual perspective, including *Artist Identification* [1], *Genre Classification* [2], *Emotion Classification* [3], *Video Synchronization* [4] or *Instrument Detection* [5]. The objectives and added value of analyzing music videos are extensively discussed in [6]. Studies showed that visual information in the context of music is music-related and contributes to ensembles of or combined models [7]. Especially through recent advancements with deep neural networks it is easier to combine acoustic and visual inputs within a single model [5]. In [2] we showed that this relationship is based on the use of a visual language consisting of music-related visual stereotypes (e.g. cowboy hats are predominant visual features in American country music). In [8] a bottom-up evaluation on the performance of various low-level visual features in classifying music videos by their music genre was

© Springer Nature Switzerland AG 2019
I. Kompatsiaris et al. (Eds.): MMM 2019, LNCS 11295, pp. 518–530, 2019.
https://doi.org/10.1007/978-3-030-05710-7_43

performed. An obvious visual feature, that also found its way into everyday language, is music video editing. Scenes in music videos are generally short, ranging in length from only a few seconds to even milliseconds. In movies such short-scene sequences are often referred to as "MTV-style editing". The intentions behind this style of editing and how it diverges from traditional movie editing have been discussed in [2]. The shot-length of music videos is a discriminatory feature to distinguish them from other video categories such as movies, news, cartoons or sports [9]. A shot in a video is defined as an unbroken sequence of images captured by a recording operation of a camera [10]. Shots are joined during editing to compose the final video. The simplest method to accomplish this, are *sharp cuts* where two shots are simply concatenated. Gradual visual effects such as *fades* and *dissolves* are common ways to smooth the transition from one shot to the other.

By inspecting the Music Video Dataset (MVD) [8] it was observed that there are characteristic styles in editing music videos for certain music genres. Also style and complexity of shot transition changed over time with new technologies available. Thus, it was intended to use state-of-the-art shot-detection approaches [11–13] to extract features such as *Shots per Minute, Average Shot Length, Variance in Shot Length* as well as further statistics. Several successful approaches reported to literature [11–13] were implemented and applied to the MVD. During this implementation and evaluation cycle it was observed, that these approaches only apply to the limited set of shot transition styles which are commonly used in movies, sport and news broadcast. Music videos utilize shot transitions in a far more artistic way and use them for example to create tension or express emotions such as distress, horror or melancholy. The biggest challenge in developing an appropriate shot-detection system for music videos is this vast number of transition styles which is further complemented by unconventional camera work such as rapid zooming or panning. A major problem in this regard is the definition of a shot-boundary or transition itself. For example in one of the videos of the MVD-VIS category *Dance* the editor used to skip three or four video frames of a recorded scene to create a rhythmic visual effect. The woman walking from left to right has an unnatural "jump" in her movement while the original scene remains the same. While some of the applied shot-detection systems identified this as shot-boundary, it is still uncertain if this can be defined as a such.

Shot boundary detection is a well researched task [11–13] and some authors consider it already to be solved [13]. In this paper we contradict this view in the context of music videos. We address the issue of missing declarations for music video transition styles and provide an extensive discussion including suggestions on how to approach various problems. In Sect. 2 we provide an overview of common transition types in music videos. Section 3 provides detailed examples of problematic or missing definitions. Section 4 provides an extensive discussion which is set in context with related work and the state-of-the-art in shot-boundary detection. Finally, conclusions and outlooks to future work are provided in Sect. 5.

Fig. 1. Example of Skip Frames. This scene was recorded in a single camera movement, starting from the left corner of the bar and panning to the right until the focus is on two women. The depicted frames show that a large segment was skipped after frame number 3 and a small segment after frame number 11. This is perceived as "jump" replaying this with 25 frames per seconds.

2   Transition-Types in Music Videos

This section lists the most common transition types found in music videos:

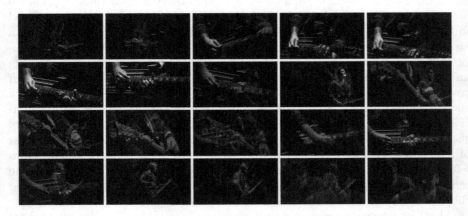

Fig. 2. Example of *Blending* video frames. Within 0.7 s (20 frames at 29 frames per seconds) 7 different scenes are blended.

Sharp Cuts: Two successive scenes are just concatenated. This is the most common transition in music videos.

Gradual Transitions: One scene gradually dissolves into the other. This common cinematic effect is also frequently used in music videos.

Fade-In/Fade-Out: These are gradual transition usually applied as the beginning (Fade-In) or end (Fade-Out) of a video. Scenes dissolve from or to a single-chromatic frame such as a blank black screen.

These effects are common cinematic types of scene transitions. As mentioned in the introduction, shot boundary detection for these types has been extensively studied. More problematic are the following types of transitions. These are artistic variations of common types or new transitions which still need to be defined.

Skip-Frames: A few video frames of a scene are skipped to create rhythmic effects or to increase the pace of the visual flow. Figure 1 depicts a 0.6 s long scene with skipped frames. The scene was originally recorded as a single camera movement. During editing a large and a small segment was removed. While the large edit can be recognized as a cut in the scene, the smaller edit is hardly recognizable in the depicted sequence of video frames. Watching the video with its defined frame-rate, the entire scene is perceived as coherent with both edits being clearly recognizable. Variations include sequences of skip-frames rhythmically aligned to a music sequence or beat.

Jumping back and forth: This effect is similar to skip-frames. The scene does not change but the order of the recorded video frames is altered. This results in perceived back- and forward jumps in the temporal progression. This effect is used intuitively and no generalizable pattern could be recognized. Examples include repetitively jumping back to visualize musical crescendos which dissolve in a new scene synchronously with the music or jumping back and forth to express confusion.

Abrupt tempo changes: The tempo of the recorded scene is altered (e.g. from normal to slow motion or high-speed). Tempo changes can last several seconds or change back quickly (e.g. speeding up for a short time or fast forward like skip-frames). Slowing down is sometimes used to emphasize on a musical transition such as the transition from pre-chorus to chorus.

Frame-Swapping/Flickering: Transition between two scenes where several frames of one video are shown, then several of the other, then again some of the first, and so on, which creates a flickering sensation. This effect is often used with build-ups in electronic dance music, which are crescendoing parts to create tension and excitement often preceding main themes or choruses.

Fast zoom in/out: This effect is partially a transition to a new shot. Within the same scene, the camera quickly zooms in to or out of a certain subject or object. Zoom levels can vary from such as zooming in to the lead singers face and zooming out again the show the entire band, to only minor zoom levels. Again, this effect can be applied several times within the same scene.

Abrupt focal changes: The focus shifts abruptly between fore- and background within a scene. Thus, one area becomes blurred and the other clears. Focus shifts could appear several times within the same scene (e.g. shift between singer and background vocals).

Split-Screen: The video frame is subdivided into multiple, usually rectangular, regions which display different scenes (see Fig. 3). These scenes can change independently and frequently within such a split-screen video scene. Also the number of split-segments can change within such a scene.

Camera Tilts: Camera tilts are fast abrupt pans by the camera. In some videos this is applied between words or lines of the lyrics, tilting away from and back to the singer.

Freezing on a frame: Slowing down to a complete halt and freezing a frame for a certain amount of time. Sometimes followed by a sped up section. A variant of this effect is to freeze in a photography, where the video frame is surrounded by a photo frame and shown for several video frames until the video progresses naturally again.

Spotlights: Spotlights or stage lighting are common equipment used in music videos, especially in videos with artists performing on a stage or in a club like environment. Spots often shining directly into the camera result in several highly or completely illuminated video frames. Some videos put the artists in front of large spots pointed directly at the camera and artistically play with the shadow thrown (see Fig. 9c).

Blending/Fading/Dissolving: Blending, fading and dissolving are effects where one scene gradually transitions to another. Music videos use of dissolves in an exaggerated artistic manner. Figure 2 shows 20 consecutive video frames of a music video. Within these 20 frames - which correspond to 0.7 s at 29 frames per seconds - 7 different scenes are blended in and out. It is not clear when one scene starts and the other ends.

Overlays: Overlays are a popular artistic tool which is applied in manifold ways such as flames blended over Heavy Metal music videos or parts of lyrics as text overlays.

Distortion Effects: Distortion overlays are visual effects applied to video frames and appear in various forms: *heavy blurring* or *distortion, diffusion, rippling, white noise* and many more. Simulation of analog TV screen errors such as *Vertical Roll* or *horizontal or vertical synchronization failures* and *vertical deflection problems* (see Fig. 4) are good examples to show the complexity of shot detection in music videos. Vertical roll is caused by a loss of vertical synchronization and results in a split screen, where the upper part of the image is shifted with the lower part.

Dropping to black: Illumination is dropped to zero over two or three frames. This effect is sometimes used in *Dance* or *Dubstep* music videos to simulate drop beats or to emphasize *drops*. These are sudden changes in the rhythm or bass line and are usually preceded by a build-up section. In music videos such drop frames do not usually indicate a scene change, although possible.

Dancing in front of Green-Box: The artist or a group of people is dancing or acting in front of a green-box. The scenery projected onto the green surface changes rapidly in music videos. While to the viewer it is clear that this is a connected dancing scene, the visual change in the background may confuse a shot-detection system.

3   Examples

This section picks some examples of music videos of the Music Video Dataset (MVD) [8] to visualize some of the introduced problems. To summarize music

Fig. 3. Example of Split-Screen scenes. The video frame is split into various, mostly geometric, regions which display different recorded scenes.

Fig. 4. Example of distortion effects. Blurring and rippling is applied to the video.

video content and visualize its progression over time a mean-color bar is generated. This is achieved by projecting the mean pixel values against the vertical axis of each video frame and each color dimension. This results in a vector representation of the mean color of a video frame in the RGB color space. The mean-color bar is then generated by concatenating the vectors of all consecutive video frames. These bars are a convenient tool and provide a rough overview of the video content. There exist a few easy to recognize patterns which can be directly related to the displayed content. Figure 5 shows examples of mean-color bars generated from music videos of the MVD.

Example 1 - Split Screens and Frame-Swapping/Flickering: Example 1 is track 92 from the *Dance* category taken from the *MVD-VIS* data-set. It is a standard electronic dance music (EDM) track. The video is situated in a dance club. The main plot of the video is to show women dancing to the music. The discussed part of the track is visualized in Fig. 6(a). The leading segment is a split-screen sequence. Figure 6(b) shows an example frame of this sequence. The screen is split horizontally and each sequence shows a different scene. This sequence is followed by a segment with interchanging slow and normal motion recording of a dancing woman which seems to serve as a preparation for the build-up which starts at about the center of the sequence. The audio part is a typical EDM build-up with dropped bass, amplified midst and a crescendoing progression towards the *drop*. The visual part mimics this progression by synchronously swapping between several scenes. An example is given in the greenish segment of Fig. 6(a). In this segment the scenes containing Fig. 6(b) and (c) are swapped six times over 12 consecutive frames. Based on the videos frame-rate of 25 frames per second (fps) this corresponds to 0.48 s or 0.08 s per scene. The hazy ascending regions between the purple and the yellow segment depict, that there is a coherent background scene, over which various different scenes are swapped. This scene is the dancing woman shown in Fig. 6(b). The build-up ends with the drop in the yellow segment - which are yellow flares that are synthetically layed over the captured video frames. After the drop the scene changes to show a crowded

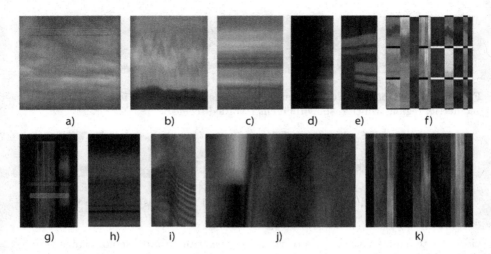

Fig. 5. Mean-color bar examples - each column of an example visualization corresponds to the mean color vector of a video frame projected against the vertical axis in RGB color space. (a) video sequence of the sky with slowly moving clouds. (b) video sequence showing trees and sky. (c) beach, sea and sky. (d) fade-in effect. (e) zooming in on object. (f) split screen video sequences. (g) object or text overlays. (h) camera fixed on object or scene. (i) moving camera focus. (j) gradual and dissolving transitions. (k) sharp cuts.

dance-floor with numerous people dancing. The same patterns of sequential highly illuminated video frames seem continues, but these illuminations originate from the synchronous disco lights in the club. This example was chosen because it addresses three problems defined in Sect. 2 - *Split-screen* sections, *frame-swapping* and *spotlights*.

Example 2 - Multiple mini-cut scenes with static camera view: Example 2 is track 64 from the *Metal* category taken from the *MVD-VIS* data-set. The video features the performing band and the scenery is reduced to a red painted room with graffiti on the wall. The discussed sequence is the bridge section of the song. The singer is in another room with clean walls painted red. The sequence is cut together of multiple independently shot takes in front of a static camera. The order of how these shots are cut together should express the distress the protagonist of the lyrics is currently in. Figure 7(b) shows video frames of a such a sequence. The singer changes abruptly position and posture. A shot lasts between 10 to 20 video frames which are 0.3–0.6 s at 30 fps or approximately 3 shots per second. This example was chosen because it illustrates the controversy towards the current definition of shot boundaries. In Fig. 7(a) large positional changes of the singer are clearly recognizable as sharp cuts. On the other hand, the static camera position creates the impression of a coherent scene. Taking into consideration that this room is only shown for the bridge of the song, this coherent impression improves further. Further, this is a good example of how cinematic techniques are used in an artistic way to express emotion and rhythm.

Example 3 - One-shot Music Videos: One-shot or one-take music videos consist literally of one long take. To present different scenes to different parts of the song, good preparation and many helping hands are required. In a usual setup different scenes are prepared along a trail on which the camera progresses. Artists and stage props move along with the camera and walk in and out of view. Example 3 is track 17 from the *Folk* category taken from the *MVD-VIS* dataset. The video opens with the investigation of a crime scene where a woman has been murdered and continues to tell the story of the curt trial, public media coverage and perception, and ends by lynching the accused. The video uses various visual effects to simulate a one-shot music video. Figure 8(b) depicts such an effect by showing an example sequence of video frames. This sequence corresponds to the mentioned opening sequence. The camera follows a photographer as he approaches the crime scene. Then the camera zooms out of this scene. While the photographer vanishes in the distance, an iris appears as frame around the image. The iris evolves to an eye and further to the face of the victim. This face turns into a photograph taken by the photographer of the previous scene. The camera still keeps zooming out until it can be recognized that the photograph is held by an attorney in a court room. This short sequence features three different scenes. Transitions are created by harnessing dark scenery which virtually hides sharp transitions. The new scene emerges out of the shadow. The other effect zooms in on small objects to hide the background scene. When zooming out again, the object is part of a different scene. These two effects are frequently used in this video. Figure 8(a) depicts that there are no sharp cuts. Further, it is hard to find the transitions at all using the mean-bar visualization.

Example 4 - Artistic Effects: This example discusses four artistic effects applied to music videos. Figure 9(a) - *Folk* 06: The example is taken from the opening of the video. The camera circles around the person while the screen is randomly illuminated by bright white flashes. These flashes are easy recognizable in the mean-color bar. Figure 9(b) - *Indie* 48: This video uses an effect that simulates the degradation of old celluloid films, as they are known from old Silence films. This results in random flickering through alternating illumination and saturation values of successive video frames (as can be seen in the mean-color bar). Figure 9(c) - *Indie* 95: In the chosen scene, a drummer plays on his drums. The camera is aimed directly at a glaring headlight, which is alternately covered by the drummer's arm when playing. The pattern visualized in the mean-color bar is very similar to sharp cut sequences. Figure 9(d) - *Hard Rock* 1: In this video sequence the camera is mounted on a drum-stick while the drummer plays the Hi-Hat cymbals. The abrupt changes create a rhythmic visual pattern depicted in the mean-color bar. The intention behind these four examples is to illustrate the influence of different effects. Naive color based approaches to shot boundary might be prone to wrong detection. While Fig. 9(a) and (b) can be solved with minor modifications, Fig. 9(c) requires dedicated approaches to distinguish this effect from real transitions.

Fig. 6. Example 1: (a) Mean-color-bar to visualize music video activity over time. (b) vertical split-screen section (first segment in a). (b) and (c) in the greenish segment of (a) the video swaps quickly between scene (b) (darker columns) and scene (c) (brighter columns). (Color figure online)

4   Discussion

The authors of summaries on shot boundary detection [11–13] list the most common shot transitions as to be *sharp Cut*, *Dissolve*, *Fade in/out* and *Wipe*. Further transition types are labeled as *Other transition types* and are stated to be difficult to detect, but are rather rare. The experience from assembling the Music Video Dataset (MVD) and the experiments performed to detect shot boundaries showed, that *Other transition types* are more commonly used in music video production including effects applied during editing or recording, which are yet not clearly defined in the context of the shot boundary detection task. Among the identified problems and challenges [12] are:

Detection of Gradual Transitions: A comprehensive overview on the difficulties of detecting dissolving transitions is provided in [14]. *Threshold-Based approaches* detect transitions by comparing similarities between frames in feature space. To detect *Fade In/out*, monochrome frame detection based on mean and standard deviation of pixel intensity values [14,15] is used. Thresholds are commonly set globally [16] which is generally estimated empirically

Fig. 7. Example 2: Cut scene of multiple independent takes with static camera. (a) Mean-color-bar visualizes recognizable shot edges for large positional changes. (b) Example frames of the consecutive shots which are not longer than a few video frames. Singer abruptly changes position and orientation with every sharp cut. (Color figure online)

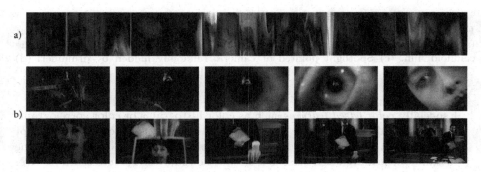

Fig. 8. Example 3: One-shot music video. (a) Mean-color-bar depicting that there are no sharp cuts in the video. (b) example video frames of the starting sequence of the music video. These frames demonstrate how zooming out is used to transition between scenes.

or adaptable [17] using a sliding window function - or a combination of both [18]. Combinations of Edge Detectors and Motion Features are used to train a Support Vector Machine (SVM) [19] which is applied in a sliding window to detect gradual changes. Most of these approaches are not invariant towards the artistic effects described in the previous section. Especially global threshold based approaches will provide inaccurate predictions on the various kinds of *Overlays* applied to music videos. Another problem is, that many blended music video sequences do not dissolve in a new shot, but the faded in sequence is faded out again and dissolves back into the original scene. Combinations with motion and audio features are reported including thresholding with Hidden Markov Models (HMM) [20]. In music videos audio features are not reliable because the transitions are not aligned nor correlated with changes in song structures such as chord changes or progressions from verse to chorus. **Disturbances of Abrupt Illumination Change:** Most features used in shot boundary detection are not invariant to abrupt changes in illumination.

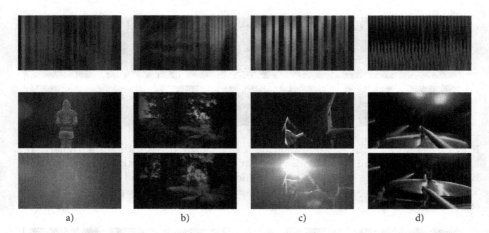

Fig. 9. Example 4: Four examples of visual effects applied to music video frames. (a) flashlights illuminating the entire video frame. (b) silent-film effect of degrading celluloid film. (c) Spotlight pointed at camera, randomly hidden by drummer. (d) Camera mounted on drum-stick while playing the Hi-Hat cymbals.

Especially *color based features* such as color histograms or color correlograms [21] are based on luminance information of different color channels. Abrupt changes such as spotlights or overlays cause discontinuities in inter-frame distances which are often classified as shot boundaries. *Texture based features* such as Tamura features, wavelet transform-based texture features or Gabor wavelet filters [22] are more robust against changes in illumination but are vulnerable to abrupt changes in textures such as motion blurring caused by fast camera panning and tilts.

Disturbances of Large Object/Camera Movement: As mentioned in the previous paragraph, fast camera movements or large moving objects in front of the camera affect the feature response of most features used in shot boundary detection, resulting in erroneous predictions of shot boundaries. Especially, fast camera movements are very frequent in music videos. Movement in any way is used to create tension or to bring a person into scene by circling around them.

Generally it can be summarized, that most approaches to shot-boundary detection presented in literature harness or rely on a wide range of rules and definitions. These may either be based on physical conditions such as spatio-temporal relationships between consecutive frames, or on rules developed by the art of film-making. For example the use of audio features [20] is based on the observation that dissolving transitions are more often used with scene changes than with transitions within the same scene. This includes a change of the sound scene, which is harnessed to augment the detector. As extensively elaborated in [2], do music videos deliberately not stick to these rules. Of course, many of the challenges listed in Sect. 2 can already be solved, but not by a general approach.

Most of them are exceptions to commonly known problems and require distinct detection approaches. For example, concerning the problem of rapid sequences of dissolving scenes as depicted in Fig. 2, one solution could be to interpret this sequence as a scene by itself. Again, a custom model or an exception handling to existing models has to be implemented for this. Further, some points listed still require a broader discussion on whether they should be considered a transition and if so, how it should be labeled.

5 Conclusions and Future Work

This paper discussed open issues of shot boundary detection for music videos. The number of shots per seconds as well as the type of transition is considered to be a significant feature for discriminating music videos by genre or mood. We listed various transition types observed in the Music Video Dataset (MVD) and discussed why those could be problematic for state-of-the-art shot boundary detection approaches. These issues are not insoluble. However, many of these effects require dedicated solutions or detectors to process them. Some issues require a broader discussion to define their category such as whether or not they are shot transitions. More problematic is, that this is only an abstract of examples and that music video creators regularly develop new creative effects. It is yet conceivable that approaches based on Recurrent Convolutional Neural Networks [23] are able to learn the different visual effects and transition types. To pursue such experiments, ground truth labels are required for the Music Video Data-set or another data-set. To facilitate the creation of such annotations we have crated an interactive tool, which is provided as open-source software[1].

For *future work* it would be required to come to mutual definition concerning labeling the various artistic effects applied in music videos and whether or not they are considered to be types of transitions. Based on these definitions, it would then be of interest to evaluate if on the one approaches can be found to detect these transitions, and on the other hand, the frequency of their application is correlated with music characteristics such as genre, style or mood.

References

1. Schindler, A., Rauber, A.: A music video information retrieval approach to artist identification. In: Proceedings of the 10th International Symposium on Computer Music Multidisciplinary Research, CMMR 2013, Marseille, France, 14–18 October 2013 (2013, to appear)
2. Schindler, A., Rauber, A.: Harnessing music-related visual stereotypes for music information retrieval. ACM Trans. Intell. Syst. Technol. 8(2), 20:1–20:21 (2016)
3. Tripathi, S., Acharya, S., Sharma, R.D., Mittal, S., Bhattacharya, S.: Using deep and convolutional neural networks for accurate emotion classification on DEAP dataset. In: Twenty-Ninth IAAI Conference, pp. 4746–4752 (2017)
4. Macrae, R., Anguera, X., Oliver, N.: MuViSync: realtime music video alignment. In: 2010 IEEE International Conference on Multimedia and Expo, ICME, pp. 534–539. IEEE (2010)

---

[1] https://blinded.for.review.

5. Slizovskaia, O., Gómez, E., Haro, G.: Musical instrument recognition in user-generated videos using a multimodal convolutional neural network architecture. In: Proceedings of the ACM on International Conference on Multimedia Retrieval, ICMR 2017, pp. 226–232 (2017)
6. Schindler, A.: A picture is worth a thousand songs: exploring visual aspects of music. In: Proceedings of the 1st International Workshop on Digital Libraries for Musicology, DLfM 2014 (2014)
7. Oramas, S., Nieto, O., Barbieri, F., Serra, X.: Multi-label music genre classification from audio, text, and images using deep features. CoRR, abs/1707.04916 (2017)
8. Schindler, A., Rauber, A.: An audio-visual approach to music genre classification through affective color features. In: Hanbury, A., Kazai, G., Rauber, A., Fuhr, N. (eds.) ECIR 2015. LNCS, vol. 9022, pp. 61–67. Springer, Cham (2015). https://doi.org/10.1007/978-3-319-16354-3_8
9. Iyengar, G., Lippman, A.B.: Models for automatic classification of video sequences. In: Storage and Retrieval for Image and Video Databases VI, vol. 3312, pp. 216–228. International Society for Optics and Photonics (1997)
10. Hampapur, A., Weymouth, T., Jain, R.: Digital video segmentation. In: Proceedings of the 2nd ACM International Conference on Multimedia, pp. 357–364. ACM (1994)
11. Cotsaces, C., Nikolaidis, N., Pitas, I.: Video shot detection and condensed representation. A review. IEEE Signal Process. Mag. 23(2), 28–37 (2006)
12. Yuan, J., et al.: A formal study of shot boundary detection. IEEE Trans. Circ. Syst. Video Technol. 17(2), 168–186 (2007)
13. Smeaton, A.F., Over, P., Doherty, A.R.: Video shot boundary detection: seven years of TRECVID activity. Comput. Vis. Image Underst. 114(4), 411–418 (2010)
14. Lienhart, R.W.: Reliable dissolve detection. In: Storage and Retrieval for Media Databases, vol. 4315, pp. 219–231. International Society for Optics and Photonics (2001)
15. Zheng, W., Yuan, J., Wang, H., Lin, F., Zhang, B.: A novel shot boundary detection framework. In: Visual Communications and Image Processing, vol. 5960, p. 596018. International Society for Optics and Photonics (2006)
16. Cernekova, Z., Pitas, I., Nikou, C.: Information theory-based shot cut/fade detection and video summarization. IEEE Trans. Circ. Syst. Video Technol. 16(1), 82–91 (2006)
17. Xia, D., Deng, X., Zeng, Q.: Shot boundary detection based on difference sequences of mutual information. In: Fourth International Conference on Image and Graphics, ICIG 2007, pp. 389–394. IEEE (2007)
18. M Quśenot, G., Moraru, D., Besacier, L.: CLIPS at TRECVID: shot boundary detection and feature detection (2003)
19. Zhao, Z.-C., Zeng, X., Liu, T., Cai, A.-N.: BUPT at TRECVID 2007: shot boundary detection. In: TRECVID (2007)
20. Boreczky, J.S., Wilcox, L.D.: A hidden Markov model framework for video segmentation using audio and image features. In: ICASSP, vol. 98, pp. 3741–3744 (1998)
21. Amir, A., et al.: IBM research TRECVID-2003 video retrieval system. NIST TRECVID-2003 7(8), 36 (2003)
22. Hauptmann, A., et al.: Confounded expectations: Informedia at TRECVID 2004. In: Proceedings of TRECVID (2004)
23. Baraldi, L., Grana, C., Cucchiara, R.: Hierarchical boundary-aware neural encoder for video captioning. In: 2017 IEEE Conference on Computer Vision and Pattern Recognition, CVPR, pp. 3185–3194. IEEE (2017)

Enhancing Scene Text Detection via Fused Semantic Segmentation Network with Attention

Chao Liu[1], Yuexian Zou[1,2(✉)], and Dongming Yang[1]

[1] ADSPLAB, School of ECE, Peking University, Shenzhen, China
zouyx@pkusz.edu.cn
[2] Peng Cheng Laboratory, Shenzhen, China

Abstract. Scene text detection (STD) in natural images is still challenging since text objects exhibit vast diversity in fonts, scales and orientations. Deep learning based state-of-the-art STD methods are promising such as PixelLink which has achieved 85% accuracy on ICDAR 2015 benchmark. Our preliminary experimental results with PixelLink have shown that its detection errors come mainly from two aspects: failing to detect the small scale and ambiguous text objects. In this paper, following the powerful PixelLink framework, we try to improve the STD performance via delicately designing a new fused semantic segmentation network with attention. Specifically, an inception module is carefully designed to extract multi-scale receptive field features aiming at enhancing feature representation. Besides, a hierarchical feature fusion module is cascaded with the inception module to capture multi-level inception features to obtain more semantic information. At last, to suppress background disturbance and better locate the text objects, an attention module is developed to learn a probability heat map of texts which helps accurately infer the texts even for ambiguous texts. Experimental results on three public benchmarks demonstrate the effectiveness of our proposed method compared with the state-of-the-arts. We note that the highest F-measure on ICADR 2015, ICADR 2013 and MSRA-TD500 has been obtained for our proposed method but the higher computational cost is required.

Keywords: Scene text detection (STD) · Semantic segmentation Hierarchical feature fusion · Attention mechanism

1 Introduction

Recently, scene text reading in the wild is an active research in the computer vision which has made tremendous progress under the development of deep convolutional neural networks (DCNNs). Scene text reading can be divided into two main sub-tasks: scene text detection (STD) and scene text recognition. We focus on the task of STD in this study which is the crucial step for robust scene reading. It is noticed that STD is still challenging since text instances often exhibit vast diversity in fonts, scales and arbitrary orientations with various illumination affects.

© Springer Nature Switzerland AG 2019
I. Kompatsiaris et al. (Eds.): MMM 2019, LNCS 11295, pp. 531–542, 2019.
https://doi.org/10.1007/978-3-030-05710-7_44

Nowadays, deep learning based methods [1–3] directly learn hierarchical features from training data, which demonstrates more accurate and efficient performance in various STD public benchmarks. From literatures, we category the DCNN based STD methods into two mainstream approaches, namely bounding box regression method (BBR-STD) and semantic segmentation method (SS-STD). BBR-STD method predicts the offsets between the bounding box proposals and the corresponding ground truth [4], e.g. SSTD [2] and CTPN [5]. It is noted that SSTD and CTPN are essentially derived from Faster-RCNN [6] and SSD [7] frameworks. Differently, SS-STD method converts the STD task into the instance-aware semantic segmentation task which predicts a category label for each pixel [1, 8].

From the recent literature study, it is clear that the SS-STD methods have achieved better performance than BBR-STD methods. For example, PixelLink [1] achieves the state-of-the art on several public benchmarks. However, our preliminary experimental results with PixelLink have shown that it did not perform well in detecting small-scale and ambiguous text objects in the scene images. Carefully evaluation on of PixelLink shows that the feature maps in the higher layers remain less detail information which is not able to maintain good representation of small-scale and ambiguous text objects. However, the lower layers remain enough detail information of the text objects. Therefore, it is easy to understand that the performance of STD can be improved by jointly using the feature information from the higher layers and lower layers simultaneously in certain manner.

In this study, we are inspired by the excellent performance of PixelLink and drive to improve its STD performance especially in detecting small-scale text and ambiguous text objects. Specifically, we designed the novel inception module and the hierarchical feature fusion module to enhance the feature representation which especially benefit in detecting small-scale text objects. Meanwhile, an attention module is proposed to improve detecting the ambiguous text objects. It is noted that the proposed attention module learns a probability heat-map of texts which provides the location information of the texts existing in the image and especially benefits for detecting ambiguous text objects. Experimental results on three public benchmarks demonstrate the effectiveness of our proposed method compared with the state-of-the-arts, where we acquire the highest F-measure on ICADR 2015, ICADR 2013 and MSRA-TD500.

The remaining of the paper is organized as follows. Section 2 introduces the related work of our study. Section 3 presents pipelines and algorithms of our proposed method. Section 4 shows the experimental results. Finally, Sect. 5 draws the conclusions.

2 Related Work

Detecting the text objects in the natural images has been extensively studied in the past few years, motivated by many real-world applications, such as photo OCR and blind navigation. Along with the development of DCNNs for object detection [6, 7], the performance of the DCNN-based text detection algorithm also improves a lot. For the STD tasks, the STD problem could be roughly divided into two categories: Horizontal text detection [9, 10] and Multi-oriented text detection [1, 2]. At present, the multi-oriented text detection has become the hottest research topic since the proposed horizontal text detection methods cannot work well when there are blurred, multi-oriented, low-resolution and small-scale texts in the natural images. It is clear that there are two mainstream methods: bounding box regression methods (BBR-STD) [2, 11–14] and semantic segmentation methods (SS-STD) [1, 3].

BBR-STD methods followed the advance of object detection frameworks such as Faster-RCNN [6] and SSD [7], they consist two steps which are object classification and bounding box regression for localization. Research showed that the rotation-invariant feature maps improve the performance of object classification but have trivial contribution on enhancing the performance of bounding box regression of text objects [14]. To balance the conflict between classification and regression, a state-of-the-art BBR-STD method [3] proposed to separate the regression task from the classification task, and achieved better performance in mainstream public STD benchmarks. However, it still has limitations on multi-oriented STD task, especially for small-scale and ambiguous text objects.

Differing from BBR-STD methods, SS-STD methods eliminate the process of regression. Thus, compared with BBR-STD methods, SS-STD methods have achieved outstanding performance on STD task since reducing the fail and miss detection during regression. SS-STD methods are normally derived under segmentation algorithms (such as the fully convolutional networks, or FCN [15]) framework to identify image areas that are likely to contain texts at pixel-level. The developed SS-STD methods [4, 16, 17] have attempted to convert text object detection task into instance-aware semantic segmentation task. It is noted that separating text objects distinctly from semantic segmentation map is difficult since text objects in images normally are very close to each other. To address this problem, a method [12] proposed to predict three different score maps are generated, including text/non-text score map, character classes score map, and character linking orientations score map. Then, this method integrated these three score maps into a semantic segmentation map to obtain words or lines detection. Another method named TextBlocks [11] proposed to generate a saliency map, and then the MSER algorithm is adopted to obtain character objects. Lately, the state-of-the-art SS-STD method named PixelLink [1] followed the FCN framework to generate two different score maps: text/non-text score map and link predicting score map, the text objects are detected by post-processing. Since SS-STD methods above eliminate the process of regression, we can obtain accurate multi-oriented location information via semantic segmentation map. It can be seen from the above observations that SS-STD methods bring the state-of-arts performance in detecting multi-oriented of text objects. From another side, we also noted that SS-STD methods employ several pipelines which are computational inefficient [17].

Utilizing the superiorities of SS-STD methods, in this study, we proposed an end-to-end trainable framework to improve the performance of STD task by focusing on effectively detecting small-scale and ambiguous texts in multi-orientated and shapes.

3 Methodology

In this section, the pipeline and algorithms of our proposed methods are described in details. The pipeline of our method is depicted in Fig. 1. From Fig. 1, it can be seen that our method mainly consists of five parts which are integrated into a FCN framework.

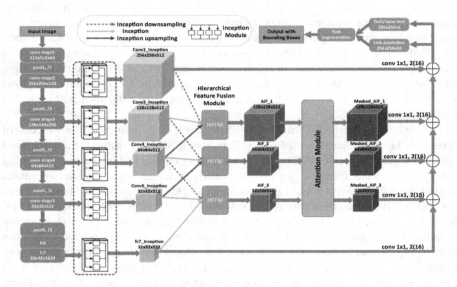

Fig. 1. The architecture of our proposed method. The inception modules are in red dotted box, the grey 2D blocks represent HFFMs, and the blue 2D block represents attention module. (Color figure online)

First part is the feature extraction where the convolutional features of the input image are extracted by VGG-16 backbone [18] as shown in green color in Fig. 1. In our design, following VGG-16, conv1 to conv5 are kept unchanged, and fc6 and fc7 are transformed into the convolutional layers. Second part is our designed inception modules (dotted box in red in Fig. 1) which targets at generating new feature maps with multi-scale receptive fields. Details of our designed inception module will be depicted in Sect. 3.1. Third part is termed as the hierarchical feature fusion module (HFFM) (blocks in grey in Fig. 1) which is proposed to enhance the feature representation to improve the detection performance on small-scale texts. The output of the HFFM is denoted as by the Aggravating multi-layer Inception Features (AIFs). Details of the HFFM will be depicted in Sect. 3.2. The fourth part is the attention module (block in blue in Fig. 1) which is carefully designed to improve the detection performance on ambiguous texts, via getting the location information of the text objects more accurately. Details of the attention module will be depicted in Sect. 3.3. Finally, the fifth part is kept the same as the PixelLink. Specifically, the Masked_AIFs in different layers are fed into the network to generate the text/non-text score map and link predicting score map, respectively. Then, the detection results are obtained by post-processing via OpenCV. Details will be depicted in Sect. 3.4.

3.1 Inception Module

Inspired by the designed inception model in GoogLeNet [19], we redesign a new Inception Module to capture multi-scale receptive field features. In our design, convolutional kernels with different size in different channel are used, which can focus on image content in a wide scope of scales. Using this approach, we need to consider the dramatic increase in computational cost caused by the convolution operation. Here, we use the dimensionality reduction strategy by employing 1×1 kernel. Meanwhile, we consider reducing the amount parameters caused by multi-channel structure and large kernel size. In this design, we adopt dilated convolutional approach [20] for implementing large kernel filters which is able to expend the area of receptive field exponentially without increase of the amount of parameters and decrease of its spatial dimensions. Therefore, our designed inception module is able to generate better features efficiently at the reasonable computational cost.

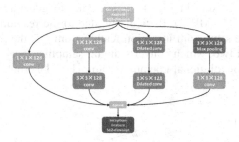

Fig. 2. Our designed inception module. The input convolutional features come from *conv2_3*, *conv3_3*, *conv4_3*, *conv5_3*, and *fc7*, respectively.

The structure of our designed Inception Module is plotted in Fig. 2. From Fig. 2, we can see that our Inception Module has four channels to process the input convolutional features in parallel. Specifically, the input of the module is a 512-dimision convolutional feature from each layer in VGG-16. The first channel is 1×1 *conv*, which has 128-dimision. The second channel is 3×3 *conv* with 1×1 *conv*, which both have 128-dimision. The third channel is 3×3 *maxpooling* with 1×1 *conv*, which both have 128-dimision. The fourth channel is 5×5 *conv* which is divided into 5×1 and 1×5 dilated convolution layers [21], which both have 128-dimision. In this study, we set the dilation rate as 2.0 for considering the computational efficiency. The final output of the inception module is a 512-dimision inception feature map which is generated by concatenating four 128-dimision features. We set five same inception modules side by side after VGG-16 as shown in Fig. 1, which can obtain five inception feature maps with 512-dimision.

3.2   Hierarchical Feature Fusion Modules (HFFM)

To further enhance the convolutional features and improve the performance of small-scale text detection, we designed the Hierarchical Feature Fusion Modules (HFFM) which are cascaded with the inception modules as we mentioned above to aggravate multi-level inception features. Our basic idea comes from the observations: for general object detection framework, the higher recall value can be achieved by employing deeper networks but the capability of object localization goes worse under this condition. Paying close attention to this phenomenon, we noted that the features in lower layers focus on image details which benefits localization, especially for small objects. Meanwhile, the higher layers contain more abstract semantic information which benefits object classification. Therefore, we design a hierarchical feature fusion module to balance this disequilibrium to capture the traits of features in lower and higher layers in the CNN, which benefits to obtain both location information and abstract semantic information. Moreover, in our design, we also take the computational cost into account.

Our detailed design is shown in Fig. 3, the output of this module is computed by three adjacent layers: the upper layer, the intermediate layer and the under layer. Down-sampling and up-sampling are utilized on the upper layer and under layer respectively, which keep the same resolution with the intermediate layer. The element-wise addition is implemented for aggravating multi-layer inception features (AIFs). There are three HFFMs are set side by side in Fig. 1, which aims to generate three AIFs of 512-dimision (AIF_1, AIF_2, AIF_3). Particularly, due to the resolution of inception feature from *conv5* is the same with inception feature from *fc7*, the third HFFM is a little different with the first two, which converts the up-sampling inception feature from *fc7* into scale-invariant convolutional operation with a 1×1 kernel.

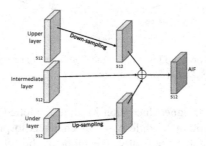

Fig. 3. The structure of proposed hierarchical feature fusion module (HFFM).

3.3   Attention Module

A large amount of ambiguous text objects exists in scene images, which greatly affect the performance of text detection. To improve the accuracy, these ambiguous texts must be considered. We designed an attention module to automatically learn rough spatial regions of text from convolutional features. Then we encoded it back into the features which suppressed the background disturbance and enhance the location information of texts in the feature map. The mechanism of this module is to learn a probability heat map of texts. Moreover, the procedure of learning the attention map is in a supervised manner, an auxiliary loss via a binary mask is adopted which indicates the text/non-text at each pixel location. Then a softmax function is used to optimize this attention map towards the provided text binary mask, explicitly encoding strong location information into the attention module.

The functions of this module are shown as follows:

$$\alpha = softmax(Conv_{1\times1}(deconv_{3\times3}(F_{AIF\_1}))) \tag{1}$$

$$F_{Masked\_AIF} = resize(\alpha^+) \odot F_{AIF} \tag{2}$$

The input images are processed by network we designed to obtain three AIFs, as shown in Fig. 1. We merely take AIF_1 as the input of Function (1), since it has more contextual information which can benefit learning attention map. Specifically, we use deconvolutional operation to up-sample AIF_1 ($R^{128\times128\times512}$) into the same resolution with original input images ($R^{512\times512\times3}$), named it as AIF_1_resized ($R^{512\times512\times512}$). After this procedure, we use a 1×1 *conv* to filter the AIF_1_resized, which is further projected to 2-channel maps ($R^{512\times512\times2}$). Then a softmax function is adopted, the positive output of softmax (α^+) is defined as the attention map. Finally, the learned attention map will be resized into appropriate resolution with three AIFs, and we fused these attention maps into AIFs to obtain three AIFs with attention, named them as Masked_AIF_1, Masked_AIF_2, and Masked_AIF_3.

The framework of this module is depicted in Fig. 4. The process of this module benefits for reducing false text detection and improves the performance of ambiguous text detection. The framework finally improves the accuracy of text detection.

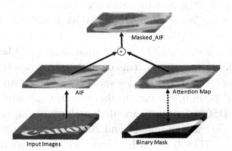

Fig. 4. The structure of attention module. We visualized the feature maps in the middle of procedures in this module. We can easily observe that contextual information in the feature map has been enhanced after this module.

3.4 FCN Framework and Post-processing

After the process of dedicated design modules we proposed above, we can obtain a new set of convolutional features, which are two original inception features and three Masked_AIF, as shown in Fig. 1. Then, we followed the PixelLink framework to acquire the final semantic segmentation maps to obtain two separate maps, filtering by two sets of 1×1 *conv* with different channels, one for text/non-text prediction (1×2), and the other (2×8) for link prediction. For link design, we followed PixelLink where every pixel has 8 neighbors if they lie within the same instance, the link between them is labeled as positive, otherwise negative. Therefore, the channel of link prediction map is 2×8. Meanwhile, the loss function followed strategy of PixelLink [1].

Post-processing procedure includes Connected Components (CC) algorithm and invoking *minAreaRect* function. CC algorithm pieces the predicted positive pixels together while invoke *minAreaRect* function in OpenCV obtains the bounding boxes of CCs as the final detection results.

4   Experiments and Analysis

To evaluate our proposed method, we conduct extensive experiments on three mainstream benchmarks: ICDAR2013 (IC13) [22], ICDAR2015 (IC15) [23], and MSRA-TD500 (TD500) [12]. Full results are compared with state-of-the-art performance on these three benchmarks.

4.1   Datasets

ICDAR 2015 Incidental Text (IC15) is the challenge 4 of ICDAR2015 Robust Reading Competition which is collected by using Google Glass. This dataset contains 1500 images in total: 1000 images for training and the remained 500 images for testing. This benchmark is designed for evaluating multi-oriented text detection. Annotations of the dataset are given in word-level quadrilaterals. This dataset is more challenging than others because it includes images with arbitrary orientations, motion blur, and low-resolution ambiguous text. We evaluate our results based on the online evaluation system.

ICDAR 2013 (IC13) consists 229 training images and 233 testing images, and the images are with word-level annotation. This dataset is designed for near-horizontal text detection which focuses on world-level evaluation. Our results were obtained by uploading the predicted bounding boxes to the official evaluation system.

MSRA-TD500 (TD500) is multi-oriented and multi-lingual both Chinese and English. It consists of 300 training images and 200 testing images. Different from IC15 and IC13, annotations of TD500 are at line level which are rotated rectangles.

SynthText in the Wild (SynthText) contains 800,000 synthetic images [10] in total. Text with random colors, fonts, scale and orientation are rendered on natural images carefully to have a realistic look. Annotations are given in character, word and line level.

We take data augmentation strategy for training sets of IC15, IC13 and TD500 before fine-tune procedure. We followed SSD [7] and PixelLink [1], which rotated images at a probability of 0.2, by a random angle of 0, $\pi/2$, π or $3\pi/2$ firstly. Then randomly crop them with areas ranging from 0.1 to 1, and aspect ratios of the images are ranging from 0.5 to 2. At last, images are resized uniformly to 512×512. As for the text instances in the processed images, the shorter side less than 10 pixels are ignored. After the procedure of data augmentation, we can obtain enough data for fine-tune.

4.2 Implementation Details

Training. Our experiments are conducted on two NVIDIA Titan X GPUs with 12 GB memory each. The whole algorithm is implemented in pyTorch-0.4.0 and python-3.6. Firstly, we pre-trained our proposed method on the subset of SynthText which contains 160,000 images for 120 K iterations, then we fine-tune the model on IC15, IC13 and TD500 respectively. The training starts from a randomly initialized VGG-16 model. The training images are all with resolution of 512×512. The well-known training manner Stochastic Gradient Descent (SGD) is used for our training. Meanwhile, momentum and weight decay are set as 0.9 and 0.0005 respectively. Base learning rate is set as 0.0001 for the first 1000 iterations and is fixed at 0.001 for the rest. As for the fine-tune procedure on three benchmarks, data augmentation strategy we mentioned above is adopted for training set. Due to implementation in pyTorch, we need to convert the ground truth of SynthText (.mat) into format of txt during pre-processing.

Testing. Input images are resized into 1280×768, 512×512 and 768×768 for IC15, IC13 and TD500 respectively. During post-processing, *minAreaRect* function in OpenCV is invoked to obtain the bounding boxes of CCs as the final detection results.

4.3 Results

Table 1 shows results of the proposed Text-Detector on IC15 compared with previous state-of-the-art methods. We use the augmentation of data from IC15 training set to fine-tune the pre-trained model on SynthText for 60K iterations. The characteristic of this dataset is multi-scale and multi-oriented. From the results shown in Table 1 we can see that our method achieves the highest score of Recall (0.85) and F-measure (0.78) which demonstrates our method is more robust for STD than previous methods.

Table 1. Results on ICDAR 2015 incidental dataset

Method	Year	Precision	Recall	F-measure
EAST [22]	2017	0.83	0.78	0.81
SegLink [17]	2017	0.73	0.77	0.75
He et al. [13]	2017	0.80	0.82	0.81
RRD + MS [23]	2018	**0.88**	0.80	0.84
PixelLink [16]	2018	0.85	0.82	0.84
Proposed	-	0.87	**0.85**	**0.86**

Results on IC13 are shown in Table 2 along with other state-of-the-art methods. We use the augmentation of data from IC13 training set to fine-tune the pre-trained model on SynthText for 15K iterations. This dataset is designed for near-horizontal text detection which focuses on world-level evaluation. It is clearly to conclude that our method is comparable for near-horizontal word-level text detection task and even provides more accurate detection results since we get the highest Recall (0.90) and F-measure (0.89).

Table 2. Results on ICDAR 2013 dataset

Method	Year	Precision	Recall	F-measure
TextBoxes [11]	2017	0.86	0.74	0.80
SegLink [24]	2017	0.88	0.83	0.85
CTPN [5]	2017	**0.93**	0.83	0.87
SSTD [2]	2017	0.88	0.86	0.87
PixelLink [1]	2018	0.87	0.89	0.88
Proposed	-	0.89	**0.90**	**0.89**

Our method also shows nice performance on MSRA-TD500 Dataset. We use the augmentation of data from TD-500 training set to fine-tune the pre-trained model on SynthText for 25K iterations. The characteristic of this data is multi-oriented and multi-lingual. We can see that our method obtains the highest F-measure (0.81) which manifests our method have better performance in multi-lingual scene images than others (Table 3).

Table 3. Results on MSRA-TD500 dataset

Method	Year	Precision	Recall	F-measure
RRPN [25]	2017	0.82	0.68	0.74
EAST [21]	2017	0.87	0.67	0.76
SegLink [24]	2017	0.86	0.70	0.77
RRD [14]	2018	**0.87**	0.73	0.79
PixelLink [1]	2018	0.73	**0.83**	0.78
Proposed	-	0.86	0.76	**0.81**

Detection results on several challenging images are shown in Fig. 5, where our text detector can localize many extremely challenging texts. It is important to point out that the word-level detection by our method is particularly accurate, especially for small-scale texts and ambiguous texts. Some challenging texts are even tough for human to point them out, but our method can detect them with appropriate rotational bounding boxes clearly.

Fig. 5. Detection results by the proposed method. Some small-scale and ambiguous texts can be detected by our proposed method.

5 Conclusion

We present an end-to-end accurate multi-oriented scene text detector, following the powerful PixelLink framework via semantic segmentation. The inception module, the hierarchical feature fusion module and the attention module are carefully designed and integrated into FCN frameworks for making full use of the properties of convolutional networks. Finally the framework improve the performance of small-scale and ambiguous text detection. Experimental results validate the effectiveness of proposed method, which outperforms previous state-of-the-art text detection approaches on three typical benchmarks. Our method achieved the both highest recall and F-measure on the on IC13 and IC15 respectively and achieve the highest F-measure on the TD500. Although we obtain excellent performance on three public benchmarks, the speed of our algorithm is not fast enough, which takes 3.2 s for detecting one image on a NVIDIA Titan X GPU. For the reason of detection efficiency of our algorithm is not meet need to real-time processing, what we're going to do is to improve the efficiency of our algorithm.

Acknowledgment. This paper was partially supported by the Shenzhen Science & Technology Fundamental Research Program (No.: JCYJ20160330095814461) & Shenzhen Key Laboratory for Intelligent Multimedia and Virtual Reality (ZDSYS201703031405467). Special Acknowledgements are given to Aoto-PKUSZ Joint Research Center of Artificial Intelligence on Scene Cognition & Technology Innovation for its support.

References

1. Deng, D., Liu, H., Li, X., Cai, D.: PixelLink: detecting scene text via instance segmentation (2018)
2. He, P., Huang, W., He, T., Zhu, Q., Qiao, Y., Li, X.: Single shot text detector with regional attention. In: IEEE International Conference on Computer Vision, pp. 3066–3074 (2017)

3. Dai, Y., Huang, Z., Gao, Y., Chen, K.: Fused text segmentation networks for multi-oriented scene text detection (2017)
4. He, W., Zhang, X.Y., Yin, F., Liu, C.L.: Deep direct regression for multi-oriented scene text detection, pp. 745–753 (2017)
5. Tian, Z., Huang, W., He, T., He, P., Qiao, Y.: Detecting text in natural image with connectionist text proposal network. In: Leibe, B., Matas, J., Sebe, N., Welling, M. (eds.) ECCV 2016. LNCS, vol. 9912, pp. 56–72. Springer, Cham (2016). https://doi.org/10.1007/978-3-319-46484-8_4
6. Ren, S., He, K., Girshick, R., Sun, J.: Faster R-CNN: towards real-time object detection with region proposal networks. IEEE Trans. Pattern Anal. Mach. Intell. **39**, 1137–1149 (2017)
7. Liu, W., et al.: SSD: single shot MultiBox detector. In: Leibe, B., Matas, J., Sebe, N., Welling, M. (eds.) ECCV 2016. LNCS, vol. 9905, pp. 21–37. Springer, Cham (2016). https://doi.org/10.1007/978-3-319-46448-0_2
8. Dai, J., He, K., Sun, J.: Instance-aware semantic segmentation via multi-task network cascades. In: Computer Vision and Pattern Recognition, pp. 3150–3158 (2016)
9. Zhang, Z., Shen, W., Yao, C., Bai, X.: Symmetry-based text line detection in natural scenes. In: IEEE Conference on Computer Vision and Pattern Recognition, pp. 2558–2567 (2015)
10. Gupta, A., Vedaldi, A., Zisserman, A.: Synthetic data for text localisation in natural images. In: IEEE Conference on Computer Vision and Pattern Recognition, pp. 2315–2324 (2016)
11. Liao, M., Shi, B., Bai, X., Wang, X., Liu, W.: TextBoxes: a fast text detector with a single deep neural network (2016)
12. Yao, C., Bai, X., Liu, W.: A unified framework for multioriented text detection and recognition. IEEE Trans. Image Process. **23**, 4737–4749 (2014)
13. Nagaoka, Y., Miyazaki, T., Sugaya, Y., Omachi, S.: Text detection by faster R-CNN with multiple region proposal networks. In: IAPR International Conference on Document Analysis and Recognition, pp. 15–20 (2017)
14. Liao, M., Zhu, Z., Shi, B., Xia, G., Bai, X.: Rotation-sensitive regression for oriented scene text detection (2018)
15. Long, J., Shelhamer, E., Darrell, T.: Fully convolutional networks for semantic segmentation. In: IEEE Conference on Computer Vision and Pattern Recognition, pp. 3431–3440 (2015)
16. He, T., Huang, W., Qiao, Y., Yao, J.: Accurate text localization in natural image with cascaded convolutional text network (2016)
17. Zhang, Z., Zhang, C., Shen, W., Yao, C., Liu, W., Bai, X.: Multi-oriented text detection with fully convolutional networks. In: Computer Vision and Pattern Recognition, pp. 4159–4167 (2016)
18. Simonyan, K., Zisserman, A.: Very deep convolutional networks for large-scale image recognition. Comput. Sci. (2014)
19. Szegedy, C., et al.: Going deeper with convolutions, pp. 1–9 (2014)
20. Yu, F., Koltun, V.: Multi-scale context aggregation by dilated convolutions (2016)
21. Zhou, X., et al.: EAST: an efficient and accurate scene text detector, pp. 2642–2651 (2017)
22. Karatzas, D., et al.: ICDAR 2013 robust reading competition. In: International Conference on Document Analysis and Recognition, pp. 1484–1493 (2013)
23. Karatzas, D., et al.: ICDAR 2015 competition on robust reading. In: International Conference on Document Analysis and Recognition, pp. 1156–1160 (2015)
24. Shi, B., Bai, X., Belongie, S.: Detecting oriented text in natural images by linking segments, pp. 3482–3490 (2017)
25. Ma, J., et al.: Arbitrary-oriented scene text detection via rotation proposals. IEEE Trans. Multimed. **PP**, 1 (2017)

Exploiting Incidence Relation Between Subgroups for Improving Clustering-Based Recommendation Model

Zhipeng Wu, Hui Tian$^{(\boxtimes)}$, Xuzhen Zhu, Shaoshuai Fan, and Shuo Wang

State Key Laboratory of Networking and Switching Technology,
Beijing University of Posts and Telecommunications, Beijing 100876, China
{wzp,tianhui,zhuxuzhen,fanss,wangshuo16}@bupt.edu.cn

Abstract. Matrix factorization (MF) has been attracted much attention in recommender systems due to its extensibility and high accuracy. Recently, some clustering-based MF recommendation methods have been proposed in succession to capture the associations between related users (items). However, these methods only use the subgroup data to build local models, so they will suffer the over-fitting problem caused by insufficient data in the process of training. In this paper, we analyse the incidence relation between subgroups of users (items) and then propose two single improved clustering-based MF models. Through exploiting these relations between subgroups, the local model in each subgroup can obtain global information from other subgroups, which can mitigate the over-fitting problem. Above all, we generate an ensemble model by combining the two single models for capturing associations between users and associations between items at the same time. Experimental results on different scales of MovieLens datasets demonstrate that our method outperforms state-of-the-art clustering-based recommendation methods, especially on sparse datasets.

Keywords: Recommender system · Clustering method
Matrix factorization · Incidence relation

1 Introduction

Recommender systems are ubiquitous in our daily life especially in multimedia online services, such as movie recommendation [1] and mobile application recommendation [3]. It can help users find valuable information from large amounts of data effectively and mitigate the problem of information overload [14]. Because recommendation algorithms have a direct impact on the performance of recommender system, researchers have proposed many improved recommendation algorithms, among which collaborative filtering (CF) is the most salient algorithm for rating prediction task in recommender systems [8].

CF-based methods exploit interactive information between users and items to predict the degree of users' interests in items which they have not interacted yet

© Springer Nature Switzerland AG 2019
I. Kompatsiaris et al. (Eds.): MMM 2019, LNCS 11295, pp. 543–555, 2019.
https://doi.org/10.1007/978-3-030-05710-7_45

[19]. Generally, there are two major categories of CF-based methods: memory-based CF and model-based CF. Memory-based CF methods find the neighbors of the target user by using similarity measurement techniques, and then aggregate the neighbors' ratings to predict the values of unrated items [2]. Although the memory-based CF methods are simple and effective, their performances are severely affected by the sparsity of datasets. To alleviate this problem, model-based CF methods use machine learning algorithms to learn from the interaction information between users and items. Among all model-based CF methods, matrix factorization (MF) has received increasingly widespread attention in recommender systems due to its extensibility and high accuracy [10].

MF factorizes the sparse rating matrix into the user latent factor matrix and the item latent factor matrix, and makes predictions for unknown ratings by the dot product between two latent factor vectors. On this basis, many improved MF approaches have been proposed, such as Bayesian probabilistic matrix factorization [16], dynamic matrix factorization [7], non-negative matrix factorization [12], etc. Although these methods have achieved good results in recommender systems, the performance of these methods may degrade among a small set of strongly related items [9]. Consequently, it's helpful to mine the local associations between users (items) for improving the accuracy of recommendation.

In order to capture the local associations from interactive information, recently, many clustering-based MF recommendation models have been proposed. O'Connor et al. [6] first apply clustering methods to memory-based CF methods, they partition the item space into several clusters for discovering relationships between items. But the performance of this method has not been significantly improved because of only using partial data will lead to over-fitting. Yuan et al. [18] consider each user has multiple types of behaviors and then divide the item latent factor into several groups, so items in each group have the same type of user behavior, but this method needs user's different behavior data such as movie ratings, music ratings and social relation. Chen et al. [5] apply the co-clustering method on the rating matrix to produce a set of different clustering results, and design an ensemble strategy to generate the final rating prediction. However, this ensemble strategy has high time complexity. Recently, Chen et al. [11] combine the global model and local model to capture the unique interests and the common interests of users, and in [4] they embed global information in local MF models to enhance the accuracy.

Different from the above methods, in this paper, we propose a new clustering-based MF model for dealing with the over-fitting problem in clustering-based methods. First, after utilizing the clustering method to divide users (items) into several subgroups, we consider the incidence relation between them, and then add the corresponding constraint term to the objective function. Therefore, when training the local model, local latent factors can be adjusted according to the information of other subgroups, which alleviates the over-fitting problem caused by insufficient data. Next, we propose an ensemble strategy to combine the two single models (user-based model and item-based model) for capturing local associations of users and items at same time. In addition, an improved clustering method is proposed based on [4], in which users (items) are divided by their rating distributions. Finally, we evaluate our models on different scales of MovieLens datasets, and our ensemble model gets better performance than other state-of-the-art MF-based methods in prediction accuracy.

2 Preliminaries

In this section, we describe the problems to be solved in recommender systems and the basic framework of MF-based recommendation algorithms.

2.1 Problem Definition

In a common recommender system, we usually have m users, n items and users' ratings on some items. Therefore, we can obtain the sparse user-item rating matrix $\mathbf{R} \in \mathbb{R}^{m \times n}$. Each value $r_{i,j} \in \mathbf{R}$ denotes the user i's rating on item j, and $\hat{r}_{i,j}$ denotes the predicted value of the user i on item j. The goal of this paper is to accurately predict users' ratings on their non-interactive items based on the rating matrix $\mathbf{R}$.

2.2 Matrix Factorization

Matrix factorization is one of the most popular techniques in recommender systems [10]. It factorizes the rating matrix $\mathbf{R}$ into two low-rank latent factor matrices $\mathbf{U} \in \mathbb{R}^{m \times f}$ and $\mathbf{V} \in \mathbb{R}^{f \times n}$ such that $\mathbf{R} \approx \mathbf{U}\mathbf{V}$. In addition, the parameter f is the number of latent factors and $f \ll \min(m, n)$. The predicted value $\hat{r}_{i,j}$ is defined as:

$$\hat{r}_{i,j} = \mathbf{u}_{i,.}\mathbf{v}_{.,j}, \tag{1}$$

where $\mathbf{u}_{i,.}$ is the i-th row of user latent factor matrix $\mathbf{U}$ and $\mathbf{v}_{.,j}$ is the j-th column of item latent factor matrix $\mathbf{V}$. The regularized squared error objective function can be written as:

$$\arg\min_{\mathbf{U},\mathbf{V}} \sum_{(i,j) \in T} (r_{i,j} - \hat{r}_{i,j})^2 + \lambda(||\mathbf{U}||_F^2 + ||\mathbf{V}||_F^2), \tag{2}$$

where λ is the parameter of regularization term, $||\cdot||_F$ denotes the Frobenius norm and T denotes the training set of the (user, item) pairs. On this basis, Paterek [13] considers that some users and items have different rating tendencies, and adds biases to the rating prediction formula:

$$\hat{r}_{i,j} = \mu + b_i + b_j + \mathbf{u}_{i,.}\mathbf{v}_{.,j}, \tag{3}$$

where μ is the global mean value, b_i and b_j denote the bias of user i and the bias of item j, respectively. This method has been widely concerned because of its good performance.

3   Proposed Method

In this section, we demonstrate our improved clustering-based MF single model and then introduce the framework of ensemble model. Moreover, we introduce the process of optimization, and propose a new clustering method for further improving the accuracy of recommendation.

3.1   Single Model

Many common clustering-based MF models [5,6,18] don't consider the incidence relation between subgroups. Although these methods can find the strong local associations between users (items), however, they will suffer the over-fitting issue due to only use partial user (item) data when training the local model. For dealing with this problem, we consider exploiting the incidence relation between subgroups to adjust the latent factors in local models for getting good performance.

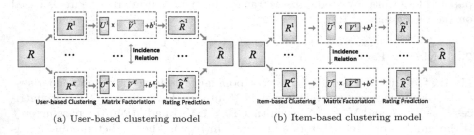

(a) User-based clustering model   (b) Item-based clustering model

Fig. 1. Framework of two single models

As it is depicted in Fig. 1(a), we first use a clustering method to divide users into K subgroups, and then generate K submatrices $\{\mathbf{R}^1, \mathbf{R}^k, \ldots, \mathbf{R}^K\}$ from the original rating matrix $\mathbf{R}$. For each submatrix $\mathbf{R}^k \in \mathbb{R}^{m_k \times n}$, m^k represents the number of users in k-th subgroup. We define the rating prediction formula as:

$$\hat{r}_{i,j}^k = b_i^k + \mathbf{u}_{i,\cdot}^k \tilde{\mathbf{v}}_{\cdot,j}^k, \tag{4}$$

where b_i^k represents the bias of user i, $\mathbf{u}_{i,\cdot}^k$ and $\tilde{\mathbf{v}}_{\cdot,j}^k$ represent i-th row of user latent factor matrix $\mathbf{U}^k \in \mathbb{R}^{m_k \times f}$ and j-th column of item latent factor matrix $\tilde{\mathbf{V}}^k \in \mathbb{R}^{f \times n}$, respectively. Different from the Eq. (3), we don't add the bias of item because the submatrix $\mathbf{R}^k$ only contains partial ratings of each item, so the bias of item will not be learned accurately in the submatrix.

The submatrix $\mathbf{R}^k$ has all the ratings made by users in k-th subgroup, so the user latent factor vector $\mathbf{u}_{i,\cdot}^k$ can be learned using the full rating data of each user. In contrast, because each submatrix $\mathbf{R}^k$ only contains partial ratings of each item, for each item latent factor vector $\tilde{\mathbf{v}}_{\cdot,j}^k$, it will suffer from insufficient data issue compared with $\mathbf{u}_{i,\cdot}^k$ in training process. For solving this problem, we consider item j's each local latent factor vector $\tilde{\mathbf{v}}_{\cdot,j}^k$ has the incidence relation in the latent space. In other words, the item j's local latent factor vectors $\{\tilde{\mathbf{v}}_{\cdot,j}^1, \tilde{\mathbf{v}}_{\cdot,j}^2, \ldots, \tilde{\mathbf{v}}_{\cdot,j}^k\}$ in different local models should be close to each other, because they represent the latent factor vectors of the same item j in latent space. Based on this idea, we add the constraint term to the overall objective function:

$$\underset{b_i^k, \mathbf{U}^k, \tilde{\mathbf{V}}^k}{\arg\min} \sum_{k=1}^{K} \Big(\sum_{(i,j)\in R^k} (r_{i,j}^k - \hat{r}_{i,j}^k)^2 w_{i,j} + \lambda_v \frac{1}{K-1} \sum_{l=1,l\neq k}^{K} \left\| \tilde{\mathbf{V}}^k - \tilde{\mathbf{V}}^l \right\|_F^2 + \lambda f_{reg}^k \Big),$$

(5)

where λ and λ_v represent the regularization parameters. $w_{i,j}$ represents the reliability of each rating and can be easily obtained from [17], f_{reg}^k represents the general regularization term to prevent the over-fitting:

$$f_{reg}^k = \left\| \mathbf{U}^k \right\|_F^2 + \left\| \tilde{\mathbf{V}}^k \right\|_F^2 + \sum_{i=1}^{m^k} (b_i^k)^2.$$

(6)

In this way, local item latent factors can be adjusted according to the incidence relation with other subgroups. We call this clustering-based model IRCMF-u.

Similarly, the framework of item-based single model (IRCMF-i) is shown in Fig. 1(b). We divide all items into C subgroups and generate C submatrices $\{\mathbf{R}^1, \mathbf{R}^c, \ldots, \mathbf{R}^C\}$ by using the clustering method. For each submatrix $\mathbf{R}^c \in \mathbb{R}^{m \times n^c}$, n^c represents the number of items in c-th item subgroup. The prediction formula for each rating in $\mathbf{R}^c$ is defined as:

$$\hat{r}_{i,j}^c = b_j^c + \tilde{\mathbf{u}}_{i,\cdot}^c \mathbf{v}_{\cdot,j}^c,$$

(7)

where b_j^c represents the bias of item j, $\mathbf{v}_{\cdot,j}^c$ and $\tilde{\mathbf{u}}_{i,\cdot}^c$ represent the item j's latent factor vector and the user i's latent factor vector of the c-th submatrix, respectively. Because each item subgroup only contains partial ratings of each user, for each user latent factor vector $\tilde{\mathbf{u}}_{i,\cdot}^c$, it will suffer from insufficient data issue compared with $\mathbf{v}_{\cdot,j}^c$ in training process. We consider the latent factor vectors $\{\tilde{\mathbf{u}}_{i,\cdot}^1, \tilde{\mathbf{u}}_{i,\cdot}^2, \ldots, \tilde{\mathbf{u}}_{i,\cdot}^c\}$ in different local models should be close to each other, because they represent the latent factor vectors of the same user i in latent space. Therefore, same as the Eq. (5), we also add the constraint term to the overall objective function:

$$\underset{b_j^c, \tilde{\mathbf{U}}^c, \mathbf{V}^c}{\arg\min} \sum_{c=1}^{C} \Big(\sum_{(i,j)\in R^c} (r_{i,j}^c - \hat{r}_{i,j}^c)^2 w_{i,j} + \lambda_u \frac{1}{C-1} \sum_{l=1,l\neq c}^{C} \left\| \tilde{\mathbf{U}}^c - \tilde{\mathbf{U}}^l \right\|_F^2 + \lambda f_{reg}^c \Big),$$

(8)

where λ, λ_u represent the regularization parameters. f_{reg}^c represents the general regularization term to prevent the over-fitting:

$$f_{reg}^c = \|\mathbf{V}^c\|_F^2 + \left\| \tilde{\mathbf{U}}^c \right\|_F^2 + \sum_{j=1}^{n^c} (b_j^c)^2,$$

(9)

3.2 Ensemble Model

The above two kinds of single models are built based on the perspective of users and items, receptively. In order to capture local associations of users and items at the same time, we propose an ensemble strategy to combine the user-based model and the item-based model.

After dividing users into K subgroups and dividing items into C subgroups, we can obtain the $K \times C$ user-item submatrices by splitting the original rating matrix $\mathbf{R}$ based on these subgroups. For each submatrix $\mathbf{R}^{k,c}$, users in $\mathbf{R}^{k,c}$ belongs to the k-th user subgroup and items in $\mathbf{R}^{k,c}$ belongs to the c-th item subgroup. We define the prediction formula $\hat{r}_{i,j}^{k,c}$ of the each rating in $\mathbf{R}^{k,c}$ as:

$$\hat{r}_{i,j}^{k,c} = (\alpha \mathbf{u}_{i,\cdot}^k + \beta \tilde{\mathbf{u}}_{i,\cdot}^c)(\beta \mathbf{v}_{\cdot,j}^c + \alpha \tilde{\mathbf{v}}_{\cdot,j}^k) + \alpha b_i^k + \beta b_j^c. \tag{10}$$

Equation (10) combines the two single models (IRCMF-u and IRCMF-i). In IRCMF-u, $\mathbf{u}_{i,\cdot}^k$ is learned from all historical records of user i, while the corresponding item latent factor vector $\tilde{\mathbf{v}}_{\cdot,j}^k$ is only learned from partial item data. In contrast, in IRCMF-i, $\mathbf{v}_{\cdot,j}^c$ is learned from all ratings of item j and $\tilde{\mathbf{u}}_{i,\cdot}^c$ is learned from user i's partial data. We combine $\tilde{\mathbf{v}}_{\cdot,j}^k$ of the user-based model and the $\mathbf{v}_{\cdot,j}^c$ of the item-based model to generate the integrated item latent factor vector $\bar{\mathbf{v}}_{\cdot,j}^{k,c} = \beta \mathbf{v}_{\cdot,j}^c + \alpha \tilde{\mathbf{v}}_{\cdot,j}^k$. Similarly, the integrated user latent factor vector $\bar{\mathbf{u}}_{i,\cdot}^{k,c} = \alpha \mathbf{u}_{i,\cdot}^k + \beta \tilde{\mathbf{u}}_{i,\cdot}^c$ is generated by $\mathbf{u}_{i,\cdot}^k$ and $\tilde{\mathbf{u}}_{i,\cdot}^c$. Consequently, each rating $r_{i,j}^{k,c}$ in submatrix $\mathbf{R}^{k,c}$ is inextricably linked with submatrices $\mathbf{R}^k$ and $\mathbf{R}^c$ through this ensemble strategy. It can capture local associations between users and local associations between items at the same time, and mitigate the problem of insufficient user (item) related data in $\mathbf{R}^{k,c}$.

In Eq. (10), we control the contribution of the two single models by adjusting the values of α and β. If we set $\alpha = 1$ and $\beta = 0$, the ensemble model becomes the user-based single model (IRCMF-u) because it only considers the subgroups of users. Obviously, when $\alpha = 0$ and $\beta = 1$, the ensemble model becomes the item-based single model (IRCMF-i), so we set $\beta = 1 - \alpha$ for simplicity. Finally, the objective function is defined as:

$$\underset{b_i^k, b_j^c, \mathbf{U}^k, \tilde{\mathbf{V}}^k, \tilde{\mathbf{U}}^c, \mathbf{V}^c}{\arg \min} \sum_{k=1}^{K} \sum_{c=1}^{C} \sum_{(i,j) \in R^{k,c}} (r_{i,j}^{k,c} - \hat{r}_{i,j}^{k,c})^2 w_{i,j} + \sum_{k=1}^{K} \left(\lambda f_{reg}^k + \right.$$
$$\left. \frac{\lambda_v}{K-1} \sum_{l=1, l \neq k}^{K} \left\| \tilde{\mathbf{V}}^k - \tilde{\mathbf{V}}^l \right\|_F^2 \right) + \sum_{c=1}^{C} \left(\lambda f_{reg}^c + \frac{\lambda_u}{C-1} \sum_{l=1, l \neq c}^{C} \left\| \tilde{\mathbf{U}}^c - \tilde{\mathbf{U}}^l \right\|_F^2 \right). \tag{11}$$

We call this ensemble model IRCMF.

3.3 Optimization

In this section, we take the ensemble model as an example to demonstrate the optimization process. Stochastic gradient descent (SGD) is a popular method to solve the optimization problem in MF-based methods due to its high efficiency and simplicity [10], so we use SGD to solve the problem in Eq. (11).

First, for each observed rating $r_{i,j}^{k,c}$ in $\mathbf{R}^{k,c}$, we should calculate the prediction error $e_{i,j}^{k,c} = r_{i,j}^{k,c} - \hat{r}_{i,j}^{k,c}$. Next, we calculate the partial derivative of each parameter when the other irrelevant parameters are fixed, and get the opposite direction of the gradient. The update rules are as follows:

$$b_i^k \leftarrow b_i^k + \eta(\alpha \bar{e}_{i,j}^{k,c} - \lambda b_i^k), \tag{12}$$

$$b_j^c \leftarrow b_j^c + \eta(\beta \bar{e}_{i,j}^{k,c} - \lambda b_j^c), \tag{13}$$

$$\mathbf{u}_{i,\cdot}^k \leftarrow \mathbf{u}_{i,\cdot}^k + \eta(\alpha \bar{e}_{i,j}^{k,c} (\bar{\mathbf{v}}_{\cdot,j}^{k,c})^T - \lambda \mathbf{u}_{i,\cdot}^k), \tag{14}$$

$$\mathbf{v}_{\cdot,j}^c \leftarrow \mathbf{v}_{\cdot,j}^c + \eta(\beta \bar{e}_{i,j}^{k,c} (\bar{\mathbf{u}}_{i,\cdot}^{k,c})^T - \lambda \mathbf{v}_{\cdot,j}^c), \tag{15}$$

$$\tilde{\mathbf{u}}_{i,\cdot}^c \leftarrow \tilde{\mathbf{u}}_{i,\cdot}^c + \eta\big(\beta \bar{e}_{i,j}^{k,c} (\bar{\mathbf{v}}_{\cdot,j}^{k,c})^T - \lambda \tilde{\mathbf{u}}_{i,\cdot}^c - \lambda_u \sum_{l=1,l\neq c}^{C} \frac{\tilde{\mathbf{u}}_{i,\cdot}^c - \tilde{\mathbf{u}}_{i,\cdot}^l}{C-1}\big), \tag{16}$$

$$\tilde{\mathbf{v}}_{\cdot,j}^k \leftarrow \tilde{\mathbf{v}}_{\cdot,j}^k + \eta\big(\alpha \bar{e}_{i,j}^{k,c} (\bar{\mathbf{u}}_{i,\cdot}^{k,c})^T - \lambda \tilde{\mathbf{v}}_{\cdot,j}^k - \lambda_v \sum_{l=1,l\neq k}^{K} \frac{\tilde{\mathbf{v}}_{\cdot,j}^k - \tilde{\mathbf{v}}_{\cdot,j}^l}{K-1}\big), \tag{17}$$

where $\bar{e}_{i,j}^{k,c} = e_{i,j}^{k,c} w_{i,j}$ and η is the learning rate. When the number of iterations reaches the maximum value or the objective function converges, we will stop updating and then make predictions on the unrated items for each user.

3.4   Clustering Method

Using appropriate clustering methods to find strongly associated users and items is crucial to the performance of our model. K-means is one of the most popular clustering methods in machine learning, but the dimension of original user (item) rating vector is high which will cost more computation time in the process of clustering. Chen et al. [4] proposed the domain-specific data-projected clustering (DSDP) method. They replaced the original rating vector with the probability distribution of the rating value's frequency to reduce the dimension of rating vectors. However, the number of ratings of each user is different, when users make new ratings, the rating probability distribution of users with a small number of ratings will be changed greatly compared with users with large number of ratings. Therefore, we consider adding the number of unrated items as a statistical parameter to alleviate this problem.

For example, if the rating scale is from 1 to 5, we use $N_i^1, N_i^2, N_i^3, N_i^4, N_i^5$ to represent the corresponding number of ratings of user i. Instead of calculating the probability distribution directly like DSDP, we add N_i^0 as a statistical parameter to represent the number of unrated items. It is defined as: $N_i^0 = N - \sum_{z=1}^{5} N_i^z$. We set N equal to the total number of items n, therefore, the probability distribution vector of user i is $[\frac{N_i^0}{N}, \frac{N_i^1}{N}, \frac{N_i^2}{N}, \frac{N_i^3}{N}, \frac{N_i^4}{N}, \frac{N_i^5}{N}]$. Certainly, if the rating scale is continuous, we should discretize each rating first. The difference of the two probability distributions is measured by the Kullback-Leibler (KL) divergence:

$$D_{KL}(p^i||q^k) = \sum_{z=0}^{Z} p_z^i log \frac{p_z^i}{q_z^k}, \tag{18}$$

where Z is the number of rating scale, p^i represents the probability distribution vector of user i and q^k represents the cluster center vector of cluster k. The clustering process of users is shown in Algorithm 1 and the clustering process of items is similar. We call this clustering method Improved DSDP (IDSDP).

Algorithm 1. IDSDP Clustering Method for Users

Input: rating matrix $\mathbf{R}$; the number of users' subgroup K; number of iterations It;
Output: K user subgroups;

1: Get the probability distribution of all users;
2: Randomly initialize K cluster center probability distribution vectors q^k; $I = 0$;
3: **while** $I < It$ or not converged **do**
4:     **for** each user probability distribution vector p^i **do**
5:         **for** each cluster center vectors q^k **do**
6:             calculate $D_{KL}(p^i||q^k)$;
7:         **end for**
8:         assign user i to the closest cluster k;
9:     **end for**
10:    **for** each cluster k **do**
11:        calculate the average distribution $\bar{q}^k$, and then $q^k \leftarrow \bar{q}^k$;
12:    **end for**
13:    $I \leftarrow I + 1$;
14: **end while**

---

4   Experiments

In this section, we introduce the information of MovieLens dataset and the evaluation metric used in our experiments, and make comprehensive experiments to measure the performance of our proposed method.

4.1   Datasets

MovieLens[1] dataset collects real ratings of the user from MovieLens website, and it is extensively used to evaluate the performance of recommendation algorithms. In our experiments, we use three different scales of MovieLens datasets: MovieLens 100K, MovieLens 1M and MovieLens 10M. Each user in MovieLens

---

[1] https://grouplens.org/datasets/movielens/.

dataset has at least 20 ratings on items, and the range of rating value is from 1 to 5. Table 1 shows the basic information of the three datasets. For each dataset, we randomly take 90% of the data as training set and the remaining as the test set. This process is carried out five times and we present the average results in our experiments.

Table 1. Statistics of datasets

Dataset	Users	Items	Ratings	Sparsity	Rating scale
MovieLens 100K	943	1,682	100,000	93.70%	{1,2,3,4,5}
MovieLens 1M	6,040	3,952	1,000,209	95.80%	{1,2,3,4,5}
MovieLens 10M	69,878	10,677	10,000,054	98.66%	{1,2,3,4,5}

4.2 Evaluation Metric

Root mean squared error (RMSE) is extensively used to evaluate the performance of recommender system. So we adopt RMSE as evaluation metric in our experiments. RMSE is defined as: $\sqrt{\sum_{(u,i) \in D} (r_{u,i} - \hat{r}_{u,i})^2 / |D|}$, where D represents the test set of (user, item) pairs and $|D|$ represents the set size.

4.3 Parameter Setting

In our experiments, we set the initial value of learning rate $\eta = 0.007$ and use grid search to find the best parameters of λ, λ_u and λ_v. Therefore, we choose $\lambda = 0.02$, $\lambda_u = 0.5$ and $\lambda_v = 0.5$ in our experiments. The maximum number of iterations is set to 150. Other parameters such as the number of clusters, α, β and the number of latent factors f will be discussed in next section.

4.4 Results and Discussion

Single Model and Ensemble Model. We first analyze the impact of the trade-off parameters α, β in ensemble model. For parameter setting, the number of latent factors $f = 20$, $K = 2$ and $C = 2$.

As shown in Fig. 2(a), the performance of ensemble model on three datasets reaches the best when α is around 0.6. When $\alpha = 0$ or $\alpha = 1$, the performance is poor due to the ensemble model becomes the single model. Therefore, we choose $\alpha = 0.7$ for Movielens 100K and $\alpha = 0.6$ for the other two datasets in ensemble model. Next, we compare the performance of single model and ensemble model on three datasets. The results are shown in Fig. 2(b), (c) and (d). We can see that the IRCMF outperforms the two single models (IRCMF-u and IRCMF-i) on all latent factors f, and the value of RMSE reaches a stable level when $f \geqslant 80$. This indicates IRCMF-u and IRCMF-i only capture one kind of associations, while IRCMF can capture both item associations and user associations for improving recommendation accuracy.

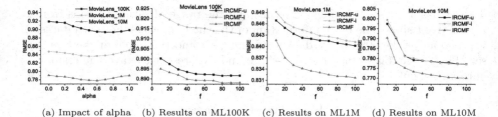

(a) Impact of alpha   (b) Results on ML100K   (c) Results on ML1M   (d) Results on ML10M

Fig. 2. Comparison between single model and ensemble model

Impact of Clustering Method. Obviously, the clustering method and the numbers of clusters K, C have significant influence on the performance of IRCMF. We compare the performance of four different clustering methods: random partition, K-means, DSDP method and our proposed IDSDP method. As for the number of clusters K, C, we set $K, C \in \{2, 3, 4\}$.

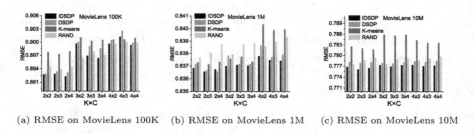

(a) RMSE on MovieLens 100K   (b) RMSE on MovieLens 1M   (c) RMSE on MovieLens 10M

Fig. 3. Performance on three datasets under different number of clusters

We can see from Fig. 3 that the values of RMSE on three datasets are lower when $K = 2$. In contrast, with the increase of K and C, the prediction accuracy of all clustering methods gradually decreases due to each subgroup contains less and less data. For the impact of clustering methods, we can see that the performance of K-means is the worst method on Movielens 10M dataset. It is because sparse user data and sparse item data make the K-means method hard to find strongly related neighbors. In addition, it can be seen from the comparison between DSDP and IDSDP that the performance of IDSDP has a certain improvement on three datasets. Especially on MovieLens 10M dataset, IDSDP obtains the best values of RMSE (0.7761) when $K = 2$ and $C = 3$, which are 0.002 and 0.0017 lower than that of DSDP. It indicates that the number of unrated users (items) is an important factor affecting the performance of clustering. Consequently, the IDSDP method can improve the recommendation accuracy of IRCMF.

Performance Comparison. We compare our ensemble model with five state-of-the-art rating prediction models: probabilistic matrix factorization (PMF) [15], biased probabilistic matrix factorization (BPMF) [13], WEMA [5], MPMA [11] and GLOMA [4]. Among them, WEMA, MPMA and GLOMA are the recent cluster-based MF models, which are closely related to our model. Because the size of three datasets is different, we set $f = 20$ for Movielens 100K and 1M datasets, and set $f = 200$ for Movielens 10M dataset. From the analysis of the previous section, we set $K = 2$ and $C = 3$ to get the best result in our model.

Table 2. Performance comparison on RMSE

Dataset	PMF	BPMF	WEMA	MPMA	GLOMA	IRCMF
MovieLens 100K	0.9097	0.9041	0.9021	0.9003	0.8975	**0.8929**
MovieLens 1M	0.8457	0.8426	0.8415	0.8389	0.8378	**0.8369**
MovieLens 10M	0.7718	0.7709	0.7705	0.7695	0.7672	**0.7668**

As it is shown in Table 2, the performance of basic MF methods (PMF and BPMF) has a certain gap compared with other clustering-based MF methods, this is because basic MF methods are hard to capture the associations between users or items. Moreover, IRCMF obtains the lowest value of RMSE on three datasets. For example, on Movielens 10M dataset, the RMSE of IRCMF is 0.7668 which is 0.0041 lower than that of BPMF and 0.0004 lower than that of state-of-the-art clustering-based method GLOMA. The reason is that IRCMF can capture both associations between users and associations between items, and use the incidence relation between subgroups to mitigate the problem of the insufficient data in local model.

5   Conclusion

In this paper, we exploit the incidence relation between subgroups for improving clustering-based recommendation model. Each local model can be adjusted according to the information of other subgroups. Based on this idea, we design the user-based single model and the item-based single model, and then combine them to generate the ensemble model for further improving the performance. In addition, an improved clustering method is proposed which considers the impact of the number of unrated users (items) on the clustering results. Experimental results show that the performance of our ensemble model is superior to the state-of-the-art clustering-based MF recommendation methods.

Acknowledgments. This work was supported by the National Natural Science Foundation of China (No. 61602048) and the Fundamental Research Funds for the Central Universities (No. NST20170206).

References

1. Basilico, J., Raimond, Y.: Recommending for the world. In: Proceedings of the 10th ACM Conference on Recommender Systems, pp. 375–375. ACM, Boston (2016)
2. Bell, R.M., Koren, Y.: Scalable collaborative filtering with jointly derived neighborhood interpolation weights. In: Proceedings of the 2007 Seventh IEEE International Conference on Data Mining, pp. 43–52. IEEE Computer Society, Washington, DC (2007)
3. Cao, D., et al.: Cross-platform app recommendation by jointly modeling ratings and texts. ACM Trans. Inf. Syst. **35**(4), 37:1–37:27 (2017)
4. Chen, C., Li, D., Lv, Q., Yan, J., Shang, L., Chu, S.: GLOMA: embedding global information in local matrix approximation models for collaborative filtering. In: AAAI Conference on Artificial Intelligence (2017)
5. Chen, C., Li, D., Zhao, Y., Lv, Q., Shang, L.: WEMAREC: accurate and scalable recommendation through weighted and ensemble matrix approximation. In: International ACM SIGIR Conference on Research and Development in Information Retrieval, pp. 303–312 (2015)
6. O'Connor, M.: Clustering items for collaborative filtering. In: ACM SIGIR Workshop on Recommender Systems: Algorithms and Evaluation (1999)
7. Devooght, R., Kourtellis, N., Mantrach, A.: Dynamic matrix factorization with priors on unknown values. In: Proceedings of the 21st International Conference on Knowledge Discovery and Data Mining, pp. 189–198. ACM (2015)
8. Hu, J., Li, P.: Collaborative filtering via additive ordinal regression. In: Proceedings of the 11th ACM International Conference on Web Search and Data Mining, pp. 243–251. ACM, Marina Del Rey (2018)
9. Koren, Y.: Factorization meets the neighborhood: a multifaceted collaborative filtering model. In: Proceedings of the 14th International Conference on Knowledge Discovery and Data Mining, pp. 426–434. ACM, Las Vegas (2008)
10. Koren, Y., Bell, R., Volinsky, C.: Matrix factorization techniques for recommender systems. Computer **42**(8), 30–37 (2009)
11. Li, D., Chen, C.: MPMA: mixture probabilistic matrix approximation for collaborative filtering. In: International Joint Conference on Artificial Intelligence (2016)
12. Luo, X., Zhou, M., Li, S., You, Z., Xia, Y., Zhu, Q.: A nonnegative latent factor model for large-scale sparse matrices in recommender systems via alternating direction method. IEEE Trans. Neural Netw. Learn. Syst. **27**(3), 579–592 (2016)
13. Paterek, A.: Improving regularized singular value decomposition for collaborative filtering. In: Proceedings of KDD Cup and Workshop (2007)
14. Ricci, F., Rokach, L., Shapira, B.: Recommender systems: introduction and challenges. In: Ricci, F., Rokach, L., Shapira, B. (eds.) Recommender Systems Handbook, pp. 1–34. Springer, Boston (2015). https://doi.org/10.1007/978-1-4899-7637-6_1
15. Salakhutdinov, R., Mnih, A.: Probabilistic matrix factorization. In: International Conference on Neural Information Processing Systems, pp. 1257–1264 (2007)
16. Salakhutdinov, R., Mnih, A.: Bayesian probabilistic matrix factorization using Markov chain Monte Carlo. In: Proceedings of the 25th International Conference on Machine Learning, pp. 880–887. ACM, Helsinki (2008)
17. Wu, Z., Tian, H., Zhu, X., Wang, S.: Optimization matrix factorization recommendation algorithm based on rating centrality. In: Tan, Y., Shi, Y., Tang, Q. (eds.) DMBD 2018. LNCS, vol. 10943, pp. 114–125. Springer, Cham (2018)

18. Yuan, T., Cheng, J., Zhang, X., Qiu, S., Lu, H.: Recommendation by mining multiple user behaviors with group sparsity. In: AAAI Conference on Artificial Intelligence, pp. 222–228 (2014)
19. Zhang, J., Chow, C., Xu, J.: Enabling kernel-based attribute-aware matrix factorization for rating prediction. IEEE Trans. Knowl. Data Eng. **29**(4), 798–812 (2017)

Hierarchical Bayesian Network Based Incremental Model for Flood Prediction

Yirui Wu[1,2], Weigang Xu[1], Qinghan Yu[1], Jun Feng[1(✉)], and Tong Lu[2]

[1] College of Computer and Information, Hohai University, Nanjing, China
{wuyirui,fengjun}@hhu.edu.cn,weigangxu@163.com,1140833939@qq.com
[2] National Key Lab for Novel Software Technology, Nanjing University, Nanjing, China
lutong@nju.edu.cn

Abstract. To minimize the negative impacts brought by floods, researchers pay special attention to the problem of flood prediction. In this paper, we propose a hierarchical Bayesian network based incremental model to predict floods for small rivers. The proposed model not only appropriately embeds hydrology expert knowledge with Bayesian network for high rationality and robustness, but also designs an incremental learning scheme to improve the self-improving and adaptive ability of the proposed model. Following the idea of a famous hydrology model, i.e., XAJ model, we firstly present the construction of hierarchical Bayesian network as local and global network construction. After that, we propose an incremental learning scheme, which selects proper incremental data to improve the completeness of prior knowledge and updates parameters of Bayesian network to prevent training from scratch. We demonstrate the accuracy and effectiveness of the proposed model by conducting experiments on a collected dataset with one comparative method.

Keywords: Incremental learning · Hierarchical Bayesian network Flood prediction

1 Introduction

Flood, as one of the most common and largely distributed natural disasters, happens occasionally and brings large damages to life and property. In the past decades, researchers have proposed a quantity of models for accurate, robust and reasonable flood prediction. We generally category models into two types, namely hydrology model [8,11,17] and data-driven model [4,6,18]. Hydrology models utilize highly non-linear mathematic systems to represent the complex hydrology processes from clues to results. However, such models are extremely sensitive to parameters [16] and require quantity of research efforts of experts to fit them for one specific river. On the contrary, data-driven models use machine learning methods to directly predict the river runoff values based on historical observed and time-varying flood factors. However, floods are complicated natural

© Springer Nature Switzerland AG 2019
I. Kompatsiaris et al. (Eds.): MMM 2019, LNCS 11295, pp. 556–566, 2019.
https://doi.org/10.1007/978-3-030-05710-7_46

phenomena affected by multiple factors. It's hard to guarantee the rationality and robustness by utilizing such data-driven models and not considering physical processes.

In this work, we pay special interests to the problem of flood prediction for small rivers, whose catchments are smaller than 3000 km. Predicting floods with either hydrology models or data-driven models for small rivers could be a hard task, since small rivers are not only complex to model and analyze, but also suffer from shortages of exhaustive historical observation data. It's an intuitive thought that we should properly utilize the strength of hydrology model to improve the accuracy, robustness and rationality of data-driven model. The hydrology expert knowledge behind the hydrology model could relieve the requirement for large amount of data, which solves the problem of not enough data at a certain extent. Moreover, we aim to construct data-driven models with "growth" ability. That is the predicting capability of models could be gradually improved with more captured data. In fact, the floods data collected in small rivers are generally lack of completeness and unevenly distributed. By involving the ability of growth, the constructed model can run ahead and converge to a finalized and robust system during the running period. Moreover, the predicting capability of models are greatly affected by the occurrence of climatic variations, human activities and other environmental changes. Models with growth ability thus should continuously process new information captured from the latest floods and make self-adaptive adjustments to ensure the accuracy of predictions.

Guided by the ideas of expertise and growth, we propose a hierarchical Bayesian network based incremental model. In order to extract the expert hydrology knowledge behind physical models, the entities and relations of the proposed model refer to the physical factors and processes extracted from a famous hydrology model, *i.e.*, the XAJ model [10,17]. Moreover, we construct an incremental learning scheme to develop the growth ability of the proposed model without changing network structures or training from the scratch.

The main contribution of the paper is to propose a hierarchical Bayesian network based incremental model for flood prediction of small rivers, which not only embeds hydrology process to improve the accuracy, robustness and rationality, but also designs an incremental learning scheme to improve the self-improving and adaptive ability. Owing to the expertise and growth ability of the proposed model, the requirements for size of training dataset could be largely reduced, which coincides with the environment and conditions of predicting floods for small rivers. The proposed method is powerful to discover the inherent patterns between input flood factors and flow rate, especially for regions whose flood formation mechanism is too complex to construct a convinced physical model.

2   Related Work

Hydrology Model. The famous XAJ model not only considers the rains and runoffs, but also takes other hydrology processes into account, such as evaporation from water bodies and surface, rain infiltrated and stored by the soil, and so on. We explain the processes of XAJ model with the following four modules:

1. Evaporation module: XAJ model firstly divide the river watershed into several local regions. Evaporation values of local regions are computed based on the soil tension water capability (referring to soil water storage capability) in three layers, i.e., upper, lower and deep soil layers.
2. Runoff generation module: The XAJ model defines local runoff is not produced until the soil water of the local region reaches its maximum of soil tension water capacity, and thereafter the excess rainfall becomes the runoff without further loss. Therefore, the local runoff of XAJ model is calculated according to the rainfall, evaporation and soil tension water capability.
3. Runoff separation module: The local runoff is subdivided into three components, including surface runoff, interflow runoff and groundwater runoff.
4. Runoff routing module: The outflow from each local region is finally routed by the Muskingum successive-reaches model [17] to calculate the outlet flow of the whole river catchment.

Sensitive parameters of the XAJ model need be adjusted by experts' experiences, which makes it difficult to apply on small rivers for predictions.

Data-Driven Model. From the views of computer scientists, floods are directly induced and affected by a set of multiple factors, including rainfall, soil category, the structure of riverway and so on. Early, Reggiani et al. [9] construct a modified Bayesian predicting system by involving numerical weather information to address the spatial-temporal variabilities of precipitation during prediction. Later, Cheng et al. [1] perform accurate daily runoff forecasting by proposing an artificial neural network based on quantum-behaved particle swarm optimization, which trains the ANN parameters in an alternative way and achieves much better forecast accuracy than the basic ANN model. Recently, Wu et al. [14] construct a Bayesian network for flood predictions, which appropriately embeds hydrology expert knowledge for high rationality and robustness. The proposed method is built on it and involves an incremental design over all steps of Bayesian network for fitting to the problem of flood predictions for small rivers.

Impressed by significant ability of deep learning architectures [5,7,15], researchers try to utilize deep learning architectures for flood prediction. For example, Zhuang et al. [18] design a novel Spatio-Temporal Convolutional Neural Network (ST-CNN) to fully utilize the spatial and temporal information and automatically learn underlying patterns from data for extreme flood cluster prediction. Liu et al. [6] propose a deep learning approach by integrating stacked auto-encoders (SAE) and back propagation neural networks (BPNN) for the predictions of stream flow. Most recently, Wu et al. [13] propose context-aware attention LSTM network to accurately predict sequential flow rate values based on a set of collected flood factors. However, the above deep learning methods require large datasets to train. Without prior knowledge and inferences extracted from hydrology models, the deep learning based models can't predict floods in a rational sense.

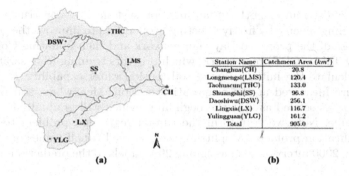

Fig. 1. Illustration of the Changhua watershed, where (a) is the map for various kinds of stations and (b) represents catchment areas corresponding to the listed rainfall stations. Note that we need predict the flow rate values of river gauging station CH and station SS functions as an evaporation station.

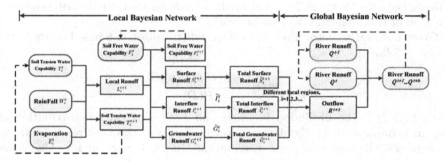

Fig. 2. Illustration of the proposed hierarchical Bayesian network based incremental model, where dotted lines refer to time-varying updating, blue and green rectangles represent incremental inputs and flood predictions, respectively. (Color figure online)

3   The Proposed Method

Take a typical small river, *i.e.*, Changhua, for an example, we show its general information in Fig. 1, where we can notice 7 rainfall stations, 1 evaporation station and 1 river gauging station. In our work, we aim to predict the flow rate values at the river gauging station CH for the next 6 h with the proposed incremental model. The input set of flood factors consists of rainfalls observed at the rainfall stations, evaporation and soil moisture observed at the evaporation station SS and former river runoff observed at CH.

Considering that XAJ model is organized with local and global steps, we follow its conception to design the proposed hierarchical Bayesian network based incremental model as shown in Fig. 2. By inferring probabilistic relations between inputting flood factors and intermediate variables extracted from the XAJ model, we embed the hydrological expert knowledge with the proposed model by first establishing relations and then improving the representations of knowledge with probabilistic distributions other than function systems. We construct the incremental learning scheme by firstly selecting proper data to improve the generative completeness of the proposed Bayesian network and then updating Conditional Probability Table (CPT) of network, which prevents training from scratch. Note that we calculate the initial value of soil tension water capability T_i^t based on soil moisture measured at the evaporation station. Meanwhile, soil free water capability F_i^t is settled as 0 at the beginning, which will gradually converge to the real value. Note we transform the run-off regression problem to a multi-label classification problem by splitting the observed runoff values of Changhua dataset into 2000 intervals, $i.e.$, assigning 2000 labels to the predictions of run-off values.

3.1   Construction of Hierarchical Bayesian Network

In this subsection, we firstly introduce the theory foundation and novelty by utilizing Bayesian Network for flood predicting. After that, we describe the construction of Hierarchical Bayesian network.

Given data D, we determine the posterior distribution of θ based on Bayesian theory as follows:

$$P(\theta|D) = \frac{L(D|\theta)P(\theta)}{P(D)} \tag{1}$$

where $L(D|\theta)$ is the likelihood function and $P(\theta)$ is the prior distribution of random variable θ. Since the denominator of Eq. 1 is a constant related only to the data set, the choice of prior distribution $P(\theta)$ is important for calculation of the posterior distribution $P(\theta|D)$. Selecting proper $P(\theta)$ generally requires to consider from the measured data and available prior knowledge. The former is named as data-based prior distribution and could be obtained from the existing data and research results, while the latter, named as non-data-based prior distribution, refers to a prior distribution resulted from subjective judgments or theory.

By extracting prior expert hydrology knowledge from the XAJ model and historic observation data, we think Bayesian Network offers an appropriate structure to joint learn the posterior distribution with the prior knowledge. Specifically, the proposed method firstly considers the given observation data D is formed by a set of hydrology attributes $\{X_i|i = 1...n\}$ and the predicting run-off value could be represented as an attribute X_0 as well. Therefore, we could represent the joint distribution of $\{X_i|i = 0...n\}$ as

$$P(X_0, X_1, X_2, ..., X_n) = \prod_{i=0}^{n} P(X_i|\zeta(Parents(X_i))) \tag{2}$$

where function $Parents()$ and $\zeta()$ represents the sets of directly precursor attributes and the corresponding joint distribution, respectively. In order to solve Eq. 4 for X_0, we utilize marginalization [3] operations to convert it as a list of conditional probabilities. We further adopt Bayesian network and the cooperating CPTs to describe conditional probabilities. During training, we use loopy belief propagation to estimate the parameters of conditional probability table. Due to the loopy structure of the network, it is difficult to check for the convergence. We thus adopt that training is terminated when 10 iterations of gradient decent go not yield averagely improved likelihood over the previous 10.

After explaining the theory of Bayesian network, we describe the construction of hierarchical Bayesian network. During the Local Bayesian Network stage, we aim to predict the runoff contribution values in the local regions. We firstly divide the total river watershed into small local regions based on hydrology principles [12] and the locations of rainfall stations. The split results of local regions are represented in Fig. 1(b). We then collect multiple kinds of inputs in each local region, $i.e.$ soil moisture T_i^t, rainfall W_i^t and evaporation E_i^t by interpolation based on observed flood factors, where i refers to the index of local region. Next, we follow the first three modules of the XAJ model as discussed in the last section, in order to embed the expert knowledge about hydrology processes into the construction of the local Bayesian network. Finally, the trained local Bayesian network could compute several hydrology intermediate variables, such as surface runoff $\widetilde{S}_i^{t+1}$, interflow runoff $\widetilde{I}_i^{t+1}$ and groundwater runoff $\widetilde{G}_i^{t+1}$. In the Global Bayesian Network stage, we utilize the last module of XAJ model to construct the global Bayesian network, which predicts the river runoff for the next$h$ hours $\{Q^t, ..., Q^{t+h}\}$ based on the output of the local Bayesian network and river runoff Q^{t-1}, Q^t in former times. To sum up, we properly embed the hydrology process and variables of the XAJ model into the hierarchical Bayesian Network.

3.2 Bayesian Network Incremental Learning

In this subsection, we firstly discuss how to select proper incremental data to improve the completeness of the proposed model and then describe steps to update CPTs of the proposed hierarchical Bayesian network.

Incremental data selection is one of the most important factors to improve efficiency of incremental learning. In fact, selecting false labeled samples will bring noise and decrease accuracy of further predictions. Generally, researchers

---

Algorithm 1. Incremental sample selection algorithm

Input: Model trained in the last iteration M, set of incremental samples S
Output: Prior incremental set $P = \emptyset$, undetermined incremental set $U = \emptyset$ and noise set $N = \emptyset$

1: **For** each $a_i \in S$, $c = gt(a_i)$
2:    **If** $c \in C_n$, $N.add(a_i)$
3:    **Else** $\beta = M(a_i)$
4:       **If** $|\beta - c| < \omega$, $P.add(a_i)$
5:       **ELSEIf** $|\beta - c| < \varepsilon$, $U.add(a_i)$
6:       **ELSE** $N.add(a_i)$

---

select incremental data by calculating model loss, defined as difference values of prediction accuracy between before and after selecting new samples for incremental learning. However, such procedure is rather low in efficiency due to time-consuming calculation. We thus propose a threshold-ruled incremental data selection algorithm for better efficiency, which is presented in Algorithm 1.

In Algorithm 1, function $gt()$ checks the ground-truth classification label from training dataset, function $add()$ adds an incremental sample into different sets, function $M()$ refers to the classification result achieved by hierarchical Bayesian Network in the last iteration, C_n represents the classification labels set in the last iteration, ω and ε are two adaptive parameters to decide the operation on the inputting incremental sample. Specifically, we define $\omega = \tilde{Q} \times 5\%$ and $\varepsilon = \tilde{Q} \times 20\%$ to avoid the induce of noise data, where $\tilde{Q}$ refers to the mean runoff value corresponding to the small river. Note that 20% is originated from the international rule for permissible range of flood prediction system error. After defining the set of P and U based on the inputting data S, we add the samples of P for incremental training at first. After then, we utilize a matrix generated from the normal distribution to expand the data in P by $\tilde{p} = L * p$. For the generated and expanded data $\tilde{p}$, we further process it as input by Algorithm 1 and utilize the corresponding results of P and U for incremental training at last.

After selection on the proper incremental data, we discuss the updating rule inside the network. When incremental data and the former training date are ruled by the same joint distribution, the training Bayesian network could be adjusted only with the parameters to fit with new data. Following this idea, we define D_0, D_+ and $D = D_0 + D_+$ as the initial dataset, incremental dataset and total dataset, respectively. We also define the number of dataset as $N_0 = |D_0|$, $N_+ = |D_+|$ and $N = N_0 + N_+$. Supposing that there are n variables $X_1, X_2, ..., X_n$ and the corresponding possible values $x_i^1, x_i^2, ..., x_i^{r_i}$, we could use

$$\theta_{ijk} = p(x_i^k | \pi_i^j, \theta_i, G) \tag{3}$$

to represent the parameters of Bayesian network with structure G, where $\pi_i^1, \pi_i^2, ..., \pi_i^{q_i}$ ($q_i = \prod_{x_m \in \pi_i} r_j, m \neq i$) are the father node set for node X_i. After adding samples for incremental learning, we thus could calculate the modified parameters as

$$\theta_{ijk}(D, G) = \frac{\theta'_{ijk}(D_0, G) + N_{ijk}(D_+, G)}{\theta'_{ij}(D_0, G) + N_{ij}(D_+, G)} \tag{4}$$

where $\theta'_{ij}(D_0, G) = \sum_{k=1}^{r_i} \theta'_{ijk}(D_0, G)$, $N_{ij}(D_+, G) = \sum_{k=1}^{r_i} N_{ijk}(D_+, G)$ and the network parameters can be defined as

$$\begin{cases} \sum_{k=1}^n \theta_{ijk} = 1 \\ \theta_{ij} = \bigcup_{k=1}^{r_i} \theta_{ijk} \\ \theta_i = \bigcup_{j=1}^{q_i} \theta_{ij} \\ \theta = \bigcup_{i=1}^{n} \theta_i \end{cases} \tag{5}$$

4   Experimental Results

4.1   Dataset and Measurements

We collect hourly data of floods happened from 1998 to 2010 in Changhua river as our dataset. The floods happened from 1998 to 2003 and from 2009 to 2010 are used as the basic training and testing dataset respectively, meanwhile floods happened from 2004 to 2008 are adopted as the incremental datasets, which are divided into five parts and marked with D_1 to D_5, respectively. We analysis the runoff values of Changhua dataset and find the values are unevenly distributed in a fixed interval, which proves the supposition for data of small rivers, *i.e.*, incomplete and highly uneven. Therefore, it's necessary to involve the incremental learning to improve the performance of flood prediction in small rivers.

To better evaluate performance of the proposed method, we adopt several quality measurements for evaluation of classification results, which could be represented as

$$FN = \frac{N_{non}}{N_{all}} \tag{6}$$

$$k - FC = \frac{N_{k,correct}}{N_{all}} \tag{7}$$

where N_{all} is the total number of testing samples and N_{non} refers to number of none deciding testing samples, which can't be assigned with labels by the proposed model due to the lack of complete prior knowledge, *i.e.*, related probability inferences. $N_{k,correct}$ refers to the number of testing samples, whose run-off prediction values are close with ground-truth values. The difference value between the prediction and ground-truth should be smaller than value represented by k splitting intervals, where k is define as 1 in our experiment. Note that FN is designed to show the ability to acquire new knowledge during the process of incremental learning, meanwhile k-FC is used to evaluate the ability for accurately flood prediction. Higher FN and k-FC value implies better performance.

4.2   Performance Analysis

We show the improvements on FN and 1-FC measurement with the proposed method in Fig. 3. We can observe great decrements of FN values during the period of incremental learning, especially for the first, third and fifth increment. This is due to the completeness of the prior knowledge is gradually increased with more training samples and the proposed method is efficient in extracting such knowledge by incremental learning. The reason for different decrement values lies in the fact that the dataset is split based on year other than the amount of new knowledge. For 1-FC, we can view an obvious decrement in prediction accuracy with larger perdition hours, which implies the task of flood prediction becomes harder when predicting for a relatively long time. With the incremental learning, we find the prediction accuracy is improved, especially for the first and fifth increment. The most obvious improvements are labeled by blue rectangles in Fig. 3, which refer to the fifth incremental learning for prediction in 4 and 5 h.

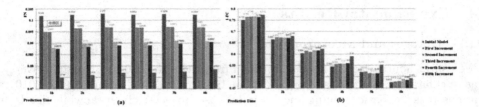

Fig. 3. Illustration of the improvements on FN and 1-FC with the proposed incremental learning scheme, where blue rectangles represent the obvious improvement on 1-FC with the fifth increment. (Color figure online)

This fact proves that the proposed method is better at predicting in a relatively long time.

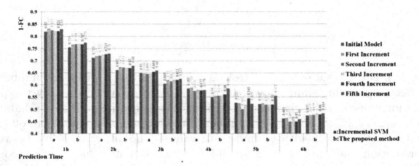

Fig. 4. Comparison of 1-FC values on Changhua dataset computed by the proposed method and incremental SVM.

In Fig. 4, we compare the 1-FC values computed by the proposed method and incremental SVM [2]. Since SVM could predict without complete prior knowledge, it's meaningless to compare FN. We implement the incremental SVM according to the instructions given in their paper. From Fig. 4, we can find the prediction accuracy achieved by the proposed method is lower than that achieved by the incremental SVM when predicting for 1 h, 2 h, 3 h and 4 h. However, the proposed method gets better performance when predicting for 5 h and 6 h, which proves the proposed method is better than incremental SVM at predicting in a relatively long time. With Incremental learning, we can find improvements achieved by either incremental SVM or the proposed method. However, the increase values gained by the proposed method are more impressive than that gained by the incremental SVM, especially when predicting for 4 h and 5 h. This proves the proposed method is more efficient than incremental SVM for tasks of incremental learning, especially for long time flood predicting.

5   Conclusion

In this paper, we propose a hierarchical Bayesian network based incremental model to predict floods for small rivers. The proposed model not only appropriately embeds hydrology expert knowledge with Bayesian network for high rationality and robustness, but also designs an incremental learning scheme to improve the self-improving and adaptive ability of the proposed model. By involving power of incremental learning, the proposed model could be gradually improved with more collected data, which makes it fit with various application scenarios. Experiment results on Changhua dataset show the proposed method outperforms several comparative methods and achieves promising prediction results on small rivers. Our future work includes the exploration on other hydrology purposes with the proposed method, for example mid-term flood predicting.

Acknowledgement. This work was supported by National Key R&D Program of China under Grant 2018YFC0407901, the Natural Science Foundation of China under Grant 61702160, Grant 61672273 and Grant 61832008, the Fundamental Re-search Funds for the Central Universities under Grant 2016B14114, the Science Foundation of Jiangsu under Grant BK20170892, the Science Foundation for Distinguished Young Scholars of Jiangsu under Grant BK20160021, Scientific Foundation of State Grid Corporation of China (Research on Ice-wind Disaster Feature Recognition and Prediction by Few-shot Machine Learning in Transmission Lines), and the open Project of the National Key Lab for Novel Software Technology in NJU under Grant K-FKT2017B05.

References

1. Cheng, C., Niu, W., Feng, Z., Shen, J., Chau, K.: Daily reservoir runoff forecasting method using artificial neural network based on quantum-behaved particle swarm optimization. Water **7**(8), 4232–4246 (2015)
2. Diehl, C.P., Cauwenberghs, G.: SVM incremental learning, adaptation and optimization. In: Proceedings of International Joint Conference on Neural Networks, vol. 4, pp. 2685–2690 (2003)
3. Friedman, N., Geiger, D., Goldszmidt, M.: Bayesian network classifiers. Mach. Learn. **29**(2–3), 131–163 (1997)
4. Han, S., Coulibaly, P.: Bayesian flood forecasting methods: a review. J. Hydrol. **551**, 340–351 (2017)
5. Jing, P., Su, Y., Nie, L., Bai, X., Liu, J., Wang, M.: Low-rank multi-view embedding learning for micro-video popularity prediction. IEEE Trans. Knowl. Data Eng. **30**(8), 1519–1532 (2018)
6. Liu, F., Xu, F., Yang, S.: A flood forecasting model based on deep learning algorithm via integrating stacked autoencoders with BP neural network. In: Proceedings of IEEE International Conference on Multimedia Big Data, pp. 58–61 (2017)
7. Nie, L., Zhang, L., Yan, Y., Chang, X., Liu, M., Shaoling, L.: Multiview physician-specific attributes fusion for health seeking. IEEE Trans. Cybern. **47**(11), 3680–3691 (2017)
8. Paquet, E., Garavaglia, F., Garçon, R., Gailhard, J.: The schadex method: a semi-continuous rainfall-runoff simulation for extreme flood estimation. J. Hydrol. **495**, 23–37 (2013)

9. Reggiani, P., Weerts, A.: Probabilistic quantitative precipitation forecast for flood prediction: an application. J. Hydrometeorol. **9**(1), 76–95 (2008)
10. Ren-Jun, Z.: The Xinanjiang model applied in China. J. Hydrol. **135**(1–4), 371–381 (1992)
11. Rogger, M., Viglione, A., Derx, J., Blöschl, G.: Quantifying effects of catchments storage thresholds on step changes in the flood frequency curve. Water Resour. Res. **49**(10), 6946–6958 (2013)
12. Villarini, G., Mandapaka, P.V., Krajewski, W.F., Moore, R.J.: Rainfall and sampling uncertainties: a rain gauge perspective. J. Geophys. Res. Atmos. **113**(D11) (2008)
13. Wu, Y., Liu, Z., Xu, W., Feng, J., Shivakumara, P., Lu, T.: Context-aware attention LSTM network for flood prediction. In: Proceedings of International Conference on Pattern Recognitions (2018)
14. Wu, Y., Xu, W., Feng, J., Shivakumara, P., Lu, T.: Local and global Bayesian network based model for flood prediction. In: Proceedings of International Conference on Pattern Recognition (2018)
15. Wu, Y., Yue, Y., Tan, X., Wang, W., Lu, T.: End-to-end chromosome Karyotyping with data augmentation using GAN. In: Proceedings on International Conference on Image Processing, pp. 2456–2460 (2018)
16. Yao, C., Zhang, K., Yu, Z., Li, Z., Li, Q.: Improving the flood prediction capability of the Xinanjiang model in ungauged nested catchments by coupling it with the geomorphologic instantaneous unit hydrograph. J. Hydrol. **517**, 1035–1048 (2014)
17. Zhao, R., Zhuang, Y., Fang, L., Liu, X., Zhang, Q.: The Xinanjiang model. In: Proceedings Oxford Symposium Hydrological Forecasting, vol. 129, pp. 351–356 (1980)
18. Zhuang, W.Y., Ding, W.: Long-lead prediction of extreme precipitation cluster via a spatiotemporal convolutional neural network. In: Proceedings of the 6th International Workshop on Climate Informatics: CI (2016)

A New Female Body Segmentation and Feature Localisation Method for Image-Based Anthropometry

Dan Wang[1,2], Yun Sheng[1,2(✉)], and GuiXu Zhang[1,2]

[1] Shanghai Key Laboratory of Multidimensional Information Processing,
East China Normal University, Shanghai, People's Republic of China
[2] The Department of Computer Science and Technology,
East China Normal University, Shanghai, People's Republic of China
ysheng@cs.ecnu.edu.cn

Abstract. An increasingly growing demand on the bespoke service for buying clothes online presents a new challenge of how to efficiently and precisely acquire anthropometric data of distant customers. The conventional 2D anthropometric methods are efficient but face a problem of imperfect body segmentation because they cannot automatically deal with arbitrary background. To address this problem this paper aimed at female anthropometry proposes to segment the female body out of an orthogonal photo pair with deep learning, and to extract a group of body feature points according to curvature and bending direction of the segmented body contour. With the located feature points we estimate six body parameters with two existing mathematical models and assess their pros and cons in this paper.

Keywords: Anthropometric methods · Deep learning · Feature points

1 Introduction

With the development of electronic commerce, there is an increasingly growing demand on the bespoke service for buying clothes online. This presents a new challenge of how to efficiently and precisely acquire anthropometric data of distant customers. The conventionally manual measurement for human circumferences needs manpower and means that different operators may have different measurement results even for the same model. Therefore, an accurate, efficient, and contactless measurement for human body parameters is desired, and multimedia technology can make such a measurement a reality.

The mainstream methods of contactless measurement are classified into three-dimensional (3D) measurement and two-dimensional (2D) measurement. The 3D methods [10,13] require special equipments, such as laser scanners, Kinect, *etc.*, to attain 3D information of the human body. As the 3D laser scanning devices are expensive and awkward, Kinect thanks to its affordability and

© Springer Nature Switzerland AG 2019
I. Kompatsiaris et al. (Eds.): MMM 2019, LNCS 11295, pp. 567–577, 2019.
https://doi.org/10.1007/978-3-030-05710-7_47

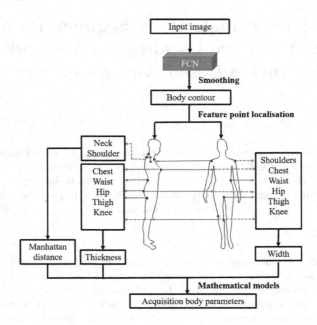

Fig. 1. The pipeline of our anthropometric method.

portability provides a highly effective solution for people to scan themselves at home [3,13,15], but needs professional skills to set up. Some researchers turned to reconstruct a 3D human model with an orthogonal-view photo pair [16,17]. They utilised the parameters derived from the frontal and lateral view images to customise a predefined generic 3D human model. Circumferences can then be calculated with the depth information of the newly customised model. Compared with the 3D methods, their 2D image-based counterparts are easier to implement and need to locate body features ahead of body parameters acquisition. For instance, Widyanti et al. located human body features by segmenting the bright ribbon-tied model from the dark background [14]. Their segmentation and localisation results heavily relied on the experimental set-up. Aslam et al. located body feature points with a peak and valley detection algorithm [1] following the body region extracted by Graphcuts [2], an interactive segmentation method. Both the above feature localisation methods were followed by the use of mathematical models to evaluate body circumferences [1,14] but cannot automatically cope with arbitrary background images. So 2D anthropometric methods may face a problem of imperfect body segmentation and this problem in body segmentation will affect further processes, such as feature point localisation and body parameter acquisition.

To address the above problem in the 2D image-based anthropometric methods, in this paper we propose to segment the female body with deep learning. The pipeline of our method is shown in Fig. 1. Differing from the extant ones, our method first adopts the Fully Convolutional Neural Network (FCN) [8] to separate the foreground, *i.e.* human body, out of the background of an orthogonal image pair, followed by the use of Fourier descriptors to smooth out the segmented body contour in the orthogonal image pair. Compared with those commonly used body segmentation methods requiring user interaction, the FCN carries out segmentation automatically for images with low contrast. In this paper we also propose to extract body feature points, such as the neck points, shoulder points, *etc.*, according to curvature and bending direction of the body contour. Our experiments show that in comparison with the conventional methods the FCN improves the precision of human body segmentation, downplays the side effect of arbitrary background, and thus is able to increase the precision of feature point localisation. Moreover, to complete our anthropometry we estimate the width and thickness for each body feature with the located feature points and then acquire the body parameters using two existing mathematical models introduced in [1,14]. We also propose a method to estimate the shoulders with a parabola in 3D space. We assess the two body parameter acquisition schemes based on the feature points localised by our method and analyse their pros and cons in this paper.

2 Body Segmentation

Since its result affects the accuracy of feature localisation as well as further calculations, body segmentation plays a crucial role in 2D anthropometric methods. There exist many image segmentation methods available for body segmentation. Some methods are edge-based, *e.g.* active contour models, where the contour curve is gradually approaching the target edge by minimising an energy function. The method of Snakes [5] employs a similar idea but may easily fall into a local minimum. The Chan-Vese method [4] is also an active contour model based on level sets, but it fails to correctly shrink or expand in the foot line of the wall where gradients change rapidly. There are also some interactive segmentation methods. For example, Grabcut [11] combining both colour and edge information minimises an energy function with a Gaussian mixture model to estimate the distribution of foreground and background colours. Nevertheless, if the background becomes complicated the robustness of this method will decline, and more user interactions will be required. Negative examples of Grabcut are shown in Fig. 2. Image matting [6] also needs some user-defined information and the matting result is a grayscale image with higher intensity values corresponding to greater possibilities of being classified as foreground. We choose 60% of the maximum intensity value whose mean IU (Intersection over Union) is the highest as the threshold to binarise the matting result, as shown in Fig. 2. We also tested the Otsu's method [9] as well as skin colour extraction [12] for body segmentation, and the results were unstable, specially when the complexity of background increased. Thus, in this paper we adopt the FCN for body segmentation.

The FCN [8] has been a powerful tool used for pixel-by-pixel semantic segmentation. Based on VGG19, we train an FCN-8s model with an iteration number set to 100000, and change the output into a dichotomy. Moreover, training

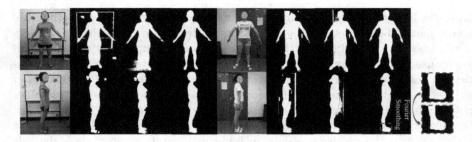

Fig. 2. Images with arbitrary backgrounds and their segmentation results of, from left to right, Grabcut, Matting (60%), and smoothing following the FCN.

set data are also a decisive aspect in this segmentation network. The commonly used datasets contain various classes, and even the datasets containing people are not specialised for anthropometry. To this end, we construct a training set of 9083 images and a validation set of 3000 images chosen from a human parsing dataset [7]. In the original dataset, the labeled people contain missing pixels. We conduct image processing, *e.g.* morphological filtering, to fill these holes and convert the label from multi-classification into dichotomy.

We input the resized images into the trained FCN and the results show that the segmentation results are more accurate than those produced by the other tested algorithms, as shown in Fig. 2, except the body contour segmented by the FCN is ragged because of the deconvolution and upsampling operations. Moreover, clothes wrinkles also lead to serrated contours, likely resulting in incorrect localisation of feature points. In order to smooth out the contour, we employ Fourier descriptors to eliminate the bulges from the point of view of the frequency domain. Taking advantage of inverse Fourier transform, we can use a few low-frequency descriptors to represent a whole human body contour, as shown in Fig. 2.

3   Localisation of Feature Points

Regarding the segmentation results, we observe that curvature variation provides a major geometric feature of the binary image. Therefore, we locate the feature points according to two properties of the body contour, the curvature and bending direction. The curvature is used to describe the bending degree while the bending direction distinguishes whether the local body contour is concave or convex. There are three steps for feature point localisation and calculation of the width and thickness for the chest, waist, hip, thigh, knee, and shoulders.

First, according to the anthropometric knowledge the body silhouette within a minimum bounding rectangle is equally divided into seven sections, as shown in Fig. 3, where L symbolises the section length, and a, b, c, d, e, and f indicate the cut-points of each section. With this division strategy we may come out with some knowledge. For example, the head generally lies in the first section

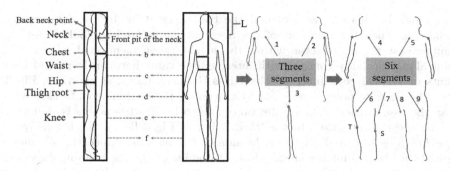

Fig. 3. Illustration of feature point localisation.

from the top. A rough estimation of feature point positions is then performed. In the frontal view, we find six salient feature points, the head point, foot points, armpit points, and thigh root point with a coarse-to-fine strategy as shown in Fig. 3. The head point and foot points are close to the bounding rectangle and can first be located. The three feature points are then used to divide the body contour into three segments. The thigh root point is concave with a maximum bending degree along the contour of Segment 3. The left armpit point and right armpit can be located similarly in Segment 1 and Segment 2, respectively. With the located feature points the whole body contour is further separated into six segments for the sake of computational efficiency. The above segmentations of the body contour can help narrow the computational scope of feature point localisation.

Second, after the above body contour partitioning, feature points of the neck, chest, and hip can be found in the side-view image, while the knee point and shoulder points can be located in the different segments of the front-view contour divided in the first step. The waist and thigh points can be obtained in both the views. Because the relative position of feature points to the whole body is fixed, for the same feature point, as long as we find its position in one view, we can readily map it from the current view into the other. However, in many cases the feature points in two orthogonal views cannot be precisely mapped because the shooting angles of two views are not absolutely orthogonal. To address this problem, we first check if it is able to locate a body feature in both the views. If not, then we carry out the mapping from one view to the other. By doing this we can reduce the error produced by mismapping. We introduce the detail of feature point localisation as follows.

In the Lateral View Image. In the lateral view image shown in Fig. 3 curvature variations for the neck, chest, waist, and hip are visually salient. The neck point should lie in the height range $[a_y - L/2, a_y + L/2]$, where y symbolises the vertical coordinate. The curvature variation along the head is more intensive than that of the back. When we traverse the contour clockwise, the curve along the back is gradually bending until the back neck point where the bending degree reaches maximum. To this end we can find the back neck point by the two contour properties. Then the front pit of the neck can be located by looking for the point closest to the bisector within the height range mentioned before. The point along the body contour with intermediate value between front and back points in vertical coordinate is selected as the neck point, as shown in Fig. 3. The other feature points are found by traversing the contour counterclockwise. Take the case of chest. The localisation of the other feature points is similar to it. The chest point shown in the lateral view of Fig. 3 lies in the height range $[b_y - L/2, b_y + L/2]$ and on the right side of the bisector. Since the silhouette around the chest point is convex, which can be judged by the bending direction, we choose the point with a maximum bending degree as the chest point. If more than one point come with the maximum bending degree, we select the one most distant from the bisector.

In the Frontal View Image. Since it is difficult to find the chest point in the frontal view, we map the chest point from the lateral view. The same applies to the hip. Sometimes we miscalculate the position due to clothes not tightly fitting into the human body, resulting in a larger estimate of the chest width. To address this issue, we use the distance between two armpits as an alternative to the chest width. As for the knees, we discover that their contours in both the lateral and frontal views are nearly straight, as shown in Fig. 3. From the thighs to knees the outer thigh contours are concave. So are the inner contours from the knees to shanks. With this knowledge, we can locate both a point T above the knee in Segment 6 of Fig. 3 and a point S below the knee in Segment 7 of Fig. 3 with a local maximum bending degree and concave bending direction. T lie in $[e_y - L/2, e_y + 2L/3]$ and S lie in $[T_y, e_y + 2L/3]$, as shown in Fig. 3. We define that the knee point is horizontally in line with the middle point of T and S. The corresponding position of the knees can also be obtained in the lateral view through mapping.

Third, according to the extracted feature points we compute the width and thickness of the body features, which will be used later in the mathematical models for body parameter acquisition.

4   Acquisition of Body Parameters

Since all the calculations thus far are carried out in the image domain, to measure real circumferences of the body features a conversion between the image system and metric system has to be performed. The conversion between the real height and the height in pixel are conducted through the camera pinhole model. Given a real height, we can calculate the real width and thickness if we have their values in pixel.

The body parameters extracted in this paper include five circumferences and one shoulder length. The circumference of each body feature is obtained by counting the length of its circumscribed curve. In this paper we adopt two mathematical models proposed in [14] and [1] for body parameters acquisition. The model in [1] uses two semi-elliptic curves to approximate the human circumferences, while the model in [14] uses linear regression to obtain the circumferences with variant thickness and width values. However, the precision of [1] is unstable and the sample quantity in [14] is also insufficient to cover different races with different body types. Thus, in this paper we compare the two body parameter acquisition methods to oversee their performance. Moreover, we regard the measuring track of the shoulders as a parabola in 3D space, as shown in Fig. 4. Let N be a half of the shoulder width, and H and M be the Manhattan distances from the shoulders to the neck point in y and x directions, respectively. The parabola in 3D space is formulated in terms of parametric equation as

$$\begin{cases} Y(X) = H - \frac{H}{N^2}X^2 \\ Z(X) = M - \frac{M}{N}X \end{cases} \tag{1}$$

The shoulder length S is calculated as

$$S = 2\int_0^N dS = \sqrt{N^2 + M^2 + 4H^2} + \frac{N^2+M^2}{4H}\ln(\frac{\sqrt{N^2+M^2+4H^2}+2H}{\sqrt{N^2+M^2+4H^2}-2H}) \tag{2}$$

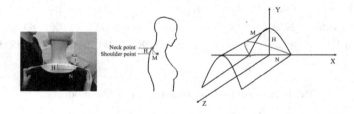

Fig. 4. The shoulder curve in red in 3D space. (Color figure online)

5   Experimental Evaluations

Our method requires that a camera is held up towards the centre of the model, and the distance between the camera and model is properly set so that the full body of the model can be taken into an image.

Evaluation of Segmentation. 51 images collected from different scenes, such as laboratory, living room, plain-background, *etc.*, are tested for segmentation. We utilise the mean IU [8] to evaluate the accuracy of three segmentation methods, involving two interactive methods generally considered as more robust than those non-interactive ones, as shown in Table 1. Ahead of assessment we need to binarise the matting results from grayscale images. We in turn choose 40%, 50%, 60%, 70%, 80%, and 90% of the maximum intensity value as thresholds. It can be seen from the table that our method with the FCN is more accurate than Grabcut. When we choose 50% or 60% of the maximum intensity value as thresholds, the mean IU values of Matting are only slightly higher than ours. But this method needs users to mark foreground and background pixels which is, however, time-consuming. Furthermore, different labeling may lead to different segmentation results and the precision of labeling heavily effects the segmentation result as well.

Evaluation of Feature Point Localisation. We conduct the following experiments mainly on five models with arbitrary backgrounds as their groundtruth data are approachable, involving one plastic model with and without clothes and four female models shown in Fig. 5. In order to quantitatively evaluate the proposed method, we calculate the average error in Euclidean distance between the manually labeled feature positions and those computed by our method for these models. For each model we take account of 12 feature points including two shoulder points, two armpit points, two knee points, and one thigh point from the frontal view, as well as the neck, chest, waist, hip and thigh points from the lateral view. The average error is 1.27 cm per feature point.

Table 1. The mean IU results

Methods	Ours	Grabcut [11]	Matting [6]					
Threshold values	N/A	N/A	40%	50%	60%	70%	80%	90%
Mean IU	96.65	91.3	96.29	96.73	96.75	96.54	95.89	94.11

Table 2. Acquired circumferences of five models

Test image	Methods	Circumference(cm)/Error(cm) to the Groundtruth					Width(cm)/Ours
		Chest	Waist	Hip	Thigh	Knee	Shoulder
Model	Method 1 [1]	84.2/**0.5**	64.4/**1.7**	80.4/-6.6	47.6/**-2.4**	29.4/**-4.6**	/
	Method 2 [14]	92.3/8.6	65.4/2.7	84/**-3**	47/-3	26.2/-7.8	/
	Groundtruth	83.7	62.7	87	50	34	41/36.1
Naked Model	Method 1 [1]	76.6/-7.1	59.5/-3.2	78.6/-8.4	49.6/**-0.4**	27.9/**-6.1**	/
	Method 2 [14]	85.4/**1.7**	60.3/**-2.4**	80.3/**-6.7**	48.8/-1.2	26.8/-7.2	/
	Groundtruth	83.7	62.7	87	50	34	41/39.2
Person 1	Method 1 [1]	79.6/**-1.9**	66.5/1	83.8/-5.2	50.1/**-0.9**	32.2/-2.8	/
	Method 2 [14]	87.2/5.7	67.7/2.2	84.7/**-4.3**	49.7/-1.3	33.9/**-1.1**	/
	Groundtruth	81.5	65.5	89	51	35	41/37.9
Person 2	Method 1 [1]	88.1/**-0.4**	70.8/**1.8**	90.5/-2	52.8/**-1.2**	35/0	/
	Method 2 [14]	97.6/9.1	72.4/3.4	93.3/**0.8**	52.5/-1.5	34.3/-0.7	/
	Groundtruth	88.5	69	92.5	54	35	37/35.6
Person 3	Method 1 [1]	82.4/**-0.6**	71.4/**3.4**	93.6/**0.6**	54.6/0.6	38.3/**-0.4**	/
	Method 2 [14]	91.6/8.6	72.5/4.5	94.2/1.2	54.4/**0.4**	37.7/-1	/
	Groundtruth	83	68	93	54	38.7	40/37.6
Person 4	Method 1 [1]	98.3/**5.3**	86/8	97.1/-1.9	54.7/**-3.3**	35/**-3.5**	/
	Method 2 [14]	108/15	88.3/10.3	100/1	54.6/-3.4	34.7/-3.8	/
	Groundtruth	93	78	99	58	38.5	41/42.2

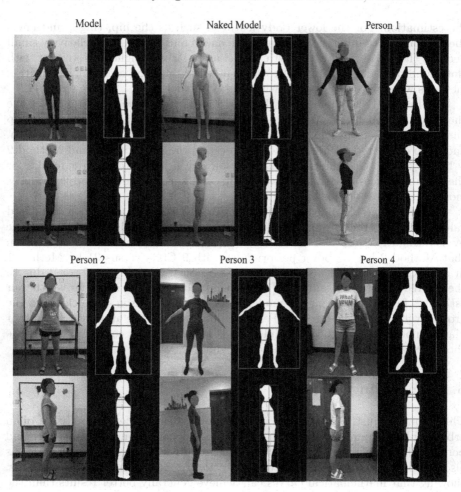

Fig. 5. Feature point localisation results of five models.

Evaluation of Body Parameter Acquisition. We evaluate two exist body parameter acquisition methods in calculating body parameters of the five models. We tabulate the estimated body parameters with the manual measured groundtruth in Table 2. The tested models consist of the plastic model with clothes named Model and without clothes named Naked Model, and the four females in Fig. 5 in turn named Person 1, Person 2, Person 3 and Person 4.

In order to find how much clothes will affect the measurement, we test the two methods with the plastic model both naked and dressed. As can be seen, for the upper body features, such as the chest and waist, the circumferences of Naked Model estimated by the two methods are understandably smaller than those with clothes. This demonstrates that clothes lend a negative impact to the estimation. For the lower body features, such as the hip, thigh, and knee, the circumference differences between the naked and dressed are relatively small because the trousers on this plastic model are relatively tighter. Note that with clothes on does not mean smaller errors because the two parameter acquisition methods were originally trained with dressed models.

For Person 1, Method 1 has the best results for the circumferences of the chest, waist, and thigh. Method 2 produces more accurate results for the hip and knee. For Person 2 and Person 4, circumferences of the chest, waist, thigh, and knee estimated by Method 1 are closest to the groundtruth and Method 2 is better for hip circumferences. For Person 3, Method 1 has better results for the circumferences of the chest, waist, hip, and knee, while Method 2 produces more accurate results for the thigh.

In Table 2, we highlight the smaller error values which mean the calculated values Closer to the Groundtruth (CtG). We perform straightforward statistic by counting the number of the values being CtG for each method. It can be seen that Method 2 has a poorer performance with 9 CtGs versus 21 by Method 1 in our experiments, because its linear regression was poorly performed due to the limited quantity of sampling [14]. When it comes to the shoulder width, our estimates for the naked plastic model, Person 2, and Person 4 are closer to the groundtruth, while the error for Person 1 and Person 3 are around 3 cm and for plastic model with cloth is around 5. This is because the contours around the shoulders with clothes are sometimes irregular.

6 Concluding Remarks

This paper has justified the use of the FCN to segment the female body out of an arbitrary background, followed by feature point localisation with curvature and bending direction in a 2D image-based anthropometric method. The paper has also compared the body parameter acquisition results of two existing methods, showing that mathematical curves can achieve generally better results than the linear regression method in more cases. Although geometric shapes, such as ellipse and circle, can be quickly fit into the body features, the linear regression model in [14] should work better if the sampling number were high enough so as to cover as many body shapes as possible. As for what to wear during the measurement, since it was uneasy to find a generic leotard tightly fit to every lady, the clothes dressed by the models came with wrinkles and thus gave rise to some obstacles in our experiments. This issue has to be tackled in the future. Moreover, our paper only considers female models, but some of the male body features, such as the neck, waist, hip, knees, shoulders, etc. can also be located and measured in a similar way.

Acknowledgements. This work was supported by the Open Research Fund of Shanghai Key Laboratory of Multidimensional Information Processing, East China Normal University.

References

1. Aslam, M., Rajbdad, F., Khattak, S., Azmat, S.: Automatic measurement of anthropometric dimensions using frontal and lateral silhouettes. IET Comput. Vis. **11**(6), 434–447 (2017)
2. Boykov, Y.Y., Jolly, M.P.: Interactive graph cuts for optimal boundary & region segmentation of objects in ND images. In: International Conference on Computer Vision, vol. 1, pp. 105–112. IEEE (2001)
3. Cui, Y., Chang, W., Nöll, T., Stricker, D.: KinectAvatar: fully automatic body capture using a single kinect. In: Park, J.-I., Kim, J. (eds.) ACCV 2012. LNCS, vol. 7729, pp. 133–147. Springer, Heidelberg (2013). https://doi.org/10.1007/978-3-642-37484-5_12
4. Getreuer, P.: Chan-Vese segmentation. Image Process. Line **2**, 214–224 (2012)
5. Kass, M., Witkin, A., Terzopoulos, D.: Snakes: active contour models. Int. J. Comput. Vis. **1**(4), 321–331 (1988)
6. Levin, A., Lischinski, D., Weiss, Y.: A closed-form solution to natural image matting. IEEE Trans. Pattern Anal. Mach. Intell. **30**(2), 228–242 (2008)
7. Liang, X., et al.: Human parsing with contextualized convolutional neural network. In: Proceedings of the IEEE International Conference on Computer Vision, pp. 1386–1394 (2015)
8. Long, J., Shelhamer, E., Darrell, T.: Fully convolutional networks for semantic segmentation. In: IEEE Conference on Computer Vision and Pattern Recognition, pp. 3431–3440 (2015)
9. Otsu, N.: A threshold selection method from gray-level histograms. IEEE Trans. Syst. Man Cybern. B Cybern. **9**(1), 62–66 (1979)
10. Roodbandi, A.S.J., Naderi, H., Hashenmi-Nejad, N., Choobineh, A., Baneshi, M.R., Feyzi, V.: Technical report on the modification of 3-dimensional non-contact human body laser scanner for the measurement of anthropometric dimensions: verification of its accuracy and precision. J. Lasers Med. Sci. **8**(1), 22–28 (2017)
11. Rother, C., Kolmogorov, V., Blake, A.: Grabcut: interactive foreground extraction using iterated graph cuts. ACM Trans. Graph. (TOG) **23**(3), 309–314 (2004)
12. Sheng, Y., Sadka, A.H., Kondoz, A.M.: Automatic single view-based 3-D face synthesis for unsupervised multimedia applications. IEEE Trans. Circuits Syst. Video Technol. **18**(7), 961–974 (2008)
13. Weiss, A., Hirshberg, D., Black, M.J.: Home 3D body scans from noisy image and range data. In: International Conference on Computer Vision, pp. 1951–1958. IEEE (2011)
14. Widyanti, A., Ardiansyah, A., Yassierli, Iridiastadi, H.: Development of anthropometric measurement method for body circumferences using digital image. In: PPCOE, The Eighth Pan-Pacific Conference on Occupational Ergonomics (2007)
15. Xu, H., Yu, Y., Zhou, Y., Li, Y., Du, S.: Measuring accurate body parameters of dressed humans with large-scale motion using a Kinect sensor. Sensors **13**(9), 11362–11384 (2013)
16. Zhou, X., Chen, J., Chen, G., Zhao, Z., Zhao, Y.: Anthropometric body modeling based on orthogonal-view images. Int. J. Ind. Ergon. **53**, 27–36 (2016)
17. Zhu, S., Mok, P., Kwok, Y.: An efficient human model customization method based on orthogonal-view monocular photos. Comput. Aided Des. **45**(11), 1314–1332 (2013)

Greedy Salient Dictionary Learning
for Activity Video Summarization

Ioannis Mademlis$^{(\boxtimes)}$, Anastasios Tefas, and Ioannis Pitas

Department of Informatics, Aristotle University of Thessaloniki,
Thessaloniki, Greece
imademlis@cds.auth.gr

Abstract. Automated video summarization is well-suited to the task of analysing human activity videos (e.g., from surveillance feeds), mainly as a pre-processing step, due to the large volume of such data and the small percentage of actually important video frames. Although key-frame extraction remains the most popular way to summarize such footage, its successful application for activity videos is obstructed by the lack of editing cuts and the heavy inter-frame visual redundancy. Salient dictionary learning, recently proposed for activity video key-frame extraction, models the problem as the identification of a small number of video frames that, simultaneously, can best reconstruct the entire video stream and are salient compared to the rest. In previous work, the reconstruction term was modelled as a Column Subset Selection Problem (CSSP) and a numerical, SVD-based algorithm was adapted for solving it, while video frame saliency, in the fastest algorithm proposed up to now, was also estimated using SVD. In this paper, the numerical CSSP method is replaced by a greedy, iterative one, properly adapted for salient dictionary learning, while the SVD-based saliency term is retained. As proven by the extensive empirical evaluation, the resulting approach significantly outperforms all competing key-frame extraction methods with regard to speed, without sacrificing summarization accuracy. Additionally, computational complexity analysis of all salient dictionary learning and related methods is presented.

Keywords: Key-frame extraction · Dictionary learning
Column Subset Selection Problem · Video summarization

1 Introduction

Videos depicting human activities may come from different sources, such as surveillance feeds or movie/TV shooting sessions. They typically extend to many hours of footage which must be manually browsed in order to retain the most

The research leading to these results has received funding from the European Union Seventh Framework Programme (FP7/2007-2013) under grant agreement numbers 287674 (3DTVS) and 316564 (IMPART).

I. Kompatsiaris et al. (Eds.): MMM 2019, LNCS 11295, pp. 578–589, 2019.
https://doi.org/10.1007/978-3-030-05710-7_48

interesting parts. Video summarization algorithms may help in automating a large part of this tedious and labour-intensive process, by producing a short summary of the video input. However, activity videos, which can be considered as temporal concatenations of consecutive activity segments, share certain properties which make automated summarization difficult compared to other video types (such as movies [17]): lack of clear editing cuts, static camera and static background resulting in heavy visual redundancy between video frames, as well as increased subjectivity in identifying important video frames (there is no clear way to proclaim a specific part of a human action as more representative than another one). Potential sources of such videos are surveillance cameras, capture sessions in TV/movie production, etc.

Video summarization algorithms are expected to achieve a balance between different needs, such as sufficient summary compactness (lack of redundancy), conciseness, outlier inclusion, semantic representativeness and content coverage. Despite the fact that many different ways to summarize a video exist (e.g., skimming [17], shot selection [16], synopsis [27], or temporal video segmentation [26,28]), *key-frame extraction*, i.e., producing a temporally ordered subset of the original video frame set that in some sense contains the most important and representative visual content, remains the most widely applicable video summarization method. In fact, it is unavoidable if the selected subset of original video frames must be retained in unprocessed form, since in such a case video synopsis (which results in synthetic video frames, each one aggregating content from multiple original video frames) cannot be applied. Moreover, simple temporal video segmentation does not result in a summary per se, but is only a substitute of shot cut/boundary detection [4], while skimming requires key-frame extraction as an initial step. Thus, in the context of this paper, the terms "video summarization" and "key-frame extraction", as well as the terms "video summary" and "key-frame set", are hereafter used as synonymous (although this is not true in general). In actual method deployment, the extracted key-frames could be temporally extended to key-segments and then concatenated, so as to form a video skim.

Although supervised key-frame extraction methods, attempting to implicitly learn how to produce static summaries from human-created manual video summaries, have recently appeared due to the success of deep learning [32], they suffer from the subjectiveness inherent in the problem (different persons may produce widely differing summaries for the same video source) and the lack of manual activity video summaries readily available for training in most use-cases. Indeed, no specific video frame of an activity video segment can be reliably considered as more important than another one from the same segment. A more natural summarization goal would be for the algorithm to select one key-frame per actual activity segment, with the video frames belonging to the same segment considered as fully interchangeable. Therefore, this paper focuses on unsupervised key-frame extraction for activity video summarization and employs an objective evaluation metric that takes the above into account.

Two main algorithm families have emerged for unsupervised key-frame extraction over the years. The first one consists in distance-based data partitioning via video frame clustering, under the assumption that video shooting focuses more on important video frames [33]. The number of clusters is either pre-defined by the user or may depend proportionally on the video length [9]. The cluster medoids are selected as key-frames, in a manner dependent on the underlying clustering algorithm. The second algorithm family consists in dictionary-of-representatives approaches, where the original video frames are assumed to be approximately composed of linear combinations of a representative subset of them. These "dictionary frames" are detected and employed as key-frames [10].

In all cases, video frames are either represented by a raw, vectorized form of their unaltered pixel values (e.g., in [8]), or they are initially described by low-level/mid-level global or local image descriptors [13,14], with sparse local descriptors typically aggregated under a representation scheme such as Bag-of-Features (BoF) [7]. High-level semantic video frame representations, learnt via deep neural networks, have also been tested [23].

Video frame clustering implicitly models summarization as a frame sampling problem, where criteria such as compactness, outlier inclusion and video content coverage should be met. Scene semantics are not considered and semantics extraction is entirely offloaded to the underlying, employed video frame description/representation scheme. Although clustering is a baseline key-frame extraction method, it still dominates the relevant literature due to its simplicity, straightforward problem modelling and relatively good accuracy.

In contrast, dictionary-of-representatives methods inherently consider scene semantics in an unsupervised manner, since they decompose the video into isolated visual building blocks. In [6,22] the video summarization problem is formulated as sparse dictionary learning, with extracted key-frames ideally enabling optimal linear reconstruction of the original video from the selected dictionary. In both cases, the outliers are entirely disregarded.

In [10] a similar approach is followed, via sparse modeling representative selection. In [8] RPCA-KFE is presented, a key-frame extraction algorithm that takes into account both the contribution to video reconstruction and the distinctness of each video frame. The idea is to select as a summary the subset of video frames that simultaneously minimizes the aggregate reconstruction error and maximizes the total distinctness. However, the distinctness term is defined very inflexibly and is bound to the reconstruction term in a complementary manner.

Very recently, salient dictionary learning was proposed as a way to generalize dictionary-of-representatives approaches for activity key-frame extraction [19]. The key-frame set is extracted by simultaneously optimizing the desired summary for maximum reconstructive ability and maximum saliency. Activity videos are especially suited to such an approach, since human activities can be easily decomposed into approximately linear combinations of elementary actions [1], but on the other hand they contain a significant number of uninteresting/non-salient video frames that, nonetheless, convey large reconstructive advantage (e.g., video frames solely depicting the static background, or containing mostly human body poses common to multiple activity segments).

Following preliminary work in [18], where no saliency term was considered, the Column Subset Selection Problem (CSSP) was selected to model the reconstruction term. This was a novel application of the CSSP, mainly employed for feature selection tasks up to that point. In [19] a fast, randomized, SVD-based two-stage algorithm for solving the CSSP was adopted from [3] and adapted to salient dictionary learning, while video frame saliency was computed using a dense inter-frame distance matrix. In [20] that saliency term was replaced with a much faster to compute Regularized SVD-based Low-Rank Approximation approach, resulting in state-of-the-art summarization accuracy at near-real-time speeds. However, with regard to the reconstruction term, a black box of non-negligible computational cost remained in the form of the deterministic second stage from [3].

This work further explores the possibilities opened up by CSSP-based modelling and adopts from [11] a different, non-randomized CSSP solution for the reconstruction term. It is a greedy, iterative algorithm, adapted here to salient dictionary learning and coupled with the fast, SVD-based saliency term from [20]. Computational complexity analysis of all salient dictionary learning and related methods is presented for the first time. Extensive empirical evaluation of the proposed method is performed under the setup described in [20]. The results indicate high speed gains while retaining state-of-the-art summarization accuracy, making the proposed algorithm especially suitable for big data pre-processing.

2   Method Preliminaries

Below, an input video composed of N frames is represented as a matrix $\mathbf{D} \in \mathbb{R}^{V \times N}$. Each column vector $\mathbf{d}_j, 0 \leq i < N$, describes a video frame. Moreover, we assume that the desired summary is a matrix $\mathbf{S} \in \mathbb{R}^{V \times C}, C << N$ containing an ordered set of video key-frames. Its columns are indicated by a binary-valued frame selection vector $\mathbf{s} \in \mathbb{N}^N$.

2.1   The Column Subset Selection Problem

In the methods this paper improves upon (the no-saliency, dictionary-of-representatives algorithm [18] and the salient dictionary learning algorithms [19,20]), the Column Subset Selection Problem (CSSP) [3] was selected for algebraically modelling the reconstruction term.

Given $\mathbf{D}$ and a parameter $C << N$, the CSSP consists in selecting a subset of exactly C columns of $\mathbf{D}$, which will form a new $V \times C$ matrix $\mathbf{S}$ that captures as much of the information contained in the original matrix as possible. The goal is to construct a matrix $\mathbf{S} \in \mathbb{R}^{V \times C}$ such that the quantity:

$$\|\mathbf{D} - (\mathbf{SS}^+)\mathbf{D}\|_F \tag{1}$$

is minimized. $\| \cdot \|_F$ is the Frobenius matrix norm and $\mathbf{S}^+$ is the pseudoinverse of $\mathbf{S}$. Obviously, $\mathbf{S}$ is entirely defined by $\mathbf{D}$ and the frame selection vector $\mathbf{s}$.

The CSSP was deemed to be especially suitable for modelling key-frame extraction, since it results in a small number C of unaltered columns of the original matrix that are significant in a dictionary-of-representatives sense, with C being strictly user-defined. However, the problem is considered to be NP-hard [2]. A fast, numerical, randomized CSSP method operating in two stages [3] was employed as a main building block in [19] and [20]. The method relied on the SVD decomposition of $\mathbf{D}$.

2.2   Salient Dictionary Learning for Activity Summarization

Salient dictionary learning entails joint optimization of a "reconstruction term" and a "saliency term", so as to avoid a summary that contains many uninteresting video frames (e.g., depicting the static background) and does not include any outliers. The related objective is defined in [19] using the CSSP for reconstruction and a vector $\mathbf{p}$ for saliency:

$$\min_{\mathbf{s}} : \|\mathbf{D} - \mathbf{S}\mathbf{S}^+\mathbf{D}\|_F - \alpha c\mathbf{s}^T\mathbf{p}, \tag{2}$$

where $\alpha \in [0, 1]$ is a user-provided parameter regulating the contribution of the saliency component and c is a scaling factor to bring per-video frame saliency value down to the scale of the dictionary component. $\mathbf{p} \in \mathbb{R}^N$ is a precomputed per-frame saliency vector, assigning a scalar saliency value to each video frame.

In [19], the approximate CSSP algorithm from [3] was coupled with a simple saliency term. Initially, the saliency term produced a precomputed, per-frame saliency vector $\mathbf{p}$. Subsequently, video data matrix $\mathbf{D}$ was suitably transformed in a manner that took into account per-frame saliency, before applying the numerical algorithm from [3] to the modified matrix. The above method implicitly solved the objective from Eq. (2).

In [20] the saliency term was replaced with a Regularized SVD-based Low Rank Approximation method that significantly reduced the computational overhead. This was due to the fact that no inter-frame distance matrix needed to be constructed, while the SVD decomposition of the video data matrix was also required by the employed CSSP algorithm and, therefore, readily available.

3   Greedy Salient Dictionary Learning

Although the method in [20] is faster and, in general, equally or more accurate than competing methods, it is still burdened by the second, deterministic stage of the numerical CSSP algorithm from [3] (Rank-Revealing QR decomposition [5] was employed in both [19] and [20]). Given that the required runtime is a quadratic function of N (as shown below), minimizing the per-frame computational cost of salient dictionary learning is essential for successful deployment in big activity video data analysis.

Towards this end, the possibilities opened up for activity video key-frame extraction by CSSP modelling were explored. In this paper, the numerical, two-stage CSSP solution for the reconstruction term is entirely replaced by an efficient, iterative, deterministic, greedy method [11], adopted from recent CSSP literature and described below.

At each iteration of the algorithm a single video frame is added to the summary, so as to greedily minimize the reconstruction error, until the key-frame set contains exactly C key-frames. The following quantities are defined for the t-th iteration:

1. $\mathbf{s}^{t-1}$: the currently extracted key-frame set/summary binary selection vector, prescribing the current summary $\mathbf{S}^{t-1}$. It holds that $\|\mathbf{s}^{t-1}\|_0 = t - 1$.
2. $\overline{\mathcal{R}}^{t-1}$: the set of the temporal indices of all video frames not contained in $\mathbf{S}^{t-1}$. It contains $N - (t - 1)$ elements, all in the interval $[0, N - 1]$.
3. l^t: the temporal index of the video frame $\mathbf{d}_{:l_t}$ that is actually selected for inclusion in $\mathbf{S}^t$ during iteration t. Obviously, $l^t \in \overline{\mathcal{R}}^{t-1}$, but $l^t \notin \overline{\mathcal{R}}^t$.

The method recursively updates two vectors, $\mathbf{f}, \mathbf{g} \in \mathbb{R}^N$. Each one keeps track of a scalar score for each video frame $\mathbf{d}_{:i}, 0 \leq i < N$. At the start of the t-th iteration, the most suitable l^t is selected for addition to the extracted key-frame set/summary in the following manner:

$$l^t = \arg \max_i \frac{f_i^{t-1}}{g_i^{t-1}}, \quad i \in \overline{\mathcal{R}}^{t-1}, \tag{3}$$

where f_i^{t-1}, g_i^{t-1} is the i-the entry of current vector $\mathbf{f}, \mathbf{g}$, respectively. Subsequently, $\mathbf{f}^t$ and $\mathbf{g}^t$ are computed, by updating $\mathbf{f}^{t-1}$ and $\mathbf{g}^{t-1}$ based on the value of l^t. The formulas for initializing and updating $\mathbf{f}$ and $\mathbf{g}$ can be found in [11].

In order to adapt the above method to the proposed framework, $\tilde{\mathbf{p}} \in \mathbb{R}^N$ is initially precomputed once. It is a slightly modified version of $\mathbf{p}$ from [20], with its entries (the per-frame saliency factors) normalized into the interval $[0, 1]$. Subsequently, the greedy CSSP algorithm is iteratively executed as described above, but Eq. (3) is modified in the following manner:

$$l^t = \arg \max_i \left((1 - \alpha) \frac{f_i^{t-1}}{g_i^{t-1}} + \alpha \tilde{p}_i \frac{f_i^{t-1}}{g_i^{t-1}} \right), \quad i \in \overline{\mathcal{R}}^{t-1}. \tag{4}$$

where $\tilde{p}_i$ is the i-th entry of $\tilde{\mathbf{p}}$. Thus, at each iteration, vectors $\mathbf{f}$ and $\mathbf{g}$ are updated based on the reconstructive advantage currently conveyed by each video frame, but the actual selection of a candidate video frame for inclusion in the summary also depends on its precomputed saliency and the provided saliency contribution parameter α. The algorithm is completed after C iterations.

4   Computational Complexity Analysis

Below, the computational complexity of all CSSP-based activity video key-frame extraction methods is briefly presented for the first time. In [18], the

CSSP objective is directly employed as a fitness function under a genetic algorithm, with no saliency term considered. Since the computation of $\mathbf{S}^+$ runs in $\mathcal{O}(min\{VC^2, V^2C\})$, the entire reconstruction term is dominated by the matrix multiplications in Eq. (1). Therefore, assuming population size P and G generations, total method complexity is either $\mathcal{O}(PGV^2N)$, if $V < C$, or $\mathcal{O}(PGVCN)$, if $V > C$.

In [19], the employed CSSP algorithm runs in $\mathcal{O}(min\{VN^2, V^2N\})$ [3], while the time complexity of the proposed inter-frame distance matrix-based saliency term is $\mathcal{O}(VN^2)$. The proposed adaptation of the CSSP method to salient dictionary learning runs in $\mathcal{O}(VN)$. Thus, the overall method complexity is $\mathcal{O}(VN^2)$.

In [20], the CSSP algorithm from [3] is retained, but a different SVD-based saliency term is proposed. Given that the SVD decomposition of $\mathbf{D}$ can be used for both the reconstruction and the saliency term, the complexity of the latter is $\mathcal{O}(VN)$. Finally, the adaptation to salient dictionary learning runs in $\mathcal{O}(VN)$, as in [19]. Thus, the overall method complexity is $\mathcal{O}(min\{VN^2, V^2N\})$.

In this paper, the initialization of $\mathbf{f}$ and $\mathbf{g}$ runs in $\mathcal{O}(VN^2)$, while the main, iterative CSSP algorithm runs in $\mathcal{O}(VNC)$ [11]. The saliency term from [20] is retained and its computation is dominated by the SVD decomposition: $\mathcal{O}(min\{VN^2, V^2N\})$. Since the per-frame saliency vector only needs to be derived once, replacing Eq. (3) with Eq. (4) does not alter its time complexity. Thus, given that $C << N$, the overall method complexity is $\mathcal{O}(VN^2)$.

For comparison purposes, the time complexities of [8,9,22] are $\mathcal{O}(VCN)$, $\mathcal{O}(CNV^2)$ and $\mathcal{O}(VCN^2)$, respectively.

5   Evaluation

In order to empirically evaluate the proposed algorithm, extensive comparisons were made against a baseline clustering approach [9], random video frame sampling over a million iterations, as well as competing state-of-the-art methods [8,18–20,22], using three human activity video datasets. The empirical evaluation setup is identical to the one found in [20]. All method implementations were in MATLAB, except [18] which was written in C++, using fast linear algebra libraries OpenBLAS [30] and Armadillo [25]. All experiments were performed on a high-end desktop PC.

Although video descriptors that have been learnt via a neural network are becoming the norm in video summarization [21], we employed a combination of traditional, hand-crafted low- and mid-level descriptors for video frame representation. Thus, three different feature descriptors were extracted for each video: LMoD [15], SIFT [13] and Improved Dense Trajectories (IDT) [29], aggregated per video frame under the Improved Fisher Vector (IFV) approach [24]. IFV codebook size was empirically set to 8, 24 and 32 visual words for IDT, SIFT and LMoD, respectively, leading to total dimensionality of video frame representation (after concatenation) $V = 17568$. In the case of [8], vectorized raw image pixel values were employed for video frame representation, due to the nature of the algorithm.

Single-view subsets of three publicly available, annotated, multi-view activity video datasets were employed. The datasets were slightly processed to better suit an activity video summarization task (e.g., several videos, each one depicting a single activity, were temporally concatenated, so as to form a long video composed of multiple consecutive activities). In each case, a specific camera angle was chosen from the original multi-view dataset for all activity sessions. The processed versions are briefly described below:

1. The IMPART video dataset [28], depicting 3 actors in 2 different settings: an outdoor one and a living-room. A total of 116 indoor and 214 outdoor activity sessions with static camera are included, where the actors perform a series of activities one after another, moving along approximately fixed trajectories via predefined waypoints. 4 different activity types were performed, namely "Walk", "Hand-wave", "Run" and "Other". The dataset consists of 6 video files with a resolution of 720×540 pixels and mean duration of about 4542 video frames.
2. The IXMAS dataset [31], depicting 10 actors in an indoor setting. A total of 467 activity sessions with static camera are included, where the actors perform a series of activities one after another, with varying/unconstrained body poses. In total, 11 different activities were performed. The dataset consists of 4 video files with a resolution of 390×290 pixels and mean duration of about 9055 video frames. This is the most challenging dataset, due to the low video resolution, the relatively high number of video frames and activity segments, as well as the very high visual similarity between video frames belonging to different activity segments.
3. The i3DPOST dataset [12], depicting 8 actors in a blue-screen backdrop. A total of 104 activity sessions with static camera are included, where either the actors perform a series of activities one after another, moving along approximately fixed trajectories, or two actors interact. In total, 12 different activities were performed. The dataset consists of 3 video files with a resolution of 640×480 pixels and mean duration of about 5358 video frames.

The objective Independence Ratio (IR) metric was employed for summarization accuracy evaluation, as in [18–20]. IR scores bypass the subjective, or semi-subjective, nature of traditionally employed video summarization metrics, by treating any two video frames belonging to the same activity segment as interchangeable and, from the aspect of its empirical evaluation, reducing activity video summarization to a variant of temporal video segmentation. Given a summary $\mathbf{s}$ of an input video $\mathbf{D}$, the number I_s of extracted key-frames derived from actually different activity segments (hereafter called *independent key-frames*) is used as an indirect indication of summarization success. Obviously, I_s equals the number of different activity segments represented in the summary $\mathbf{s}$. Thus, the IR score is defined as follows:

$$IR(\mathbf{s}) = \frac{I_s}{C},$$ (5)

Table 1. Mean IR for all competing methods across all datasets (higher is better).

	Random	**Proposed**	[20]	[18]	[19]	[9]	[22]	[8]
IMPART	58.86%	**77.17%**	72.16%	75.85	72.02%	72.94%	68.03%	50.17%
i3DPOST	59.01%	**77.78%**	75.64%	72.56%	74.39%	72.65%	65.81%	44.87%
IXMAS	59.40%	65.72	**66.38%**	62.00%	66.22%	65.29%	66.16%	46.66%

where C is the total number of requested key-frames. IR scores indicate the percentage of extracted key-frames derived from actually different activity segments, among the entire extracted key-frame set (computed using the ground truth).

Tables 1 and 2 present the mean IR scores obtained by all competing methods, across all datasets, as well as the mean execution times per video frame. For [8,19,20] and the proposed method, only the highest IR results across five tested values of the saliency contribution parameter ($\alpha = 0$, 0.25, 0.50, 0.75, 1.00) are reported per dataset.

Algorithm [8] completely fails to handle activity summarization, simple clustering from [9] performs relatively well, while the proposed method achieves state-of-the-art IR accuracy on two out of three datasets, at the lowest computational penalty. On IMPART, [20] seems to be faster (although with significantly lower IR score), but this stems from the fact that [20] achieved its best IR score (for that particular dataset) with $\alpha = 0$, i.e., without computing the saliency term at all.

Table 2. Mean runtime per video frame (in milliseconds) for all competing methods across all datasets (lower is better).

	Proposed	[20]	[18]	[19]	[9]	[22]	[8]
IMPART	28.86	**17.90**	552.92	232.21	76.85	4043.82	427.84
i3DPOST	**31.67**	42.05	517.80	262.26	70.01	2544.20	385.35
IXMAS	**49.07**	80.82	734.34	461.15	225.45	8594.31	891.95

Therefore, Table 3 details the evaluation results of [20] and the proposed method for all tested values of α, on the IMPART dataset. As it can be seen, the proposed method is significantly faster for any given α, while for $\alpha = 1$ (where the corresponding, adapted CSSP algorithm is executed as a reconstruction term, but only video frame saliency is actually taken into account for key-frame selection) the proposed method achieves almost 14% better IR score than [20]. On IXMAS, [20] performs slightly better than the proposed method, at a significantly higher computational cost.

Table 3. Mean IR and runtime per video frame for the fastest methods, on the IMPART dataset.

α	Proposed-IR	[20]-IR	Proposed-Time	[20]-Time
0.00	75.21%	**72.16%**	**1.26**	**17.90**
0.25	75.18%	69.86%	28.77	45.96
0.50	76.00%	70.40%	28.91	45.28
0.75	**77.17%**	68.80%	28.86	44.98
1.00	70.30%	56.09%	28.13	36.14

6   Conclusions

A fast approach to salient dictionary learning for activity video key-frame extraction is proposed. The method retains the SVD-based saliency term from the fastest relevant algorithm available up to now, but replaces the numerical CSSP method employed for reconstruction with a greedy, iterative algorithm, properly adapted to salient dictionary learning. The result is a very rapid approach that, in general, achieves state-of-the-art summarization accuracy, while simultaneously significantly outperforming all competing methods in terms of speed. The proposed algorithm seems especially suitable for pre-processing large video streams, while greater performance gains are expected in the future, by employing neurally derived video descriptors and by integrating constraints in the optimization problem.

References

1. Aggarwal, J.K., Ryoo, M.S.: Human activity analysis: a review. ACM Comput. Surv. **43**(3), 16:1–16:43 (2011)
2. Arai, H., Maung, C., Schweitzer, H.: Optimal column subset selection by A-star search. In: AAAI Conference on Artificial Intelligence (2015)
3. Boutsidis, C., Mahoney, M.W., Drineas, P.: An improved approximation algorithm for the column subset selection problem. In: Symposium on Discrete Algorithms, pp. 968–977 (2009)
4. Cernekova, Z., Pitas, I., Nikou, C.: Information theory-based shot cut/fade detection and video summarization. IEEE Trans. Circuits Syst. Video Technol. **16**(1), 82–91 (2006)
5. Chan, T.F., Hansen, P.C.: Low-rank revealing QR factorizations. Numer. Linear Algebra Appl. **1**(1), 33–44 (1994)
6. Cong, Y., Yuan, J., Luo, J.: Towards scalable summarization of consumer videos via sparse dictionary selection. IEEE Trans. Multimed. **14**(1), 66–75 (2012)
7. Csurka, G., Dance, C., Fan, L., Willamowski, J., Bray, C.: Visual categorization with bags of keypoints. In: European Conference on Computer Vision (ECCV), pp. 1–2 (2004)
8. Dang, C., Radha, H.: RPCA-KFE: key frame extraction for video using robust principal component analysis. IEEE Trans. Image Process. **24**(11), 3742–3753 (2015)

9. De Avilla, S.E.F., Lopes, A.P.B., Luz, A.L.J., Araujo, A.A.: VSUMM: a mechanism designed to produce static video summaries and a novel evaluation method. Pattern Recogn. Lett. **32**(1), 56–68 (2011)

10. Elhamifar, E., Sapiro, G., Vidal, R.: See all by looking at a few: Sparse modeling for finding representative objects. In: Proceedings of the IEEE Conference on Computer Vision and Pattern Recognition (CVPR) (2012)

11. Farahat, A.K., Ghodsi, A., Kamel, M.S.: Efficient greedy feature selection for unsupervised learning. Knowl. Inf. Syst. **35**(2), 285–310 (2013)

12. Gkalelis, N., Kim, H., Hilton, A., Nikolaidis, N., Pitas, I.: The i3DPOST multiview and 3D human action/interaction database. In: Proceedings of the IEEE Conference for Visual Media Production (CVMP), pp. 159–168 (2009)

13. Lowe, D.G.: Object recognition from local scale-invariant features. In: International Conference on Computer Vision (ICCV), pp. 1150–1157. IEEE(1999)

14. Mademlis, I., Nikolaidis, N., Pitas, I.: Stereoscopic video description for key-frame extraction in movie summarization. In: European Signal Processing Conference (EUSIPCO), pp. 819–823. IEEE (2015)

15. Mademlis, I., Tefas, A., Nikolaidis, N., Pitas, I.: Compact video description and representation for automated summarization of human activities. In: Angelov, P., Manolopoulos, Y., Iliadis, L., Roy, A., Vellasco, M. (eds.) INNS 2016. AISC, vol. 529, pp. 18–28. Springer, Cham (2017). https://doi.org/10.1007/978-3-319-47898-2_3

16. Mademlis, I., Tefas, A., Nikolaidis, N., Pitas, I.: Movie shot selection preserving narrative properties. In: Proceedings of the IEEE International Workshop on Multimedia Signal Processing (MMSP) (2016)

17. Mademlis, I., Tefas, A., Nikolaidis, N., Pitas, I.: Multimodal stereoscopic movie summarization conforming to narrative characteristics. IEEE Trans. Image Process. **25**(12), 5828–5840 (2016)

18. Mademlis, I., Tefas, A., Nikolaidis, N., Pitas, I.: Summarization of human activity videos via low-rank approximation. In: Proceedings of the IEEE International Conference on Acoustics, Speech and Signal Processing (ICASSP) (2017)

19. Mademlis, I., Tefas, A., Pitas, I.: Summarization of human activity videos using a salient dictionary. In: Proceedings of the IEEE International Conference on Image Processing (ICIP) (2017)

20. Mademlis, I., Tefas, A., Pitas, I.: Regularized SVD-based video frame saliency for activity summarization. In: Proceedings of the IEEE International Conference on Acoustics, Speech and Signal Processing (ICASSP) (2018)

21. Mahasseni, B., Lam, M., Todorovic, S.: Unsupervised video summarization with adversarial LSTM networks. In: Proceedings of the IEEE International Conference on Computer Vision and Pattern Recognition (CVPR) (2017)

22. Mei, S., Guan, G., Wang, Z., Wan, S., He, M., Feng, D.D.: Video summarization via minimum sparse reconstruction. Pattern Recogn. **48**(2), 522–533 (2015)

23. Otani, M., Nakashima, Y., Rahtu, E., Heikkilä, J., Yokoya, N.: Video summarization using deep semantic features. arXiv preprint arXiv:1609.08758 (2016)

24. Perronnin, F., Sánchez, J., Mensink, T.: Improving the fisher kernel for large-scale image classification. In: Daniilidis, K., Maragos, P., Paragios, N. (eds.) ECCV 2010. LNCS, vol. 6314, pp. 143–156. Springer, Heidelberg (2010). https://doi.org/10.1007/978-3-642-15561-1_11

25. Sanderson, C., Curtin, R.: Armadillo: a template-based C++ library for linear algebra. J. Open Source Softw. **1**, 26 (2016)

26. Sener, F., Yao, A.: Unsupervised learning and segmentation of complex activities from video. arXiv preprint arXiv:1803.09490 (2018)

27. Song, X., Sun, L., Lei, J., Tao, D., Yuan, G., Song, M.: Event-based large scale surveillance video summarization. Neurocomputing **187**, 66–74 (2016)
28. Theodoridis, T., Tefas, A., Pitas, I.: Multi-view semantic temporal video segmentation. In: Proceedings of the IEEE International Conference on Image Processing (ICIP) (2016)
29. Wang, H., Schmid, C.: Action recognition with improved trajectories. In: Proceedings of the IEEE International Conference on Computer Vision (ICCV) (2013)
30. Wang, Q., Zhang, X., Zhang, Y., Yi, Q.: AUGEM: automatically generate high performance dense linear algebra kernels on x86 CPUs. In: Proceedings of the International Conference on High Performance Computing, Networking, Storage and Analysis. ACM (2013)
31. Weinland, D., Ronfard, R., Boyer, E.: Free viewpoint action recognition using motion history volumes. Comput. Vis. Image Underst. **104**(2), 249–257 (2006)
32. Zhang, K., Chao, W.-L., Sha, F., Grauman, K.: Video summarization with long short-term memory. In: Leibe, B., Matas, J., Sebe, N., Welling, M. (eds.) ECCV 2016. LNCS, vol. 9911, pp. 766–782. Springer, Cham (2016). https://doi.org/10. 1007/978-3-319-46478-7_47
33. Zhuang, Y., Rui, Y., Huang, T., Mehrotra, S.: Adaptive key frame extraction using unsupervised clustering. In: International Conference on Image Processing (ICIP), pp. 866–870. IEEE (1998)

Accelerating Topic Detection on Web for a Large-Scale Data Set via Stochastic Poisson Deconvolution

Jinzhong Lin[1], Junbiao Pang[2], Li Su[1], Yugui Liu[1], and Qingming Huang[1,3(✉)]

[1] School of Computer and Control Engineering,
University of Chinese Academy of Sciences, Beijing, China
lin_jin_zhong@outlook.com, {suli,liuyg,qmhuang}@ucas.ac.cn
[2] Faculty of Information Technology, Beijing University of Technology,
Beijing, China
junbiao_pang@bjut.edu.cn
[3] Institute of Computing Technology, Chinese Academy of Sciences,
Beijing, China

Abstract. Organizing webpages into hot topics is one of the key steps to understand the trends from multi-modal web data. To handle this pressing problem, Poisson Deconvolution (PD), a state-of-the-art method, recently is proposed to rank the interestingness of web topics on a similarity graph. Nevertheless, in terms of scalability, PD optimized by expectation-maximization is not sufficiently efficient for a large-scale data set. In this paper, we develop a Stochastic Poisson Deconvolution (SPD) to deal with the large-scale web data sets. Experiments demonstrate the efficacy of the proposed approach in comparison with the state-of-the-art methods on two public data sets and one large-scale synthetic data set.

Keywords: Large-scale · Poisson Deconvolution
Unsupervised ranking · Web topic detection · Surrogate function

1 Introduction

With the rapid development of information technology and mobile internet, social media websites greatly facilitate both the generation and the propagation of User-Generated Content (UGC). Consequently, the unprecedented explosion in the volume of UGC [10] data makes people difficult to quickly grasp "hot" contents. Driven by this practical requirement, topic detection from web [10,11,26] is such an effort to organize webpages into meaningful topics automatically. Different from the traditional Topic Detection and Tracking (TDT) [5] that aims at discovering topics from professionally edited news articles, web topic detection faces a large-scale UGC data which never evolve into any hot topics. In this paper, web topic detection is formally defined as the task of discovering of a

© Springer Nature Switzerland AG 2019
I. Kompatsiaris et al. (Eds.): MMM 2019, LNCS 11295, pp. 590–602, 2019.
https://doi.org/10.1007/978-3-030-05710-7_49

tiny fraction of webpages strongly connected by a seminal hot event from a large amount of social media [10].

The state-of-the-art approach for web topic detection is to rank the interestingness of topics on a similarity graph [10,12]. Concretely, PD allocates an weight to each topic by diffusing the similarities between webpages [10]. Although a similarity graph is not only efficiently constructed by online k-Nearest Neighborhood Graph (k-N^{2}G) [23] but also is efficiently stored as a sparse matrix, one pressing problem is that PD is not efficiently scalable for a large-scale data set. The reason is that PD has to reconstruct a $N \times N$ float matrix at each iteration where N is the number of webpages.

It is natural to ask: *can we exploit a small fraction of data at each iteration for PD?* One of the simple and yet efficient approaches is stochastic optimization [14]. There are at least two potential benefits of this approach: reducing the requirement of the physical memory, and avoiding the reconstruction of a $N \times N$ scale similarity graph. However, PD optimized by EM algorithm has to maintain a hidden variable which has the same scale of the similarity graph.

In this paper, we propose a Stochastic Poisson Deconvolution (SPD) approach to handle a large-scale data set for web topic detection. It iteratively builds a surrogate of the expected objective function when only a small fraction of data are observed at each iteration. Meanwhile, only a few small stochastically sampled data are used to update the surrogate function. Therefore, avoiding loading all data into memory, SPD significantly reduces the running time.

To the best of our knowledge, this is the first to handle the scalability of PD for web topic detection. The proposed method is conceptually simple and yet efficiently. On a large-scale data set, SPD leads to drastic training-time improvement, *e.g.*, approximate 12.6× speedup on a toy data set with about 200,000 webpages. Meanwhile, SPD can achieve the similar performances to that of PD on two public data sets.

The rest of this paper is organized as follows: Sect. 2 reviews the related work. We describe the details of our approach in Sect. 3. Experimental results are presented in Sect. 4, and the paper is concluded in Sect. 5.

2   Related Work

Detect Web Topic from Multi-modal Data. Recognizing that webpages are the typical heterogeneous data, many literatures consider web topic detection as the clustering task from the multi-modal data. There are two important research threads. One is the multi-modal-based method [2,4], and the other is the similarity graph-based method [22].

In the former thread, topic detection extends the single-modality based approaches into multi-modal data. For instance, multi-modal LDA [4], a variation of LDA [3], is proposed to detect topics from both the images and their tags. In the similarity graph-based method, multi-modal information is fused into the edges of a graph, where the vertexes are clustered into different topics. For instance, Wu *et al.* [24] detect topics of news videos by fusing the similarities from Nearly-Duplicated Keyframes (NDKs) and the speech transcripts.

Compared with the multi-modal-based topic modelings [4], similarity graph-based approach is easily extendable for the other algorithms [6,16,22]. SPD belongs to the similarity graph-based approach. However, our method does not aim at improving accuracy of the detection system, but rather making PD scalable for a large scale data set.

Despite many approaches propose to detect topics in social media, to the best of our knowledge, only a few solutions try to parallelize LDA, *e.g.*, [7,25,27]. As discussed in [10,11], LDA assumes that each webpage should belong to a topic. In fact, in terms of web topic detection, almost 90% webpages would not evolve into any hot topics. Therefore, the paralleled LDAs are incapable to remove the low-valued webpages which do not develop into hot topics.

Stochastic Optimization. Stochastic optimization refers to the minimization (or maximization) of a function in the presence of randomness. The randomness may be presented as noises in measurements, Monte Carlo randomness during the search, or both [14]. For instance, Stochastic Gradient Descent (SGD) and its variants [8,18,20] has been popular in machine learning due to their efficiency and effectiveness. However, the objective function of PD is iteratively changed at each expectation step. This makes SGD unusable for the EM-based PD.

Majorization-Minimization (MM) [13], a generalization of EM [19,21], iteratively minimizes a surrogate function that is the upper bound of the objective function. Many approaches can be interpreted as MM, such as variational Bayes [17] and proximal algorithms [1]. Recently, Stochastic MM (SMM) [9] is proposed to make MM scalable.

Inspired by the success of warm restart and SMM [9], our proposed method additively updates a surrogate function. The resulting SPD not only stores a few random sampled edges, but also significantly speeds up the convergence speed in practice. To the best of our knowledge, this paper is first to apply the surrogated-based method to accelerate PD for web topic detection.

3   Stochastic Poisson Deconvolution

3.1   Revisit Poisson Deconvolution

Given a set of webpages $\mathcal{X} = \{\mathbf{x}_1, \ldots, \mathbf{x}_N\}$, we convert these webpages into a similarity graph $G = (V, E, A)$, where the vertex set V corresponds to the webpages $\mathcal{X}$, the elements of affinity matrix A ($a_{ij} \in A$) corresponds to the scaled and truncated similarities between webpages $\mathcal{X}$, and the edge set E ($e_{ij} \in E$) corresponds to the similarities between webpages $\mathcal{X}$. The details about how to build a similarity graph can be founded in [11].

A set of multi-granularity topics C_k ($k = 1, \ldots, K$) are generated from a similarity graph G, where a topic C_k is represented as:

$$C_k = c_k^\top \circ c_k, \tag{1}$$

in which the indicator vector $c_k \in \{0,1\}^{1 \times N}$, where 1 or 0 means that whether the topic C_k contains the webpage $\mathbf{x}_i$ or not. The operation $\circ$ means that the diagonal of the matrix $c_k^\top c_k$ is set to be zero.

Given a set of topics $\{C_1, \ldots, C_K\}$ and a similarity Graph $G = (V, E, A)$, the topic-wise weight μ_k of a topic C_k is learned under Poisson noise as follows:

$$w_{ij} \sim \text{Poisson}(a_{ij})$$
$$\text{where } w_{ij} = \sum_{k=1}^{K} \mu_k C_{k_{ij}}. \tag{2}$$

The interestingness of a topic is estimated as $i_k = \mu_k \cdot |C_k|$, where $|C_k|$ is the number of webpages in the topic C_k.

By applying EM algorithm, PD (2) is iteratively solved as follows:

$$\mu_k = \frac{\sum_{a_{ij} \in C_k} a_{ij} P_{k_{ij}}}{\sum_{a_{ij} \in C_k} C_{k_{ij}}}, \tag{3}$$

where $P_{k_{ij}}$ ($\sum_{k=1}^{K} P_{k_{ij}} = 1$) are the hidden variables, i.e., $P_{k_{ij}} = \frac{\mu_k C_{k_{ij}}}{\sum_{m=1}^{K} \mu_m C_{m_{ij}}}$ [10].

The Drawback of Poisson Deconvolution: Equation (3) needs to reconstruct all edges in a similarity graph G at each iteration. In practice, a float $N \times N$ matrix has to be allocated in memory; besides, at each iteration, each element of the $N \times N$ matrix has to be updated. Therefore, the time complexity of PD is $O(TN^2)$ where T is the number of iterations; meanwhile, the space complexity of PD is $O(N^2)$. The polynomial complexity handicaps the scalability of PD for a large-scale data set. This problem looms as long as the computation-intensive $N \times N$ matrix is required to be allocated and reconstructed.

3.2   Stochastic Poisson Deconvolution

We present SPD for a large-scale data set in Algorithm 1. At each iteration, by assuming that the edges in a similarity graph are *i.i.d.* from an unknown distribution, we draw a mini-batch edges $\bar{A}^t$ from a similarity graph at the t-th iteration. However, in practice, the mini-batch edges are computed by cycling on a randomly permuted training set [15], since it is often difficult to obtain true *i.i.d.* samples.

Concretely, the objective function of PD (2) is equal to the following problem:

$$\max \ln \prod_{a_{ij} \in \bar{A}^t} \text{Poisson}(a_{ij})$$
$$\Leftrightarrow \min \frac{1}{b} \underbrace{\sum_{a_{ij} \in \bar{A}^t} \left(\sum_{k=1}^{K} \mu_k C_{k_{ij}} - a_{ij} \ln \sum_{k=1}^{K} \mu_k C_{k_{ij}} \right)}_{f^t(\bar{A}^t, \boldsymbol{\mu})}, \tag{4}$$

where b is the number of rows in a mini-batch $\bar{A}^t (\bar{A}^t \in \mathbb{R}^{b \times N})$.

Algorithm 1: Stochastic Poisson Deconvolution

Input: G (Similarity Graph), C_k $k = 1, \ldots, K$ (Topics), b (Batch size), T
   (Number of iteration);
Initialization: cumulative intermediates:$\bar{B}^0 = \bar{D}^0 = 0^{K \times 1}$; $W = 0^{K \times 1}$; β, α; $\boldsymbol{\mu}^0$;
for $t = 1, \ldots, T$ **do**

> Randomly draw a few rows of G: $\bar{A}^t$;
> compute the weight by (9);
> compute the temporary variable B_k^t, D_k^t by (6);
> update the cumulative intermediates:
> $$\bar{B}_k^t = (1 - w_k^t)\bar{B}_k^{t-1} + w_k^t B_k^t;$$
> $$\bar{D}_k^t = (1 - w_k^t)\bar{D}_k^{t-1} + w_k^t D_k^t;$$
>
> update the current estimate: $\mu_k^t = \frac{\bar{B}_k^t}{\bar{D}_k^t}$;

end
Output: $\boldsymbol{\mu}$;

Using Jensen's inequality, the upper bound of likelihood function in (4) is used as the surrogate function:

$$f^t(\bar{A}^t, \boldsymbol{\mu}) \leqslant \underbrace{\frac{1}{b} \sum_{a_{ij} \in \bar{A}^t} \left(\sum_{k=1}^K \mu_k C_{k_{ij}}^t - a_{ij} \sum_{k=1}^K P_{k_{ij}}^t \ln \frac{\mu_k C_{k_{ij}}^t}{P_{k_{ij}}^t} \right)}_{J^t(f^t, \mu^{t-1})}. \tag{5}$$

where $C_{k_{ij}}^t$ means the k-th topic contracted by sampled webpages, $P_{k_{ij}}^t (\sum_{k=1}^K P_{k_{ij}}^t = 1)$ is the hidden variable for the t-th iteration, *i.e.*, $P_{k_{ij}}^t = \frac{\mu_k^{t-1} C_{k_{ij}}^t}{\sum_{k=1}^K \mu_k^{t-1} C_{k_{ij}}^t}$.

The gradient of $J^t(f^t, \mu^{t-1})$ with respect to μ_k is as follows:

$$\frac{d}{d\mu_k} J^t(f^t, \boldsymbol{\mu}^{t-1}) = \underbrace{\frac{1}{b} \sum_{a_{ij} \in \bar{A}^t} C_{k_{ij}}^t}_{D_k^t} - \underbrace{\frac{\frac{1}{b} \sum_{a_{ij} \in \bar{A}^t} a_{ij} P_{k_{ij}}^t}{\mu_k}}_{B_k^t}, \tag{6}$$

where $D_k^t \in \mathbb{R}^{1 \times 1}$ and $B_k^t \in \mathbb{R}^{1 \times 1}$ are the temporal variables.

Proposition 1 *(Iterative Update Process). Given the temporal variables B_k^t and D_k^t, μ_k can be iteratively updated as follows:*

$$\mu_k^t = \frac{\bar{B}_k^t}{\bar{D}_k^t}, \quad s.t. : \quad k \in \{k | \exists C_{k_{ij}}^t \neq 0\} \tag{7}$$

where

$$\bar{B}_k^t \leftarrow (1 - w_k^t)\bar{B}_k^{t-1} + w_k^t B_k^t,$$
$$\bar{D}_k^t \leftarrow (1 - w_k^t)\bar{D}_k^{t-1} + w_k^t D_k^t, \tag{8}$$

where the weight w_k^t for the t-th iteration is as follows:

$$w_k^t = \beta \sqrt{\frac{1+\alpha}{W_k + \alpha}}, \tag{9}$$

in which $W_k = W_k + 1$, $\beta \in (0,1]$, $\alpha \geq 0$.

Proof. Following the suggestions in SMM [9], the combination of the approximate surrogate and the current estimation is as follows:

$$\bar{J}_k^t \leftarrow (1 - w_k^t)\bar{J}_k^{t-1} + w_k^t J_k^t, \tag{10}$$

μ_k is optimized by minimizing (10), *i.e.*, $\mu_k^t = \arg\min \bar{J}_k^t(\mu)$. This process can be derived like following:

When $t = m$, solving for μ_k^m in (10) by (6) (7) (8) can get

$$\mu_k^m = \frac{(1 - w_k^m)\bar{B}_k^{m-1} + w_k^m B_k^m}{(1 - w_k^m)\bar{D}_k^{m-1} + w_k^m D_k^m} = \frac{\bar{B}_k^m}{\bar{D}_k^m}. \tag{11}$$

Finally, without loss of generality, we can get μ_k^t in the iterative update process (7) (8).

The weight w plays a role of Exponentially Weighted Moving Average (EWMA) in approximate surrogate (10). The EWMA is a type of infinite impulse response filter that represents the exponentially decreased weighting factor. Note that the weight of each older surrogate decreases exponentially but never reaches to zero. The w reflects the importance of the current surrogate; meanwhile $1 - w$ reflects the importance of the previous surrogates. Consequently, the older the surrogate is, the smaller the weight should be.

4   Experiments and Discusses

4.1   Data Sets, Features and Evaluation Criteria

Datasets: In the experiments, we evaluate our method on two public data sets, *i.e.*, *MCG-WEBV* [6] and *YKS* [26]. MCG-WEBV is first proposed to detect web video topics from the video sharing websites, being downloaded from the "Most viewed" videos of "This month" on *YouTube*. This data set contains video clips and their titles, tags and descriptions on *Youtube* from Dec. 2008 to Feb. 2009. YKS is a cross-media and cross-platform data set crawled from *YouKu* and *Sina*, respectively. The meta data of YKS contains news articles on *Sina* and titles, tags and descriptions web videos on *YouKu* from May 2012 to June 2012. The statistics of data sets are summarized in Table 1.

Features: During the pre-processing, MCG-WEBV and YKS are tokenized by *NLTK*[1] package. We simply use TF-IDF to encode the textual features. That

---
[1] www.nltk.org.

Table 1. Summary of data sets in the experiments

Data sets	#Webpage	#Topics	k	Sparsity(%)
MCG-WEBV	3660	4240	100	2.73
YKS	7332	5252	20	0.273

is, the surrounding text of each video is considered as a set of words. The cosine distance is used to measure the similarity.

Evaluation Criteria: There are two evaluation methods, *i.e.*, top-10 F_1 versus Number of Detected Topics (NDT) [6] and Accuracy versus False Positive Per Topic (FPPT) [10]. Note that if two methods have the same top-10 F_1 or accuracy score, the one with smaller NDT or FPPT has better performance.

– **Top-10 F_1 versus NDT:** A detected topic is matched with the ground truth, and then the top 10 F_1 scores are averaged to measure the performance of a system:

$$F_1 = \frac{2 \times Precision \times Recall}{Precision + Recall},$$ (12)

where $Precision$ is $\frac{|DT \cap GT|}{|DT|}$, $Recall$ is $\frac{|DT \cap GT|}{|GT|}$, in which DT is a detected topic, GT is a ground truth topic, and $|\cdot|$ denotes the number of webpages in a topic.

– **Accuracy versus FPPT:** if a topic is correctly detected, FPPT is the number of false positive topics caused by a detection system. In this paper, accuracy is defined as follows:

$$Accuracy = \frac{\#Successful}{\#Groundtruth},$$ (13)

where $Successful$ means a detected topic DT is successfully discovered, if Normalized Intersected Ratio (NIR) $\frac{|DT \cap GT|}{|DT \cup GT|}$ is larger than a threshold. Following the previous work [10], 0.5 is used as the threshold of NIR in our experiments.

For the time efficiency, the curve about the objective function versus the used time is used. More specially, the one with less time to reach convergence has better performance.

Enviroment Setting: To fairly compare our algorithm to the state-of-the-art method, we follow the same setting (*i.e.*, similarity graph and topics) to demonstrate the efficiency of our approach. All experiments are implemented in python with a 3.6 GHz processer and 32G RAM.

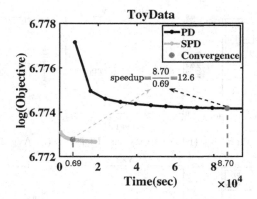

Fig. 1. Comparison between PD and SPD on ToyData (best viewed in color).

4.2   Analysis of Time Complexity and Space Complexity

For PD, a float $N \times N$ matrix has to be allocated in memory to store the reconstructed similarity graph. Therefore, the space complexity and time complexity of PD is $O(N^2)$ and $O(TN^2)$, respectively. In contrast, SPD only updates a small fraction of the reconstructed similarity graph at each iteration. Therefore, SPD only maintains a float $b \times N$ matrix in memory, where $b \times N$ means the size of mini-batch edges (*i.e.*, $\bar{A}^t \in \mathbb{R}^{b \times N}$). The space complexity of SPD is $O(bN)$ ($b \ll N$).

4.3   Evaluation on Toy Dataset

To evaluate the efficientness of SPD, we construct a large-scale toy data set by duplicating MCG-WEBV 50 times. The resulting toy data set has approximate $200,000$ webpages. In this paper, an algorithm converges to a local minimum, if the change of the log likelihood between two consecutive iterations is less than 10^{-5}. The speedup is a ratio of CPU time taken to converge to a local minimum between two algorithms.

Figure 1 shows that SPD significantly outperforms PD in terms of the convergence speed. In our evaluation, SPD achieves about 12.6× speedup. Moreover, at each iteration, although the decrease of the objective function of PD is larger than that of our method, our stochastic approach costs a fewer training time than that of the batch approach. This is because that PD uses all data to perform an accurate update while SPD only uses a small fraction of data to perform an approximate update at each iteration. When training a large-scale toy dataset, PD will cost more time than SPD with one epoch of data due to the problems of computational efficiency and memory limitations. Therefore, SPD converges much faster than PD in large-scale data sets. It validates the advantage of the loss (10): one should not spend too much effort on accurately minimizing the

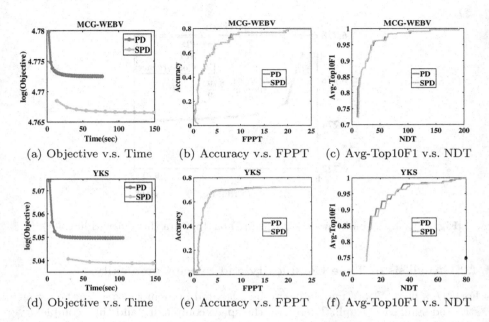

Fig. 2. Comparisons between PD and SPD on MCG-WEBV and YKS.

empirical loss. In addition, just like gradient descent, PD suffers from local minima issue while SPD can avoid it, which make SPD can converge to a smaller value than PD.

4.4 Comparisons with State-of-the-Art Algorithms

Figure 2 shows the comparisons between PD and SPD on both MCG-WEBV and YKS data sets. Figures 2(b), (e), (c), and (f) illustrate that SPD achieves the similar performances to that of PD. Figures 2(a) and (d) show that SPD can get a lower log likelihood than PD. It means that SPD can converge to a smaller value with no drop in performance. Due to these two data sets are all small, PD costs fewer time than SPD with one epoch of data. Therefore, PD converges faster than SPD in small-scale data sets.

4.5 Parameter Analysis

The Size of Mini-Batch: Figure 3 shows the effectiveness of different mini-batch size in SPD on MCG-WEBV. As shown in Fig. 3, objective values of different settings all converge to a local minimum; besides, the smaller the mini-batch is, the lower the log likelihood is. One possible reason is that a smaller mini-batch will bring a larger randomness, which may make SPD escape worse local minima and arrive at a relatively reasonable local minimum. Interestingly, the different sizes of mini-batch obtain very similar results in terms of accuracy v.s. FPPT and top-10 F_1 v.s. NDT. Therefor, the size of the mini-batch does not affect the effectiveness of SPD.

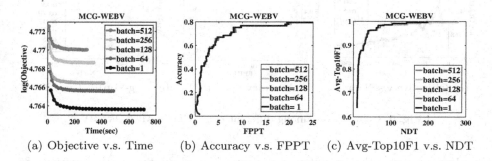

(a) Objective v.s. Time   (b) Accuracy v.s. FPPT   (c) Avg-Top10F1 v.s. NDT

Fig. 3. Comparisions between different batch size on MCG-WEBV.

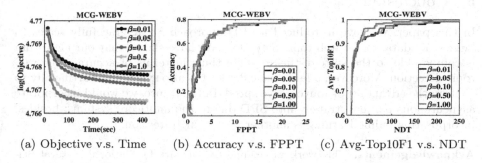

(a) Objective v.s. Time   (b) Accuracy v.s. FPPT   (c) Avg-Top10F1 v.s. NDT

Fig. 4. Comparisons among different β in SPD on MCG-WEBV.

Weight Parameters α and β: In our implementation, we use a decreasing weight in (9), where β is a initial weight, and α is a decay factor. Figure 4 shows comparisons among various β when other parameters are fixed, *i.e.*, $\alpha = 0$, mini-batch $= 128$, and *epoch* $= 30$. Figure 4(a) illustrates the effectiveness of β on the convergence rate. As expected, the larger β is, the faster the convergence speed of SPD is. Because a larger β will make the surrogate function quickly adapt to the latest surrogate one. From Fig. 4(b) and (c), we find that a larger β not only results in a faster convergence speed, but also obtains a better performance.

Figure 5 shows comparisons among various α when the other parameters are fixed, *i.e.*, $\beta = 1$, mini-batch $= 128$, *epoch* $= 30$. Figure 5(a) shows that a smaller α leads to a smoother objective function curves. Because a smaller α not only makes β decay faster, but also makes SPD stable to the latest surrogates. These different settings of α converges to a local minimum.

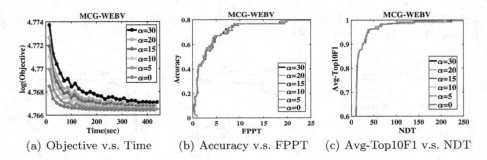

(a) Objective v.s. Time   (b) Accuracy v.s. FPPT   (c) Avg-Top10F1 v.s. NDT

Fig. 5. Comparison among different α in SPD on MCG-WEBV.

In summary, although different settings of α and β influence the convergence speed of SPD, both accuracy v.s. FPPT and top-10 F_1 v.s. NDT are robust to these parameters.

5   Conclusion

In this paper, we have introduced a SPD approach Sthat gracefully scales to large-scale data set for web topic detection. We have shown that our algorithm is comparable to the state-of-the-art algorithms in terms of accuracy for web topic detection. Moreover, a large-scale data set is also synthesized artificially to confirm the advantage of convergence speed. In the future, we would incorporate asynchronous parallel strategy into SPD due to the multicore systems; besides, incorporating online learning is another interesting direction.

Acknowledgements. This work was supported in part by National Natural Science Foundation of China: 61332016, 61472389, 61672069, 61872333, 61650202 and U1636214, in part by Key Research Program of Frontier Sciences, CAS: QYZDJ-SSW-SYS013.

References

1. Beck, A., Teboulle, M.: A fast iterative shrinkage-thresholding algorithm for linear inverse problems. SIAM J. Imaging Sci. **2**(1), 183–202 (2009)
2. Blei, D., Lafferty, J.: A correlated topic model of science. Ann. Appl. Sci. **1**, 17–35 (2007)
3. Blei, D., David, M., Ng, A., Jordan, M., Lafferty, J.: Latent Dirichlet allocation. J. Mach. Learn. Res. **3**, 993–1022 (2003)
4. Putthividhy, D., Attias, H.T., Magarajan, S.S.: Topic regression multi-modal latent Dirichlet allocation for image annotation. In: Computer Vision and Pattern Recognition, vol. 1, pp. 3408–3415 (2010)
5. Allan, J., Carbonell, J., Doddington, G., Yamron, J., et al.: Topic detection and tracking pilot study final report. In: Proceedings of the DARPA Broadcast News Transcription and Understanding Workshop, pp. 194–218 (1998)

6. Cao, J., Ngo, C., Zhang, Y., Li, J.: Tracking web video topics: discovery, visualization, and monitoring. IEEE Trans. Circuits Syst. Video Technol. **21**(12), 1835–1846 (2011)
7. Chen, J., Li, K., Zhu, J., Chen, W.: WarpLDA: a cache efficient o(1) algorithm for latent Dirichlet allocation. Proc. VLDB Endow. **9**(10), 744–755 (2015)
8. Mairal, J.: Optimization with first-order surrogate functions. In: ICML (2013)
9. Mairal, J.: Stochastic majorization-minimization algorithms for large-scale optimization. In: International Conference on Neural Information Processing Systems, vol. 2, pp. 2283–2291 (2013)
10. Pang, J., Jia, F., Zhang, C., Zhang, W., Huang, Q., Yin, B.: Unsupervised web topic detection using a ranked clustering-like pattern across similarity cascades. IEEE Trans. Multimed. **17**(6), 843–853 (2015)
11. Pang, J., Tao, F., Zhang, C., Zhang, W., Huang, Q., Yin, B.: Robust latent poisson deconvolution from multiple features for web topic detection. IEEE Trans. Multimed. **18**(12), 2482–2493 (2016)
12. Pang, J., Tao, F., Li, L., Huang, Q., Yin, B., Tian, Q.: A two-step approach to describing web topics via probable keywords and prototype images from background-removed similarities. Neurocomputing **275**, 478–487 (2018)
13. Lange, K., Hunter, D.R., Yang, I.: Optimization transfer using surrogate objective functions. J. Comput. Graph. Stat. **9**(1), 1–20 (2000)
14. Hannah, L.A.: Stochastic optimization. Int. Encycl. Soc. Behav. Sci. **5**(5), 473–481 (2015)
15. Bottou, L., Bousquet, O.: The tradeoffs of large scale learning. In: International Conference on Neural Information Processing Systems, pp. 161–168 (2007)
16. Aiello, L.M., et al.: Sensing trending topics in Twitter. IEEE Trans. Multimed. **15**(6), 1268–1282 (2013)
17. Wainwright, M.J., Jordan, M.I.: Graphical models, exponential families, and variational inference. Found. Trends® Mach. Learn. **1**(1-2), 1–305 (2008)
18. Roux, N.L., Schmidt, M., Bach, F.: A stochastic gradient method with an exponential convergence rate for finite training sets. In: International Conference on Neural Information Processing Systems, vol. 2, pp. 2663–2671 (2012)
19. Cappé, O., Moulines, E.: On-line expectation-maximization algorithm for latent data models. J. R. Stat. Soc. **71**(3), 593–613 (2009)
20. Johnson, R., Zhang, T.: Accelerating stochastic gradient descent using predictive variance reduction. In: International Conference on Neural Information Processing Systems, vol. 1, pp. 315–323 (2013)
21. Neal, R.M., Hinton, G.E.: A view of the EM algorithm that justifies incremental, sparse, and other variants. In: Jordan, M.I. (ed.) Learning in Graphical Models. ASID, vol. 89, pp. 355–368. Springer, Dordrecht (1998). https://doi.org/10.1007/978-94-011-5014-9_12
22. Papadopoulous, S., Zigkolis, C., Kompatsiaris, Y., Vakali, A.: Cluster-based landmark and event detection on tagged photo collections. IEEE Multimed. **18**(1), 52–63 (2011)
23. Debatty, T., Michiardi, P., Mees, W.: Fast online K-NN graph building. CoRR (2016)
24. Wu, X., Hauptmann, G., Ngo, C.: Novelty detection for cross-lingual news story with visual duplicates and speech transcripts. In: ACM Multimedia, pp. 168–177 (2007)
25. Wang, Y., Bai, H., Stanton, M., Chen, W.-Y., Chang, E.Y.: PLDA: parallel latent Dirichlet allocation for large-scale applications. In: Goldberg, A.V., Zhou, Y. (eds.)

AAIM 2009. LNCS, vol. 5564, pp. 301–314. Springer, Heidelberg (2009). https:// doi.org/10.1007/978-3-642-02158-9_26

26. Zhang, Y., Li, G., Chu, L., Wang, S., Zhang, W., Huang, Q.: Cross-media topic detection: a multi-modality fusion framework. In: 2013 IEEE International Conference on Multimedia and Expo (ICME), pp. 1–6 (2013)

27. Liu, Z., Zhang, Y., Chang, E.Y., Sun, M.: PLDA+: parallel latent Dirichlet allocation with data placement and pipeline processing. ACM Trans. Intell. Syst. Technol. **2**(3), 26:1–26:18 (2011)

Automatic Segmentation of Brain Tumor Image Based on Region Growing with Co-constraint

Siming Cui[1,3], Xuanjing Shen[1,3], and Yingda Lyu[2(✉)]

[1] College of Computer Science and Technology, Jilin University,
Changchun, China
[2] Center for Computer Fundamental Education, Jilin University,
Changchun, China
ydlv@jlu.edu.cn
[3] Key Laboratory of Symbolic Computation and Knowledge
Engineering of Ministry of Education, Jilin University, Changchun, China

Abstract. Image segmentation remains an ongoing challenge in medical image processing research. Owing to brain tumor's inhomogeneous structure and blurred boundary, the segmentation of brain tumor image is not always ideal. Therefore, we propose a novel region growing model that enables to segment the brain tumor image accurately and automatically. The model mainly improves the selection of seed points and the growth rules. Using the method of fusion information with multimodal MRI images is described to select the seed point automatically, which makes the segmentation algorithm more robust. Furthermore, in order to mostly remain the local feature and the boundary information of brain tumor, a spatial texture feature is constructed in this study. Based on the above model, an automatic brain tumor image segmentation algorithm is established, which uses the region growing with the Co-constraint of intensity and spatial texture. In terms of performance evaluation, the proposed method not only outperforms other segmentation algorithms in the accuracy of results, but also has lower computational cost. This is undoubtedly a worthy method of brain tumor image segmentation.

Keywords: Image segmentation · Spatial texture · Region growing

1 Introduction

Medical image segmentation is an important research in the field of image processing. Brain tumor image segmentation plays a crucial role in the auxiliary diagnosis of diseases and follow-up surgical treatment programs. Applying computer image processing technology to provide more detailed information for clinicians. MRI (Magnetic Resonance Imaging) is clear solution for soft tissue, such as brain, spinal cord, heart, etc. [1]. What's more, MRI has the characteristics of multi-mode imaging. Therefore, researching the segmentation of brain tumor image has become a hotspot.

In recent years, many experts have made greatly progress in the research of brain tumor image segmentation. However, the clustering [2] and threshold methods [3] are

© Springer Nature Switzerland AG 2019
I. Kompatsiaris et al. (Eds.): MMM 2019, LNCS 11295, pp. 603–615, 2019.
https://doi.org/10.1007/978-3-030-05710-7_50

not ideal for brain tumor segmentation. Salman et al. [4] indicated that region growing was better applied to the brain tumor image segmentation. Region growing method mainly consists of two steps: firstly, the initial point is manually selected as a "seed", and then some similarity properties (such as gray value, texture, color) between the seed and the neighboring pixels are used as growth constraint to obtain region of interest (ROI).

The selection of the initial seed is the first and foremost for region growing, which is usually selected manually [5]. Manually selecting seed points is not only time-consuming, but is also likely to be mis-selected because of the partial volume effect. Developing an automatic seed selection method would make the algorithm more efficient. Sarathi et al. [6] proposed that the feature points of wavelet transform was utilized as the seed points, but the unmatched points need to be eliminated, which made it cumbersome. Ho et al. [7] used the distribution and intensity values of various regions of the brain tissue to determine the selection of seed points, but this requires the prior knowledge of brain map structure and intensity information. For MRI, radiofrequency pulse signals of different frequencies can be applied to form images of different contrast levels. There are different information in the resulting of multimodal images. This paper uses the fusion of multi-modal images to obtain information to select the initial seed automatically.

The setting of similarity criteria determines the quality of the regional growth process. However, the specificity of tumor leads to the uneven grayscale of imaging, the traditional method of region growing relies on grayscale information during seed growth, which can result in insufficient or excessive segmentation [8]. Texture feature was extracted as similarity criterion, which made up for the limitation of single grayscale [9]. Recently, many improvements for the region growing method have emerged. Viji et al. [10] proposed a method based on region growing with modified Local Binary Patterns (LBP) texture to fragment MR brain images. Although this method adds more neighborhood information, it does not take into account the directional gradient similarity between the central pixel and the neighboring pixel. And Charutha et al. [11] integrated the approach [10] and the edge detection to segment tumor. Viji et al. [12] made further efforts in the previous method [10] to add "orientation" on the growth restrictions. The orientation feature was used as the growth conditions, but the spatial relation between pixels was ignored. For tumors with edema, the exact segmentation is not achieved. Though texture feature of image is an inherent property, for the heterogeneity structure and blurred boundary of diseased tumor tissue, no specific texture feature extraction has been to describe the image information uniformly. Machine learning is also used for feature extraction in image segmentation [13, 14]. These learning-based methods are mainly classified by sample training. And it is a challenge to optimizing calculation methods. Especially, the parameters optimization and computational complexity make scholars feel powerless and frustrated. Hamamci et al. [15] proposed a graph cut method based on cellular automata (CA) to segment tumor used region growing. But the state transition process of the automatic cell machine causes energy loss, which affects the final segmentation quality. Sompong et al. [16] proposed a gray level co-occurrence matrix method based on cellular automaton (GLCM-CA) approach to improve Tumor-Cut [15], which coped the ambiguous tumor boundaries effectively. We need to fully consider the contextual information of the tumor to describe its characteristics, so as to obtain a more accurate segmentation.

In this paper, we propose an automatic region growing method for brain tumor image segmentation. The proposed mainly include three contributions: (1) According to the analysis of the modal imaging characteristics, two model images are fused. And the initial seed point is selected automatically from the results. (2) In order to eliminate the mismatching initial seed points, the sliding window is used to filter the fusion result, which provides reliability for the selection of initial seed points. (3) We fully consider the characteristics of brain tumor and define a texture feature extraction based on the pixel spatial information, which is used as the growth constraint of region growing. The tumor is separated by region growing with co-constraint of spatial texture and intensity. The proposed method has obtained fantastic segmentation results on the BraTS 2012.

The structure of the paper is as follows: Sect. 1 introduces the research background; Sect. 2 describes the proposed method in detail; Sect. 3 gives the experimental results and analysis; Sect. 4 concludes the work.

2 Proposed Method

In order to solve the problem of structural inhomogeneity and edge blurring for the brain tumor image segmentation. An automatic region growing method is proposed, which based on the constraints of intensity and spatial texture. The framework is shown in Fig. 1. Overview of the proposed brain tumor segmentation method Fig. 1:

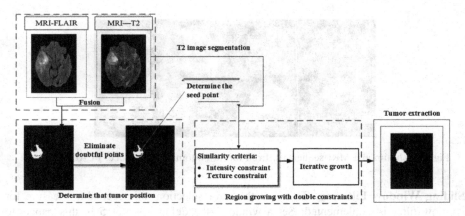

Fig. 1. Overview of the proposed brain tumor segmentation method

The tumor segmentation algorithm mainly includes the following parts:

1. The image is preprocessed by Gaussian filter so as to provide its quality for further image processing.
2. Fuse the two modal images to select the initial seed point.
3. Filter removes redundant initial candidate seed points.
4. Calculate intensity constraint and spatial texture constraint.
5. Extract the tumor in image based on region growing method.

2.1   Automatic Selection of the Seed Point

We present an outgoing approach of the selection seeds using the fusion information of MRI multimodal images.

Multimodal Image Fusion. Multi-modality sequence images can be formed by the MRI imaging technology. As shown in Fig. 2, the T2 weighted image (T2) can highlight the lesion site, but it also presents a high-intensity signal for cerebrospinal fluid. In contrast, the fluid attenuated inversion recovery (FLAIR) image is capable of suppressing fluids. The cerebrospinal fluid portion exhibits a low signal in the FLAIR when it maintains a high signal in the T2. So the T2 and FLAIR images are fused.

The fusion rule of T2 and FLAIR is:

$$R_I = \begin{cases} 1: & if\ p \in T2 \cap FLAIR \\ 0: & otherwise \end{cases} \quad (1)$$

Where R_I is fusion result, and p represents the highlighted pixel position in an image.

The result serves as the location of the tumor and the initial seed is automatically selected form this. We make best of the advantages of multi-modal T2 and FLAIR information fusion to select the initial seed.

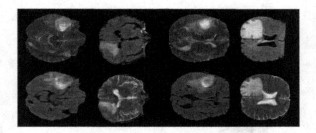

Fig. 2. Multimodal MRI sequences, from top to bottom: T2 sequence, FLAIR sequence

Sliding Window Filtering. To avoid the error selection, an acceptable measure for window filter is implemented: Set a window (the default is 5×5 in this paper) to remove the points with zero pixel in neighbor.

Figure 3 illustrates the process of the initial seed automatically. For the convenience of display, we enlarge the fusion results (red dotted frame). T2 and FLAIR are fused by the above rules (1), there are still some isolated points (orange circle). Filter operation eliminates isolated points and preserves most seed point selections. Next, randomly selecting a point as the initial seed.

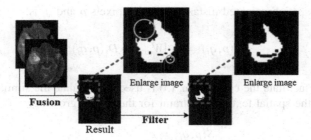

Fig. 3. The process of selecting the initial seed automatically (Color figure online)

In this way, the selection of the initial seed achieves two effects: (1) The highest probability of a pixel belongs to the tumor region must be marked as a seed (2) The selection of seed is automatic and random, which reduces the chance of artificial selection.

2.2   Extraction of the Spatial Texture Feature

Another factor affecting region growing is the setting of growth rules. Texture feature can better reflect the variety of local areas in the image, which represents the relationship between pixels. For the non-homogeneity and boundary ambiguity of the tumor, the proposed algorithm extracts the spatial texture feature based on weighted distance.

The following shows the detailed calculation:

Set a pixel p in the image I, q_j is the neighborhood of p, the spatial distance between pixels p and q_j is:

$$D_s(p, q_j) = \frac{1}{N_P} |C(x, y) - C(x_n, y_n)| \tag{2}$$

Where, $C(x, y)$ is a 3×3 matrix, which contains 8-neighbor pixel values centered on pixel (x, y). $N(p)$ is the number of elements' in C.

Next, we assign a corresponding weight to each spatial distance, and the spatial weighted distance is more limited to distinguish the similarity between pixels.

The weight of each distance difference is given:

$$W_{(p,q_j)} = \frac{e^{-\gamma D_s(p,q_j)}}{\sum_{j=1}^{N_p} e^{-\gamma D_s(p,q_j)}} \tag{3}$$

Here, γ is a constant, which is the influence value of the weight.

Define the spatial weighted distance between pixels p and q_j is:

$$D_w(p, q_j) = \frac{1}{N_p} |W_{(p,q_j)} \bullet D_s(p, q_j)| \tag{4}$$

In order to facilitate the calculation, (5) is used to calculate the similarity function, which defines the spatial texture constraint for the region growing:

$$S(p, q_j) = e^{-\alpha D_w(p,q_j)} \tag{5}$$

Here, α is a constant, which is the influence value of the similarity function.

2.3   Region Growing with Co-constraint of Spatial Texture and Intensity

The traditional region growing method always using a single threshold constrain. For example, Fig. 4 displays the simulation of the region growing.

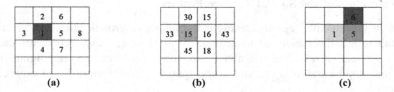

Fig. 4. The simulation process of the region growing, (a) is the pixel label, and (b) is the corresponding pixel intensity value. During the region growing process, the seed point is compared with all its neighbor pixels, the point with the smallest gray scale difference is merged into the seed region (c), and then the average of the divided regions is used to update the value of the seed point.

However, most brain tumor imaging has noise or uneven intensity. We enlarge the tumor structure by 300 times to illustrate, as shown in Fig. 5, There is no significant difference in the pixel values in the grayscale image between "boundary blur" and "internal heterogeneity", a single growth condition leads to insufficient or excessive segmentation. For effectively resolving the drawbacks of the traditional region growing and making tumor segmentation more accurate. The improved region growing method is described, and its growth criterion is under the constraints of both intensity threshold and spatial texture feature. We take a pixel from the inside of the tumor to explain the necessity of setting spatial texture constraint in region growing. Figure 6 shows the simulation of the region growing with co-constrained.

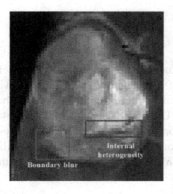

43	143	167
62	161	135
86	167	139

(a)

118	18	6
99	0	26
75	6	22

(b)

0.33	0.85	0.78
0.39	1	0.39
0.48	0.90	0.78

(c)

Fig. 5. The map of tumor structure, the red box indicates "internal heterogeneity", the green box indicates "boundary blur". (Color figure online)

Fig. 6. The simulation of region growing with co-constrained, (a) Pixel values, (b) Difference intensity, (c) Texture similarity

We can see in Fig. 6 that under the same intensity difference, texture similarity can illustrate more pixel-to-pixel relationships. The proposed spatial weighted distance not only fully considers the context information, but also distinguishes the similarity between pixels. For images with uneven gray scale, in the process of region growing, the respective spatial weighted distance between pixels is used as the similarity criterion, and sufficient context information will compensate for the partial volume effect of the image. At the same time, for the fuzzy boundary of the tumor, the distance to each of the 8 neighborhoods also provides a certain directional gradient constraint effect. Therefore, the both of constrains in region growing provide a stronger guarantee for growth conditions, which makes the growth direction more accurate.

The pseudocode of the proposed algorithm as follows:

Algorithm: Region growing with co-constrained of spatial texture and intensity.
Input: MRI image T2, FLAIR

Output: segmentation results (J)

Method:

1   Gaussian filter preprocessed image;
2   Fuse *T2* and *FLAIR* images and use *5×5* window filtering
3   Select the initial seed S
4   Initialize intensity threshold: $J_{mean} = Mean(N(p))$
5   Set pixel pending list: *List*
6   **For** each $p \in list$ **do**
7   **For** each $q_j \in N(p)$ **do**
8   Calculate intensity difference $D(p, q_j)$ and similarity value $S(p, q_j)$
9   **End do**
10   **If** $D(p, q_j) < T_D$ && $S(p, q_j) < T_S$
11   Let $q_j \in J$
12   **End if**
13   **End for**
14   Update seed, J_{mean}
15   ROI=J

3 Experimental Results and Analysis

3.1 Database and Evaluation Metrics

Our experimental data is derived from multi-modal MRI brain tumor databaseB-raTS2012 [17]. The dataset provides MRI scans of more than 20 real patients with ground truth values for image segmentation. All the algorithm programs of our method were running in Windows 7 system of 3.6 GHz CPU, 8 G RAM with Matlab2014a.

Three metrics is used to evaluate the segmentation results objectively in this paper. (1) *Accuracy:* The probability of correct segmentation. (2) *Sensitivity:* The probability that the tumor area is correctly judged. (3) *Misclassification Error:* The probability that the pixel is misclassified.

3.2 Parameter Optimization

Suitable parameter setting is the key for achieving the pleased experimental results. Experiments have shown that the difference between the intensity values of tumor and non-tumor regions is around 0.15. Due to the blurred tumor edges and internal highlights, we set the range of the intensity threshold is $[0, 0.2]$, a step is 0.01, Fig. 7 shows the sensitivity and accuracy curve of the threshold segmentation.

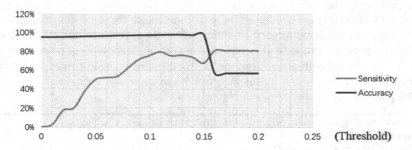

Fig. 7. The segmentation effect affected by the threshold

As we can see in Fig. 7, there is obviously lacking segmentation when $T_D < 0.08$, and over-segmentation occurs on $T_D > 0.15$. We select $T_D = 0.1$ as the optimal intensity threshold to segment the image. At this time, both evaluation indicators reach the maximum. Other parameter settings as shown in Table 1:

Table 1. Parameter setting

Parameter description	The value
The influence of the weight γ	0.05
The influence of similarity function α	0.5
Intensity constraint threshold T_D	0.1
Spatial texture constraint threshold T_S	0.85

3.3 Segmentation Results and Data Analysis

The proposed algorithm to is experimented on MRI brain tumor images provided by BraTS2012. The images in the dataset contain three cases according to the shape and location of the brain tumor. To illustrate the generalization of the algorithm, two images in each type are randomly selected to display the experimental results. It can be seen from Fig. 8:

- Tumors in image 1 and 2 are independent, uniform shape and structure.
- Tumors in image 3 and 4 are not independent, uniform shape, uneven structure.
- Tumors in image 5 and 6 are not independent, random shape, uneven structure.

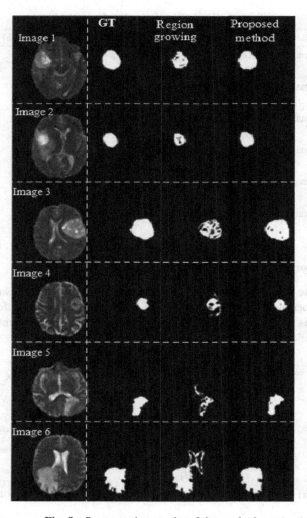

Fig. 8. Segmentation results of the methods

To observe the experimental results, the corresponding image ground truth is used as the segmentation standard and the traditional algorithm segmentation results is used as a comparative test. It can be seen from Fig. 8, the proposed method is more accurate in the segmentation than traditional region growing. Especially, for image 4, 5, 6, the effect of inhibition on the edge is incisively and vividly. For further quantitative comparison, the evaluation indicators of the above results is calculated. The detailed data refer to Table 2.

From Table 2, these data strongly prove that the proposed method is superior, compare to the traditional region growing, which in the case of automatic segment ion, the average accuracy is higher than 2%, up to 30% increases in sensitivity, and effectively reduces the error rate.

Table 2. Evaluation metrics of the methods.

The image	The method	Auto	Acc (%)	Sen (%)	ME (%)
Image 1	Region growing	N	98.42	67.69	1.58
	The proposed	Y	99.60	94.39	0.40
Image 2	Region growing	N	98.61	58.09	1.39
	The proposed	Y	99.75	94.38	0.25
Image 3	Region growing	N	98.03	54.22	1.97
	The proposed	Y	99.31	84.71	0.69
Image 4	Region growing	N	95.15	97.79	4.85
	The proposed	Y	98.53	99.37	1.47
Image 5	Region growing	N	97.74	67.13	2.26
	The proposed	Y	98.47	97.59	1.53
Image 6	Region growing	N	98.37	60.83	1.63
	The proposed	Y	98.80	99.14	1.20

3.4   The Algorithm Performance Analysis

To illustrate the performance of the proposed algorithm. Under the same parameter setting, 20 experiments on the same image are implemented by different the seed selection means. Taking image 1 as a representative, the experimental results are explained in following curves (Fig. 9):

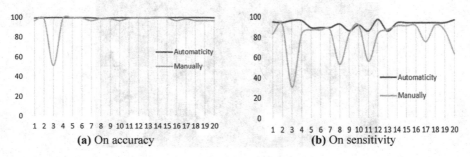

(a) On accuracy   (b) On sensitivity

Fig. 9. The segmentation effect affected by the selection of seed point

From Fig. 9, the following conclusions can be obtained:

(1) From a global perspective: When automatic selecting seed points, accuracy and sensitivity are greater than manually selection. The cause of this fluctuation is that the manually selection of seed point uncertainty, which leads to the short or excessive of image segmentation.

(2) From a local perspective: Compared with accuracy, the sensitivity has more fluctuation range. The reason for this phenomenon is that the non-tumor area is much larger than the tumor in the brain tumor image. This objective fact makes sensitivity more reflective of the correctness of tumor segmentation.

3.5   Comparison with Other Algorithms

To further argument the performance of the proposed algorithm, several algorithms of brain tumor image segmentation are compared. The experimental results of 20 patient images in this paper are averaged. The accuracy is counted as follows (Table 3):

Table 3. Accuracy of the other theses

Algorithm	Accuracy (%)	Time (ms)
IBTRG [10]	93.16	6943
IOBTRG [12]	93.17	8327
AM-CWT&DT-CWT [14]	96.10	1400
GLCM-CA [16]	91.00	3×10^4
The proposed	99.12	1670

From Table 3, compare with other improved region growing [10, 12, 16], the proposed not only improve the accuracy but also reduce computational costs. Especially in [16], this paper has a significant improvement in time complexity. For other segmentation method [14], the proposed increases the accuracy by 3% while maintaining the same level of time complexity. However, leaving aside the proportion of non-tumor area larger than the tumor, our average sensitivity is as high as 97%. Therefore, experiments have proved that the proposed algorithm has achieved encouraging results.

4   Conclusion

The paper presents an effective segmentation method for the MRI brain tumor image, and it has been proved by experiments. Two innovations have been proposed using to improve the normal region growing method. On the one hand, for growth constraints, extracting the texture future of spatial information is an extremely correct choice, which has a better description of the tumor features, such as borderless and non-uniform shapes. In particular, the region growing with the co-constraint of spatial texture and intensity provides sufficient information during the growth process, using it can obtain more accurate tumor image segmentation results. Besides, compared with the extraction of other texture features, our method greatly reduces the computational complexity. On the other hand, in order to reduce the intervention of manually selecting the seed point, we use the approach of multi-modal images fusion to detect the tumor location and then determine the initial seed point, which also has obviously improved the robustness of the region growing algorithm. To generalize, the method proposed in this paper is novel and lower cost, which makes it more versatile. In our future research topics, the role of multimodal information should be more fully utilized than just to detect the location of tumor.

Acknowledgement. This research is supported by the National Natural Science Foundation of China (61672259, 61602203), Key Projects of Jilin Province Science and Technology Development Plan (20180201064SF), and Outstanding Young Talent Foundation of Jilin Province (20170520064JH, 20180520020JH).

References

1. Arabi, H.: Magnetic resonance imaging-guided attenuation correction in whole-body PET/MRI using a sorted atlas approach. Med. Image Anal. **31**, 1 (2016)
2. Abdel-Maksoud, E.: Brain tumor segmentation based on a hybrid clustering technique. Egypt. Inform. J. **16**(1), 71–81 (2015)
3. Feng, Y., Shen, X., Chen, H., Zhang, X.: Internal generative mechanism based Otsu multilevel thresholding segmentation for medical brain images. In: Ho, Y.-S., Sang, J., Ro, Y.M., Kim, J., Wu, F. (eds.) PCM 2015. LNCS, vol. 9314, pp. 3–12. Springer, Cham (2015). https://doi.org/10.1007/978-3-319-24075-6_1
4. Salman, Y.: Validation techniques for quantitative brain tumors measurements. In: 2005 IEEE Engineering in Medicine and Biology 27th annual Conference, pp. 7048. IEEE, Shanghai (2006)
5. Thiruvenkadam, K.: Brain tumor segmentation of MRI brain images through FCM clustering and seeded region growing technique. Int. J. Appl. Eng. Res. **10**(76), 427–432 (2015)
6. Sarathi, M.P.: Automated brain tumor segmentation using novel feature point detector and seeded region growing. In: 2013 36th International Conference on Telecommunications and Signal Processing, pp. 648–652. IEEE, Rome (2013)
7. Ho, Y.L., Lin, W.Y., Tsai, C.L., et al.: Automatic brain extraction for T1-weighted magnetic resonance images using region growing. In: 2016 16th International Conference on Bioinformatics and Bioengineering, pp. 250–253. IEEE, Taichung (2016)
8. Suri, J.S., Wilson, D., Laxminarayan, S.: Handbook of Biomedical Image Analysis. Springer, New York (2005). https://doi.org/10.1007/b104805
9. Jafari, M.: Automatic brain tissue detection in MRI images using seeded region growing segmentation and neural network classification. Aust. J. Basic Appl. Sci. **34**(1), 577–582 (2011)
10. Viji, K.S.A.: Modified texture based region growing segmentation of MR brain images. In: 2013 IEEE Conference on Information and Communication Technologies, pp. 691–695. IEEE, Thuckalay (2013)

11. Charutha, S.: An efficient brain tumor detection by integrating modified texture based region growing and cellular automata edge detection. In: 2014 International Conference on Control, Instrumentation, Communication and Computational Technologies, pp. 1193–1199. IEEE, Kanyakumari (2014)

12. Viji, A.: Modified texture, intensity and orientation constraint based region growing segmentation of 2D MR brain tumor images. Int. Arab J. Inf. Technol. **13**(6A), 723–731 (2016)

13. Havaei, M.: Brain tumor segmentation with deep neural networks. Med. Image Anal. **35**, 18–31 (2017)

14. Nabizadeh, N.: Automatic tumor segmentation in single-spectral MRI using a texture-based and contour-based algorithm. Expert Syst. Appl. **77**, 1–10 (2017)

15. Hamamci, A.: Tumor-cut: segmentation of brain tumors on contrast enhanced MR images for radiosurgery applications. IEEE Trans. Med. Imaging **31**(3), 790 (2012)

16. Sompong, C.: An efficient brain tumor segmentation based on cellular automata and improved tumor-cut algorithm. Expert Syst. Appl. **72**, 231–244 (2017)

17. DTU Compute. https://www.imm.dtu.dk/projects/BRATS-2012/data.html

Proposal of an Annotation Method for Integrating Musical Technique Knowledge Using a GTTM Time-Span Tree

Nami Iino[1,2,3](✉)🆔, Mayumi Shimada[1], Takuichi Nishimura[2]🆔,
Hideaki Takeda[3,4]🆔, and Masatoshi Hamanaka[1]

[1] RIKEN (Institute of Physical and Chemical Research), Saitama, Japan
nami.iino@riken.jp
[2] National Institute of Advanced Industrial Science and Technology,
Ibaraki, Japan
[3] SOKENDAI (Graduate University for Advanced Studies), Kanagawa, Japan
[4] National Institute of Informatics, Tokyo, Japan

Abstract. This paper proposes an annotation method for integrating the knowledge of musical techniques and musical structures. We have attempted to support musical instrument performances from the viewpoint of knowledge engineering. We focused on classical guitar, which requires many techniques, and developed guitar rendition ontology that can serve as a guideline for classical guitar performances at teaching and learning sites. In order to effectively use ontology knowledge at the sites, we need to connect it with musical structures so that the ontology data can be integrated with musical score information. Therefore, we propose a method that annotates the knowledge related to musical techniques to time-span trees obtained from time-span analysis based on the generative theory of tonal music (GTTM). We experimented with several bars of four guitar pieces and investigated how much the knowledge, which is executed with more than two notes, can add to time-span trees. Our results showed that about 76% of the ontology knowledge corresponded with the structure of time-span trees.

Keywords: Guitar rendition ontology · Musical technique · GTTM
Time-span tree

1 Introduction

Interest in musical activities that enhance vitality and relieve stress has been increasing. Musical training provides a wide variety of multisensory experiences, including exercising motor functions and reading of musical notation [1, 2]. These health promotion activities are built on extensive knowledge and are supported by many technologies. However, the knowledge acquired in a community varies depending on the characteristics of the participants, making it difficult to share knowledge between them [3].

We focused on classical guitar because acquiring its techniques, including rendition, is quite difficult. The current form of classical guitar was established in the late 19th century, so its history is shorter than that of other instruments such as the piano or

© Springer Nature Switzerland AG 2019
I. Kompatsiaris et al. (Eds.): MMM 2019, LNCS 11295, pp. 616–627, 2019.
https://doi.org/10.1007/978-3-030-05710-7_51

the violin. Classical guitar requires many renditions (modes of playing) that have changed and developed over time and reflect a high level of performance. However, these changes and developments have led to a lack of standardization for even basic techniques, causing people to interpret guitar renditions differently on individual level and across generations. Such confusion could hinder learners' progress.

To resolve this issue, our previous work systematized classical guitar knowledge. First, we collected the knowledge of classical guitar renditions from people and textbooks and organized it by using a goal-oriented form of description [4]. However, it is difficult to use as the basis of knowledge-based systems because the knowledge is not so clear. Therefore, we developed "guitar rendition ontology" by refining the goal-oriented knowledge [5]. The ontology consists of 96 concepts that are hierarchically classified classical guitar renditions and 18 properties that explain the concepts. We significantly improved the machine-readability and machine-processability of guitar rendition knowledge by using computer languages like the Web Ontology Language (OWL).

Traditional music analysis of western music is based on harmonics. However, some theories and methods on the cognitive sciences of music have been proposed to objectively and cognitively structure music [6–9]. One is, a generative theory of tonal music (GTTM) analysis that can represent the hierarchical structure of a piece of music by the melody, rhythm, and harmony, and express their relationships using a tree structure-style. The rules of GTTM describe musical insight and knowledge so that a person can understand, and it is possible to translate into a computer program. In particular, the time-span analysis based on GTTM provides suitable analysis results from fundamental musical elements such as phrases and metrics. Moreover, automatic time-span tree analyzer (ATTA) has been developed [10].

Connecting knowledge of guitar rendition ontology with musical score information is necessary in order to effectively use it at teaching and learning sites. Figure 1 shows our approach for integrating guitar rendition ontology and tree structures. First, we improve the OWL data of guitar rendition ontology. Next, we acquire time-span trees and store this data with the Extensible Markup Language (XML). Then, we annotate the knowledge of musical techniques including the ontology knowledge on the trees. Finally, we integrate the annotated knowledge with information about the notes. For this study, we used time-span analysis to obtain time-span trees of four guitar pieces and defined several rules for annotating the knowledge on those trees. Experimental results indicated that the rate of knowledge annotated on the trees was high.

This paper is organized as follows. We describe our previous work on guitar rendition ontology and provide an outline of GTTM in Sect. 2. We discuss the expression of the tree structure obtained by time-span analysis of a classical guitar piece in Sect. 3. Then, we describe the annotation rules and the experimental results and conclusion in Sects. 4 and 5.

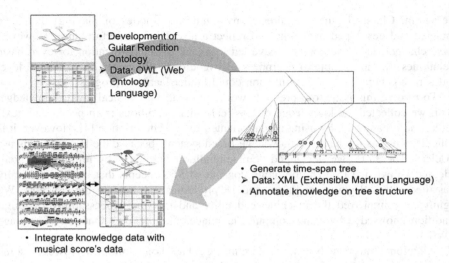

Fig. 1. Use of guitar rendition ontology by using GTTM time-span tree.

2 Related Work

In this section, first, we describe our previous work that systematized classical guitar knowledge. Then, we outline the time-span analysis based on GTTM, which has several approaches from a musical element point of view.

2.1 Guitar Rendition Ontology

Classical guitar is one of the most difficult instruments to play because it has many renditions and requires complex motions[1]. First, we must gather information from professional guitarists and teachers in order to collect and systematize such knowledge as common information. Therefore, we previously collected the knowledge from books [11] and teachers and systematized the knowledge by using a goal-oriented form of description [4]. However, describing the knowledge presents some difficulties; i.e., the structure is not applicable to knowledge-based systems. Therefore, we developed guitar rendition ontology through refining the goal-oriented knowledge [5]. We used Protégé[2], an ontology editor and a knowledge management system that supports OWL[3].

Guitar rendition ontology consists of 96 concepts that classify renditions into several groups and 18 properties that explain the concepts (Fig. 2). We chose guitar rendition as a concept and roughly divided it into two purposes related to sound and movement. The first category has seven types of rendition: *Percussive rendition* imitating percussion instruments without using strings; *Chord rendition*, methods of

---

[1] https://github.com/guitar-san/Guitar-Rendition-Ontology.

[2] https://protege.stanford.edu.

[3] https://www.w3.org/OWL/.

playing chords; *Ornament rendition*, adding notes to "decorate" sounds; *Note value rendition*, changing the length of the note value; *Articulation rendition*, altering the way of notes are connected; *Timbre rendition*, changing the timbre using strings; and *Harmony rendition*, changing the sounds. The second category is the *Fingering rendition*, which is classified further into the following three renditions: *Set rendition*, which indicates placing fingers on strings to stably pluck them; *Press string rendition*, which is the form of the hand when pressing strings; and *Pluck string rendition*, which is the way of plucking. Then, we described all specific concepts (e.g., *Pizzicato* and *Sul ponticello*) as subclasses of each type of rendition by an is–a relationship. When specific concepts had no name, we distinguished them by number, like *Natural harmonics1* and *Natural harmonics2*, which are both subclasses of *Natural harmonics*. Moreover, we defined identical renditions (i.e., synonymous) as equivalent concepts such as *Set* and *Planting*, which are both subclasses of *Set rendition*.

In order to explain specific concepts, we defined a description form by properties. As the core structure of a guitar rendition concept, we defined three properties that describe the process of the action of concepts: "action," "primary-action," and "conditional-action." Figure 3 shows an example of a concept and its OWL expression. *Pizzicato*, which is a subclass of *Timbre rendition*, follows. In the "action1," a player plucks a string with the hand on the guitar-body side while touching the strings on the bridge side with the palm of the same hand. Here, the playing-action of the "primary-action" is *pluck_string_body*, and the playing-action of the "conditional-action" is *touch_string_body* with properties related to the placement and the part of the hand.

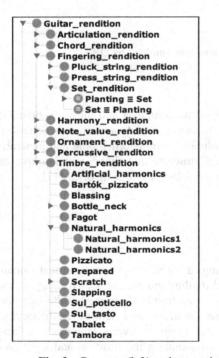

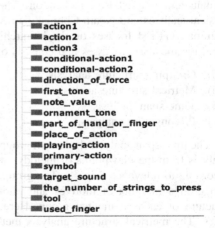

Fig. 2. Concepts (left) and properties (right) of guitar rendition ontology.

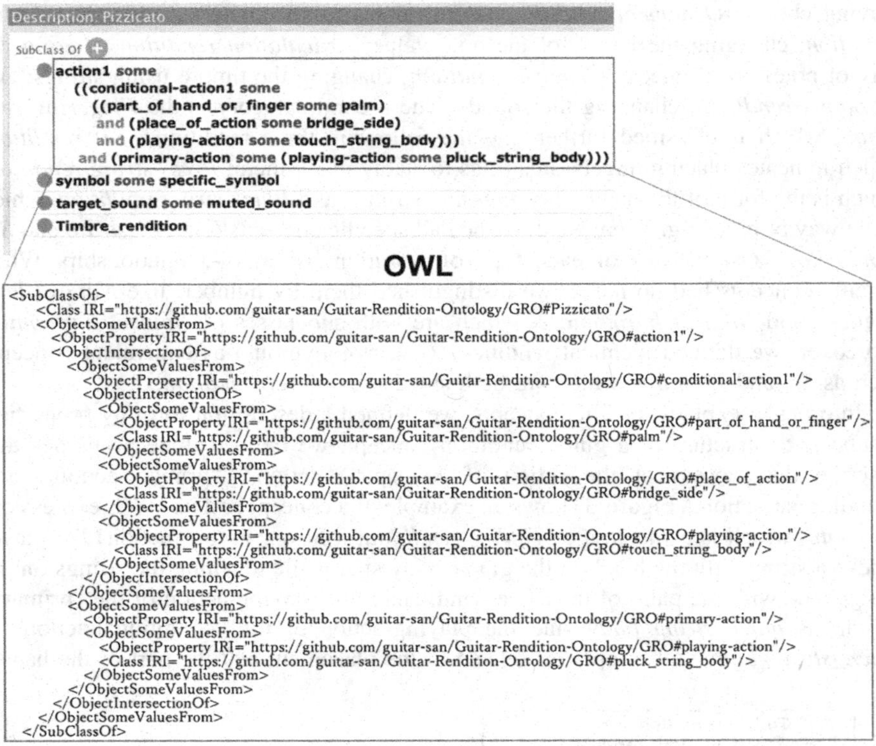

Fig. 3. Description of guitar rendition ontology by OWL.

2.2 Generative Theory of Tonal Music

GTTM is a theory of music analysis conceived by composer and music theorist Fred Lerdahl and linguist Ray Jackendoff. The theory is based on Heinrich Schenker's musical analysis and Noam Chomsky's revolutionary transformational and generative grammar. GTTM focuses on the hierarchical structure that shapes our intuitive and cognitive musical processes and consists of the following four theories [12].

 (i) Grouping structure analysis
 (ii) Metrical structure analysis
(iii) Time-span analysis
(iv) Prolongation analysis.

The time-span analysis deals with grouping structure analysis and metrical structure analysis from the viewpoints of melody and rhythm and hierarchically arranges notes according to relevance (Fig. 4). The grouping structure analysis method divides notes into groups of units of motives and phrases in music and defines the hierarchical structure of each segmented group. Here, the group is several temporally adjacent notes. The metrical structure analysis method estimates the position and strength of each beat and determines the strong beats and the weak beats. The tree structure obtained by time-span analysis is called the "time-span tree". Prolongation analysis is a method of generating a tree structure from a harmonic viewpoint.

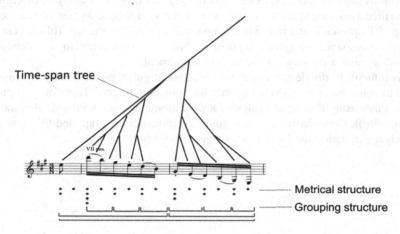

Fig. 4. Time-span tree with grouping structure and metrical structure.

3 Time-Span Analysis of Classical Guitar Pieces

Here, we discuss the expression of the time-span tree for classical guitar music. Classical guitar music is generally homophonic (which consists of a single note sequence with chords), but sometimes polyphonic (which consists of two or more simultaneous lines of independent melodies). However, several rules in the theory of GTTM only allow monophony, which consists of a melody line. Therefore, we describe the time-span analysis for homophonic music and polyphonic music.

3.1 Time-Span Analysis of Polyphony

To acquire the time-span tree automatically, Hamanaka et al. have been constructing a music analysis system [10]. They proposed an additional novel rule of time-span analysis for homophonic music and polyphonic music so that a time-span tree can be consisted all notes [13]. First, musicologists arrange polyphonic music to homophonic music by dividing the notes into two parts: a melody and an accompaniment. This process is similar to time-span reduction, which acquires a time-span tree by obtaining an abstracted melody line, except for ornamental notes. Then, the musicologists analyze the musical structure based on GTTM and acquire the time-span tree, adding the branches of the omitted notes. The notes that the omitted notes connect to can be detected in from the following two cases: when one is the head of the smallest time-span that includes any omitted notes, and the other is the head of another voice time-span that is the same as or similar to the time-span that includes any omitted notes.

3.2   Expression of Time-Span Tree of Classical Guitar

We extracted 8 bars of homophonic music from the classical guitar piece "Caprice No. 7" composed by L. Legnani. First, musicologists divided the notes into two parts: a prior melody and an accompaniment. Then, they did time-span analysis of each part and acquired two time-span trees. Figure 5(a) shows a time-span tree of the melody, and Fig. 5(b) presents two individual time-span trees of the melody (black branches) and the accompaniment (green branches). The note connected to the dotted line functions as both a melody and as an accompaniment.

It is difficult to divide the voice part in classical guitar music clearly because it is limited to notes that are played using only four plucking fingers. Therefore, we put two parts together using time-span analysis for polyphony, and acquired a single time-span tree (Fig. 5(c)). Considering classical guitar performances, we applied this single tree style when annotating the knowledge of guitar rendition ontology.

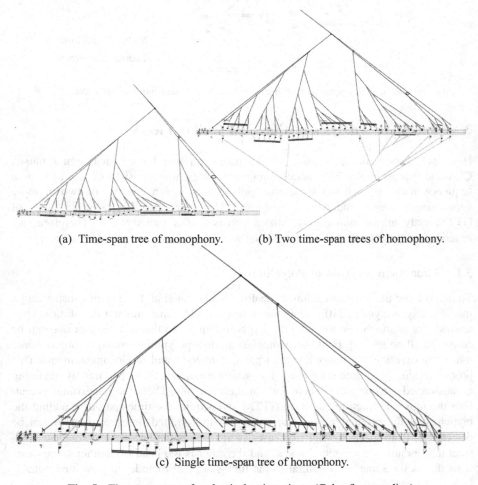

(a) Time-span tree of monophony.   (b) Two time-span trees of homophony.

(c) Single time-span tree of homophony.

Fig. 5. Time-span tree of a classical guitar piece. (Color figure online)

Generating time-span trees is a subjective process because it depends on the interpretation and ability of music analyst. Therefore, we considered the interpretation and ability of a player when analyzing a piece so that tree structures can closely relate to musical techniques. For example, we interpreted *Slur* as not musical articulation, but specific rendition of classical guitar.

4 Experiment

In this section, we define some rules for annotating knowledge on time-span trees of guitar pieces and investigate the relationship between knowledge of musical techniques and musical structure. We chose four guitar pieces that require many guitar techniques and used several bars from each of them. In the experiment, we used the knowledge of a guitarist, who is the top author of this study.

4.1 Annotation Rules

We acquired the knowledge of each pieces using the following processes:

Process 1. Acquiring the knowledge written in the musical score.
Process 2. Describing the fingering information.
Process 3. Acquiring the knowledge obtained from observing performances.
Process 4. Checking the vocabulary against guitar rendition ontology.

First, we acquired the knowledge of a musical score as a primary information (Process 1). In practical sites, professional players often change articulations written in the musical score depending on their musical interpretations and suitable motions. Therefore, we collected the fingering information of a guitarist to understand her interpretation of music and movement (Process 2). Next, we observed the guitarist's performance and acquired the practical knowledge to modify the knowledge of Process 1 (Process 3). Finally, we checked the vocabulary of the knowledge against guitar rendition ontology for standardization (Process 4). If some knowledge was not defined in the ontology, we described the action.

The rules for annotating acquired knowledge on time-span trees are as follows:

Rule 1. The annotation describes knowledge executed with more than two notes.
Rule 2. The annotation is placed on the intersection of branches.
Rule 3. The annotated knowledge propagates along the notes of the lower branch.

Figure 6 shows an example of annotation. *Slur* is an articulation symbol in western musical notation indicating that the sequence of notes is to be played without separation. On the other hand, it means a specific action of classical guitar rendition, in which players make sounds without using plucking fingers. *Slur* has two types of playing: *Hammer-on* (or, an "*Ascending slur*"), which is performed by firmly putting a finger down on a string, and *Pull-off* (or a "*Descending slur*"), which can be done by quickly pulling the finger off a string while the notes are still ringing. Such knowledge executed with two notes is annotated at the intersection of branches following Rules 1 and 2.

Set is also called *"Planting,"* where a player places fingers on the strings before plucking to stabilize the finger's movements [16]. This rendition is implicit knowledge that is not notated on a musical score. In Fig. 6, it was described only at the intersection of the branches of note A and note C following Rule 3.

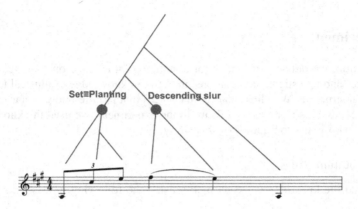

Fig. 6. Example of annotation.

4.2   Results and Discussion

Here, we discuss whether the knowledge acquired from a guitarist was annotated properly on time-span trees that were acquired by time-span analysis for polyphonic music. We selected four guitar pieces and used several bars from each of them. Figures 7 and 8 are two time-span trees with annotations. The blue numbers represent the fingering information, the red circles and text on the time-span tree represent annotations, and the text and red lines under the score represent other knowledge performed by a guitarist.

There were many *Slurs* and *Sets* among the annotated knowledge, and *Slurs* were annotated in all pieces. Some knowledge (e.g., *Arpeggio* and *Set*) was annotated on the intersections of branches of melodies and accompaniments. Moreover, we acquired two pieces of implicit knowledge that were not included in the guitar rendition ontology: "Slide finger while touching string" and "Mute open string." To provide further information on how "Mute open string" is performed, we added detailed actions, such as "Touch string by p (thumb of right hand)," "Touch string by 4 (little finger of left hand)," etc. We need to improve guitar rendition ontology considering these actions.

Table 1 shows the matching rate between annotated knowledge and each guitar piece. Our results show that about 76% of all knowledge could be annotated on a time-span tree. The piece with the highest matching rate was "Variation on a Theme by Mozart," composed by F. Sor during the classical period. On the other hand, the matching rate of "Introduction and Rondo" composed by D. Aguado in the same period was the lowest because several "Mute open string"s could not be annotated. Using the open strings tended to decrease the matching rate.

In the experiment, we found several problems related to the annotation rules. Because time-span analysis does not recognize rests, we could annotate the knowledge performed at a rest time. Moreover, we must need to improve the rules for applying the knowledge executed by one note.

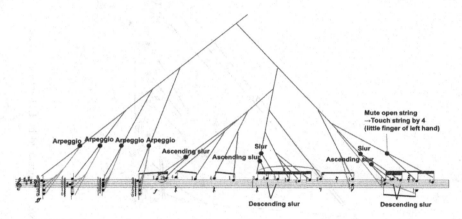

Fig. 7. Time-span tree of classical guitar piece "Fandango," composed by J. Rodrigo. (Color figure online)

Table 1. Rate of annotated knowledge.

Piece	Composer	Period	Bar	All knowledge	Annotated knowledge	Matching rate
Caprice No. 7	L. Legnani	Classical	8	21	15	**71%**
Introduction and Rondo	D. Aguado	Classical	8	18	11	**61%**
Variation on a Theme by Mozart	F. Sor	Classical	8	20	17	**85%**
Fandango from Tres piezas espanolas	J. Rodrigo	Modern	3	13	11	**85%**
Average			6.75	17.75	13.25	**76%**

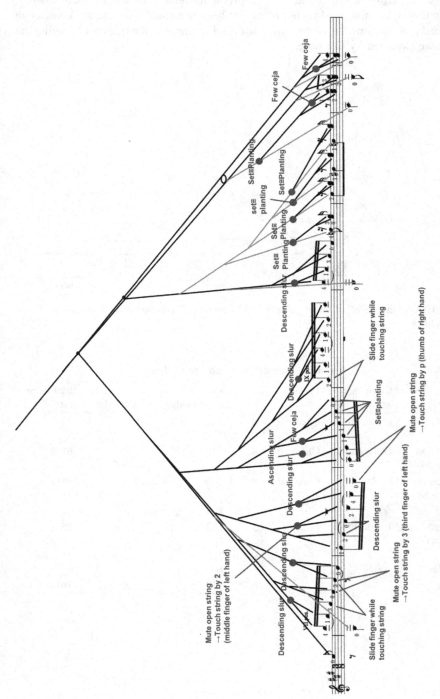

Fig. 8. Time-span tree of classical guitar piece "Caprice No. 7," composed by L. Legnani. (Color figure online)

5 Conclusion

In this paper, we proposed a method that annotates classical guitar knowledge to time-span trees obtained from time-span analysis based on the generative theory of tonal music (GTTM). This method makes it possible to integrate the guitar rendition ontology we developed with musical structures, and it provides us efficient teaching and learning of classical guitar. As a first step, we investigated how much the knowledge of the ontology can be annotated on tree structures. To treat classical guitar music, we applied time-span analysis for polyphonic music and acquired the time-span trees of four guitar pieces. Then, we annotated the knowledge executed with more than two notes on the tree structure. Experimental results showed that we acquired implicit knowledge that is not included in the guitar rendition ontology, and about 76% of all knowledge corresponded with the tree structure. In future studies, we will investigate more guitar pieces and compare this annotation method with other existing methods; then, we will integrate the data of knowledge and musical scores to provide rich information for teaching and learning support.

Acknowledgements. This work was supported by JSPS KAKENHI, Grant Numbers 17H01847 and 16H01744.

References

1. Zatorre, R.J., McGill, J.: Music, the food of neuroscience? Nature **434**(7031), 312–315 (2005)
2. Schlaug, G., Norton, A., Overy, K., Winner, E.: Effects of music training on the child's brain and cognitive development. Ann. N. Y. Acad. Sci. **1060**, 219–230 (2005)
3. Nishimura, S., et al.: Employee driven approach to "knowledge explication" in elderly care service. Trans. Jpn. Soc. Artif. Intell. **32**(4), C-G95_1-15 (2017)
4. Iino, N., Nishimura, S., Fukuda, K., Watanabe, K., Jokinen, K., Nishimura, T.: De-velopment and use of an activity model based on structured knowledge – a music teaching support system. In: IEEE International Conference on Data Mining Workshop, pp. 576–581 (2017)
5. Iino, N., Nishimura, S., Nishimura, T., Fukuda. K., Takeda, H.: A Development of Guitar Rendition Ontology for Knowledge Sharing. SIG-SWO-044-09 (2018)
6. Cooper, G., Meyer, L.B.: The Rhythmic Structure of Music. The University of Chicago Press, Chicago (1960)
7. Narmour, E.: The Analysis and Cognition of Basic Melodic Structure. The University of Chicago Press, Chicago (1990)
8. Tempeley, D.: The Cognition of Basic Musical Structures. The MIT Press, Cambridge (2001)
9. Lerdahl, F., Jackendoff, R.: A Generative Theory of Tonal Music. The MIT Press, Cambridge (1983)
10. Hamanaka, M., Hirata, K., Tojo, S.: Implementing "a generative theory of tonal music". J. New Music Res. **35**(4), 249–277 (2006)
11. Gendai Guitar Co. Ltd.: All About the Guitar Renditions. Gendai guitar, No. 595 (2013)
12. Nagashima, Y., Hashimoto, S., Hiraga, Y., Hirata, K.: Computer and music. Kyoritsu Shuppan Co., Ltd. (1999)
13. Hamanaka, M., Hirata, K., Tojo, S.: Time-span tree analyzer for polyphonic music. In: Proceedings of the 10th International Symposium on Computer Music Multidisciplinary Research, pp. 886–893 (2013)

A Hierarchical Level Set Approach
to for RGBD Image Matting

Wenliang Zeng$^{(\boxtimes)}$ ⓘ and Ji Liu ⓘ

College of Computer Science,
NO. 174, Shazheng Street, Shapingba Street, Chongqing, China
{wliang,liujiboy}@cqu.edu.cn

Abstract. This paper presents a novel method for the image matting of
RGBD data, using a Hierarchical Level Set. The approach has four main
steps. First of all, the color and depth channel is preprocessed. Noise
is eliminated by using a Directional Joint Bilateral Filter and holes are
removed from the depth map. Secondly, color cues and depth cues are
integrated to segment the image using a Hierarchical Level Set Framework. After this, the segmentation of the color and depth cues is used to
generate a trimap. Finally, an extended alpha matting approach is used
to obtain the final matting result, with the color image, depth image
and trimap serving as input. Experiments using complex natural images
demonstrate that the proposed RGBD matting approach is able to generate good matting results.

Keywords: Image matting · Depth image · Hierarchical level set

1 Introduction

Image matting is a fundamental aspect of computer vision. It has become a crucial part of the accurate extraction of foregrounds and is widely used throughout
the academic community. It is also used extensively for visual effects production,
object detection, and 3D reconstruction. The weight loss scene at the beginning
of the film Avatar is a typical example of visual effects Blue Screen Matting [1],
whilst the method for salient object detection using spectral matting proposed by
Naqvi et al. [2] provides a typical example of how it is used for object detection.
As matting is used throughout the afore-mentioned areas, it forms an important
part of computer vision research. Here the focus is on computing foreground
information, background information and opacity [3]. The key objective here
was to be able to compute α in the following equation:

$$I = \alpha F + (1 - \alpha)B \tag{1}$$

where I is the image, F is the foreground, B is the background and α is the
opacity. This problem is highly under-constrained, with three unknowns and only
one known, making it very difficult to solve. Smith et al. therefore suggested what

I. Kompatsiaris et al. (Eds.): MMM 2019, LNCS 11295, pp. 628–639, 2019.
https://doi.org/10.1007/978-3-030-05710-7_52

is known as the Triangulation Matting method. Assuming I is known and B is known, then is it possible to get F. Although matting is an under-constrained problem, user input in the form of trimaps or scribbles [4], can be an effective way to solve it. Taking trimaps as an example, trimaps partition the original image into three parts: a background region; a foreground region; and an unknown region. There are many color-based methods that can work well if an accurate trimap is provided.

For instance, in Bayesian approaches [3], a trimap is used to estimate the α, F and B simultaneously for each foreground and background pair in a Bayesian framework. This is effective if the color distribution of the foreground and the background do not overlap. Most state- of-the-art natural image matting algorithms [see Chuang et al. [3]; Sun et al. [5]; Levin et al. [4]; Aksoy et al. [6]] rely on trimaps provided by the user. Previous research has confirmed that the more accurate the trimap, the better the result. However, using just a trimap and color channels does not cover the following situations: (i) where the foreground is quite similar to the background; (ii) where the trimap is not as accurate as expected. This has resulted in existing methods not always doing as well as might be hoped. Obtaining more accurate trimaps and extra cues therefore seems to be the best way to proceed.

Depth information is one such potential extra cue. Depth sensors appeared in 2006, offering a new way to deal with the matting problem. Since the depth map can provide valuable depth information, it helps with situations that cannot be solved by color information alone. Crabb et al. [9] were the first to approach the computation of a trimap by assigning to each depth map pixel the probability of it belonging to the foreground. Pitie et al. [11] extended the closed-form matting approach [4] where they treated the depth as an extra channel and used it as a diffusion guide for matting. In order to solve the trimap problem and other similar problems, in this paper we present a Hierarchical Level Set based approach to image matting using RGB-D data (see the final matting result, it can produce in Fig. 1(d)). Our own approach is inspired by the method proposed in [17], which can be divided into two parts: (1) Using a Level Set, a trimap is automatically generated using a binary segmentation result that is based on the depth image; (2) A Bayesian matting method is used to obtain the final matting result. Our proposed method differs from [17] in several ways.

First of all, a trimap is generated that combines the color and depth cues using a Hierarchical Level Set. In [17] only the depth channel was used to generate the trimap. Then, based on [10] we extend the alpha matting and take depth as an extra channel to obtain a matting result that uses the trimap and the color image. The paper offers three novel contributions:

- Integration of color and depth cues using a Hierarchical Level Set framework to obtain a binary segmentation result;
- Generation of trimaps based on segmentation results for color and depth data;
- Obtaining a final matting result by taking trimaps, color images, and depth images as input for depth-assisted alpha matting.

Fig. 1. The input data and matting result using our method. (a) Color channels image, (b) Depth channel image, (c) Ground truth, (d) Our result.

2   Related Work

2.1   Matting with RGB

Previous work regarding matting with RGB was discussed in the *Introduction*. Most state-of-the-art natural image matting methods using RGB require some form of user interaction, e.g. trimaps or scribbles. A key outcome of this work is the observation that trimap accuracy is positively correlated with the matting results. So, the more accurate the trimap, the better the quality of the matting result.

2.2   Level Set Method

The Level Set method is a form of active contouring that has been widely used in image segmentation. It was first proposed in 1988 by Osher and Sethian [28]. Due to the advantages of handling various topological changes automatically, the Level Set method is generally regarded to be an effective approach to object detection and image segmentation. Thus, Memar et al. [12] suggest an object detection method that uses active contour modeling with depth cues.

In another paper that focuses on region-based active contour modeling and uses the variational Level Set method for image segmentation [17], a local Gaussian is defined that distributes fitting energy with Level Set functions and local means and variances as variables. Meanwhile, Ping et al. [19] offered an efficient approach to object detection that combines the Level Set method with deep learning.

Beyond this, as already mentioned, the variational Level Set method was applied in [25] to color and depth information for image matting. A difference from our own method, here, is that we use an image pyramid to refine the boundary and use a Level Set for both depth and the color image.

2.3 Matting with RGBD

As mentioned above, image matting based on the joint use of color and depth information has been the subject of a considerable amount of research [21]. For instance, [8] describes a different approach that deals with pixels instead of objects. This kind of pixel-based method makes it possible to limit the number of assumptions about the scene and ignores the notion of any 3D model, aiming to directly analyze the dynamic content of a scene by applying a background subtraction technique to a depth map.

Generally speaking, state-of-the-art approaches for image matting using color and depth can be divided into two main frameworks: (1) those that treat depth as a fourth channel with the color channels and modify the algorithm to cope with it; (2) those that treat depth as an independent channel and build a confidence map combining depth and matte. However, there are some inevitable problems with depth information, such as low resolution, noisy signals, and imprecise distance measurements [14]. Neither of the frameworks can perform well when confronted with poor quality depth data. In order to get a higher-quality depth map, our own method uses a Directional Joint Bilateral Filter [23].

Beyond the approaches mentioned so far, Ling et al. [16] have suggested a novel interactive method using color and depth in the Graph Cut framework. The main drawback with this approach is that it still requires user interaction. The approach in [17] gives a lower depth weight to pixels close to the boundaries, at the same time increasing the depth weights when the foreground and background color are similar. In our own approach, we first of all generate a trimap using a Hierarchical Level Set that draws upon color and depth cues together. In [17] only the depth channel is used to generate the trimap and there is no image pyramid. After this, we extend the alpha matting approach discussed in [7] and treat depth as an extra channel to obtain the matting result along with the trimap and color image (see Fig. 2).

3 Materials and Methods

Figure 2 shows an overview of our method. The method has four components. Firstly, the RGBD data is preprocessed using the color image and depth image as input. This includes things like image resizing, denoising and hole filling. Secondly, the depth and color channels are integrated using the Hierarchical Level Set method to obtain the RGBD segmentation result, together with an image pyramid to refine the boundary of the result. Next, a trimap is generated using the RGBD data segmentation result. Finally, depth-assisted alpha matting is used to arrive at the final matting result. These elements are discussed in more detail below.

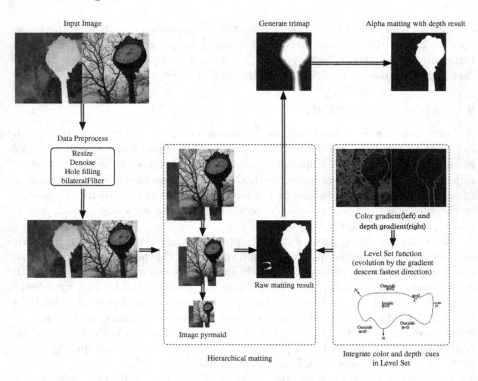

Fig. 2. An overview of our method.

3.1 Preprocessing the Depth Map

To fill holes in the depth image, this paper adopts a method presented in [23]. For the non-hole regions, noise was removed by a Joint Trilateral Filter [23]. Blurring in the object boundary of the non-hole was removed by a Directional Joint Bilateral Filter [23]. Otherwise, holes in non-edge regions were filled by a Partial Directional Joint Bilateral Filter [23] the edge regions were filled by a Directional Joint Bilateral Filter [23].

3.2 Formulating the Level Set Function

Level Set approaches to image matting have been widely used of recent times, especially for binary segmentation. Using a Level Set provides the segmentation result, which can be used to generate the desired trimap. The segmentation task can be described as follows: given an image I, define the Ω as the 2D space for I and the interface $C \subset \Omega$ for the boundary of a subset $\Omega_o \subset \Omega$. C is equal to

$\partial\Omega_o$ and represents all the points on the boundaries.

$$\phi(x, y, 0) = \begin{cases} 0 & C \\ -\rho & inside(C) \\ \rho & outside(C) \end{cases} \tag{2}$$

The contour is the zero level set of function $\phi(x, y, t)$ formulated as in Eq. (2), ρ is a constant specified by a user, $inside(C)$ and $outside(C)$ represent the regions inside and outside of $\partial\Omega_o$. According to [25], the evolution of C can be written as follows:

$$\frac{\partial\phi}{\partial t} = V |\nabla\phi| \tag{3}$$

V is the speed of evolution. Thus, the key for the Level Set method is to solve V. The sequence of the Level Set method is written as follow:

1. Initialize the function $\phi(x, y, 0)$;
2. Evolve the curve using Eq. (3);
3. Calculate and extract iteratively the zero level set until it has converged.

During the process of evolving the level set, the contour can be found by minimizing an appropriate energy function. For this paper, the energy function is as follows:

$$E^{cv}(c_1, c_2, C) = \mu \cdot Length(C) + \lambda_1 \cdot \int_{inside(C)} |u_0 - c_1|^2$$
$$dxdy + \lambda_2 \cdot \int_{outside(C)} |u_0 - c_2|^2 dxdy \tag{4}$$

where μ, λ_1 and λ_2 are positive constant values, u_0 is the zero level set, c_1 is the inside of C, c_2 is the outside of C, and $\lambda_1 = \lambda_2 = 1$. Taking $\phi(x, y)$ into consideration, Eq. (4) can be rewritten the as Eq. (5):

$$E^{cv}(c_1, c_2, C) = \mu \cdot \int_{\Omega} \delta_\varepsilon(\phi(x, y)) |\nabla\phi(x, y)| \, dxdy$$
$$+ \lambda_1 \cdot \int_{\Omega} |u_0 - c_1|^2 H_\varepsilon(\phi(x, y)) dxdy \tag{5}$$
$$+ \lambda_2 \cdot \int_{\Omega} |u_0 - c_2|^2 (1 - H_\varepsilon(\phi(x, y))) dxdy$$

$H(z)$ represents the Heaviside function and $\delta(z)$ is the Dirac delta function. These can be formulated, respectively, as follows:

$$H(z) = \begin{cases} 1 & z \geq 0 \\ 0 & z < 0 \end{cases} \tag{6}$$

$$\delta(z) = \frac{d}{dz} H(z) \tag{7}$$

Evolution of the process needs a stop condition. Evolution is stopped here using an edge indicator function, with G_σ being the Gaussian kernel with σ standard deviation.

$$g = \frac{1}{1 + |\nabla G_\sigma \cdot I|^2} \tag{8}$$

Additionally, there needs to be a penalty to obtain the final curve. This is good for controlling the level set function as an approximate signed distance function. The penalty is expressed as follows:

$$P(\phi) = \int_\Omega \frac{1}{2}(|\nabla \phi(x,y)| - 1)^2 dx dy \tag{9}$$

3.3 Integrating Color and Depth to Generate the Trimap

When it comes to generating the trimap, there are three steps to follow:

1. Preprocess the color image and the depth image;
2. Integrate the color and depth segmentation results;
3. Perform morphological operations (dilation, erosion and edge-detection) on the fused result in step two to obtain the final trimap.

The color channels and depth channel are segmented using the Hierarchical Level Set method. In other words, the image pyramid is used according to the Level Set framework. Different scales of an image have a similar appearance but contain different matting results on the boundary, so the image pyramid helps to re-define the boundary. In this paper, there is a scale space, $\{I_1, I_2, I_3, \ldots, I_n\}$, for every RGBD image I, and each image contains the color and depth channels. We can define the I_c to be the binary segmentation result of the color image and I_d to be the binary segmentation result of the depth image. The color and depth cues can be integrated as follows:

$$R(I) = \sum_{i=1}^{N} \omega_i \cdot I_i^p \cdot \delta < p^c, p^d > \tag{10}$$

$$\delta < i, j >= \begin{cases} 1 & \text{i=j} \\ 0 & \text{otherwise} \end{cases} \tag{11}$$

where R is the fusion of the segmentation results for the color and depth channels, N equals the levels of the image pyramid, I_i^p represents the pixel p in the ith level image, p^c is a the color pixel of I_c and p^d is a depth pixel of I_d, ω_i represents the weight of every level of I and $\sum_{i=1}^{N} \omega_i = 1$.

3.4 Extended Alpha Matting with Depth to Obtain the RGBD Matting Result

Integrating the depth cue matting result and the color cue matting result to generate the trimap. The method used here extends on the approach adopted in [7] and takes depth as an extra channel to obtain an accurate matting result, using the trimap and the color image. The key step in color-based alpha matting is to estimate α_c, which can be computed as follows:

$$\alpha_c = \frac{(C_p - B_p)(F_p - B_p)}{||F_p - B_p||} \tag{12}$$

where the C_p is the unknown region of the input color image, F_p is the foreground region and B_p is the background region of the input color image. Eq. (12) can also be applied to the depth image. Depth-based alpha matting seeks to estimate α_d in the same fashion. The color matting and depth matting results are shown in Fig. 3. The regions in color-based alpha matting results have a high confidence if the foreground is not similar to the background. However, the confidence is poor if there are similar regions and those regions are adopted as a part of the depth-based alpha matting result. To combine the color and depth matte, difference of color can be used. A threshold λ representing the distance between the background and the foreground of the color image is defined to decide whether to replace the color matte with the depth matte. The distance between two pixels is as follows:

$$d_i = \frac{1}{|\Omega|} \sum_{j \in \Omega} ||I_i^c - I_j^c|| \tag{13}$$

For every pixel, the distance is supported by the average of eight nearest neighbors result. When the color difference is less than the defined λ, the color matte can be adopted. Otherwise the depth matte is adopted. This can be written as follows:

$$R(I_i) = \omega_i \cdot I_i^c + (1 - \omega_i) \cdot I_i^d \tag{14}$$

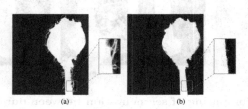

(a)   (b)

Fig. 3. The color-based alpha matting result and depth-based alpha matting result. (a) The color-based alpha matting result; and (b) The depth-based alpha matting result.

$$\omega = \begin{cases} 1 & d_i < \lambda \\ 0 & \text{otherwise} \end{cases} \tag{15}$$

To define the Ω for the eight nearest neighbors of each pixel, $\omega = 1$ when the $d_i < \lambda$ otherwise $\omega = 0$.

4   Experiment Results and Discussion

In this section, common setting is presented for all the experiment and experimental steps and the parameters are elaborated. To validate the performance of matting result, the $NJU2000$ [26] (http://mcg.nju.edu.cn/resource.html) is used in experiments. The proposed matting system is implemented in C++ and Matlab 9.0, and all the experiments are executed on a Mac with the two-core 1.4 GHz Intel Core i5 and 4 GB memory. In the process of matting, the RGBD data are resized to multiples of 2^N, where N is the level of the image pyramid and $N = 3$ in our experiment. The performance is measured by MSE (Mean Squared Error) and $PSNR$ (Peak Signal to Noise Ratio) in the experiment, and ground truth is the baseline.

In order to evaluate and assess the performance of the proposed matting system, this paper makes two comparisons: (1) comparison of segmentation, (2) comparison of matting result. For the comparison of segmentation, the segmentation of this paper is compared to the segmentation GrabCut (implemented in OpenCV) and the segmentation in Ge [16] method, as shown in Fig. 4. As for Fig. 4(e), it represents the segmentation using hierarchical level set. Form Fig. 4, it's clear that the segmentation in this paper is good enough.

(a)   (b)   (c)   (d)   (e)

Fig. 4. **Examples comparing of segmentation between our matting method, GrabCut and method in** [16]. From left to right: (a) color channels and depth channels of RGBD images, (b) ground truth, (c) segmentation using GrabCut implemented in OpenCV, (d) segmentation using the method in [16], (e) segmentation generated by our method.

Fig. 5. Examples of the matting result. From left to right: (a) color channels and depth channels of RGBD images, (b) ground truth, (c) matting using the method in [5], (d) matting using the method in [17], (e) matting using the method in [29], (f) matting using the method in [30], (g) matting result generated by our method.

Table 1. Evaluation of matting results

Method	MES		PSNR	
	Bell	*Tower*	*Bell*	*Tower*
Close-form solution [5]	35.02	24.55	32.68	34.22
Lu [17]	5.88	46.25	40.43	31.47
Ehsan [29]	3.31	5.62	42.94	40.63
Li [30]	3.48	5.86	42.70	40.44
Ours	**2.97**	**2.66**	**43.39**	**43.87**

For the comparison of matting result, we compare the matting result in Lu [17], matting using tradition Bayesian and matting using close-form solution with our matting result, matting using using Weighted Color and Texture Matting [29] (rank 21.6 in www.alphamatting.com), matting using Three-layer graph [30] (rank 10.8 in www.alphamatting.com). The examples is shown in Fig. 5. From Fig. 5 and Table 1, it can be seen that our method was able to provide a high-quality matting result without shadow, demonstrating that our method can generate a good matting result.

5   Conclusion

This paper has proposed an efficient method for RGBD image matting. Depth information is taken into consideration and integrated with the color information to get a raw matting result using a Hierarchical Level Set method. After that, a trimap is generated using the raw matting result. Finally, the final matting result is computed using depth-assisted alpha matting where the color image, depth image, and trimap are used together as input. The method?s performance is not only better than where just color cues are adopted but also better than where just depth cues are used. This is especially the case when the foreground is very similar to the background. The advantages of the method can be summarized as follows: a fusion of the color information and depth information significantly improves the matting result; the more accurate trimap that is therefore generated is able to provide a much better alpha matting result.

6   Competing Interests

The authors have declared that no competing interests exist.

Acknowledgments. This work is supported by the National Natural Science Foundation of China (No. 61502060), National Natural Science Foundation of China (No. 61701051).

References

1. Smith, A.R., Blinn, J.F.: Blue screen matting. In: International Conference on Computer Graphics and Interactive Techniques, pp. 259–268 (1996)
2. Naqvi, S.S., Browne, W.N., Hollitt, C.: Salient object detection via spectral matting. Pattern Recogn. **51**, 209–224 (2016)
3. Chuang, Y., Curless, B., Salesin, D., Szeliski, R.: A Bayesian approach to digital matting, vol. 2, pp. 264–271 (2001)
4. Sun, J., Jia, J., Tang, C., Shum, H.: Poisson matting. In: International Conference on Computer Graphics and Interactive Techniques (2004)
5. Levin, A., Lischinski, D., Weiss, Y.: A closed-form solution to natural image matting. IEEE Trans. Pattern Anal. Mach. Intell. **30**(2), 228–242 (2008)
6. Cho, J., Ziegler, R., Gross, M.H., Lee, K.H.: Improving alpha matte with depth information. IEICE Electron. Express **6**(22), 1602–1607 (2009)
7. Gastal, E.S.L., Oliveira, M.M.: Shared sampling for real-time alpha matting. In: Computer Graphics Forum, vol. 29, no. 2, pp. 575–584 (2010)
8. Pollefeys, M., Aksoy, Y., Aydin, T.O.: Designing effective inter-pixel information flow for natural image matting (2017)
9. Crabb, R., Tracey, C., Puranik, A., Davis, J.: Real-time foreground segmentation via range and color imaging, pp. 1–5 (2008)
10. Wang, O., Finger, J., Yang, Q., Davis, J., Yang, R.: Automatic natural video matting with depth. In: Pacific Conference on Computer Graphics and Applications, pp. 469–472 (2007)
11. Pitie, F., Kokaram, A.: Matting with a depth map. In: IEEE International Conference on Image Processing, pp. 21–24 (2010)
12. Osher, S., Sethian, J.A.: Fronts propagating with curvature-dependent speed: algorithms based on Hamilton-Jacobi formulations. J. Comput. Phys. **79**(1), 12–49 (1988)
13. Xu, L., Sun, W., Au, O.C., et al.: Adaptive depth map assisted matting in 3D video. In: IEEE International Conference on Multimedia and Expo, pp. 1–6 (2011)
14. Lee, S.W., Seo, Y.H., Yang, H.S.: Efficient foreground extraction using RGB-D imaging. Kluwer Academic Publishers (2016)

15. Wang, L., Gong, M., Zhang, C., Yang, R., Zhang, C., Yang, Y.H.: Automatic real-time video matting using time-of-flight camera and multichannel poisson equations. Int. J. Comput. Vision **97**(1), 104–121 (2012)
16. Ge, L., Ju, R., Ren, T., Wu, G.: Interactive RGB-D image segmentation using hierarchical graph cut and geodesic distance. In: Ho, Y.-S., Sang, J., Ro, Y.M., Kim, J., Wu, F. (eds.) PCM 2015. LNCS, vol. 9314, pp. 114–124. Springer, Cham (2015). https://doi.org/10.1007/978-3-319-24075-6_12
17. Lu, T., Li, S.: Image matting with color and depth information, pp. 3787–3790 (2012)
18. Memar, S., Jin, K., Boufama, B.: Object detection using active contour model with depth clue. In: Kamel, M., Campilho, A. (eds.) ICIAR 2013. LNCS, vol. 7950, pp. 640–647. Springer, Heidelberg (2013). https://doi.org/10.1007/978-3-642-39094-4_73
19. Hao, W., Zheng, S., Guo, C., Xie, Y.: Level set contour extraction based on data-adaptive Gaussian smoother, pp. 11–15 (2012)
20. Hu, P., Shuai, B., Liu, J., Wang, G.: Deep level sets for salient object detection. In: IEEE Conference on Computer Vision and Pattern Recognition (2017)
21. Chan, T.F., Vese, L.A.: Active contours without edges. IEEE Trans. Image Process. **10**(2), 266–277 (2001)
22. Zanuttigh, P., Marin, G., Dal Mutto, C., Dominio, F., Minto, L., Cortelazzo, G.M.: Time-of-Flight and Structured Light Depth Cameras. Springer, Cham (2016). https://doi.org/10.1007/978-3-319-30973-6
23. Chen, L., Lin, H., Li, S.: Depth image enhancement for kinect using region growing and bilateral filter. In: International Conference on Pattern Recognition, pp. 3070–3073 (2013)
24. Le, A.V., Jung, S., Won, C.S.: Directional joint bilateral filter for depth images. Sensors **14**(7), 11362–11378 (2014)
25. Jung, S.: Enhancement of image and depth map using adaptive joint trilateral filter. IEEE Trans. Circuits Syst. Video Technol. **23**(2), 269–280 (2013)
26. Li, C., Xu, C., Gui, C., Fox, M.D.: Level set evolution without re-initialization: a new variational formulation. In: 2005 IEEE Computer Society Conference on Computer Vision and Pattern Recognition, CVPR 2005, vol. 1, pp. 430–436 (2005)
27. Ju, R., Liu, Y., Ren, T., Ge, L., Wu, G.: Depth-aware salient object detection using anisotropic center-surround difference. Signal Process. Image Commun. **38**(C), 115–126 (2015)
28. Leens, J., Piérard, S., Barnich, O., Van Droogenbroeck, M., Wagner, J.-M.: Combining color, depth, and motion for video segmentation. In: Fritz, M., Schiele, B., Piater, J.H. (eds.) ICVS 2009. LNCS, vol. 5815, pp. 104–113. Springer, Heidelberg (2009). https://doi.org/10.1007/978-3-642-04667-4_11
29. Varnousfaderani, E.S., Rajan, D.: Weighted color and texture sample selection for image matting. IEEE Trans. Image Process. **22**(11), 4260–4270 (2013)
30. Li, C., Wang, P., Zhu, X., Pi, H.: Three-layer graph framework with the sumD feature for alpha matting. Comput. Vis. Image Underst. **162**, 34–45 (2017)

A Genetic Programming Approach to Integrate Multilayer CNN Features for Image Classification

Wei-Ta Chu[✉] and Hao-An Chu

National Chung Cheng University, Chiayi, Taiwan
wtchu@ccu.edu.tw

Abstract. Fusing information extracted from multiple layers of a convolutional neural network has been proven effective in several domains. Common fusion techniques include feature concatenation and Fisher embedding. In this work, we propose to fuse multilayer information by genetic programming (GP). With the evolutionary strategy, we iteratively fuse multilayer information in a systematic manner. In the evaluation, we verify the effectiveness of discovered GP-based representations on three image classification datasets, and discuss characteristics of the GP process. This study is one of the few works to fuse multilayer information based on an evolutionary strategy. The reported preliminary results not only demonstrate the potential of the GP fusion scheme, but also inspire future study in several aspects.

Keywords: Genetic programming · Convolutional neural networks
Multilayer features · Image classification

1 Introduction

Convolutional neural networks have been widely adopted in visual analysis, such as image classification and object detection. A common network structure includes a sequence of convolutional blocks followed by several fully-connected layers. Each convolutional block usually consists of one or more convolutional layers followed by a pooling layer. With vary-sized convolutional kernels and pooling, different convolutional layers extract visual features at various levels. A sequence of convolutional blocks thus can be viewed as a powerful feature extractor, and the extracted features are then fed to a classification network or a regression network to accomplish the targeted task.

Features extracted from the first few layers more likely describe basic geometric patterns, while features extracted from the last few layers more likely describe higher level object parts. Though high-level features may be preferable in recognizing visual semantics, in some domains low-level features and high-level features are better jointly considered to achieve better performance. For example, Li et al. [10] integrated features extracted from multiple CNN layers

© Springer Nature Switzerland AG 2019
I. Kompatsiaris et al. (Eds.): MMM 2019, LNCS 11295, pp. 640–651, 2019.
https://doi.org/10.1007/978-3-030-05710-7_53

based on the Fisher encoding scheme, and demonstrated very promising performance in remote sensing scene classification. In [16], multilayer features from CNNs were also jointly considered by the Fisher encoding scheme, and multiple CNNs were employed to extract features from multiple modalities to facilitate video classification.

To improve image classification performance, we introduce a novel way to integrate features extracted from multiple CNN layers based on *genetic programming* [8]. Both genetic programming (GP) and genetic algorithm (GA) [6] are evolutionary strategies motivated by biological inheritance and evolution. They both work by iteratively applying genetic transformations, such as crossover and mutation, to a population of individuals, in order to create better performing individuals in subsequent generations. Different from GA, individuals in GP iterations are not limited to fixed-length chromosomes. More complex data structures like tree or linked lists can be processed by GP. In our work, we take features extracted from CNN layers as the population of individuals, and attempt to find better representation by integrating individuals with GP.

Contributions of this paper are twofold:

- We introduce a multilayer feature fusion method based on genetic programming. To our knowledge, this would be the first work adopting genetic programming in integrating deep features extracted from different CNN layers.
- We demonstrate that this approach yields better image classification performance on three image benchmarks. Extensive discussions are provided to inspire future studies in several aspects.

2   Related Works

2.1   Multilayer Features

Many studies have been proposed to integrate features derived from multiple models. In this subsection, we simply review those integrating features derived from multiple layers of a single model, especially for image/video classification. To classify remote sensing scene images, i.e., aerial images, Li et al. [10] extracted visual features based on pre-trained deep convolutional neural networks. The models they used include AlexNet [9], CaffeNet [7], and variants of VGG [2, 13]. From an input image, a series of images at different scales is produced by the Gaussian pyramid method. These images are fed to a CNN to get convolutional features, which are then concatenated and encoded as a Fisher vector. Basically, the idea of combining multilayer features in [10] is concatenation of convolutional features encoded by the Fisher kernel.

Yang et al. [16] extracted features from multiple layers and from multiple modalities to do video classification. Given a sequence of video frames, each frame is first fed to a CNN separately. The filter responses over time but corresponding to the same (pre-defined) spatial neighborhood are then encoded into Fisher vectors. In [16], Fisher vectors corresponding to different spatial locations are further weighted differently to improve the effectiveness. Basically, jointly considering feature maps from multiple layers in the representation of Fisher vectors is the idea of combining multilayer features.

In [15], a directed acyclic graph structure was proposed to integrate features extracted from different CNN layers. Feature maps from each layer are processed with pooling, normalization, and embedding, and the processed features from all layers are element-wisely added to form the final representation. This representation is then fed to a softmax layer to achieve scene image classification.

In most of these works, the operations to combine multiple layers are concatenation or addition. We will study how to automatically find more complex operations to fuse multilayer information based on GP.

2.2   Genetic Programming

Genetic programming is a branch of evolutionary computation that iteratively manipulates the population using crossover and mutation according to some fitness function, and attempts to find the individual that achieves the best performance. This strategy has been adopted in various domains. In this subsection, we simply review studies on the ones related to visual analysis.

Shao et al. [12] proposed to use GP in feature learning for image classification. Simple features like RGB colors and intensity values are extracted from images, which are viewed as the basic primitives. To generate better representations, a set of functions is defined to process these primitives, like Gaussian smooth, addition/subtraction, and max pooling. Basic primitives are processed by a sequence of pre-defined functions, and then integrated representations can be generated. Taking classification error rate as the fitness function, each integrated representation is evaluated, and better representations are selected to generate the next-generation individuals at the next iteration.

Liang et al. [11] formulated foreground-background image segmentation as a pixel classification problem. From each pixel, the Gabor features representing gradient information at a specific scale and a specific orientation are extracted. A binary classifier categorizing pixels as foreground or background is then constructed by the GP process.

Al-Sahaf et al. [1] learnt rotation-invariant texture image descriptors by GP. The statistical values like mean and max of a window centered by a pixel are viewed as the basic primitives, and a code is generated by a series of operations on the primitives to represent information derived from a pixel. The codes of pixels over the entire image are then quantized to be the image descriptor.

Inspired by the requests of designing a CNN structure for a specific task, Suganuma et al. [14] adopted the GP search strategy to find better CNN structures. Taking common components in CNNs, like convolutional block and max pooling, as the basic primitives, the proposed method automatically learns a series of CNN structures. This work would be one of the first studies linking CNN structure design with GP.

In our work, the basic idea is more like feature learning presented in [12]. However, the primitives are feature maps derived from pre-trained CNNs, and we want to verify that the automatically learnt representation can yield better performance in image classification. Different from [10] and [16], the operations to combine multilayer features are automatically learnt by GP.

3   Overview of Genetic Programming

The three components in GP are the terminal set, the function set, and the fitness function. The terminal set includes basic primitives to be manipulated. Each single primitive itself usually is a simple solution, but we want to learn to manipulate primitives to generate a better solution. For example, the terminal set of [12] simply contains RGB colors and intensity values of pixels, and in our work we take feature maps derived from a pre-defined CNN as the terminals.

The GP algorithm dynamically selects parts of the terminals, and sequentially processes or combines them to form an integrated presentation. A sequence of processing can be illustrated as a tree, as shown in Fig. 1(a) and (b). In Fig. 1(a), the terminal T_1 is first processed with F_1, and then is combined with T_2 by the function F_2. Then it is combined with T_3 by the function F_3 to form the final integrated representation. Notice that the terminal nodes and the function nodes are automatically selected by the GP algorithm, given the constraint of tree height. The same terminal nodes or function nodes may be selected multiple times in the same tree, as shown in Fig. 1(b).

At each iteration of the GP algorithm, a set of S integrated representations are generated. Each integrated representation can be described by a tree and can be evaluated by the fitness function. Parts of the representations that yield higher fitness values would be selected in the mating pool. The representations in the mating pool are potential *parents* that generate children representations by genetic operations like *crossover* and *mutation* at the next iteration.

Taking trees in Fig. 1(a) and (b) as the parents, Fig. 1(c) and (d) show two generated children by the crossover operation. Figure 1(c) is generated from Fig. 1(a) by replacing the leaf node T_2 with a subtree from Fig. 1(b). Conversely, Fig. 1(d) is generated from Fig. 1(b) by replacing a subtree by the leaf node T_2 of Fig. 1(a). We intentionally draw subtrees from Fig. 1(a) and (b) in blue and green, respectively, to clarify the idea. To conduct mutation, a tree is randomly generated as the basic element, as shown in Fig. 1(e). A mutation result from Fig. 1(a) is generated by replacing a subtree rooted at F_2 by the one shown in Fig. 1(e), yielding the illustration in Fig. 1(f).

We keep combining selected parents to generate children representation until the number of children is the same as that of the previous population, i.e., the number S mentioned above. Fitness values of the representations in the newly-generated population are then evaluated, and then better ones are selected in the mating pool for generating the next population. The same process keeps iterating until some stop criterion meets. Finally, the best-so-far representation is picked as the final representation.

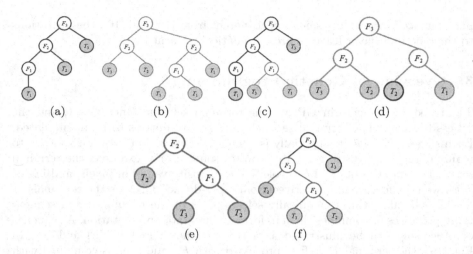

Fig. 1. Illustrations of the GP processes. (a)(b) Trees describing sequences of processes to generate integrated representations. (c)(d) Two children representations generated by applying the crossover operation on trees in (a) and (b). (e) The randomly-generated tree to conduct the mutation operation. (f) A tree generated from (a) with the mutation operation shown in (e). (Color figure online)

4   GP-Based Combination

This section provides details of how we employ GP in integrating features extracted from different CNN layers. Although the proposed integration method is not limited to any specific CNN models, we take the VGG-S model [2] as the main example in this section.

Assume that there are N_i feature maps of size $M_i \times M_i$ from the ith CNN layer, and there are N_j feature maps of size $M_j \times M_j$ from the jth CNN layer. For each layer, we flatten the feature maps into vectors, and thus the ith terminal T_i is represented as N_i vectors of dimensionality $M_i \times M_i$.

When the two terminals T_i and T_j are to be combined with element-wise addition, for example, we would first ensure that vectors from two terminals are comparable. Assume that $M_i > M_j$ and $N_i > N_j$, we first reduce dimensionality (M_i) of vectors in T_i into M_j by the principal component analysis method, and then concatenate all of them to form a ($N_i \times M_j \times M_j$)-dimensional vector $\boldsymbol{t}_i$ to represent T_i. For the terminal T_2, we first concatenate all vectors and get a ($N_j \times M_j \times M_j$)-dimensional vector $\boldsymbol{t}_j$. Two different addition operations are designed to make $\boldsymbol{t}_j$ compatible with $\boldsymbol{t}_i$, which are denoted as AddPad and AddTrim, respectively. If $\boldsymbol{t}_j$ and $\boldsymbol{t}_i$ are combined with the AddPad operation, we pad zeros at the end of $\boldsymbol{t}_j$ such that the dimensionality of $\boldsymbol{t}_j$ is increased to ($N_i \times M_j \times M_j$). This dimensionality transformation strategy follows the setting mentioned in [14]. If $\boldsymbol{t}_j$ and $\boldsymbol{t}_i$ are combined with the AddTrim operation, appropriate numbers of items at the end of $\boldsymbol{t}_i$ are trimmed, such that the dimensionality of $\boldsymbol{t}_i$ is decreased to ($N_j \times M_j \times M_j$). Similarly, the element-wise subtraction, multiplication, and division operations all have the padded version and trimmed version. The GP process determines whether the padded version or the trimmed version is more effective automatically.

Pre-defined operations to combine two nodes are element-wise addition, subtraction, multiplication, division, and taking maximum/minimum/absolute values. Another operation is concatenation, which is also one of the most common operations used in previous works [3, 10]. Taking the terminals T_i and T_j as the example, we concatenate the N_i $(M_i \times M_i)$-dim vectors with the N_j $(M_j \times M_j)$-dim vectors, and finally form a $(N_i M_i M_i N_j M_j M_j)$-dimensional vector.

A sequence of processes on terminal nodes and internal nodes can be described as a tree like Fig. 1(a), and the root node represents the final integrated descriptor. To evaluate goodness of the final representation, we define the classification error rate as the fitness value. For an evaluation dataset like the Caltech-101 image collection [4], we divide it into three parts: training set, validation set, and test set. From the training set, we feed images into the VGG-S model and extract feature maps from CNN layers. Integrated representations $\{f_1, f_2, ..., f_N\}$ are generated by N sequences of processes, each of which is described by a tree. Based on the ith integrated representations $\{f_i\}$ extracted from the training images, we construct a multi-class classifier based on a support vector machine. The ith integrated representations extracted from the validation set are then used to test the classifier, and then the classification error rate can be calculated. The training set and the validation set are in fact shuffled based on the five-fold cross validation scheme. Overall, the average classification error rate after five runs of training and validation is viewed as the fitness value, which is the clue for selecting better integrated representations into the mating pool.

One important parameter to generate an integrated representation is the height of a tree. A tree of larger height means more processes are involved in generating the integrated representation. Conceptually, if higher trees are allowed, larger search space is allowed to find better representations, but the GP algorithm is more computationally expensive. We thus dynamically increase the heights of trees in the GP algorithm. Let H_{max} denote the maximum height allowed to generate a tree, and H_{cur} denote the height of the highest tree at the current iteration. Starting from the parents selected from the tth iteration, if a children tree T_c is generated by crossover or mutation for the $(t+1)$th iteration, and its height is H_c, then it is filtered by the following process.

- If $H_c \leq H_{cur}$, take the tree T_c into consideration at the $(t+1)$th iteration. The representation described by T_c will be evaluated.
- If $H_c > H_{cur}$ and $H_c \leq H_{max}$, the representation described by T_c is evaluated. If the solution described by T_c is better than all existing solutions, we set H_{cur} as H_c. Otherwise, we discard the tree T_c.
- If $H_c > H_{max}$, discard the tree T_c.

The idea of the aforementioned filtering process is that we increase the search space only when better solutions can be obtained by higher trees. This guarantees a reasonable computational cost when we conduct the GP process.

5   Experiments

5.1   Evaluation Settings and Datasets

We conduct experiments on the Caltech-101 dataset [4], the Caltech-256 dataset [5], and the Stanford-40 action dataset [17]. The Caltech-101 dataset consists of 101 widely varied object categories, and each category contains between 45 to 400 images. The Caltech-256 dataset consists of 256 object categories, and each category contains between 80 to 827 images. The Stanford-40 dataset contains 9,532 images in total with 180–300 images per action class. For the Caltech-101 dataset, we follow the experimental protocol mentioned in [12]. The first 20 images from each category are selected as the training data, the following 15 images from each category are taken as the validation data, and the remaining is taken as the testing data. For the Caltech-256 dataset, the first 45 images from each category are selected as the training data, the following 15 images from each category are taken as the validation data, and the remaining is taken as the testing data. For the Stanford-40 dataset, the first 80 images from each action class are selected as the training data, the following 20 images from each class are the validation data, and the remaining is the testing data.

Table 1. Configurations of the baseline models [2].

Arch.	conv1	conv2	conv3	conv4	conv5	full6	full7	full8
VGG-S	$96 \times 7 \times 7$ st. 2, pad 0 LRN, x3 pool	$256 \times 5 \times 5$ st. 1, pad 1 x2 pool	$512 \times 3 \times 3$ st. 1, pad 1 –	$512 \times 3 \times 3$ st. 1, pad 1 –	$512 \times 3 \times 3$ st. 1, pad 1 x3 pool	4096 dropout	4096 dropout	1000 softmax

To generate GP-representations, we search for good GP-representations based on information extracted by the VGG-S model [2]. Table 1 shows the configurations of the VGG-S model. The first sub-row of each cell denotes the number of convolution filters and their receptive field as "number × size × size". In the second sub-row, the notation "st" stands for the convolution stride, and "pad" stands for spatial padding. In the third sub-row, LRN stands for Local Response Normalization [9], followed by the max-pooling downsampling factor. For the fully-connected layers, we specify the number of nodes. The layers full6 and full7 are regularized using dropout, and the output of the full8 layer is activated by a softmax function. Activation function of all layers is ReLU.

In the GP process, we take responses of all layers (including convolutional layers and fully-connected layers) as the input, and iteratively combine them with predefined operations. The GP process runs for 20 generations, and at each generation, 100 trees are built and evaluated. After 20 generations, the best-so-far representation is picked as the final GP representation, which is then used to construct an SVM classifier to do image classification. The mean class accuracy is reported in the following experiments.

5.2   Performance on the Caltech-101 Dataset

We first evaluate the GP representation determined based on the VGG-S model on the Caltech-101 dataset. Table 2 shows mean class accuracies obtained based on various image representations. The first sub-table lists performance yielded by handcrafted features, including HOG, SIFT, LBP, Texton histogram, and Centrist. At most 75% accuracy can be achieved by handcrafted features.

Table 2. The mean class accuracies obtained by handcrafted features, learned features, and the proposed GP representation, based on the Caltech-101 dataset.

	Handcrafted features				
	HOG	SIFT	LBP	Texton his.	CENTRIST
Accuracy	60.7	63.3	58.3	73.4	75.1
	Learnt features				
	DBN	CNN	MOGP [12]	VGG-S (w/o fine-tuning)	VGG-S (with fine-tuning)
Accuracy	78.9	75.8	80.3	72.4	87.8
	GP representation				
Accuracy	**90.4**				

The second sub-table shows performance obtained based on three types of learning features. The DBN item stands for a deep brief network consisting of three layers with 500, 500, and 2000 nodes, respectively. Responses of the final layer are taken as the image representation, and an SVM classifier is constructed to do image classification. The CNN item stands for a convolutional neural network consisting of five convolutional layers. Responses of the final convolutional layer are taken as the image representation to construct an SVM classifier. These two learnt features yield performance better than handcrafted features. The MOGP (Multi-Objective Genetic Programming) [12] is a GP-based method that integrates simple handcrafted features, i.e., pixel's RGB values and intensity, by genetic programming. We see that over 80% accuracy can be achieved, even better than the DBN or CNN features, though only very simple features are used as the foundation for feature fusion.

Our main idea is that we would like to further improve performance by fusing multilayer learnt features by GP. In this experiment, the baseline learnt features are from the output of the last layer of the VGG-S model. The last two items in the second sub-table show performance yielded by the baseline features. Without fine-tuning, the VGG-S features do not work well. By fine-tuning with the Caltech-101 dataset, the classification accuracy is largely boosted to 87.8%, conforming to the trend shown in [2]. The third sub-table shows that the determined GP representation yields the best performance, i.e., 90.4% mean class accuracy. This verifies that the proposed GP method can effectively integrate multilayer information and boost performance.

Figure 2(a) shows that how the classification error rate gradually decreases as the number of iteration increases. This shows appropriately fusing multilayer

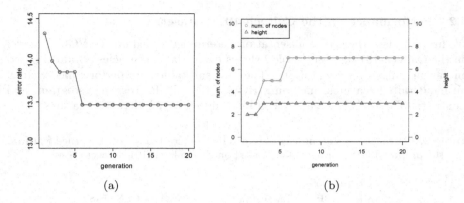

(a)   (b)

Fig. 2. (a) The evolutions of error rate as the number of generation increases. (b) The evolutions of number of tree nodes and number of tree height as the number of generation increases.

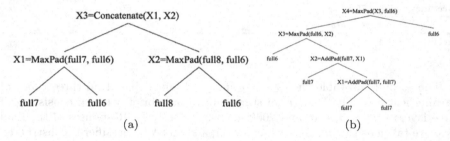

(a)   (b)

Fig. 3. (a) The tree representing the final fusion result yielding the best performance in Table 2. (b) The tree representing the final fusion result yielding the best performance in Table 3.

features by GP really yields better classification performance. Figure 2(b) shows that, as the number of GP iteration increases, how the number of tree nodes and the number of tree height change. From the orange curve, we see that generally the number of nodes increases as the number of iteration increases. This means the GP process tends to fuse more features as the evolution proceeds. From the red curve, we see that trees grow higher as the evolution proceeds. The height of the tree yielding the best performance in Table 2 is three.

Figure 3(a) shows the final fusion result that yields the best performance. As shown in the tree, information extracted by full7 and full6 is first combined by the MaxPad operation (taking element-wise maximum after padding) to generate the internal representation X1. Another subtree shows that full8 and full6 are also combined by the MaxPad operation to generate X2. The international representations X1 and X2 are then concatenated to form the final GP representation X3. Notice that information from the same layer may be adopted multiple times to form the GP representation, e.g., full6 in this case. The ways to combine multilayer information and the information to be fused are all determined by the genetic programming automatically.

5.3   Performance on Other Datasets

We evaluate the GP representation determined based on the VGG-S model on the Caltech-256 dataset. Table 3 shows mean class accuracies obtained by the baseline model and the GP representation. Notice that the setting for fine tuning in Table 3 is different from that used in [2]. In [2], 60 images from each class were selected for fine tuning, while in our work, only 45 images are selected for fine tuning, and the remaining 15 images are used for validation in the GP process due to hardware limit of our implementation. With such setting, Table 3 again shows the superiority of the GP representation. The performance gain is around 1%. Figure 3(b) shows how the GP representation is constructed. The internal node X2 is actually the result of multiplying full7 by three. This simple process is done by adding full7 three times. The internal node X3 is obtained by finding the maximum of X2 and full6 element-wisely. Finally, the final GP representation X4 is obtained by finding the maximum of X3 and full6 element-wisely.

Table 3. The mean class accuracies obtained by the baseline and the proposed GP representation, based on the Caltech-256 dataset.

	VGG-S (with fine-tuning)	GP representation
Accuracy	70.32	71.78

We also evaluate the determined GP representation on the Stanford-40 action dataset. Table 4 shows mean class accuracies obtained by the baseline model and the GP representation. We see that, based on the GP representation, around 2% performance improvement can be obtained.

Table 4. The mean class accuracies obtained by the baseline and the proposed GP representation, based on the Stanford-40 dataset.

	VGG-S (with fine-tuning)	GP representation
Accuracy	59.76	61.80

5.4   Discussion

We make discussion based on the experiments on the Caltech-101 dataset. Figure 4(a) shows the number of times different layers' information used in fusion as the evolution proceeds. We count how many times a layer's output is used at each iteration. As can be seen in Fig. 4(a), the outputs of full6, full7, and full8 are much frequently utilized in combination. Interestingly, this trend conforms to previous studies that show deeper layers of a neural network extract high-level semantics and are usually used to do image classification and many other tasks.

Figure 4(b) shows the number of times different operations used to combine multiplayer information as the GP process proceeds. Overall, the operations of MaxPad, MaxTrim, and Concatenation are more frequently utilized to fuse multilayer information. We think this characteristic may pave a way to improve the commonly-used neural networks, but the reason why these operations are utilized more frequently still needs further investigation in the future.

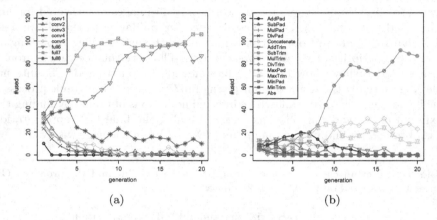

(a)   (b)

Fig. 4. (a) The number of times different layers' information used in fusion as the number of generation increases. (b) The number of times different operations used to combine multilayer information as the number of generation increases.

6   Conclusion

We have presented a fusion method based on genetic programming to integrate information extracted from multiple layers of a neural network. We verify the effectiveness of the proposed GP method by showing that the automatically determined representation yields better performance than the output of the best single layer. In addition, we also discuss the characteristics of the trees embodying the determined GP representation, and the trends of utilized operations and layers as the evolution proceeds. A few directions can be investigated in the future, such as conducting evaluation based on a large-scale collection, and considering more basic operations in the GP process.

Acknowledgement. This work was partially supported by the Ministry of Science and Technology under the grant 107-2221-E-194-038-MY2 and 107-2218-E-002-054, and the Advanced Institute of Manufacturing with High-tech Innovations (AIM-HI) from The Featured Areas Research Center Program within the framework of the Higher Education Sprout Project by the Ministry of Education (MOE) in Taiwan.

References

1. Al-Sahaf, H., Al-Sahaf, A., Xue, B., Johnston, M., Zhang, M.: Automatically evolving rotation-invariant texture image descriptors by genetic programming. IEEE Trans. Evol. Comput. **21**(1), 83–101 (2017)
2. Chatfield, K., Simonyan, K., Vedaldi, A., Zisserman, A.: Return of the devil in the details: delving deep into convolutional networks. In: Proceedings of British Machine Vision Conference (2014)
3. Dosovitskiy, A., et al.: FlowNet: learning optical flow with convolutional networks. In: Proceedings of IEEE International Conference on Computer Vision (2015)
4. Fei-Fei, L., Fergus, R., Perona, P.: Learning generative visual models from few training examples: an incremental Bayesian approach tested on 101 object categories. In: Proceedings of CVPR Workshop of Generative Model Based Vision (2004)
5. Griffin, G., Holub, A., Perona, P.: Caltech-256 object category dataset. Technical report, California Institute of Technology (2007)
6. Holland, J.H.: Adaptation in Natural and Artificial Systems: An Introductory Analysis with Applications to Biology, Control and Artificial Intelligence. MIT Press, Cambridge (1992)
7. Jia, Y., et al.: Caffe: convolutional architecture for fast feature embedding. In: Proceedings of ACM International Conference on Multimedia, pp. 675–678 (2014)
8. Koza, J.R.: Genetic Programming: On the Programming of Computers by Means of Natural Selection. MIT Press, Cambridge (1992)
9. Krizhevsky, A., Sutskever, I., Hinton, G.E.: ImageNet classification with deep convolutional neural networks. In: Proceedings of International Conference on Neural Information Processing Systems, pp. 1097–1105 (2012)
10. Li, E., Xia, J., Du, P., Lin, C., Samat, A.: Integrating multilayer features of convolutional neural networks for remote sensing scene classification. IEEE Trans. Geosci. Remote Sens. **55**(10), 5653–5665 (2017)
11. Liang, Y., Zhang, M., Browne, W.N.: Figure-ground image segmentation using genetic programming and feature selection. In: Proceedings of IEEE Congress on Evolutionary Computation (2016)
12. Shao, L., Liu, L., Li, X.: Feature learning for image classification via multiobjective genetic programming. IEEE Trans. Neural Netw. Learn. Syst. **25**(7), 1359–1371 (2014)
13. Simonyan, K., Zisserman, A.: Very deep convolutional networks for large-scale image recognition. In: Proceedings of International Conference on Learning Representation (2015)
14. Suganuma, M., Shirakawa, S., Nagao, T.: A genetic programming approach to designing convolutional neural network architectures. In: Proceedings of the Genetic and Evolutionary Computation Conference, pp. 497–504 (2017)
15. Yang, S., Ramanan, D.: Multi-scale recognition with DAG-CNNs. In: Proceedings of IEEE International Conference on Computer Vision (2015)
16. Yang, X., Molchanov, P., Kautz, J.: Multilayer and multimodal fusion of deep neural networks for video classification. In: Proceedings of ACM Multimedia Conference, pp. 978–987 (2016)
17. Yao, B., Jiang, X., Khosla, A., Lin, A.L., Guibas, L., Fei-Fei, L.: Human action recognition by learning bases of action attributes and parts. In: Proceedings of IEEE International Conference on Computer Vision (2011)

Improving Micro-expression Recognition Accuracy Using Twofold Feature Extraction

Madhumita A. Takalkar⬥, Haimin Zhang⬥, and Min Xu[✉]⬥

School of Electrical and Data Engineering,
Faculty of Engineering and Information Technology,
University of Technology Sydney, Ultimo, NSW 2007, Australia
{madhumita.a.takalkar,haimin.zhang}@student.uts.edu.au, min.xu@uts.edu.au

Abstract. Micro-expressions are generated involuntarily on a person's face and are usually a manifestation of repressed feelings of the person. Micro-expressions are characterised by short duration, involuntariness and low intensity. Because of these characteristics, micro-expressions are difficult to perceive and interpret correctly, and they are profoundly challenging to identify and categorise automatically.

Previous work for micro-expression recognition has used hand-crafted features like LBP-TOP, Gabor filter, HOG and optical flow. Recent work also has demonstrated the possible use of deep learning for micro-expression recognition. This paper is the first work to explore the use of hand-craft feature descriptor and deep feature descriptor for micro-expression recognition task. The aim is to use the hand-craft and deep learning feature descriptor to extract features and integrate them together to construct a large feature vector to describe a video. Through experiments on CASME, CASME II and CASME+2 databases, we demonstrate our proposed method can achieve promising results for micro-expression recognition accuracy with larger training samples.

Keywords: Micro-expression recognition · Deep learning
Local binary pattern-three orthogonal planes (LBP-TOP)
Convolutional neural network (CNN) · Small training data
Data augmentation

1 Introduction

Facial expression plays an essential role in people's daily communication and emotion expression. Typically, a full facial expression last from (1/2) to 4 s and can be easily identified by humans. The psychological studies, indicate that the recognition of human emotion based on facial expressions may be misleading [15]. In other words, someone may try to hide his or her emotion by exerting an opposite facial expression.

As early as in 1969, Ekman [2] observed micro-expressions when he analysed an interview video of a patient with depression. The patient who tried to commit

© Springer Nature Switzerland AG 2019
I. Kompatsiaris et al. (Eds.): MMM 2019, LNCS 11295, pp. 652–664, 2019.
https://doi.org/10.1007/978-3-030-05710-7_54

suicide showed brief yet intense sadness but resumed smiling quickly. Such micro-expressions only last for less than 1/12 s. In the following decades, Ekman and his colleague continued researching micro-expressions. Their work had drawn increasing interests from both academic and commercial communities.

For its authenticity and objectivity, subtle emotions in humans has a broad range of applications in different domains. In the clinical work, to detect and recognise micro-expression is vital to assist psychologists in the diagnosis and remediation of patients with mental diseases such as autism and schizophrenia. Micro-expressions are also useful in affect monitoring [1], serving as a vital clue in law enforcement, evidence collection, criminal investigations. As such, machine-automated recognition of facial micro-expressions would be enormously valuable.

While research towards micro-expressions has seen the significant exertion in the previous decades in the discipline of psychology, research into micro-expressions is only starting to thrive in the train of pattern recognition, computer vision, multimedia and machine learning. Recently the deep learning has become popular in computer vision, also in affective computing. This motivates us to develop promising deep learning methodology for improving the performance of micro-expression recognition.

Our contributions are listed as follows:

- To the best of our knowledge, this is the first attempt to combine the temporal hand-craft LBP-TOP feature descriptor and spatial CNN deep feature to extract features from all facial regions preventing loss of even the most minute micro-expression details. Our method is more straightforward than most of the traditional hand-craft feature descriptors.
- Experiments are performed on widely used CASME and CASME II databases and also on CASME+2 [14] database. Our method outperformed the state-of-the-art recognition methods.
- Our work is the first to use CASME database for fine-tuning the VGG Face network to obtain deep learning results. Due to a smaller number of samples in CASME as compared to CASME II, there are no deep learning results demonstrated on CASME database. The experiment have accomplished more prominent result than state-of-the-art methods for CASME database.

The structure of the paper is organised as follows: in Sect. 2 reviews related work in the field of micro-expression recognition using hand-craft features and deep learning features. The outline of the proposed method is briefed in Sect. 3 and detailed in Sect. 4. Section 5 presents the experimental setup and results. Finally, the future directions in the field and conclusions are summarised in Sect. 6.

2   Related Work

In this section, we present a review of previous work on micro-expression recognition. For a more comprehensive summary of related work on facial micro-expressions, we refer the reader to a survey in [13]. We introduce the related

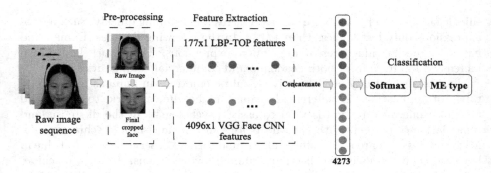

Fig. 1. Framework of the proposed model.

work in two aspects. Hand-crafted features are first reviewed followed by deep learning features.

2.1   Hand-Crafted Features

For addressing micro-expression recognition problem, some low-level features were proposed at an early stage. Pfister et al. [12] proposed to use local binary pattern from three orthogonal planes (LBP-TOP) to describe micro-expression video clips for micro-expression recognition task. Subsequently, lots of spatio-temporal descriptors are developed for micro-expression recognition tasks, such as spatio-temporal LBP with integral projection (STLBP-IP) [4], histogram of oriented gradient-TOP (HOG-TOP) [7].

It is worth noting the works of [8,18], in which Liu et al. and Xu et al. respectively designed novel features, i.e., main directional mean optical (MDMO) and facial dynamics map (FDM), to describe micro-expressions. On the other hand, Wang et al. [16] also proposed a colour space decomposition method called tensor independent colour space (TICS) to utilise the colour information for micro-expression recognition.

Out of all the above-reviewed methods, we are using state-of-the-art feature descriptor LBP-TOP that achieves highest recognition accuracy.

2.2   Deep Learning Features

Lately, deep learning methods have also been applied to micro-expression recognition. For example, Kim et al. [6] proposed a deep learning framework consisting of the popular convolutional neural network (CNN) and long short-term memory (LSTM) recurrent network for micro-expression recognition. In this framework, the representative expression-states frames of each micro-expression video clip are first selected to train a CNN and the CNN feature of is extracted to train an LSTM network. Similarly, Patel et al. [10] attempted to explore the potential purpose of deep learning for micro-expression recognition task. They used transfer learning from objects and facial expression based CNN models.

The aim is to use feature selection to remove the irrelevant deep features. Peng et al. [11] also addresses the database limitation by selecting data from CASME and CASME II to form the experiment dataset CASME I/II. They proposed a Dual Temporal Scale Convolutional Neural Network (DTSCNN) for spontaneous micro-expressions recognition. The DTSCNN is a two-stream network to adapt to the different frame rate of micro-expression video clips.

2.3 Discussions

The aforementioned hand-craft works make a substantial contribution to automatic micro-expression recognition. However, there is still scope to enhance the techniques. Firstly, most of the feature selection process relies intensively on the involvement of researchers. Secondly, the recognition accuracy of the methods is not sufficiently high for practical applications. Therefore, a more efficient method that can generate high-level feature automatically for micro-expressions recognition is desired.

In the successful works of CNN, the large dataset is expected to train the network. However, the micro-expression database that we can utilise so far is significantly smaller than conventional database fed to CNN. A severe overfitting problem would occur if we directly apply CNN on the existing micro-expression database.

Spatial feature learning by CNN improves the expression class separability of the learned micro-expression features. LBP-TOP learns the timescale dependent information (temporal characteristics) that resides along the video sequences. Our proposed approach is the first method designed to cascade LBP-TOP with CNN to extract spatio-temporal features from video sequences an capture more evident differences in micro-expression classes. The CASME+2 database used for experiments provide comparatively large data to train the network. The experiment results on CASME, CASME II and CASME+2 databases demonstrate that our proposed method gave higher recognition accuracy as compared to some state-of-the-art recognition methods.

3 Method Outline

Figure 1 shows the outline of the proposed model. The proposed model comprises of five modules: Pre-processing, feature extraction by (1) LBP-TOP; (2) CNN, concatenation of LBP-TOP and CNN features, and finally passing feature vector to Softmax for classification. The tasks of each module can be explained as below.

Module 1: Pre-processing module corrects the head pose, if any, in the image sequence and crops it to contain only the face region. It does so to make the input suitable for feature extraction.

Module 2: The cropped pre-processed face images generated from the pre-processing module are given to the LBP-TOP feature descriptor to extract the three orthogonal feature matrices. The feature matrices from LBP-TOP are normalised to form one feature vector.

Module 3: The extraction of feature vector using CNN's VGG-Face architecture is a separate module independent of LBP-TOP feature extraction where the input are again the pre-processed face images. The VGG-Face network is initially fine-tuned on micro-expressions to generate a micro-expression trained VGG-Face network.

Module 4: The extracted features from LBP-TOP and VGG-Face are concatenated to form a single feature vector.

Module 5: Newly created feature vector represents the input video sequence which is fed to the Softmax. The softmax is a classifier which recognises the micro-expression in the input.

Our work contributes to encouraging the idea of LBP-TOP and CNN feature fusion to achieve improved micro-expression recognition accuracy. The detailed description about the modules are discussed below.

4   Method Description

In this section, each module of the proposed method is described in detail.

4.1   Data Pre-processing

Pre-processing makes the input video sequence appropriate to be given to our proposed network. Initially, faces are detected using the classic histogram of oriented gradients (HOG) feature combined with the linear classifier, an image pyramid and sliding window detection scheme. The detected face regions are cropped and then processed for head pose correction by computing the angle between the centroid of both eyes and later applying the affine transformation. The aligned face image is again passed through the face detector to crop and save the more certain face region. Figure 1 presents the face detection and initial processing steps in Pre-processing module.

All the micro-expression databases being relatively small in size, there is a high chance of overfitting. To overcome overfitting issue, we architect our proposed deep CNN by using VGG-Face deep CNN model pretrained for face recognition and fine-tune it to perform micro-expression recognition. Deep networks need a significant amount of training data to achieve good performance. To build a robust image classifier using very little training data, image augmentation is usually required to boost the performance of deep networks. Image augmentation artificially creates training images in different ways of processing or combination of multiple processing, such as random rotation, shifts, shear and flips, etc.

To train VGG-Face network for our experiments, we have used the vertical flipping data augmentation technique. Vertically flipping creates a mirror image of the original face image. The data augmentation is done only for the training set to lift the number of samples for training the deep network. In our case, image augmentation doubles the training set for CASME, CASME II and CASME+2 databases.

4.2   Features Extraction

(1) Temporal feature descriptor: Local Binary Pattern-Three Orthogonal Planes (LBP-TOP) operator

Facial feature extraction is the most crucial step in expression recognition. Because of the short duration and the small intensity of the micro-expressions, micro-expression feature extraction based on dynamic image sequence becomes a challenging task. LBP-TOP is an algorithm that is designed for describing videos' dynamic texture, and LBP is a robust method to describe the texture features.

LBP-TOP method combines the temporal and spatial features of an image sequence by LBP and extracts the dynamic texture features of image sequences from three orthogonal planes. These dynamic texture features are used to express the spatial, temporal and motion characteristics of image sequences.

(2) Spatial feature descriptor: Finetuned VGG-Face Convolutional Neural Network (CNN)

CNN is a biologically-inspired model. The input layer receives normalised images with identical size. The convolutional layer will process a set of units in a small neighbourhood (local receptive field) in the input layer and creates a feature map. Rectified Linear (ReLU) is a non-linear operation. Each feature map has only one convolutional kernel. This design of CNN can mainly save calculation time and make specific feature stand out in a feature map. There usually is more than one feature map in a convolutional layer, so that includes multiple features in the layer.

To make the feature invariant to the geometrical shift and distortion, a pooling layer that can subsample the feature maps follows the convolutional layer. Max pooling function is used for subsampling. The first convolutional layer and the pooling layer would acquire low-level information of the image, while the stack of them would enable high-level feature extraction.

The output layer acts as an input to the Fully connected layer that uses a Softmax activation function in the output layer. The purpose of the fully connected layer is to use these features for classifying the input image into respective classes depending on the training dataset.

Putting it all together, the Convolutional + Pooling layers act as Feature Extractors while Fully Connected layer acts as a Classifier.

The VGG-Face CNN descriptors are computed using CNN implementation based on the VGG-Very-Deep-16 CNN architecture as described in [9]. The network is composed of a sequence of convolutional, pool, and fully connected (FC) layers. The convolutional layers of dimension three while the pool layers perform subsampling with a factor of two.

In our experiments, we utilize a pre-trained VGG-Face CNN model. The VGG-Face is a network trained on a very large-scale face image database (2.6M images, 2.6k people) for the task of face recognition. The VGG-Face can be utilized as a feature extractor for any subjective face image by operating the image through the whole network, then extracting the output of the fully connected layer FC-7. The extracted feature is exceedingly discriminative, minimal, and interoperable encoding of the input image. Once the features are acquired from FC-7 layer of the VGG-Face CNN, they can be utilized for training and testing subjective face classifier.

4.3   Classification

The fully connected layer is a traditional multi-layer perceptron that uses softmax activation function in the output layer (other classifiers like SVM can also be used, but we will stick to softmax for our experiment). The summation of output probabilities from the fully connected layer is 1. This is guaranteed by utilising the softmax activation function in the output layer of the fully connected layer. The Softmax function takes a vector of absolute real-valued scores and vectorises elements between zero and one that sums to one.

5   Implementation and Results

A few techniques to improve the recognition were implemented. The head pose is estimated by computing the angle between the eye centroid and then using affine transformation.

5.1   Datasets

There are a very few well-developed micro-expression databases, which impeded the development of micro-expression recognition research. Currently, several spontaneous databases with micro-expression labels are available SMIC, CASME, CASME II. They all were recorded in laboratory conditions. The subjects were recorded in the frontal head pose while watching emotional videos being asked to keep as much neutral expression as possible. Moreover, to stimulate the stress factor, a reward CASME, CASME II or a punishment SMIC followed, filling a dull form in case of apparent failure of suppressing the emotions. Table 1 lists the key features of existing micro-expression databases.

For our experiments, we consider the most comprehensive datasets CASME and CASME II, which were created by Chinese Academy of Sciences and publicly available for research use, to validate the performance of our proposed technique. CASME contains 195 micro-expression videos, and CASME II contains 247 videos. All labelled by two professional coders (to the acceptable reliability of 0.846) [17] into eight and seven emotion classes for CASME and CASME II respectively.

Takalkar et al. in [14] aggregated CASME and CASME II databases to form a new CASME+2 database with a large number of samples to train the CNN model. On the similar grounds, in our experiment, we will combine the CASME and CASME II databases to form CASME+2 database to work with videos.

For our experiments, we trained the deep convolutional neural networks on CASME, CASME II and CASME+2 databases. We categorised the databases into six classes: Disgust, Fear, Happiness, Neutral, Sadness and Surprise.

Table 1. Details of existing micro-expression databases [13]

Database		Frame rate (fps)	Subjects	Samples	Emotion class
SMIC	HS	100	20	164	3 (Negative, Positive, Surprise)
	VIS	25	10	71	
	NIR	25	10	71	
CASME		60	35	195	8 (Contempt, Disgust, Fear, Happiness, Repression, Sadness, Surprise, Tense)
CASME II		200	35	247	7 (Disgust, Fear, Happiness, Others, Repression, Sadness, Surprise)

We used the data augmentation technique on the training set to increase the number of training samples by vertical flipping. The CASME, CASME II and CASME+2 databases are randomly divided into two datasets as Training comprises of 80% videos and Testing with remaining 20% videos respectively.

5.2 Experiment Settings

(1) Face detection and pre-processing. An OpenCV DLib library that includes facial landmark predictions, face detector, and face aligner packages is used for the face detection and pre-processing of the input video frames before they are given for feature extraction. The input frames are cropped to a 224×224 size and then converted to grayscale. These grayscale frames are given for LBP-TOP and CNN features extraction.

(2) Use LBP-TOP to extract temporal features. A micro-expression sequence is seen as a whole block. Then we extract dynamic features of the sequences according to the following steps:

(a) Suppose that a centre pixel of a frame in the sequence is (x, y, t). Then extract its LBP features from the three orthogonal planes. Calculate the decimal value of the LBP features and record them as:

$$f_0(x_c, y_c, t_c), f_1(x_c, y_c, t_c), f_2(x_c, y_c, t_c) \tag{1}$$

(b) For each pixel, the histogram of the local binary patterns of the dynamic image sequence in each orthogonal plane can be defined as:

$$H_{i,j} = \sum_{x,y,t} I\{f_j(x,y,t) = i\}, \ i = 0, ..., n_j - 1; j = 0, 1, 2 \tag{2}$$

where n_j is the number of different labels processed by LBP operator in the jth plane (j = 0: XY, 1: XT, 2: YT), $f_i(x,y,t)$ is the LBP code of central pixel (x, y, t) in the jth plane, and $I(A) = \begin{cases} 1, & if \ A \ is \ true; \\ 0, & if \ A \ is \ false. \end{cases}$

(c) Finally, cascade the histograms of three orthogonal planes and get the LBP-TOP feature of the whole sequence.

In this paper, the characteristics extracted are 3×59 matrices. We normalise them to 177×1 dimensional vectors to calculate conveniently. In XT and YT plane, the fluctuations are much more significant and also contain many features than the XY plane. It proves that the XT and YT planes are essential for feature classification and expression recognition. So combining features extracted from three orthogonal planes is reasonable.

(3) Use VGG-Face CNN to extract spatial deep features.

We implemented the deep convolutional neural network based on Caffe [5], a fast open framework for deep learning and computer vision. It took five days for each of the databases to fine-tune the VGG-Face network. The fine-tuned models on each of the databases (CASME, CASME II and CASME+2) were then used to extract the features from the fully connected layer FC-7.

The overall process of the Convolutional Network (ConvNet) can be summarised as below:

(a) Initialize all filters and parameters/weights with random values.

(b) The network takes a training image as input, goes through the forward propagation step (convolution, ReLU and pooling operations along with the forward propagation in the fully connected layer) and finds the output probabilities for each class.

(c) Calculate the total error at the output layer.

(d) Use backpropagation to calculate the gradients of error concerning all weights in the network and use gradient descent to update all filter values/weights and parameter values to minimise the output error.

(e) Iterate through steps 2–4 for every image in the training set.

When a new (unseen) image is input into the ConvNet, the network will devour the forward propagation step and output a probability for each class (for a fresh image, the output probabilities are computed using the weights which have been optimised to classify all the previous training samples correctly).

In our experiment, the feature vector of dimension (4096×1) is extracted from the feature extraction layer and stored separately for further processing. Figure 1 depicts the CNN feature extraction process.

(3) Our Proposed Spatio-Temporal feature extraction method (LBP-TOP + CNN)

LBP-TOP features were extracted to describe micro-expressions from the temporal point of view, and CNN is used to extract deep spatial features. As mentioned in (1) above, the normalised vector of dimension 177×1 is extracted from the input video frames. As mentioned in (2) the feature vector of dimension 4096×1 extracted from CNN FC-7 layer. The proposed network model works on extracting more number of features from hand-craft and deep learning methods together. The extraction of more features leads to effective training of the classifier, which in turn results in better micro-expression recognition accuracy.

The resultant feature vector after concatenation is a 4273×1 dimension matrix for each video. Such feature vectors for all the videos from the Training

Table 2. Micro-expression recognition accuracy for LBP-TOP and CNN with Softmax

Database	CASME		CASME II		CASME+2	
Features	LBP-TOP	FC7	LBP-TOP	FC7	LBP-TOP	FC7
Testing accuracy	0.428	0.761	0.448	0.758	0.477	0.818

dataset are generated and given to the classifier for training. The Softmax is trained using these features from respective micro-expression classes and ready for testing.

5.3   Micro-expression Recognition Results

We tested our proposed network on two publicly available micro-expression datasets CASME and CASME II and a combined dataset CASME+2 to verify the effectiveness of our proposed micro-expression recognition method. The proposed method is evaluated using the 20% Testing dataset created earlier.

We have performed the experiments to evaluate the results of individual feature extraction methods (LBP-TOP and CNN) with Softmax. Table 2 shows the results of each feature extractor with Sofmax.

Table 3 illustrates the micro-expression recognition accuracy of our proposed method which is the concatenation of LBP-TOP and FC7 features with Softmax on CASME, CASME II and CASME+2 databases. We expand our results to F1 score, precision and recall metrics as presented in the Table 3. It can be observed from the table that the best performance of our proposed model is achieved on the more substantial database CASME+2. It can be interpreted that the larger the training set is, the higher the recognition accuracy is attained.

Table 3. Micro-expression recognition accuracy, F1, precision and recall metrics for proposed method

Dataset	Accuracy	Metric	Micro-expression					
			Disgust	Fear	Happy	Neutral	Sad	Surprise
CASME	76.19%	F1	0.90	0	0	0.75	0.66	0.75
		Precision	0.81	0	0	0.60	1.00	0.75
		Recall	1.00	0	0	1.00	0.50	0.75
CASME II	79.31%	F1	0.88	0	0.87	0	0.66	0.60
		Precision	0.85	0	0.77	0	1.00	0.60
		Recall	0.92	0	1.00	0	0.50	0.60
CASME+2	84.09%	F1	0.93	0	0.80	1.00	0.66	0.70
		Precision	0.90	0	0.72	1.00	1.00	0.75
		Recall	0.95	0	0.88	1.00	0.50	0.66

Comparing results in Tables 2 and 3 it is observed that, except for CASME dataset using CNN+Softmax, experiments on CASME II and CASME+2 datasets have improved recognition accuracy by approximately 2–3%.

Table 4 shows a comparison to some existing approaches for micro-expression recognition. It ought to be noticed that the outcomes are not specifically comparable due to distinctive experimental setups (number of expression classes and number of sequences), but they still indicate the discriminating power of each approach.

Table 4. Performance comparison with the state-of-the-art methods on different databases. Results in bold correspond to our method

Database	Method	Recognition accuracy (%)
CASME	FHOFO + LSVM [3]	71.57%
	MDMO + SVM [8]	68.86%
	LBP-TOP + SVM [16]	61.85%
	Our method	**76.19%**
CASME II	LBP-TOP + SVM [17]	75.30%
	MDMO + SVM [8]	67.37%
	FHOFO + LSVM [3]	64.06%
	CNN + LSTM [6]	60.98%
	CNN + SVM [10]	47.3%
	Our method	**79.31%**
CASME+2 CASME I/II	DSTCNN + SVM [11]	66.67%
	Our method	**84.09%**

Due to the larger number of samples in CASME II database compared to CASME database, most of the researchers opted to demonstrate deep learning results on CASME II database. In our research, as we have applied data augmentation to increase the number of samples in all the databases used. After data augmentation, the CASME training set also contains an adequate amount of training samples to train our deep network. Hence, we are the first to utilise CASME database for the deep network training. From Table 3, it can be seen that our model outperformed the state-of-the-art methods for CASME database with the recognition accuracy of 76.19%. A significant amount of research is done on CASME II database using hand-craft descriptors and recently a few using deep learning. Our experiment on CASME II database obtains recognition result of 79.31% which is higher than the existing hand-craft descriptors and deep learning methods. The combined databases increase the number of training samples and also increases the probability of improved recognition accuracy. This is reflected in our experiment on CASME+2 with the efficiency of 84.09%.

6   Conclusion and Future Work

In the recent few years, some research groups have attempted to improve the accuracy of micro-expression recognition by designing a variety of feature extractors that can best capture the subtle facial changes. In this paper, we select a new combination of methods and database and recognise micro-expression successfully.

In our work, we proposed an innovative method for recognising micro-expressions by learning a spatio-temporal feature representation with LBP-TOP and CNN.

In pre-processing, the first step was to align head pose in the video frames and crop the face region. The second was to use the data augmentation technique to increase the number of training samples for CNN fine-tuning. In feature extraction part, we use the most efficient local texture descriptor in combination with deep learning feature descriptor. The features extracted by both the descriptor were normalised to form one vector representing the input and was given to the classifier. Finally, in the classification part, we used the Softmax function to compare the extracted characteristics directly.

In this paper, the best facial micro-expression recognition rate obtained is 84.04% for CASME+2 database. However, there is still a scope for improvement in the recognition accuracy.

For future work, further evaluation of the proposed method is to be conducted on real-time spontaneous facial micro-expressions with various kinds of metrics (i.e. F1 score, precision and recall).

References

1. Bernstein, D.M., Loftus, E.F.: How to tell if a particular memory is true or false. Perspect. Psychol. Sci. **4**(4), 370–374 (2009)
2. Ekman, P., Friesen, W.V.: Nonverbal leakage and clues to deception. Psychiatry **32**(1), 88–106 (1969)
3. Happy, S., Routray, A.: Fuzzy histogram of optical flow orientations for micro-expression recognition. IEEE Trans. Affect. Comput. (2017)
4. Huang, X., Wang, S.J., Zhao, G., Piteikainen, M.: Facial micro-expression recognition using spatiotemporal local binary pattern with integral projection. In: Proceedings of the IEEE International Conference on Computer Vision Workshops, pp. 1–9 (2015)
5. Jia, Y., et al.: Caffe: convolutional architecture for fast feature embedding. In: Proceedings of the 22nd ACM International Conference on Multimedia, pp. 675–678. ACM (2014)
6. Kim, D.H., Baddar, W.J., Ro, Y.M.: Micro-expression recognition with expression-state constrained spatio-temporal feature representations, pp. 382–386. ACM (2016)
7. Li, X., et al.: Towards reading hidden emotions: a comparative study of spontaneous micro-expression spotting and recognition methods. IEEE Trans. Affect. Comput. (2017)

8. Liu, Y.J., Zhang, J.K., Yan, W.J., Wang, S.J., Zhao, G., Fu, X.: A main directional mean optical flow feature for spontaneous micro-expression recognition. IEEE Trans. Affect. Comput. **7**(4), 299–310 (2016)
9. Parkhi, O.M., Vedaldi, A., Zisserman, A., et al.: Deep face recognition. In: BMVC, vol. 1 (2015)
10. Patel, D., Hong, X., Zhao, G.: Selective deep features for micro-expression recognition. In: 2016 23rd International Conference on Pattern Recognition (ICPR), pp. 2258–2263. IEEE (2016)
11. Peng, M., Wang, C., Chen, T., Liu, G., Fu, X.: Dual temporal scale convolutional neural network for micro-expression recognition. Front. Psychol. **8**, 1745 (2017)
12. Pfister, T., Li, X., Zhao, G., Pietikäinen, M.: Recognising spontaneous facial microexpressions. In: 2011 IEEE International Conference on Computer Vision (ICCV), pp. 1449–1456. IEEE (2011)
13. Takalkar, M., Xu, M., Wu, Q., et al.: A survey: facial micro-expression recognition. Multimed. Tools Appl. **77**, 19301 (2018). https://doi.org/10.1007/s11042-017-5317-2
14. Takalkar, M.A., Xu, M.: Image based facial micro-expression recognition using deep learning on small datasets. In: 2017 International Conference on Digital Image Computing: Techniques and Applications (DICTA), pp. 1–7. IEEE (2017)
15. Vasconcellos, S.J.L., Salvador-Silva, R., Gauer, V., Gauer, G.J.C.: Psychopathic traits in adolescents and recognition of emotion in facial expressions. Psicologia: Reflexão e. Crítica **27**(4), 768–774 (2014)
16. Wang, S.J., Yan, W.J., Li, X., Zhao, G., Fu, X.: Micro-expression recognition using dynamic textures on tensor independent color space. In: 2014 22nd International Conference on Pattern Recognition (ICPR), pp. 4678–4683. IEEE (2014)
17. Wang, Y., et al.: Effective recognition of facial micro-expressions with video motion magnification. Multimed. Tools Appl. **76**(20), 21665–21690 (2017)
18. Xu, F., Zhang, J., Wang, J.Z.: Microexpression identification and categorization using a facial dynamics map. IEEE Trans. Affect. Comput. **8**(2), 254–267 (2017)

An Effective Dual-Fisheye Lens Stitching Method Based on Feature Points

Li Yao[1,2(✉)], Ya Lin[1], Chunbo Zhu[3], and Zuolong Wang[3]

[1] School of Computer Science and Engineering, Southeast University,
Nanjing 211189, People's Republic of China
Yao.li@seu.edu.cn
[2] Key Laboratory of Computer Network and Information Integration,
Southeast University, Ministry of Education,
Nanjing 211189, People's Republic of China
[3] Samsung Electronics, Suwon, South Korea

Abstract. Fisheye lens is a super-wide-angle lens which is very light. Usually two cameras can shoot 360-degree panoramic images. However, the limited overlapping field of views make it hard to stitch in the boundaries. This paper introduces a novel method for dual-fisheye camera stitching based on feature points. And we also put forward the idea of expanding to video. Results show that this method can be used to produce high-quality panoramic images by stitching the original images of the dual-fisheye camera Samsung Gear 360.

Keywords: Dual-fisheye · Stitching · Panorama-video · Virtual reality

1 Introduction

Dual-fisheye lens cameras are becoming popular for 360-degree video capture. The focal length is very short and a single lens's viewing angle can approach even more than 180°. Compared to the traditional and professional 360-degree capturing systems such as [1] and [2], their portability and affordability make them available for live streaming. It has been widely used in safety monitoring, video conference, panoramic parking because of its large viewing angle and small size.

However, the limited overlapping filed of views and misalignment between the two lenses increase the difficulty of stitching. For stitching of images from the multiple cameras, a classic method is autostitch [3], which extract features from the images being stitched and calculate the homography matrix to transform them to the same plane. This method relies on accurate feature points and cannot be directly applied to the dual-fisheye camera. Gao et al. [4] use two homographies per image to produce a more seamless image. Lin et al. [5] use more affine transformations which have stronger alignment capabilities. Although these two methods improve the stitching results, they are heavily dependent on feature points having high computational complexity and cannot be used in real-time image processing. In video stitching, He et al. [6] present a parallax-robust video stitching technique for timely synchronized surveillance video. But this algorithm requires that the camera position and background remain unchanged. Lin et al. [7] presented a algorithm that can stitch videos captured

© Springer Nature Switzerland AG 2019
I. Kompatsiaris et al. (Eds.): MMM 2019, LNCS 11295, pp. 665–677, 2019.
https://doi.org/10.1007/978-3-030-05710-7_55

by hand-held cameras and can get good results, but the efficiency is too low. Ho [8] et al. proposed a two-step alignment method for dual-fisheye lens using fast template matching as a substitute for feature points, but fast template matching is considered to be computationally expensive [9]. There are many problems with these methods directly applied to the dual-fisheye lens.

In this paper, we propose a feature point-based stitching method whose efficiency can meet the requirements of real-time performance. This algorithm contains four steps: color correction, unwarping, alignment and blending. Our contributions are:

(1) A simple and effective color correction is used to correct the color inconsistency between two lenses which can easily meet the requirement of real-time.
(2) In the spherical model, we map the image outside the 180° view to the other hemisphere of the sphere and expand the entire sphere. We can easily find overlapping areas which help calculate color differences and detect feature points.
(3) By matching feature points in sliding window, we make it possible to match the feature points in the dual-fisheye image.
(4) By grading the homography, we can align the left and right sides of the fish-eye image separetely using different rotation matrices.
(5) We optimized the method of multi-band blending [10] to make it more suitable for fisheye image, which is faster but never reduce the image quality.

2 Dual-Fisheye Stitching

Figure 1 shows the processing flow of our approach. There are 4 steps in total, where the overlapping area mapping matrix and the affine warping matrix could be precomputed and remain unchanged. We will generate a new warping matrix according to the rotation angle in the process of alignment. If we need, the new one could also be precomputed because the range of the rotation angle is small, so the speed of our algorithm could be very fast.

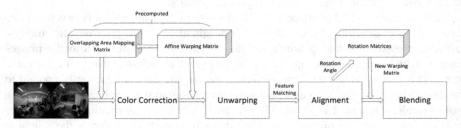

Fig. 1. The processing flow of this paper.

2.1   Color Correction

Due to the uneven brightness of the ambient light, the camera will inevitably have inconsistent hue and brightness when imaging. Ho et al. [11] solved the problem of vignetting through intensity compensation. Because there are also nuances in different cameras, it is difficult to accurately quantify the difference in color. In the process of stitching, a simple and efficient method is to correct the color of the image in different color spaces. For two images with large color difference, we assume that the overlap area after registration is A, then the two images to be stitched must have the same number of pixels in A. In general, the two images in the overlapping area are under the same scene, so we can quantify the color difference with the statistics of this area.

Take the Samsung Gear 360 as an example, we calculate the sum of the two images on the RGB three channels respectively. On different channels, the greater the difference between the sum, the greater the error. Figure 2(a) shows the original image with a large color difference, from which we can see that the fisheye image on the left is yellowed compared to the right one. The stitching result showed in Fig. 1(b) also proved this. From the results showed in Table 1, we can see that the gap between the channels is not very significant. But when converting to the HSV model [12], we can clearly see the difference between the two images in the S channel. So we only need to scale all the pixels in the S channel. and the result is shown in Fig. 2(e).

Such a color correction method only needs to perform a calculation operation on a specific area as a whole, and can meet the requirements of real-time performance (Table 2).

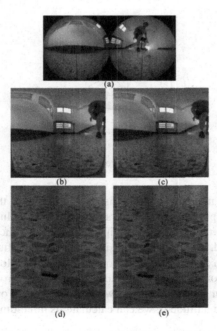

Fig. 2. (a) Original image taken by Samsung Gear 360. (b) Stitch without color correction. (c) Stitch using the color correction method we proposed. (d), (e) are the enlarged parts of (b), (c).

Table 1. Cumulative sums of RGB channels in overlapping regions.

	R	G	B
Left image	8.01446e + 07	8.45898e + 07	8.3173e + 07
Right image	7.91371e + 07	8.47454e + 07	7.79583e + 07
SumL/SumR	0.886	0.998	1.067

Table 2. Cumulative sums of HSV channels in overlapping regions.

	H	S	V
Left image	5.8555e + 07	2.65566e + 07	8.65651e + 07
Right image	5.44479e + 07	3.91667e + 07	8.53828e + 07
SumL/SumR	1.075	0.678	1.014

2.2 Fisheye Unwarping

The ability of a fisheye lens to capture large viewing angles is at the expense of the intuitiveness of the image, the most serious being barrel distortion [13]. Most of the algorithms cannot perform well on a distorted image. In addition, the original fisheye image cannot be stitched directly. Spherical perspective model [14] is commonly used to describe the imaging process of a fisheye lens. This model can be used not only to correct distortion but also to convert the shape of fisheye images.

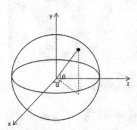

Fig. 3. Fisheye unwarping.

The first step is to map the original fisheye image to a three-dimensional unit sphere. Create a unit spherical model as shown in Fig. 3. In order to reduce the calculation for filling in the blank pixel points and facilitate the expansion, a reverse mapping method is used. Assume that the size of the image after expansion from the sphere is $h \times w$, let x-axis positive direction be the starting longitude and establish w warps at intervals from the angle $-\pi$ to $+\pi$. Similarly, from $-\pi/2$ to $+\pi/2$, we establish h wefts. We can get a total of h × w intersections. For one point on the sphere whose longitude is α and latitude β, we can calculate its three-dimensional coordinates:

$$x = \cos \alpha \times \cos \beta$$
$$y = \sin \beta \tag{1}$$
$$z = \sin \alpha \times \cos \beta$$

Each intersection needs to be mapped to a point on the fisheye image. Let f be the camera's field of view (FOV), and we assume the camera's FOV is uniform. For a fisheye camera with a 180-degree FOV, it maps perfectly to a hemisphere. Then the projection of the original image on the sphere will exceed the hemisphere when the FOV exceeds 180°, so for the part beyond 180°, it should be mapped to the other side of the sphere.

For a point on the sphere with coordinates (x, y, z), we can calculate its deviation from the x axis:

$$\theta = \arccos x \tag{2}$$

Then we can get the scale factor from the center in the original fisheye image:

$$\varphi = \frac{\theta}{\pi} \times \frac{180}{f} \times r \tag{3}$$

Where r is the radius of the original fisheye image. Finally the corresponding point on the fish-eye image is:

$$(z \times \varphi, y \times \varphi) \tag{4}$$

if we assume that the center coordinates of the fisheye image are $(0, 0)$.

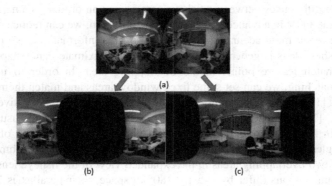

Fig. 4. Fisheye unwarping results.

Now we can map any point on the sphere to the original fisheye image, we need to map the points on the sphere to a plane that is easy to stitch. We have chosen a plane of size $h \times w$, the number of points on the sphere is also $h \times w$, although their distribution on the sphere is not uniform. Points at the same latitude should be on the same line of the expanded image, the same is true for longitude. Knowing this, when expansion, it can be segmented from any one of the longitude lines, and the pixels can be arranged in the expansion view in order. Figure 4 (b), (c) show the expanded images of original image (a) Photographed by Gear 360.

In general, the spherical model is only a rough description of the fisheye imaging process. There may be various types of distortion in the imaging process, and the FOV of the lens may not be uniform. So we need more accurate alignment.

2.3 Alignment

By mapping the fisheye image of the circular area to the image shown in Fig. 4, we can clearly see the overlapping region of the two images, its shape is roughly as shown in Fig. 5. Before blending them together, we adopted a alignment process to make the same objects as close as possible. The method of computing homography matrix based on feature points is very mature, but a lot of adjustments are needed when performing on the fisheye images.

Fig. 5. Overlapping area (Marked with black).

One of the differences between a fisheye camera and an ordinary camera is that we can measure the FOV in advance and the value will remain, we can reduce calculations and make the result more accurate by taking use of this information. The overlapping area of the fisheye lens is generally small which is approximate band shape. We only search and match feature points in the overlapping area. In order to improve the accuracy of matching, we can set some fixed window areas and match them within the window pairs [15]. The wrong point pairs will undoubtedly have a negative impact on the RANSAC [16] algorithm. The matching points on fisheye images usually do not differ much in horizontal direction, so we can manually remove some of the points where the angles are very different before performing RANSAC algorithm (Fig. 6).

There are two overlapping areas in the expanded view of the fisheye lens. Since the two overlapping regions differ by exactly 180° in space, their parallax is likely to be different. In order to get a panoramic image with size $h \times w$, and leave no blanks on the border, we stitch the two overlapping areas separately, and handle conflicting parallax conflicts properly.

For a set of matching point pairs (x_1, y_1) and (x_2, y_2), the pixel difference in the vertical direction between them is $y_2 - y_1$. Return to the spherical model and the angle difference between them is:

(a)　　　　　　(b)

Fig. 6. Feature points matching results. (a) Matching results on the left side. (b) Matching results on the right side.

$$X = \arcsin(y_2 - y_1) \tag{5}$$

In order to get more accurate angle, we take the average value of the angle difference of n pairs of matched points.

With the angle difference, we just need to rotate one image on the sphere by (X, Y, Z). Here we don't consider Y and Z for the time being). Convert it to a normalized quaternion (a, b, c, d), and then create rotation matrix R from the quaternion [17]:

$$R = \begin{pmatrix} a^2 + b^2 - c^2 - d^2 & 2bc - 2ad & 2bd + 2ac \\ 2bc + 2ad & a^2 - b^2 + c^2 - d^2 & 2cd - 2ab \\ 2bd - 2ac & 2cd + 2ab & a^2 - b^2 - c^2 + d^2 \end{pmatrix} \tag{6}$$

We would only align one side if we rotate the entire image. However, the calculated rotation angles on both sides may be inconsistent, so we make a smooth process for the rotation matrix in order to make the two sides do not affect each other. Assume that the original rotation matrix is R', we build a series of evenly changing matrices $(R_0, R_1, R_2, ..., R_k ... R_n)$ from R to R', where the number of matrices can be equal to $w/4$ (Roughly half of a single image). From edge to center, multiply each column of pixels by the corresponding rotation matrix(the kth column pixels multiply by R_k). In this way, we only stitch one side without affecting the other, and this uniform gradient matrix does not have an adverse effect on the visual. The same method can be used for horizontal correction which affects angle Z.

2.4   Blending

Blending is the last step of the stitching, which can make smoother transition in overlapping area. A common practice is to find the best seam [18], and then perform the multi-band blending method on the images on both sides of the seam.

The multi-band blending method can eliminate the seam well, but it reduces the image quality [19]. Here we use the method proposed by Xiao [19] et al. In this way we perform multi-band blending only on the overlapping area which is very narrow in a fisheye image. When we get our best seam showed in Fig. 7(a), then we take a small piece of each image on the left and right side of the image for blending. After that, we get Fig. 7(b). Calculate the weighted average pixel value between the original left and right image we used last step and Fig. 7(b) according to the distance from the seam. Let (r, c) be the pixel at row r and column c in the overlapping region and we assume that one point where the seam passes is $S(r', c')$. Then the blended pixel $B(r, c)$ on the left side of S can be calculated as follows:

$$B(r,c) = \frac{c' - c}{d} \times L(r,c) + (1 - \frac{c' - c}{d}) \times O(r,c) \tag{7}$$

whereas d represents the distance from the point of furthest to $S(r', c')$ to $S(r', c')$, and $O(r, c)$ represents the point in the temporary blending region such as Fig. 7(b). Finally, we get our final result showed in Fig. 7(c).

This approach accelerates the speed of blending without degrading image quality. In the example of Fig. 7, the size of the panorama we eventually get is 2048 × 4096. On the side we show in Fig. 7, the size of our blending area is 2048 × 600. So the total

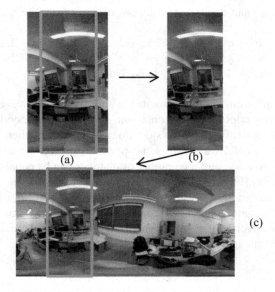

Fig. 7.   Blending only on the overlapping region.

size of blending area is 2048 × 1200, which is about one quarter of the whole image. This means saving three-quarters of the computing time in the blending stage.

3   Extend to Video

The method described above is for images, and it is time-consuming if we directly perform it on a video, there will also be discontinuities between frames. For the problem of discontinuities, we only recalibrate when objects are moving in the over-lapping area. Algorithm 1 illustrates our method of maintaining the temporal coherence for the sequence. And for the improvement of time performance, we use some special techniques. We use ORB [20] for feature matching, which is proved to be faster than SIFT [21] and SURF [22]. The alignment process is the most time-consuming, which requires a lot of matrix operations to correct the offset angle. During the tests, we found that the offset angle has a fixed range and this range is not so wide because the position of our lenses is fixed. Therefore, the converted mapping matrix can be calculated in advance and corresponds to the angle. In the alignment process, we only need to find the best-fit mapping matrix according to the rotation angle calculated by the matching feature points.

Algorithm 1 Video Stitching

$i \leftarrow 0$
$xAngle, yAngle, zAngle \leftarrow 0$
$isRotating \leftarrow$ False
$rotMat \leftarrow defaultRotMat$
$scale \leftarrow defaultRotScale$
for $frame$ **in** real-time video stream **do**
    if $i\%N = 0$ **or** $isRotating$ **or** $SceneChanged()$ **then**
        // We recalculate the rotation matrix in three cases:
        // 1. When this is the initial frame, where i = 0,
        // And every fixed frame N. Maybe the scene
        // changes slowly but the parallax changes.
        // 2. When it is rotating now.
        // 3. When scene changes.
        $xAngleCur, yAngleCur, zAngleCur \leftarrow$ Recompute the x, y, z angle
        // We don't adjust to the final state instantly.
        $xAngle \leftarrow$ adjust min($scale, xAngleCur - xAngle$) along gradient
        $yAngle \leftarrow$ adjust min($scale, yAngleCur - yAngle$) along gradient
        $zAngle \leftarrow$ adjust min($scale, zAngleCur - zAngle$) along gradient
        if $xAngle = xAngleCur$ **and** $yAngle = yAngleCur$
        and $zAngle = zAngleCur$ **then**
            $isRotating \leftarrow$ True
        else
            $isRotating \leftarrow$ False
        end if
        $rotMat \leftarrow$ calculate the rotation matrix with x, y, z angle
    end if
    warp with rotMat
    $i \leftarrow i + 1$
end for

---

4 Experiments and Analysis

First, we show the comparison result of color correction between Samsung Gear 360 software (Fig. 8(a)) and our algorithm (Fig. 8(b)). We use the black line to mark the stitching line in the result. It can be clearly seen from the left and right sides of the line

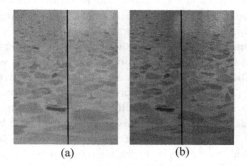

(a)   (b)

Fig. 8. Color correction result. (a) Enlarged result of Gear 360 software. (b) Enlarged result of our method.

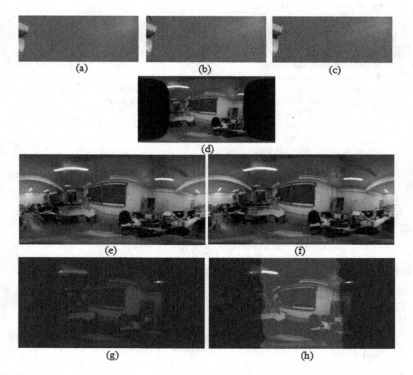

Fig. 9. Comparison of blending results. (d) Left lens original expanded image. (e) Stitching result of multi-band blending. (f) Stitching result of our method. (a–c) are enlarged parts of (e–f). (g), (h) are results of comparing (e, f) with (d) using Beyond Compare. (Color figure online)

that Gear360 has a poor correction effect on the color, and our method basically makes the color consistent.

In order to verify the advantages of the blending method used in this paper in image quality, we enlarge the projecting part of the light on the wall in Fig. 9(d). Figure 9(a), (b), and (c) are correspond to the region of (e), (d) and (f), respectively. It can be found that (c) has remained almost the same and (a) has become blurred. Besides, we use software Beyond Compare [23] to analyze pixel differences. We use the right expanded image as the standard for comparison because the right image of the original fisheye remains unchanged before and after alignment. We use the results of multi-band blending and our results to compare with Fig. 9(a) respectively. The comparison results are showed in Fig. 9(d), (e). Gray color means that the pixel value is the same here, and red means different. From the results we see that the multi-band blending algorithm changed the value of some pixels, but our method only changes the pixel value of the stitching area, which keeps the details of the image.

In Fig. 10, we showed the stitching results of two sets of videos using our stitching method. Each row in the figure is consecutive frames in the video, where the first row and the third row are the results of Gear 360 software, and the second and the last one are ours. From the results, we can see that the alignment ability of our method is better than that of Gear 360 software in both indoor and outdoor scenarios.

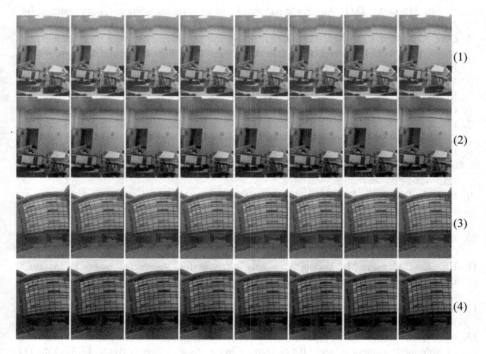

Fig. 10. Stitching boundary in consecutive frames. Row (1) and (3) are results of Gear 360. Row (2) and (4) are results this paper.

5 Discussion and Future Work

This paper has introduced a novel method for stitching the images generated by the dual-fisheye lens cameras. This method overcomes the shortcomings of small and severe distortion in the overlapping area of dual-fisheye images, enables feature points to be found and matched correctly, and the stitching of left and right side will not affect each other by making the rotation matrix gradual. Meanwhile, Based on the color correction of Gear 360, a new idea of quickly solving the color difference of stitching images is put forward. Our method can be applied to video through pre-calculation, and have the ability to adapt to the scenes changing slowly. But for fast-changing scenes, there are still no simple and effective strategies to meet real-time requirements. More work will be carried out about video in the future.

Acknowledgement. This work is supported by natural science foundation of Jiangsu Province under Grant No. BK20181267.

References

1. GoPro Odyssey. https://gopro.com/odyssey. Accessed 27 April 2018
2. Facebook Surround360. https://facebook360.fb.com/facebook-surround-360. Accessed 27 April 2018
3. Brown, M., Lowe, D.G.: Automatic panoramic image stitching using invariant features. Int. J. Comput. Vis. **74**(1), 59–73 (2007)
4. Gao, J., Kim, S.J., Brown, M.S.: Constructing image panoramas using dual-homography warping. In: IEEE Conference on Computer Vision and Pattern Recognition, pp. 49–56. IEEE Computer Society (2011)
5. Matsushita, Y.: Smoothly varying affine stitching. In: Computer Vision and Pattern Recognition, pp. 345–352. IEEE (2011)
6. He, B., Yu, S.: Parallax-robust surveillance video stitching. Sensors **16**(1), 7 (2015)
7. Lin, K., Liu, S., Cheong, L.F.: Seamless video stitching from hand-held camera inputs. In: Computer Graphics Forum, pp. 479–487 (2016)
8. Ho, T., et al.: 360-degree video stitching for dual-fisheye lens cameras based on rigid moving least squares. In: IEEE International Conference on Image Processing, pp. 51–55. IEEE (2017)
9. Bay, H., Tuytelaars, T., Van Gool, L.: SURF: speeded up robust features. In: Leonardis, A., Bischof, H., Pinz, A. (eds.) ECCV 2006. LNCS, vol. 3951, pp. 404–417. Springer, Heidelberg (2006). https://doi.org/10.1007/11744023_32
10. Burt, P.J.: A multiresolution spline with applications to image mosaics. ACM Trans. Comput. Graph. **2**(4), 217–236 (1983)
11. Ho, T., Budagavi, M.: Dual-fisheye lens stitching for 360-degree imaging. In: IEEE International Conference on Acoustics, Speech and Signal Processing, pp. 2172–2176. IEEE (2017)
12. Stricker, A.M.A., Orengo, M.: Similarity of color images. In: Proceedings of SPIE Storage & Retrieval for Image & Video Databases, vol. 2420, pp. 381–392 (1995)
13. Ngo, H.T., Asari, V.K.: A pipelined architecture for real-time correction of barrel distortion in wide-angle camera images. IEEE Trans. Circuits Syst. Video Technol. **15**(3), 436–444 (2005)

14. Ying, X.H.: Fisheye lense distortion correction using spherical perspective projection constraint. Chin. J. Comput. (2003)
15. Sharghi, S.D., Kamangar, F.A.: Geometric feature-based matching in stereo images. In: 1999 Proceedings of IEEE Information, Decision and Control, IDC 1999, pp. 65–70 (1999)
16. Fischler, M.A., Bolles, R.C.: Random sample consensus. Commun. ACM **24**(6), 381–395 (1981)
17. comp.graphics.algorithms Frequently Asked Questions. www.faqs.org/faqs/graphics/algorithms-faq2. Accessed 27 April 2018
18. Gao, J., Li, Y., Chin, T.J., Brown, M.S.: Seam-driven image stitching. In: Eurographics (2013)
19. Xiao, J.S., Rao, T.Y.: An image fusion algorithm of Laplacian pyramid based on graph cuting. J. Optoelectron. Laser **25**(7), 1416–1424 (2014)
20. Rublee, E., et al.: ORB: an efficient alternative to SIFT or SURF. In: International Conference on Computer Vision, Barcelona, pp. 2564–2571 (2011)
21. Lowe, D.G.: Distinctive image features from scale-invariant keypoints. Int. J. Comput. Vis. **60**(2), 91–110 (2004)
22. Li, Y., et al.: A fast rotated template matching based on point feature. In: MIPPR 2005: SAR and Multispectral Image Processing, 60431P–60431P-7 (2005)
23. Beyond Compare. http://www.beyondcompare.cc. Accessed 6 May 2018

3D Skeletal Gesture Recognition via Sparse Coding of Time-Warping Invariant Riemannian Trajectories

Xin Liu and Guoying Zhao[✉]

Center for Machine Vision and Signal Analysis, University of Oulu,
90014 Oulu, Finland
{xin.liu,guoying.zhao}@oulu.fi

Abstract. 3D skeleton based human representation for gesture recognition has increasingly attracted attention due to its invariance to camera view and environment dynamics. Existing methods typically utilize absolute coordinate to present human motion features. However, gestures are independent of the performer's locations, and the features should be invariant to the body size of performer. Moreover, temporal dynamics can significantly distort the distance metric when comparing and identifying gestures. In this paper, we represent each skeleton as a point in the product space of special orthogonal group $SO3$, which explicitly models the 3D geometric relationships between body parts. Then, a gesture skeletal sequence can be characterized by a trajectory on a Riemannian manifold. Next, we generalize the transported square-root vector field to obtain a re-parametrization invariant metric on the product space of $SO(3)$, therefore, the goal of comparing trajectories in a time-warping invariant manner is realized. Furthermore, we present a sparse coding of skeletal trajectories by explicitly considering the labeling information with each atoms to enforce the discriminant validity of dictionary. Experimental results demonstrate that proposed method has achieved state-of-the-art performance on three challenging benchmarks for gesture recognition.

Keywords: Gesture recognition · Manifold · Sparse coding

1 Introduction

Human gesture analysis is emerging as a central problem in computer vision applications, such as human-computer interfaces and multimedia information retrieval. 3D skeleton-based modeling is rapidly gaining popularity due to it simplifies the problem caused by replacing monocular RGB camera with more sophisticated sensors such as the Kinect. It can explicitly localize gesture performer and yield the trajectories of human skeleton joints. Compared to RGB data, skeletal data is robust to varied background and is invariant to camera view-point. In the past decade, a considerable number of 3D skeleton-based

© Springer Nature Switzerland AG 2019
I. Kompatsiaris et al. (Eds.): MMM 2019, LNCS 11295, pp. 678–690, 2019.
https://doi.org/10.1007/978-3-030-05710-7_56

recognition methods [2–5,7,13–16,19–24] have been proposed. Although there have been significant advancements in this area, accurate recognition of the human gesture in unconstrained settings still remains challenging. There are two issues need to be thoroughly discussed:

* One important issue in gesture recognition is the feature representation of models to capture variability of 3D human body (skeleton) and its dynamics. Existing methods typically utilize absolute (real world) coordinate to present human motion features. However, activities are independent of performer's locations, and the feature should be invariant to the size of the performer.
* Another issue of human gesture recognition lies in the temporal dynamics. For instance, even the same actions or gestures performed by the same person can have different implementation rates and different starting/ending points, let alone different performers.

A common way to deal with the first problem is to transform all 3D joint coordinates from the world coordinate system to a performer-centric coordinate system by placing the hip center at the origin, but the accuracy heavily depends on the precise positioning of the human hip center. Another solution is to consider the relative geometry between different body parts (bones), such as the Lie Group [19], which utilize rotations and translations (rigid-body transformation) to represent the 3D geometric relationships of body parts. However, the translation is not a scale-invariant representation since the size of skeleton varies from subject to subject.

To account for the second issue, a typical treatment is using the graphical model to describe the presence of sub-states, where the time series are reorganized by a sequential prototype, and the temporal dynamics of gestures are trained as a set of transitions among these prototypes [2]. The typical model is the hidden Markov model (HMM) [22]. However, in these models, the input sequences have to be previously segmented on the basis of specific clustering metrics or discriminative states, which itself is a challenging task. With the development of deep learning, plenty of researches [5,13,14] addressing the problem of temporal dynamics by recurrent neural networks (RNN), such as the long short-term memory (LSTM). Although LSTM is a powerful framework for modeling sequential data, it is still arduous to learn the information of the entire sequence with many sub-events. In fact, the most common solution to temporal dynamics is the Dynamic Time Warping (DTW) [7,19], which needs to choose a nominal temporal alignment, and then all sequences of a category are warped to that alignment. However, the performance of DTW is highly depends on the selection of a reference, which is commonly computed by experience.

Aiming to tackle above issues, in this paper, a novel method for gesture recognition is proposed. The main contributions are summarized as follows:

(1) we represent a human skeleton as a point on the product space of special orthogonal group ($SO3$), which is a Riemannian manifold. This representation is independent to the performer's location, and can explicitly models

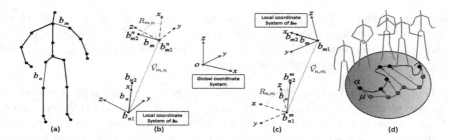

Fig. 1. (a) Illustration of a 3D skeleton, (b) Representation of bone b_m in the local coordinate system of b_n, (c) Representation of b_n in the local coordinate system of b_m, (d) Pictorial of the warped trajectory α on a manifold according to a reference μ.

the 3D geometric relationships between body parts using rotations. Then a gesture (skeletal sequences) can be represented by a trajectory composed of these points (see Fig. 1(d)). The gesture recognition task is formulated as the problem of computing the similarity between the shapes of trajectories.

(2) we extend the transported square-root vector field (TSRVF) representation for comparing trajectories on the product space of $SO(3) \times \cdots \times SO(3)$. Therefore, the temporal dynamic issue of gesture recognition can be solved by this time-warping invariant feature.

(3) we present a sparse coding of skeletal trajectories by explicitly considering the labeling information with each atom to enforce the discriminant validity of dictionary. The comparison experimental results on three challenging datasets demonstrated the proposed method have achieved state-of-the-art performances.

2   Related Works

Over the last few years, plenty of 3D skeletal human gesture recognition models have been explored in various routines. In this section, we limited our review on the relevant manifold-based solutions. A representative work is the Lie group [19], which utilized the special Euclidean (Lie) group $SE(3)$ to characterize the 3D geometric relationships among body parts. A convenient way of analyzing Lie group is to embed them into Euclidean spaces, with the embedding typically obtained by flattening the manifold via tangent spaces, such as the Lie algebra $\mathfrak{se}(3)$ at the tangent space identity I_4. In that way, former classification tasks in manifold curve space are converted into the classification problems in a typical vector space. Then, the authors of [19] employed the DTW and Fourier temporal pyramid (FTP) to deal with the temporal dynamics issues of gesture recognition. However, as discussed in Sect. 1, the success of DTW is heavily related to the choice of the nominal temporal alignment empirically. And the FTP is restricted by the width of the time window and can only utilize limited contextual information [5]. Following the same representation, Anirudh *et al.* [3] introduced the framework of transported square-root velocity fields (TSRVF)

[18] to encode trajectories lying on Lie groups, as such, the distance between two trajectories is invariant to identical time warping. Since the final feature is a high-dimensional vector, the principal component analysis (PCA) is used to reduce the dimension and learn the basis (dictionary) for representation. While PCA is an unsupervised model and thus the discriminant of dictionary cannot be boosted through a labeled training. Based on the square root velocity (SRV) framework [17], in [4], trajectories are transported to a reference tangent space attached to the Kendall's shape space at a fixed point, which may introduce distortions in the case points are not close to the reference point. In [8], Ho *et al.* proposed a general framework for sparse coding and dictionary learning on Riemannian manifolds. Different to [17] which using the fixed point for embedding, the [8] working on the tangent bundle, namely, each point of manifold is coded on its attached tangent space into which the atoms are mapped.

3   Product Space of $SO(3)$ for 3D Skeleton Representation

Inspired by the rigid body kinematics, any rigid body displacement can be realized by a rotation about an axis combined with a translation parallel to that axis. This 3D rigid body displacements forms a Lie group, which is generally referred to as $SE(3)$, the special Euclidean group in three dimensions:

$$P(R, \boldsymbol{v}) = \begin{bmatrix} R & \boldsymbol{v} \\ 0 & 1 \end{bmatrix} \tag{1}$$

where $R \in SO(3)$ is a point in the special orthogonal group $SO(3)$, denotes the rotation matrix, and $\boldsymbol{v} \in \mathbb{R}^3$ denotes the translation vector.

The human skeleton can be modeled by an articulated system of rigid segments connected by joints. As such, the relative geometry between a pair of body parts (bones) can be represented as a point in $SE(3)$. More specifically, given a pair of bones b_m and b_n, their relative geometry can be represented in a local coordinate system attached to other [19]. Let $b_{i1} \in \mathbb{R}^3$, $b_{i2} \in \mathbb{R}^3$ denote the starting and ending points of bones b_i respectively. The local coordinate system of bone b_n is calculated by rotating with minimum rotation and translating the global coordinate system so that b_{n1} act as the origin and b_n coincides with the $x-$axis, Fig. 1 give an example to explain this pictorially. As such, at time t, the representation of bone b_m in the local coordinate system of b_n (Fig. 1(b)), the starting point $b_{m1}^n(t) \in \mathbb{R}^3$ and ending point $b_{m2}^n(t) \in \mathbb{R}^3$ are given by

$$\begin{bmatrix} b_{m1}^n(t) & b_{m2}^n(t) \\ 1 & 1 \end{bmatrix} = \begin{bmatrix} R_{m,n}(t) & \boldsymbol{v}_{m,n}(t) \\ 1 & 1 \end{bmatrix} \begin{bmatrix} 0 & l_m \\ 0 & 0 \\ 0 & 0 \\ 1 & 1 \end{bmatrix} \tag{2}$$

where $R_{m,n}(t)$ and $\boldsymbol{v}_{m,n}(t)$ respectively denote the rotation and translation measured in the local coordinate system attached to b_n, and l_m is the length of b_m.

According to the theory of rigid body kinematics, the lengths of bones do not vary with time, thus, the relative geometry of b_m and b_n can be described by

$$P_{m,n}(t) = \begin{bmatrix} R_{m,n}(t) & v_{m,n}(t) \\ 1 & 1 \end{bmatrix} \in SE(3), \quad P_{n,m}(t) = \begin{bmatrix} R_{n,m}(t) & v_{n,m}(t) \\ 1 & 1 \end{bmatrix} \in SE(3)$$

$$(3)$$

One restriction of this motion feature is the translation v is relative to the size of performer (subject). But as we known it is very important to obtain a scale-invariant skeletal representation for recognition task in an unconstrained environment. To remove the skeletons scaling variability, in this paper, we discard the translation from motion representation, then the relative geometry of b_m and b_n at time t can be described by rotations $R_{m,n}(t)$ and $R_{n,m}(t)$, and expressed as elements of $SO(3)$. Then, let M denotes the number of bones, the resulting feature for an entire human skeleton is interpreted by the relative geometry between all pairs of bones, as a point $C(t) = (R_{1,2}(t), R_{2,1}(t), \ldots, R_{M-1,M}(t), R_{M,M-1}(t))$ on the curved product space (see Fig. 1(d)) of $SO(3) \times \cdots \times SO(3)$, and the number of $SO(3)$ is $2C_M^2$, where C_M^2 is the combination formula.

4   Trajectories Identification on Riemannian Manifold

As presented above, gesture recognition is formulated as the problem of computing the similarity between shapes of trajectories. The basis for these comparability determinations are related to a distance function on the shape space.

To be specific, let α denote a smooth oriented curve (trajectory) on a Riemannian manifold M, and let $\mathcal{M}$ denote the set of all such trajectories: $\mathcal{M} = \{\alpha : [0,1] \to M | \alpha \text{ is smooth}\}$. Re-parameterizations will be represented by increasing diffeomorphisms $\gamma : [0,1] \to [0,1]$, and the set of all these orientation preserving diffeomorphisms is denoted by $\Gamma = \{\gamma \to [0,1]\}$. In fact, γ plays the role of a time-warping function, where $\gamma(0) = 0, \gamma(1) = 1$ so that preserve the end points of the curve. More specifically, if α in the form of time observations $\alpha(t_1), \ldots, \alpha(t_n)$, is a trajectory on M, the composition $\alpha \circ \gamma$ in the form of time-warped trajectory $\alpha(\gamma(t_1)), \ldots, \alpha(\gamma(t_n))$, is also a trajectory that goes through the same sequences of points as α but at the evolution rate governed by γ [18].

For classify trajectories, a metric is needed to describe the variability of a class of trajectories and to quantify the information contained within a trajectory. A directly and commonly solution is to calculate point-wise difference, since M is a Riemannian manifold, we have a natural distance d_m between points on M [18]. Then, the distance d_x between any two trajectories: $\alpha_1, \alpha_2 : [0,1] \to M$:

$$d_x(\alpha_1, \alpha_2) = \int_0^1 d_m(\alpha_1(t), \alpha_2(t)) \, dt \tag{4}$$

Although this quantity describes a natural extension of d_m from M to $M^{[0,1]}$, it suffers from the issue that $d_x(\alpha_1, \alpha_2) \neq d_x(\alpha_1 \circ \gamma_1, \alpha_2 \circ \gamma_2)$. As discussed in the Sect. 1, in the task of recognition, the temporal dynamics is a key issue that need to be solved when a trajectory (gesture) α is observed as $\alpha \circ \gamma$, for a random temporal evolution γ. That is, for arbitrary temporal re-parametrizations γ_1, γ_2 and arbitrary trajectories α_1, α_2, a distance $d(\cdot, \cdot)$ is wanted that enable

$$d(\alpha_1, \alpha_2) = d(\alpha_1 \circ \gamma_1, \alpha_2 \circ \gamma_2) \tag{5}$$

A distance that is particularly well-suited for our goal is the one used in the Square Root Velocity (SRV) framework [17]. Based on the concept of elastic trajectories in [17], Su [18] proposed a Transported Square-Root Vector Field (TSRVF) to represent trajectories, and the original Euclidean metric based SRV has been generalized to the manifold space based framework. Specifically, for a smooth trajectory $\alpha \in \mathcal{M}$, the TSRVF is a parallel transport of a scaled velocity vector field of α to a reference point $c \in M$ according to

$$h_\alpha(t) = \frac{\dot{\alpha}(t)_{\alpha(t) \to c}}{\sqrt{|\dot{\alpha}(t)|}} \in T_c(M) \tag{6}$$

where $\dot{\alpha}(t)$ is the velocity vector along the trajectory at time t, and $\dot{\alpha}(t)_{\alpha(t) \to c}$ is its transport from the point $\alpha(t)$ to c along a geodesic path, and $|\cdot|$ denotes the norm related to the Riemannian metric on M and $T_c(M)$ denotes the tangent space of M at c. Especially, when $|\dot{\alpha}(t)| = 0$, $h_\alpha(t) = 0 \in T_c(M)$. Since α is smooth, so is the vector field h_α. Let $\mathcal{H} \subset T_c(M)^{[0,1]}$ be the set of smooth curves in $T_c(M)$ obtained as TSRVFs of trajectories in M, $\mathcal{H} = \{h_\alpha | \alpha \in \mathcal{M}\}$ [18]. By means of TSRVF, two trajectories such as α_1 and α_2, can be mapped into the tangent space $T_c(M)$, as two corresponding TSRVFs, h_{α_1} and h_{α_2}. The distance among them can be measured by ℓ_2-norm on the typical vector space

$$d_h(h_{\alpha_1}, h_{\alpha_2}) = \sqrt{\int_0^1 |h_{\alpha_1}(t) - h_{\alpha_2}(t)|^2 dt} \tag{7}$$

The motivation of TSRVF representation comes from the following fact. If a trajectory α is warped by γ, to result in $\alpha \circ \gamma$, the TSRVF of $\alpha \circ \gamma$ is given by

$$h_{\alpha \circ \gamma}(t) = h_\alpha(\gamma(t)) \sqrt{\dot{\gamma}(t)} \tag{8}$$

Then, for any $\alpha_1, \alpha_2 \in \mathcal{M}$ and $\gamma \in \Gamma$, the distance d_h satisfies

$$d_h(h_{\alpha_1 \circ \gamma}, h_{\alpha_2 \circ \gamma}) = \sqrt{\int_0^1 |h_{\alpha_1}(s) - h_{\alpha_2}(s)|^2 ds} = d_h(h_{\alpha_1}, h_{\alpha_2}) \tag{9}$$

where $s = \gamma(t)$. For the proof of equality, we refer the interested reader to [17,18]. From the geometric point of view, this equality implies that the action of Γ on $\mathcal{H}$ under the ℓ_2 metric is by isometries. It enable us to develop a fully invariant distance to time-warping and use it to properly register trajectories [18]. Also, this invariability in execution rates is crucial for statistical analyses, such as sample means and covariance. Then, we define the equivalence class $[h_\alpha]$ (or the notation $[\alpha]$) to denote the set of all trajectories that are equivalent to a given $h_\alpha \in \mathcal{H}$ (or $\alpha \in \mathcal{M}$).

$$[h_\alpha] = \{h_{\alpha \circ \gamma} | \gamma \in \Gamma\} \tag{10}$$

Clearly, such an equivalent class $[h_\alpha]$ (or $[\alpha]$) is associated with a category of gesture. In this framework, the task of comparison two trajectories is performed by comparing their equivalence classes, in other words, an optimal re-parametrization γ^* is need to be found to minimize the cost function $d_h(h_{\alpha_1}, h_{\alpha_2 \circ \gamma})$. Let $\mathcal{H}/\sim$ be the corresponding quotient space, this can be bijectively identified with the set $\mathcal{M}/\sim$ using $[h_\alpha] \mapsto [\alpha]$ [3]. The distance d_s on $\mathcal{H}/\sim$ (or $\mathcal{M}/\sim$) is the shortest d_h distance between equivalence classes in $\mathcal{H}$ [18], given by:

$$d_s([\alpha_1], [\alpha_2]) \equiv d_s([h_{\alpha_1}], [h_{\alpha_2}]) = \inf_{\gamma \in \Gamma} d_h(h_{\alpha_1}, h_{\alpha_2 \circ \gamma})$$
$$= \inf_{\gamma \in \Gamma} \left(\int_0^1 |h_{\alpha_1}(t) - h_{\alpha_2}(\gamma(t)) \sqrt{\dot{\gamma}(t)}|^2 dt \right)^{1/2} \quad (11)$$

In practice, the minimization over Γ is solved for using dynamic programming [17,18]. One important parameter of TSRVF is the reference point c, which should remain unchanged in the whole process of computing. Since the selection of c can potentially affect the results, typically, a point is a natural candidate for c if most of trajectories pass close to that one. In this paper, the Karcher mean [11] as Riemannian center of mass is selected, since it is equally distant from all the points thereby minimizing the possible distortions. Given a set $\{\alpha_i(t)_{t=1,\dots,n}\}_{i=1}^m$ of sequences (trajectories), its Karcher mean $\mu(t)$ is calculated using the TSRVF representation with respect to d_s in $\mathcal{H}/\sim$, defined as

$$h_\mu = \arg \min_{[h_\alpha] \in \mathcal{H}/\sim} \sum_{i=1}^m d_s([h_\alpha], [h_{\alpha_i}])^2 \quad (12)$$

As a result, each trajectory is recursively aligned to the mean $\mu(t)$, thus, another output of Karcher mean computing is the set of aligned trajectories $\{\tilde{\alpha}_i(t)_{t=1,\dots,n}\}_{i=1}^m$. For each aligned trajectory $\tilde{\alpha}_i(t)$ at time t, the shooting vector $v_i(t) \in T_{\mu(t)}(M)$ is computed so that a geodesic that goes from $\mu(t)$ to $\tilde{\alpha}_i(t)$ in unit time [18] with the initial velocity $v_i(t)$

$$v_i(t) = \exp_{\mu(t)}^{-1}(\tilde{\alpha}_i(t)) \quad (13)$$

Then, the combined shooting vectors $V(i) = [v_i(1)^{\mathrm{T}} \ v_i(2)^{\mathrm{T}} \ \dots \ v_i(n)^{\mathrm{T}}]^{\mathrm{T}}$ is the final feature of a trajectory α_i.

5 Discriminative Sparse Coding of Riemannian Trajectories

Since the final feature of a trajectory (gesture sequence) lies on a high dimensional vector, a common solution is to utilize the principal component analysis (PCA) to reduce the dimension and learn the basis for representation, such as [17,18] did. As we know, PCA is an unsupervised learning model without labeled training. Compared to the component analysis techniques, the sparse coding model with labeled training has superior capability to capture inherent relationship among the input data and label information. To the best of our knowledge, few manifold representation-based models considered the connection between the labels and the dictionary learning. In this paper, we try to associate label information with each dictionary atom to enforce the discriminability of sparse codes during the dictionary learning process.

Given a set of observations (feature vectors of gestures) $\mathcal{Y} = \{y_i\}_{i=1}^{N}$, where $y_i \in \mathbb{R}^n$, and let $\mathcal{D} = \{d_i\}_{i=1}^{K}$ be a set of vectors in $\mathbb{R}^n$ denoting a dictionary of K atoms. The learning of dictionary $\mathcal{D}$ for sparse representation of $\mathcal{Y}$ can be expressed as

$$<\mathcal{D}, X> = \arg\min_{\mathcal{D}, X} \|\mathcal{Y} - \mathcal{D}X\|_2^2 \qquad s.t. \; \forall i, \; \|x_i\|_0 \leq T \qquad (14)$$

where $X = [x_1, ..., x_N] \in \mathbb{R}^{K \times N}$ represents the sparse codes of observation $\mathcal{Y}$, and T is a sparsity constraint factor. The construction of D is achieved by minimizing the reconstruction error $\|\mathcal{Y} - \mathcal{D}X\|_2^2$, and satisfying the sparsity constraints. The K-SVD [1] algorithm is a commonly used solution to (14).

Inspired by [10, 25], the classification error and label consistency regularization are introduced into the objective function:

$$<\mathcal{D}, W, A, X> = \arg\min_{\mathcal{D}, W, A, X} \|\mathcal{Y} - \mathcal{D}X\|_2^2 + \beta\|L - WX\|_2^2$$
$$+ \tau\|Q - AX\|_2^2 \qquad s.t. \; \forall i, \; \|x_i\|_0 \leq T \qquad (15)$$

where $W \in \mathbb{R}^{C \times K}$ denotes the classifier parameters, and C is the number of categories. $L = [l_1, ..., l_N] \in \mathbb{R}^{C \times N}$ represents the class labels of observation $\mathcal{Y}$, and $l_i = [0, ..., 1, ..., 0]^T \in \mathbb{R}^C$ is a label vector corresponding to an observation y_i, where the nonzero position (index) indicates the class of y_i. Then, the additional term $\|L - WX\|_2^2$ denotes the classification error for label information.

For the last term $\|Q - AX\|_2^2$, where $Q = [q_1, ..., q_N] \in \mathbb{R}^{K \times N}$ and $q_i = [0, ..., 1, ..., 1, ..., 0]^T \in \mathbb{R}^K$ is a sparse code corresponding to an observation y_i for classification, the purpose of setting nonzero elements is to enforce the "discriminative" of sparse codes [10]. Specifically, the nonzero elements of q_i occur at those indices where the corresponding dictionary atom d_n share the same label with the observation y_i. The A denotes a $K \times K$ transformation matrix, which is utilized to transform the original sparse code x to be a discriminative one. Thus, the term $\|Q - AX\|_2^2$ represents the discriminative sparse code error, which enforces that the transformed sparse codes AX approximate the discriminative sparse codes Q. It forces the signals from the same class to have similar sparse representations. β and τ are regularization parameters which control the relative contributions of the corresponding terms. Equation (15) can be rewritten as:

$$<\mathcal{D}, W, A, X> = \arg\min_{\mathcal{D}, W, A, X} \left\| \begin{pmatrix} \mathcal{Y} \\ \sqrt{\beta}L \\ \sqrt{\tau}Q \end{pmatrix} - \begin{pmatrix} \mathcal{D} \\ \sqrt{\beta}W \\ \sqrt{\tau}A \end{pmatrix} X \right\|_2^2 \qquad s.t. \; \forall i, \; \|x_i\|_0 \leq T$$
$$(16)$$

Let $\mathcal{Y}' = (\mathcal{Y}^{\mathrm{T}}, \sqrt{\beta}L^{\mathrm{T}}, \sqrt{\tau}Q^{\mathrm{T}})^{\mathrm{T}}$, $\mathcal{D}' = (\mathcal{Y}^{\mathrm{T}}, \sqrt{\beta}W^{\mathrm{T}}, \sqrt{\tau}A^{\mathrm{T}})^{\mathrm{T}}$. Then, the optimization of Eq. (16) is equivalent to solving the (14) (replace $\mathcal{Y}$ and $\mathcal{D}$ with $\mathcal{Y}'$ and $\mathcal{D}'$ respectively), this is just the problem that K-SVD [1] solves. In this paper, a similar initialization and optimization solution of K-SVD described in [10] is adopted. For parameter settings, the maximal iteration equals to 60, the sparsity factor $T = 50$ is used, and β and τ are set to 1.0 in our experiments.

6   Experiments

In this section, the proposed 3D skeletal gesture recognition method is evaluated in comparison to state-of-the-art methods using three public datasets, namely, ChaLearn 2014 gesture [6], MSR Action3D [12], and UTKinect-Action3D [23].

In order to testify the effectiveness of the proposed method, eighteen state-of-the-arts are compared, we simply divided these methods into three groups. The first group is the methods most related to us, including four Lie group based algorithms, the Lie group using DTW [19] (Lie group-DTW), Lie group with TSRVF [18] (Lie group-TSRVF) and using PCA for dimensionality reduction [3] (Lie group-TSRVF-PCA), and K-SVD for sparse coding [1] (Lie group-TSRVF-KSVD). And also including two TSRVF related methods, the body part features with SRV and k-nearest neighbors clustering [4] (SRV-KNN), TSRVF on Kendall's shape space [2] (Kendall-TSRVF). The methods in second group are based on classic feature representations, like histogram of 3D joints (HOJ3D) [23], EigenJoints [24], actionlet ensemble (Actionlet) [20], histogram of oriented 4D normals (HON4D) [16], rotation and relative velocity with DTW (RVV+DTW) [7], naive Bayes nearest neighbor (NBNN) [21]. The last group including seven deep learning methods, namely the convolutional neural network based ModDrop (CNN) [15], HMM with deep belief network (HMM-DBN) [22], LSTM [9], hierarchical recurrent neural network (HBRNN) [5], spatio-temporal LSTM with trust gates (ST-LSTM-TG) [13], and global context-aware attention LSTM (GCA-LSTM) [14]. The baseline results are reported from their original papers.

To verify the effectiveness of the TSRVF on product space of $SO(3) \times \cdots \times SO(3)$ (SO3-TSRVF), we present its discriminative performance without any further step (such as PCA or sparse coding) on three datasets. For comparison of dictionary learning ability, we also report the results of the classic coding such as K-SVD [1] (SO3-TSRVF-KSVD) and the proposed sparse coding scheme (SO3-TSRVF-SC). In order to fairly comparison, we follow the same classification setup as in [1–3,18,19] , namely, we utilized an one-vs-all linear SVM classifier (the parameter C set to 1.0). All experiments are carried out on an Intel Xeon CPU E5-2650 PC with a NVIDIA Tesla K80 GPU.

The ChaLearn 2014 [6] is a gesture dataset with multi-modality data, including audio, RGB, depth, human body mask maps, and 3D skeletal joints. This dataset collects 13585 gesture video segments (Italian cultural gesture) from 20 classes. We follow the evaluation protocol provided by the dataset which assigns 7754 gesture sequences for training, 3362 sequences for validation, and 2742

Table 1. Comparison of recognition accuracy (%) with existing 3D skeleton-based methods on ChaLearn 2014 [6], MSR Action3D [12] and UTKinect-Action3D [23] Datasets (best: bold, second best: underline).

Methods	ChaLearn 2014	MSR Action3D	UTKinect-Action3D
Lie group-DTW [19]	79.2	92.5	97.1
Lie group-TSRVF [18]	91.8	87.7	94.5
Lie group-TSRVF-PCA [3]	90.4	88.3	94.9
Lie group-TSRVF-KSVD [1]	91.5	87.6	92.7
SRV-KNN [4]	-	92.1	91.5
Kendall-TSRVF [2]	-	89.9	89.8
EigenJoints [24]	59.3	82.3	92.4
Actionlet [20]*	-	88.2	-
HOJ3D [23]	-	78.9	90.9
HON4D [16]*	-	88.9	90.9
RVV-DTW [7]	-	93.4	-
NBNN [21]	-	**94.8**	98.0
ModDrop (CNN) [15]*	<u>93.1</u>	-	-
HMM-DBN [22]	83.6	82.0	-
LSTM [9]	87.1	88.9	72.7
HBRNN [5]	-	94.5	-
ST-LSTM-TG [13]	92.0	**94.8**	97.0
GCA-LSTM [14]	-	-	**98.5**
Ours (SO3-TSRVF)	92.1	93.4	96.8
Ours (SO3-TSRVF-KSVD)	92.8	93.7	97.2
Ours (SO3-TSRVF-SC)	**93.2**	<u>94.6</u>	<u>98.1</u>

* The method use skeleton and RGB-D data.

sequences for testing. The detailed comparison with other approaches is shown in Table 1 (second column). It can be seen that the proposed method achieves the highest recognition accuracy as 93.2%. Compared to Lie group based methods, the effectiveness of SO3-TSRVF has been proved by the experimental results. It is noted that Lie group-DTW [19] is only 79.2%, this is due to the performance of DTW is highly depends on the reference sequences for each category, and that empiric selection task turn to difficult as the size of dataset get larger. It also can be observed that the accuracy of the LSTM [9] is 6 percents less than the proposed method. Although LSTM is designed for perceiving the contextual information, it is still challenging to model the sequence with temporal dynamics, especially when training data is limited. It is noted that the ModDrop [15] ranked the first place in Looking at People challenge [6]. While our method can achieve a higher score than ModDrop but without using RGB-D and audio data.

The MSR Action3D [12] is a commonly used dataset, where actions are highly similar to each other and have typical large temporal misalignments. This dataset comprises of 567 pre-segmented action instances, and 10 people performing 20 classes of actions. For a fair comparison, the same evaluation protocol, namely the cross-subject testing as described in [12] is followed, where half of the subjects are used for training (subjects number 1, 3, 5, 7, 9) and the remainder for testing

(2, 4, 6, 8, 10). We compare the proposed method with the state-of-the-arts, the recognition accuracies on MSR Action3D dataset are recorded in Table 1 (third column). We can see that the proposed method achieves better performance than Lie group based and classical feature representation approaches. And again, the performance of proposed sparse coding is superior than K-SVD and PCA based coding methods. Actually, the recognition accuracy of the proposed is only 0.2% inferior to the NBNN [21] and ST-LSTM-TG [13], which are recently proposed.

The UTKinect-Action3D [23] is a difficult benchmark due to its high intra-class variations. This dataset collects 10 types of actions using the Kinect. We follow [23] and use the *Leave-One-Sequence-Out Cross Validation* setting which selects each sequence as the testing sample in turn, regards others as training samples and calculates the average (20 rounds of testing) recognition rate. Table 1 (fourth column) reports the comparisons of the proposed to state-of-the-art methods. Obviously, our approach outperforms other methods except the GCA-LSTM [14] which is a sophisticated deep learning model proposed recently.

7   Conclusion

In this paper, a new human gesture recognition method is proposed. We represented a 3D human skeleton as a point in the product space of special orthogonal group $SO3$, as such, a human gesture can be characterized as a trajectory in the Riemannian manifold space. To consider re-parametrization invariance properties for trajectory analysis, we generalize the transported square-root vector field to obtain a time-warping invariant metric for comparing trajectories. Moreover, a sparse coding scheme of skeletal trajectories is proposed by thoroughly considering the labeling information with each atom to enforce the discriminant validity of dictionary. Experiments demonstrate that proposed method has achieved state-of-the-art performances. Possible directions for future work include studying on an end-to-end deep network architecture in the manifold space to handle the issues of 3D skeletal gesture recognition.

Acknowledgments. This work is supported by Academy of Finland, Tekes Fidipro Program, Infotech, Tekniikan Edistamissaatio, and Nokia Foundation.

References

1. Aharon, M., Elad, M., Bruckstein, A.: K-SVD: an algorithm for designing overcomplete dictionaries for sparse representation. IEEE Trans. Signal Process. **54**(11), 4311–4322 (2006)
2. Amor, B.B., Su, J., Srivastava, A.: Action recognition using rate-invariant analysis of skeletal shape trajectories. IEEE Trans. Pattern Anal. Mach. Intell. **38**(1), 1–13 (2016)
3. Anirudh, R., Turaga, P., Su, J., Srivastava, A.: Elastic functional coding of human actions: from vector-fields to latent variables. In: Proceedings of the IEEE Conference on Computer Vision Pattern Recognition, pp. 3147–3155 (2015)

4. Devanne, M., Wannous, H., Berretti, S., Pala, P., Daoudi, M., Del Bimbo, A.: 3D human action recognition by shape analysis of motion trajectories on Riemannian manifold. IEEE Trans. Cybern. **45**(7), 1340–1352 (2015)
5. Du, Y., Wang, W., Wang, L.: Hierarchical recurrent neural network for skeleton based action recognition. In: Proceedings of the IEEE Conference on Computer Vision and Pattern Recognition, pp. 1110–1118. IEEE (2015)
6. Escalera, S., et al.: ChaLearn looking at people challenge 2014: dataset and results. In: Agapito, L., Bronstein, M.M., Rother, C. (eds.) ECCV 2014. LNCS, vol. 8925, pp. 459–473. Springer, Cham (2015). https://doi.org/10.1007/978-3-319-16178-5_32
7. Guo, Y., Li, Y., Shao, Z.: RRV: a spatiotemporal descriptor for rigid body motion recognition. IEEE Trans. Cybern. **48**, 1513–1525 (2017)
8. Ho, J., Xie, Y., Vemuri, B.: On a nonlinear generalization of sparse coding and dictionary learning. In: Proceedings of the International Conference on Machine Learning, pp. 1480–1488 (2013)
9. Hochreiter, S., Schmidhuber, J.: Long short-term memory. Neural Comput. **9**(8), 1735–1780 (1997)
10. Jiang, Z., Lin, Z., Davis, L.S.: Label consistent K-SVD: learning a discriminative dictionary for recognition. IEEE Trans. Pattern Anal. Mach. Intell. **35**(11), 2651–2664 (2013)
11. Karcher, H.: Riemannian center of mass and mollifier smoothing. Commun. Pure Appl. Math. **30**(5), 509–541 (1977)
12. Li, W., Zhang, Z., Liu, Z.: Action recognition based on a bag of 3D points. In: Proceedings of the IEEE Conference Computer Vision and Pattern Recognition Workshops, pp. 9–14. IEEE (2010)
13. Liu, J., Shahroudy, A., Xu, D., Wang, G.: Spatio-temporal LSTM with trust gates for 3D human action recognition. In: Leibe, B., Matas, J., Sebe, N., Welling, M. (eds.) ECCV 2016. LNCS, vol. 9907, pp. 816–833. Springer, Cham (2016). https://doi.org/10.1007/978-3-319-46487-9_50
14. Liu, J., Wang, G., Hu, P., Duan, L.Y., Kot, A.C.: Global context-aware attention LSTM networks for 3D action recognition. In: Proceedings of the IEEE Conference Computer Vision and Pattern Recognition, pp. 1647–1656 (2017)
15. Neverova, N., Wolf, C., Taylor, G., Nebout, F.: ModDrop: adaptive multi-modal gesture recognition. IEEE Trans. Pattern Anal. Mach. Intell. **38**(8), 1692–1706 (2016)
16. Oreifej, O., Liu, Z.: HON4D: histogram of oriented 4D normals for activity recognition from depth sequences. In: Proceedings of the IEEE Conference Computer Vision and Pattern Recognition, pp. 716–723 (2013)
17. Srivastava, A., Klassen, E., Joshi, S.H., Jermyn, I.H.: Shape analysis of elastic curves in Euclidean spaces. IEEE Trans. Pattern Anal. Mach. Intell. **33**(7), 1415–1428 (2011)
18. Su, J., Kurtek, S., Klassen, E., Srivastava, A.: Statistical analysis of trajectories on Riemannian manifolds: bird migration, hurricane tracking and video surveillance. Ann. Appl. Stat. **8**, 530–552 (2014)
19. Vemulapalli, R., Arrate, F., Chellappa, R.: Human action recognition by representing 3D skeletons as points in a Lie group. In: Proceedings of the IEEE Conference Computer Vision and Pattern Recognition, pp. 588–595. IEEE (2014)
20. Wang, J., Liu, Z., Wu, Y., Yuan, J.: Learning actionlet ensemble for 3D human action recognition. IEEE Trans. Pattern Anal. Mach. Intell. **36**(5), 914–927 (2014)

21. Weng, J., Weng, C., Yuan, J.: Spatio-temporal Naive-Bayes nearest-neighbor (ST-NBNN) for skeleton-based action recognition. In: Proceedings of the IEEE Conference Computer Vision and Pattern Recognition (2017)
22. Wu, D., Shao, L.: Leveraging hierarchical parametric networks for skeletal joints based action segmentation and recognition. In: Proceedings of the IEEE Conference Computer Vision and Pattern Recognition, pp. 724–731. IEEE (2014)
23. Xia, L., Chen, C.C., Aggarwal, J.K.: View invariant human action recognition using histograms of 3D joints. In: Proceedings of the IEEE Conference Computer Vision and Pattern Recognition Workshops, pp. 20–27. IEEE (2012)
24. Yang, X., Tian, Y.: Eigenjoints-based action recognition using Naive-Bayes-nearest-neighbor. In: PProceedings of the IEEE Conference Computer Vision and Pattern Recognition Workshops, pp. 14–19. IEEE (2012)
25. Zhang, Q., Li, B.: Discriminative K-SVD for dictionary learning in face recognition. In: Proceedings of the IEEE Conference Computer Vision and Pattern Recognition, pp. 2691–2698. IEEE (2010)

Efficient Graph Based Multi-view Learning

Hengtong Hu[✉], Richang Hong, Weijie Fu, and Meng Wang

HeFei University of Technology, HeFei 230009, People's Republic of China
hfut.hht@qq.com

Abstract. Graph-based learning methods especially multi-graph-based methods have attracted considerable research interests in the past decades. In these methods, the traditional graph models are used to build adjacency relationships for samples within different views. However, owing to the huge time complexity, they are inefficient for large-scale datasets. In this paper, we propose a method named multi-anchor-graph learning (MAGL), which aims to utilize anchor graphs for the adjacency estimation. MAGL can not only sufficiently explore the complementation of multiple graphs built upon different views but also keep an acceptable time complexity. Furthermore, we show that the proposed method can be implemented through an efficient iterative process. Extensive experiments on six publicly available datasets have demonstrated both the effectiveness and efficiency of our proposed approach.

Keywords: Semi-supervised learning · Multi-graph-based learning Anchor graph

1 Introduction

Semi-supervised learning that exploits the prior knowledge from unlabeled data to improve classification performance, has been widely used to handle datasets where only a portion of data are labeled. These methods mostly are developed based on the cluster assumption [16], which means nearby points are likely to have the same labels. In recently years, semi-supervised learning methods have various applications based on above assumption, such as co-training, semi-supervised support vector machines, and graph-based methods.

In this paper, we focus on the family of graph-based semi-supervised methods, which usually utilize a weighted graph to capture the label dependencies among data points. Generally, these approaches construct a graph where the vertices are images and the edges reflect their pairwise similarities. As we all know, the type of the most effective features should vary across data points. Therefore, employing multiple features can be a solution to improve classification performance.

Recently the development of multi-view learning [3,4] is noteworthy, which is concerned with the problem where data is represented with multiple distinct feature views. Multi-view learning methods have been applied into various

© Springer Nature Switzerland AG 2019
I. Kompatsiaris et al. (Eds.): MMM 2019, LNCS 11295, pp. 691–703, 2019.
https://doi.org/10.1007/978-3-030-05710-7_57

fields, including dimensionality reduction, semi-supervised learning, supervised learning. The multi-view classification built upon graph-based learning is named multi-graph-based learning [14], which fuses multiple views to improve the performance of algorithms. Similar to graph-based learning, the framework of these methods also consists of the smoothness constraint and the fitting constraint. In addition, many of them intend to assign appropriate weights to different graphs.

However, most above methods remain challenging mainly due to the underlying time complexity. Recently some works seek to employ anchors in scaling up graph-based learning models, such as anchor graph regularization [7]. As the number of anchors is much smaller than data points, both the memory costs and time costs can get a significant drop. In this paper, we propose a novel approach named multi-anchor-graph learning (MAGL) for efficient multi-view learning. Different from above methods, our MAGL can sufficiently explore the complementation of multiple graphs and keep an acceptable time complexity. The main contributions of our work are as follows.

(1) We propose the MAGL algorithm for multi-view classification with a well compromise between classification performance and computational efficiency. The effects of different views can be adaptively modulated in our learning scheme.
(2) We adopt the anchor graph to estimate the adjacency relationships between data points for each view and integrate the obtained multiple graphs into a regularization framework. We also give a detailed analysis on its storage costs and computational complexity.
(3) For the purpose of simultaneously optimizing the anchor label variables and the weight variables, we propose an efficient iterative method.

2   Related Work

2.1   Semi-supervised Learning

In recent years, with the availability of large data collections associated with only limited human annotation, semi-supervised learning has gained a lot of research efforts. Many semi-supervised learning algorithms have been proposed. In [8], Nigam et al. demonstrated that algorithms explicitly leveraging a natural independent split of the features outperform algorithms that do not. In [6], Joachims applied transductive support vector machines to text classification.

More recently, graph-based methods have attracted the interest of researchers in this community. Many works have demonstrated that the these methods are efficient to deal with many tasks. In [1], Felzenszwalb et al. applied them to solve the problem of image segmentation. [2] proposed a bilayer graph-based learning framework to address the problem of hyperspectral image classification with limited number of labeled pixels. However, these methods mostly adopt single view to optimize the model, while the real-world images are often represented by multiple feature views. Later we will show that, different from their approaches, our proposed method explores multiple complementary graphs in the manner of semi-supervised learning.

2.2   Multi-view Learning

In many real-world applications the data is often derived from serval different sources, therefore, many multi-view learning methods have been proposed to deal with those kind of data. The applications of multi-view learning range from dimensionality reduction and semi-supervised learning to active learning and so on. [13] proposed algorithms for performing canonical correlation analysis. In [12], Sindhwani et al. proposed a co-regularization framework where classifiers are learnt in each view through forms of multi-view regularization.

Here we focus on one of its applications on semi-supervised learning, which is named as multi-graph-based learning. These methods have widespread applications in many fields. For example, [15] introduced a web image search reranking approach that explores multiple modalities in a graph-based learning scheme. In [14], Wang et al. proposed a method which aims to simultaneously tackle the difficulties plaguing video annotation in a unified scheme.

However, many of above methods usually have difficulties in handling large-scale datasets. This blocks widespread applicability to real-life problems. In this paper, we introduce anchor graph models to address the scalability issue plaguing those methods. We will show that the proposed MAGL method adaptively learns the weighting parameters to effectively integrate multiple anchor graphs. Figure 1 illustrates the schemes of the MAGL-based image classification process. Experimental results will demonstrate the superiority of this approach.

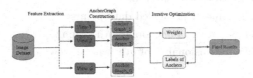

Fig. 1. Schematic illustration of the MAGL-based image classification process.

3   Multi-graph-Based Learning

3.1   Problem Definition

Given an image dataset, $\mathcal{D}=\{(\mathbf{x}_1,y_1),(\mathbf{x}_2,y_2),\ldots,(\mathbf{x}_l,y_l),\mathbf{x}_{l+1},\ldots,\mathbf{x}_n\}$, where there are n samples and l samples are labeled, the semi-supervised learning aims to classify each unlabeled sample into one specific class. In particular, in the setting of multi-view learning, the feature of each sample $\mathbf{x}_i$ consists of G types of views $\mathbf{x}_i=(\mathbf{x}_{v_1},\mathbf{x}_{v_2},\ldots,\mathbf{x}_{v_G})$, $\mathbf{x}_{v_g} \in \mathbb{R}^{d_g \times 1}$, where the dimension of the view v_g is d_g. Multi-graph-based learning first constructs a series of undirected weighted graphs $\mathscr{G}_g(\mathscr{V}_g,\mathscr{E}_g)$, where $\mathscr{V}_g$ is a set of nodes corresponding to the representation of the gth view, $\mathscr{E}_g$ is a set of edges connecting these adjacent node with a weight matrix $\mathbf{W}_g$. Then multi-graph-based learning formulate the objective function based on the cluster assumption, and optimizes it to obtain the labels of unlabeled data points $\mathbf{f}$. For convenience, some important notations used throughout the paper and their explanations are listed in Table 1.

Table 1. Notations and definitions

Notation	Definition
$\mathscr{G}(\mathscr{V}, \mathscr{E})$	An undirected weighted graph, where $\mathscr{V}$ indicates data points, and $\mathscr{E}$ is a set of edges connecting adjacent nodes
$\mathbf{W}_g$	The adjacency matrix of gth graph used in label smoothness regularization
$\mathbf{D}_g$	The diagonal matrix for gth graph, in which the ith diagonal element equals to the sum of the ith row of $\mathbf{W}_g$
$\mathbf{Z}_g$	The local weight matrix of gth graph that measures the relationship between data points and anchors
Y_l	The class indicator matrix on labeled data points
$\mathbf{A}_g$	The soft label matrix of anchors in gth graph
$\mathbf{f}$	The soft label matrix of data points
G	The number of graphs
T	The number of iterations in the corresponding iterative optimization process
n	The number of data points
l	The number of labeled data points
m_g	The number of anchors of gth graph
d_g	The dimensionality of gth feature view

3.2   Formulation of Multi-graph-Based Learning

Graph-based learning is a large family among the existing semi-supervised methods. It is conducted on a graph where the vertices are labeled and unlabeled samples, and the edges reflect the similarities between datapoint pairs. In this section, we introduce a multi-graph-based method which denoted as MGL. Denote $\mathbf{W}$ as an affinity matrix with W_{ij} indicating the similarity between the ith and jth sample. The similarity is often estimated based on

$$W_{ij} = \begin{cases} \exp(-\frac{\|\mathbf{x}_i - \mathbf{x}_j\|^2}{2\sigma^2}) & \text{if } i \neq j \\ 0 & \text{otherwise} \end{cases} \tag{1}$$

where σ is the radius parameter of a Gaussian function that converts distance to similarity.

Suppose we construct G graphs $\mathbf{W}_1, \mathbf{W}_2, \ldots, \mathbf{W}_G$ for G views. There are two items for each view in this regularization scheme, where the first item implies the smoothness of the labels on the graph and the second item indicates the constraint of training data. Then we integrate G graphs into a regularization framework by the weight parameter $\boldsymbol{\alpha} = [\alpha_1, \alpha_2, \ldots, \alpha_G]$

$$Q(\mathbf{f}, \boldsymbol{\alpha}) = \sum_{g=1}^{G} \alpha_g^r$$

$$\left(\sum_{i,j} W_{g;ij} \left| \frac{f_i}{\sqrt{D_{g;ii}}} - \frac{f_j}{\sqrt{D_{g;jj}}} \right|^2 + u_g \sum_i |f_i - y_i|^2 \right) \quad (2)$$

$$[\mathbf{F}, \boldsymbol{\alpha}] = \operatorname{argmin}_{\mathbf{f}, \boldsymbol{\alpha}} Q(\mathbf{f}, \boldsymbol{\alpha}), \text{s.t.} \sum_{g=1}^{G} \alpha_g = 1$$

where $\mathbf{D}_g$ is a diagonal matrix for gth graph, in which the ith diagonal element equals to the sum of the ith row of $\mathbf{W}_g$, f_i can be regarded as a relevance score, y_i is the label of ith sample, r is a parameter which modulates the effect of the smoothness difference of graphs, $u_g > 0$ is a trade-off parameter.

As a consequence, we can solve the above problem by updating two variables iteratively. That is, we first fix $\mathbf{f}$ and optimize $\operatorname{argmin}_{\alpha} Q(\mathbf{f}, \boldsymbol{\alpha})$, s.t. $\sum_{g=1}^{G} \alpha_g = 1$, which can be solved with

$$\alpha_g = \frac{\left(\frac{1}{\mathbf{f}^T \mathbf{L}_g \mathbf{f} + u_g |\mathbf{f} - \mathbf{y}|^2} \right)^{\frac{1}{r-1}}}{\sum_{g=1}^{G} \left(\frac{1}{\mathbf{f}^T \mathbf{L}_g \mathbf{f} + u_g |\mathbf{f} - \mathbf{y}|^2} \right)^{\frac{1}{r-1}}} \quad (3)$$

Then, we fix $\boldsymbol{\alpha}$ and optimize $\operatorname{argmin}_f Q(\mathbf{f}, \boldsymbol{\alpha})$, which can be solved as

$$\mathbf{f} = \left(\mathbf{I} + \frac{\sum_{g=1}^{G} \alpha_g^r \mathbf{L}_g}{\sum_{g=1}^{G} \alpha_g^r u_g} \right)^{-1} \mathbf{y} \quad (4)$$

3.3 Analysis of Multi-graph-Based Learning

MGL consists of the following steps: (1) constructing affinity matrix $\mathbf{W}_g$ for each graph, and computing the normalized Laplacian matrix $\mathbf{L}_g$; (2) solving the object function via an iterative solution according to Eqs. (3) and (4); (3) predicting the hard labels on unlabeled data points. The time complexities of step 1 and step 2 are $O\left(\sum_{g=1}^{G} d_g n^2\right)$ and $O(Tn^3)$, where d_g is the dimension of gth view and T is the number of iterations. As we can see, MGL will lead to huge time costs and storage costs as n gets large, so it will be too slow for large-scale applications. Therefore, reducing storage costs and time costs constitutes a major work for multi-graph-based learning.

4 The Proposed Approach

4.1 Construction of Anchor Graphs

In this paper, we propose a novel multi-view learning approach, which can efficiently employ features from different views for higher classification accuracies on large-scale datasets. To achieve this requirement, we first construct anchor graphs which use a small set of points called anchors to approximate the data distribution structure. First, we generate m_g anchor points $U_g = \{u_1, u_2, \ldots, u_{m_g}\} \in \mathbb{R}^{d_g \times m_g}$ from the training dataset, which can be done by running K-means, where m_g is the number of anchors for gth view, and d_g is the dimension of gth view.

We design a regression matrix $\mathbf{Z}$ that measures the underlying relationship between data points and anchors, which usually is defined based on a kernel function $K_h()$ with a bandwidth h:

$$Z_{ik} = \frac{K_h(\mathbf{x}_i, \mathbf{u}_k)}{\sum_{k' \in \langle i \rangle} K_h(\mathbf{x}_i, \mathbf{u}_k)} \ \forall k \in \langle i \rangle \tag{5}$$

Only the s nearest anchors are computed for each datapoint $\mathbf{x}_i$ in $\mathbf{Z}$, which are saved in the notation $\langle i \rangle \subset [1 : m]$. Typically, we may adopt the Gaussian kernel $K_h(\mathbf{x}_i, \mathbf{u}_k) = \exp(-\frac{\|\mathbf{x}_i - \mathbf{u}_k\|^2}{2h^2})$for the kernel regression.

According to $\mathbf{Z}$, the anchor graph provides a powerful approximation to the original adjacency matrix $\mathbf{W}$ as follows:

$$\mathbf{W} = \mathbf{Z}\mathbf{\Lambda}^{-1}\mathbf{Z}^T \tag{6}$$

where the diagonal matrix $\mathbf{\Lambda} \in \mathbb{R}^{m \times m}$ is defined as $\Lambda_{kk} = \sum_{i=1}^{n} Z_{ik}$, $k = 1, \ldots, m$.

4.2 Multi-anchor-Graph Regularization

Similar to MGL, our MAGL model consists of two important aspects, including the design of the smoothness constraint and that of the fitting constraint. First, we suppose that the predicted labels of nearby data points in each independent view should be similar. Therefore, we propose the following unified constraint for label smooth in manifold regularization:

$$\sum_{g=1}^{G} \alpha_g \sum_{i,j} W_{g;ij} \left| \frac{\mathbf{Z}_{g;i}\mathbf{A}_g}{\sqrt{D_{g;ii}}} - \frac{\mathbf{Z}_{g;j}\mathbf{A}_g}{\sqrt{D_{g;jj}}} \right|^2 \tag{7}$$

where $\boldsymbol{\alpha} = [\alpha_1, \alpha_2, \ldots, \alpha_G]$ is a weight vector which satisfies $\alpha_g \geq 0$ and $\sum_{g=1}^{G} \alpha_g = 1$, $\mathbf{A}_g$ is the prediction label matrix on the anchor set for the gth graph, and $\mathbf{Z}_{g;i}$ is the ith row of $\mathbf{Z}_g$.

Second, we suppose that the fused predicted labels should not change too much from the initial label assignment. $\mathbf{Y}_L \in \mathbb{R}^{l \times c}$ denotes a class indictor matrix on labeled samples. Hence, we present the fitting constraint as follows:

$$\sum_i \left| \sum_{g=1}^{G} \alpha_g \mathbf{Z}_{g;i\cdot} \mathbf{A}_g - \mathbf{Y}_{i\cdot} \right|^2 \tag{8}$$

Finally, our algorithm can be formulated as the following optimization problem

$$[\mathbf{A}, \boldsymbol{\alpha}] = \mathrm{argmin}_{\mathbf{A}, \alpha} Q\left(\mathbf{A}, \boldsymbol{\alpha}\right), \text{ s.t. } \sum_{g=1}^{G} \alpha_g = 1 \tag{9}$$

where

$$Q\left(\mathbf{A}, \boldsymbol{\alpha}\right) = \sum_{g=1}^{G} \alpha_g \sum_{i,j} W_{g;ij} \left| \frac{\mathbf{Z}_{g;i\cdot} \mathbf{A}_g}{\sqrt{D_{g;ii}}} - \frac{\mathbf{Z}_{g;j\cdot} \mathbf{A}_g}{\sqrt{D_{g;jj}}} \right|^2$$

$$+ \frac{u}{2} \sum_i \left| \sum_{g=1}^{G} \alpha_g \mathbf{Z}_{g;i\cdot} \mathbf{A}_g - \mathbf{Y}_{i\cdot} \right|^2 \tag{10}$$

$$= \frac{1}{2} \sum_{g=1}^{G} \alpha_g tr(\mathbf{A}_g^T \tilde{\mathbf{L}}_g \mathbf{A}_g) + \frac{1}{2} \left\| \sum_{g=1}^{G} \alpha_g \mathbf{Z}_g \mathbf{A}_g - \mathbf{Y}_L \right\|_F^2$$

where

$$\tilde{\mathbf{L}}_g = \mathbf{Z}_g^T \mathbf{L}_g \mathbf{Z}_g$$

$$= \mathbf{Z}_g^T \left(\mathbf{I} - \mathbf{Z}_g \boldsymbol{\Lambda}^{-1} \mathbf{Z}^T \right) \mathbf{Z}_g \tag{11}$$

$$= \mathbf{Z}_g^T \mathbf{Z}_g - \mathbf{Z}_g^T \mathbf{Z}_g \boldsymbol{\Lambda}^{-1} \mathbf{Z}_g^T \mathbf{Z}_g,$$

is the reduced Laplacian matrix for gth graph, $\mathbf{Z}_{g;L} \in \mathbb{R}^{l \times m}$ is the sub-matrix according to the labeled part of the local weight matrix $\mathbf{Z}_g$, and $u > 0$ is a trade-off parameter.

We alternatively update $\mathbf{A}$ and $\boldsymbol{\alpha}$ to solve Eq. (9). When α_g is fixed, we optimize $\mathrm{argmin}_{\mathbf{A}_g} Q(\mathbf{A}, \boldsymbol{\alpha})$ and obtain,

$$\mathbf{A}_g = -u \left(\tilde{\mathbf{L}}_g + u\alpha_g \mathbf{Z}_{g;L}^T \mathbf{Z}_{g;L} \right)^{-1} \mathbf{Z}_{g;L}^T \left(\sum_{k=1}^{G} \alpha_k \mathbf{Z}_{k;L} \mathbf{A}_k - \mathbf{Y}_L \right) \tag{12}$$

When $\mathbf{A}_g$ is fixed, the problem turns to $\mathrm{argmin}_{\alpha} Q(\mathbf{A}, \boldsymbol{\alpha})$, s.t. $\sum_{g=1}^{G} \alpha_g = 1$. In this case, we optimize α_g with convex optimization tools, such as CVX.

Table 2 shows the iterative process for MAGL. We use $\mathbf{A}^t$ and $\boldsymbol{\alpha}^t$ to denote the values of $\mathbf{A}$ and $\boldsymbol{\alpha}$ in tth repetition in the process, then we have

$$Q\left(\mathbf{A}^{t+1}, \boldsymbol{\alpha}^{t+1}\right) < Q\left(\mathbf{A}^t, \boldsymbol{\alpha}^{t+1}\right) < Q\left(\mathbf{A}^t, \boldsymbol{\alpha}^t\right) \tag{13}$$

Table 2. Iterative solution method for MAGL

Input: local weight matrix $\mathbf{B}_{g;L}$ which measures the relationships between anchors and data points, Local weight matrix $\mathbf{Z}_g$, reduced Laplacian matrix $\tilde{\mathbf{L}}_g$, parameter u.
1: Initialize $\mathbf{A}_g = \mathbf{B}_{g;L}\mathbf{Y}_L, \alpha_g = \frac{1}{G}$.
2: for t=1:T
for g=1:G
update $\mathbf{A}_g$ according to (13).
update α_g by the CVX toolbox.
end
end
Output: weight vector $\boldsymbol{\alpha}$, anchor label matrix $\mathbf{A}_g$.

which implies our cost function $Q(\mathbf{A}, \boldsymbol{\alpha})$ converges monotonically.

As we can see, MAGL is superior to MGL in terms of both memory cost and time costs. Besides, we list the storage costs and the computational complexities of several graph-based algorithms in Tables 3 and 4.

Table 3. Comparison of storage costs of three graph-based methods

Approach	Storage
Anchor Graph Regularization (AGR)	$O(mn)$
Optimized Multigraph-Based Semi-supervised Learning (MGL)	$O(Gn^2)$
Multi-anchor-Graph-Based Learning (MAGL)	$O\left(\sum_{g=1}^{G} m_g n\right)$

Table 4. Comparison of computational complexities of three graph-based methods

Approach	Find anchors	Design Z	(reduced) Graph Laplacian L	Optimization
AGR	$O(mndT)$	$O(dmn)$	$O(m^2 n)$	$O(m^2 n + m^3)$
MGL	-	-	$O\left(\sum_{g=1}^{G} d_g n^2\right)$	$O(GTn^3)$
MAGL	$O\left(n \sum_{g=1}^{G} m_g d_g T\right)$	$O\left(\sum_{g=1}^{G} m_g d_g n\right)$	$O\left(\sum_{g=1}^{G} m_g^2 n\right)$	$O\left(T \sum_{g=1}^{G} m_g^2 n + T \sum_{g=1}^{G} m_g^3\right)$

5 Experiment

5.1 Experiment Settings

To evaluate the performance of the proposed approach, we conduct experiments on six publicly available datasets: Coil-20, Corel1000, Caltech101, Caltech256, Cifar-10, and Tiny-imagenet. The attributes of these datasets are listed in Table 5. All the experiments are implemented on a PC with E5-2620 v2 @2.1GHz and 64 GB RAM. Following the setting in multi-view fusion tasks, we design the following feature channels.

1. Bag of features (BoF) [5]: It counts the number of visual words within one image. We use this method to get a 500-dimensional vector to represent an image.
2. GIST [9]: It is one kind of feature description about scene. We calculate a 512-dimensional GIST descriptor for each image.
3. HSV: We generate a 256-dimensional HSV color histogram feature.
4. CNN: We use a pretrained AlexNet network to get the feature representations of the dataset. Then conducting PCA to deal with the result to get a 256-dimensional feature.

Table 5. Details of the datasets

Datasets	Coil-20	Corel1000	Caltech101	Caltech256	Cifar-10	Tiny-imagenet
Of instances	1,440	1,000	9,135	30,608	60,000	100,000
Of categories	20	10	102	257	10	200

In our experiments, we classify the above datasets into small and large sizes. Specifically, we regard Coil-20 and Corel1000 as small-size datasets, Caltech101, Caltech256, Cifar-10 and Tiny-imagenet as large-size datasets. Here we further compare the proposed MAGL approach with the following methods. (1) MGL, optimized multi-graph-based semi-supervised learning. (2) AGR with multiple views, which denoted by "AGR_{mv}". (3) AGR with the single best view, which denoted by "AGR_{bv}". (4) KNN with multiple views, which denoted by "KNN_{mv}". (5) KNN with the single best view, which denoted by "KNN_{bv}". (6) SVM with multiple views, which denoted by "SVM_{mv}". (7) SVM with the single best view, which denoted by "SVM_{bv}".

5.2 Experiment Results

We first conduct experiments on two small datasets on three different features: BoF, GIST and HSV. For convenience, we set the number of anchors to 100 for implementing k-means for each feature. Of note, a more adaptive setting of the number of clustering centers can be found in [10] sindhwani2005co. As for the setting of semi-supervised learning, we vary the number of labeled samples $l = \{5, 6, \ldots, 15\}$, while the rest samples remain as unlabeled data. The average classification accuracies over 10 trials are illustrated in Fig. 1.

From these results, we obtain the following observations. Firstly, as a general trend, as the number of labeled data increases, the performances of all methods become better. Secondly, two multi-graph-based methods stay at a higher Level than both AGR_{mv} and AGR_{bv} when the number of labeled data points is small. Thirdly, compared with MGL, the proposed MAGL obtains comparable or better classification accuracies. Results on small-size datasets show the good performance of MAGL for image classification (Fig. 2).

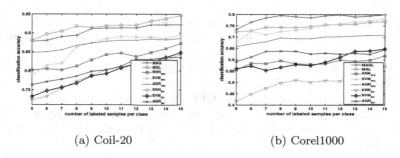

(a) Coil-20   (b) Corel1000

Fig. 2. Classification accuracy versus the number of labeled samples on small datasets

Then we conduct experiments on four large datasets. Here we use four views to conduct our experiments: BoF, GIST, HSV, and CNN. For convenience, we set the number of anchors to 900, 3,000, 700 and 5000 for implementing k-means. Of note, a more adaptive setting of the number of clustering centers can be found in [11]. For these large-size datasets, we vary the number of labeled samples $l = \{5, 10, \ldots, 30\}$, $l = \{10, 20, \ldots, 60\}$ and $l = \{1, 2, \ldots, 10\}$. Averaged over 10 trials, we calculate the classification accuracies for the referred methods. We do not conduct MGL method for Cifar-10 and Tiny-imagenet because of it's huge time costs. The results of large size datasets are shown in Fig. 3. The time costs of the above algorithms with 10 labeled samples per class are in Table 6.

From these results, the following observations can be obtained. Firstly, compared with AGR_{mv} and AGR_{bv}, the accuracies of MAGL and MGL are higher, as the latter two methods can exploit the complementation of multiple graphs. Secondly, the results of MAGL can be comparable or even higher than MGL in most cases. This demonstrates that the effectiveness of our proposed method. Thirdly, the time costs of MAGL are apparently lower than MGL. The results demonstrate the efficiency of MAGL for image classification.

Table 6. Time costs (seconds) of the compared learning algorithms on large-size datasets

	AGR_{mv}	AGR_{bv}	MAGL		MGL
			K-means	Optimization	
Caltech101	2.1409	1.2669	14.7394	90.5945	846.2607
Caltech256	83.7451	68.0878	150.8944	259.1304	4836.9325
Cifar-10	122.0299	22.5077	79.1551	99.0917	–
Tiny-imagenet	854.3696	135.4208	832.9362	1092.0058	–

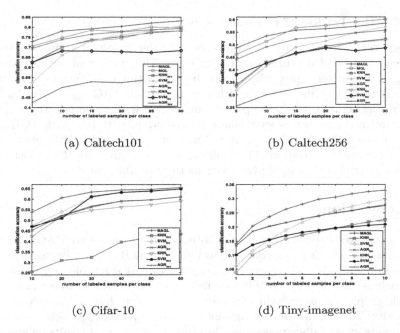

(a) Caltech101

(b) Caltech256

(c) Cifar-10

(d) Tiny-imagenet

Fig. 3. Classification accuracy versus the number of labeled samples on large datasets

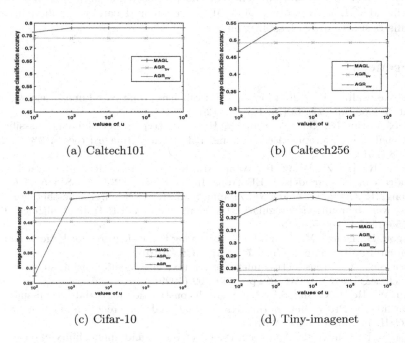

(a) Caltech101

(b) Caltech256

(c) Cifar-10

(d) Tiny-imagenet

Fig. 4. Average performance curves of MAGL with respect to the variation of u. Here, the number of labeled samples is set to 10 per class.

5.3   On the Trade-Off Parameters u

We also test the sensitivity of parameter u in the proposed approach. We set the number of labeled samples to 10 per class. The number of anchors and the setting of parameter s just follows the above experiments. We vary u from 10^2 to 10^6. Here we also illustrate the other methods, i.e., "AGR_{mv}", "AGR_{bv}", for comparison. Figure 4 shows the performance curve with respect to the variation of u. From the figure, we observe that our method outperforms both AGR_{mv} and AGR_{bv} in most cases and the performances stay at a stable level over a wide range of parameter variation. These observations demonstrate the robustness of the parameter selection in applying our method to different datasets.

6   Conclusion

In this paper we proposed a multi-graph-based algorithm called MAGL, which is able to integrate multiple anchor graphs into a regularization framework. Specifically, our approach employs anchor graphs to build tractable large adjacency relationships. In this way, MAGL can not only explore the complementation of multiple graphs to improve the classification accuracies but also reduce the time complexity. To evaluate the performance of the proposed approach, we conduct experiments on six publicly available datasets. Experimental results demonstrate both the effectiveness and efficiency of the proposed method. It is noteworthy that the MAGL is actually a general approach and can be applied in many domains besides image classification.

References

1. Felzenszwalb, P.F., Huttenlocher, D.P.: Efficient graph-based image segmentation. Int. J. Comput. Vis. **59**(2), 167–181 (2004)
2. Gao, Y., Ji, R., Cui, P., Dai, Q., Hua, G.: Hyperspectral image classification through bilayer graph-based learning. IEEE Trans. Image Process. **23**(7), 2769–2778 (2014)
3. Hong, R., Hu, Z., Wang, R., Wang, M., Tao, D.: Multi-view object retrieval via multi-scale topic models. IEEE Trans. Image Process. **25**(12), 5814–5827 (2016)
4. Hong, R., Zhang, L., Zhang, C., Zimmermann, R.: Flickr circles: aesthetic tendency discovery by multi-view regularized topic modeling. IEEE Trans. Multimed. **18**(8), 1555–1567 (2016)
5. Jégou, H., Douze, M., Schmid, C.: Improving bag-of-features for large scale image search. Int. J. Comput. Vis. **87**(3), 316–336 (2010)
6. Joachims, T.: Transductive inference for text classification using support vector machines. In: ICML, vol. 99, pp. 200–209 (1999)
7. Liu, W., He, J., Chang, S.F.: Large graph construction for scalable semi-supervised learning. In: Proceedings of the 27th International Conference on Machine Learning (ICML-10), pp. 679–686 (2010)
8. Nigam, K., Ghani, R.: Analyzing the effectiveness and applicability of co-training. In: Proceedings of the Ninth International Conference on Information and Knowledge Management. pp. 86–93. ACM (2000)

9. Oliva, A., Torralba, A.: Modeling the shape of the scene: a holistic representation of the spatial envelope. Int. J. Comput. Vis. **42**(3), 145–175 (2001)

10. Pelleg, D., Moore, A.W., et al.: X-means: extending k-means with efficient estimation of the number of clusters. In: Icml, vol. 1, pp. 727–734 (2000)

11. Ray, S., Turi, R.H.: Determination of number of clusters in k-means clustering and application in colour image segmentation. In: Proceedings of the 4th International Conference on Advances in Pattern Recognition and Digital Techniques, Calcutta, India, pp. 137–143 (1999)

12. Sindhwani, V., Niyogi, P., Belkin, M.: A co-regularization approach to semi-supervised learning with multiple views. In: Proceedings of ICML Workshop on Learning with Multiple Views, vol. 2005, pp. 74–79. Citeseer (2005)

13. Thompson, B.: Canonical correlation analysis. Encycl. Stat. Behav. Sci. (2005)

14. Wang, M., Hua, X.S., Hong, R., Tang, J., Qi, G.J., Song, Y.: Unified video annotation via multigraph learning. IEEE Trans. Circ. Syst. Video Technol. **19**(5), 733–746 (2009)

15. Wang, M., Li, H., Tao, D., Lu, K., Wu, X.: Multimodal graph-based reranking for web image search. IEEE Trans. Image Process. **21**(11), 4649–4661 (2012)

16. Zhou, D., Bousquet, O., Lal, T.N., Weston, J., Schölkopf, B.: Learning with local and global consistency. In: Advances in Neural Information Processing Systems, pp. 321–328 (2004)

DANTE Speaker Recognition Module.
An Efficient and Robust Automatic
Speaker Searching Solution
for Terrorism-Related Scenarios

Jesús Jorrín[✉] and Luis Buera[✉]

Nuance Communications, Inc., Madrid, Spain
{jesus.jorrin,luis.buera}@nuance.com

Abstract. The vast amount of data crossing the net with terrorism-related content, including voice, is so immense that the use of powerful filtering/detection tools with great discriminative capacities becomes essential. Although the analysis of this content often ends with some manual inspection, a first filtering process becomes basic. In this direction, we propose a speaker clustering solution based on a speaker identification system. We show that both the speaker clustering and the speaker recognition solution can be used individually to efficiently solve searching tasks in several terrorism-related scenarios.

Keywords: Automatic speaker recognition · Speaker identification
Speaker verification · Automatic speaker clustering

1 Introduction

With the rise of online resources in the last decades, terrorist organizations have found these environments as one of their most effective facets of their recruitment efforts. By spreading their ideology online, they can reach significantly more people than they ever could before. In every terrorist organization, the most consequential factor for its sustainability is manpower. Considering this, terroristic organizations often distribute propagandistic content on the Web for alluring potential individuals that are prone to be radicalized. But propaganda is not the only activity these organizations perform on the net. For example, fund-raising terroristic activities are nowadays established in online sites that are publicly available to others in order to obtain as many funds as possible. Since Social Media has rapidly grown and gained much popularity, it is used for touting fundraising campaigns so as to elicit the money of persons that are potentially "mesmerized" by its ideological scope. Also, the increasing availability of online sources make the finding of digital training material very easy.

Active searching of potential terrorists online is a challenging issue for Law Enforcement Agencies (LEAs). For many scenarios, LEAs are forced to monitor, sometimes manually, hundreds of digital contents to follow their online

© Springer Nature Switzerland AG 2019
I. Kompatsiaris et al. (Eds.): MMM 2019, LNCS 11295, pp. 704–715, 2019.
https://doi.org/10.1007/978-3-030-05710-7_58

activities. With the goal of supporting LEAs in their struggle against online terrorist-related activities, the DANTE project was born [1]. In this way, the DANTE project aims to deliver an effective, efficient, and automated data mining and analytics solution. This system will be used to detect, retrieve, collect and analyze huge amounts of heterogeneous and complex multimedia and multi-language terrorist-related contents, from both the Surface and the Deep Web, including Darknets. The envisaged tool will assist officers in their everyday operations, as it will provide an automated and quick way for reliable detection of terrorist-related content on the Web.

Voice is one of the most commons means the terrorists use to transmit messages. Videos, telephonic conversations, or pod-casts are examples of this multimedia content that LEAs must deal with in their daily work. Since listening hundreds of audios to extract information is not feasible, speaker recognition (SR) tools are used to enable these analyses. Speaker recognition consists of identifying a person from their voice characteristics. It is important to notice the difference between the act of authentication (commonly referred to as speaker verification or speaker authentication) and identification. Effectively, speaker verification involves a comparison between two pieces of speech and we have to detect whether they were uttered by the same person or not. However, speaker identification involves a comparison between a piece of audio and some other pieces of audio and we have to detect if the former was uttered by one of the speakers considered in the latter ones or not.

Speaker recognition is a mature technology with a history dating back some decades [2,3]. Speaker recognition uses the acoustic features of speech that have been found to differ between individuals. These acoustic patterns reflect both anatomy (e.g., size and shape of the throat and mouth) and learned behavioral patterns (e.g., voice pitch, speaking style). These patterns are captured into the voice templates called "speaker voiceprints" or "speaker models". These voiceprints are later used by pattern recognition systems to decide if the underlying speech came from the same speaker or not.

We can find many applications for the voice biometrics technology: forensic scenarios, intelligent domotic environments, bank/financial operations, or the counter-terrorism tools covered in this work are a few examples of them. But also, many are the technologies/tools that are built on top SR systems. A good example of them are the speaker clustering techniques. The term cluster analysis, first used by Tryon in 1939 [4], encompasses a number of different algorithms and methods for grouping objects of similar kind into respective categories. In other words cluster analysis is an exploratory data analysis tool which aims at sorting different objects into groups in a way that the degree of association between two objects is maximal if they belong to the same group and minimal otherwise. Given the above, cluster analysis can be used to discover structures in an unsupervised method. In the case of speaker clustering, the goal is to classify speech segments into clusters such that each cluster contains speech from one single speaker and also speech from the same speaker is classified into the same cluster.

DANTE platform has many different modules, depending on the multimedia content they analyze. Particularly, two are the modules related to the speaker recognition of multimedia voice files. Both modules are based on a common SR system, but they offer different functionalities. The first module provides an identification/verification tool, while the second one covers speaker clustering scenarios. The goal of these two modules is no other than facilitate LEAs searching activities when they try to find potential terrorists over a set of suspicious audios. In this work, we present, analyze and evaluate these voice related modules in the context of terrorism scenarios. The document is structured as follows. First, Sects. 2 and 3 describe the speaker recognition module and the speaker clustering module respectively. Then, in Sect. 4 we introduce the experiments performed to evaluate each of the previously described solutions. A description of a real database considered for this work and the metrics used to evaluate the results are also introduced in this section. Later, results are presented in Sect. 5. Finally, Sect. 6 summarizes the conclusions extracted from the experiments.

2   Speaker Recognition

The SR engine included in the DANTE platform combines the results provided by several SR systems (subsystems). Particularly, we have subsystems rooted in i-vectors technology [5], whether they are based on Gaussian Mixture Models (GMMs) or Deep Neural Network (DNN) models. Each subsystem exploits different acoustic front-end parameters that differ by feature type and dimension. In this section, we cover the main modules for each of those subsystems. Particularly, the ones responsible for the Voice Activity Detection (VAD), the feature extraction, the feature normalization, the classifier, the score normalization, and the score fusion. These components are described in the following subsections.

2.1   Voice Activity Detection

A VAD model based on Neural Network (NN) phonetic decoding is used. The decoders are hybrid HMM-NN models trained to recognize 11 phone classes, as the one presented in [6], or detailed English-US acoustic units. The Neural Network used for the VAD is Multilayer Perceptrons that estimates the posterior probability of phonetic units (or classes), given an acoustic feature vector.

2.2   Feature Extraction and Normalization

Two types of features are considered: Mel-frequency cepstral coefficients (MFCC) features, and Perceptual Linear Predictive (PLP) features. They exploit feature warping and cepstral mean and variance normalization over the segments detected by the VAD.

Analysis bandwidth, window lengths, number of Mel filters, liftering, etc., have been configured with different values for the considered feature extractors, in order to maximize the feature orthogonality. Apart from the static coefficients, delta and delta-delta coefficients are also considered.

2.3 I-Vector Extractor and Classifier

The SR engine considers the combination of different models, for i-vector extraction:

GMM-IVector with Pairwise SVM: The GMM-IVector extractors follow the standard paradigm proposed in [5]. Gender independent UBMs are trained with 2048 diagonal covariance matrices, and total variability T matrices with 500 factors are computed via Expectation-Maximization iterations. The speaker recognition raw scores have been obtained by using a Pairwise Support Vector Machine (PSVM) [7,8].

DNN-IVector with Pairwise SVM: The DNN-IVector extractors are based on the hybrid Deep Neural Network/GMM approach for extracting Baum-Welch statistics proposed in [9]. The final Softmax layer produces the posterior probability of the output senone based units. Based on the DNN posterior probabilities, Baum-Welch statistics for extracting i-vectors are computed.

2.4 Score Normalization and Score Combination

The raw scores obtained from all our subsystems are subject to score normalization. In particular, the GMM and DNN i-vector systems use Adaptive Symmetric Normalization (AS-Norm) [10].

The combination of the subsystems scores was obtained by linear fusion of such scores.

3 Speaker Clustering

We can find many approaches that solve the clustering problem; for example, sequential, hierarchical, or cost function optimization implementations [11]. DANTE clustering module considers a bottom-up Agglomerative Hierarchical Clustering (AHC), [12]. This is a greedy algorithm that starts with a number of clusters equal to the number of speech segments and it merges the closest clusters iteratively until a stopping criterion is met. There are several ways of implementing these kind of algorithms, such as those based on matrix theory or graph theory [11]. For our purpose, we use an approach based on matrix theory. The input for these kind of implementations is a proximity matrix $P(X)$, where $X = \{x_i\}, i = 1...N$ is the set of elements to be clustered. $P(X)$ is an $N \times N$ square matrix with (i, j) component equal to the similarity $s(x_i, x_j)$, or dissimilarity $d(x_i, x_j)$ between the elements x_i and x_j. In this paper we only consider similarity measures. Particularly, the used similarity is the SR score provided by the SR engine described in Sect. 2. So, to fill in the proximity matrix, the scores of the all vs all segments considered in the clustering task are computed. Once the proximity matrix is created, the clustering process starts. At each iteration

t, of the clustering process, the clusters with the highest value in the similarity matrix are merged. After this merger, a new similarity matrix P_t is computed. To obtain the new matrix P_t, we start from P_{t-1} and we proceed as follows (note that P_0 is the $N \times N$ square matrix at the beginning of the clustering process): (1) delete the two columns and rows associated with the merged clusters, and (2) add a new row and column with the distances between the new cluster and the old ones. We can find many approaches to compute these new distances such as single/complete/average linkages or centroids methods [11]. In this work we consider the average linkage algorithm. This process is repeated until no more mergers are available. As output of the clustering process, a dendrogram tree is obtained. A dendrogram tree is graphical representation used to illustrate the arrangement of the clusters produced at each step of a clustering process.

4   Experiments

There are two major applications of speaker recognition technologies and methodologies. If the speaker claims to be of a certain identity and the voice is used to verify this claim, this is called verification or authentication. On the other hand, identification is the task of determining an unknown speaker's identity from a pool of voiceprints. Speaker verification is also called a 1:1 match where one speaker's voice is matched to one voiceprint, whereas speaker identification is a 1:N match where the voice is compared against N templates. From a security perspective, identification is different from verification. Thus, it makes sense to consider different experiments and metrics according to each scenario. In the following subsections, these two tasks are considered separately. We also present a third experiment to evaluate the speaker clustering scenario.

4.1   Database

The database used for this work was provided by LEAs during the first stages of the DANTE project. LEAs provided audios coming from a real terrorism case, so we could evaluate the speaker recognition modules with real field data. Particularly the dataset contains audios pulled from different propaganda video documentaries that were extracted from the Web by LEAs. The audio labels needed to measure the performance of the system were obtained by visual inspection over the original video documentaries. The dataset contains 48 speakers and 89 audios whose durations go from few seconds (5–10 s) up to 2–3 min, with an average duration of about 30 s. Apart from this, is worth to notice that some of the documentaries were taped under noisy conditions, as they were recorded in the street with different types of noise such as crowd, car; or even with background music. The considered audios have an average signal to noise ratio (SNR) of 15.1 dB. Table 1 summarizes the audios per speaker distribution, which is a representation of the number of speakers with a specific amount of audios. This distribution is a key point while characterizing a speaker clustering problem [13].

Table 1. Audios per speaker distribution.

Number of audios per speaker	1	2	3	4	5	6
Number of speakers	25	14	5	1	1	2

4.2 Speaker Verification Scenario

In this experiment for each audio in the database, we create a voiceprint. Then, these voiceprints are used to perform a set of verifications between themselves. The output of these verifications are the scores provided by the SR engine. All the scores are gathered to evaluate the performance of the SR engine. To characterize this experiment, we consider the following numbers: (a) the number of trials, where a trial is a comparison between two of the previous voiceprints, (b) number of target trials, a trial is classified as target when the identity of both voiceprints is the same, and (c) number of speaker models, the number of generated voiceprints. These numbers are compiled for the tested database in Table 2.

Table 2. Speaker verification experiment characterization. Number of trials, target trials, and speaker models.

Trials	Target trials	Speaker models
7728	46	89

Performance Metrics. As a metric we use detection error tradeoff (DET) which is a graphical plot of error rates for binary classification systems, plotting the false rejection (FR) rate vs. false acceptance (FA) rate. In this work, we will not consider the whole curve, but three specific working points: (a) Equal Error Rate (EER), point where $FA = FR$, (b) FR at 1% FA, and (c) FR at 0.5% FA. The EER is usually computed when measuring the performance of SR systems as it is a good representation of the behavior of the system. On the other hand, the two other working points are selected because SR systems usually work there.

4.3 Speaker Identification Scenario

While dealing with identification scenarios we find a speaker voiceprint (target speaker/model) that is faced against a set (searching list) of N other voice templates, and we have to conclude about the presence of the target speaker in the searching list. To reproduce this scenario, from the already created voiceprints from previous scenario, we select those having more than one voiceprint per speaker as our target models. Then, to create the searching list, for each of the target models, we select a set of N other voiceprints (coming from the pool of 89 voiceprints). We consider two cases, $N = 10$ and $N = 50$. When dealing with identification scenarios, we can find two situations: a closed-set identification, if the target speaker is always on the searching list; or an open-set identification, when the target speaker may appear or not in the searching list. Once the target models and their searching lists are defined, for each of these pairs (model + list) an identification task is performed. To do this, N verifications are performed (the target model vs all the elements in the searching list). The output of the identification is a sorted list of scores. We characterize this experiment with the number of identifications. These number are shown in Table 3.

Table 3. Speaker identification experiment characterization. Number of identifications including a target model (T) and not including it (NT)

Task	Identifications (T)	Identifications (NT)
Open-set	46	46
Closed-set	46	0

Performance Metrics. When considering closed-set identification tasks, we can evaluate the performance by using a Cumulative Match Characteristic (CMC) curve [14]. CMC graphs represent the probability of finding the target score in the list, among the topX positions of the list. This metric cannot be considered for the open-set scenario since not all the lists will have target scores. In this case, we will select a threshold value, and we will count the number of scores upper this threshold when the lists have a target score and when they do not. Additionally, we define the detection probability as the ratio between the number of lists with targets upper the threshold value and all the lists with target scores.

4.4   Speaker Clustering Scenario

In this experiment we consider all the 89 audios from the database, and we use them to run a clustering process. The output would be a dendrogram used to conclude about the common speakers found in the database.

Performance Metrics. Some common quality measures to evaluate the performance of a clustering task are: the rand index, F-measure, the mutual information or purity measures [15]. In this work, we consider the latter. The purity is a measure of cluster cleanness: clusters containing data from a single speaker. Particularly, we will consider speaker impurity (SI) and cluster impurity (CI) measures defined in [12]. The first one measures how spread the speakers are between the different clusters in a single partition. The second one measures to what extent clusters contain audios from different speakers. We will use these two measures, since they evaluate the trade-off between grouping audios from common speakers and having pure clusters; i.e., clusters containing audios from one unique speaker.

To evaluate a complete dendrogram, which is the output of our clustering algorithm, we compute the CI and SI values for all the partitions and plot them in one single graph where each point represents the speaker and cluster impurity for a certain iteration of the clustering process. These graphics are known as Impurity trade-off (IT) curves [13]. While working with the trade-off impurity curves we can reach conclusions if we make an analysis based on these graphics trends. Although these curves offer us an interesting review, in real scenarios specific working points are used as a performance measure. Despite this, some of them are most commonly used as a reference while analyzing clustering tasks:

- Equal Impurity (EI): The point where Cluster and Speaker Impurities are equal. This operating point assumes that merging two different speakers is as critical as obtaining two different clusters for a single speaker.
- Speaker impurity (SI) for null cluster impurity (CI = 0% or first error point): This operating point assumes that merging two speakers is unacceptable. The SI also represents the value before two different speakers merge into the same cluster for the first time. A low Speaker impurity will indicate that for every speaker there is a cluster that contains most of the recordings where the speaker is present.

5   Results

5.1   Speaker Recognition Task

Table 4 shows the results for the verification task. These results should be understood as a measure of the performance of the SR engine. Since the SR engine is later used to cover different scenarios, such as the identification one, or the speaker clustering one, having lower rates (both in FA and in FR) will ensure a higher performance in the mentioned scenarios.

Table 4. Speaker recognition results. False rejection rates for several false acceptance rates.

EER	FR@1%FA	FR@0.5%FA
4.38%	30.43%	34.78%

5.2   Speaker Identification Task

Figure 1 shows the results for the closed-set identification tasks and the two considered sizes of searching list (N = 10 and N = 50). First of all, these results allows us to measure the influence of the size of the searching list in an identification task. If we compare results for both sizes, we observe higher performance when

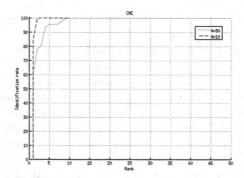

Fig. 1. Speaker identification results (closed-set). CMC curve. Percent of time (%) the target score is found among the top1, top5 or top10 scores, when the size of the list is N = 10 or N = 50.

the size of the searching list decreases. This is the expected behavior, as the size of the searching list increases, we get a larger number of nontarget scores, having in consequence a higher chance of finding greater nontarget scores among them. Apart from this, and if we focus, for example, on the N = 50 results, we find that an identification rate of 100% is reached at top8. Let's assume LEAs need to perform an identification task over a set of 50 suspicious audios they collected from the Web. Considering the obtained results, it would be enough for LEAs to manually inspect the 8 audios related with the top8 scores, instead of checking all the 50 audios to find the target speaker among the database. As an extreme situation, if they just keep one single audio (the top score), they would find the target speaker 62% of the times. If we analyze results for N = 10, we confirm better results are obtained since for the top1 this 62% raises to 84%.

Results for the open-set identification are gathered in Fig. 2 and Table 5. Figure 2 shows the trend for all working points, while in Table 5 some relevant working points are shown.

In a first analysis, we should check that the numbers of scores upper the threshold, sizeT and sizeNT, should have a difference of approximately one, meaning that the target score is responsible for the change in the number of scores above the threshold for the two types of lists (those with and without target score). From Table 5 we observe this is met.

Secondly, if we analyze pT, we are able to relate the number of nontarget scores we find over the threshold value (false alarms) at the cost of detecting the target score with a certain probability. In Table 5 we present two interesting working points (threshold values). If we consider Th = 2, we found that if the searching list contained a target speaker, the engine always detected it. Also, apart from correctly detecting the target speaker, the engine produced 5.82 false alarms on average. On the other hand, for Th = 3.5, we had no false alarms, but the target speaker was detected in 56% of the searches. We can see there is a clear trade-off between the false alarms and the false rejections. This trade-off is the

Table 5. Speaker identification results (open-set). N = 50. Average number of scores in the lists above the threshold value (th) when the list has a target score (sizeT) and when it does not (sizeNT). Percentage of the lists with the target the target score above the threshold value (pT)

Th	sizeT	sizeNT	pT
2	6.78	5.82	100%
2.25	4.95	4.02	95%
3.5	1	0.43	56%

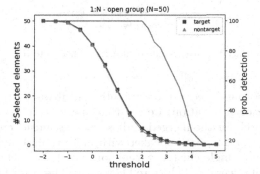

Fig. 2. Speaker identification results (open-set). N = 50. Threshold values against the number of scores above the threshold when the lists do not have target scores (red) and when they do (blue). Percentage of the lists with target the target score upper the threshold value (green) (Color figure online)

measure of goodness of a SR system. This aspect was covered in the verification scenario (Sect. 5.1).

5.3 Speaker Clustering Task

Figure 3 summarizes the performance of the clustering engine at each iteration of the clustering process. If we focus on the considered working points, the following analysis can be made:

- Before the first error, we have a speaker impurity of 10.11%. This occurs at the 33rd iteration. This means we made 33 merges out of 89 without making any errors, having 56 perfect clusters (containing audios from one single speaker). With the obtained SI rate, we have that about 90% of the audios from each speaker are in a unique cluster. So, keeping the largest clusters will ensure most of the audios from such speakers are kept.
- We have an EER of 6.17%. With this rate, on average we have that about 95% of the audios contained in each cluster belongs to the same speaker, but also all the speakers have about 95% of the audios contained in a single cluster.

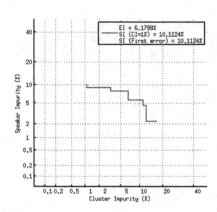

Fig. 3. Speaker clustering results. IT curve.

Apart from the considered working points, and if we study a bit the audios and the merges at each iteration, we see that the first errors are due to noisy conditions that match for the merged audios, such as music, crowd or car noise. Also, before the first error, each speaker with more than 4 audios had all their audios contained in a single cluster, except for one of the speakers with 6 audio files, where 5 out of 6 were still clustered correctly. The rest of the speakers had 1,2 audios per cluster. This is something we could expect from the analysis at the CI $= 0\%$ working point.

6   Conclusions

In this work, we presented the SR modules integrated into DANTE platform. We showed how these modules are used to solved different LEAs scenarios. For this purpose real field audios, coming from terrorism scenarios, were collected and used to model three different cases.

The first one is a speaker identification task, where two audios are compared to decide if they were uttered by the same speaker. The SR engine showed robust performance, despite the noisy recording conditions, with an EER of 4.38%

The second scenario is an identification case, where LEAs need to check if a suspicious speaker is found among a set of audios. It was showed that LEAs could save time by reducing the duration of their manual inspection sessions by 84%. For this scenario it was also showed that the selection of different threshold modulated the trade-off between the time the speaker is found and the number of false alarms. It was showed that under no false alarms, the target speaker was detected 56% of the times. On the other hand, with a detection rate of 100%, on average 5.82 false alarms were detected. If we consider terrorism use cases, since LEAs work usually ends with some manual inspection, it is better for them to select a lower threshold value, as they'll miss less number of targets, and all the possible false alarms will be manually discarded.

The final scenario was a speaker clustering one, where the whole set of audios was used to conclude about the presence of common speakers in such database. It was shown that the presented algorithm was able to satisfactory detect audios belonging to common speakers, even before the first merge errors.

Acknowledgements. The work presented in this paper was supported by the European Commission under contract H2020-700367 DANTE [1].

References

1. DANTE project homepage. http://www.h2020-dante.eu/. Accessed July 2018
2. Atal, B.S.: Automatic recognition of speakers from their voices. Proc. IEEE **64**, 460–475 (1976)
3. Doddington, G.R.: Speaker recognition-identifying people by their voices. Proc. IEEE **73**, 1651–1664 (1985)
4. Tryon, R.: Clustering Analysis (1993)
5. Dehak, N., Kenny, P., Dehak, R., Dumouchel, P., Ouellet, P.: Front-end factor analysis for speaker verification. IEEE Trans. Audio Speech Lang. Process. **19**(4), 788–798 (2011)
6. Castaldo, F., Colibro, D., Dalmasso, E., Laface, P., Vair, C.: Compensation of nuisance factors for speaker and language recognition. IEEE Trans. Audio Speech Lang. Process. **15**(7), 1969–1978 (2007)
7. Cumani, S., Laface, P.: Training pairwise support vector machines with large scale datasets. In: 2014 IEEE International Conference on Acoustics, Speech, and Signal Processing ICASSP 2014, Florence (Italy), pp. 1664–1668 (2014)
8. Cumani, S., Laface, P.: Large scale training of pairwise support vector machines for speaker recognition. IEEE/ACM Trans. Audio Speech Lang. Process. **22**(11), 1590–1600 (2014)
9. Lei, Y., Scheffer, N., Ferrer, L., McLaren, M.: A novel scheme for speaker recognition using a phonetically-aware deep neural network. In: Proceedings of ICASSP 2014, pp. 1714–1718 (2014)
10. Cumani, S., Batzu, P.D., Colibro, D., Vair, C., Laface, P., Vasilakakis, V.: Comparison of speaker recognition approaches for real applications. In: Interspeech 2011, Florence, Italy, pp. 2365–2368 (2011)
11. Theodoridis, S., Koutroumbas, K.: Pattern Recognition, 4th edn. Academic Press, Cambridge (2008)
12. Leeuwen, D.A.V.: Speaker linking in large datasets. In: Odyssey 2010, the Speaker Language and Recognition Workshop, Brno, Czech Republic, pp. 202–208 (2010)
13. Jorrín-Prieto, J.., Vaquero, C., García, P.: Analysis of the impact of the audio database characteristics in the accuracy of a speaker clustering system. In: Odyssey 2016, the Speaker Language and Recognition Workshop, Bilbao, Spain, pp. 393–399 (2016)
14. Bolle, R.M., Connell, J.H., Pankanti, S., Ratha, N.K., Senior, A.W.: The relation between the ROC curve and the CMC. In: Fourth IEEE Workshop on Automatic Identification Advanced Technologies (AutoID 2005), pp. 15–20 (2005)
15. Manning, C.D., Raghavan, P., Schütze, H., et al.: Introduction to Information Retrieval, vol. 1, 1st edn. Cambridge University Press, Cambridge (2008)

Author Index

Printed in the United States
By Bookmasters